Artificial Intelligence and Knowledge Management

Artificial Intelligence and Knowledge Management

Edited by **Akira Hanako**

WILLFORD PRESS

New York

Published by Willford Press,
118-35 Queens Blvd., Suite 400,
Forest Hills, NY 11375, USA
www.willfordpress.com

Artificial Intelligence and Knowledge Management
Edited by Akira Hanako

International Standard Book Number: 978-1-68285-182-1 (Hardback)

Printed in the United States of America.

Contents

Preface IX

Chapter 1 **Sphericall: A Human/Artificial Intelligence Interaction Experience** 1
Frack Gechter, Bruno Ronzani, Fabien Rioli

Chapter 2 **From Management Information System to Business Intelligence: The Development of Management Information Needs** 11
Rimvydas Skyrius, Gėlytė Kazakevičienė, Vytautas Bujauskas

Chapter 3 **Auto-Adaptative Robot-Aided Therapy Based in 3D Virtual Tasks Controlled by a Supervised and Dynamic Neuro-Fuzzy System** 18
L. D. LLedo, A. Bertomeu, J. Díez, F. J. Badesa, R. Morales, J. M. Sabater, N. Garcia-Aracil

Chapter 4 **Business and Social Behaviour Intelligence Analysis Using PSO** 24
Vinay S. Bhaskar, Abhishek Kumar Singh, Jyoti Dhruw, Anubha Parashar, Mradula Sharma

Chapter 5 **Global Collective Intelligence in Technological Societies: As a Result of Collaborative Knowledge in Combination with Artificial Intelligence** 30
Juan Carlos Piedra Calderón, J. Javier Rainer

Chapter 6 **A Constraint-Based Model for Fast Post -Disaster Emergency Vehicle Routing** 35
Roberto Amadini, Imane Sefrioui, Jacopo Mauro, Maurizio Gabbrielli

Chapter 7 **Reality and Perspectives of a Model for the Population that Obtains its Income with the use of an Animal-Drawn Vehicle in the City of Bogota** 44
Sánchez Aparicio, Ismael Fernando., Romero Villalobos, Oswaldo Alberto

Chapter 8 **Recognition of Emotions using Energy Based Bimodal Information Fusion and Correlation** 49
Krishna Asawa, Priyanka Manchanda

Chapter 9 **Approach for Solving Multimodal Problems Using Genetic Algorithms with Grouped into Species Optimized with Predator-Prey** 54
Pablo Seoane, Marcos Gestal, Julián Dorado

Chapter 10 **SketchyDynamics: A Library for the Development of Physics Simulation Applications with Sketch-Based Interfaces** 62
Abílio Costa, João P. Pereira

Chapter 11 **Legal Issues Concerning P2P Exchange of Educational Materials and their Impact on E-Leaninging Multi-Agent Systems** 70
Eugenio Gil, Andrés G. Castillo Sanz

Chapter 12   **Big Data and Learning Analytics in Blended Learning Environments: Benefits and Concerns**   **76**
Anthony G. Picciano

Chapter 13   **Dissemination Matters: Influences of Dissemination Activities on User Types in an Online Educational Community**   **85**
Min Yuan, Mimi Recker

Chapter 14   **Model Innovation of Process Based on the Standard E-Commerce International GS1**   **93**
Giovanny Mauricio Tarazona Bermúdez, Luz Andrea Rodríguez Rojas, Cristina B Pelayo, Oscar Sanjuan Martínez

Chapter 15   **L.I.M.E. A Recommendation Model for Informal and Formal Learning, Engaged**   **99**
Daniel Burgos

Chapter 16   **Our System IDCBR-MAS: From the Modelisation by AUML to the Implementation Under JADE Platform**   **107**
Abdelhamid Zouhair, El Mokhtar En-Naimi, Benaissa Amami, Hadhoum Boukachour, Patrick Person, Cyrille Bertelle

Chapter 17   **Confidentiality of 2D Code using Infrared with Cell-Level Error Correction**   **117**
Nobuyuki Teraura, Kouichi Sakurai

Chapter 18   **Engineering Education through Elearning Technology in Spain**   **126**
Juan Carlos Fernández Rodríguez, José Javier Rainer Granados, Fernando Miralles Muñoz

Chapter 19   **BROA: An Agent-Based Model to Recommend Relevant Learning Objects from Repository Federations Adapted to Learner Profile**   **131**
Paula A. Rodríguez, Valentina Tabares, Néstor D. Duque, Demetrio A. Ovalle, Rosa M. Vicari

Chapter 20   **Fusing Facial Features for Face Recognition**   **137**
Jamal Ahmad Dargham, Ali Chekima, Ervin Gubin Moung

Chapter 21   **Improved Differential Evolution Algorithm for Parameter Estimation to Improve the Production of Biochemical Pathway**   **144**
Chuii Khim Chong, Mohd Saberi Mohamad, Safaai Deris, Mohd Shahir Shamsir, Yee Wen Choon, Lian En Chai

Chapter 22   **Integration of Multiple Data Sources for Predicting the Engagement of Students in Practical Activities**   **152**
Llanos Tobarra, Salvador Ros, Roberto Hernández, Antonio Robles-Gómez, Agustín C.Caminero, Rafael Pastor

Chapter 23   **A Multi-Agent System Model to Integrate Virtual Learning Environments
and Intelligent Tutoring Systems**   162
Giuffra P., Cecilia E., Silveira Ricardo A.

Chapter 24   **Improving Web Learning through Model Optimization using Bootstrap
for a Tour-Guide Robot**   170
Rafael León, J. Javier Rainer, José Manuel Rojo, Ramón Galán

Chapter 25   **A Grammatical Approach to the Modeling of an Autonomous Robot**   176
Gabriel López-García, A. Javier Gallego-Sánchez, J. Luis Dalmau-Espert,
Rafael Molina-Carmona, Patricia Compañ-Rosique

Chapter 26   **Mining Social and Affective Data for Recommendation of Student
Tutors**   184
Elisa Boff, Eliseo Berni Reategui

Chapter 27   **Comparative Study on Feature Selection and Fusion Schemes for Emotion
Recognition from Speech**   191
Santiago Planet, Ignasi Iriondo

Chapter 28   **Conceptualizing the E-Learning Assessment Domain using an Ontology
Network**   199
Lucía Romero, Milagros Gutiérrez, María Laura Caliusco

Chapter 29   **DEVELOP-FPS: A First Person Shooter Development Tool for Rule-Based
Scripts**   208
Bruno Correia, Paulo Urbano, Luís Moniz

Chapter 30   **An Agent -Based Approach for Evaluating Basic Design Options of
Management Accounting Systems**   216
Friederike Wall

Chapter 31   **Review of Current Student-Monitoring Techniques used in
Elearning-Focused Recommender Systems and Learning Analytics.
The Experience API & LIME Model Case Study**   225
Alberto Corbi, Daniel Burgos

Permissions

List of Contributors

Preface

Over the recent decade, advancements and applications have progressed exponentially. This has led to the increased interest in this field and projects are being conducted to enhance knowledge. The main objective of this book is to present some of the critical challenges and provide insights into possible solutions. This book will answer the varied questions that arise in the field and also provide an increased scope for furthering studies.

Artificial intelligence and knowledge management have transformed the process of knowledge circulation and database management in different business enterprises and corporate organizations. Some of the significant topics discussed in the chapters of this book are AI planning strategies and tools, AI tools for information processing, data mining, knowledge-based systems, etc. It explores the innovative concepts and advancements in these emerging fields. The book is an invaluable source of knowledge for students and researchers involved in this field at various levels.

I hope that this book, with its visionary approach, will be a valuable addition and will promote interest among readers. Each of the authors has provided their extraordinary competence in their specific fields by providing different perspectives as they come from diverse nations and regions. I thank them for their contributions.

Editor

Sphericall: A Human/Artificial Intelligence interaction experience

Frack Gechter[1], Bruno Ronzani[2], and Fabien Rioli[3]

[1]IRTES-SET, UTBM, Belfort Cedex, France
[2]Oyez Digital Agency
[3]Tharsis Evolution

Abstract — **Multi-agent systems are now wide spread in scientific works and in industrial applications. Few applications deal with the Human/Multi-agent system interaction. Multi-agent systems are characterized by individual entities, called agents, in interaction with each other and with their environment. Multi-agent systems are generally classified into complex systems categories since the global emerging phenomenon cannot be predicted even if every component is well known. The systems developed in this paper are named reactive because they behave using simple interaction models. In the reactive approach, the issue of Human/system interaction is hard to cope with and is scarcely exposed in literature. This paper presents Sphericall, an application aimed at studying Human/Complex System interactions and based on two physics inspired multi-agent systems interacting together. The Sphericall device is composed of a tactile screen and a spherical world where agents evolve. This paper presents both the technical background of Sphericall project and a feedback taken from the demonstration performed during OFFF Festival in La Villette (Paris).**

Keywords — **Live demonstration, Human/complex system interactions, Multi-agent systems, Physics inspired behaviours.**

I. INTRODUCTION

MULTI-AGENT systems are now widespread in scientific works and in industrial applications. They are characterized by individual entities, called agents, in interaction with each other and with their environment. Each agent is autonomous. It behaves following a set of rules that can be based on a complex representation of individual goals (cognitive agents) or based on simple stimulus/response local actions (reactive agents). In this context, local phenomena (interaction, behaviours...) lead together to a global system response that can be defined as intelligent. Multi-agent systems are generally classified into complex systems. The emerging phenomena cannot be predicted even if every component is well known.

Multi-agent systems are used in a wide range of applications such as artificial life/complex system simulation [11], [14], mobile robots [12], [13] and intelligent vehicle behaviour [17],

smart energy networks [16]... Agents behaviours are generally inspired by physics [18] or biology, especially by social insects such as ants [19], termites, spiders [20]... This last inspiration source is also known as swarm intelligence [5], [6], [7].

Few articles deal with the Human/Reactive multi-agent system interaction issue. However, some recent works that deal with this issue in various contexts such as Human activity recognition [22] or Human/multiple robots interactions definition [23], start to appear. This scarce representation of this issue in literature is mainly due to the complex character of these kinds of systems where the global emergent properties are not easily predictable. In these kinds of applications, the main problem is to determine at which the level (local or global) the Human/agency interaction must take place. The local Human/agent interaction is easy to set up but its influence on the agency is hard to determine/predict. A global Human/agency interaction is hard to put into practice but is more easily predictable. Moreover, this interaction can be direct, modification of the agent behaviours, or indirect by modifying the environment perceived by the agents.

Sphericall has been developed to study the link between the Human being and the agency. It can be considered as a Human/Artificial Intelligence interaction experience, which puts the focus on several sensitive abilities (visual, tactile, and hearing).

The Sphericall device is composed of two main elements:
• A tactile surface aimed at modifying the music (effect, volume, pan,...) diffused to the intelligent system.
• The work of art, as itself, which emerges from interaction between music, which is controlled by a Human, and a reactive multi-agent system.

Agents, spread on a sphere, are autonomous entities which build/destroy skyscrapers, organic trees... depending on their musical perception. The artist can influence, but not totally control, the work of art by modifying the sounds and the music, which is sent to the system.

This paper presents both the technical background of the Sphericall project and a feedback taken from the demonstration performed during OFFF Festival (Online Flash-Film-Festival) and from a poll made among students, which have the habit of manipulating multi-agent systems.

The paper is structured as follows. First, section II draws a state of the art of multi-agent and of the Human/multi-agent system interaction issue. Then, section III will present the technical aspects of Sphericall project, dealing with the interactive interface on the one side and with the intelligent system on the other. Then, section IV exhibits results obtained after OFFF festival demonstration in La Villette (France). Finally, section V concludes by giving some future work.

II. STATE OF THE ART

A. Multi-agent systems

Since a couple of decades multi-agent systems have been used in a wide range of problem solving, modelling and simulation applications. These approaches are characterized by their capability to solve complex problems, while maintaining functional and conceptual simplicity of involved entities called agents. In many cases, multi-agent based approaches exhibit effectiveness in various fields such as life simulation [24], crowd simulation, robots cooperation [25] or vehicle control related to devices such as obstacle avoidance systems. The multi-agent systems design generally focuses on agents' definition (internal states, perception and behaviour,...) and/or on the interactions between agents and their environment using biological [19], [26], [27], [28] or physical inspiration sources [29], [30], [31]. One can find two main trends in multi-agent design: the cognitive and the reactive approaches. The cognitive approaches focus mainly on the agent definition and design. In this context, each agent is defined with high level reasoning capabilities and interacts with its mates in using high-level interactions such as explicit communication for instance. Among these approaches one can cite the consensus methods [41] or the belief-desire-intention (BDI) agents as used in [42]. Cognitive agent systems rely generally on a small number of agents. By contrast, reactive agent approaches are based on numerous agents, with small cognitive abilities (generally based on simple stimulus-response behaviours), and interacting intensively with each other and with their evolving area named environment. The role of the environment and its characteristics (dynamics, topology,...) are crucial in reactive approaches. As it has been explained in [32], [33], [34] the environment plays a key role in reactive multi-agent systems. Indeed, a reactive agent can neither handle a representation of the global goal of the system nor compute a solution to reach it. The environment can thus be considered as the place where the system computes, builds and communicates. Then, one can say that the intelligence of the system is not contained into the population of agents but emerges from the numerous interactions between agents and with their environment. This notion of emergence is central in reactive multi-agent systems and explains the interest of such systems for complex system control, observation or simulation. In [35], a system is defined to present emergent properties when phenomena appear dynamically on a macroscopic point of view as a result of interactions between system components at microscopic level.

Moreover one can find several definition of emergence from the nominal emergence to the weak emergence and the strong emergence [36]. The main problem encountered is linked to the evaluation, measurement and prediction of emerging organization and/or properties. On the Human/system interactions point of view, the notion of emergence is the key element. Indeed, the challenge of designing a control interface for complex system relies on the ability to propose to the user an abstract interface, which enables him to manipulate and to understand the evolution of the system without knowing the interaction that occurs at microscopic level.

B. The Human/Multi-agent system interaction issue

The Human/multi-agent system interaction problem, and more generally, the Human/complex system interaction problem is a tough issue, which has been dealt with for a couple of years [1]. In multi-agent systems, one can consider two different categories depending on the reactive/cognitive aspect of the considered agents as described in the previous paragraph. The Human interaction, from the cognitive agent point of view, is more natural and easy to analyse. Since the cognitive approach tends to design agents which behave using high-level reasoning, decisional and/or perceptive abilities, it is then logical to consider the behaviour of the interacting Human at the same level of intelligence as one agent in [2]. Another way to specify the Human/Agency interaction is to consider the Human as a supervisor able to interpret the information furnished by each agent [3] or to translate Human gestures into control primitives [4]. The key indicator in such systems is the fan-out of a Human-agents team as defined by Olsen and Wood in [37], [38] to be the number of agents that a Human can control simultaneously. The examples, found in literature, deal mainly with Human-multiple robot interaction/control [23], [39]. In this context the fan-out for a Human/robots team can reach 18 homogenous robots [40].

In the reactive approach this issue is harder to cope with, since the number of agents involved can be as many as hundreds of elements. Indeed, the reactive multi-agent systems are based on numerous agents, the behaviours of which are triggered by numerous interactions. Generally, such systems are considered to be complex as referred to the definition given in [8]. Thus, it's hard to interact with the system because its complex nature makes its understanding impossible even if all local aspects are well known. In this situation, the external interaction has to be linked to the emergent properties because the influence is not directly measurable. In [9], several interaction strategies are defined. The Human/complex system interactions can be made by explicit control or by implicit cooperation. Explicit cooperation correspond to direct interactions with the local element of the system such as agents' behaviours or agent-agent interaction mechanisms. Implicit cooperation can be considered to indirect interaction through modification of the agents' environment. The feedback of these interactions is always made through global and indirect indicators. Finally, [10] studies the relation that can be brought to Humans by swarm systems.

Thus, one can separate the interaction effectors and the feedback representation on the one side and the complex system on the other. Effectors and feedbacks are abstractions of the real system for a better Human understandability. For instance, when driving a car, we manipulate abstract effectors (wheel, pedals...), which have a direct or indirect influence on the global system (engine, gearbox, wheels, tyres...). In this example, the feedback is made through a Human perception of the car behaviour. Following this two-side separation concept, the device presented in this paper is split into a tactile device, which plays the abstract effector role and the Sphere, which represents a visual feedback of what happens in the multi-agent system.

III. PRINCIPLE

As previously said, Sphericall is composed of two devices.
- A tactile device, based on a multipoint capacitive screen. This screen can be considered as a mixing interface used by the Human so as to interact indirectly with the agency by modifying music characteristics (volume, pan...).
- A video screen representing a 3D sphere, which is the work of art built thanks to Human/multi-agent system interactions.

The next sections will describe in detail these two elements.

A. Interactive Interface

1) Technical tools

The tactile interactive interface is based on two libraries developed by Tharsis Software: SimpleSound and SimpleUI.

SimpleSound is a library aimed at managing sound devices. It provides programming elements to develop real time mixing tools. Thanks to this library several audio files can be read at the same time (In this case, the audio files are merged into an audio group). Their characteristics (volume level, pan...) can be modified during the reading of audio files as it can be made with a classical hardware or a software-mixing console. In addition, effects and information filters can be added. Information filters allow specific information on the signal such as output level, Fourier transform, band pass... to be obtained.

SimpleUI is a graphic library developed by Tharsis Software (see http://www.tharsis-software.com/ for more details) and based on OpenSceneGraph (OSG). This library allows adding, removing and manipulating various types of widgets such as buttons, images... For this project a physical layer, using Box2d, has been added in order to provide widgets with coherent physical behaviours such as inertia, collision management...

2) Appearance and behaviours

In the designed mixing interface, a circle represents each channel. Channel circles are grouped into a Group Channel. The volume of a circle is linked to its vertical position, its horizontal position defining the stereo position of the audio source (pan left/right). A short touch on a circle triggers the activate on/off function. Each group Channel has its own colour (blue and green for keyboards, bass and drums, pink

and orange for the orchestra and the voices). The final interface used for the demonstration is composed of 21 channels spread into 5 groups. The circle can interact with each other through collisions. Thus, one can send one group in the direction of another. When the collision occurs the groups react as snooker balls, which collide each other and involve changes in volume and pan position. The same interaction can be made with channel circles inside each group (cf. Figure 1).

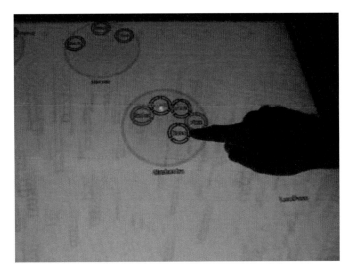

Fig. 1. Interactive Interface: Groups

Sound effects are represented by little coloured square buttons. The activation of them is the same as the one for the circles. The position of the square button in the interface field is linked to two parameters specific to each effect.

Finally, four classical buttons have been placed at the top left corner of the interface. These are for general purpose such as the rebooting of the Sphere and/or the rebooting of the mixing interface, sound effects visible on/off toggle, and 8-band equalizer on/off toggle (cf. Figure 2).

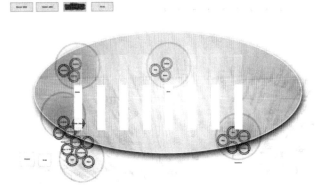

Fig. 2. Interactive Interface: Equalizer

3) Comparison with similar devices

The appearance of the sound control part can appear to be similar to some commercial tactile mixers such as Line6 StageScape or digital audio workstation tablet interfaces (V-Control, AC-7 Core...). However, these are generally a transposition, within a tactile screen of the functionalities of a standard mixer. In some exceptions, as in [15] for instance, the tactile mixer is coupled with a haptic device enabling the user to "sense" the sound.

The key difference in our proposal is the fact that the mixer already includes a multi-agent system. Each mobile element is an agent and behaves following interaction rules with other agents. For the moment the interactions between mixer-agents are simple collisions, but one can imagine changing them to use other interaction models such as gravitation-based repulsions. In this case, the interaction model will lead to an emergent behaviour of the channels and the groups similar to satellite orbits and involving influences on the diffused sound.

For the moment, we decided to use simple collision to make the mixer easier to use. Hence, the influence on the sound can still be considered as the product of the direct Human interaction (as in a regular mixer).

B. Sphere world
1) Environment

Instead of using classical planar environment for this experiment, we chose to provide to agents a spherical environment. This kind of environment is not widespread in agent related work because it requires the expression of influence forces, distances,... into spherical coordinate system which is not necessarily adequate in agents systems.

Since all agents move on the surface of the sphere, their coordinates consist only in a couple of angles θ and ϕ, ρ being always equal to sphere radius. (cf. Figure 3). The gravity relies then only on the variations of ρ. Thus, every element (perceptions, acceleration, speed, position...) is defined using a spherical coordinate system.

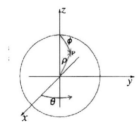

Fig. 3. Spherical representation of agent positions

For the localisation of the elements, and for the frustum culling, a QuadTree has been developed to manage the (θ, Φ) plane. (cf. Figure 4). This structure is generally used for 2D worlds. The main interest, in this application, is to allow a localisation of any entity with a logarithmic complexity. Moreover, even while maintaining a 3D representation of the world, the computation cost is very low since everything is computed as in a 2D world.

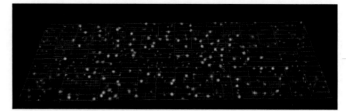

Fig. 4. Quadtree planar representation

Of course, the choice of such an environment implies several drawbacks. First of all, the management of the values of the angle on the limits of the cosinus and sinus functions make the continuity of the world hard to maintain when computing agents' movements. Besides, even if there is a bijection between the sphere and the (θ, Φ) plane, it is required to define a transformation function to translate measurements made on the plane into their equivalent in the sphere world.

2) Agents: role and interactions

Figure 5 represents the sphere agency organization using a RIO (Role, Interaction, Organization) diagram as defined in [21]. This diagram represents the different roles that can be played by agent (μ, γ, β, δ roles) and the interactions between these. The next paragraphs detail these elements.

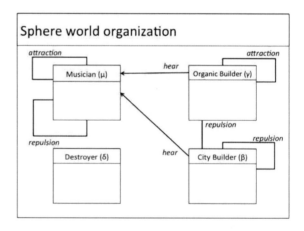

Fig. 5. RIO diagram of Sphere world

➢ Agents roles

• **µ role**

This role corresponds to the musician's role. Each musician is linked to an audio channel and emits the sound of it into the sphere world. This role can be considered as the link between the sound world (the mixing console) and the visual world (the sphere).

The agents which play this role, are attracted by other µ agents of the same mixing group. By contrast, all other agents, including µ agents of other mixing groups, are repulsed by them.

• **γ role**

This role corresponds to an **organic builder** role. Agents, which play this role, build organic structures (vegetable) into the sphere world. This role is sensitive to one specific μ role (i.e. one specific sound channel) by which it is attracted. The behaviour is similar to fireflies. A gauge is fed by the sounds that came from the associated musician. The nearest the musician is to the γ agent, the more the gauge is fed. When the gauge reaches its maximum value, an organic structure is built. During the construction of the structure, the γ agent is inactive. After this, the agent disappears and let the place to a new γ agent created randomly on the sphere.

The agents, which endorse this role, are attracted by the organic structure and repulsed by β agents (defined in the next item) and by their constructions (buildings).

• **β role**

This role is similar to the role of γ. The main differences are the following:
1. The structures built are big buildings similar to skyscrapers.
2. Agents, which endorse the β role, are repulsed by both β and γ agents.

• **δ role**

This role corresponds to destructors. Agents, which endorse this role, are attracted by skyscrapers, which they destroy when they are on them. When there are no buildings left, δ agents move randomly on the sphere.

In order to obtain good visual results, β agents are associated to bass, keyboard and drum sounds. Voices and strings are associated to γ agents. Hundreds of agents of each type are created to obtain the results shown in figures 7 and 8.

➤ Interactions

This section described in detail the different interactions used between agents. After this description, a summary of all interactions used in the sphere world is made in table 1.

• **Attraction**

The attraction law is a standard linear equation. The more the attracted agents are near to each other the less the attraction is important. This law is described by the following equation:

$$\overrightarrow{F_{A_iA_j}} = \beta . m_{A_i} . m_{A_i} \overrightarrow{A_iA_j} \tag{1}$$

This equation represents the attraction force applied to agent A_i due to the presence of agent A_j. In this equation β is a scalar multiplier, m_{Ai} and m_{Aj} are respectively the mass of agent A_i and A_j.

• **Repulsion**

Repulsion can be treated as a negative gravitationnal force between two weighted elements. As with natural gravitational force, repulsion depends on the $1/r^2$ value, where r is the distance between agents.

The following equation shows the analytic expression of the repulsion force applied to agent A_j taking into account the influence of agent A_i. α is a scalar multiplier that takes into account the environmental gravitational constant and the proportion of attraction compared with the other forces.

In practice, since the agents' environment is virtual, this constant allows us to tune the importance of the repulsion behaviour relative to the other forces. In this equation, m_i and m_j are respectively the weight of the agents A_i and A_j.

$$\overrightarrow{R_{ij}} = \alpha . m_i m_j \frac{\overrightarrow{A_iA_j}}{\left\|\overrightarrow{A_iA_j}\right\|^3} \tag{2}$$

TABLE 1
SUMMARY OF INTERACTIONS BETWEEN SPHERE ELEMENTS

	μ agent	γ agent	δ agent	β agent
μ agent	attraction/ repulsion	hear	x	hear
γ agent	x	x	x	repulsion
organic structures	x	attraction	x	repulsion
δ agent	x	x	x	x
β agent	x	repulsion	x	repulsion
buildings	x	repulsion	attraction	repulsion

3) Resolving dynamical equations

The position, speed and acceleration for each agent are computed in a continuous world.

The agents' dynamical characteristics are computed following the laws of the classical Newtonian physics. Each behaviour, applied to an agent, corresponds to a force, which influences its movement. The behaviour is selected according to the role endorsed by the agent and the roles of its nearest mates.

By applying the fundamental law of dynamics, we can compute the acceleration of each agent (cf. equation 3). Here, $\vec{\gamma}$ represents acceleration, m the agent's mass, and $\overrightarrow{F_b}$ the force resulting from behaviour b.

$$\vec{\gamma} = \frac{1}{m} \sum_{behaviors} \overrightarrow{F_b} \tag{3}$$

Introducing a fluid friction force defined, and integrating twice we obtain the following equations:

$$\vec{V}_t = \vec{V}_{t-1} + \frac{\delta t}{m}\left(\overrightarrow{F_{attraction}} + \overrightarrow{F_{repulsion}} + \overrightarrow{F_{friction}}\right) \qquad (4)$$

$$\vec{V}_t\left(1 + \frac{\delta t}{m}\lambda\right) = \vec{V}_{t-1} + \frac{\delta t}{m}\left(\overrightarrow{F_{attraction}} + \overrightarrow{F_{repulsion}}\right) \qquad (5)$$

$$\vec{X}_t = \vec{X}_{t-1} + \left(\vec{V}_{t-1}\delta t + \frac{(\delta t)^2}{2m}\left(\vec{F}_{attraction} + \vec{F}_{repulsion}\right)\right)\left(\frac{1}{(1 + \frac{\delta t}{m}\lambda)}\right)$$

$$(6)$$

where $\vec{X}_t$ is the position of the considered agent at time t, $\vec{V}_t$ its speed, $\vec{F}_{repulsion}$ the sum of all repulsion forces applied to the agent, $\vec{F}_{attraction}$ the sum of all attraction forces and λ the fluid friction coefficient of the environment.

C. Software implementation

The software implementation has been made under C++ following the class diagram presented in figure 6. Each agent involved in the sphere world inherits from the abstract class Agent, which defines the live() method. This method corresponds to the behaviour of the agent. Its purpose is to compute the equations (3) to (6). This method is overloaded in each specific agent so as to embed specific characteristics such as the forces involved by the role. The scheduler class is a thread loop that calls the live() method of each agent one after the other. The agent are linked to the Environment class which manage the positions of the agents on the sphere. The GUI part (not detailed in the class diagram) corresponds to the set of classes aimed at managing the graphical interface of the sphere. The link between the sphere and the tactile interface is made through the µ agents, which are associated to audio channels. They have state values named pitch and level, reachable by γ and β agents. Depending on these values, γ and β agents will react if it corresponds to their behaviours. A low pitch value is associated to low frequencies, triggering β agents behaviour and a high pitch value is associated to high frequencies so as to trigger γ agents behaviours. The level value is used to feed the gauge of the agents.

On the dynamical point of view, the live() method starts by sending the position of its associated agent to the environment. As an answer, the environment sends back a list of the nearest agents with their characteristics (position, type, pitch,…). Using this list, the agent chooses the forces to be applied and computes its acceleration, speed and position. Then, it updates its position in the environment. The scheduler can now loop on other agents.

The link between the sphere and the tactile device is asynchronous. The thread of the tactile device updates the pitch and the level values of µ agents each time it is possible

depending on the music timeline. The time schedule of the sphere world is faster than the music time schedule so as to ensure a better reactivity of the sphere.

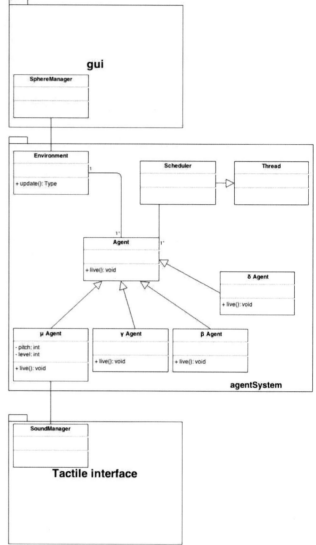

Fig. 6. Agents system class diagram

IV. OFFF FESTIVAL PRESENTATION

After a presentation of OFFF Festival, this section will draw on the results obtained during the demonstration.

A. OFFF Festival

Since 2001, OFFF (http://www.offf.ws/) festival has been held in Barcelona, becoming the globally recognized and trendsetting event it is today. OFFF Festival was initially the Online Flash-Film-Festival. After 3 years of existence, it became the International festival for the post-digital creation culture but kept the short initial designation. OFFF is spreading the work of a generation of creators that are breaking all kind of limits, those separating the commercial arena from the worlds of art and design; music from illustration, or ink and chalk from pixels. Artists, those have grown with the web and receive inspiration from digital tools, even when their canvas is not the screen came to the festival. □□□

Fig. 7. Sphericall device

B. Sphericall demonstration

1) Global feeling

Our set fits perfectly with the general appearance of the festival area. The design of the device and the appearance of the Sphere are very attractive to the audience. The public doesn't hesitate to manipulate the device. The feedback on the mixing console use and on appearance is very good. The casual users succeed in manipulating the device easily and seem to adapt quickly to the relationship between the audio part and the mixing device. The use of the circular shaped buttons, which can collide with each other, adds an entertaining aspect as compared to the classical use of a mixing console. □

Fig. 8. Global illustration of the 3D sphere (reversed colors)□

After a couple of minutes, the question on the link between the mixing console and the sphere arrives. Indeed, the link between the manipulation of the mixing console and the appearance of the sphere is not as direct as the link between the sound and the mixing console part. The relationship between these two components has thus to be explained. After a short explanation of the whole system, the casual users return on the table so as to try to figure out the side effects that occur on the sphere when manipulating the sounds. We estimate that almost 85% of the users found the interface easy to use even if in 70% of the cases they took more than 10 minutes to understand the relationships between the music controller and its effects on the sphere well. After 10 minutes, all the users were able to play with the sphere making abstraction from the tactile interface. After this, the user no longer looked at the mixing console but stared at the sphere world. If some effects are natural and easy to find (bass levels...) some other are subtler and need a deep investment in the use of the system.

From the technical point of view, the questions we encountered concern mainly the agents and their characteristics as compared to other techniques. Some artists, having already the habit of using interfaces such as *Processing* (http://processing.org/), *openFrameworks* (http://www.openframeworks.cc/) or *Cinder* seem to be very interested by the concept we have developed.

2) Analyse of the users' behaviour

The main innovation is in the way the user can interact indirectly with the system. By controlling, via this simple interface, the music and sounds produced, the user is actually linked with the whole artificial intelligence of the system, and, like a conductor, smoothly leads how the agents will act - and interact - thus how the scene is rendered. This is quite different from a standard "visualisation" plugin, where most of the time the colours and shapes rendered are directly calculated from the sound waveform.

The user faces a two-level interaction: as he may be used to, he directly hears the changes he makes in the music, but he also focuses on the consequences of his choices. This is different from a real-time strategy video game, where he knows how to control each unit, and expects them to behave exactly as he orders or from a passive 3D visualisation plugin, where everything is computed. His choices directly influence the behaviours of the agents, but without dictating them: the global result can be guided, but never predicted.

There is a permanent curiosity lightened in the user: it's a new approach for building interactions between Humans and computers, which leaves, when necessary, some parts of the decision process to the computer. We can for instance think about an interface with intelligent and independent components, which adapt to the user choices and habits.

The result obtained visually is the interaction between the Human and the Artificial Intelligence (AI) of the system. This experiments shows that, even without training sessions, the Human player is able to interact with a complex system provided the interaction device is simple enough. Moreover, the interaction device has to be based on notions and feelings already experienced by the user in another context. In our application, the visual result is obtained making the user play with sounds and not directly with the parameters of the AI.

So as to have more details on the use of the Sphericall device, other experiments were made with a set of students who used to manipulate multi-agent systems. We firstly proposed to the students a direct control through agents parameters manipulations. In this situation the control is less easy and the students, despite their knowledge in multi-agent system, had some difficulties to well understand the implication of each parameter change. By contrast, using the tactile device and the sound feedback, untrained users were able to easily manipulate the system. After this experiment, the students had filled out a short questionnaire. The goal of this questionnaire was to rate the easiness of the interface in terms of understandability of the link between manipulators and sphere. The questions were the following:

1. Is the manipulation of the agents parameters easy to understand?
2. Is the link between the parameters and the sphere appearance easy to understand?
3. Is the manipulation of the mixing control device easy to understand?
4. Is the link between the mixing control device and the sphere easy to understand?
5. Are the modifications of sphere appearance logical in relation with the change performed on the sound device?
6. Which kind of control do you prefer?

Students had to give an answer between 1 and 5 for the first 5 questions. (1 corresponds to fully disagree and 5 to fully agree). The results obtained with a set of 35 students are presented in table 2.

TABLE 2
RESULTS OF THE STUDENTS QUESTIONNAIRE.

Question	1	2	3	4	5
1	20%	26%	43%	8,5%	2,5%
2	43%	48,5%	8,5%	0%	0%
3	8,5%	14%	20%	34%	23,5%
4	2,5%	14%	26%	28,75%	28,75%

Table 2 shows clearly that not only the mixing console is easier to manipulate but also that it allows students to better understand the correlation between the sphere world and their manipulations. Of course, for question #5, more than 90% of the students prefer the mixing console to the direct parameter manipulation. These results show that the mixing console device helps the user to better understand the complex world of the sphere. In most of the cases, the user better understands the system with the abstraction as compared to the whole explanation of the entire system. Consequently, providing a well-chosen abstract interface makes the task of understanding the complex system easier. The example chosen there is a little biased because it is based on elements that are based on common knowledge and easy to understand. However, we think that this experiment gives interesting enough results to be explored in other fields more deeply.

Fig. 9. Details of the sphere

V. CONCLUSION

This paper presented Sphericall, an application aimed at studying Human/agency interactions. The Sphericall device, composed of a tactile screen and a sphere world where agents evolve, has been deployed during the OFFF festival in La Villette. The two devices are developed based on the multi-agent paradigm. The tactile device differs from commercial tactile mixers on the fact that the result in music control is obtained taking into account both user manipulations and interaction behaviours of graphical elements. This tactile mixer can be considered as an abstraction of the complex world of the Sphere. The Sphere as itself is represented in 3D and allows the result of Human/System interactions to be shown. This deployment was a public success and allows having a great feedback on the deployment of such a device. The application is intuitive enough to permit a non-scientific public to interact with the artificial intelligence. Indeed, it's hard to handle the complexity of such systems. The solution presented in this paper relies on an interface aimed at translating the complexity of the Sphere world into a more easily understandable effector unit. The feedback, as itself, is made through the Sphere representation. On the artistic point of view the results obtained were really appreciated by the public. A movie of this event is available at http://www.youtube.com/watch?v=iDEkBE6Cbz8.

We now plan to use the knowledge acquired through this experiment to other application fields such as authority sharing in complex decision systems. The two main targets we plan to deal with are the following: (1) Trying to increase the fan-out of Human-robot team using abstract multimodal interfaces such as the one used in Sphericall. To that way, we will focus our research work on the nature of the representation of the data and on the observation/interpretation of the Human behaviour. We are now exploring interfaces based on natural gesture recognition. (2) Trying to enable the manipulation of big databases using Sphericall-like interfaces. The main issues encountered are linked to the representation/manipulation of the data and to the introduction of queries using an abstract interface.

REFERENCES

[1] D. Fass, "Putting in Perspective Human-Machine System Theory and Modeling: From Theoretical Biology to Artifacts Integrative Design and Organization", Digital Human Modeling and Applications in Health, Safety, Ergonomics, and Risk Management. Healthcare and Safety of the Environment and Transport, Lecture Notes in Computer Science Volume 8025, 2013, pp 316-325.

[2] I. Lacko, Z. Moravek, J.-P. Osterloh, F. Rister, F. Dehais, and S. Scannella, "Modeling approach to multi-agent system of Human and machine agents: Application in design of early experiments for novel aeronautics systems", Industrial Informatics (INDIN), 2013 11th IEEE International Conference on Industrial Informatics (INDIN), pp.786,789, 29-31 July 2013, doi: 10.1109/INDIN.2013.6622984

[3] J.Y.C Chen, S. Quinn, J. Wright, M. Barnes, D. Barber, D. Adams, "Human-agent teaming for robot management in multitasking environments", Human-Robot Interaction (HRI), 2013 8th ACM/IEEE International Conference on , vol., no., pp.103,104, 3-6 March 2013 doi: 10.1109/HRI.2013.6483522

[4] M. Tornow, A. Al-Hamadi, V. Borrmann, "A multi-agent mobile robot system with environment perception and HMI capabilities", Signal and Image Processing Applications (ICSIPA), 2013 IEEE International Conference on , vol., no., pp.252,257, 8-10 Oct. 2013 doi: 10.1109/ICSIPA.2013.6708013

[5] M. Dorigo, "Swarm-Bots and Swarmanoid: Two Experiments in Embodied Swarm Intelligence", Web Intelligence and Intelligent Agent Technologies, 2009. WI-IAT '09. IEEE/WIC/ACM International Joint Conferences on , vol.2, no., pp.2,3, 15-18 Sept. 2009 doi: 10.1109/WI-IAT.2009.377

[6] Y-F Zhu and X-M Tang, "Overview of swarm intelligence", Computer Application and System Modeling (ICCASM), 2010 International Conference on , vol.9, no., pp.V9-400,V9-403, 22-24 Oct. 2010 doi: 10.1109/ICCASM.2010.5623005

[7] J. Duan, Y. Zhu, and S. Huang, "Stigmergy agent and swarm-intelligence-based multi-agent system", Intelligent Control and Automation (WCICA), 2012 10th World Congress on , vol., no., pp.720,724, 6-8 July 2012 doi: 10.1109/WCICA.2012.6357972

[8] T. Moncion, P. Amar, and G. Hutzler, "Automatic characterization of emergent phenomena in complex systems".In Journal of Biological Physics and Chemistry 10, p. 16?23. url : http://hal.inria.fr/hal-00644627. 2010.

[9] G. Zambrano Rey, M. Carvalho, D. Trentesaux, "Cooperation models between Humans and artificial self-organizing systems: Motivations, issues and perspectives", Resilient Control Systems (ISRCS), 2013 6th International Symposium on , vol., no., pp.156,161, 13-15 Aug. 2013 doi: 10.1109/ISRCS.2013.6623769

[10] M. Goodrich, S. Kerman, B. Pendleton, P.B. Sujit, "What Types of Interactions do Bio-Inspired Robot Swarms and Flocks Afford a Human?", Robotics: Science and Systems VIII, Sydney 2012.

[11] N. Gaud, S. Galland, F. Gechter, V. Hilaire, A. Koukam, "Holonic multilevel simulation of complex systems: Application to real-time pedestrians simulation in virtual urban environment", Simulation Modelling Practice and Theory 16(10): 1659-1676 (2008)

[12] A. Drogoul and J. Ferber, "From Tom-Thumb to the Dockers: Some Experiments with Foraging Robots", proceedings of From Animals to Animats II, MIT Press, Cambridge, pp 451-459, 1993

[13] O. Simonin, and J. Ferber, "Modeling Self Satisfaction and Altruism to handle Action Selection and Reactive Cooperation", Simulation of Adaptive Behavior (SAB2000), From Animals to Animats, Paris, Int. Soc. For Adaptive Behavior, pp. 314-323, 2000.

[14] O Lamotte, S Galland, JM Contet, F Gechter, "Submicroscopic and physics simulation of autonomous and intelligent vehicles in virtual reality", Advances in System Simulation (SIMUL), Second International Conference pp 28-33 2010

[15] S. Merchel, M.E. Altinsoy, M. Stamm, "Touch the Sound: Audio-Driven Tactile Feedback for Audio Mixing Applications", in Journal of the Audio Engineering Society, 60(1/2), pp. 47-53. 2012

[16] G. Basso, N. Gaud, F. Gechter, V. Hilaire, and F. Lauri. "A Framework for Qualifying and Evaluating Smart Grids Approaches: Focus on Multi-Agent Technologies", In Smart Grid and Renewable Energy, vol. 4(4), 2013. DOI: 10.4236/sgre.2013.44040.

[17] J.-M. Contet, F. Gechter, and L. Lefoulon. "Autonomous Emergent Painting Triggered by Music and Motion" In International Journal of Arts and Technology, 2013.

[18] B. Dafflon, F. Gechter, P. Gruer, and A. Koukam, "Vehicle Platoon and Obstacle Avoidance: a Reactive Agent Approach" In IET Intelligent Transport Systems, (3), pp. 257-264(7), Institution of Engineering and Technology, 2013. ISSN: 1751-956X.

[19] S. Brueckner, "Return from the ant : Synthetic Eco-systems for Manufacturing Control", Thesis at Humboldt University Berlin, Department of Computer Science, 2000.

[20] C. Bourjot and V. Chevrier and V. Thomas, "How social spiders inspired an approach to region detection", proceedings of AAMAS 2002, pp 426-433,

[21] Y. Lin, and V. Hilaire, and N. Gaud, and A. Koukam, "K-CRIO: an ontology for organizations involved in product design", Digital Information and Communication Technology and Its Applications, pp 362-376 Springer 2011.

[22] J. P. Gupta, and P. Dixit and, B. S. Vijay, "Analysis of Gait Pattern to Recognize the Human Activities", Special Issue on Multisensor User Tracking and Analytics to Improve Education and other Application Fields, International Journal of Artificial Intelligence and Interactive Multimedia, volume 2, pp 7-16. 2014

[23] M. Lichtenstern, and M. Frassl, and B. Perun, and M. Angermann, "A prototyping environment for interaction between a Human and a robotic multi-agent system,",7th ACM/IEEE International Conference on Human-Robot Interaction (HRI), pp.185,186, 5-8 March 2012

[24] H.V.D. Parunak, R. Bisson, S. A. Brueckner, "Agent interaction, multiple perspectives, and swarming simulatio", AAMAS '10 Proceedings of the 9th International Conference on Autonomous Agents and Multiagent Systems}, Volume 1, International Foundation for Autonomous Agents and Multiagent Systems, Richland, SC, 549-556.

[25] A. Glad, O. Simonin, O. Buffet, F. Charpillet, "Influence of different execution models on patrolling ant behaviors: from agents to robots", \In Proceedings of the 9th International Conference on Autonomous Agents and Multiagent Systems, Volume 3 (AAMAS '10), International Foundation for Autonomous Agents and Multiagent Systems, Richland, SC, 1173-1180.

[26] E. Bonabeau, M. Dorigo, G. Theraulaz, "Swarm Intelligence: From Natural to Artificial Systems", M. Dorigo and M. Birattari, Swarm intelligence, Scholarpedia (1999)

[27] J. Bajo, D. Tapia, S. Rodriguez, A. Luis, and J. Corchado. "Nature inspired planner agent for health care", International Work-Conference on Artificial and Natural Neural Networks IWANN 2007: 1090-1097.

[28] G. DiMarzo-Serugendo, A. Karageorgos, O.F. Rana, and F. Zambonelli. "Engineering Self-Organising Systems: Nature-Inspired Approaches to Software Engineering", Lecture notes in Artificial intelligence}, 2004, vol. 2977, 299 p.

[29] J-M. Contet, F. Gechter, P. Gruer, A. Koukam. "Reactive Multi-agent approach to local platoon control: stability analysis and experimentations", International Journal of Intelligent Systems Technologies And Application. 2010. 231-249

[30] F. Gechter, J-M. Contet, P. Gruer, A. Koukam, "Car-driving assistance using organization measurement of reactive multi-agent system", Procedia Computer Science 1(1): 317-325., 2010.

[31] C.W. Reynolds. "Flocks, herds, and schools: A distributed behavioral model in computer graphics". SIGGRAPH Conference Proceedings, pages 25-34, 1987.

[32] K. Zeghal and J. Ferber. "A reactive approach for distributed air traffic control", in international conference on artificial intelligence and expert systems (1994), pp. 381-390.

[33] H.V.D. Parunak, "Go to the Ant: Engineering Principles from Natural Agent Systems``, \it{Annals of Operations Research}, Vol. 75, No. 1. (1997), pp. 69-101

[34] D. Weyns, H.V.D. Parunak, F. Michel, T. Holvoet, J. Ferber: "Environments for Multiagent Systems State-of-the-Art and Research Challenges``, \it{E4MAS} 2004: 1-47.

[35] De Wolf, Tom and Holvoet, Tom, "Emergence versus self-organisation: different concepts but promising when combined", Engineering Self Organising Systems: Methodologies and Applications, Lecture Notes in Computer Science, vol. 3464 pages 1-15, 2005.

[36] M. A. Bedau, "Downward Causation and the Autonomy of Weak Emergence", Principia, pp 5-50 2002.

[37] D. R. Olsen, B. Wood: "Fan-out: Measuring Human Control of Multiple Robots" CHI '04, ACM, (2004).

[38] D. R. Olsen, B.Wood, J. Turner: "Metrics for Human Driving of Multiple Robots" International Conference on Robots and Automation, ICRA '04, IEEE, (2004).

[39] J. W. Crandall, M.A. Goodrich, D.R. Jr Olsen, C.W. Nielsen, "Validating Human-robot interaction schemes in multitasking environments," Systems, Man and Cybernetics, Part A: Systems and Humans, IEEE Transactions on , vol.35, no.4, pp.438,449, July 2005.

[40] P. Velagapudi, P. Scerri, K. Sycara, Huadong Wang, M. Lewis, Jijun Wang, "Scaling effects in multi-robot control," Intelligent Robots and Systems, 2008. IROS 2008. IEEE/RSJ International Conference on , vol., no., pp.2121,2126, 22-26 Sept. 2008.

[41] S. Abhinav, G. Binetti, A. Davoudi, F.L. Lewis, "Toward consensus-based balancing of smart batteries," Applied Power Electronics Conference and Exposition (APEC), 2014 Twenty-Ninth Annual IEEE , vol., no., pp.2867,2873, 16-20 March 2014.

[42] S. Korecko, T. Herich, B. Sobota, "JBdiEmo — OCC model based emotional engine for Jadex BDI agent system," IEEE 12th International Symposium on Applied Machine Intelligence and Informatics (SAMI), pp.299,304, 23-25 Jan. 2014 doi: 10.1109/SAMI.2014.6822426.

## 2

From Management Information Systems to Business Intelligence: The Development of Management Information Needs

Rimvydas Skyrius, Gėlytė Kazakevičienė, and Vytautas Bujauskas

Economic Informatics Department, Vilnius University, Lithuania

Abstract — Despite the advances in IT, information systems intended for management informing did not uniformly fulfil the increased expectations of users; this can be said mostly about complex information needs. Although some of the technologies for supporting complicated insights, like management decision support systems and technologies, experienced reduction in interest both from researchers and practitioners, this did not reduce the importance of well-supported business informing and decision making. Being attributed to the group of intelligent systems and technologies, decision support (DS) technologies have been largely supplemented by business intelligence (BI) technologies. Both types of technologies are supported by respective information technologies, which often appear to be quite closely related. The objective of this paper is to define relations between simple and complex informing intended to satisfy different sets of needs and provided by different sets of support tools. The paper attempts to put together decision support and business intelligence technologies, based on common goals of sense-making and use of advanced analytical tools. A model of two interconnected cycles has been developed to relate the activities of decision support and business intelligence. Empirical data from earlier research is used to direct possible further insights into this area.

Keywords — management decision support, business intelligence, information needs

I. INTRODUCTION

THE job of informing business managers and other people in charge of running organizations stays on the agenda of many researchers and practitioners around the information systems and information management community. While the advances in technological foundations of management information systems have been impressive, the advances in efficient satisfaction of management information needs have been less impressive. The development of systems for managerial information needs, while having a rich history of several decades, has been based on a heterogeneous set of needs: some of these needs stay stable (developing, implementing and adjusting strategy; keeping track of own activities), and some evolve or have a turbulent life cycle:

monitoring close environment; looking out for threats and opportunities. Information environment (support infrastructure) is driven by the nature of business activities. On one hand, this nature is recurrent and cyclical, supported mostly by the function of a MIS. On the other hand, this nature is turbulent and unpredictable, requiring intelligent and insightful support; this is a function of a BI system and related applications – decision support, competitive intelligence, operational intelligence, early warning systems and other types of systems to support monitoring, sense-making and problem solving.

The recent research on complex information needs including decision support and business intelligence has been diversified into quite a few related areas; far from being an exhaustive set, several examples follow. Lemieux and Dang [7] have researched the issues of accountability for decision making, and suggested tools for tracking the decision-making reasoning of human agents, thus adding to the research on a problem of experience management. Thorleuchter and Van den Poel [17] have investigated the use of website content analysis in partner search for improved research and technology collaboration planning, adding to the body of research on information integration. Saad et al [11] have researched a conceptual framework for early warning information systems for crisis situations, expanding the research on intelligence technologies for monitoring and detection. Castano [1] has researched the possibility of putting together business process management (BPM) and data mining techniques to provide intelligent BPM management functions. Redondo-Garcia et al [10] have researched information integration tasks when using disparate (heterogeneous) information sources.

The sample of research directions presented above for a long time has been attributed to the area of decision support systems and technologies, serving the complex or high-end side of user information needs. In the field of technologies for satisfying complex information needs, the once-prominent area of management decision support systems (DSS) apparently has settled to stable levels of both academic and practitioner activities [9]. However, a somewhat faded interest in decision support systems does not imply any reduction in importance of well-supported decision making, as well as general awareness of the state of internal and external business environment. On the contrary, the current economic situation in most settings demands an efficient and reliable, „military grade" management environment to support decisions, insights, recovery or mere survival.

Decision support alone, being reactive and activated only when a problem is encountered, eventually proved to be insufficient. The problem solving context received IT-based support mostly from the resources of a regular information system, therefore of a limited nature and in most cases complicated by time pressures. An alternative use of decision support, if coupled to a proactive monitoring of the environment, ensured better understanding of the problem context, leading to higher decision quality. A term "business intelligence" came into use, serving as an umbrella term for tools and technologies that let business information users stay aware of changes in internal and external environments.

The research problem of this paper is centered around how the current array of technologies and approaches provides support for functions of insight building. Currently there is a confusion in defining whether management information systems overlap with intelligence systems, and whether business intelligence is a part of decision support function, or vice versa; eventually this confusion spreads to business management community which at all times has expressed the need for insight building and reliable decision support which would justify substantial investments into support technologies. In this paper, the authors have decided to use the results of their earlier research to make an attempt in developing a model positioning business intelligence and decision support functions.

The paper is structured as follows. Section 1 defines the dimensions of the problem and the goal of the paper. Section 2 clarifies the definition of business intelligence and its information needs. Section 3 defines a relation between the areas of decision support and business intelligence. Section 4 presents empiric data on user responses towards decision support anad business inteligence functions. Finally, Section 5 presents conclusions and directions for further research.

II. BUSINESS INTELLIGENCE AND INFORMATION NEEDS

Although business intelligence is regarded as a relatively new term, with authorship assigned to Howard Dressner of Gartner Group in 1989, we can have a retrospective look at the mission of management information systems (MIS), whose role of keeping management aware of the state of business has never been downplayed, and mission definitions for MIS sound very much like the mission definitions for business intelligence today. A few explanations of MIS role from earlier sources are presented below:

- "Two types of information for strategy implementation are in use. The first one is the external information, used for strategy development. The second type is internal information, used to monitor strategy execution" [14].

- "A management information system refers to many ways in which computers help managers to make better decisions and increase efficiency of an organization's operation" [7].

- "For information to be useful for managerial decision making, the right information (not too much and not too little) must be available at the right time, and it must be presented in the right format to facilitate the decision at hand" [4].

- "A management information system is a business system that provides past, present, and projected information about a company and its environment. MIS may also use other sources of data, particularly data about the environment outside of the company itself." [6].

- "The systems and procedures found in today's organizations are usually based upon a complex collection of facts, opinions and ideas concerning the organization's objectives. … For an organization to survive, it must learn to deal with a changing environment effectively and efficiently. To accomplish the making of decisions in an uncertain environment, the firm's framework of systems and procedures must be remodeled, refined, or tailored on an ongoing basis." [3].

There are definitions of business intelligence that do not differ much from the above definitions; e.g., Vuori [20] states that "… business intelligence is considered to be a process by which an organization systematically gathers, manages, and analyzes information essential for its functions". In order to have a more precise definition of business intelligence, we have to decide whether all informing functions are „intelligence" because they increase awareness, or does BI have a clear separation from other (lower level) informing functions. If so, the separation criteria between BI systems and any other management information systems have to be defined. For the purposes of this paper, we will use the division of management information needs along two dimensions – their simplicity or complexity, and common or specific focus, as presented in the Table 1 and based on earlier work by one of the authors [14]:

TABLE 1.
RELATION OF SIMPLE-COMPLEX AND COMMON-SPECIAL INFORMATION NEEDS

	Simple needs	Complex needs
Special needs (problem-specific)	Simple special needs	Complex special needs
Common needs (available permanently)	Simple common needs	Complex common needs

The mission of BI becomes clearer if weighted against the types of served information needs. Regarding the positioning of these needs against the axis of simple-complex information needs, they usually fall into the more sophisticated part of the information needs complexity spectrum. Same can be said about the process of decision making, which often requires sophisticated tools to support awareness, communication, sense-making and evaluation of risks. The dimension of common and special information needs separates decision making from the rest of business intelligence in a sense that while decision support activities are directed towards a certain problem which has been recognized and has created a task of its solving, business intelligence can be considered an activity which, apart from encompassing decision support, has a permanent nature and allows the discovery of problems and general awareness about the state of activities.

III. DECISION SUPPORT AND BUSINESS INTELLGENCE PROCESSES

A. Structure of Decision SupportProcess

A decision support process includes a number of stages, and if accumulation and subsequent use of experience is included, the process takes a cyclical nature (Fig. 1, from [13]):

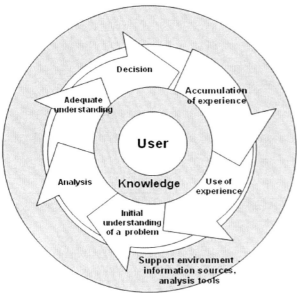

Fig. 1. The decision support process

The structure of the decision support process can be related to relevant information needs:

1. Monitoring (using previous experience): the environment, both internal and external, is being watched to notice things worth attention; *simple* and *common* information needs prevail.

2. In the case of recognizing a situation of interest (initial understanding of a problem or opportunity) the situation is evaluated and given extra attention to achieve desired understanding. At this stage *special* information needs arise.

3. Additional analysis and decision development is required if the situation is complex enough (semi-structured or unstructured); *simple* needs are complemented by *complex* needs; more information is brought into decision making environment; specific problem-solving tools such as formal approaches and

models are likely to be used to achieve an adequate understanding of a problem.

4. The decision-making stage involves formerly available as well as newly gained understanding of the situation, and the decision maker or makers will use all possessed knowledge to arrive at the best possible decision, time or other circumstances permitting. In this paper, the term "knowledge" is deliberately avoided most of the time, but here it serves to show that data or information alone are insufficient for decision making; all that is known will be used in its entirety, and new knowledge most likely will be gained.

5. The experience accumulation stage records the newly gained experience from both decision making and its implementation, and keeps it for possible reuse. *Special needs* become *common*, adding new material to the already available body of experience, and the need to capture the essential features of the recorded case keeps this sort of information need in the complex segment. This phase should also include the practical experience in decision implementation, which can sometimes reveal additional circumstances of the problem.

6. The use of new experience, along with that formerly accumulated, brings the process back to stage 1 – monitoring.

Stage 1 of the above process is directly related to (or can be considered a part of) business intelligence, because that's where the actual monitoring of the business environment is being done. Stage 2 is a principal point of joining business intelligence and decision support.

As we can see, during the decision making process the focus of information needs moves around the quadrants of Table 1: stage 1 concentrates in the simple/common sector; stage 2 moves on to simple/special sector, stages 3 and 4 concentrate in the special/complex sector, stage 5 moves into complex common sector, and finally stage 6 brings the focus back to simple/common sector.

B. Structure of Business Intelligence Process

The business intelligence process, too, takes a cyclical nature (Fig. 2., from [20]), and includes the stages of information needs definition, information collection, information processing, analysis, information dissemination, information utilization and feedback. The cycle structure is justified if the received feedback helps to reevaluate or redefine information needs.

In business intelligence process, there's usually no clear concentration on a specific topic or problem, and the resources of a BI system are used for constant monitoring of internal and external business environment. In other words, such systems serve *common* information needs to keep users informed about the state of business environment, often combining a monitoring function with alerts, exception reports and other tools to draw attention to changes or inconsistencies. Therefore, an important feature of BI systems is their ability to produce a complete composite view that would help avoiding surprises.

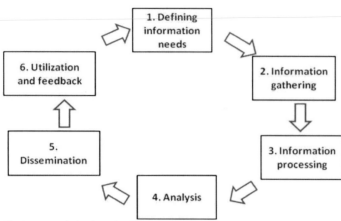

Fig. 2. A generic business intelligence process model [20]

The business intelligence cycle, as presented in Fig. 4., raises several questions. First of all, it does not disclose the difference between regular management information systems or their current incarnation, ERP systems, and business intelligence systems. It is unclear, for example, whether external information is used in the cycle, and if so, in what ways. Secondly, the cyclical feedback should invoke the re-evaluation of information needs, as business conditions change, or some needs have been incorrectly assessed from previous cycles (inclusion of irrelevant information or omission of important information).

From the above descriptions of technologies and processes for both decision support and business intelligence we can define two different but interrelated cycles: cycle 1 for business intelligence process, and cycle 2 for decision support process (Fig. 3).

As cycles 1 and 2 unfold, the focus moves around different types of information needs. In cycle 1, the steps of information gathering and processing can be attributed to the *common* and *simple* part of information needs. The analysis step uses processed information and produces derivative results that produce additional insight and move from *simple* to more *complex* needs. If a problem situation is recognized, *special* needs arise, and cycle 2 is activated. For a problem analysis, *special* needs may be both of *simple* and *complex* nature, depending upon the severity of a problem. A problem-specific model is developed for better understanding of the problem and evaluating the alternatives. Decision implementation brings in valuable experience that is saved for later reuse and, together with other experience, satisfies *common* information needs important both for future business intelligence and decision making.

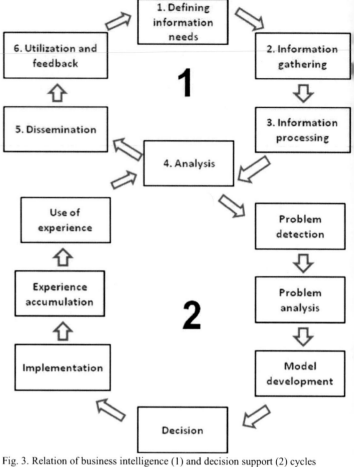

Fig. 3. Relation of business intelligence (1) and decision support (2) cycles

IV. User Responses on IT Use for Decision Support and Business Intelligence

The opinions on IT role in supporting the sophisticated side of information needs can be roughly split into deterministic approaches and behavioural, human-centered approaches. The former assign prime importance to IT performance and ability to automate complex analytical procedures [2], while the latter assign prime importance to human skills and creative powers ([16], [5], [19]), at the same time stating that the majority of existing decision support and analytical tools are technology-centric rather than user-centric. The conflicting attitudes have initiated a survey, performed earlier by one of the authors [14], where issues like monitoring of internal and external environment, IT role in the monitoring process, and experience management have been researched to gain insight on IT use to support the compl;ex side of management information needs, including DS and BI. The survey had yielded 250 responses from a convenience sample of managers of small and medium businesses in a Central-Eastern Europe country.

Regarding the *monitoring of internal organization environment*, the users appeared to be quite comfortable using IT for monitoring key data about their organization's activities. Such information is contained within their in-house information system that has been created to monitor these activities. The absolute majority of responders (161 or 64.4%) have indicated that IT is used to monitor all issues relating to an organization's internal information needs; such needs are attributed mostly to the simple common needs. The information system-based information tasks are largely routine, and satisfaction of this type of information needs does not pose any significant problems.

For *external monitoring* the use of IT is significantly lower; the number of responders having indicated that they use IT to monitor all external issues has been 125, or 50%; 122 responders, or 48.8%, had stated that they use IT for some of the external monitoring issues. The lower numbers of use do not point to second-rate importance of external monitoring; rather, they indicate that the sources of external information are not under the control of a single own information system, as it is in the case of internal information sources. The external environment, being an important source of changes, opportunities and risks, is much more turbulent, and there is a greater variety of issues to be monitored, information sources, formats, and access modes; this variety significantly complicates the use of IT for external monitoring.

Supporting the detection of important changes, IT had been considered a helpful aid in monitoring and detecting changes, but rather limited in supporting information needs for sense-making. The absolute majority of responses (105 out of 207 responders having indicated that IT has some role in detecting important changes, or about 51%) stressed the role of IT as a principal technical support tool. No responses stated that IT had significantly supported the function of sense-making (revealing important changes in the environment).

The reuse of experience and competence information is one of the most important functions in the process chains of BI and DS; this statement can be supported by a seemingly growing number of published work on experience management systems. The results of the survey have indicated that the reuse of important problem-solving and decision making experience is of mixed success; recorded practice is reused – in most cases conditionally, as situations change and information needs have to be constantly re-evaluated. The survey had also shown that experience records are recorded in all convenient ways: free text format in digital media, structured format (with some standardized features and values) in digital media, and same on paper. IT role can be seen mostly in arranging, managing structures, imposing standards, and allowing easy filtering and retrieval. Level of reuse is limited due to changing context, although the reuse of templates, structures, models and other procedural issues is commonplace.

Decision-making information needs are hard to plan because of their variety and unstructuredness. Regarding this issue, the respondees have been asked about:

- decision making infomation needs that are known beforehand, and the principal types of such information;

- decision making information needs that are not known beforehand and emerge in the process of developing a decision, and the principal types of such information.

The *known* information needs relate to information whose content and location are known and accessible because of earlier experience, or this information is already available. This information or tools for its access can be placed in close proximity to the decision makers. The distribution of responses between the different types of this information is given in Table 2.

TABLE 2
KNOWN INFORMATION NEEDS FOR DECISION MAKING

Type of information	No. of cases	Percent
Market information (customers, sales, needs, opportunities)	49	19,6%
Competition information (competitors' status, strength, intentions, actions)	29	11,6%
Internal information (financials, capacity, inventory)	27	10,8%
Legal information (laws, regulations, standards)	26	10,4%
No such cases	26	10,4%
Technical information	2	0,8%
Did not specify	91	36,4%
Total:	**250**	**100,0%**

A separate important group of information needs is the *unexpected* information needs, which emerge mostly because of turbulent business nature, are hard to plan, and the use of programmed solutions is rather limited. The distribution of responses between the different types of this information is given in Table 3.

TABLE 3
UNEXPECTED INFORMATION NEEDS FOR DECISION MAKING

Type of information	No. of cases	Percent
No such cases	86	34,4%
Yes, there have (without specifying the information)	46	18,4%
Market information	23	9,2%
Internal information	15	6,0%
Competition information	14	5,6%
Legal information	14	5,6%
Technical information	14	5,6%
Informal, "soft" information (e.g., opinions, foresights)	12	4,8%
Confidential information (e.g., customer reliability checks)	5	2,0%
Did not specify	21	8,4%
Total:	**250**	**100,0%**

The distribution of both responses is not much different, and suggests that often decision makers have to look deeper into existing issues ("more of the same"). However, the significant presence of unexpected information needs might require a set of support tools that would allow tailored approaches using assorted decision support techniques – e.g., modeling, data mining, text mining, information integration and others.

The above separation of information needs into known and unexpected roughly corresponds to the related cycles pictured in Fig.5, where the business intelligence cycle is performed mostly against known information needs. If a specific problem is detected, the known needs together with readily available information move to the decision support cycle, where additional information needs of unexpected nature are likely to emerge. This approach can be useful in designing business intelligence environments incorporating a sub-level for decision support, with generic functionality contained mostly in the 1st cycle, and the problem-specific tools and techniques in the 2nd cycle.

V. DISCUSSION AND CONCLUSIONS

There's no doubt that the need for well-informed business decisions, as well as for general awareness of developments in the business environment, will remain acute. The current state of management decision support gets more complicated as rapidly changing conditions often require swift reaction, information overload is commonplace, and additional issues arise regarding information quality [9]. Under these conditions, a need for right information at the right time and in the right place remains essential, and the well-aimed and reasonable use of support technology can increase decision making quality and efficiency, regardless of whatever name this technology is bearing at the moment.

We suggest here to use here the arguments presented in this paper, regarding the development of an efficient information environment for decision makers. It has been proposed that such environment should be split into two tiers:

- the first tier containing a simple set of support tools that are close and easy to use;
- the second tier containing more distant and more complicated information sources and processing techniques that are required much less often;
- manageable support environment that allows easy switching of items between tiers, similar to the form of managerial dashboards with interchangeable items on display.

The items contained in the first ("lite") tier would be required most of the time, simple to use and able to be configured to the users' needs:

- basic data on internal and external environment: sales, market share, cash-at-hand, order or project portfolio, comparative figures by time/place/product etc.;
- information access tools: simple search in own sources – databases and data warehouses, simple search in public sources, tools for arranging search results (e.g., by relevance or size), easy classification and annotation;
- tools for simple calculations: templates, financial models, other simple models.

The second ("heavy") tier might include:

- access to more distant and complex information sources with advanced search tools;
- modelling tools for forecasting, simulation, scenario development;
- data analysis and presentation technologies – drill-down tools, OLAP queries, data and text mining facilities, graphing and visualization tools.

Such split of functionality would roughly reflect required functions for generic business intelligence and decision support cycles respectively. It would also allow for required cross-functionality in the cases when simple decision support needs would be well-served by first tier functions alone, or when business intelligence needs would required more advanced tools. The more defined set of features for both tiers of the support environment could lead to a possible set of requirements for the interface design of an information environment for decision makers.

The further research is planned in several related and more specific directions. Firstly, it is important to research what part of business decisions are adequately supported by the first tier of the support environment, thus possibly defining an efficient and economical set of support tools. Secondly, the issues of handling experience information and providing experience support should be investigated in more specific terms of what key information on decisions already made should be recorded to create brief yet essential context, and what is the reusability and relevance rate for different types of experience records.

REFERENCES

[1] Castano A. P. Prototype of assignment intelligent adaptive of service providers inside of ESB with data mining. International Journal of Artificial Intelligence and Interactive Multimedia, 1(2), 39-43 (2012).

[2] Davenport T. Competing on analytics. Harvard Business Review, January 2006, 99-107 (2006).

[3] FitzGerald J., FitzGerald A., Stallings W. Fundamentals of systems analysis. New York, NY: John Wiley & Sons (1981).

[4] Gremillion L., Pyburn P. Computers and information systems in business. New York, NY: McGraw-Hill (1988).

[5] Johnstone D., Bonner M., Tate M. Bringing human information behaviour into information systems research: an application of systems modelling. Information Research, 9(4), paper 191 (2004). http://InformationR.net/ir/9-4/paper191.html.

[6] Kroenke D., McElroy M., Shuman J., Williams M. Business computer systems. Santa Cruz, CA: Mitchell Publishing (1986).

[7] Lemieux V., Dang T. Building Accountability for Decision Making into Cognitive Systems. WorldCIST 2013, March 27-30, Algarve, Portugal (2013).

[8] Pick J. Computer systems in business. Boston, MA: PWS Publishers (1986).

[9] Power D. Decision Support Basics. Business Expert Press (2009).

[10] Redondo-Garcia J.L., Botón-Fernandez V., Lozano-Tello A. Linked Data Methodologies for Managing Information about Television Content. International Journal of Artificial Intelligence and Interactive Multimedia, 1(6), 36-43 (2012).

[11] Saad M., Mazen Sh., Ezzat E., Zaher H. Towards a Conceptual Framework for Early Warning Information Systems (EWIS) for Crisis Preparedness. WorldCIST 2013, March 27-30, Algarve, Portugal (2013).

[12] Shim J.P., Warkentin M., Courtney J., Power D., Sharda R., Carlsson C. Past, present, and future of decision support technology. Decision Support Systems, 33, 111-126 (2002).

[13] Skyrius R. Satisfying Complex End of User Information Needs: User Experiences. The Business Review, Cambridge, 6(2), December 2006, 132-138 (2006).

[14] Skyrius R. The current state of decision support in Lithuanian business. Information Research, 13(2), paper 345 (2008). http://InformationR.net/ir/31-2/paper345.html.

[15] Skyrius R., Bujauskas V. Business intelligence and competitive intelligence: separate activities or parts of integrated process? The Global Business, Economics and Finance Research Conference. London (2011).

[16] Sjoberg L. The distortion of beliefs in the face of uncertainty. SSE/EFI Working Paper Series in Business Administration, 2002:9. (2002).

[17] Thorleuchter D., Van den Poel D. Analyzing Website Content for Improved R&T Collaboration Planning. WorldCIST 2013, March 27-30, Algarve, Portugal (2013).

[18] Tom P. Managing information as a corporate resource. Glenview, IL: Scott, Foresman and Company (1987).

[19] Turpin M., & du Plooy N. Decision-making biases and information systems. In The 2004 IFIP International Conference on Decision Support Systems (DSS2004), pp. 782-792, Prato, Italy (2004).

[20] Vuori V. Methods of Defining Business Information Needs. Frontiers of e-Business research conference. Tampere University of Technology, Tampere, Finland (2006).

## 3

Auto-adaptative Robot-aided Therapy based in 3D Virtual Tasks controlled by a Supervised and Dynamic Neuro-Fuzzy System

L. D. LLedo, A. Bertomeu, J. Díez, F. J. Badesa, R. Morales, J. M. Sabater, N. Garcia-Aracil

Miguel Hernández University of Elche, Elche, Spain

Abstract — **This paper presents an application formed by a classification method based on the architecture of ART neural network (Adaptive Resonance Theory) and the Fuzzy Set Theory to classify physiological reactions in order to automatically and dynamically adapt a robot-assisted rehabilitation therapy to the patient needs, using a three-dimensional task in a virtual reality system. Firstly, the mathematical and structural model of the neuro-fuzzy classification method is described together with the signal and training data acquisition. Then, the virtual designed task with physics behavior and its development procedure are explained. Finally, the general architecture of the experimentation for the auto-adaptive therapy is presented using the classification method with the virtual reality exercise.**

Keywords — **Rehabilitation robotics; Physiological state; Neural networks; Fuzzy logic system; Virtual reality; Collision detection.**

I. INTRODUCTION

THERE are a great number of literature about the growing importance of the use of robotic systems in the neurorehabilitation field [1] , [2]. Particularly in the assisted robotic devices for motor retraining in subjects who have suffered neurological injuries such as stroke or Parkinson. It is known that this kind of rehabilitation therapies produce a beneficial effects in those patients [3]. Many researchers intend to include them in a control loop [4] to increase the efficiency and effectiveness of such systems. Thus, robot-assisted systems are able to decide the difficulty level that can be made during the different rehabilitation therapies taking into account the emotional and physiological aspects of the subject.

Currently, the adaptation of the robotic systems behavior using psycho-physiological measures is analyzed by the scientific community. A large number of classification methods and emotional estimation are compared in [5]. However, there are few studies about the utilization of neuro-fuzzy methods in these subjects. The hypothesis that neural network help us to estimate the emotional state of the patients is supported due to the network theory can be applied into the neural computing of the emotions, as is described conceptually in [6], and the architecture of cognitive networks, affective networks and evaluation layers is proposed in [7].

Furthermore, the virtual reality is a technology that allows developing rehabilitation environments such as virtual therapies based on activities of daily living (ADL), intended for stroke patients [8]. In other research, it was compared the virtual rehabilitation with the classical rehabilitation with two different post stroke groups [9]. The result was that the group exposed to the virtual rehabilitation shown a better improvement in the motor deficits of the upper limb than the other group. For this reasons, the adaptive robot-assisted rehabilitation therapy can be beneficial for the patient.

This paper proposes a neuro-fuzzy architecture combined with 3D virtual reality in the development of an upper-limb rehabilitation application to study the potential usefulness of neural networks, fuzzy logic and three-dimensional environments based in physical principles. This method can be dynamically modify and can adapt the robot-assisted rehabilitation therapy according to the emotional state of the patient, following the psycho-physiological computing processing as defined in [5].

II. CLASSIFICATION METHOD

In this section, an analysis of the classification method, used to differentiate the emotional state of the user during the proposed robot-assisted rehabilitation therapy, the acquisition data process and the extraction features of physiological signals are explained. Further information about the learning algorithm and validation test is also presented.

A. Neuro-fuzzy System: S-dFasArt

S-dFasArt [10] is a classification method based on the architecture provided by the ART neural network [11], where fundamentals of the Fuzzy Sets theory are applied in the different processing stages of the classification algorithm. The neuro-fuzzy architecture takes the advantages of both techniques, the learning and adaptability capacity of the neural networks, and the robustness, the interpretability and the fault tolerance of the fuzzy systems.

To improve the convergence speed and the update mode of the fuzzy weights dynamical equations are used. Moreover, this classification method allows a fast, supervised and competitive learning, keeping the accumulated knowledge. All nodes or output categories are actuated by the input data due to its competitive property, but only the neuron with the highest response level is activated. Therefore, the winner category generates the classifier output on the current input pattern.

The architecture of the proposed method is shown in Fig. 1. This model is formed by three layers or levels and an orientation subsystem.

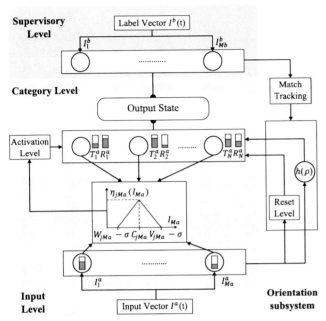

Fig. 1 S-dFasArt Architecture.

- The Input Level is used to receive the input data in a vector form, with the most important features of the physiological signals. Furthermore, in this level it is also applied an activation-membership function to determine the membership degree of each input attribute on the generated categories [12].
- The Supervisory Level presents the output pattern for the association with the input pattern.
- The Category Level is formed by a several nodes that represent the fuzzy units or categories and it contains the classification results with activation and reset levels. This level stores the association between the input sequences and its corresponding supervision vector.
- The Orientation Subsystem is responsible to create categories during the learning and the generalization of the similar categories.

B. Training data acquisition

To test the possibilities of the proposed classification method it is necessary the acquisition of the training data. The process to obtain the physiological signals is done as it is

explained in [14] A robotic device designed for upper-limb assisted therapy called PUPArm, which is commercialized by Instead Technologies Inc, is used during the therapy. It has a signal acquisition system provided by g.tec medical engineering GmbH with different sensors and a virtual reality system. The physiological signal of the subject, such a pulse rate, respiration rate, skin conductance level (SCL), skin conductance response (SCR) and skin temperature [15], were recorded in real-time.To test the possibilities of the proposed classification method it is necessary the acquisition of the training data. The process to obtain the physiological signals is done as it is explained in [14]. A robotic device designed for upper-limb assisted therapy called PUPArm, which is commercialized by Instead Technologies Inc, is used during the therapy. It has a signal acquisition system provided by g.tec medical engineering GmbH with different sensors and a virtual reality system. The physiological signal of the subject, such a pulse rate, respiration rate, skin conductance level (SCL), skin conductance response (SCR) and skin temperature [15], were recorded in real-time.

The integrated virtual reality system encourages different psycho-physiological states of the patient. The activity is formed by a series of rectangular elements of different sizes that they move randomly across the screen with different speeds inside a defined area. Meanwhile, the user control a pointer with the robotic device in order to avoid the collision with the rectangular elements. Three different levels of difficulty (relax level, medium level and stress level) were defined using the number and speed of the rectangular elements shown in screen.

Once the physiological signals are acquired, a data processing, based on normalization of the features, was performed to get the final set of training data with its respective supervision measures. The emotional states of the patient are collected in these supervision data.

C. Learning algorithm

In this section, the S-dFasArt neuro-fuzzy learning algorithm is explained briefly showing the required steps to train the neuro-fuzzy network nodes. Detailed explanation about this algorithm can be found in [13].

$$\frac{dT_j}{dt} = -A_T T_j + B_T \prod_{i=1}^{M} \eta_{ji}\left(I_i^a(t)\right) \quad (1)$$

$$l_{ji} = max\left(V_{ji}, I_i^a\right) - min\left(W_{ji}, I_i^a\right))$$
$$\frac{dR_j}{dt} = \left(-A_R R_j + B_R dreset\right)\left(R_{max} - R_j\right) \quad (2)$$
$$R_j(0) = 0$$

The input training data and its corresponding supervision labels are received through the classifier at the Input Level and Supervisory Level respectively. Next, the activation level (1) and the reset level (2) of all nodes that form the Category Level are calculated.

Then, the winner category is determined by comparing the activation levels values (3) and selecting the node with the highest value. If this activation value is null the classifier add a new uncommitted category.

$$T_J = max\{T_j; \quad j = 1...N\} \tag{3}$$

In the next step, it is necessary to check the reset level to determinate if the winner category accomplishes the necessary conditions of similarity with the input vector using a vigilance threshold. If it overtakes the threshold, the category whose level activation is the next highest, is searched. Once the winner category exceeds activation and reset conditions, its supervision label is compared with the supervision label received to confirm if it is a correct prediction. If it is not satisfied, the next category is sought.

To perform the update of the weights nodes of the neuro-fuzzy network the following dynamic equations (4) are used in case of an existing category.

$$\frac{dW}{dt} = -A_W W + B_W min\left(I^a(t), W\right)$$
$$\frac{dC}{dt} = A_C\left(I^a(t) - C\right) \tag{4}$$
$$\frac{dV}{dt} = -A_V V + B_V max\left(I^a(t), V\right)$$

In case of a new category, the weights nodes are initialized (5) using the input vector.

$$W = C = V = I^a(t) \tag{5}$$

D. Validation Test

At this point, a functional classification model has been implemented to distinguish correctly in real time the input patterns generated by the physiological signals of the patient and they are processed for features extraction. To get this functional model, an adjustment process of the SdFasArt neuro-fuzzy classifier have been applied following three phases [10]:

1. Initialization of the static value parameters linked to the dynamic equations.
2. Learning the weights whose values represent the diffuse categories generated by the presentation of the input pattern data to the classifier, using the learning algorithm explained in the previous subsection.
3. Setting the most influential parameters of the neuro-fuzzy network, σ and A_T, related to the diffuse character and the activation speed of the classifier categories, checking the values that provide better classification results.

Once the possible values of σ y A_{T} are analyzed, the functional classification model is completed. This model has been tested using the Leave-one-out validation technique to evaluate the classification results and ensure that they are independent of the partition between training and test data. Finally, the accuracy level has been calculated obtaining a performance results of 92.38% with 34 diffuse categories.

III.   3D Visual Tasks Architecture

The virtual task developed to perform the robot-assisted rehabilitation therapy has been designed following the scheme of programming routines. The general architecture is shown in Fig. 2. The graphic content required for the virtual scene is generated using Blender [16], a modeling software. This modeling tool can generate 3D meshes files with an appropriate format for an easy installation. Thus, the polygon mesh of the stage and the interacting elements are obtained. A file with the distribution of all scene elements is also generated.

These visual elements implemented are interpreted by the application core to build the virtual environment providing a characteristic behavior to each element. The core is responsible for controlling the application execution to organize all components of each of the blocks of the general scheme. The open source software called Ogre3D [17] has been used as a graphics engine. Ogre3D provides a flexible and object-oriented programming and, through its high level interface written in C++, it offers a series of intuitive methods that facilitates the preparation of 3D visualization applications with quite realistic, interactive and real-time environments on any kind of platform.

The physical engine is an important component that has been added. In this case, to simulate elements with some realism degree the NVIDIA PhysX \cite{physx} has been used. This engine tries to predict the physics effects within a scene subject to various conditions of speed, force, friction, mass and many more physics variables. Its main function is the collision detect algorithms able to calculate the interaction between all elements of the physics scene and the forces generation. Then, the rendering loop of the graphic engine updates the temporal evolution of the physics elements. It is also responsible for the visual representation of the behavior of each physics model by moving its corresponding graphical model. Each physics model consists in a simplified geometry of each specific graphical model to provide the main core the collision detect within the simulated physics space.

A sounds engine has been also incorporated to play sound effects depending on the task objectives. This engine helps in realism of the application and immerse the user in the virtual environment. The robotic system is controlled by the patient to manage the position of a virtual tool, whose movement affects in the collisions detect generated by the physics engine, depending of the simulated tool geometry. Meanwhile, the user has a visual feedback of everything happening in the application.

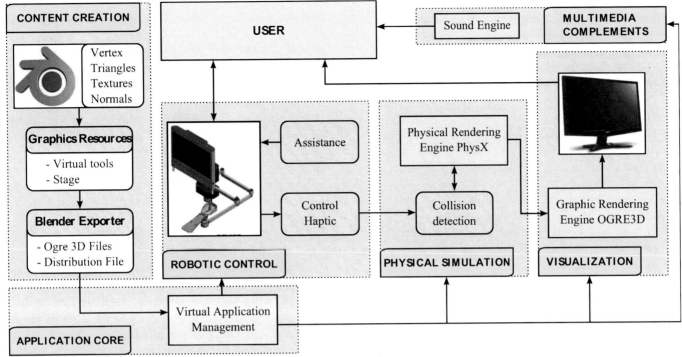

Fig. 2 General architecture of virtual reality applications.

A. Whack a Rabbit

In this paper, an example of virtual task has been designed using the procedure explained previously. The main objective of this task is to find items, in this case rabbits, which appear randomly on the scene. The user should use the robotic system to control the virtual tool and hit these targets. In Fig. 3 the implemented virtual task is shown.

To complete the experimentation different difficulty levels have been implemented in the virtual task for automatic level changes depending of the emotional state of the patient.

- Only one rabbit appears and stays on stage for 10 seconds.
- Only one rabbit appears and stays ion stage for 5 seconds.
- Two rabbits appear at the same time, and they stay on stage for 10 seconds.
- Two rabbits appear asynchronously, and everyone stays on stage for 5 seconds.
- Three rabbits appear at the same time, and they stay on stage for 10 seconds.
- Three rabbits appear asynchronously, and everyone stays on stage for 5 seconds.

The physic and visual elements used to develop the virtual task are explained in the following subsections.

Fig. 3 Virtual task screenshot

1) Static bodies

The static bodies are the elements of PhysX that are used in this application. These elements are placed in a particular localization in the scene and they are kept immobile during all simulation, while the remaining elements are influenced by the collision forces inside the stage during the exercise. In this virtual task the static elements have been designed to represent a garden with lawn, a wooden fence and 9 rabbit burrows. Also, a garden tools have been added to introduce the patient on the virtual reality.

2) Kinematic bodies

The kinematic bodies are objects that the user can freely

move within defined work range, and do not act under the influence of forces response, gravity and collisions. The movement of the kinematic bodies are produced getting the coordinates generated by the robotic system. In this task, a hammer has been designed as kinematic body, which generates an hit animation when the hammer is closed to the target.

3) Soft bodies

To provide more realism when the collision with the target occurs, the PhysX feature of soft bodies generating has been used. These deformable and volumetric elements have a elastic topology formed structurally by tetrahedral meshes that encapsulate all the 3D object surfaces. The stretching and bending constraints maintain subjected the vertices of this mesh type. The vertex positions are modified because of the internal forces of the soft body and the external forces generated in the physical engine.

Each tetrahedron of the soft body involves a number of vertices in the visual mesh. These vertices are attached to the behavior of the corresponding tetrahedron. Once the physics are updated, the new vertices positions are calculated and the graphic engines change the vertices positions of the visual mesh depending on the displacement suffered by the soft body. Thus, the 3D soft visualization body is updated. Also, PhysX offers different parameters that influence the internal physics of these bodies such as density, friction or damping, whose values can cause varying impact on the overall response of the element.

In this task, the bodies that move randomly in the scene are the soft bodies and they are shaped like a rabbit. Whenever a body is hit by the virtual tool, it color changes to indicate the success. Therefore, thanks to this functionality, the user is aware of the impact moment against the target and force direction.

IV. AUTOADAPTATIVE EXPERIMENTATION

The final application, based on adaptive robot-assisted rehabilitation therapy according with the specific psycho-physiological state of each patient, is defined in this section. A good performance has been observed in the classification method used in this experimentation, explained in the section II.

The general diagram of the autoadaptive experimentation is shown in Fig. 4, it is formed by four functional blocks. The sensors are connected to the user to record his/her physiological signals while controlling the interaction system. The explained rehabilitation robotic device and the virtual reality subsystem are included in this interaction system. The user has three feedback types (visual, audio and force). When the user starts using the robotic system, his physiological signals are processed to extract the most important features. These features are sent to the functional model of the neuro-fuzzy classifier. Three possible states are generated by the classification block processing, the input information to check the psycho-physiological state of the user and decide the

modification to be made in the deployed task (up level, down level or maintain level). This proportionate classification state is sent to the interaction system to complete the experiment of automatic difficulty level changes in the virtual task explained in section II, where six levels have been defined. The aim of the experimentation is to maintain an intermediate difficulty level along the task period.

The extraction and processing of the signals features have been performed in a Simulink scheme, while the classification block has been designed with Matlab. A UDP protocol is used to communicate the classifier with the virtual task software. This communication is applied every 30 seconds to send three possible action commands and changing the difficulty level of the virtual task:

1. If the user has an over-stressed level, one difficulty level is reduced in the virtual task.
2. If the user has stable state, the virtual task does not change the difficulty level.
3. If the user is relaxed, the actual difficulty level is increased.

Currently, several subjects are doing these experiments, who were informed of the work purpose. The subjects must perform an adaptation period of few minutes. Then, the subjects signals in relaxed state for 5 min are recorded to obtain baseline measurements. Finally, the subjects perform the task for 10 minutes, starting in the first difficulty level of the virtual task.

V. CONCLUSSION

In this paper, a classification model based on a neural network architecture and the fuzzy logic is presented to classify three different states of the user's reactions physiological in an assisted system of robotic rehabilitation. This method has obtained a quite good performance results (92.38% in LOOCV) that allow an efficient classification in real-time.

On the other side, a graphical application based on 3D virtual reality has been implemented. The aim of this issue is to increase the sense immersion of the user inside of the virtual environment, checking the patients behavior in front of scenes in three dimensions. Ogre3D has been used for visualization. The physics engine adds realism to the scene providing performance energies on elements that have different physical behaviors. These software tools offer a great versatility and flexibility to implement all type of virtual exercises with visually and physically realistic environments.

ACKNOWLEDGMENT

This work has been supported by the Spanish Government through the project ``Interpretation of the human intention and performance through biomedical signals and analysis of kinematic and dynamic motion'' (DPI2011-29660-C04-04), by CIBER BBN and by MAT2012-39290-C02-01.

Auto-adaptative Robot-aided Therapy based in 3D Virtual Tasks controlled by a Supervised and Dynamic...

23

REFERENCES

[1] E. L. Miller, L. Murray, L. Richards, R. D. Zorowitz, T. Bakas, P. Clark
, S. A. Billinger, "On behalf of the American Heart Association Council on Cardiovascular Nursing, and the Stroke Council. Comprehensive
overview of nursing and interdisciplinary rehabilitation care of the
stroke patient: A scientific statement from the American Heart
Association", Stroke 41(10), pp. 2402-2448, 2010.

[2] "The Management of Stroke Rehabilitation Working Group on behalf
of the Department of Veterans Affairs, Department of Defense, and The
American Heart Association/American Stroke Association, VA/DoD
Clinical Practice Guideline for the Management of Stroke Rehabilitation". Available: www.healthquality.va.gov. Accessed 25 Feb 2014.

[3] N. Norouzi-Gheidari, P. S. Archambault, J. Fung, "Effects of robot-
assisted therapy on stroke rehabilitation in upper limbs: systematic
review and meta-analysis of the literature",Journal of Rehabilitation
Research and Development 49(4), pp. 479496, 2012.

[4] A. Duschau-Wicke, A. Caprez, R. Riener, "Patient-cooperative control
increases active participation of individuals with SCI during robot-aided
gait training", Journal of NeuroEngineering and Rehabilitation 7(43),
2010.

[5] D. Novak , M. Mihelj, M. Munih, "A survey of methods for data fusion
and system adaptation using autonomic nervous system responses in
physiological computing", Interacting with Computers 24(3), pp. 154-
172, 2012.

[6] L. Pessoa, "On the relationship between emotion and cognition",Nature
Reviews Neuroscience 9(2), pp. 148-158, 2008.

[7] F. Shu, A. H. Tan, "A biologically-inspired affective model based on
cognitive situational appraisal", Neural Networks (IJCNN), The 2012
In- ternational Joint Conference, doi: 10.1109/IJCNN.2012.6252463,
2012.

[8] K. Laver, S. George, S. Thomas, J. Deutsch, M. Crotty, "Virtual reality
for stroke rehabilitation", Cochrane Database Syst Rev 9:CD008349,
2011.

[9] A. Turolla, M. Dam, L. Ventura, P. Tonin, M. Agostini, C. Zucconi, P.
Kiper, A. Cagnin, L. Piron, "Virtual reality for the rehabilitation of the
upper limb motor function after stroke: a prospective controlled trial",
Journal of NeuroEngineering and Rehabilitation, pp.10:85, 2013.

[10] J. M. Cano-Izquierdo, J. Ibarrola, M. Almonacid M, "Improving Motor
Imagery Classification with a new BCI Design using Neuro-Fuzzy
SdFasArt", IEEE Transactions on Neural Systems and Rehabilitation
Engineering 10(1), pp. 2-7, 2012

[11] G. Carpenter, S. Grossberg, N. Markuzon, N. Reynolds, D. Rosen,
"Fuzzy ARTMAP: A neural network architecture for incremental supervised learning of analog multidimensional maps", IEEE Transactions
on Neural Networks 3(4), pp. 698-713, 1992.

[12] J. M. Cano-Izquierdo, Y. A. Dimitriadis, E. Gomez-Sanchez, J. Lopez-
Coronado, "Learning from noisy information in FasArt and FasBack
neuro-fuzzy systems", Neural Networks 14(4-5), pp. 407-425, 2001.

[13] J. M. Cano-Izquierdo, M. Almonacid, M. Pinzolas, J. Ibarrola, "dFasArt:
Dynamic neural processing in FasArt model", Neural Net- works 22(4),
pp. 479-487, 2009.

[14] F. J. Badesa, R. Morales, N. Garcia-Aracil, J. M. Sabater, A. Casals, L.
Zollo, "Auto-adaptive robot-aided therapy using machine learning
techniques", Computer Methods and Programs in Biomedicine 116(2),
pp. 123-130, 2014

[15] F. J. Badesa, R. Morales, N. Garcia Aracil, J. M. Sabater, C. Perez-
Vidal, E. Fernandez, "Multimodal interfaces to improve therapeutic
outcomes in robot-assisted rehabilitation", IEEETransactions on
Systems, Man, and Cybernetics, Part C 42(6), pp. 11521158, 2012.

[16] Gonzalez-Crespo, R., S. Rios-Aguilar, R. Ferro-Escobar, and N. Torres,
"Dynamic, ecological, accessible and 3D Virtual Worlds-based Libraries
using OpenSim and Sloodle along with mobile location and NFC for
checking in", IJIMAI, vol. 1, issue Regular Issue, no. 7, pp. 62-69,
12/2012

Business and Social Behaviour Intelligence Analysis Using PSO

Vinay S Bhaskar[1], Abhishek Kumar Singh [2], Jyoti Dhruw[3,] Anubha Parashar[4], Mradula Sharma[5]

[1]*Human Resource Manager, Electro Equipment, Roorkee, India*
[2]*IIIT Allahabad*
[3]*Chhatrapati Shivaji Institute of Technology (CSIT, Durg, Chhattisgrah*
[4]*Maharshi Dayanand University, Rohtak*
[5]*MNNIT Alllahabad*

Abstract — **The goal of this paper is to elaborate swarm intelligence for business intelligence decision making and the business rules management improvement. The paper introduces the decision making model which is based on the application of Artificial Neural Networks (ANNs) and Particle Swarm Optimization (PSO) algorithm. Essentially the business spatial data illustrate the group behaviors. The swarm optimization, which is highly influenced by the behavior of creature, performs in group. The Spatial data is defined as data that is represented by 2D or 3D images. SQL Server supports only 2D images till now. As we know that location is an essential part of any organizational data as well as business data: enterprises maintain customer address lists, own property, ship goods from and to warehouses, manage transport flows among their workforce, and perform many other activities. By means to say a lot of spatial data is used and processed by enterprises, organizations and other bodies in order to make the things more visible and self-descriptive. From the experiments, we found that PSO is can facilitate the intelligence in social and business behaviour.**

Keywords — **PSO, Map, Artificial Intelligence, Geography, Optimization.**

I. INTRODUCTION

SWARM describes a behavior of an aggregate of animals of similar size and body orientation [1]. Swarm intelligence (SI) is based on the collective behavior of a group of animals. Collective intelligence emerges via grouping and communication, resulting in successful foraging (the act of searching for food and provisions) for individual in the group, for examples Bees, ants, termites, fishes, birds etc. The perform the following sequence of activity in group: Marching of ants in an army, Birds flocking in high skies, Fish school in deep waters, Foraging activity of micro-organisms.In the context of AI, SI systems are based on collective behavior of decentralized, self-organized systems [2]. Typically made up of a population of simple le agents interacting with one another locally and with their environment causing coherent functional global pattern to emerge. Distributed problem solving model without centralized control. Even with no centralized control structure dictating how individual agents should behave, local interactions between agents lead to the emergence of complex global behavior [3]. Swarms are powerful which can achieve things which no single individual could do.

An intelligent technology is the duplication of human thought process by machine. It learn from experience, interpreting ambiguities, rapid response to varying situations, applying reasoning to problem-solving and manipulating by applying knowledge, thinking and reasoning [4]. Different from traditional optimization technique, evolutionary computation techniques work on a population of potential solutions (points) of the search space. The most commonly used population-based evolutionary computation techniques is PSO [5]. It is a cost optimized solution. Organizations generate and collect large volumes of data, which they use in daily operations. Yet despite this wealth of data, many organizations have been unable to fully capitalize on its value because information implicit in the data is not easy to distinguish. However, to compete effectively today, taking advantage of high-return opportunities in a timely fashion, decision-makers must be able to identify and utilize the information. These requirements imply that an intelligent system must interact with a data warehouse and must interface with decision support systems (DSS), which are used by decision-makers in their daily activities. There is a substantial amount of empirical evidence that human intuitive judgment and decision-making can be far from optimal, and it deteriorates even further with complexity and stress. Because in many situations the quality of decisions is important, aiding the deficiencies of human judgment and decision-making has been a major focus of science throughout history [6] [7]. Disciplines such as statistics, economics, and operations research developed various methods for making rational choices. More recently, these methods, often enhanced by a variety of techniques originating from information science, cognitive psychology, and artificial intelligence, has been implemented in the form of computer programs as integrated computing environments for complex decision making. Such environments are often given the common name of decision support systems (DSS) [20] [21].

The development and deployment of managerial decision support system represents an emerging trend in the business and organizational field in which the increased application of Decision Support Systems (DSS) can be compiling by

Intelligent Systems (IS). Decision Support Systems (DSS) are a specific class of computerized information system that supports business and organizational decision-making activities [18] [19]. A properly designed DSS is an interactive software-based system intended to help decision makers compile useful information from raw data, documents, personal knowledge, and/or business models to identify and solve problems and make decisions. Competitive business pressures and a desire to leverage existing information technology investments have led many firms to explore the benefits of intelligent data management solutions such as Particle Swarm Optimization (PSO). This study proposes a new PSO (SPSO)-model based on product mix model for optimizing Constraint values as well as objective function. The formulations of the objective function for the minimization problem. This technology is designed to help businesses to finding multi objective functions, which can help to understand the purchasing behavior of their key customers, detect likely credit card or insurance claim fraud, predict probable changes in financial markets, etc. Keywords: Linear problem, Intelligent System, particle swarm optimization, simplex method. The Sql Server Spatial Database is designed to make the storage, retrieval, analysis and manipulation of spatial data easier and natural to users. Once we have data we can perform any operation easily like retrieve all data related to our concern, manipulate it as par requirement [17]. Spatial data is the main need for graphic visualization to make useful result about. It is useful to guess of localization i.e. longitude and latitude. Now we have Microsoft SQL Server 2008 which is including simple feature graphical representation of location data as location in the map by firing query for location in query results   area which was not available in the previous version of Microsoft SQL Server i.e. Microsoft SQL Server 2000 and 2005. This visualizer works with a geography column in the query results and in graph by plotting location data and if multiple location column in appearing in as a query result we can select one to visualize [22] [23] [24]. For example suppose we have a location data then we have a choice to flexible plot the diagram of the map either it is rectangle or any other polygon shape for projection purpose on graph but we are assuming out projection should not be overlaid with default projection. By this technique we can easily and very convenient overlay a graph on map if we have the table of map outline data which we can use to do UNION ALL between the row set and the row set that have the map location [8]. Spatial data is useful in lots of cases because every customer has its own address. We usually think of addresses as street, city, state, country and ZIP code and in other words spatial data can use for finding the exact position of real world entity like suppose we have the database of customer where we are storing address which not merely containing which we are supposing street, city or state but actually it is showing the latitude and longitude. As technically by address we mean part of territory which can draw by polygon for convenient we are assuming single point not a polygon and by this we can guess about longitude and latitude for the answer of query like here:

- Find the nearest branch of bank for client info.

- And who is the representative or concern person for that particular client.
- And we can also retrieve the client information within a particular boundary i.e. how many clients are there in particular organisation of any business.

We can guess client information related to position within the range and outside so it is not just maintain the branch location of our office but also allowing to put information of client related to us. To make whole system and process convenient, reliable, to speedup of process, robust by storing data and analyzed data and get information and by exchanging information we can assure all the above mention benefit in our work. As we know that reliability, speed and robustness is only the required feature; here we will consider. Another important aspect or we can say the further advancement of spatial techniques is the visualization of spatial data using maps. The methods used for retrieval problem [9] [10], human activity and face recognition problem [11] [12], location estimation, [13] and scalable replica estimation problem [14] can also be integrated with proposed PSO based approach. After all, location information is all about maps, and to paraphrase a common saying, a map is certainly worth 1,000 words. A better choice is to use a visualizer that provides map overlay by default [15] [16]. SQL Server Studio 2008 use a map overlay for showing spatial data. Some other approaches are also used for similar task [25] [26] [27] [28]. The Advantages of proposed method are as follows: (1) Adaptability - Self-organizing, (2) Robustness - Ability to find a new solution if the current solution becomes invalid, (3) Reliability - Agents can be added or removed without disturbing behavior of the total system because of the distributed nature, (4) Simplicity, and (5) No central control. The rest of the paper is organized in further four section: section 2 discuss some background concepts which are used in our problem such as spatial data, visulizers and spatial index; section 3 introduced the proposed methodology of business intelligence using the concept of particle swarm optimization; section 4 shows some practical application of introduced work with result; finally section 5 conclude the paper with future remark of the paper.

II. BACKGROUND CONCEPTS

A. Spatial data

Spatial data is data which is use for finding the position of the real world entity like we have to find the position of sea sore, restaurant, hotel, tourist palace, historical important location and some territory. In spatial database is the combination of all the data types, statics and indexing of location. For fast accessing, the location information from spatial database done by spatial function and spatial indexing. We can retrieve it through Sql.

```
    DECLARE  @addr  nvarchar(256)  =  'Some
sample address, City, State, Zip';
    DECLARE @addr_as_xy nvarchar(30);
    DECLARE @g geography;
    SET @addr_as_xy = dbo.Geocoder(@addr);
    SET                                    @g=
geography::STPointFromText(@addr_as_xy,
4326);
```

Fig. 1. Code for location initialization

We have an instance of a location type with a sql variable declaration (@p position) or a column of table, and we have a number of way to initialize data type let's us take an example we have geographical data type who is using to show the instance of location point, the easier way to do it by use of STPointfromText() method of the location type. The STPointFromText() method is using for SRID (spatial reference identifier) with other feature textual representation of point that is POINT(x,y) in open Geospatial boundary. SRID identifier is the spatial reference system for use of either shape of earth whether flat or round mapping and it is enough to know the MapPoint geocoder Web Service uses coordinates of GPS to related to SRID 4326 so for location initialization our code will look something like in Figure 1:

B. Visualizers

Microsoft SQL Server 2008 provides a feature to visualize location result in either query result area or window. Microsoft SQL Server 2008 shows the spatial data as a graph plot in query result area to represent the longitude and latitude related to geography and we can select one column if we have lot of spatial column appearing in same time by query result. And column to display should be in SQL Server binary format, the ToString() method or STAsText() method not work with visualizer.

C. Spatial Indexes

After growing our enterprise to calculate the position between client and every entrepreneur and every salesman and every client might be too slow. Microsoft SQL Server 2008 has also spatial indexing. And here spatial indexing is based on ordinary B-tree index to make it faster like as relational indexes in SQL Server 2000 and 2005.If we have geographical data type, then we are dividing the entire globe into hemisphere and projecting each hemisphere onto a plane. And if we have geometrical data type, because we are specifying our own rectangular coordinate system, we can specify the boundaries that our spatial index covers the whole area. To return to the customer system, you could define a spatial index on the geog column in your customer table with the following data definition language (DDL):

```
CREATE SPATIAL INDEX cust_geog_idx
ON dbo.customer(geog)
```

GRIDS
=(LEVEL1=HIGH,LEVEL2=HIGH,LEVEL3=HIGH,LEVEL4=HIGH)).

III. METHODOLOGY

A. Swarm inspired methods

Particle Swarm Optimization (PSO): PSO is a population based stochastic optimization technique developed by Eberhart and Kennedy in 1995. It is inspired by social behaviour of flocks of birds and school of fish. It is a set of agents (similar to ants), search in parallel for good solutions and co-operate through the pheromone-mediated indirect method of communication. They belong to a class of meta-heuristics. These systems started with their use in the Travelling Salesman Problem (TSP). They have applications to practical problems faced in business and industrial environments. The evolution of computational paradigm for an ant colony intelligent system (ACIS) is being used as an intelligent tool to help researchers solve many problems in areas of science and technology.

Particle Swarm Intelligent Systems: Originated with the idea to simulate the unpredictable choreography of a bird flock with Nearest-neighbour velocity matching, Multi-dimensional search, Acceleration by distance, and Elimination of ancillary variables. PSO shares many similarities with Genetic Algorithms (GA). The system is initialized with a population of random solutions (called *particles*) and searches for optima by updating generations. Each particle is assigned a randomized velocity. Particles fly around in a multidimensional search space or problem space by following the current optimum particles. However, unlike GA, PSO has no evolution operators such as crossover and mutation. Compared to GA, the advantages of PSO are that it is easy to implement and there are few parameters to adjust. Each particle adjusts its position according to its own experience and the experience of a neighboring particle. Particle keeps track of its co-ordinates in the problem space which are associated with the best solution/ fitness achieved so far along with the fitness value (*pbest ← partcle best*). Overall best value obtained so far is also tracked by the global version of the particle optimizer along with its location (*gbest*). There are two versions exist (according to acceleration): (1) Global - At each time step, the particle changes its velocity (*accelerates*) and moves towards its **pbest** and **gbest** and (2) Local - In addition to **pbest**, each particle also keeps track of the best solution (**lbest/nbest** – neighbour best) attained within a local topological neighbourhood of the particle. The acceleration thus depends on **pbest, lbest**, and **gbest**.

B. Problem solution

Conceptual framework of sense making (Psychological Systems): A psychological system can be thought of as an "information-processing" function. We measure psychological systems by identifying points in psychological space. Usually the psychological space is considered to be multidimensional.

A swarm is a large number of homogenous, simple agents interacting locally among themselves, and their environment, with no central control to allow a global interesting behavior to emerge. Swarm-based algorithms have recently emerged as a family of nature-inspired, population-based algorithms that are capable of producing low cost, fast, and robust solutions to several complex problems. This indirect type of interaction is referred to as stigmergy, which essentially means communication through the environment.

"Philosophical Leaps" Required:
  i. Individual minds = a point in space
  ii. Multiple individuals can be plotted in a set of coordinates
  iii. Measuring the individuals result in a "population of points"
  iv. Individuals near each other imply that they are similar
  v. Some areas of space are better than others Location.

Applying Social Psychology: Individuals (points) tend to move towards each other and influence each other. This is why; individuals want to be in agreement with their neighbors. Individuals (points) are influenced by their previous actions/behaviors and the success achieved by their neighbors. Figure 2 illustrates the working algorithm of particle swarm optimization. First the particle is initialized randomly. Then for each particle a fitness value is calculated. If the current fitness value is better than previous personal best then personnel based is set to current fitness value. The global best is also updated with the best fitness value. After updating the personnel best and global best, particle velocity is calculated using equation (a) of Figure 3 and [particle position is also updated using equation (b) of Figure 3. These steps are repeated until the convergence criteria is met (i.e. optimized solution or maximum iteration).

IV. Practical Work and Results

Human being is a social animal and one of intelligent creation of god. The Human being whose behavior is strongly inspired by and govern my group activity like some animal fish schooling, bird flocking swam optimization. Whose behavior is influence by group .As there is a population which has their own knowledge of intelligence and best fit of cost of their daily need but if some trend can show them a different need and arise some tread which can motivate or can given some general scene about our prediction. Particle Swarm is an evolutionary computation based technique. There is a substantial amount of empirical evidence that human intuitive judgment and decision-making can be far from optimal, and it deteriorates even further with complexity and stress. Because in many situations the quality of decisions is important, aiding the deficiencies of human judgment and decision-making has been a major focus of science throughout history. Disciplines such as statistics, economics, and operations research developed various methods for making rational choices. More recently, these methods, often enhanced by a variety of techniques originating from information science, cognitive

psychology, and artificial intelligence, has been implemented in the form of computer programs as integrated computing environments for complex decision making. Such environments are often given the common name of decision support systems (DSS).

```
For each particle
     Initialize particle
END

Do
   For each particle
        Calculate fitness value
        If the fitness value is better than its peronal best
        set current value as the new pBest
   End

   Choose the particle with the best fitness value of all as gBest
   For each particle
        Calculate particle velocity according equation (a)
        Update particle position according equation (b)
   End
While maximum iterations or minimum error criteria is not attained
```

Fig. 2. Working algorithm of PSO

```
Equation (a)
v[] = c0 *v[]
    + c1 * rand() * (pbest[] - present[])
    + c2 * rand() * (gbest[] - present[])
(in the original method, c0=1, but many
   researchers now play with this parameter)

Equation (b)
present[] = present[] + v[]
```

Fig. 3. Velocity updating of a swarm in PSO

A PSO based algorithm is developed to define the bi-level pricing model. Experiments illustrate that thus PSO based algorithm can achieve a profit increase for buyers or vendors, if they are treated as leader under some situation (see Figure 4).

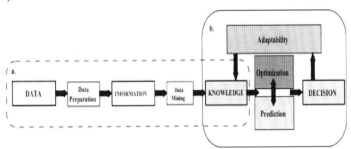

Fig. 4. PSO based Algorithm

Figure 5 shows points representing a set of more than 700 cities from the Mondial database in the SQL Server Management Studio visualizer.

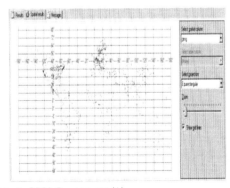

Fig. 5. Output of SQL Server query (A)

Following are the two SQL server queries and its output.
The SQL Server query (A): (see output in Figure 5)
SELECT geog, name
FROM Mondial.dbo.city
WHERE geog IS NOT NULL
The SQL Server query (B): (see output in Figure 6)
SELECT geo, name
FROM Mondial.dbo.cityname
WHERE geo IS NOT NULL
UNION ALL
SELECT geo, cntry_name
FROM SpatialSamples.dbo.cntry

An even better choice is to use a commercial or shareware visualizer that provides map overlay by default, as shown in Figure 5. We see that the Spatial Results tab in MS SQL Server 2008 shows a rowset of more than 600 points with a map overlay.

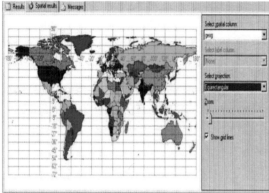

Fig. 6. Output of SQL Server query (B)

A. Application to Common Table Expression (CTE)

A CTE can be thought of as a temporary result set and are similar to a derived table in that it is not stored as an object and lasts only for the duration of the query. A CTE is generally considered to be more readable than a derived table and does not require the extra effort of declaring a Temp Table while providing the same benefits to the user. However; a CTE is more powerful than a derived table as it can also be self-referencing, or even referenced multiple times in the same query.

The basic syntax structure for a CTE is shown below:
WITH MyCTE
AS (SELECT EmpID, FirstName, LastName, ManagerID
FROM Employee
WHERE ManagerID IS NULL)
SELECT *
FROM MyCTE
Building a Recursive CTE

In the following examples, we will show how to harness the power of a recursive CTE query by fulfilling a common business requirement, retrieving hierarchical data. By the time the final query is complete you will be able to easily determine how many levels from the top executive each employee is. A recursive CTE requires four elements in order to work properly.

1. Anchor query (runs once and the results 'seed' the Recursive query)
2. Recursive query (runs multiple times and is the criteria for the remaining results)
3. UNION ALL statement to bind the Anchor and Recursive queries together.
4. INNER JOIN statement to bind the Recursive query to the results of the CTE.

The syntax structure is as follows,
WITH MyCTE
AS (SELECT EmpID, FirstName, LastName, ManagerID
FROM Employee
WHERE ManagerID IS NULL
UNION ALL
SELECT EmpID, FirstName, LastName, ManagerID
FROM Employee
INNER
JOIN MyCTE ON Employee.ManagerID = MyCTE.EmpID
WHERE Employee.ManagerID IS NOT   NULL   )
SELECT *
FROM MyCTE.

V. CONCLUDING REMARKS

The above literature covers the spatial data and tools that are used to tackle the visualization aspect of spatial database. The tools include SQL SERVER 2008. In addition, the different concepts that these tools use are also mentioned. The effective and advanced applications can be developed using the features of SQL SERVER Spatial like ship tracking system and city bus management system.

REFERENCES

[1] A. Janecek, T. Jordan and F. B. Lima-Neto, "Agent-Based Social Simulation and PSO," *Advances in Swarm Intelligence*. Springer Berlin Heidelberg, pp. 63-73, 2013.

[2] J. Kennedy, "Particle swarm optimization," In *Encyclopedia of Machine Learning*, Springer US, pp. 760-766, 2010.

[3] M. G. Epitropakis, P. P.Vassilis and N. V. Michael, "Evolving cognitive and social experience in particle swarm optimization through differential evolution," *IEEE Congress on Evolutionary Computation (CEC)*, 2010.

[4] P. Soni and M. Choudhary, "Hybrid Computational Intelligence for Optimization Based On PSO and DE," *International Journal of Advanced Research in Computer Engineering & Technology*, pp-265, 2012.

[5] H. Ahmed and G. Janice, "*Swarm Intelligence: Concepts, Models and Applications*," Technical Report, 2012-585. Queen's University, Kingston, Ontario, Canada K7L3N6, 2012.

[6] S.R. Dubey and A.S. Jalal, "Robust Approach for Fruit and Vegetable Classification", *Procedia Engineering*, 38, pp. 3449-3453, 2012.

[7] A. E. Yilmaz, "Swarm Behavior of the Electromagnetics Community as regards Using Swarm Intelligence in their Research Studies," *Acta Polytechnica Hungarica*, 2010.

[8] S.R. Dubey and A.S. Jalal, "Detection and Classification of Apple Fruit Diseases Using Complete Local Binary Patterns", In *Third International Conference on Computer and Communication Technology*, pp. 346-351, 2012.

[9] J. P. Gupta, N. Singh, P. Dixit, V. B. Semwal, and S. R. Dubey, "Human Activity Recognition using Gait Pattern," *International Journal of Computer Vision and Image Processing*, vol. 3, no. 3, pp. 31 – 53, 2013.

[10] M. Sati, V. Vikash, V. Bijalwan, P. Kumari, M. Raj, M. Balodhi, P. Gairola and V.B. Semwal, "A fault-tolerant mobile computing model based on scalable replica", *International Journal of Interactive Multimedia and Artificial Intelligence*, 2014.

[11] K.K. Susheel, V.B. Semwal and R.C. Tripathi, "Real time face recognition using adaboost improved fast PCA algorithm," *arXiv preprint arXiv:1108.1353* (2011).

[12] K.S. Kumar, V.B. Semwal, S. Prasad and R.C. Tripathi, "Generating 3D Model Using 2D Images of an Object," *International Journal of Engineering Science*, 2011.

[13] N. Singh, S.R. Dubey, P. Dixit and J.P. Gupta, "Semantic Image Retrieval by Combining Color, Texture and Shape Features," *In the Proceedings of the International Conference on Computing Sciences*, pp. 116-120, 2012.

[14] V.B. Semwal, V.B. Semwal, M. Sati and S. Verma, "Accurate location estimation of moving object in Wireless Sensor network," *International Journal of Interactive Multimedia and Artificial Intelligence*, vol. 1, no. 4, pp. 71-75, 2011.

[15] S.R. Dubey and A.S. Jalal, "Adapted Approach for Fruit Disease Identification using Images," *International Journal of Computer Vision and Image Processing*, vol. 2, no. 3, pp. 44-58, 2012.

[16] S. Singh and V. Bijalwan, "Design Of Wireless Sensor Network Node On Zigbee For Water Level Detection", Vol. 3, No. 8, 2013.

[17] A. Bijalwan and V. Bijalwan, "Examining the Crimninology using Network Forensic", *National Conference USCSTC*, 2013.

[18] V. Bijalwan, V. Kumar, P. Kumari and J. Pascual, "KNN based Machine Learning Approach for Text and Document Mining", *International Journal of Database Theory and Application*, Vol. 7, No. 1, pp. 61-70, 2014.

[19] P. Kumari and V. Pareek, "RAKSHITA- A Novel web based Approach for Protecting Digital Copyrights Using Public Key Digital Watermarking and Human Fingerprints", *International conference on methods and models in computer science*, 2010.

[20] P. Kumari and A. Vaish, "Instant Face detection and attributes recognition" *International Journal of Advanced Computer Science and Applications*, 2011.

[21] P. Kumari and A. Vaish, "A Comparative study of Machine Learning algorithms for Emotion State Recognition through Physiological signal", *Advances in Intelligent Systems and Computing*, Vol. 236, 2013.

[22] P. Kumari and A. Vaish, "Brainwave's Energy feature Extraction using wavelet Transform", proceeding of IEEE SCEECS, 2014.

[23] V.B. Semwal, K.S. Kumar, V.S. Bhaskar and M. Sati, "Accurate location estimation of moving object with energy constraint & adaptive update algorithms to save data", *arXiv preprint arXiv:1108.1321*, 2011.

[24] J.P. Espada et al., "Virtual Objects on the Internet of Things", *International Journal of Interactive Multimedia and Artificial Intelligence*, 2011.

[25] R.G. Crespo, S.R. Aguilar, R.F. Escobar and N. Torres, "Dynamic, ecological, accessible and 3D Virtual Worlds-based Libraries using OpenSim and Sloodle along with mobile location and NFC for checking in", *International Journal of Interactive Multimedia & Artificial Intelligence*, Vol. 1, No. 7, 2012.

[26] K.S. Kumar et al, "Sports Video Summarization using Priority Curve Algorithm", *International Journal on Computer Science & Engineering*, 2010.

[27] R.G. Crespo et al., "Use of ARIMA mathematical analysis to model the implementation of expert system courses by means of free software OpenSim and Sloodle platforms in virtual university campuses", *Expert Systems with Applications*, Vol. 40, No. 18, pp. 7381-7390, 2013.

[28] S.R. Dubey, P. Dixit, N. Singh, and J.P. Gupta, "Infected fruit part detection using K-means clustering segmentation technique", *International Journal of Artificial Intelligence and Interactive Multimedia*, Vol. 2, No. 2, 2013.

Vinay S. Bhaskar has been severed as a PCC member in several International conferences and Journals. He is graduated from IIMS pune and serving birla tyre as HR&PR manager. Previously he served the organization named ITc, Malva Machine Tool etc.

Abhishek Kumar Singh is presently working as Software Engineer, Honeybell, India. He completed his M.Tech form Indian Institute of Information Technology, Allahabad, his major research work Interest in Image Processing, computer sensor network & Pattern Recognition.

Jyoti Dhruw presently working as Assistant Professor, India. She is B.Tech from *CSIT, Durg, Chhattisgrah* and pursing M.Tech from NITTR Chandigrah. Her major research work Interest in Image Processing, Sensor Network, Design and Analysis of Algorithm, Data Structure.

Anubha Parashar received her B.Tech in Computer Science and Engineering from [4]*Maharshi Dayanand University, Rohtak*. Her research interests include Pattern recognition, Cloud Computing, Big Data and Distributed Database.

Mradula Sharma is currently working as assistant professor at JERC, Jaipur and she completed her M.tech. from MNNIT Allahabad. Her majors are data structure, business intelligency.

## 5

Global Collective Intelligence in Technological Societies: as a result of Collaborative Knowledge in combination with Artificial Intelligence

Juan Carlos Piedra Calderón, J. Javier Rainer

Universidad Pontificia de Salamanca, Spain

Abstract — **The big influence of Information and Communication Technologies (ICT), especially in area of construction of Technological Societies has generated big social changes. That is visible in the way of relating to people in different environments. These changes have the possibility to expand the frontiers of knowledge through sharing and cooperation. That has meaning the inherently creation of a new form of Collaborative Knowledge. The potential of this Collaborative Knowledge has been given through ICT in combination with Artificial Intelligence processes, from where is obtained a Collective Knowledge. When this kind of knowledge is shared, it gives the place to the Global Collective Intelligence.**

Keywords — **Collective intelligence, knowledge managenemt, artificial intelligence, intelligent systems, collaborative multimedia, ICT.**

I. INTRODUCTION

The inclusion of the Technology in normal live has meaning big changes in society. If ones can see to the past through ICT, in one minute could see: more than eleven millions of sending instant messages, more than fifty eight shopping web transaction, more than twenty thousand app downloads for mobile, more than six hundred and fifty new smartphone functioning, more than twenty four hours in video are uploaded in YouTube, more than three thousand tweets are sending, more than two millions searches in google and many more [1].

The use of ICT has been the key factor through the use of information and knowledge has introduced to society in the way to conform part of the Technological Societies. In fact, the European and Information Global Society report [2], talks about how new technologies, telecommunication and information has made an important global revolution which is comparable or even superior to the industrial revolution. In this new revolution, knowledge is recognizing as a technical factor that has made transformations in social, economic, political and institutional dimension.

As a result of this technological revolution and the network telecommunication advances has created a necessity to introduce new concepts and processes. The most important are collaboration, cooperation and sharing information and knowledge with the objective to give them an added value through acquisition, absorption, processing and communication of these elements [3]. This encouraged the introduction of two growth technical and economic factors which are innovation and investigation. That when both are enriched by continuous learning processes and once led to a global society forms a *Collective Intelligence*.

This concept is also directly linked to some dimensions of human development, such as: social, cultural, economic, political, technological and environmental. That produces institutional and plural perspectives changes in development of dynamism of the global society changes [4]. In fact, members of countries in the World Summit of Information Society[9] emphasize that the most important thing to consider is the commitment and desire to build a people-center society, focused in a global technological integration with an orientation to help and to a sustainable develop. Being important creation, search, use, and sharing of information and knowledge, creating a mutual participation on communities and people to help improve the quality of life [4].

II. DIGITAL AND COLLABORATIVE LEARNING

Every knowledge form inside Technological Societies in combination with the trend to collaborate and to share, shows learning as an important factor in the assimilation and transmission of an improved knowledge taking from information and knowledge received. Digital and Collaborative learning is superior than traditional learning in the way that a person can access and learn better from his own contents and the other people that share their more specific information and knowledge [5].

This create a sense of *global collaborative learning* where everyone has the same level to learn and to access to information in every place in the world, that means for example that an African young can access to the same knowledge that other young that is studying in the best university [6]. People from more collaborative environments learn more complex technological abilities with great facility and familiarity [7]. For this reason educative model built through more collaborative environments help to develop more creativity and potential in people which are growing up in more technicians environments [8][9].

This fundamental role of ICT in this new form of learning is based in a tendency toward "learning to learn" [10], that through adaptive methods and a greater appreciation of knowledge and collaboration between individuals [11]. It will be of great contribution to be transmitted, shared and especially compared to other thoughts, scientists and with Artificial Intelligence systems that process natural language, in the way to generate true global solution shared. These gradually improve the perception of complexity (in positive sense) of life in this Technological society.

One way to donate potential to this kind of collaborative learning is through the use of methodologies that strategically combine traditional learning techniques with new learning techniques based in new knowledge creation through Artificial Intelligence technics as intelligence tutorial systems that do processes allowing form an own strategy and molds as other Artificial Intelligence systems to learning needs. Being this interaction very propitious to conform the *collaborative learning* [12].

III. COLLABORATIVE KNOWLEDGE

There is no doubt that the best promoter of *collaborative knowledge* has been telecommunications networks. What at first had a useful of interchange and interconnection finally has being a space where collaboration between users and intelligent systems has become in a growing and daily trend. This is because adaptive learning of Artificial Intelligence through machine learning systems join with human learning has created a new model of collaborative learning based in cooperation between individual and devices [13], which helps to acquire and to build new knowledge giving potential development of new technologies and that helps to build a new *collaborative knowledge*.

At an organizational level this vision of a collaborative society allows the development of new knowledge in groups that function as knowledge production networks, which allows the creation of methodologies that encourage cooperative working form, assuming responsibility on self-learning and in knowledge transmission [14]. Thanks to connectivity this network society is itself a communication system globalized that have the capacity to join people from different cultures and languages through one and unique technological architecture [15].

Many tools used in this moment have been designed in a collaborative way, which aided by Artificial Intelligence processes such as intelligence systems, expert systems and recognition systems, based in knowledge engineering technics, obtaining a new assessment and dimension of this

collaborative knowledge that is capable to increase technology experience [16]. Many of these tools have taken the development to a new way of perception of the new Semantic Web environment and App giving a way to the new construction of Cloud computing.

TABLE I
TRANSMISSION TYPE OF KNOWLEDGE

Knowledge element	Transmission Type
Individual Knowledge	One way
Collaborative Knowledge	Biderectional
Collective Knowledge	Bidirectonal
Cloud Contribution	One way
AI Contribution	Bidirectional

The thought called "knowledge paradox" says that according more knowledge is developed, it will lose its current value, therefore, it will be necessary creating new concepts such as *technological wisdom*. That means every new concept will be related with concepts in the ICT age based in a collective wisdom, and will be used to the growth of society [17], follow the way to the global technical revolution.

IV. COLLECTIVE KNOWLEDGE

This technological age is expanding through combination of social, human and technological factors. Mainly through two purely intellectual processes: knowledge and intelligence. Where collaboration and cooperation in large scale, in union with interconnection that allows the interchange of these intellectual elements, conform a global network of knowledge, that are concentrate in form as a greater knowledge inside the *global brain* where the thought of every person works as a neuron and the synapses accurse through Artificial Intelligences technics as Bayesian networking and fuzzy logic, directly on the Cloud.

A scientific study of the Technical Institute of Massachusetts in EEUU, says that the more efficient work is "group work". That is because collective knowledge involves flexibility in allocating activities, and individual and group participation to give solution to problems. These allows the creation of a sensitivity social dynamic among team members. The result of these dynamics shows the existence of a collective intelligence as a joint ability, which is defined by the same ability of the individual intelligence and his relations with others [18].

This does not mean the discovery of collective knowledge concept, because it have already been used for long time in teams, however, is in the technological age, thanks to the Artificial Intelligence systems and ICT when it really started to have a real and potential meaning. Being the potential of this collective intelligence the creation of new knowledge networks [18], where an important element is the complexity that has arrived these knowledge networks as a collaborative system that interconnects equal intelligence and are implicated with sharing and developing of the new knowledge. This has changed the way to work in three types of knowledge networks: investigation, business and education [13].

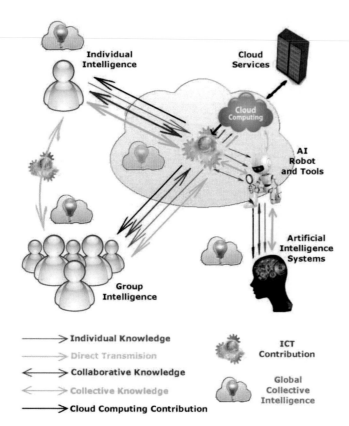

Fig. 1. Global Collective Intelligence.

Until few years ago, wisdom was concentrated and represented just by lone geniuses, but now it is represented and performed by collaborating people which sharing their knowledge arrive to an enriched knowledge that generated *collective intelligence*. That does not mean that there is no longer talented people and geniuses, but ICT evolution allows global participation creates the possibility of new developments, in short term, through this new technical-social element, as is *global collective intelligence*, which allows the creation of global and community wisdom [17].

All of these have transform human mindset from individual thinking to global thinking [20] which allows build a new intellectual level called *global collective intelligence*. These new kind of collective intelligence is giving by the direct relationship between normal collective knowledge processes with aids of Artificial Intelligence systems, in addition to ICT technologies [31].

V. ARTIFICIAL INTELLIGENCE CONTRIBUTION

Artificial Intelligence has been presented as a desire to get a better comprehension of human behavior through multidisciplinary information processes that involves complex aspects of own people cognitions and social processes that lead to acquire knowledge through collaborative processes [21]. Also the desire of imitate cognitive human behavior has made that in this half of century of application of Artificial

Intelligence, it has passed from simple theories and assumptions to have intelligent systems that follow algorithms created from logical models. Which with the help of different engineering techniques increasing the resemblance of the complex human thought.

Inside of ICT field, Artificial Intelligence has contributed significantly in last years in conformation and concretion of virtualization tools that give a delocalization service in real time. For this it has become very popular the use of Cloud Computing [22], which allows to cover the necessities of software and web services demand through the Cloud, in a bigger scale and lower cost that invest in an own technical infrastructure.

The creation of a collaborative platform can helps to collective absorption of the risk and a greater flexibility to give effectively solutions to the market [23]. Cloud Computing has allowed developing of a digital economy, which has allowed organization to obtain a key element over global economy. This is to increase the competitiveness and other benefits as: improve demand attention on infrastructure and services, stimulating activity and guarantee sustainability, process optimization, creating new market opportunities, business stability, and return of investment, among others [24].

The interaction between business, society and Technology though the creation, use and storage of large amounts of multimedia information inside the *Big Global Data* [10], which will need more and more sophisticated Artificial Intelligence Systems and equipped with operational intelligence and data mining, which help to have a faster and personalized access to all information helped by knowledge engineering [25]. And likewise through intelligent agents it is possible to learn to recognize patterns to obtain suggestions from access information systems [26], which help to increase in collaborative knowledge and the growth in collective intelligence.

TABLE II
ARTIFICIAL INTELLIGENCE SYSTEMS THAT CONTRIBUTE TO THE CREATION OF
GLOBAL COLLECTIVE KNOWLEDGE

AI System	Field
Machine Learning	Automatic Learning
Tutorial Systems	Learning Help
Knowledge Engineering	Expert Systems Develop
Bayesian Networks	Networking Assignation
Computational Linguistic	Voice Recognizing
Natural language Processing	Communication
Data Mining	Data Exploration
Software Agents	Information Treatment
Fuzzy Logic	Decision-making
Operational Intelligence	Real Time Information Management

VI. COLLABORATIVE MULTIMEDIA IMPORTANCE

In the past years, the arrival of mature has had both Cloud Computing and Smartphone technologies have had a big

10Big Global Data is a concept of a large global database.

influence in society. Which allowed to introduce agile changes enhanced by the large interconnection between people and technologies [27]. The combination of digital social media with the set of Artificial Intelligence techniques as a computational linguistic and natural languages processing, integrated in digital devices and app with transmission and communication networks have changed the way that people socialize. Relationships include a new compromise concept in communication [28], reflecting a better communication, comprehension quality and optimizing knowledge exchange [29].

Maybe it is here, where more Artificial Intelligence techniques as a software agents have been used to process all collaborative knowledge given by multimedia through tools as robots applied to the Cloud, expert and predictive tools that attempt to predict knowledge preferences, which joined with patterns recognized tools can suggest the best information options obtaining a more dynamic knowledge [30]. This helps to grow in a more *Collaborative Multimedia* experience that becomes more and more in a collective knowledge storage tool from which it is possible to learn in a global and collaborative way.

VII. CONCLUSION

The contribution received by the human elements as knowledge and intelligence, that have been maximize by ICT and their big influence in Technological Societies have begun to transcend human frontiers. The emergence and maturation of Artificial Intelligence has made human individual and collective cognitive elements creates and improves a new enriched knowledge. Which when it can be shared through communication network and processed by collaborative tools, generates an individual intelligence.

This individual intelligence sharing with others and transmitted as a Collaborative Knowledge and also process by Artificial Intelligence tools form a new Collective Intelligence that thanks to telecommunication networks becomes into a *Global Collective Intelligence.*

REFERENCES

[1] Ericsson. (2011). *Networked Society – Shaping Ideas* [Online]. Ericsson Channel. Available: http://www.youtube.com/watch?NR=1&v=-tHoh2ilSQs&feature=endscreen. [03/12/12]

[2] European Commission. (1994). *Europe and the Global Information Society* [Online]. Report of European Commission. Luxemburg. pp. 5 – 40. Available: http://aei.pitt.edu/1199/1/info_society_bangeman_report.pdf. [30/09/13]

[3] Lévy, P. (2004). *Inteligencia Colectiva: Por una Antropología del Ciberespacio* [Online]. Traducción por Organización Panamericana de la Salud. Available: http://inteligenciacolectiva.bvsalud.org/public/documents/pdf/es/inteligenciaColectiva.pdf. [30/09/13]

[4] Torres, R M. (2005). *Sociedad De La Información / Sociedad Del Conocimiento* [Online]. Universidad de Barcelona. pp. 1 – 3. Available: http://www.ub.edu/prometheus21/articulos/obsciberprome/socinfsocon.pdf. [27/12/12]

[5] Cisco. (2012). *Collaborative Learning Inside the Classroom* [Online]. Cisco Channel. Available: http://www.youtube.com/watch?v=gaLzoc3MhG0. [10/12/12]

[6] Ericsson. (2012). *Learning & education – the future of learning* [Online]. Portal Web Available: Ericsson. http://www.ericsson.com/thinkingahead/networked_society/learning_education. [10/12/12]

[7] Vázquez N. & Alonso V. & Sernández A. & Santos M & Rodrigo C. (2011). *Replicación de Sistemas Virtualizados para la aplicación de Servivios en un Entorno Virtual Multiusuario en la UNED* [Online]. Revista Boletín de la Red Nacional de I+D RedIRIS. Nº 90. pp. 55 – 62. Available: http://www.rediris.es/difusion/publicaciones/boletin/90/ponencia8.B.pdf. [30/09/13]

[8] Ericsson. (2010). *A Vision Of A 2015 Multimedia Experience* [Online]. Ericsson Channel. Available: http://www.youtube.com/watch?feature=endscreen&NR=1&v=uJpr-dpLm8w. [01/12/12]

[9] Ericsson. (2011a). *Get ready to join the ride towards a networked society!* [Online]. Ericsson Channel. Available: http://www.youtube.com/watch?v=_aET8-JTRI. [12/12/12]

[10] Coursera. (2012). *E-Learning And Digital Cultures* [Online]. Portal Web de Coursera. Sección Courses. Available: https://www.coursera.org/course/edc. [19/12/12]

[11] Piattini V, M. (2009). *Pasado, Presente y Futuro de la Fabricación de Software.* Lección inaugural del solemne acto de apertura del curso 2009/2010 de la Universidad de Castilla - La Mancha. pp. 5 – 38.

[12] Urrietavizcaya L, M. (2001). *Sistemas Inteligentes en el ámbito de la Educación* [Online]. Revista Iberoamericana de Inteligencia Artificial. Vol 5. Nº 12. ISSN-e: 1988-3064. Available: http://cabrillo.lsi.uned.es:8080/aepia/Uploads/12/132.pdf. [30/09/13]

[13] Valentín L-, Carrasco A, Konya K, Burgos D. (2013). *Emerging Technologies Landscape on Education. A review.* International Journal of Interactive Multimedia and Artificial Intelligenece (IJIMAI).Vol.2 Special Issue on Improvements in Information Systems and Technologies pp. 55-70. DOI: 10.9781/ijimai.2013.238.

[14] Moreno C, M. (2005). *Comunidades de la Sociedad del Aprendizaje* [Online]. Universidad de Guadalajara. pp. 3 – 6. Available: http://mail.udgvirtual.udg.mx/biblioteca/bitstream/123456789/180/1/XEI-Comunidades.pdf. [14/01/13]

[15] Castells, M. & Cardoso, G. (2005). *The Network Society From Knowledge to Policy.* Center for Transatlantic Relations. Washington, DC. pp. 3 – 5.

[16] García F, R. (2008). *Sistemas Basados en Tecnologías del Conocimiento para Entornos de Servicios Web Semánticos* [Online]. Tesis Doctoral. Universidad de Murcia. pp. 50 – 90. Available: http://hdl.handle.net/10201/154. [30/09/13]

[17] Tasaka, H. (2009). *La paradoja de la sociedad del conocimiento* [Online]. Entrevista en Infonomiatv. Available: http://www.youtube.com/watch?v=FzbO8NdD86g. [23/12/12]

[18] Malone, T W. (2010). *Collective Intelligence* [Online]. MITNewsOffice Channel. Available: http://www.tendencias21.net/Demostrada-la-existencia-de-la-inteligencia-colectiva_a4929.html. [06/01/13]

[19] Turiera, T. (2007). Conversando Con Hiroshi Tasaki [Online]. Portal Web Infonomia. http://www.infonomia.com/if/articulo.php?id=111&if=54. [08/01/2013]

[20] Sánchez B, J M. (2011). *La Era De La Infancia: Una Nueva Ética Del Futuro* [Online]. Web La infancia y la Sociedad del Conocimiento. Available: http://infanciasociedadconocimiento.blogspot.fr/2011/11/la-era-de-la-infancia-una-nueva-etica.html. [09/01/13]

[21] Escolano R, F. & Cazorla Q, M A. & Alfonso G, M I. & Colomina P, O. & Lozano O, M A. (2003). Inteligencia Artificial: Modelos, Técnicas y Áreas de Aplicación. Homson Ediciones Spain. Parainfo S.A. pp. Prólogo, 1 – 7. ISBN: 84-9732-183-9.

[22] Buckley, D. & Kaliski, B. & O'Sullivan, B. &. Artificial Intelligence for Data Center management and Cloud Computing. AAAI Workshop Journal. pp. 44. ISBN: 978-1-57735-524-11-08.

[23] Oxford Economics. (2011). *The New Digital Economy – How It Will Transform Business* [Online]. Oxford Economics, At&T, PwC, Cisco, Citi, Sap. pp. 5 – 8. Available: http://www.pwc.com/gx/en/technology/publications/assets/the-new-digital-economy.pdf. [16/03/13]

[24] Cámara de Comercio España. (2012). *SPAIN 2020: La Economía*

Digital, Clave Para Retomar El Crecimiento [Online]. Cámara de Comercio de EE en España. Available: http://www.amchamspain.com/sites/default/files/La%20Econom%C3% ADa%20Digital%20clave%20para%20el%20crecimiento.pdf. [17/03/13]

[25] Imhoff., C. (2013). Converging Technologies: Real-Time Business Intelligence and Big Data [Online]. Intelligent Solution, Inc. Available: http://www.vitria.com/pdf/WP-Extending-Data-Warehouse-Architecture.pdf?submissionGuid=6a4c4eac-fe3b-4f16-bf4e-4fd4a208e98e. [01/10/13]

[26] Ferraté T. (2013). *The Near Future of Robotics: Cloud Robotics* [Online]. Portal Web de Robotica Educativa y Personal. Available: http://www.robotica-personal.es/2013/04/the-near-future-of-robotics-cloud.html. [30/09/13]

[27] Ericsson. (2010a). *Operator Revenue Growth* [Online]. Ericsson Chanel. Available: http://www.youtube.com/watch?v=SKhb2cyDdLU. [12/12/12]

[28] Ericsson. (2012a). *Thinking Cities Networked Society* [Online]. Ericsson Chanel. Available: http://www.youtube.com/watch?v=6ctxP6Dp8Bk. [12/12/12]

[29] Corningin. (2012). *A Day Made of Glass 2: Unpacked. The Story Behind Corning's Vision* [Online]. Corningin Corporated Channel. Available: http://www.youtube.com/watch?v=X-GXO_urMow. [13/12/12]

[30] Ferraté T. (2012). *Cloud Robotics New Paradigm is Near* [Online]. Portal Web de Robotica Educativa y Personal. Available: http://www.robotica-personal.es/2013/01/cloud-robotics-new-paradigm-is-near.html. [30/09/13]

[31] Flor Nancy Díaz Piraquive, Víctor Hugo Medina García, Rubén González Crespo (2014*). ICT as a Means of Generating Knowledge for Project Management*. Springer Proceedings in Complexity, pp. 617-629, ISBN: 978-94-007-7286-1, DOI: 10.1007/978-94-007-7287-8_50

A Constraint-Based Model for Fast Post-Disaster Emergency Vehicle Routing

Roberto Amadini [1], Imane Sefrioui [2], Jacopo Mauro [1], Maurizio Gabbrielli [1]

[1] Department of Computer Science and Engineering/Lab. Focus INRIA.
University of Bologna, Italy
[2] Computer Science, Operational Research and Applied Statistics Lab.
Faculty of Sciences, Abdelmalek Essaadi University, Tetuan, Morocco

Abstract — **Disasters like terrorist attacks, earthquakes, hurricanes, and volcano eruptions are usually unpredictable events that affect a high number of people. We propose an approach that could be used as a decision support tool for a post-disaster response that allows the assignment of victims to hospitals and organizes their transportation via emergency vehicles. By exploiting the synergy between Mixed Integer Programming and Constraint Programming techniques, we are able to compute the routing of the vehicles so as to rescue much more victims than both heuristic based and complete approaches in a very reasonable time.**

Keywords — **Disaster Recovery, Decision Support Systems, Constraint Programming, Mixed Integer Programming.**

I. INTRODUCTION

Disasters are unpredictable events that demand dynamic, real-time, effective and cost efficient solutions in order to protect populations and infrastructures, mitigate the human and property loss, prevent or anticipate hazards and rapidly recover after a catastrophe. Terrorist attacks, earthquakes, hurricanes, volcano eruptions *etc.* usually affects a high number of persons and involve a large part of the infrastructures thus causing problems for the rescue operations which are often computationally intractable. Indeed, these problems have been tackled by using a *pletora* of different approaches and techniques, ranging from operational research to artificial intelligence and system management (for a survey please see [1]).

Emergency response efforts [2] consist of two stages: pre-event responses that include predicting and analyzing potential dangers and developing necessary action plans for mitigation; post-event response that starts while the disaster is still in progress. At this stage the challenge is locating, allocating, coordinating, and managing available resources.

In this paper we are concerned with post-event response. We propose an algorithm and a software tool that can be used as a decision support system for assigning the victims of a disaster to hospitals and for scheduling emergency vehicles for their transportation. Even though our algorithm could be used to handle daily ambulance responses and routine emergency calls, we target specifically a disaster scenario where the number of victims and the scarcity of the means of transportation are usually overwhelming. Indeed, while for normal daily operations the ambulances can be sent following the order of the arrival of emergency calls, when a disaster happens this First In First Out policy is not more acceptable. In these cases, the number of victims involved and the quantity of damages require a plan and a schedule of rescue operations, where usually priority is given to more critical cases, trying in any case to maximize the number of saved persons. In this context there are clearly also essential ethical issues which we do not address in this paper (for example, is ethically acceptable not to save a person immediately if this behavior allow us to save more persons later on?).

Our tool then assumes a simplified scenario where the number, the position and the criticality of victims is known.

The tool computes solutions that try to maximize the global number of saved victims. In many practical cases finding the optimal solution in not computationally feasible, hence we use a relaxation of the pure optimization problem. Our approach uses a *divide-et-impera* technique that exploits both Mixed Integer Programming (MIP) and Constraint Programming in order to solve the underlining assignment and scheduling problems.

To evaluate the effectiveness of our approach we have compared it against two alternative approaches: on one hand, a greedy algorithm based on the heuristic that send the ambulances first to the most critical victims and later to the others and, on the other hand, a complete algorithm that tries to find the optimal solution in terms of number of rescued victims.

Empirical results based on random generated disaster scenarios show that our approach is promising: it is able to compute the schedule usually in less than half a minute and almost always save more victims than other approaches.

Paper Structure. In Section II we define the model we are considering while in Sections III and IV we present the algorithms and the tests we have conducted. In Section V we present some related work. We conclude giving some directions for future work in Section VI.

II. MODEL

In the literature a lot of models have been proposed to abstract from a concrete disaster scenario. Some of them are extremely complex and involve a lot of variables or probability distributions [3], [4]. For the purposes of this paper we adapt one of the simplest models, following [5], which considers only three entities: victims, hospitals, and ambulances. However, note that the flexibility of the Constraint Programming paradigm would also allow to handle more sophisticated models. Formally, we consider three disjoint sets:

- the set of the ambulances $Amb := \{A_1, ..., A_m\}$;
- the set of the victims $Vict := \{V_1, ..., V_n\}$;
- the set of the hospitals $Hosp := \{H_1, ..., H_p\}$;

and we assume to know the following data:

- the spatial coordinates $sa_i \in \mathbb{R}^2$ of every ambulance A_i;
- the spatial coordinates $sv_j \in \mathbb{R}^2$ of every victim V_j;
- the spatial coordinates $sh_k \in \mathbb{R}^2$ of every hospital H_k;
- the capacity $ca_i \in \mathbb{N}$ of every ambulance A_i;
- the capacity $ch_k \in \mathbb{N}$ of every hospital H_k;
- the estimated time to death $ttd_j \in \mathbb{N}$ of every victim V_j;
- the estimated dig-up time $dig_j \in \mathbb{N}$ of every victim V_j, i.e. the time needed by the rescue team to be able to rescue the victim as soon as the ambulance arrives on the spot;
- the a function $T : \mathbb{R}^2 \times \mathbb{R}^2 \to \mathbb{N}$ that estimates the time needed by an ambulance to move between two given points;
- the initial time $start_i \in \mathbb{N}$ an ambulance become available (an ambulance may be dismissed or already busy when the disaster strikes).

We are well aware that, especially in a disaster scenario, these data may be difficult to retrieve, imprecise and unreliable. Nevertheless our model can exploit these data to compute a first solution and then later, when the information become more precise, it can be rerun to improve the computed solution. Moreover, in order to get these information one can use the results of such works like [6], [7] that allow to esteem the time to death of a civilian or to find the best routes to reach the victims.

Assuming that all the above information are known, our goal is then to find as quickly as possible an optimal scheduling of the ambulances in order to bring the maximal number of alive victims to the hospital. Of course, solving optimally such a scheduling may be computationally unfeasible, especially in the case of a large number of victims.

Moreover, in our scenario, a fast response of the scheduling algorithm is important for different reasons. First of all, the quicker the response is, the faster we can move the ambulances and therefore more victims may be saved. In addition, waiting for a long time may be useless because usually information rapidly changes (i.e. more victims come, the criticality of the patients vary, the hospitals may have damages or emergencies, ambulances can be broken). Hence, spending a lot of time for computing an optimal solution that in few seconds could become non optimal may result in a waste of resources and then lead to the impossibility of saving some victims. On the other hand, a purely greedy approach that at each stage makes the locally optimal choice (according to heuristics such as the seriousness or the location of the victims) would be definitely faster, but could result in a smaller global number of victims saved.

III. PROCEDURE

As previously mentioned, our aim is to find the best possible compromise between the optimality of the ambulances scheduling and the time it takes to find it.

For this reason, we propose an approach that at the same time allows to compute a solution within a reasonable time limit and still allows us to save more victims than greedy strategies. Motivated by the success of hybrid algorithms on problems of resource assignment and scheduling [8], we developed a mixed approach that basically lies in the interaction of two phases: the *allocation phase*, in which we try to allocate as many victims as possible to ambulances and hospitals, and the *scheduling phase*, in which we compute the path that each ambulance must follow in order to bring the victims to the hospitals. In this section we first detail these two phases and then we show the pseudo-code explaining the interplay needed between the allocation and scheduling phase to solve the problem.

A. Allocation

In the allocation phase, we relaxed some constraints of the problem assuming that every ambulance can save in parallel all the victims it contains (in other terms, each ambulance with capacity c can be seen as the union of c distinct ambulances with capacity 1). The allocation of every victim to an ambulance and a hospital is performed by solving a Mixed Integer Programming problem by using two kind of binary variables, denoted by $a_{i,j}$ and $h_{j,k}$. The variable $a_{i,j}$ is set to 1 if and only if the victim V_j is assigned to the ambulance A_i, while $h_{j,k} = 1$ if and only if the victim V_j is assigned to the hospital H_k. The constraints that we enforced are the followings:

- $\sum_{i=1}^{m} a_{i,j} \leq 1$ (for each $j = 1, ..., n$ a victim V_j can not be assigned to more than one ambulance);
- $\sum_{k=1}^{p} h_{j,k} \leq 1$ (for each $j = 1, ..., n$ a victim V_j can not be assigned to more than one hospital);

- $\sum_{j=1}^{n} a_{i,j} \leq ca_i$ (for each $i = 1, ..., m$ the maximum number of patients on an ambulance A_i must not exceed its capacity);
- $\sum_{j=1}^{n} h_{j,k} \leq ch_k$ (for each $k = 1, ..., p$ the maximum number of victims in a hospital H_k must not exceed its capacity);
- $\sum_{i=1}^{m} a_{i,j} = \sum_{k=1}^{p} h_{j,k}$ (for each $j = 1, ..., n$ a victim V_j is assigned to an ambulance A_i if and only if V_j is assigned to an hospital H_k: there must not be 'dangling' victims);
- $\sum_{i=1}^{m} \sum_{k=1}^{p} (start_i + T(sa_i, sv_j)) \cdot a_{i,j} + dig_j + T(sv_j, sh_k) \cdot h_{j,k} < ttd_j$ (for each $j = 1, ..., n$ the time an ambulance A needs to reach a victim V_j, dig up and bring her to an hospital H is enough to save her).

Since the objective of the MIP problem is to try to maximize the number of rescued victims, we defined an objective function which takes into account both the seriousness and the location of the victims. Specifically, we require the maximization of the following objective function:

$$\sum_{i=1}^{m} \sum_{j=1}^{n} \frac{1}{\alpha_{i,j}} \cdot a_{i,j} + \sum_{j=1}^{n} \sum_{k=1}^{p} \frac{1}{\eta_{j,k}} \cdot h_{j,k}$$

where:

$$\alpha_{i,j} := (ttd_j - dig_j) \cdot (start_i + T(sa_i, sv_j))$$
$$\eta_{j,k} := (ttd_j - dig_j) \cdot T(sv_j, sh_k).$$

Recall that solving this problem does not necessarily mean to solve the overall problem: the solution found gives an esteem of the victims that could be saved and a preliminary allocation of every victim to an ambulance and a hospital. Indeed, since this is a relaxation of the original problem, it may be possible that not all the victims allocated to an ambulance may be saved. Anyway, it is worth noticing that the allocation guarantees that at least one victim for ambulance can be rescued. Also, there are no restrictions on the number of hospitals that an ambulance can visit.

B. Scheduling

Once the victims have been allocated by the first phase, the scheduling phase allows to define the path that each ambulance must follow in order to maximize the number of victims saved. After solving the above MIP we can assume that the allocation phase identifies a partition $\Pi := \{A_1^*, ..., A_m^*\}$ where for each $i = 1, ..., m$ we define:

$$A_i^* := \{(V_j, H_k) : V_j \text{ is transported to } H_k \text{ by } A_i\}.$$

The ambulance scheduling for each ambulance A is then obtained by computing a *minimal Hamiltonian path* in a weighted and direct graph derived from A_i^*. Given such an A_i^*, let us consider the graph $\mathcal{G}_i := (\mathcal{N}_i, \mathcal{A}_i, \omega_i)$ where:

- the set of nodes $\mathcal{N}_i$ corresponds to a set of spatial coordinates, in particular each node represents either:
  - the initial position sa_i of the ambulance A_i;
  - the position of the victims $sv_1, ..., sv_{n_i}$ that A_i transports;
  - the position of the hospitals $sh_1, ..., sh_{p_i}$ that A_i visits;
- the set of arcs $\mathcal{A}_i \subseteq \mathcal{N}_i \times \mathcal{N}_i$ corresponds to the movements that A can do from one node to another and it is defined as follows:
  - $(sa_i, sv_j) \in \mathcal{A}_i$ (A can go to any assigned victim V from its initial position);
  - if V is assigned to H, then $(sv_j, sh_k) \in \mathcal{A}_i$ (A can bring a victim to its assigned hospital);
  - if $V \neq V$ are assigned to the same hospital, then $(sv_j, sv_{j'}) \in \mathcal{A}_i$ (A can move from an assigned victim to another one, but no victims assigned to different hospitals can be simultaneously on A);
  - if V is not assigned to H, then $(sh_k, sv_j) \in \mathcal{A}_i$ (A can move from an hospital to a victim only if she is not assigned to such hospital);
  - no other arcs belongs to $\mathcal{A}_i$ (no other move is allowed).
- the weight function $\omega_i : \mathcal{N}_i \times \mathcal{N}_i \to \mathbb{R}$ corresponds to the estimated time for moving from one point to another, including dig-up time:
  - $\omega_i(sa_i, sv_j) := start_i + T(sa_i, sv_j) + dig_j$
  - $\omega_i(sv_j, sh_k) := T(sv_j, sv_k)$
  - $\omega_i(sv_j, sv_{j'}) := T(sv_j, sv_{j'}) + dig_{j'}$
  - $\omega_i(sh_k, sv_j) := T(sh_k, sv_j) + dig_j$

Therefore, if A has assigned n victims and has to visit p hospitals, the number of nodes will be $|\mathcal{N}_i| = 1 + n_i + p_i$ while the number of arcs will be $|\mathcal{A}_i| = n_i^2 + n_i \cdot p_i$.

The scheduling of each ambulance A can be computed by finding the minimum cost Hamiltonian path $P_1 \to P_2 \to \cdots \to P_{n_i}$ in $\mathcal{G}_i$ where:

- P corresponds to the initial location sa_i of A;
- P^1 for each $1 < j < n$, corresponds either to the location of a victim or the location of an hospital;
- P is the location of an hospital of A_i^*;
- $\Omega^{n_i} < ttd$, where Ω is the total cost of the path and ttd the time-to-death of each victim of A_i^*.

The scheduling phase can therefore be mapped into a *Constraint Optimization Problem* (COP) with the goal of minimizing Ω and solved by using constraint programming techniques.

As already stated, it may be the case that not all the victims allocated to an ambulance may be saved, since differently to what happen in the relaxed problem now an ambulance has to save the victims sequentially. When this happens we have to compute a schedule that saves a maximal subset of such victims. However, instead of considering as maximal subset the one which contains the greater number of elements, we choose the one which has the maximum *priority value* that is calculated as follows. We first compute the remaining time $RT := ttd - dig$ of each victim by subtracting her dig-up time from the expected time to death. Then, given a subset of victims $W \subseteq Vict$, we set its priority to $w = \sum_{V_j \in W} \frac{1}{RT_j}$ (bigger values of w means higher priority). We decided to use this sum to evaluate the priority because, analogously to what happens for the harmonic average, the sum of the reciprocal gives priority to the victim having least remaining time and it mitigates at the same time the influence of large outliers (i.e. victims with big remaining time that can be easily saved later).

When an ambulance is scheduled, the model is updated accordingly and the allocation phase is possibly restarted in order to try to allocate the victims which have not yet been assigned. The procedure ends when no more victims can be saved.

C. A&S Algorithm

Listing 1: A&S Algorithm

```
1   ALLOCATE_AND_SCHEDULE(Amb, Vict, Hosp):
2     while  Vict ≠ ∅:
3       REMOVE_NOT_RESCUABLE_VICTIMS(Vict)
4       Π = ALLOCATE(Amb, Vict, Hosp)
5       sorted_ambs = SORT_AMBS_BY_PRIORITY(Π)
6       foreach  Aᵢ ∈ sorted_ambs:
7         V = VICTIMS(Aᵢ,Π)
8         if  V ≠ ∅:
9           (Σ, Ω) = SCHEDULE(Aᵢ,V,Π)
10          if Σ is not feasible:
11            w = 0
12            Ω = +∞
13            foreach  k ∈ [|V| − 1,...,1]:
14              foreach  h ∈ [1,...,(|V| k)]:
15                V' = GET_SUBSET(h,k,V)
16                w' = ∑_{vₗ∈V'} 1/ttdₗ
17                if  w' ≥ w:
18                  (Σ', Ω') = SCHEDULE(Aᵢ,V',Π)
19                  if Σ' is feasible ∧
20                    (w' == w → Ω' < Ω):
21                    w = w'
22                    Ω = Ω'
23                    Σ = Σ'
24          startᵢ = Ω
25          foreach  Hₖ ∈ Hosp:
26            chₖ = chₖ − NO_OF_VICTIMS(Σ, Hₖ)
27          saᵢ = LAST(Σ)
28          Vict = Vict \ VICTIMS(Σ)
29          schedule[Aᵢ].append(Σ)
30          if VICTIMS(Σ) ≠ V:
31            break
32  return schedule
```

The main procedure called Allocate & Schedule (A&S) and presented in Listing 1 takes as input the set of ambulances *Amb*, the set of victims *Vict*, and the set of hospitals *Hosp*. It consists of a cycle where, first of all, the victims that can not be saved (*i.e.* victims with a remaining time less than or equal to 0) are removed. This operation is performed by the external function REMOVE_NOT_RESCUABLE_VICTIMS at line 3.
The ALLOCATE function solves the MIP problem described in Section III-A and returns the allocation of every victim to one ambulance and one hospital. The ambulances are then sorted by the function SORT_AMBS_BY_PRIORITY according to the sum of the priority values of the victims assigned to each ambulance; in this way, the schedule of the ambulances which transport victims with higher priority is performed earlier.

The nested loop starting at line 6 is responsible to compute the schedule of all the ambulances. Considering the ambulance A, in line 7 the variable V is defined to be the set of the victims assigned to A. If V is not empty then SCHEDULE(A,V,Π) returns a possible schedule Σ and its cost Ω for the ambulance A. This is done following the procedure described in Section III-B. If the schedule problem has no solution (line 10) then another solution that involves less victims is computed (lines 11-23). In particular, the priority of the set of the victims w is initialized to 0, while the cost of the solution Ω to $+\infty$ (lines 12-13).

The loops enclosed between lines 13 and 23 have the aim of calculating a maximum eligible subset of victims, *i.e.* a subset V' of V that both maximizes the value of $\sum_{v_l \in V'} \frac{1}{ttd_l}$ and admits a feasible schedule. In order to compute all the subsets of V we exploit the function GET_SUBSET(i, k, A) that returns the i-th subset (*w.r.t.* lexicographic order) among all the $\binom{|A|}{k}$ subsets of A with cardinality k. Note that computing all the subsets is in general exponential on the capacity of the ambulances. However, in real cases, this can be computationally feasible since the capacity of the ambulances is usually small. In line 15 a subset V' is retrieved and its weight is computed in line 16. In case the weight is greater than the weight of the current solution, a schedule of the ambulance A for victims in V' is computed (line 18). If the schedule is feasible and has a lower cost in case of equal weight then the current schedule Σ, the current weight w and the current cost Ω are updated.

By construction, once exiting from the above loops a schedule that involves at least a victim is always found. Then, we just need to update the model. First, we update the start time of the ambulance A with the total cost of the schedule Σ (line 24). Then, for each hospital H we decrease the hospital capacity ch_k according to the number of victims that A brings to them (lines 25-26). The new spatial location of A is set to the value of the last hospital it visits (line 27) and we remove from *Vict* all the victims that A has rescued. Finally, the schedule Σ is added to the associative array *schedule* that is the output of the A&S procedure.

In case only a part of the victims allocated to the ambulance A were saved (line 30) the cycle starting at line 6 is interrupted in order to compute a new allocation that may allocate the remaining victims to other ambulances.

The algorithm terminates when no more victims can be saved. From the computational point of view this algorithm cyclically solves MIP and COP problems, which are well known NP-hard problems. However, by exploiting the relaxation of the MIP problem, on one hand, and the limited size of the COP problems, on the other, it is possible to get quickly optimal solutions by exploiting current MIP and COP solvers. An empirical proof of this is provided in the next section.

IV. TESTS

We did not find in the literature suitable and extensive benchmarks of disaster scenarios that we could use to evaluate and compare the performances of our approach. For this reason, in order to evaluate our algorithm we extended the methodology used in [9]. In particular, we built random generated scenarios obtained by varying the number of hospitals in the set $\{1, 2, 4\}$, the number of ambulances in $\{4, 8, 16, 32, 64\}$, and the number of victims in $\{8, 16, 32, 64, 128, 256, 512\}$. The position of each entity was randomly chosen in a grid of 100×100 by using the Euclidean distance to estimate the time needed for moving from one point to another.

The capacities of the ambulances and the hospitals were selected randomly in the intervals $[1..4]$ and $[300..1000]$, respectively, while the dig-up time and the time to death of every victim were randomly chosen in $[5..30]$ and $[100..1000]$, respectively. For $i = 1, ..., m$ we considered initially $start_i = 0$.

Listing 2: GREEDY Algorithm

```
1   GREEDY(Amb, Vict, Hosp):
2     REMOVE_NOT_RESCUABLE_VICTIMS(Vict)
3     sorted_victs = SORT_VICTS_BY_PRIORITY(Vict)
4     while sorted_victs ≠ []:
5       V_j = sorted_victs.pop()
6       A_i = CLOSEST_AMB(V_j)
7       schedule[A_i].append((start_i, sv_j))
8       H_k = CLOSEST_HOSP(V_j)
9       deadline = ttd_j
10      position = sv_j
11      victims = 1
12      time = start_i + T(sa_i, sv_j) + dig_j + T(sv_j, sh_k)
13      hosp_time = T(sv_j, sh_k)
14      foreach V_l ∈ sorted_victs
15        t = T(position, sv_l) + dig_l + T(sv_l, sh_k) - hosp_time
16        if victims < ca_i ∧ victims < ch_k ∧
17          time + t < deadline ∧ time + t < ttd_l:
18            hosp_time = T(sv_l, sh_k)
19            sorted_victs.remove(V_l)
20            schedule[A_i].append((position, sv_l))
21            deadline = min(deadline, ttd_l)
22            victims = victims + 1
23            time = time + t
24            position = sv_l
25        schedule[A_i].append((position, sh_k))
26      start_i = time
27      sa_i = sh_k
28      ch_k = ch_k - victims
29      REMOVE_NOT_RESCUABLE_VICTIMS(sorted_victs)
30    return schedule
```

To increase the accuracy and the significance of the results we tested our approach by running the experiments 20 times for each different scenario and by measuring the average number of rescued victims as well as the time required to solve the problem. In total we tested then 105 different scenarios.

For every different scenario we compared the results of A&S w.r.t. a greedy approach GREEDY and a complete approach COMP that are used as baselines. In the following, before reporting the results, we briefly explain the algorithms we used as baselines.

A. GREEDY

GREEDY is a heuristic based algorithm that at each time tries to assign the most critical victims to the closest available ambulance and then such ambulance to the closest available hospital. Moreover, GREEDY also looks if in the path from the ambulance to the hospital it is possible to save other critical victims.

The pseudo-code of GREEDY is summarized in Listing 2. As in Listing 1, the main procedure takes as input the ambulances, the victims, and the hospitals. After removing all the non rescuable victims (line 2), it sorts all the victims by decreasing priority (line 3). At line 4 it starts the main loop, which is repeated until no more victims can be saved. First, the most critical victim is extracted into the variable V (line 5): this is the victim that the ambulance will save first. In line 6 the function CLOSEST_AMB is used to retrieve the closest free ambulance A to victim V while CLOSEST_HOSP is a function that returns the closest available hospital to V. In lines 9-13 we define some auxiliary variables for computing the schedule of the ambulance. In particular deadline, position, and victims are used to store respectively the minimum time to death of the transported victims, the position of the last victim of the schedule, and the total number of victims on the ambulance. The variable hosp keeps track of the total cost of the path from the ambulance to the hospital while hosp_time represents instead the cost of the last segment of the path, i.e. time needed for moving from the last victim to the hospital H.

The ambulance A is immediately sent to hospital H unless there are other victims that can be saved along the way. In order to look for such additional victims, we use a loop that scans each remaining victim V of sorted_victs (line 14). Within the cycle, in line 15 we evaluate the cost t needed for carrying the victim V to H. If such a transportation is possible, that is the capacity of A and H is not exceeded and there is enough time for saving all the victims of A (lines 16-17) then in lines 18-25 we update the ambulance schedule by updating the corresponding variables.

When the foreach cycle terminates, all the victims that could be saved by A (according to the heuristic) have been considered and therefore the ambulance is sent to the hospital. Therefore, in lines 26-28 we update the start-time of A, its location and the capacity of the hospital. Finally, in line 29 we remove all the not rescuable victims and the while cycle starts again until no more victims can be saved.

B. COMP algorithm

COMP is an algorithm that maps the rescue problem into a COP and computes the schedule of every ambulance without a pre-allocation phase. COMP is a complete algorithm: it tries to maximize the number of rescuable victims and when it terminates with success it always returns an optimal solution.

COMP assigns to all the ambulances, victims, and hospitals an unique identifier. In particular all the ambulances of *Amb* have an identifier $i \in D_a := [0..m]$, all the victims of *Vict* have an identifier $j \in D_v := [m+1..m+n]$ and all the hospitals in *Hosp* have an identifier $k \in D_h := [m+n+1..m+n+p]$.

The schedule of ambulance A_i at its *j*-th *round* (where by round we mean a path from its starting point to exactly one hospital) was encoded with an array $R_{i,j}$ of integer variables indexed from 0 to $ca_i + 2$. We then defined $m \cdot n$ arrays containing the identifiers of the victims and the hospital that each ambulance should visit in sequence.

$R_{i,j}[0] \in \{i\} \cup D_h$ is the index corresponding to the location of the ambulance A_i at the beginning of the *j*-th round. Since in the first round the starting point of A is always *start* and in the following rounds the starting point is always the location of a hospital, we have $R_{i,1}[0] = i$ and $R_{i,j}[0] \in D_h$ for $i = 1,..., m$ and $j = 2,..., n$.

$R_{i,j}[1],...,R_{i,j}[ca_i] \in \{0\} \cup D_v$ are instead the indexes of the victims that A can rescue. In case the ambulance round was not filled completely one or more elements of $R_{i,j}$ are set to 0, signaling for every element set to 0 that a place was not used.

The last two elements of the arrays contain the index of the hospital where the ambulance ends its round and the total cost of the round. Note that each $R_{i,j}$ definition also entails that a victim can not be assigned to more than one hospital and that the maximum number of victims on A must not exceed its capacity ca_i. Additional constraints are needed in order to achieve the soundness of the solution and to reduce the search space. In particular, we added constraints enforcing that:

- the total cost of each round $R_{i,j}$ has to be lower than the time to death of each victim of $R_{i,j}$;
- if $R_{i,j}$ does not save any victim then all the subsequent rounds will not save any victim;
- the maximum number of victims in a hospital H_k must not exceed its capacity ch_k;

- a victim can occur in at most one round.

The objective of the COP is maximize the number of rescued victims, *i.e.* maximize the cardinality of the disjoint union of the victims assigned to each round. In order to encode the problem, we used basic constraints (such as <, +, ...) as well as *global constraints* [10] (namely, *element*, *alldifferent_except_0*, and *count*).

As can be imagined, solving such a problem may consume too many resources. In order to conduct the experiments using scenarios of nontrivial size we imposed some limitations that in some cases may result in a loss of completeness. We first limited the number of rounds for each ambulance to the ratio between victims and ambulances whenever the number of victims was greater than the number of ambulances. Then, during the computation of the solutions, we have limited the use of the virtual memory to 50% of the total available space and set a timeout of 300 seconds keeping the best solution founded up to that time if no solution was proven optimal.

C. Results

Fig. 1 shows the average percentage of rescued victims obtained by using A&S, GREEDY, and COMP approaches. The x-axis values represent scenarios sorted lexicographically by increasing number of victims, ambulances, and hospitals (labels are omitted for the sake of readability, since each x-value is actually a triple of values).

Our approach is in average able to rescue the 87.08% of the victims (from a minimum of 18.02% to a maximum of 100%). Considering the median value, in half of the scenarios we are able to rescue more than 99.38% of the victims.

In only 2 cases (0.02% of the scenarios) GREEDY is better than our approach, while in only one case COMP is better than A&S. However, in these few cases the difference of saved victims is minimal (between 0.31% and 1.48%) while the gap between A&S and GREEDY or COMP can reach peaks of about 78% and 100% respectively. In average, A&S is able to rescue about 31.03% of victims more than GREEDY and 59.38% more than COMP.

From the plot we can also see that our approach is

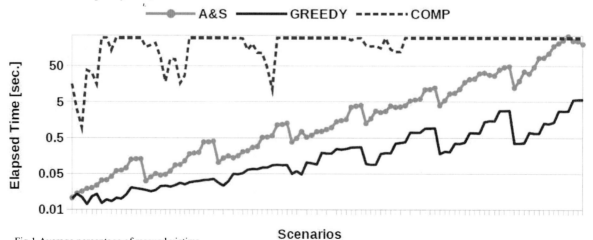

Fig.1 Average percentage of rescued victims.

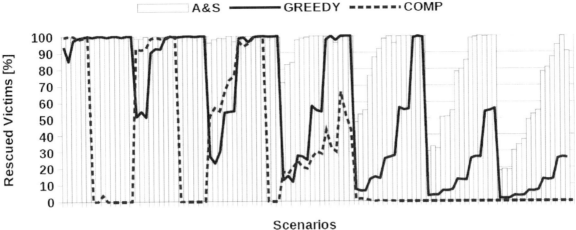

Fig.2 Average scheduling time.

especially better for scenarios involving a large number of victims. In particular, COMP algorithm can not find a solution within the timeout when the number of victims is greater than 128. It is therefore clear that this approach, although conceptually complete, is not scalable to large sizes. This can be a significant problem in scenarios like ours: it is not permissible to wait 5 minutes and having no solutions. GREEDY usually makes local choices that have a huge impact on the total number of the victims that could be saved. Although better than COMP for scenarios with many victims, the gap between GREEDY and A&S is significant. On the other hand, our approach in these cases tries to come up with a better global choice and therefore it can be far superior than a simple heuristic based approach.

In Fig. 2 we show the time needed to compute the entire schedule of the ambulances (please note the logarithmic scale). Although it is not surprising that GREEDY is faster while COMP is slower (the timeout expired often), it can however be observed that our approach takes reasonable times. In fact, in average the ambulances are allocated in 24.48 seconds, which means that on average in less than half a minute all the ambulances will be able to know the path that should be followed. Moreover, the median value indicates that for half of the scenarios the entire schedule is computed in less than 1.17 seconds.

Technical details. All the experiments were conducted by using an Intel Core™ 2.93 GHz computer with 6 GB of RAM and Ubuntu operating system. The code for COMP and GREEDY algorithms was fully developed in Python. In particular, GREEDY algorithm exploits Gurobi [11] optimizer for solving the MIP problem and Gecode [12] solver for the COP problems. The code for the subsets generation is instead taken from [13]. Differently, for COMP algorithm we used Python for generating a MiniZinc [14] model solved by using the G12/FD solver of the MiniZinc suite. All the code developed to conduct the experiments is available at http://www.cs.unibo.it/~amadini/ijimai_2013.zip

V. RELATED WORK

In the literature many techniques from operational research and artificial intelligence have been used to tackle different aspects of the disaster management problem. Most of the approaches are trying to develop and study pre-event solution to decrease the severity of the disaster outcome. As an example, in [15] the authors study the best allocation of deposits that allows to handle in the most efficient way the rescue operations in case natural disaster happens. In [4], the authors use MIP in order to schedule the operation rooms and the hospital facilities in case of a disaster. These paper however have a different goal from ours: we are not concerned with considering preventing measures that could allow to mitigate the consequences of future disasters. We are instead concerned with saving more victims, after the disaster happened.

There is also a large literature related to the problem of deciding the initial location of ambulances in order to decrease the average response time for ambulance calls. However, very few papers deal with the computation of the schedule for an ambulance. Some authors focus just on computing the best path for an ambulance toward the victim. For instance in [6] the authors use graph optimization algorithms in order to find a path for an ambulance. In our work we assume to have such a path and we are concerned with the problem of defining the order of the victims that an ambulance should pick up. In [16] the authors propose a routing algorithm for ambulances but, differently from our case, their model is probabilistic and it has been applied just for two small scenarios (*i.e.* scenarios containing few ambulances and victims).

In [5] the authors proposed the use of an interactive learning approach which allows rescue agents to adapt their preferences following strategies suggested by experts. The decision of the ambulance is based on a utility function incrementally improved through expert intervention.

Differently from our approach the authors here use an heuristic to dispatch the ambulances which rely on expert decision makers, while we rely only on optimization techniques.

In [17] is solved a task scheduling problem in which

rescuing a civilian is considered as a task and the ambulances are considered as resources that should accomplish the task. The goal is to perform as many tasks as possible by using the Hogdson's scheduling algorithm to compute the solutions. Differently from our case, the authors considered here only the execution cost of the task and its deadline, ignoring important constraints such as the capacity of the hospitals and ambulances.

Combinatorial auctions are used in [18], [19], [20] to perform task allocation for ambulances, fire brigades and police forces. An ambulance management center is represented as the auctioneer while ambulances bid for civilians to save. Each free ambulance makes several bids and the auctioneer determines the winners using a Branch and Bound algorithm. A drawback of this approach is that it is difficult for bidders to estimate the cost for bids containing many tasks. Moreover, as pointed out in [21], if bidders bid on each and every possible combination of tasks the computation of satisfactory results is computationally expensive.

The authors in [22], [23] proposed a model based on a Multi-Objective Optimization Problem. They adjust controllable parameters in the interaction between different classes of agents (hospitals, persons, ambulances) and resources, in order to minimize the number of casualties, the number of fatalities, the average ill-health of the population, and the average waiting time at the hospitals. Then, they use Multi-Objective Evolutionary algorithms (MOES) for producing good emergency response plans. Their underline model is completely different from ours and we argue that is not very adaptable to deal with continuous changes and unexpected situations.

In [20], authors proposed partitioning the disaster environment in homogeneous sectors and assigning an agent to be responsible for each sector. Similarly, in [24], the city areas are partitioned and assigned to an ambulance. The number of clusters is determined by the size of the city. Such solutions could lead to unfair partitioning and inefficient assignment of agents to partitions. A more powerful partitioning strategy based on the density of blockades on the roads was used in [25]. This approach however requires a real-time information of the environment that is costly and sometimes difficult to retrieve.

Similarly to the GREEDY algorithm that we use as baseline, in [26] an heuristic is used to allocate the victims giving priority to the civilian with the highest probability of death. The shortcoming of this approach is that the cost of travel of the ambulance from one civilian to another could be very large; this could lead to a huge loss of lives if the size of the map is too large as in real-world situations.

In [27] Earliest Deadline First algorithm is also used to form coalition for rescuing victims. The victim with earliest deadline is selected and the number of ambulances needed to rescue this candidate in time is computed and called coalition. The use of coalition formation however works well when a task cannot be performed by a single agent, which is not the case for the task of saving a victim.

Finally we are aware of the existence of commercial applications for Emergency Dispatching (*e.g.* [28], [29]). The technical details explaining how these software are working unfortunately are always missing.

VI. CONCLUSIONS

In this work we have described a procedure that can be used as a decision support tool for a post-disaster event when a big number of victims need to be transported to the hospitals.

The proposed algorithm takes into account the position of the victims and their criticality, and schedules the ambulances in order to maximize the number of saved victims. Even though there is no guarantee that the solution obtained is the optimal one, experimental tests confirm that the number of saved victims is greater than the one that could be obtained by using, on one hand, a greedy priority-based heuristic and, on the other hand, a complete algorithm with a reasonable timeout of 5 minutes. Moreover, the proposed solution is usually fast enough to assign all the available ambulances in less than half a minute.

As a future work it would be interesting to evaluate our approach in a more dynamic and realistic scenario since assuming that the whole model is known a priori is not very realistic. A dynamic approach needs to adapt itself to context changes (*e.g.* new incoming victims, ambulances out of service, the critical state of victims, etc...).

In the event of significant changes the solution may be quickly updated exploiting the current allocation of ambulances without recomputing from scratch everything.

Moreover we would like to integrate the model with heuristics developed by domain experts.

Adopting these heuristics will allow the system to be able to react to a change very quickly, by using a default behavior that later can be changed if a better solution is found solving the optimiztion problem.

Another direction worth investigating is to study the performance and the scalability of the algorithm proposed taking into account also the robustness of the solutions (i.e. how the solutions vary depending on small changes of the initial model).

VII. REFERENCES

[1] N. Altay and W. G. Green, "OR/MS research in disaster operations management," European Journal of Operational Research, vol. 175, no. 1, pp. 475–493, 2006.

[2] S. Tufekci and W. Wallace, "The Emerging Area Of Emergency Management And Engineering," Engineering Management, IEEE Transactions on, vol. 45, no. 2, pp. 103–105, 1998.

[3] G. Erdogan, E. Erkut, A. Ingolfsson, and G. Laporte, "Scheduling ambulance crews for maximum coverage," JORS, vol. 61, no. 4, pp. 543–550, 2010.

[4] I. Nouaouri, N. Jean-Christophe, and J. Daniel, "Reactive Operating Schedule in Case of a Disaster: Arrival of Unexpected Victims," in WCE, ser. Lecture Notes in Engineering and Computer Science. International Association of Engineers, 2010, pp. 2123–2128.

[5] T.-Q. Chu, A. Drogoul, A. Boucher, and J.-D. Zucker, "Interactive Learning of Independent Experts' Criteria for Rescue Simulations," J. UCS, vol. 15, no. 13, pp. 2701–2725, 2006.

[6] N.A.M. Nordin, N. Kadir, Z.A. Zaharudin, and N.A. Nordin, "An application of the A* algorithm on the ambulance routing," IEEE Colloquium on Humanities, Science and Engineering (CHUSER), 2011, pp. 855–859.

[7] S. A. Suarez and C. G. Quintero, and J. L. de la Rosa, "A Real Time Approach for Task Allocation in a Disaster Scenario," PAAMS, 2010, pp. 157–162.

[8] M. Lombardi, and M. Milano, "Optimal methods for resource allocation and scheduling: a cross-disciplinary survey," Constraints, vol. 17, no. 1, pp. 51–85, 2012.

[9] R. Amadini

[10] , I. Sefrioui, J. Mauro, and M. Gabbrielli, "Fast Post-Disaster Emergency Vehicle Scheduling," Distributed Computing and Artificial Intelligence, ser. Advances in Intelligent Systems and Computing, Springer International Publishing, 2013, vol. 217, pp. 219–226.

[11] N. Beldiceanu, M. Carlsson, S. Demassey, and T. Petit, "Global Constraint Catalogue: Past, Present and Future," Constraints, vol. 12, no. 1, pp. 21–62, 2007.

[12] "Gurobi - The overall fastest and best supported solver available," http://www.gurobi.com

[13] "GECODE - An open, free, efficient constraint solving toolkit," http://www.gecode.org

[14] J. McCaffrey, "Improved Combinations with the BigInteger Data Type," http://visualstudiomagazine.com/Articles/2012/08/01/BigInteger-Data-Type.aspx?Page=3, 2013.

[15] N. Nethercote, P. J. Stuckey, R. Becket, S. Brand, G. J. Duck, and G. Tack, "MiniZinc: Towards a Standard CP Modelling Language," in CP, 2007.

[16] T. Andersson, S. Petersson, and P. Värbrand, "Decision Support for Efficient Ambulance Logistics," ser. ITN research report. Department of Science and Technology (ITN), Linköping University, 2005.

[17] K. Ufuk, T. Ozden, and T. Saniye, "Emergency Vehicle Routing in Disaster Response Operations," in Proceedings of the 23rd Annual Conference on Production and Operation Management Society, 2012.

[18] S. Paquet, N. Bernier, and B. Chaib-draa, "Multiagent Systems Viewed as Distributed Scheduling Systems: Methodology and Experiments," in Advances in Artificial Intelligence, ser. Lecture Notes in Computer Science, Springer Berlin Heidelberg, 2005, vol. 3501, pp. 43–47.

[19] S. Suarez and B. Lopez, "Reverse Combinatorial Auctions for Resource Allocation in the Rescue Scenario," in ICAPS Workshop on Constraint Satisfaction Techniques for Planning and Scheduling Problems, 2006.

[20] B. Lopez, S. Suarez, and J. D. L. Rosa, "Task allocation in rescue operations using combinatorial auctions," in Proceedings of the sixth Catalan Congress on Artificial Intelligence. IOS Press, 2003.

[21] M. Sedaghat, L. Nejad, S. Iravanian, and E. Rafiee, "Task Allocation for the Police Force Agents in RoboCupRescue Simulation," in RoboCup 2005, ser. Lecture Notes in Computer Science. Springer Berlin Heidelberg, 2006, vol. 4020, pp. 656–664.

[22] Nair, Ranjit and Ito, Takayuki and Tambe, Milind and Marsella, Stacy, "Task Allocation in the RoboCup Rescue Simulation Domain: A Short Note," in RoboCup 2001, Springer-Verlag, 2002, pp. 751–754.

[23] N. Giuseppe, M. Venkatesh, N. Lewis, R. Dianne, T. Marc, H. Liza, P. Ian, and M. Bud, "Complexities, Catastrophes and Cities: Unraveling Emergency Dynamics," in InterJournal of Complex Systems, vol. 4068, no. 1745, 2006.

[24] G. Narzisi, V. Mysore, and B. Mishra, "Multi-objective evolutionary optimization of agent-based models: An application to emergency response planning," in Computational Intelligence, 2006, pp. 228–232.

[25] M. Nanjanath, A. J. Erlandson, S. Andrist, A. Ragipindi, A.A. Mohammed, A. S. Sharma, and M. Gini, "Decision and coordination strategies for robocup rescue agents," in SIMPAR, Springer-Verlag, 2010, pp. 473–484.

[26] S. Paquet, N. Bernier, and B. Chaib-draa, "Comparison of Different Coordination Strategies for the RoboCupRescue Simulation," in Innovations in Applied Artificial Intelligence, ser. Lecture Notes in Computer Science. Springer Berlin Heidelberg, 2004, vol. 3029, pp. 987–996.

[27] J. Habibi, S. H. Yeganeh, M. Habibi, A. Malekzadeh, A. Malekzadeh, S. H. Mortazavi, H. Nikaein, M. Salehe, M. Vafadoost, and N. Zolghadr, "Impossibles08 Team Description RoboCup Rescue Agent Simulation," July 2008.

[28] O. A. Ghiasvand, and M. A. Sharbafi, "Using earliest deadline first algorithms for coalition formation in dynamic time-critical environment," Education and Information Tech, vol. 1, no. 2, pp. 120–125, 2011.

[29] "Odyssey website," http://www.plain.co.uk/index.php?option=com_content&task=view&id=67&Itemid=98

[30] "GeoFES,website," http://www.dhigroup.com/MIKECUSTOMISEDbyDHI/GeoFES.aspx

Roberto Amadini received a Bachelor (2007) and Master (2011) degree in Computer Science from the University of Parma. He has worked as a Laboratory Assistant at I.I.S. "G. Romani" of Casalmaggiore (CR) from 2007 to 2009 while in January 2012 he started his Ph.D. program in Computer Science at the University of Bologna. Currently is a Ph.D. student working on theory and application of *Constraint (Logic) Programming* for modeling and solving combinatorial problems. He is also member of of the Focus Research Group at INRIA (France).

Imane Sefrioui received a graduate degree in Computer Science "Diplôme d'Ingénieur d'Etat" in 2011 from "Ecole Nationale des Sciences Appliquées" in Tangier. In January 2012, she started her Ph.D. program in Computer Science at the Faculty of Sciences of Tetuan in Abdelmalek Essaadi University. She is currently a Ph.D. student working on the techniques and algorithms for modeling and solving combinatorial optimization problems.

Maurizio Gabbrielli Maurizio Gabbrielli is professor of Computer Science at the University of Bologna and is director of the Ph.D. program in Computer Science. He received his Phd. in Computer Science in 1992 from the University of Pisa and worked at CWI (Amsterdam) and at the University of Pisa and of Udine. His research interests include constraint programming, formal methods for program verification and analysis, service oriented programming.

Jacopo Mauro received a bachelor and master degree in computer science from Udine University. In 2012 he receive a PhD in computer science from the University of Bologna. Since 2010 he is member of the Focus Research Group at INRIA (France). He has been involved in numerous Italian, French, and European research projects and a visiting student at CWI (Netherlands). He is currently working at INRIA and interested in Concurrent Languages, Service Oriented Computing, Constraint Programming, Constraint Handling Rules and AI Planning.

## 7

Reality and perspectives of a model for the population that obtains its income with the use of an animal-drawn vehicle in the city of Bogota

Sánchez Aparicio, Ismael Fernando., Romero Villalobos, Oswaldo Alberto.

Universidad Distrital Francisco José de Caldas, Bogotá, Colombia

Abstract — **This paper analyzes the structure of the data collected in the population dependent or receives its revenues in the use of animal-drawn vehicle, to extract an economic model for the development of this activity (which is currently done with these vehicles and is unbusinesslike) introducing formal parameters, as well as replacement of the vehicle analyzes the development of this activity in this population.**

Keywords — **mobility, animal-drawn vehicles, traffic and transport, Management Models.**

I. INTRODUCTION

The District University in partnership with the District Department of Transportation developed the project "Technical, legal, financial and social withdrawal project drawn vehicles - Development of socioeconomic characteristics of the population of wheelwrights (VTA) in the city of Bogotá, including proposed scenarios viable and sustainable economic projects that replace and/ or technify animal-drawn vehicle (ATV) - Phase One" within the project results were compiled economic data how dependent people or receive their income from the use of animal-drawn vehicle, these data allowed, once processed, extracting an economic model for the development of this activity, yes, without neglecting the activity currently being undertaken with these vehicles is unbusinesslike, and it is necessary to begin entering parameters formalization of this activity, and it is also necessary to think of replacing the vehicle that is currently used for the development of this activity in this population.

II. MODEL FEATURES

A. Population profile (VTA)

According to the results of the census conducted within the scope of the project and correspondence analysis conducted, it was concluded that the population of wheelwrights (VTA) is median age (35 years), with a level of education that is among the final years of primary school and early high school, living primarily in family, which has been established by cohabitation and share your home with children, siblings and parents.

The wheelwright (VTA) has chosen activity to the extent that his inner circle develops the same activity and in many cases, family members are jointly involved in the development of the tasks associated with the management of the wagon.

Those who engage in this activity are owners of his wagon and horses have it and not only a single set, which kept in proper condition. They live primarily in rented house and have access to basic services of water and energy, but do not have access to natural gas. Managing your garbage is done by the utility company, which shows the coverage of these services by district entities.

They usually work 8 to 12 hours or so and they do between Monday and Friday, but work on Saturday's noon. The wheelwrights made between 1 and 2 daily trips and their activity is directed mainly to recycling (glass, paper, plastic and metal mostly).

B. Current function of expenses (FAE)

Once the wheelwrights population profile (VTA), we found that this population group to perform an informal activity, manages its economy in the same way, though it was established that despite this, this population based his scheme of aggregate expenditures on two parameters, namely, home maintenance costs and maintenance of animal-drawn vehicle on one hand the cost of upkeep of the home, are part of the function of expenses, because the administrative, planning logistics and marketing strategies are developed within the family, where family members, act as administrators and managers in this task, so the costs of maintenance of the home are part of the expenditure function.

On the other hand, despite having no formal, expenditures for home maintenance costs resemble those of a home at any lower layer 3 and its calculation is based on:
Public services (SP), financing of housing ownership (AV), Food and cleanliness (AA), Education and Entertainment (EE) and Health and other minor expenses (SG). With the foregoing the calculation represented:

$$SO_n = SP_n + AV_n + AA_n + EE_n + SG_n, n = 1,2,3,...etc.$$

For the schema of the function and its components, you can see that this equation tends to be constant, since a home tends to stabilize and maintain their support costs at a fixed interval of low variability, this situation is familiar to the road population, however in certain periods or the result of uncontrolled events, this equation may have variations from one period to another, in circumstances such as new household members, housing changes, external situations, etc.., so is must set the value of the equation to the conditions of the period, for the calculation of the function.

Moreover, within the expenditure function can find another cost parameter, and this is the maintenance of animal-drawn vehicle (MVTA), which as its name suggests answers to the calculation of the expenses incurred by animal-drawn vehicle , but unlike the upkeep of the home to calculate this equation, vary according to the use of animal-drawn vehicle in the period, because, for the calculation takes the following variables: Rent a manger + parking (APP), wagon rent + horse (ACE), horse maintenance expenses (GME) and expenses of the wagon (GMC), and the calculation is:

$$MVTA_n = APP_n + ACE_n + GME_n + GMC_n, n = 1,2,3 ... etc.$$

Equation $MVTA_n$, can be divided into two parts viz, the first of these variables is associated with APP and ACE, which tend to assume positive values constant indifferent of using animal-drawn vehicle, ie tend to assume the same value period becoming a constant period at different times, but still and knowing this, these variables may fluctuate permanent possibilities event such as: horse change, change of parking, etc.., on the other hand have cost variables GMC and GME, unlike the first, these variables, as they tend to vary in relation to the use of animal-drawn vehicle in the period, since its value responds to the calculation of variables associated with the use of animal-drawn vehicle, so such as the fittings are costs to be incurred in the extent to which greater use of horses, the animal disease can become the occasion of contact with other horses or sites stay low hygiene, is more prone to traffic accidents in the extent to which the vehicle share the road with other vehicles, etc.

Having stated the above, the function of expenses $f(FAE)$, responds to the sum of the variables discussed above, adding the two groups given above, we can say that $f(FAE)$ it is equal to the sum of SO_n and $MVTA_n$, thus:

$$f(FAE) = SO_n + MVTA_n, n = 1,2,3 ... etc$$

C. Current Income Function (FIA)

For the calculation of the income is part of the way the wheelwrights carry out their work, ie, what was found, once the information was collected, is that this population operates in an informal way, that its main activity is the collection of materials for recycling, that in addition to this recycling, also dedicated to the transport of debris or construction material, but despite this, payment is due on sale in gathering place of the weight in kilos of transported material, so as FIA current income due to the amount of trips transporting different types of materials on the day x the number of days worked in the period, being affected this relationship by the number of hours that a wheelwrights works on an ordinary day, the income also vary according to the mix of materials animal drawn vehicle transport to the collection center, the results of the field work showed that the main materials transported by the population (VTA) are: Glass (VI), paper (PA), Plastic (PLA) and metal (ME) for the most part, also found that some of them and in some specific days a week, can transport crates (GU), rubble (ES) or other not so frequently, the above revenue function, is given by the sum of the different materials in kilos put into the collection center or place of sale, multiplied by the sales price of the same:

$$f(FIA) = \sum_{i=1}^{n} P_i x MT_i$$

In equation P is the selling price per kilo material and MT is the type of material transported, on the other hand, this function has a restricted income, which refers to the ability of the animal-drawn vehicle in kilograms to transport material, as well as the carrying capacity of the wagon is associated with the ability to have the animal shot in the fieldwork, it was found that the majority of animals used in this work are light horses (under 650kg) and heavy, and although not common, were also found mules and other animals for these studies, we also found that animals for this work are mostly race called creoles and in a few cases were found mixed breeds animals as the percheron and Creole, apart from this, the capacity of these animals will vary according to the weight of the animal, the size of it, race horse over the animal, on the other hand, we also found that the cart, also influences the total load capacity, details such as the type of tires used, type mechanism in which the tires are mounted (bearings, etc.), the material of the structure and the slab; with the foregoing, the revenue function is:

$$f(FIA) = \sum_{i=1}^{n} P_i x MT_i$$

Subject to:

$$\sum_{i=1}^{n} MT_i \leq (k \; x \; PE) - (c \; x \; PC)$$

Where k is the coefficient associated with the load you can drag the equine, PE equine weight, c is the coefficient of the structure of the wagon (This will vary according to the maintenance of the wagon and supplies it) and finally PC the weight of the wagon.

Moreover wheelwrights population, despite developing its work in the informal, is no stranger to market behavior and the conditions thereof, so as the price of kilo of material at the point of collection will vary according to demand the same experience in the period, so as to offer more the price will tend to fall and less supply of the same the effect is opposite, that is, the price will tend to rise, the equation for this situation is first degree (linear) and can be generally represented as follows:

$$P = e \times MT + P_{min}$$

Where the price will vary according to e who is modulus of elasticity, this is multiplied by the amount of material to sell, the equation is complemented with a minimum price or zero price of units, the behavior of the function vary according to the value of elasticity, which determines the slope of the same and the minimum price, the graph of the function behaves as in Figure 1, where the slope of the linear function defined by the falling price of the material with respect to the higher volume thereof.

Returning to the role of income and considering the variations with respect to prices previously explained, the new function of income will be:

$$f(FIA) = \sum_{i=1}^{n} (e \times MT + P_{min})_i \times MT_i$$

Subject to:

$$\sum_{i=1}^{n} MT_i \leq (k \times PE) - (c \times PC)$$

Operating, finally revenue function is:

$$f(FIA) = \sum_{i=1}^{n} (e_i \times MT_i^2) + (P_{min\ i} \times MT_i)$$

Subject to:

$$\sum_{i=1}^{n} MT_i \leq (k \times PE) - (c \times PC)$$

But the market volume is finally defined by all potential revenue to be gained by selling materials and are tied to the demand function, this says that the market will have a maximum value, this maximum is the highest possible income that given material could produce.

For this value, the point of maximum revenue, would derive revenue function. This concept is called Marginal Revenue and the point of maximum income will be given when the value of the marginal revenue function is equal to 0 (zero), that is:

$$\frac{df(FIA)}{dMT} = \sum_{i=1}^{n} 2e_i\ MT_i + P_{min\ i}$$

Where the value of the function is zero, find the maximum amount of material that can be sold without causing a decline in revenue.

D. Cash Flow Model

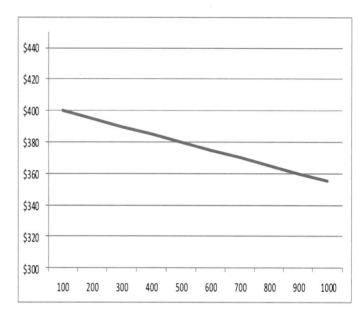

Fig 1. Sample materials demand function for A

Based on the income and expenses, we propose a cash flow model for recycling activity developed by the population of VTA wheelwrights, in this model is considered SO, MVTA as part of FIA expenditures and revenues as part of this is illustrated in Table 1.

This enclosure leads us to define the population of wheelwrights and to the activity as such the equation that helps us to establish the sustainability of the business and that is:

$$\frac{(f\ (FIA)_{n-1} - (SO_{n-1} + MVTA_{n-1})) + f\ (FIA)_n}{SO_{n+1} + MVTA_{n+1}}$$

Where should ensure that the income of the period plus the remaining amount of prior period do not exceed the amount of income in the period under review, according to information collected in the field and testimonials from community members themselves, is some periods sustainability of the activity tends to be below the minimum support value, a situation that forces people to wheelwrights to use strategies such as reducing maintenance costs of home sale or disposition of goods, loans informally with moneylenders, etc.

TABLE 1

CASH FLOW MODEL FOR POPULATION OF WHEELWRIGHTS (VTA)

	Month n	Month n+1	Month n+2
Income	$f\,(FIA)_n$	$f\,(FIA)_{n+1}$	$f\,(FIA)_{n+2}$
Functional Expenses	SO_n	SO_{n+1}	SO_{n+2}
Operating Expenses	$MVTA_n$	$MVTA_{n+1}$	$MVTA_{n+2}$
Total expenses	$SO_n + MVTA_n$	$SO_{n+1} + MVTA_{n+1}$	$SO_{n+2} + MVTA_{n+2}$
Cash	$f\,(FIA)_n - (SO_n + MVTA_n)$	$f\,(FIA)_{n+1} - (SO_{n+1} + MVTA_{n+1})$	$f\,(FIA)_{n+2} - (SO_{n+2} + MVTA_{n+2})$

E. Management Model

The population of wheelwrights uses a management model based on the immediate response to emerging needs, that is, the administrative management of money management is done in an informal way, no records of any kind logistics management is very poor or non-there since the horse-drawn vehicle begins the workday without fixed route plan, on the other hand the work of marketing and product advertising is not because the carters client is always the same and if generated these changes do not correspond to planning but rather for casual events, management of portfolio (by the way of work) is nonexistent and not allow credit sales, no inventory and manage transformation processes do not.

Therefore, management model of these business units is reduced to a daily revenue management, for these his two cost parameters: one for family and one for the vehicle, the savings are nonexistent, so no money reserves for contingencies and for modernization of the team, or for innovation or development.

The current management model that caused the population (VTA), carrying out business at a disadvantage with the rest of the population is engaged in the transportation of material, gradually forcing them to transform their business, in addition to this the animal-drawn vehicles are causing various problems such as traffic difficulties (low travel speeds faster avenues), accidents with horse (to force the horse to higher loads and work with food deficiency), the oversized loads, Insecurity (carts used in criminal acts, etc.).

Discussed above, we propose a management model should be based on the organization and distribution of income according to their obligations, they also organized into two categories: administrative and operating expenses. In the first should be organized and should include payroll and leases own activity and marketing efforts work and payments of financial obligations on the other hand, operating expenses must be related to logistics costs and vehicle maintenance costs.

III. RECOMMENDATIONS

When formalizing the processes, policies and tools oriented to the management and development of intellectual assets of the organization (in this case the District Department of Transportation Bogotá), with the aim of transforming the knowledge accumulated in value and benefits tangible to the organization and its stakeholders (other offices of the Mayor), we are talking about Knowledge Management.

We could say that the initial stage arose from the need of the District Department of Transportation to analyze the current situation and future projection VTA of resources and capacities of the city, designed to meet different scenarios, along with establishing a vision of the potential current and future (replacement) which will be based on the strategic development of the city traffic.

Given the importance of knowledge at a strategic level within the organization, there a next step that has generated the need for the development of a 'knowledge strategy', which forms the foundation for the success of the project in the organization. For this, being understood the context of the needs and projections set out in the strategy of knowledge and recognizing the degree of technological adaptability necessary for a development project.

Of course everything must start from the need for the wheelwrights to improve their working conditions and for this we examined the possibility technify your working tool, and this modernization is to change the binomial (wagon and horse) by a motorized means of transport base gasoline (motorcar) in addition to this is low power, high performance, reduce their travel time, increase their average speed, reduce operating costs, reduce maintenance costs and allow wheelwrights VTA, continue to make its core business, which at a later stage would be implementation.

In a globalized, knowledge management can be considered the organizational structure and culture that facilitates working together, sharing knowledge and information, physically and virtually, so that we are able to develop innovative products and services, new solutions and be more effective and effective.

Properly manage knowledge does not necessarily mean

being more innovative, but it involves a solid foundation (in terms of culture, processes, policies and technologies) that can and should be used by the city as a lever for innovation and change

CONCLUSIONS

The model presented seeks to better explain the existing the way it performs the activity of the population derives its income from the use of animal-drawn vehicle, in addition to this, the model should also serve as input for the analysis retirement convenience or modernization of the working tool currently used wheelwrights (VTA).

With the above model can be analyzed as changes come to affect the activity of the population currently wheelwrights (VTA), this analysis can be performed independently of both the revenue of the activity, as the expenses of the same, with this you can develop strategies or mitigation and monitoring plans when making changes to the development of the activity.

Without proper knowledge management from top management enhanced with instruments suitable motivation and involvement, innovation becomes a process even more difficult, more distant and therefore much more expensive.

ACKNOWLEDGMENT

A large part of the changes made on the ground mentioned is due to the excellent leadership of those who have been part of the team of the Agreements between the District Department of Transportation and the University District. Special thanks to the General Conventions for trusting our talents for this project as well as its diverse team of advisers who supported us with information, and you should not forget our direct team tirelessly prepared the field logistics, collected and helped to classify the various sources of information and to Dr. Ingrid Campos who attended and supported the social management.

REFERENCES

[1] Convenio Interadministrativo 2009-1252 SDM-UD, *Estructuración técnica, legal, financiera y social del proyecto retiro de vehículos de tracción animal - Elaboración de la caracterización socioeconómica de la población de carreteros (VTA) en la ciudad de Bogotá, D.C., incluidos escenarios propuestos de proyectos económicos viables y sostenibles que reemplacen y/o tecnifiquen el vehículo de tracción animal (VTA) - Fase uno,* Parte 1, Bogotá - Colombia., 2009

[2] Convenio Interadministrativo 2009-1252 SDM-UD, *Estructuración técnica, legal, financiera y social del proyecto retiro de vehículos de tracción animal - Elaboración de la caracterización socioeconómica de la población de carreteros (VTA) en la ciudad de Bogotá, D.C., incluidos escenarios propuestos de proyectos económicos viables y sostenibles que reemplacen y/o tecnifiquen el vehículo de tracción animal (VTA) - Fase uno,* Parte 2, Bogotá - Colombia., 2009

[3] Convenio Interadministrativo 2009-1252 SDM-UD, *Estructuración técnica, legal, financiera y social del proyecto retiro de vehículos de tracción animal - Elaboración de la caracterización socioeconómica de la población de carreteros (VTA) en la ciudad de Bogotá, D.C., incluidos escenarios propuestos de proyectos económicos viables y sostenibles que reemplacen y/o tecnifiquen el vehículo de tracción animal (VTA) - Fase uno,* Parte 3, Bogotá - Colombia., 2009

[4] Fox, Robert ; Technological Change: Methods and Themes in the History of Technology, Routledge Group Edition, New York, 2009

[5] Crisman, Kevin J. & Cohn, Arthur B; When horses walked on water: horse-powered ferries in nineteenth-century America, Smithsonian Institution Press, Whashington, 1998

[6] McShane, Clay & Tarr, Joel A; The horse in the city: Living machines in the nineteenth Century; The Johns Hopkins University Press, Baltimore, 2007

[7] Lizet, Bernadette; La bête noire: à la recherche du cheval parfait; Editions MSH, Paris, 1989

[8] Mavré, Marcel; Attelages te attelées: un siècle d'utilisation du cheval de trait; Editions France Agricole, París, 2004

[9] J. J. Goñi. *¿Un innovador o muchos innovadores?* [Online]. Available: http://www.gestiondelconocimiento.com/leer.php?id=339&colaborador =jjgoni

[10] N. Aramburu, *Aprendizaje Organizativo,* Tesis de Grado "Un Estudio del Aprendizaje Organizativo desde la Perspectiva del Cambio: Implicaciones Estratégicas y Organizativas.", Universidad de Deusto, San Sebastián - España, 2000. Avalaible: http://www.gestiondelconocimiento.com/documentos2/nekane/GCcam. PDF

[11] Alejandro Andrés Pavez Salazar, Tesis de Grado: *"Modelo de implantación de Gestión del Conocimiento y Tecnologías de Información para la Generación de Ventajas Competitivas",* Universidad Técnica Federico Santa María, Valparaíso - Chile, 2000. Avalaible: http://www.gestiondelconocimiento.com/documentos2/apavez/zip/apave z.pdf

## 8

Recognition of Emotions using Energy Based Bimodal Information Fusion and Correlation

Krishna Asawa, Priyanka Manchanda[1]

[1]Department of Computer Science Engineering and Information Technology
Jaypee Institute of Information Technology, Noida, India

Abstract — **Multi-sensor information fusion is a rapidly developing research area which forms the backbone of numerous essential technologies such as intelligent robotic control, sensor networks, video and image processing and many more. In this paper, we have developed a novel technique to analyze and correlate human emotions expressed in voice tone & facial expression. Audio and video streams captured to populate audio and video bimodal data sets to sense the expressed emotions in voice tone and facial expression respectively. An energy based mapping is being done to overcome the inherent heterogeneity of the recorded bi-modal signal. The fusion process uses sampled and mapped energy signal of both modalities's data stream and further recognize the overall emotional component using Support Vector Machine (SVM) classifier with the accuracy 93.06%.**

Keywords — **Bimodal Fusion, Emotion Recognition, Intelligent Systems, Machine Learning, Energy Mapping**

I. INTRODUCTION

MULTI-SENSOR information fusion is a rapidly developing area of research and development which forms the foundation of intelligent robotic control. It comprises of methods and techniques which collect input from multiple similar or dissimilar sources and sensors, extract the required information and fuse them together to achieve improved accuracy in inference than that could be achieved by the use of a single data source alone. In this contribution, we discuss a novel approach to fuse heterogeneous datasets obtained from multiple sensors with the aim of analyzing the human's emotional behavior.

Emotions play an important role in human-to-human communication and interaction, allowing people to express themselves beyond the verbal domain. The ability to understand human emotions is desirable for the computer in some applications such as computer-aided learning or user-friendly on-line help. During an interaction, an individual uses multiple modalities such as eye gaze, hand gestures, facial expressions, body posture, and tone of voice. Human behavior is thus, inherently multimodal. In addition to its multimodal nature, the emotional state of an individual is also an integral component of human experience and plays a significant role in developing intelligent systems for human computer communication. It influences numerous phenomenons such as cognition, perception, learning, creativity and decision-making. Besides the problem solving, reasoning, perception and cognitive tasks, emotion recognition also plays a pivot role in functions which are essential for artificial intelligence.

Considering these two aspects of human behavior, we have designed and developed a technique to analyze and correlate bimodal data sets and further recognize the emotional component from these fused data sets. This new technology ensures a proper balance between emotion recognition and cognition tasks.

The existing fusion methods as listed in the section- related work, do not address how to bridge the heterogeneity present in the captured data, which corresponds to the individual modality. The energy based mapping method inspired from how the different sensed stimuli signals by humans, mapped to the corresponding energy onto designated areas of the brain. This method brings homogeneity among heterogeneous emotional cues by transforming them onto their corresponding energy levels. The achieved fusion accuracy of 93.06% can ensures a proper balance between emotion recognition and cognition tasks.

The rest of the paper has been organized in the following manner: in Section II, along with existing fusion approaches, we discuss an energy based method for fusion of multimodal data sets. In Section III, we explain the architectural framework of our model. The implementation of the solution is delineated in Section IV. Section V outlines the applications of this model. Lastly, we conclude the research study in Section VI.

II. RELATED WORK

The wide use of multimodal data fusion technologies in versatile areas of application has invoked an ever increasing interest of researchers all over the globe. Multimodal data fusion techniques are used in numerous areas such as intelligent systems, robotics, sensor networks, video and image processing and many more. Multimodal data fusion can be performed at three levels: feature, decision and hybrid level fusion.

Feature level fusion has been used in [1] for fusing range of spatial cues with the relative assignment of linear weight to them. But they have unable to resolve the issue of how weights should be assigned to justify relevance and importance of different cues.

Neti [2] have been performed decision level fusion for speaker recognition and speech event detection. They have analyzed audio features (e.g. phonemes) and visual features (e.g. visemes) independently to arrive at recognized decision according to single modality. Thereafter they have employed a linear weighted sum strategy to fuse these individual decisions. The authors have used the training data to determine the relative reliability of the different modalities and accordingly adjusted their weights. Where as in [3], for speaker identification, they have considered the results of different classifier at decision level fusion. From the speech corpora, a set of patterns are identified for each speaker on the basis of predefined features by two different classifiers. The majority decision regarding the identity of the unknown speaker is obtained by fusing the output scores of all the classifiers using a late integration approach.

A multimodal integration approach using custom defined rules has been suggested by, Holzapfel et al. [4]. They have shown smooth human - robot interaction in the kitchen setting by fusing results of speech and 3D pointing gestures. This multimodal fusion which is performed at the decision level based on the n-best lists generated by each of the event parsers. A close correlation in time of speech and gesture has been proved by this approach, but this is leading to the process time overhead to determine the best action based on n-best fused input.

In [5] two techniques viz (1) Gradient-descent-optimization linear fusion (GLF) and (2) the super-kernel nonlinear fusion (NLF) are suggested. Each of which does the optimal combination of multimodal information for video concept detection. In GLF, an individual kernel matrix is first constructed and then fused together based on a weighted linear combination scheme. Unlike GLF, the NLF method does nonlinear combination of multimodal information.

In [6], the authors have used NLF method and first construct an SVM for the individual modality as a classifier. Thereafter, for optimal combination of the individual classifier models a super kernel non-linear fusion is applied. Experiments conducted on TREC-2003 Video Track benchmark shows NLF has on average 3.0% better performance than GLF.

To classify image, Zhu et al. [7] have given a hybrid level multimodal fusion framework. They have used SVM to classify the images with embedded text within their spatial coordinates. The fusion process is done in two steps. Firstly, on the basis of low-level visual features, a bag-of-words model [8] is used to classify the given image. At the same time, the text detector records the existence of text in the image using text color, size, location, edge density, brightness, contrast, etc. In the second step, for fusing the visual and textual features together a pair-wise SVM classifier is used.

A time-delayed neural network employed by Cutler and Davis [9] for feature level multimodal data fusion in for locating the speaking person in the scene. This is being done by identifying the correlation between audio and visual streams.

In another work, related to detecting human activities Gandetto et al. [10] have used the Neural Network decision level fusion method to combine sensory data. An environment equipped with a heterogeneous network of state sensors for sensing CPU load, login process, and network load and cameras for sensing observation along with computational units working together in a LAN is considered for the experiment. Human activity is monitored by fusing the data from these two types of sensors at the decision level.

A framework is given in [16] which fuse textual and visual information. Author has proposed additional preprocessing before combining these modalities in a linear weighted fashion at the feature and scoring levels. The pre-processing called as latent semantic mixing, takes care about overlapping information among both modalities by mapping the bimodal feature space onto low dimensional semantic space.

In this paper, we propose a feature level linear weighted fusion model based on a human-inspired concept of brain energy mapping model. Humans collect sensory data via human biological senses (sight, hearing, touch, smell and taste) and map this data as energy stimuli onto designated regions of the brain. The brain then fuses them together to obtain an inference. This analogy is employed in designing the architectural framework of our work. This phenomenon is depicted in Fig 1.

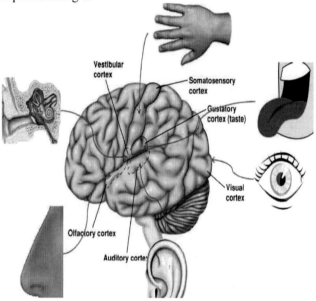

Fig. 1. The Brain Energy Mapping Model

III. ARCHITECTURAL FRAMEWORK

Figure 2 shows the overall architectural framework and computation stages as listed below.

- Step1: Obtain Bi-Modal Input stream
- Step 2: Split Bi-Modal Input into Audio and Video Components
- Step 3: Synchronized Sampling and processing of Audio and Video Components

- Step 4: Run two parallel process, each for audio and video.
- Audio thread performs segmentation and feature extraction for audio sample using praat tool.
- Video thread performs segmentation and facial feature extraction for video sample DAFL library.
- Step 5: Estimation of Audio and Video features energy.

- Step 6: Perform one of the following depending on user's input:
- Train SVM
- Test an unknown sample with trained SVM to predict emotion
- Step 7: Display emotion to the user

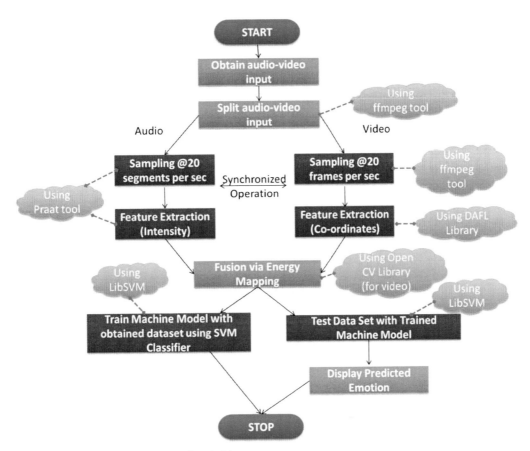

Fig 2. Architectural Framework of Bimodal Energy Based Fusion Model

Stage I – Data Pre-Processing

The bimodal inputs obtained and then split into two components – audio and video. Thereafter, audio processing and video processing is performed simultaneously and in synchronization. The synchronization is necessary to ensure that no data is lost and the audio and video samples at any particular instance are processed simultaneously.

The audio component is segmented at the rate of 20 samples (utterances) per second. Video Sampling is done at the rate of 20 frames per second.

Stage II – Feature Extraction

The prosodic feature mean intensity of the audio component between time 't1' and 't2' is computed as:

$$\frac{1}{(t2-t1)} \int_{t1}^{t2} x(t)\,dt \qquad (1)$$

where x(t) is intensity as function of time (in dB).

To compute the intensity, the values in the sound are first squared, then convolved with a Gaussian analysis window (Kaiser-20; sidelobes below -190 dB). The effective duration of this analysis window is 3.2 / (minimum_pitch), which guarantee that a periodic signal is analysed as having a pitch-synchronous intensity ripple not greater than 0.00001 dB.

The processing of video frames is done in two steps:

- Facial Feature extraction using the Discrete Area Filters (DAF) Library used to extract coordinates of 15 facial feature points. [13]
- Energy (gradient) computation (Fig 3) of extracted facial features co-ordinates using OpenCV Library.

A	B	C
D	E	F
G	H	I

$$energy(E) = \sqrt{xenergy^2 + yenergy^2}$$
$$xenergy = a + 2d + g - c - 2f - i$$
$$yenergy = a + 2b + c - g - 2h - i$$

Fig 3. Energy (Gradient) Computation

In Fig. 3, each lowercase letter represents the brightness (sum of the red, blue, and green values) of the corresponding pixel. To compute the energy of edge pixels, we consider that the image is surrounded by a 1 pixel wide border of black pixels (with 0 brightness).

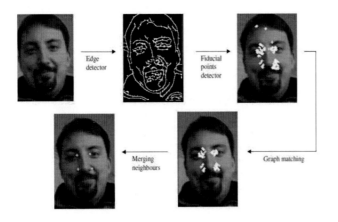

Fig 4. Facial Feature Detection using Discrete Area Filters

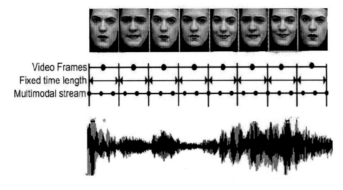

Fig 5. Bi-modal Input Processing

Stage III – Fusion via Energy Mapping

Our framework uses the technique of feature level linear weighted fusion. Consider a feature set <Ev, Ea>, where Ev is the total energy of video features and Ea is the total energy of audio features. The feature set is computed at intervals of 1 second for the bi-modal input.

$$E_a = wE_{a1} + wE_{a2} + \ldots\ldots\ldots + wE_{an} \quad (2)$$

where,
E_a is the audio energy of the audio sample of 1sec duration.

E_{ai} is the audio energy of ith sub-sample
w is the weight assigned to each sub-sample.
n is the number of sub samples = 20

$$(3)$$
$$E\_vi = w\_1 \ (E\_vio + E\_vi1 + E\_vi2 + E\_vi3) + w\_2 \ (E\_vi4 + E\_vi5 + E\_vi6 + E\_vi7) + w\_3 \ (E\_vi8 + E\_vi9 + E\_vi10) + w\_4 \ (E\_vi11 + E\_vi12 + E\_vi13 + E\_vi14)$$
where,
E_{vi} is the energy of ith frame of the video sub-sample.
w_1 is weight assigned to left eye fiducial points.
w_2 is weight assigned to right eye fiducial points.
w_3 is weight assigned to nose fiducial points.
w_4 is weight assigned to mouth fiducial points.

$$w_4 > w_1, w_2 > w_3$$

$$E_v = wE_{v1} + wE_{v2} + \ldots\ldots\ldots + wE_{vn} \quad (4)$$
where,
E_v is the combined energy of the video sub-samples.
E_{vi} is the energy of ith video sub-sample.
w is the weight assigned to each sub-sample.
n is the number of sub samples = 20

We further label the feature set with appropriate class (1 – Happy, 2 – Anger, 3 – Fear) depending on the emotional state of the user. This feature set is then used to train the machine model designed for predicting the mood of the user.

Stage IV – Emotion Prediction

The Support Vector Machine (SVM) classifier is used to predict the emotional state of the bimodal input. We use LibSVM[14] to develop the C-SVC (C - Support Vector Classification) SVM having RBF (Radial Basis Function - exp(-gamma*|u-v|^2)) kernel.

We further develop a machine model using C-SVC SVM and train it using the feature sets obtained in Stage III. The feature sets of the input to be tested are then labeled with an arbitrary label. These are then tested using the trained machine model. Finally, the predicted emotional state of the bi-modal input is displayed to the user.

IV.   RESULTS AND ACCURACY CALCULATION

The energy based bimodal data fusion model was tested for the eNTERFACE[15] database with 3 discrete emotions that are happy, anger and fear. The specifications of the database are as follows:
- 648 samples
  - 43 subjects enacting 5 sentences of each of 3 emotions (happy, anger and fear)
- Samples having both male and female subject
- Frontal views with moderate lighting conditions
- Single person input

The 80: 20 ratios of the training and testing samples are considered for cross validation. The total samples for each emotion are 215. Three times process has been repeated with different sets of training and testing in the ratio of 80:20. On average in each round 485 samples are classifies correctly on the basis of 518 samples. The average percentage of classification for the three emotions is shown in the table 1.

TABLE 1. CONFUSION MATRIX (IN %)

Predicted Emotion				
		Happy	**Anger**	**Fear**
Actual Emotion	**Happy**	92.59%	4.17%	3.24%
	Anger	1.85%	94.44%	3.70%
	Fear	1.85%	6.02%	92.13%

The model shows 93.06% accuracy for emotion recognition of Happy, Anger and Fear Emotions using energy mapping model.

V. CONCLUSION

In this research study, we have developed a tool to analyze and correlate bimodal data sets of emotional cues using energy based fusion model and further recognized the emotional component from these bimodal data sets using Support Vector Machine classifier. We have mapped the audio and video features of bimodal input to their corresponding energy levels. The model is tested for eNTERFACE 2005 database and an accuracy of 93.06% is obtained recognition of happy, anger and fear emotions. The tool developed for bimodal energy based fusion model can further be used as a wrapper tool to develop intelligent applications which require multimodal data fusion and emotion recognition, such as Real Time Emotion Recognition, Expressive Embodied Conversational Agent, Virtual Tutor, Questionnaire which analyse verbal and non-verbal behavior.

ACKNOWLEDGMENTS

The work reported in this paper is supported by the grant received from All India Council for Technical Education; A Statutory body of the Govt. of India. vide f. no. 8023/BOR/RID/RPS-129/2008-09.

REFERENCES

[1] Wang, J., Kankanhalli, M. S., Yan, W., & Jain, R. (2003). Experiential sampling for video surveillance. In First ACM SIGMM international workshop on Video surveillance (pp. 77-86).

[2] Neti, C., Maison, B., Senior, A. W., Iyengar, G., Decuetos, P., Basu, S., &Verma, A. (2000). Joint processing of audio and visual information for multimedia indexing and human-computer interaction(pp. 294-301).

[3] Radová, V., & Psutka, J. (1997). An approach to speaker identification using multiple classifiers. In Acoustics, Speech, and Signal Processing, ICASSP-97 (Vol. 2, pp. 1135-1138).

[4] Holzapfel, H., Nickel, K., & Stiefelhagen, R. (2004). Implementation and evaluation of a constraint-based multimodal fusion system for speech and 3D pointing gestures. In Proceedings of the 6th international conference on Multimodal interfaces (pp. 175-182).

[5] Wu, K., Lin, C.K., Chang, E., Smith, J.R. (2004) Multimodal information fusion for video concept detection. In: IEEE International Conference on Image Processing, Singapore (pp. 2391–2394).

[6] Adams, W. H., Iyengar, G., Lin, C. Y., Naphade, M. R., Neti, C., Nock, H. J., & Smith, J. R. (2003). Semantic indexing of multimedia content

using visual, audio, and text cues. EURASIP Journal on Advances in Signal Processing (pp. 170-185).

[7] Zhu, Q., Yeh, M. C., & Cheng, K. T. (2006). Multimodal fusion using learned text concepts for image categorization. In Proceedings of the 14th annual ACM international conference on Multimedia (pp. 211-220).

[8] Li, F.F., Perona, P. (2005). A bayesian hierarchical model for learning natural scene categories. In: IEEE Computer Society Conference on Computer Vision and Pattern Recognition, Washington (vol. 2, pp. 524–531)

[9] Cutler, R., & Davis, L. (2000). Look who's talking: Speaker detection using video and audio correlation. In Multimedia and Expo, 2000. ICME 2000 (Vol. 3, pp. 1589-1592).

[10] Gandetto, M., Marchesotti, L., Sciutto, S., Negroni, D., Regazzoni, C.S. (2003). From multi-sensor surveillance towards smart interactive spaces. In: IEEE International Conference on Multimedia and Expo, Baltimore (pp. I:641–644).

[11] Bellard, F., & Niedermayer, M. (2012). FFmpeg. http://ffmpeg.org

[12] Boersma, Paul &Weenink, David (2014). Praat: doing phonetics by computer [Computer program]. Version 5.3.77, retrieved 18 May 2014 from http://www.praat.org/.

[13] Naruniec, J., &Skarbek, W. (2007). Face detection by discrete gabor jets and reference graph of fiducial points. In Rough Sets and Knowledge Technology Springer Berlin Heidelberg (pp. 187-194).

[14] Martin, Olivier, et al. 2006. The eNTERFACE' 05 Audio-Visual Emotion Database. Data Engineering Workshops, Proceedings.

[15] Chih-Chung Chang and Chih-Jen Lin (2006). LIBSVM : a library for support vector machines. Software available at http://www.csie.ntu.edu.tw/~cjlin/libsvm

[16] [16] Nam Khanh Tran (2012) Multimodal Fusion for Combining

[17] Textual and Visual Information in a Semantic mode, Thesis submitted to Universitat Des Saarlandes.

Dr. Krishna Asawa presently working with Jaypee Institute of Information Technology (JIIT), Deemed to be University, NOIDA, INDIA in the capacity of Associate Professor. Dr. Krishna awarded Doctor of Philosophy (CSE) in 2002 from Banasthali Vidyapith, Deemed to be University, Banasthali, INDIA. Her area of interest and expertise includes Soft Computing and its applications, Information Security, Knowledge and Data Engineering. Before joining to the JIIT she worked with National Institute of Technology, Jaipur, INDIA and with Banasthali Vidyapith.

Ms. Priyanka Manchanda has completed her graduation in Computer Science and Engineering from Jaypee Institute of Information Technology (JIIT), Deemed to be University, NOIDA, INDIA in 2014. She is currently pursuing MS at Columbia University, New York.

## 9

Approach for solving multimodal problems using Genetic Algorithms with Grouped into Species optimized with Predator-Prey

Pablo Seoane, Marcos Gestal, Julián Dorado

Departament of Information and Communications Technologies, University of A Coruña, A Coruña, Spain

Abstract —**Over recent years, Genetic Algorithms have proven to be an appropriate tool for solving certain problems. However, it does not matter if the search space has several valid solutions, as their classic approach is insufficient. To this end, the idea of dividing the individuals into species has been successfully raised. However, this solution is not free of drawbacks, such as the emergence of redundant species, overlapping or performance degradation by significantly increasing the number of individuals to be evaluated. This paper presents the implementation of a method based on the predator-prey technique, with the aim of providing a solution to the problem, as well as a number of examples to prove its effectiveness.**

Key words—**Genetic Algorithms, Multimodal Problems, Species Evaluation, Predator-Prey Approach**

I. INTRODUCTION

In the Genetic Algorithms [1] there is a simulation of a population of individuals that evolves until reaching a solution within a given search space. With the aim of achieving various solutions in a multimodal environment, that is, with several optimal valid values, a division of the population into species is carried out, so that each can specialize in a solution of the problem. Using this technique, the obtained results were satisfactory [2]. However, it has some drawbacks. Due to the fact that new species are created with each generation, and therefore new individuals, the population grows exponentially. The immediate consequences are an increased consumption of computational resources, as well as a slowing down of the whole system.

To avoid the created drawbacks, the concept of predator-prey [3] is introduced in the system applying it to species in the area. The technique is firstly designed to distribute individuals behaving as prey randomly in an area and then do the same with some individuals called predators, which, according to some rules, deal with deleting some of the prey in the neighborhood. The deleted individual is replaced by another, obtained as a result of a mutation of a randomly chosen nearby prey and predators move around, looking for a new victim.

This technique could be used in a similar way when dealing with grouping into species, so that species could compete against each other, as preys or predators, according to some previously defined rules. The role is assigned dynamically, after the meeting of the two species. In the same way, the species which enhances the values of the chosen rule is helped to continue its evolution, whereas the individuals of the other species disappear. The species and individuals that are considered dispensable for obtaining solutions will be removed from the system.

The predator-prey method is aimed at overcoming the limitations that arise when applying the technique of the Genetic Algorithms grouped into species to a multimodal problem, obtaining the best results provided by the grouping of species, but using the fewest elements possible, so that the species could maintain their numbers or even suffer losses during the development of the method and as a result the total amount of individuals decreases. Hence, the method implementation is optimized.

A first approximation is performed to test the system using a multimodal Rastrigin function. This is a preliminary study whose aim will be to apply the solution to complex problems.

II. MULTIMODAL PROBLEMS

Multimodal problems are problems with multiple local optima and/or multiple global optima. In the real world, we usually wish to know the largest possible number of solutions to a problem. This may be due to various factors. On the one hand, we may not have total knowledge of the problem and when we find a solution, we may ignore how good it really is because we cannot be certain that no better solutions are available in our search space. On the other hand, we may know that our solution is the best response to a problem, but other solutions turn out to be better in global terms because they are cheaper, simpler, less cumbersome, etc. The classical functions of Rastrigin and Ackey, among others, present this behaviour.

III.   GENETIC ALGORITHMS

Genetic Algorithms are adaptive methods that are generally applied to the search and optimization of parameters and based on "sexual" reproduction and the survival of the most apt specimen. Following the schemes proposed by C. Darwin [4], an initial set of individuals or "population" is created, who evolve in the course of several generations, each individual representing the solution to a problem. After several evolutions, the best individuals are maintained, but so are other specimens of less quality, in order to respect diversity and guarantee the existence of individuals with diverse features that may adapt to possible changes in the environment.

1)   Origins and Biological Bases of Genetics Algorithms

In nature, the most adapted individuals have the best chances to reproduce themselves. Genetic inheritance provides descendants with the features of the most adapted progenitors and allows the species to evolve. Evolutionary Computation arises when researchers try to emulate the good results for problem solving offered by nature and is based on certain facts of biological evolution with strong experimental evidence:

- Evolution takes place in the chromosomes, not in the individuals.
- Natural selection is the tool that relates chromosomes to their efficiency. The most efficient individuals have more possibilities to reproduce themselves.
- Evolutionary processes take place in the reproductive stage (even though some aspects, such as mutation, may occur in other stages).

Traditional Genetic Algorithms do not contemplate the possibility of dividing individuals into species in order to reach solutions. This article proposes to open up this behaviour.

2)   Classification of Genetic Algorithms

There are several ways of classifying Genetic Algorithms. The most common solution consists in classifying them according to the obtaining of new generations, which leads to the following categories:

- Generational Genetic Algorithms: the parent generation is eliminated in the course of the last reproductive phase, and only the new population is maintained.
- Steady-state Genetic Algorithms: the parents of one generation coexist with the children of the next generation. Population substitution algorithms are used to determine who must be eliminated.
- Another classification of Genetic Algorithms focuses on methods of execution:
- Sequential Genetic Algorithms: This is the usual way of executing an algorithm: one population tries to solve a problem by crossing its individuals over several generations and evolving towards a solution.
- Parallel Genetic Algorithms: In nature, when populations are geographically isolated from each other, they tend to

evolve and originate different responses to evolutionary pressure. This originates two models that use multiple populations concurrently: the Island model and the Cellular Model [8].

In the *Island Model* the population of individuals is divided into subpopulations that evolve separately, like a normal Genetic Algorithm. In the *Cellular Model* each individual is placed in a matrix where it can only reproduce itself with the individuals that surround it, choosing at random or picking those that are most adapted.

3)   Problem codification

Any potential solution for a problem can be presented by giving values to a series of parameters. All these parameters (*genes* in the Genetic Algorithms terminology) are codified into a chain of values called *chromosome*. This codification tends to be carried out, if possible, with binary values, although real and entire values are also used. Each bit that belongs to a gene is called *allele*.

4)   Main Algorithm

The generic functioning of a sequential generational Genetic Algorithm is the following one:

```
Initiate current population arbitrarily
WHILE the termination criterium is not fulfilled
  create empty temporary population
  WHILE temporary population does not fulfil
      select parents
      cross parents with probabilty Pc
      IF crossing has ocurred
         -Mutate one of the descendants with
         probability Pm
         -evaluate descendants
         -add descendant to the temporary
         population
      OTHERWISE
         -add parents to the temporary
         population
      END IF
  END WHILE
increase generations counter
establish the temporary population as new
current population
END WHILE
```

The pseudocode of a steady-state Genetic Algorithm would be similar to the above, except that the temporary population would be absent and we would have to use substitution algorithms.

One generation is created from a previous generation by means of two types of reproduction operators: cross-over and copy. Cross-over is a sexual reproduction that originates new descendants by exchanging the genetic information of the parents; copy consists in passing a certain number of individuals to the next generation without any variation. Once the new individuals are generated, mutation takes place with a *Pm* probability, and the errors of the genetic copy process are imitated.

The process finishes when there are sufficiently good solutions in the shape of better individuals, when all the individuals converge towards a similar value, or when the largest possible number of generations is reached.

In order for a Genetic Algorithm to function correctly, it must dispose of a method that indicates whether or not the individuals of the population represent good solutions to a given problem. This is the task of the evaluation function, which establishes a numeric measurement of the quality of a solution. This measurement is called adjustment or fitness.

IV. TECHNIQUES OF GROUPING INTO SPECIES WITH GENETIC ALGORITHMS

The Genetic Algorithm-based approach is able to obtain a good approximation to the solution of the problem to be solved within a few generations. However, the tendency of finding a single solution becomes a disadvantage when dealing with multimodal problems, since in such cases it is preferred to find several solutions.

One of the options to try to solve this drawback involves using the technique of grouping into species which, broadly speaking consists of grouping the initial population of individuals into classes with similar characteristics [2]. Hence, the aim is that each group will be specialized in a particular area of search space. Thus, each species will tend to find an existing solution in its area, other than those provided by other species. This is an attempt of modeling the species distribution of individuals in the natural environment, and their evolution separately. For example, there are individuals adapted to live in cold areas, others in dry or hot ones, etc. Each group manages life in a given environment, adapting to this end specific characteristics that differentiate it from the other groups.

However, this technique has its drawbacks. Thus, certain conditions are required for proper operation, conditions which are not usually obtained in the initial distribution of the problem. For example, it would be recommended that the population should be evenly distributed throughout the search space, and moreover, that groups should be well distributed and in accordance with the number of solutions to the problem. If there are no such characteristics, there may be unexplored areas in contrast to others that are highly explored and in which, depending on how the groups are formed, several species can coexist.

To overcome these drawbacks, we use the crossing of individuals from different species through several generations. In doing so, the offspring resulting from these crosses mix knowledge of their predecessors' species and there emerges the possibility of creating a new species in an area different from their parents'. In this way, stagnation of species is avoided, new areas are explored and new knowledge emerges, that is, diversity is achieved in the environment. Once again, individuals' behavior is being modeled in their natural environment, whereas migration or expulsion of individuals takes place and if they find compatible individuals of other groups, they end up creating new species.

For the implementation of these techniques an initial population is created. The overall process - starting from creating the initial population - is to carry out successive iterations in which the following steps are required:

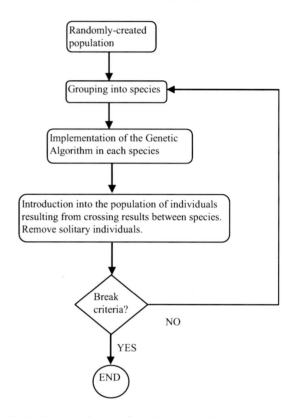

Fig. 1. Operation diagram of grouping into species

One of the main criteria is to check whether the number of iterations, also called evolutions, reaches the maximum number allowed; another is to check whether the population reaches its upper bound of individuals. If either of these conditions is met, the implementation of the algorithm is concluded. Another possible break criterion is that the error value of individuals had fallen below a threshold set in advance.

For the second step of the algorithm, there is no standard way to divide the population of the Genetic Algorithms into species. To solve this problem, techniques of unsupervised grouping of individuals are employed, as there is no a priori knowledge but simply an input data set. The classification is carried out according to some specific parameters of each grouping algorithm type. Two of these techniques that could be used are the Adaptive Method [5], which is a simple and efficient incremental heuristic method using only two parameters and Batchelor and Wilkins' algorithm or the Maximum Distance algorithm [6]. In this case, we also deal with an incremental heuristic method, but it uses a single parameter.

V. PREDATOR-PREY INTERACTION METHOD

Biologically, predation occurs when one of the animals (the predator) devours another living animal (the prey) to use the energy and nutrients in the body of the prey for growth, maintenance or reproduction. Using the predator-prey idea, a model was proposed, adapting the predator-prey concept to Genetic Algorithms [7].

There are software projects dedicated to designing and analyzing predator-prey models. One of them is PEPPA [8], which is a framework for such purpose. The user can work with different operating environments as well as set up the predators' behavior and preys' adaptability. In addition, PEP0050A provides tools for visualization and parallelization of the program running.

The original operation consists of the fact that each individual representing a solution in the genetic population plays the role of prey and of the fact that other individuals in the system play the role of predators, choosing their prey according to the objective function and the fitness of each prey. The method imitates the natural phenomenon in which a predator eliminates the weaker prey, which means that a predator eliminates the most unfit individual in the environment, which corresponds to the worst value obtained in such individuals with the objective function.

To implement this idea a network was proposed, in which the prey are randomly distributed at each node and wherein one or more predators are also placed randomly at some of the nodes.

From that moment, each predator evaluates all prey in its area and deletes the prey corresponding to the worst objective value. Then, a nearby prey is chosen and mutated. The mutated individual replaces the deleted prey and the predator moves to one of the neighboring nodes. This procedure is followed for all predators. As follows, a diagram is shown in Figure 2 [11] presenting the network created with prey and predators.

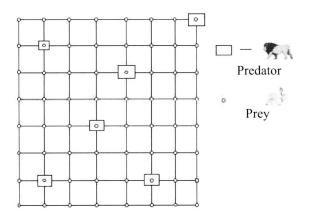

Fig. 2. Representation of prey and predators

The use of this method is widely associated with the multi-objective Genetic Algorithms [9]. These are Genetic Algorithms which are aimed at finding solutions that optimize

several objective functions simultaneously. In such a case, one or more predators are created for each of the objective functions involved; or even a predator that takes into account several objective functions involved in the system is created. The initial diagram regarding the operation of the classical algorithm of the predator-prey approach had already taken this aspect into account. Although modifications and optimizations have been made since its inception, the diagram we have broadly followed is classical [3], as detailed below.

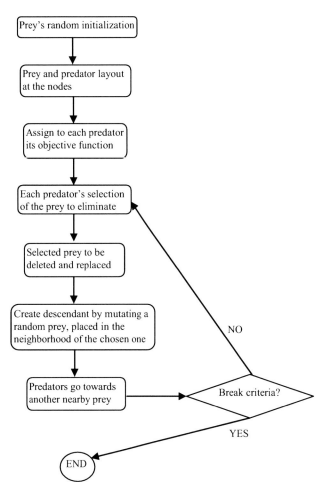

Fig. 3. Operation diagram of the predator-prey approach

The break criterion is either a maximum number of generations or the fact that the objective functions to be optimized have an error below a certain threshold.

Several set-up changes can be performed, as using more predators for every objective function, mutate the best neighbor after predation or move the predator to the box of the best neighbor, instead of moving it randomly. In some cases [9], the outcome of the overall population is improved.

VI. PREDATOR-PREY APPLICATION IN GENETIC ALGORITHMS WITH GROUPING INTO SPECIES

In spite of the fact that the Genetic Algorithms provide optimal solutions to many problems, they have some drawbacks when used to find several solutions in scenarios with multiple optimal points. With the aim of trying to overcome these drawbacks, other solutions were searched for. Among these solutions we mention the grouping the population of individuals into species.

However, it is verifiable that, in the implementations of grouping into species carried out, there are some drawbacks which arise due to the fact that both the number of species and number of individuals tend to continue to grow indefinitely throughout the different evolutions [2]. Such an increased number of individuals and species leads to a continuous increase of the necessary computational resources.

In order to optimize the number of elements used in computing, we suggest applying the benefits of the predator-prey approach to the system made up of Genetic Algorithms grouped into species. This new system is aimed at reducing the number of elements involved in computing, allowing the predation of individuals and, if the choice of which ones should be deleted is made correctly, maintaining similar results to those obtained without the predator-prey approach.

In order to apply the predator-prey approach to the developed system, some changes are necessary, using the main idea of the method as base. Thus, the elements involved are as follows:

- Space for action. This refers to the search space itself, where individuals are distributed.
- Prey. Any species in the system can become prey, being devoured by a predator, which would mean the removal of the species and individuals within it.
- Predator. Any species in the system can become predatory. A prey species devours other prey species. As a benefit, individuals of the species that devours, as well as the species itself, will be able to continue to evolve.
- Objective Function. In this approach, the system will use only the objective function that the Genetic Algorithm employs in each case to calculate the fitness of individuals if necessary.
- Interaction criterion. While in the classical predator-prey algorithm the predator devoured the worst prey in the neighborhood, in this case we need to know the criterion involved so that a species can try to devour another. An example in this sense would be when the species is close enough to the area of another species.
- Role determination criterion. Besides the classical players of the predator-prey approach, it is necessary to define a new concept, the winning rules. In the classical algorithm, some individuals behaved as prey and others as predators. In this case, the same entity – a species – can behave as predator on some occasions and as prey on others. It is necessary, therefore, to define a rule specifying, when appropriate, which of the species will behave as predator and which as prey, and therefore to know which species will survive (predator) and which will be deleted (prey). To this end, the concept of role determination criterion is defined. The role determination criterion refers to a series of algorithms by which it is decided which species would behave as

predator and which as prey. The direct consequence is that the predator species will devour the prey species, the latter disappearing from the system. An example in this regard would be that the predator species (and therefore the survivor) is the one whose individual has the best possible fitness.

The general operation is described below. Once the grouping of individuals into species is performed, and before applying the Genetic Algorithm to each of them, the predator-prey algorithm is applied as follows. The flow chart of the method is detailed in Figure 4.

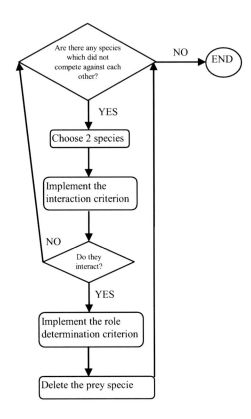

Fig. 4. Flow chart of the predator-prey approach and grouping into species

As shown, two species are chosen from the set created by grouping into species. Then, the interaction criterion is applied. If the species meet the criterion so that the predator-prey approach could be applied, we continue with the next step; otherwise, we should check again whether there are still species that do not meet the interaction criterion. If the species interact, the next step is to apply the role determination criterion to see the role each species assumes, predator or prey. Finally, the predator species is maintained and the prey species is deleted. Individuals belonging to the prey species are marked for removal. The process is repeated until there are no more species that could compete with each other.

To be able to work with this approach, a type of rules should be defined. There will be a more in depth discussion on interaction criterion, providing some examples to decide when two species should behave as predator and prey, and on role determination criterion to indicate how the decision is made regarding which species should be prey and which predator.

1) Examples Interaction criteria.

By grouping the individuals of the population into species, it is not known whether they should interact so that one becomes a prey and the other predator. Thus, the interaction criteria are used to decide when two species in the environment should establish a predator-prey relationship.

If the interaction criterion implemented for two species in the environment decides which species behave as predator and prey, we continue with the next step where it is decided which will behave as prey and which as predator. If the criterion is not met, the search is continued among the total number of species, until finding a pair to which the interaction criterion has not been applied yet. If there is no such pair of species, the proceedings will be completed.

An example of interaction criterion is making two species face each other if the distance between them is below a certain threshold.

In order to observe an example of interaction criterion of distance between species, a hypothetical scenario is shown in Figure 5, where a decision is made regarding which species will interact with the "E1" specie. With a threshold value of 5, only the "E3" specie is below the threshold, so this would be the only species that E1 interacts with.

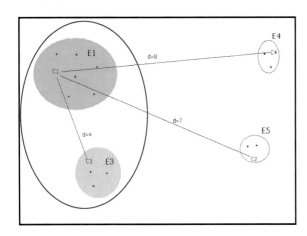

Fig. 5. Example of interaction criterion of distance between species

2) Examples Role determination criteria.

Unlike the original algorithm of the predator-prey approach in which the roles of individuals are static, as there are prey and predators from the beginning in the system and there will be as long as they are used, in this case we are dealing with a dynamic allocation, since any species can behave as prey or predator.

A role determination criterion is an algorithm that decides which of the two interacting species survives and behaves as a predator and which one behaves as prey and is therefore deleted. These rules can be usually generalized to any number of species.

A possible Role Determination Criterion is that of the Best

Individual. Using this criterion, the winner is the species that has the best individual out of the two species. This rule could be generalized to choose a predator from any number of species. In Figure 6 it is shown an example where the species with the best individual is the predator and the one with the worst individual is the prey, being thus deleted. In this example, the greater is the fitness of the individual, the better it is. E3 is the predator specie.

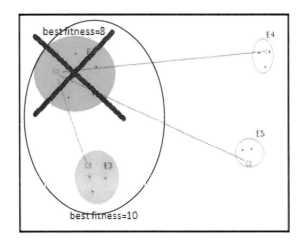

Fig. 6. Example of role determination criterion - the Best Individual

VII. Tests

To check the performance of the predator-prey approach, we use a Genetic Algorithm with Grouping into Species and the corresponding algorithms of the method are applied throughout each evolution.

Before starting the application, we need on the one hand to choose the problem to be solved and on the other hand, considering the problem in question, to select the parameters to be used both to group the individuals into species and for the Genetic Algorithm to be applied to each species in each evolution step. The values selected are in the Figure 7.

FEATURES GENETIC ALGORITHM	
Parameter	**Value**
Algorithm Selection 1/ Algorithm Selection 2	*Roulette-wheel/ Arbitrary*
Cross-over algorithm	*1 point*
Substitution Algorithm	*Worse*
Initial size population	*200*
Mutation probability/ Cross-over probability	*2%/90%*
Number of generations of each species in each evolution	*100*

Fig. 7. Features of Genetic Algorithm

Hence for a first approximation, the Rastrigin function [10] is chosen, which is widely used to show the effectiveness and study of the multimodal problem solving methods. This is a function that has many local minimum and maximum values. In this test are sought maximums. In Figure 8 it is shown a 3D representation of the Rastrigin function. As observed, it has many local maximum values (shown in red) and minimum values (shown in blue).

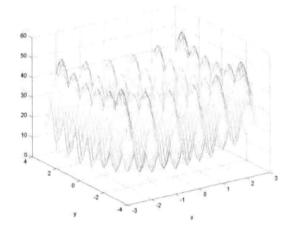

Fig. 8. 3D Representation of the Rastrigin Function

To work with the predator-prey approach, the values previously used in the Genetic Algorithm as well as the Grouping one are set. These are values that obtain satisfactory results in the system of Genetic Algorithms with Grouping into Species. Once set, we compare the results obtained when using or not using the predator-prey approach.

To show the results of applying the predator-prey approach, we implement the distance between species as interaction criterion and the best individual as role determination criterion. The results are compared to those obtained after running the system without using this method.

Once implemented the predator-prey system, it is run. Are only required 10 evolutions to show good results. As follows we present the solutions in the contour plot of the Rastrigin function. The red dots represent the best individuals of each species (the individuals with the least error). Red and green contours are maximum.

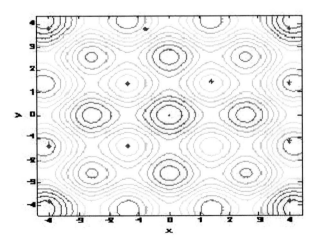

Fig. 9. Solutions found with the predator-prey approach

To obtaining such results, practically identical to those obtained without applying the predator-prey approach, it was necessary to employ a number of species and individuals at all times lower than those employed in the execution without the predator-prey approach, as shown in Figure 7. It is noted that in this case the trend in the number of individuals is increasing, but to a much lesser extent than when the method is not used, since in this case there are deletions of entire species. In Figure 10, we can see the decrease in the number of species and individuals throughout the various evolutions after using the predator-prey approach and in Figure 11 the error evolution.

Evolution	Without predator-prey		With predator-prey	
	Species	Individuals	Species	Individuals
1	15	70	12	49
2	19	84	12	61
5	22	129	16	86
10	17	210	11	123

Fig. 10. Increased number of individuals and species

Evolution	Without predator-prey		With predator-prey	
	Average	Individual	Average	Individual
1	2,5	1,9	2	1,4
2	2,5	1,7	1,9	1,4
5	2,6	1,3	1,7	1,4
10	2	1,3	1,7	1,4

Fig. 11. Evolution of the error and of the best individual's error

Note that the error persists, and the number of individuals and species is much lower, decreasing approximately 40%. The number of solutions reached in this case is slightly lower than in the case of not using the predator-prey approach.

Therefore, the objectives of reducing the number of species and individuals under study are fulfilled, maintaining the error and optimizing the number of necessary resources. Similarly, we found a large number of solutions in any of the two executed cases, approaching to the one found without applying the predator-prey approach.

VIII. CONCLUSION

The tests conducted showed that efficiency Genetic Algorithm with Grouping into Species for multimodal problems was improved. Only a few evolutions were necessary to verify the benefits of the application of predator-prey.

In general, the results were maintained or even improved since species in which individuals did not provide good solutions and increased the error were deleted of the environment.

After checking the adequacy of the proposed solution, the next step would consist of implementing new role determination and interaction criteria that should be more appropriate for a specific problem.

In addition, in each interaction there is a prey species and a predator species. This could be extrapolated, so that there could be an interaction with several preys and/or several predators, as well as a number of objective functions to be optimized, using them for selecting prey or predators.

After this preliminary study the next step is to perform extensive testing in variable selection problems. Specifically, a chemometric problem with previous results in different approaches related with the work performed [2].

REFERENCES

[1]   D. E. Goldberg, "Genetic Algorithms in Search, Optimization and Machine Learning" in Addison-Wesley, Reading, 1989.

[2]   M. Gestal Pose, *Computación evolutiva para el proceso de selección de variables en espacios de búsqueda multimodales*. PhD Thesis, 2010.

[3]   M. Laumanns, G. Rudolph, H.P.Schwefel, H. P.. *A spatial predator-prey approach to multi-objective optimization: A preliminary study. In Proceedings of the Parallel Problem Solving from Nature*, 1998.

[4]   C. Darwin, "On the Origin of Species by Means of Natural Selection", 1859.

[5]   F.J. Cortijo Bon, *Técnicas no Supervisadas: Métodos de Agrupamiento*. 2001.

[6]   B.G.Batchelor, B.R.Wilkins,*Method for location of clusters of patterns to initialise a learning machine*. Electronic Letters, p. 481-483. 1969.

[7]   H.Chen, M.Li, X.Chen, *A Predator-Prey Cellular Genetic Algorithm for Dynamic Optimization Problems*. Information Engineering and Computer Science (ICIECS). 2010.

[8]   H.Blom, C.Küch, K.Losemann, *PEPPA: a project for evolutionary predator prey algorithms*. GECCO '09. 2009.

[9]   D.Kalyanmoy, U.Bhaskara, *Investigating predator-Prey Algorithms for Multi-Objective Optimization*. Department of Mechanical Engineering Indian Institute of Technology Kanpur. 2005.

[10] A.Torn, A.Zilinskas, "Global Optimizacion". Springer-Verlag. 1989.

[11] K. Deb, U.Bhaskara Rao, *Investigating predator-Prey Algorithms for Multi-Objective Optimization*. 2005

SketchyDynamics: A Library for the Development of Physics Simulation Applications with Sketch-Based Interfaces

Abílio Costa[1], João P. Pereira[1,2]

[1] *Computer Science Department, School of Engineering (ISEP), Polytechnic of Porto, R. Dr. António Bernardino de Almeida 431, Porto, Portugal*
[2] *Knowledge Engineering and Decision Support Group (GECAD), School of Engineering, Polytechnic of Porto, R. Dr. António Bernardino de Almeida 431, Porto, Portugal*
amfcalt@gmail.com, jjp@isep.ipp.pt

Abstract — **Sketch-based interfaces provide a powerful, natural and intuitive way for users to interact with an application. By combining a sketch-based interface with a physically simulated environment, an application offers the means for users to rapidly sketch a set of objects, like if they are doing it on piece of paper, and see how these objects behave in a simulation. In this paper we present SketchyDynamics, a library that intends to facilitate the creation of applications by rapidly providing them a sketch-based interface and physics simulation capabilities. SketchyDynamics was designed to be versatile and customizable but also simple. In fact, a simple application where the user draws objects and they are immediately simulated, colliding with each other and reacting to the specified physical forces, can be created with only 3 lines of code. In order to validate SketchyDynamics design choices, we also present some details of the usability evaluation that was conducted with a proof-of-concept prototype.**

Keywords — **Gesture Recognition, Physics Simulation, Rigid Body Dynamics, Sketch-Based Interfaces.**

I. INTRODUCTION

USING pen and paper to draw or sketch something in order to express an idea is very common and also very natural for us. By using this concept in user interfaces one can make the interaction process more natural and spontaneous.

In this paper we propose SketchyDynamics, a programing library to aid in the creation of applications for 2D physics simulations in which the user interacts directly with the scene using a "pen and paper" style interaction. Thus, instead of selecting from a menu which objects compose the scene to be simulated, the user can simply draw them directly into the scene. We hope that developing this library will provide a boost for developers to create new applications around this concept, be they for educational purposes, like an application used to teach physics with an interactive whiteboard, or for entertainment purposes, such as a physics-based game where the user draws parts of the scene in order to reach a goal.

The library supports three gestures to draw rigid bodies and other three to define connections between them. The first three gestures are used to produce rectangles, triangles and circles, which can be created by drawing these symbols directly. Also, the user can draw a zigzag to connect two bodies with a spring, an alpha to pin a body over another and a small circle to define a rotation axis between two bodies. Since both the circle body and the rotation axis relation use the same gesture, we only have in fact five gestures to recognize, presented in Fig. 1.

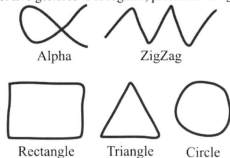

Fig. 1. Set of gestures used in our library

Although there are already several applications that combine physics simulation with a sketch-based interface, most of them have a specific scope and audience. As a library, SketchyDynamics is intended to be used in different types of applications and does not have a definite scope. We hope that our work helps developers create new and exciting applications with little effort in combining the physics simulation with the sketch-based interface.

In the next section we present an overview of the results achieved in the sketch recognition field and also works that combine sketch-based interfaces with rigid body physics simulation. Section 3 gives a little insight into a previous evaluation whose purpose was to select the sketch recognizer that best integrates with our library. In section 4 we present our library, its technical characteristics, along with its functionality. Section 5 discusses a preliminary informal evaluation and section 6 concludes this paper and presents potential future work.

II. RELATED WORK

This section presents some of the related work in the sketch-based interfaces domain and is divided into two subsections. The first subsection will address the work done in the sketch recognition field, while the second presents some examples of applications that result from the combination of sketch-based interfaces with rigid body physics simulation.

A. Sketch Recognizers

Given the potential of automatic sketch recognition, a lot of work has been done in order to develop recognizers capable of dealing with the intrinsic ambiguity of hand-drawn sketches. Since there is a wide variety of sketch recognition algorithms, it is only natural that there's also diversity in their characteristics. Examples of these characteristics are the ability to be trained to recognize new gestures, the capacity to recognize multi-stroke gestures or the sensitivity to the gesture's orientation, scale or drawing direction.

Rubine's recognizer [1], a trainable gesture recognizer, classifies each gesture using a linear classifier algorithm with a set of distinct features. The recognizer is very flexible since features can be easily added or removed to make the recognizer fit the application needs, as proven by Plimmer and Freeman [2]. The major limitations of Rubine's recognizer are its sensitivity to the drawing direction, scale, and orientation and inability to identify multi-stroke sketches. Pereira et al. [3] made some modifications to Rubine's recognizer in order to make the algorithm accept multi-stroke sketches, but only when drawn with a constant set of strokes, as pointed out by Stahovich [4]. Pereira et al. also present a way to make the algorithm insensitive to drawing direction.

CALI [5] is an easy to use multi-stroke recognizer that uses Fuzzy Logic and geometric features to classify gestures independently of their size or orientation. CALI divides gestures into two types: shapes and commands. Shapes can be drawn (and recognized) using solid, dashed and bold lines, while commands are only recognized with solid lines. Since CALI is not trainable, adding new gestures is not an easy task, involving analysis of which features characterize and distinguish the new gesture and hand-coding these features. To solve this limitation the authors also present a trainable recognizer but it has a lower recognition rate and requires numerous training templates for each gesture class[1].

Wobbrock et al. [6] present the $1 Recognizer which aims to be easy to understand and quick to implement. It is insensitive to scale and orientation of sketches, but sensitive to their drawing direction. One major advantage of $1 Recognizer is the simplicity to add support for new gestures, requiring only one training template per gesture class to be effective. Furthermore, the authors also explain how to make the recognizer sensitive to scale or orientation, for some or all gesture templates.

In order to solve some of the limitations of the $1

Recognizer, such as not being able to recognizing multi-stroke gestures, sensitivity to the drawing direction, and problems recognizing uni-dimensional gestures such as lines, Anthony & Wobbrock extended it and created the $N Recognizer [7]. Despite the improvements over the $1 Recognizer, $N has problems recognizing gestures made with more strokes than those used in the training templates. Also, it is not well suited to recognize "messy" gestures like a scratch-out, commonly used for erasing-like actions.

Lee et al. [8] present a trainable graph-based recognizer that is insensitive to orientation, scale and drawing direction and is able to recognize multi-stroke gestures. Since the recognizer uses statistical models to define symbols, it handles the small variations associated with hand-drawn gestures very well. Despite being a trainable recognizer, it requires all training templates of a gesture class to be drawn with a consistent drawing order or consistent orientation.

Vatavu et al. [9] present a trainable recognizer that uses elastic deformation energies to classify single-stroke gestures. The recognizer is naturally insensitive to gesture scale and orientation, since the same gesture has similar curvature functions independently of the drawing orientation or size, but is sensitive to drawing direction and starting point within the gesture.

Sezgin and Davis [10] present a multi-stroke sketch recognizer, based on Hidden Markov Models (HMM), that is capable of recognizing individual sketches in complex scenes even if the scene is not yet completed, i.e. while it is being drawn, and without the need to pre-segment it. On the other hand it can only recognize sketches in their trained orientations, thus being sensitive to orientation. Since the recognition relies on the stroke order of the trained templates, it is not well suited for domains where the stroke ordering cannot be predicted. Also, because HMMs are suited for sequences, it cannot recognize single-stroke sketches, unless they are pre-segmented.

B. Physics Simulation with Sketch-Based Interfaces

The idea of using a sketch-based interface to create and manipulate a simulated scene is not something new. For example, ASSIST [11] is able to recognize sketches and convert them to mechanical objects which can then be simulated. The system recognizes circles and straight-line polygons (simple or complex) made of single or multiple strokes. The recognition is done incrementally, while the user is drawing, which makes the system feel quicker and also gives an instantaneous feedback to the user, since hand-drawn lines are converted to straight lines and colored according to the type of object recognized. When an improper interpretation of a gesture is made, the user is able to correct it using a list of alternative interpretations. In ASSIST, users can also pin one object over another with a rotational axis by drawing a small circle, or anchor objects to the background by drawing a small cross. After finishing the sketch, the user can press a "Run" button to transfer his design to a 2D mechanical simulator that runs and displays a simulation of the designed scene.

---

[1] A gesture class represents a unique gesture, but can be made from multiple representations of that gesture, i.e. multiple templates.

Another application, "Free-Hand Sketch Recognition for Visualizing Interactive Physics" [12] enables users to draw simple 2D objects and simulate how these objects behave in 3D. The application is able to recognize four types of objects: lines, circles, rectangles, and triangles. When the gesture cannot be recognized a small dialog is presented, requesting the user to specify the desired gesture. After creating an object, the user is able to anchor it so that it remains static during the simulation. The design process consists of three modes: the "Ink" mode where the user can draw new objects; the "Select" mode, where a circle selects the enclosed objects; and the "Erase" mode, used to remove objects. Despite the designing being done in 2D, the physics simulation is 3D and the user is able to move the camera and also move objects in 3D space.

There are also games that take advantage of a sketch-based interface and a physics simulated environment to entertain the player. One popular example is Crayon Physics Deluxe [13], a puzzle game where the main objective is to guide a ball so that it touches all the stars in each level. Instead of controlling the ball directly, the user needs to draw objects that influence the ball, leading it to the stars. The user can draw rigid bodies with any shape and connect them with pivot points and ropes. Since the simulation is always running, sketched objects are simulated and interact with other objects right after being drawn. The game has a "children's drawing" theme, with a background that resembles a yellow paper sheet and crayon-like sketches, both characteristics that make it successfully adopt the pen-paper paradigm. Crayon Physics Deluxe also includes a level editor and an online playground, so users can create their own levels and submit them online.

III. Sketch-Based Recognition Evaluation

Due to the high importance of having good gesture recognition, since the user must feel the interaction to be as natural and unrestrictive as drawing with a pen on a paper, the gesture recognizer used in SketchyDynamics was selected based on previous evaluation [14] [15]. The evaluation was conducted using real gesture samples drawn by 32 subjects, with a gesture set specifically arranged for our library (Fig. 1).

For the evaluation process we developed an application to collect gesture samples from the subjects, process them, and compute the recognition results. With this tool we evaluated Rubine's recognizer, CALI and the 1$ Recognizer, concluding that for our gesture set CALI achieved the highest recognition rates.

With this evaluation we were also able to improve recognition rates by tweaking the templates and the recognizer's implementation to our specific gesture set.

IV. The SketchyDynamics Library

SketchyDynamics is a programing library that aims to simplify the implementation of 2D physics simulation applications with sketch-based interfaces. Using 2D graphics and physics simulation means that the user sketch (in 2D) produces a 2D object, which resembles the pen-paper paradigm and simplifies user interaction.

Out of the box, SketchyDynamics provides an interface for the user to interact with an application along with recognition and processing of user actions such as drawing, moving, scaling and removing rigid bodies and their joints. SketchyDynamics also deals with the physics simulation of these elements and visually represent them on the computer screen along with other user interface elements. Thus, a developer can integrate these features in an application with almost no effort.

A. Architecture

A major concern when designing SketchyDynamics was to make it versatile, so that developers can create all kind of applications, but at the same time simple enough to enable rapid prototyping. For example, with only 3 lines of source code a developer can create a simple test application where the user can draw objects and see their simulation, while they collide with each other and react to the specified "gravitational force". With a dozen more lines the developer is able to add a background body where the user is able to attach objects, or a ground body so that drawn bodies have something to fall onto.

As stated previously, we use CALI as the gesture recognizer since it yielded the best results in our evaluations.

For the physics simulation SketchyDynamics uses the Box2D physics engine. Despite using Box2D, SketchyDynamics does not encapsulate it or hide it from the programmer. Instead programmers have access to all Box2D objects and functionality so they are able to parameterize them according to the application's needs.

Although bodies and joints are created automatically by the library when the user draws them, the application is also able to programmatically create and remove them (along with their visual representations). Furthermore, SketchyDynamics also gives the application full control over the simulation state.

To render the bodies simulated by Box2D and any other visual elements we used the OpenGL API. Despite that, SketchyDynamics was designed so that a developer can easily use another API. This is achieved by ensuring that all OpenGL-specific code is encapsulated in a few classes, thus creating a conceptual abstraction layer.

While implementing the OpenGL abstraction we took the opportunity to add some "graphics library" functionality. For example, a programmer can easily create polygons by defining their vertices and then apply geometric transformations to them, toggle their visibility on screen, among other operations, all done in an object-oriented manner. Additionally, the library provides scene query functionality and easy texture management for the developer. To render each object SketchyDynamics offers three rendering queue layers so that each individual object can be drawn on the background, on the front (as a user interface element) or in the middle of these two layers. Furthermore, the depth or order of each object inside each layer can also be specified.

Another design decision that resulted from the OpenGL abstraction was the incorporation of the window creation process inside SketchyDynamics, thus reducing the effort on the developer's side. Moreover, SketchyDynamics delivers events received by the window, like mouse and keyboard inputs, to the application using the observer pattern, thus letting the developer take actions based on the user input.

B. User Interaction

In order to best represent the pen-paper paradigm, the user interaction was designed to take advantage of systems with a touchscreen and stylus. Thus, the user only needs to press and move the stylus to interact with the system, without needing extra buttons[2]. Furthermore, no menus are used and most of the interaction is done by sliding the stylus across the screen. Although it was designed with that type of devices in mind, SketchyDynamics also works well with a traditional computer mouse.

There are two types of objects the user is able to create: bodies and joints. Bodies are rigid objects that are simulated according to physics laws while joints are used to connect bodies. Fig. 2 shows various bodies and three types of joints.

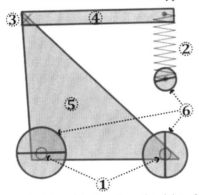

Fig. 2. Various types of joints and bodies: 1) revolute joints; 2) spring joint; 3) weld joint; 4) rectangular body; 5) triangular body; 6) circular bodies.

It is also important for the user to be able to manipulate the objects to a certain degree so SketchyDynamics lets the user change an object's position, scale, and orientation, or even delete it.

1) Creating

The creation of an object, be it a body or a joint, is done by drawing it. So, for example, if users want to create a rectangle body, they simply draw the rectangle on the screen. SketchyDynamics then recognizes the rectangle and its properties, like size and orientation, and creates the physical and visual representations of it.

SketchyDynamics supports four types of bodies: rectangles, triangles, circles and freeform bodies. When the user input is recognized as a rectangle, triangle or circle, it is represented in a beautified manner, as illustrated in Fig. 3. Otherwise, when the input is not recognized, it is interpreted as a freeform and represented in a simplified manner (with fewer vertices) for performance reasons.

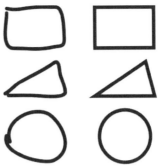

Fig. 3. Example of drawn shapes (left) and respective beautified representations (right).

The user can also connect two bodies with three different joint types: weld, revolute and spring. Weld joints connect two bodies at a specific anchor point, preventing any relative movement between them. Like weld joints, a revolute joint connects two overlapping bodies at a specific point but allows the bodies to rotate freely around that point. Spring joints try to keep a constant distance between two connected bodies, based on the distance at the time the joint was created, stretching and shrinking like a real spring.

Just like creating bodies, the creation of joints is done by drawing them. Drawing an alpha gesture over two bodies connects them with a weld joint with an anchor at the gesture's intersection, while drawing a small circle creates a revolute joint anchored at the circle's center. To create a spring joint, the user draws a zigzag gesture starting in one body and ending in another one, defining the two spring's anchor points as the start and end points of the gesture.

Regarding the visual representation of joints, the weld and revolute joints are represented by a small cross and by a small circle, respectively, on the joint anchor point while the spring joint is displayed as a zigzag line starting in one anchor point and ending on the other, stretching and shrinking subject to the distance between the bodies. The object presented in Fig. 2 was constructed using joints of the three types.

In order to better deal with the ambiguity in hand-drawn gestures, a guesses list is presented whenever the user executes a gesture. The guesses list shows all the available objects so that the user can choose an object other than the recognized one. The objects corresponding to gestures identified as matching by CALI recognizer appear bigger and first in the list, since they are the most probable choices, followed by the remaining objects. The guesses list feature can be disabled by the developer, in which case the most probable object is always selected.

Depending on the application-specific setup passed to SketchyDynamics, objects can be created while the physics simulation is in a paused state or while it is running and thus making other objects react instantly to the new object. This instantaneous simulation mode is useful for applications where the user interacts with a live environment as usually happen in games.

---

[2] In a traditional mouse system this means that only the left mouse button is needed.

2) Selecting

For an object to be manually manipulated by the user, it first needs to be selected. When any object is selected the physics simulation is paused so that the user can easily edit it without being interrupted by other moving bodies. If the simulation was running before the selection of an object, it will resume after all objects are unselected.

Objects are selected by tapping on them with the stylus (or left-clicking them with a mouse), and can be deselected with the same action. This makes selecting multiple objects an intuitive process since users only need to keep tapping on the objects they want to select. It is also possible to unselect individual objects when there are multiple objects selected. When an object is selected, its lines assume a distinctive color, returning to the original color after being unselected. As shown in Fig. 4, this gives a clear feedback regarding the object's state. Also, tapping on an area of the screen with no objects or on an object configured as non-selectable, deselects all selected objects. Non-selectable objects are useful to create the application's scenery, which the user cannot manipulate but may be able to interact with, for example by connecting a user-made body to a scenery object.

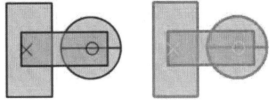

Fig. 4. Set of objects in unselected (left) and selected (right) states

When there are multiple bodies connected by joints and one of them is selected, all the other connected bodies are automatically selected, as long as they are selectable objects. This feature was introduced in order to improve the usability of the system, since we found that when multiple bodies are connected the user typically wants to manipulate them as a whole.

3) Moving

A selected body or joint can be moved by pressing over it and dragging the stylus. The object will move in sync with the stylus as long as the user keeps it pressed on the screen.

When there are multiple objects selected they all move in a synchronized manner, regardless of which object was pressed by the stylus.

4) Scaling and Rotating

Scaling and rotation of bodies is done simultaneously in a single action. As the action to move an object, scaling and rotation is done by pressing and dragging the stylus, but instead of pressing inside the selected body, the user needs to press outside it. As the user drags the stylus, the selected bodies scale and rotate based on the stylus initial and current positions. Only bodies can be rotated or scaled, so this operation is not applicable to joints.

The scale factor is calculated based on the current distance from the stylus position to the body center and the initial distance (before dragging the stylus). Regarding rotation, it is done based on the angle between two imaginary lines: the line from the current stylus position to the body's center, and the initial line (before dragging the stylus). Thus, moving the stylus closer or farther from the body scales it while moving the stylus around the body rotates it.

When multiple bodies are selected, they are all subject to the same rotation and scaling factor, but instead of using the body's center point as the reference point, the geometric average of all individual center points is used.

In order to aid the user during a scaling and rotation operation, SketchyDynamics displays a rectangle enclosing the selected objects, which rotates and scales along with them. Also, a small circle is displayed on the center reference point, along with a line connecting that point to the mouse cursor, so that the user can clearly perceive the operation being done. These visual cues are displayed in Fig. 5.

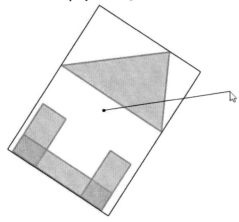

Fig. 5. Set of objects being subject to simultaneous rotation and scaling operations

5) Removing

Since removing objects is an important operation that contributes to user's creative freedom, it was designed to be simple, intuitive, and to have a low impact on the user's cognitive load. In fact, removing an object is a just special case of moving it.

When an object starts being moved by the user, a large rectangle with a trash bin icon slides down from the top of the screen, sliding back up and off-screen when the object cease to be moved. If the stylus enters the trash bin area while moving any object, the trash bin icon turns red. If the user lifts the stylus while on this rectangle, all the selected objects are removed. Fig. 6 shows the trash bin area in context of a simple, almost empty, application, and also the trash bin icon representations before and after the stylus drags an object onto it. We choose to keep this area hidden unless the user starts moving objects to improve the use of screen real estate, since objects can only be deleted when they are being moved by the user.

Joints can also be removed by simply being moved outside any of the two bodies they connect, without the need to move them to the trash bin rectangular area, although the trash bin works for joints too.

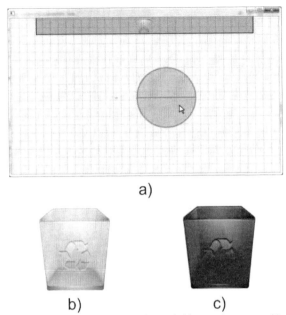

a)

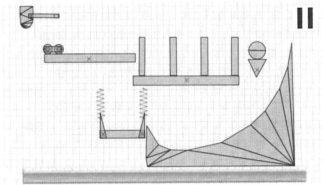

Fig. 7. Scene reproduced by subjects during the efficiency test (the ruler, at the bottom, along with the pause indicator, at the top-right corner, are part of the prototype and not user-made objects)

b) c)

Fig. 6. a) simple application showing the trash bin area in context; b) trash bin icon in its normal state; c) trash bin icon when an object is dragged inside the trash area.

V. USABILITY EVALUATION

In order to validate SketchyDynamics' features and also to better understand what needs improvement, we conducted a usability evaluation session that was attended by 8 subjects (2 females and 6 males), comprising students, teachers and researchers from the Computer Science field. During the session, participants experienced SketchyDynamics' functionalities using a traditional mouse but also using an interactive display with a stylus (Wacom Cintiq 15X).

Using a prototype application developed with SketchyDynamics, each subject performed an efficiency test by creating a complex scene[3], consisting of 17 bodies and 11 joints (Fig. 7). Before beginning the execution of the efficiency test, 5 subjects had a few minutes to experiment with the prototype. Also, during the test, the session coordinator clarified doubts raised by each of the 5 subjects. Regarding the remaining 3 subjects, they executed the test in a slightly different manner: they all done the test simultaneously, using only one computer; the experience was timed from the moment they had contact with the prototype; and had no help from the session coordinator. With this group we hope to evaluate the usability of SketchyDynamics when users are in a more adverse situation: for example, when they have no access to touchscreen and stylus, and/or have no time to get familiar with the application.

Considering the complexity of the scene to reproduce along with the inexperience of the subjects with the SketchyDynamics library prototype, the results of the efficiency tests are very encouraging. The first 5 subjects completed the test on an average of 9 minutes and 12 seconds, with a standard deviation of 3 minutes and 34 seconds.

Regarding the remaining 3 subjects, who performed the test together, it took them about 24 minutes to complete the test, which we consider to be a positive result since these 24 minutes include the time they spent learning how to use the system and discovering its functionalities. Fig. 8 presents the time taken by each subject to complete the efficiency test. Note that since subjects 6, 7 and 8 executed the test together, their results are unified.

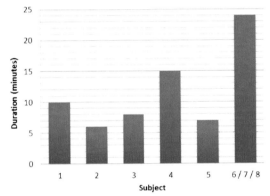

Fig. 8. Time spent per subject in the efficiency test

After the efficiency test, each subject filled out a survey form regarding their experience with the prototype. All the questions in the survey achieved average results above 1 point, in a scale from -3 (awful) to +3 (excellent), where 0 represents a neutral response, showing that SketchyDynamics pleased the users and is on the right track.

In order to know if the selected gestures were successful, one section in the survey asked about the suitability of each gesture in the creation process. As shown in Fig. 9, the average results for the majority of the gestures were equal or above 2 points, except for the gesture used to create weld joints. This lower result can be explained by the difficulty to draw an alpha gesture using a traditional computer mouse.

---

[3] A video demonstrating the creation of such scene can be found at http://youtu.be/1niigTt_m_I

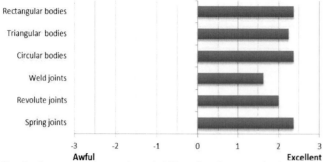

Fig. 9. Average results on the suitability of each gesture in the creation process

Fig. 11. Average results on the object removal process

Regarding the object transformation process, we found the results to be very positive (Fig. 10), since the only action that achieved an average score lower than 2 points was the continuous selection of multiple objects. By observing the subjects during the interaction with the prototype, it was evident that the action to select multiple objects caused some trouble, since it conflicts with the usual experience users have with computer applications. While in most applications a click over an object selects it and deselects any other object that was previously selected, in SketchyDynamics clicking over an object selects it but does not deselects the remaining objects. As a result of this conflict, participants would misguidedly apply transformations on objects that they thought to be deselected. Despite that, the overall opinion of the participants in relation to the object transformation process was very good, with an average score greater than 2 points.

Regarding the overall perception of SketchyDynamics, the results showed that subjects feel that it is easy to use and is also adequate for creating physically simulated scenes (Fig. 12). Concerning the stimulus, which achieved a lower result, certain participants demonstrated frustration when using the stylus, due to hardware problems. Also, some participants complained about the impossibility to undo operations. In relation to flexibility, participants have suggested that SketchyDynamics should support a larger number of object types.

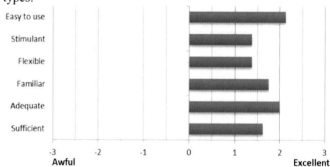

Fig. 12. Average overall results on SketchyDynamics' functionalities

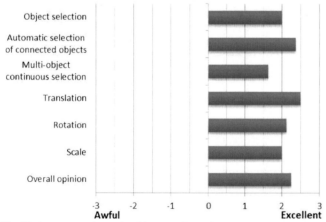

Fig. 10. Average results on the object transformation process

In addition to these questions, the survey also inquired subjects about the interaction devices, the arrangement of the user interface, and also about the manipulation of the simulation. Further discussion on the usability evaluation and also on the SketchyDynamics library can be found on [15].

VI. CONCLUSIONS

We have presented a library capable of speeding up the development of applications by providing developers a sketch-based interface combined with physics simulation. The library also provides facilities in managing the graphical side of the application and dealing with user input.

In an effort to make the library suitable for the widest range of applications we are working on adding more functionality into it, such as a new rope-like joint.

One useful feature would be the ability to select an individual body from a set of connected bodies and transform it using the joint anchor point as a reference. This poses some design problems since an object can have multiple joints (which one should be used?). The problem further increases if there is more than one selected object. Before implementation, further study on how to overcome these problems is needed.

Although subjects found that it was useful to remove a joint by simply displacing it out of the bodies it connects, the results presented in Fig. 11, despite being very encouraging, show that there is still some room for improvement in regards to the object removal process. One of the criticisms mentioned by several subjects was the impossibility to remove and object by pressing the "Delete" key. In fact, this is a feature that is present in most computer applications for the operation of removing or deleting an object.

Another interesting feature would be the existence of object hierarchies, in which transformations applied to one object are propagated onto its child objects, but not the opposite. The construction of this hierarchy could be based on the depth of the objects.

As noticed during the usability evaluation, implementing common functionalities such as clipboard to duplicate objects and undo/redo capabilities is extremely important to improve the system's usability and reduce user's frustration

Another requested feature is the ability to perform a scale or rotation operation individually. A possible and familiar solution would be the use of a modifier key to restrict the action to a single operation. Every time this key is pressed, the system could check if the mouse movement was mainly radial or tangential, doing only a scale or rotation operation, respectively. This concept could also be applied to restrict the movement of objects to horizontal, vertical and 45 degree translations.

Nevertheless, we think that current state of SketchyDynamics already enables it to be integrated and used to develop exciting applications.

REFERENCES

[1]   Rubine, D.: Specifying Gestures by Example. SIGGRAPH Computer Graphics, Volume 25 Issue 4, 329 -337 (1991)

[2]   Plimmer, B., Freeman, I.: A toolkit approach to sketched diagram recognition. Proceedings of the 21st British HCI Group Annual Conference on People and Computers: HCI.but not as we know it (BCS-HCI '07) 1, 205-213 (2007)

[3]   Pereira, J., Branco, V., Jorge, J., Silva, N., Cardoso, T., Ferreira, F.: Cascading recognizers for ambiguous calligraphic interaction. Eurographics Workshop on Sketch-Based Interfaces and Modeling (2004)

[4]   Stahovich, T.: Pen-based Interfaces for Engineering and Education. Sketch-based Interfaces and Modeling, 119-152 (2011)

[5]   Fonseca, M., Pimentel, C., Jorge, J.: CALI: An online scribble recognizer for calligraphic interfaces. AAAI Spring Symposium on Sketch Understanding, 51-58 (2002)

[6]   Wobbrock, J., Wilson, A., Li, Y.: Gestures without libraries, toolkits or training: a $1 recognizer for user interface prototypes. 20th annual ACM symposium on User interface software and technology (UIST '07), 159-168 (2007)

[7]   Anthony, L., Wobbrock, J.: A lightweight multistroke recognizer for user interface prototypes. Graphics Interface 2010 (GI '10), 245-252 (2010)

[8]   Lee, W., Kara, L., Stahovich, T.: An efficient graph-based recognizer for hand-drawn symbols. Computers & Graphics 31, 554-567 (2007)

[9]   Vatavu, R.-D., Grisoni, L., Pentiuc, S.-G.: Gesture Recognition Based on Elastic Deformation Energies. Gesture-Based Human-Computer Interaction and Simulation 5085, 1-12. (2009)

[10] Sezgin, T., Davis, R.: HMM-based efficient sketch recognition. 10th international conference on Intelligent user interfaces (IUI '05), 281-283 (2005)

[11] Alvarado, C., Davis, R.: Resolving Ambiguities to Create a Natural Computer-Based Sketching. Proceedings of IJCAI-2001, 1365-1371 (2001)

[12] Kamel, H., Shonoda, M., Refeet, M., Nabil, R.: Free-Hand Sketch Recognition For Visualizing Interactive Physics. (Accessed 2012) Available at: http://code.google.com/p/sketch-recognition-simulation-tool

[13] Purho, P.: Crayon Physics Deluxe. (Accessed 2012) Available at: http://crayonphysics.com

[14] Costa, A., Pereira, J.: SketchTester: Analysis and Evaluation of Calligraphic Gesture Recognizers. 20º Encontro Português de Computação Gráfica (20ºEPCG) (2012)

[15] Costa, A.: SketchyDynamics: Apoio à Produção de Sistemas Baseados em Interfaces Caligráficas para a Simulação da Dinâmica de Corpos Rígidos (M.S. thesis). School of Engineering (ISEP), Polytechnic of Porto, Portugal (2012)

Abílio Costa received his MSc in Computer Science Engineering at the School of Engineering, Polytechnic of Porto (ISEP-IPP), in 2012, where he also accomplished his graduation. Currently working on the graphics and rendering engine of a new product at NDrive, he has experience in user interfaces and computer graphics.

João P. Pereira earned his BSc, MSc and PhD in Electrical and Computer Engineering from the Faculty of Engineering of the University of Porto (FEUP).
He is currently teaching at the Computer Science Department of the School of Engineering, Polytechnic of Porto (ISEP-IPP), and researching at the Knowledge Engineering and Decision Support Research Center (GECAD). His main areas of interest are Computer Graphics and Human-Computer Interaction.

## 11

Legal Issues Concerning P2P Exchange of Educational Materials and Their Impact on E-Learning Multi-Agent Systems

Eugenio Gil and Andrés G. Castillo Sanz,
University Pontifical of Salamanca, Madrid Campus, Spain

Abstract — **The last years have known an impressive change in the use of technologies for the sharing and dissemination of knowledge, thus affecting deeply all the traditional means used by education in all its shapes and levels. This transformation has not been fully understood by the society at large for its immense impacts and its short life. This paper describes in the question emerging from the clash of the rights to education in a wide sense and the rights derived from authorship and how that issue is affecting the design of e-learning multi-agent tools.**

Keywords — **Education, Law, Multi-agent Systems for eLearning, Intelligent Knowledge Sharing**

I. INTRODUCTION

In the last years we have fully entered in a social environment generally known as Information and Knowledge Society (IKS), which is essentially characterized in that it is a society that is largely driven by technology and technological advances that occur almost daily.

This new society which we refer to has received over recent years different names such as Cibersociety or Networked Society [5], but it is from a legal point of view that a greater uniformity has been achieved in the sense that both the different agencies of the European Union and those of Spain have preferred to use a broader concept such as the Information Society when legislating, which leads to the concept mentioned above of the Information and Knowledge Society, taking into account what Professor Davara [3] affirms, that information is an element that gives great power to its owners already from the beginning of time, emerging therefore a class of people: the owners of information.

It's not enough to own pieces of information, it is mandatory to know how to look for it and how to handle it, it becoming stronger who knows better how to handle with it, it being an asset which does not get exhausted with their consumption but it is enriched instead by its being used. This allows that its expansion is taking place with the creation of more information by means of the development of telecommunication systems.

This concept of information should be put in touch with another concept that has been widely used in recent years under the context of the Information Society, such as it is that of Knowledge, because the latter is no more than stored information, which is preserved and treated by its recipients the same, i.e. the people.

The study of this IKS begun already in the late nineteen-sixties and early 70's by various thinkers. Those studies were consolidated in the two decades following the 80 and 90, in which a key event took place in the development IKS too, such as the emergence of the PC. In recent years of present decade, the expansion of the IKS has been so voracious by means of the monstrous development of computer technology that have led the personal, social, economic and cultural relationships to be influenced to a greater or lesser extent by such information technologies or information technologies.

No field of knowledge, from economics to law, have been untouched by this technology boom, including of course the field of Education, whose study we will address here, although we will be analyzing in it from a legal point of view the impact that it is produced by the emergence of different technologies. All this has given rise to what some authors have called Information Processing and Digital Competence, that is, the skills that a student should have acquired by the end of their educational years and which involves being more than a simple user of ICT. It involves being an autonomous, efficient, responsible, critical and reflective person at the time of processing, selecting, and using the information, its sources and its supporting media [7].

Teaching is no longer just a platform through which the teacher discloses his knowledge using lectures as it was the case until recently. It has become an area in which both the teacher and the student form an inseparable element, through which they are jointly engaged in the task of teaching and learning both connected via ICT, whose mastering brings about the possibility of using them as a tool for searching, processing, communication ... in short, as a basic tool for knowledge acquisition. This is how the concept of digital natives emerges, as persons who are characterized by the following [4]:

They receive information quickly
They like to work in parallel and multitasking
They prefer images to text
They prefer random access

They work best when they work in a network
They thrive on instant gratification and frequent rewards
They prefer to play games than to work seriously

At this point we must highlight a key element for the development of digital natives, that is, the emergence, consolidation and development of Internet usage (essential piece of the new Information Society), which has caused a transformation unimaginable a few years ago in the customs of students in their academic habits. The digital text analysis, the search of online resources or the monitoring of teaching through virtual campuses have become hallmarks of our society that has led us in many cases to a delocalization of the University, the student has access to it at any time and from any place she wishes to.

Apparently the new digital world in which we live offers many advantages in education, and certainly so, but we should not forget to keep in mind that misused technology can cause major problems especially in regard to the effects that it may have in the fundamental rights of the people.

An instrument that offers many possibilities is file sharing networks. These networks allow users to exchange information and documentation so that they disseminate what we have previously called Knowledge. It seems clear that from an educational point of view we may encounter tools that have immense potential. The problem arises at the moment that technology allows us to perform (via these networks) file sharing (e.g. textbooks or reference books) that are protected by intellectual property rights. At this point we should question if these networks are a valid tool in education since access to culture is above the right of the author, or if on the contrary we should curtail the use of them (in the case we just find the a mechanism to do so).

But what are these file sharing networks?

At the end of the decade of the 90s emerged the so-called peer to peer (P2P) or networks among friends or individuals. It is a network that allows the exchange of information among peers which has had an extraordinary boom with the advent of the Internet and that is closely linked with the MP3 format. The MP3 is simply a format for data compression, a standard developed by the Fraunhofer Institute in 1987, with which you get that a minute of music with quality similar to an audio CD occupies only a megabyte, reducing its size by about 12 times [8].

At present P2P networks operate as a decentralized network that has neither fixed clients nor servers, but it has a number of nodes that behave simultaneously as both clients and servers of the other nodes in the network. The emergence of these networks has been opposed not only by the authors of these works and holders of intellectual property rights, but also of the Managing Entities of Intellectual Property Rights, which argue the great losses suffered by the industry as a result of these actions. In contrast to the detractors of the use of these

networks is an important part of Internet users who postulate the law as fundamental argument that everybody should have free access to culture and knowledge, and the necessary adaptation of the legal rules to the new possibilities offered by technology.

One of the first cases of P2P was Napster. It was a file download program created by Shawn Fanning, a student of Computer Science in 1999. Its main problem was that it had a centralized directory from which could be known both existing files on the computers of users and the members that were online. A user accessed the directory, and if the requested file was there and the user who had it was connected, the download proceeded. The existence of this directory or central server provided the basis for considering that it was breaking the rules on copyright, and in July 2001 a U.S. judge ordered the closure of Napster servers. If Napster was closed primarily by the existence of a central server, the goal was clear: to provide the same service as Napster through a decentralized network. Thus numerous programs were created that managed to achieve this purpose: KaZaA, eDonkey, Morpheus, eMule, etc. [1]. They obviously omitted to use a central server and all computers connected to the system functioned simultaneously as both clients and servers, that way as new users download the software, the network grows exponentially.

The emergence of these networks allows the enjoyment of music or books for free (although they have many more utilities such as sharing and file search, internet telephony systems, scientific computing to process large databases, etc..) , and it has been opposed not only by the authors of these works and holders of intellectual property rights on them, who have seen it as an element giving away the result of their work for free in breach of current legislation intellectual property, but also of the Managing Entities of intellectual property Rights, which argued the heavy losses suffered by the sector as a result of these actions, and that has made recently in the month of May 2009 that a class action from several management institutions against Pablo Soto Bravo was filed in Spain as the creator of a number of P2P programs (Blubster, Piolet and Manolito [6]) on the grounds that it violates the rules of intellectual property and claiming a significant compensation for damages. Without delving further into this matter, it should be noted that one thing is that the file download behavior may constitute a crime, and another one is that the software that allows such activity must be given the same consideration, which in principle is difficult to share with the claimants of the aforementioned process.

The 'case Soto' started in June 2008 when, for civil proceedings, the recording industry, represented by Promusicae, Warner, Universal, EMI and Sony sued the software developer of Pablo Soto for 13 million euro in damages, for they considered that his programs Blubster, Piolet and ManolitoP2P were developed under the MP2P protocol, and that they were intended for illegal sharing of copyrighted music between individuals. Recently, the final decision in this case acquitted Pablo Soto considering that no offense was committed.

II. SANCTIONABLE BEHAVIORS?

We have certainly made ourselves this question more than once, when we download a book for following a study subject or simply a reference book. Of course if we make the download paying the amounts that we are required, this download will be perfectly legal, but if we do it through a file sharing network which I accessed through a links page to? Do I commit any offense? What can happen to me? And what about the administrator of website who hosts the links page?

The answer to be given is that nothing can happen to us, or at least that was the situation we were before the famous so-called Sinde Law. And I say nothing on the grounds that I shall try to summarize below.

In the Spanish legal system the possibilities for action against the user or against the administrator of the site is focused on two areas, criminal matters (for the commission of a crime) or civil (for the infringement of a right arising damages, in this case the author's rights).

III. THE CRIMINAL SCOPE

In criminal cases the starting point is the first paragraph of Article 270 of the penal code, which states: "It shall be punished with imprisonment from six months to two years and a fine of 12 to 24 months who, for financial gain and to the detriment of third, reproduce, plagiarize, distribute or communicate publicly, in whole or in part, a literary, artistic or scientific work or processing, interpretation or performance fixed in any medium or communicated by any means without the consent of the holders of the relevant intellectual property rights or assigns."

The debate in this area focuses on the existence of profit in file downloading behavior, because if it did not exist, such conduct hardly could be criminalized.

It seems clear that when a person downloads a book through a P2P network, he gets something that somehow could match that profit, because of the fact that it saves the money it would cost that product on the market. Traditionally the doctrine and the courts have been considering that profit amounts to obtaining any benefit, advantage or utility2 as a result of an activity, so that the mentioned savings could be considered comparable to profit. However, this concept of profit has been developed mainly in the field of criminal offenses against property (robbery, theft, fraud, misappropriation ...) in which it is easier to appreciate and value the gain, and it should not be applicable to those behaviors in which the new tools offered by technology play a key role.

In short, the application of Article 270 of the penal code to the conduct described in the absence of profit would be at least against two basic principles that should govern international penal matters, on one hand the principle of minimum intervention of the criminal law according to which latter

should act only in cases of extraordinary gravity and where imposed sanctions are the most severe, and on the other hand the principle of proportionality, clearly perverted if we consider the different sanction which involves a minor theft of a music CD in front of downloading that CD through the mentioned networks (imprisonment under Article 270 of the Spanish penal Code). This position has been followed also by Spanish courts, which have chosen not to include these offenses in Article 270 in the absence of the subjective element of profit. Thus, the Court of Cantabria3 on appeal and, in a supposed Internet download of exact copies of music albums, has held that the defendant's conduct is atypical and therefore not criminally punishable when it had not been proved that he acted with trading profit because he did not collect nor was enriched beyond his personal savings.

The Court of Cantabria takes upon itself a concept of commercial profit that had been used two years ago by the Attorney General's Office's Circular 1/2006, understanding it as a form of profit and thus giving rise to an interpretation of profit in strict sense. In this sense, the memo cited is very enlightening to note that the alleged violation of rights should be relegated to the realm of civil violations in which the purpose of obtaining some advantage or benefit other than commercial may be implicit.

At the same time we must keep in mind that if we access the file sharing network through a page of links, the links page itself is not committing any criminal offence it does not perform the objective behaviour that describes the aforementioned Article 270 since they do not distribute or reproduce or publicly communicate the files, simply because they do not have them. What it does is to allow us to access the network exchange from which in turn we access the files, this conduct does not constitute a crime in our penal code. The Spanish courts have stated so in various resolutions, as it could be illustrated in the Order of July 2, 2009 the Commerce Court of Barcelona and the Order of November 13, 2009 of the Commerce Court of Huelva.

IV. THE CIVIL SCOPE

Having abandoned the criminal procedure it should be considered the possibility of acting in civil proceedings against the users of these networks as a result of the infringement of copyright and therefore in their case demanding compensation for damages.

Within the general rights that are recognized to the authors and leaving aside moral rights (for its unalienable4 nature), it is important to emphasize that among the exploitation rights is fundamentally one which can be inflicted by users of these networks, such as the right of reproduction and also as the case that of public communication.

The regulation of the reproduction right is located in Article 18 of the Spanish TRLPI which qualifies it as "direct or indirect, temporary or permanent fixation by any means and in

---

2 Judgment of the Supreme Court of Spain of March 25, 2004.

3 Judgment of the Court of Cantabria of February 18, 2008.

any form of the whole work or part thereof, which makes possible its communication or the production of copies."

In relation to the injury of this right of reproduction whose ownership belongs to the author, there seems no doubt as to those websites that facilitate the direct download of books. Certainly there would be major problems with the downloading activity performed by users of P2P networks, basically for two reasons, firstly the difficulties regarding their identification and secondly the possible inclusion of the downloading activity in any of limiting or exception assumptions collected by the Spanish Law of Intellectual Property.

The first proposed assumption, such as the downloading of files directly through a web, was treated by the Barcelona Provincial Court in its judgment of September 29, 2006, which condemned to compensation for damages to the owner of www.redmp3.com and www.servidormp3.com websites for infringement of intellectual property rights by carrying out acts of reproduction and making works available without permission, that judgment stating that reproducing a work is " incorporating and attaching it into a physical hardware that enables communication and production of copies of all or part of the work." "que queda incluido en el concepto de reproducción la carga y almacenamiento de material digitalizado en la memoria muerta de un ordenador u otro sistema o aparato electrónico que lo retenga de modo estable; de modo que cuando se digitaliza una obra y se fija en un medio que permita su comunicación y la obtención de copias, se ejecuta un acto de reproducción5". Thus, based on Article 9.1 of the Berne Convention which refers that the playback can be performed under any procedure or any form, the abovementioned judgment concludes "that it is included in the concept of reproduction the download and storing of digitized material in the ROM of a computer or other electronic device system which stably holds it, so that when a work is digitalized and fixed in a medium that makes possible its communication and the obtaining of copies, it occurs an act of playback6 ".

In relation to the second mentioned case, the identification of users, it is necessary to know who are the people doing the aforementioned downloads, or in this case the holders of the IP addresses from which such downloads are made, so as to direct against them the corresponding actions. This work of identification encounters many obstacles, mainly derivatives of the right to secrecy of communications and the right to

privacy, regulated both in almost all modern constitutional texts, where constant reference is made to the necessary judicial intervention required to act against this right, a judicial intervention which does not occur because the absence of crime (as we saw in the previous section). The judges put before the right to privacy of the user against the prejudice caused to the author

Whereupon and in short, we face a situation in which the performance of file download of books or music through a file-sharing network does not constitute a criminal offence, and therefore the courts do not allow to take action against users based on their right to privacy (thus excluding them also against civil proceedings). But common sense seems to indicate that this reproduction activity injures or impairs the right of someone (the author) who should somehow be protected.

V. THE SINDE LAW

In the area of the European Union it has been sought to advance in this matter through the creation of new laws, and in this regard a French Law was approved in May, known as Hadopi law, which permits to disconnect from the Internet those users who persist in downloading files after being warned twice through an ad hoc set up body such as the High Authority for the Dissemination of Works and Protection of Rights on the Internet. Contested this law before the French Advisory Council (a body similar to our Constitutional Court), this one has shown to be contrary to it by saying that if it is true that a sanction should be imposed if the existence of illegal downloads is discovered (which seems logical and which is covered by this Council by means of limiting thus the right to privacy of the users), also points out that this High Authority is not competent to impose the penalty, since only a judge may order the cut of the connection to potential offenders.

In similar terms the European Parliament has recently manifested in a report on September 2011, but later and surprisingly on November 5 of that year it changed its position authorizing such disconnections without prior judicial authorization while referring to some concepts that we believe will lead us in any case to the necessary involvement of a judge. The European Parliament states that in order to avoid abuses in the restrictions, they "may only be imposed if they are appropriate, proportionate and necessary for a democratic society," then stating that "we must respect the presumption of innocence and the right to privacy".

In the Spanish case and given the impossibility to act against users, there has been raised in our legal system the possibility of closing the pages of links that provide access to exchange networks for the users. In order to achieve this aim, the so-called Sinde Law have been developed, changing through the Draft Law on Sustainable Economy the Services Information Society and Electronic Commerce Act in its Article 8, establishing the possibility of closing by an organ belonging to

---

[4] Article 14 of the Spanish Law of Intellectual Property 1996.

[5] The above considerations led to the conclusion that the defendant has committed an act of reproduction invading the sphere of the author in accordance with the provisions of articles 17 et seq. of Intellectual Property Law, Article 11 of the WIPO Treaty on December 20, 1996 and Article 2 of Directive 2001/29/EC on the harmonization of certain aspects of copyright, thus corresponding compensation of damages.

[6] The above considerations led to the conclusion that the defendant has committed an act of reproduction invading the sphere of the author in accordance with the provisions of articles 17 et seq. of Intellectual Property Law, Article 11 of the WIPO Treaty on December 20, 1996 and Article 2 of Directive 2001/29/EC on the harmonization of certain aspects of copyright, thus corresponding compensation of damages.

the Ministry of Culture those websites that violate intellectual property rights as set out in point 4.4 of the First Final Provision of the said Draft.

This law has been developed through the RD 1898/2011 of 30 December. It has been a very controversial and widely criticized regulation by users the Internet.

Without wishing to dwell on the specific rules governing this regulation, we believe that the main problem that frames the norm is the attribution to an administrative body such as the 2nd Section of the Copyright Commission to decide whether there has been or not a breach of the copyright. This brings us to cases in which a judge has considered that there is no offence in a specific conduct, while this Commission believes otherwise.

After the appearance of the first voices against this lack of legal certainty, there was given a new formulation to the regulation itself now introducing the necessary judicial intervention in two moments. Firstly to ask the intermediary service provider to identify the owner of the links service provider, if not known, and secondly to allow or not the measure of closing the links page which has been taken by the Commission. It is the second case which continues to pose the greatest problems, because the judge's decision will not be determined by the assessment of whether or not there is infringement, because he or she is not allowed get into assessing the facts in deep [2]. He can only pronounce on the implementation of the measure by analyzing the proportionality between the infringement of the intellectual property rights and the rights of Article 20 of the Constitution which may be affected due to the closure of the page, essentially the freedom of expression and the seizure of publications.

VI. IMPACT ON MAS

It is well known that the success of multi-agent systems is largely linked with the solution of security problems associated with its use. The autonomous character of agent behavior implies that the users that give them important tasks must trust them with confidential data. The design of the system must ensure that no other person or agent can access illegally the data carried by the owner's agent [13]. Whereas organizational agents are confronted with general security risks of network-oriented applications, the adoption of open and mobile agents in e-learning tasks introduces a new dimension.

The aforementioned legal issues concerning the downloading of educational material from p2p networks and links pages add a new level of complexity to the design of multi-agent systems which would be able to help students in their tasks [9].

In our prototype e-learning multi-agent system we have added one ontology [10] for the agents to know and learn when a links page is legally reliable, and an ancillary agent role which autonomously questions the explorer agents and web search applications to keep a register of sure pages updated.

Every student is encouraged to keep a repository of downloaded educational materials, such as books, shorter documents, databases, images, videos, audio files, etc… in which the copyright issues can be legally certified [12]. We think that if the tools provided are used to search and bring back that material for everywhere on the Internet, the students would agree to a reasonable degree of control on legal materials.

VII. CONCLUSIONS AND FUTURE WORK

On top of unresolved security problems affecting multi-agent systems, the design of multi-agent systems as e-learning tools has encountered the new educational landscape created along with the tremendous explosion of educational (multimedia and every other type) at the disposal of students. Form childhood on every student counts on the possibility of getting every imaginable document at a few clicks of distance. Mobile or navigational agents are the perfect tool for facilitating the students the task of search and retrieving of knowledge in any form [11]. We should make our agents more copyright-violation conscious than our students likely will be. We are therefore including that ability from the very beginning of their design.

REFERENCES

[1] J. P. Aparicio Vaquero, El intercambio de archivos en redes de pares a la luz del derecho vigente. En: Revista Aranzadi de Derecho y Nuevas Tecnologías No.8. Madrid. pp. 55-72 2005. ISSN: 1696-0351.

[2] J. Carbonel, Josep; M. Sabates, La controvertida Disposición Final Cuadragésimo Tercera: "Ley Sinde". Madrid: Economist & Jurist (150), 2011 pp. 26-31.

[3] M. A. Davara Rodríguez, Manual de Derecho Informático. Madrid: Aranzadi, p.23. ISBN: 84-9767-018-3, 2001.

[4] A. Fumero, Jóvenes e Infotecnologías. Madrid: Instituto de la Juventud, Ministerio de Sanidad, Política Social e Igualdad, 2012, p.17.

[5] L. Joyanes, Cibersociedad. Madrid: McGraw-Hill. p.4 ISBN: 84-481-0943-0, 1997.

[6] R. J. Millán Tejedor, Domine las Redes P2P. Madrid: Creaciones Copyright S.L. p.234. ISBN: 84-96300-20-X, 2006.

[7] A. Perez Sanz,Escuela 2.0. Educación para el mundo digital. Madrid: Instituto de la Juventud, Ministerio de Sanidad, Política Social e Igualdad (92) 2011, pp.63,86.

[8] L. J. Rodríguez Baena, Luis José, Transmisión de la cultura en la era digital. Tesis Doctoral (Doctor en Ciencias Políticas y Sociología.). Madrid: Universidad Pontificia de Salamanca. Facultad de Ciencias Políticas y Sociología, 2001 p. 206.

[9] P. A. Rodríguez, V. Tabares, N. D. Duque, D. A. Ovalle, and R. M. Vicari, "BROA: An agent-based model to recommend relevant Learning Objects from Repository Federations adapted to learner profile", in International Journal of Interactive Multimedia and Artificial Intelligence, Vol. 2, March 2013, pp. 6-11.

[10] G. A. Isaza, A. G. Castillo, M. López, L. F. Castillo, M. López, "Intrusion Correlation Using Ontologies and Multi-agent Systems", In proceeding of: Information Security and Assurance - 4th International Conference, ISA 2010, Miyazaki, Japan, June 23-25, 2010. Proceedings 01/2010; pp.51-63.

[11] J. C. Fernandez-Rodriguez, J. Rainer, and F. Miralles-Muñoz, "Engineering Education through eLearning technology in Spain", in International Journal of Interactive Multimedia and Artificial Intelligence, Vol. 2, March 2013, pp. 46-50.

[12] Y. Villuendas-Rey, C. Rey-Benguría, Y. Caballero-Mota, and M. M. García-Lorenzo, "Improving the family orientation process in Cuban

Special Schools trough Nearest Prototype classification", in *International Journal of Interactive Multimedia and Artificial Intelligence*, Vol. 2, March 2013, pp. 12-22.

[13] G. Isaza, A. Castillo, M. López, L. Castillo, "Towards Ontology-Based Intelligent Model for Intrusion Detection and Prevention", Computational Intelligence in Security for Information Systems Advances in Intelligent and Soft Computing Volume 63, Springer, 2009, pp 109-116 (Book Chapter).

## 12

Big Data and Learning Analytics in Blended Learning Environments: Benefits and Concerns

Anthony G. Picciano[1]

[1] *Graduate Center and Hunter College, City University of New York (CUNY)*

Abstract — **The purpose of this article is to examine big data and learning analytics in blended learning environments. It will examine the nature of these concepts, provide basic definitions, and identify the benefits and concerns that apply to their development and implementation. This article draws on concepts associated with data-driven decision making, which evolved in the 1980s and 1990s, and takes a sober look at big data and analytics. It does not present them as panaceas for all of the issues and decisions faced by higher education administrators, but sees them as part of solutions, although not without significant investments of time and money to achieve worthwhile benefits.**

Keyworkds — **Blended learning, data-driven decision making, big data, learning analytics, higher education, rational decision making, planning.**

I. INTRODUCTION

IN May 2014, I was at North-West University in South Africa to lecture and conduct workshops on blended learning in higher education. The topics of my workshops related to conducting research in instructional technology, design of blended learning environments, MOOCs, and technology planning. For the technology planning session, administrators at North-West University shared with me a document that outlined its plan for integrating more technology, and specifically blended learning, into its academic programs. Among the strategies to be considered was the effective use of learning analytics to profile students and track their learning achievements in order to:

- identify at-risk students in a timely manner;
- monitor student persistence on a regular basis; and
- develop an evidence base for program planning and learner support strategies.

During the session, I was specifically asked to give my opinion about whether North-West University should invest in learning analytics technology at this time.

On May 28, 2014, one week after I returned to my home institution at the Graduate Center of the City University of New York (CUNY), I received an email from the University Director of Academic Technology, asking if I would comment on a white paper entitled, Blackboard Analytics and CUNY. This white paper outlined the potential for implementation of learning analytics software into the University's course/learning management system. It was sent to members of a committee examining the feasibility of this software for the university. The email specifically asked for one of the following responses:

- I think this is worth pursuing.
- I don't think this is worth pursuing.
- I am not sure.

and to provide comments in support of the choice.

North-West University and CUNY are 8,000 miles apart, on different continents, with very different missions, organizational structures, and academic programs. Yet, with regard to the acquisition and development of learning analytics software they were pretty much in the exact same situation.

Instructional technology is at the center of many discussions on college and university campuses across the globe. The Internet has permeated every aspect of our societies by its ubiquity, and has changed higher education as well. Online and blended learning, specifically, are being utilized with increasing regularity and are changing the way instruction is provided. In the United States, more than seven million students, approximately one-third of the higher education population, were enrolled in fully online college courses in 2013. [1] Millions more are enrolled in blended courses, although precise data on the extent of blended learning in American higher education is not to be found because of problems with definition and accurate data reporting at the individual college level. Precision aside, the changes brought on by online access to instruction is affecting the way our colleges and universities are being administered. Infusions of technology infrastructure, large-scale databases, and demands for timely data to support decision making have seeped into all levels of college leadership and operations. Data-driven decision making is evolving into a vastly more sophisticated concept known as big data which relies on software approaches generally referred to as learning analytics. Big data and learning analytics for instructional applications are still evolving and will take a few years to mature, although their presence is already being felt and cannot be ignored. While big data and learning analytics are not panaceas for all of the issues and decisions being faced by higher education administrators, the hope is that they can become part of solutions and gracefully integrated into administrative and instructional functions. The purpose of this article is to examine the evolving world of big data and learning analytics in blended learning environments. Specifically, it will look at the nature of these concepts, provide basic definitions, and identify the benefits and concerns related to their development, implementation, and growth in higher education environments.

Administrative decision making processes have been evolving for decades and as more data were made available from integrated information systems, decisions became more rational, using data to support alternative courses of action. A new phenomenon, generally termed online learning, emerged in the 1990s and the early 2000s, that changed the way many faculty teach and students learn. As mentioned earlier, millions of students are learning online and entire colleges have been "built" to offer the entirety of their academic programs online. In addition, for most institutions, online technology is being integrated with face-to-face instruction in what is commonly being referred to as blended learning. The utilization of data-driven decision making in online learning environments has opened up new approaches and avenues for collecting and processing data on students and course activities whereby instructional transactions can be immediately recorded and added to an institutional database. Academic administration and evaluation, which in the past occurred away from the classroom, can now be integrated more closely into instructional activities.

II. BLENDED LEARNING

Blended learning environments present unique challenges to implementing learning analytics mainly because they have so many different facets and are difficult to define. They combine face-to-face instruction and online technology in myriad ways.

Blended learning is not one thing but comes in many different flavors, styles, and applications. It means different things to different people. The word "blended" implies a mixture rather than simply an attaching of components. When a picture is pasted above a paragraph of text, a presentation is created that may be more informative to the viewer or reader, but the picture and text remain intact and can be individually discerned. On the other hand, when two cans of different colored paints are mixed, the new paint will look different from either of the original colors. In fact, if the new paint is mixed well, neither of the original colors will continue to exist. Similar situations exist in blended learning. The mix can be a simple separation of part of a course into an online component. For instance, in a course that meets for three weekly contact hours, two hours might take place in a traditional classroom while the equivalent of one weekly hour is conducted online. The two modalities for this course are carefully separated, and

although they may overlap, they can still be differentiated. In other forms of blended courses and programs, the modalities are not so easily distinguishable. Consider an online program that offers three online courses in a semester that all students are required to take. The courses meet for three consecutive five week sessions. However, students do a collaborative fifteen-week project that overlaps the courses. The students are expected to maintain regular communication with one another through email and group discussion boards. They are also required to meet face-to-face once a month on Saturdays where course materials from the online courses are further presented and discussed and some sessions are devoted to group project work. These activities begin to blur the modalities in a new mixture or blend where the individual parts are not as discernable as they once were. Add to this the increasing popularity of integrating videoconferencing, podcasting, YouTube videos, wikis, blogs, and other media into class work and the definition of blended learning becomes very fluid.

In the broadest sense, blended learning (see Figure 1) can be conceptualized as a wide variety of technology/media integrated with conventional, face-to-face classroom activities. This conceptualization serves as a guideline and should not be viewed as an absolute, limiting declaration. Also, it can apply to entire academic programs as well as individual courses.

III. DATA-DRIVEN DECISION MAKING, BIG DATA, AND LEARNING ANALYTICS

The focus of this article is technology-based approaches that support decision making in blended learning environments. The simplest definition of the popular term "data-driven decision making" is the use of data analysis to inform courses of action involving policy and procedures. Inherent in this definition is the development of reliable and timely information resources to collect, sort, and analyze the data used in the decision making process. It is important to note that data analysis is used to inform and does not mean to replace entirely the experience, expertise, intuition, judgment, and acumen of competent educators. While decision making may be singly defined as choosing between or among two or more alternatives, in a modern educational organization, decision making is an integral component of complex management processes such as academic planning, policy making, and budgeting. These processes evolve over time, require participation by stakeholders, and most importantly, seek to include information which will help all those involved in the decision process.

Fundamental to data-driven decision making is a rational model directed by values and based on data. It is well-recognized, however, that a strictly rational model has limitations. An individual commonly associated with this concept and whose work is highly recommended for further reference, is Herbert Simon [2,3,4,5,6]. Simon was awarded the Nobel Prize in economics in 1978 for his research on decision making in organizations. His theory on the limits of

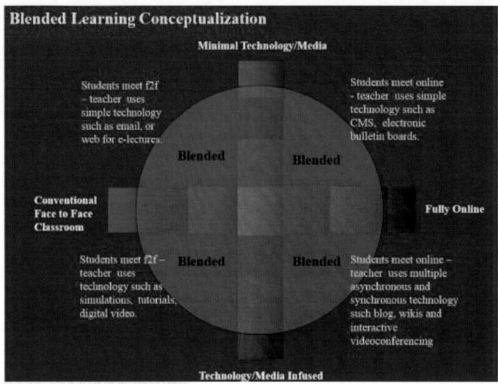

Fig. 1. Blended Learning Conceptualization

rationality, later renamed "bounded rationality," has as its main principle that organizations operate along a continuum of rational and social behaviors mainly because the knowledge necessary to function strictly according to a rational model is beyond what is available. Although first developed in the 1940s, this theory has withstood the test of time and is widely recognized as a fundamental assumption in understanding organizational processes such as decision making and planning [7,8,9]. More recently, modern computerized information systems are facilitating and instilling a greater degree of rationality in decision making in all organizations including colleges and universities. They support organizations and help them to adjust, adapt, and learn in order to perform their administrative functions. [10] While these systems are not replacing the decision maker, they surely are helping to refine the decision-making process.

Figure 2 illustrates the basic data-driven decision-making process. It assumes that decision making in education environments is fundamentally part of a social process. It also assumes that an information system is available to support the decision process, that internal and external factors not available through the information system are considered, and that a course or courses of action are determined. The information system in Figure 2 is a computerized database system capable of storing, manipulating, and providing reports from a wide variety of data. The decision process concludes with decision makers reflecting on and evaluating their decisions.

Terms related to data-driven decision making include data

warehousing, data mining, and data disaggregation. Data warehousing essentially refers to a database information system that is capable of storing, integrating and maintaining large amounts of data over time. It might also involve multiple database systems. Data mining is a frequently used term in research and statistics which refers to searching or "digging into" a data file for information to understand better a particular phenomenon. Data disaggregation refers to the use of software tools to break data files down into various characteristics. An example might be using a software program to select student performance data by gender, by major, by ethnicity, or by other definable characteristics.

In recent years, two other terms, big data and analytics, have become important. Big data is a generic term that assumes that the information or database system(s) used as the main storage facility is capable of storing large quantities of data longitudinally and down to very specific transactions. For example, college student record keeping systems have maintained outcomes information on students such as grades in each course. This information could be used by institutional researchers to study patterns of student performance over time, usually from one semester to another or one year to another. In a big data scenario, data would be collected for each student transaction in a course, especially if the course was delivered electronically online. Every student entry on a course assessment, discussion board entry, blog entry, or wiki activity could be recorded, generating thousands of transactions per student per course. Furthermore, this data would be collected in real or near real time as it is transacted and then analyzed to suggest courses of action. Analytics software is evolving to assist in this analysis.

The generic definition of analytics is similar to data-driven decision making. Essentially it is the science of examining data to draw conclusions and, when used in decision making, to present paths or courses of action. In recent years, the definition of analytics has gone further, however, to incorporate elements of operations research such as decision trees and strategy maps to establish predictive models and to determine probabilities for certain courses of action. It uses data mining software to establish decision processes that convert data into actionable insight, uncover patterns, alert and respond to issues and concerns, and plan for the future. This might seem to be an overly complicated definition but the term "analytics" has been used in many different ways in recent years and has become part of the buzzword jargon that sometimes seeps into new technology applications and

products. Goldstein and Katz (2005) in a study of academic analytics admitted that they struggled with coming up with a name and definition that was appropriate for their work. They stated that they adopted the term "academic analytics" for their study but that it was an "imperfect label."[11] Alias (2011) defined four different types of analytics that could apply to instruction including web analytics, learning analytics, academic analytics, and action analytics. [12] The trade journal, Infoworld, referred to analytics as:

"One of the buzzwords around business intelligence software...[that]...has been through the linguistic grinder, with vendors and customers using it to describe very different functions.

The term can cause confusion for enterprises, especially as they consider products from vendors who use analytics to mean different things..." [13]

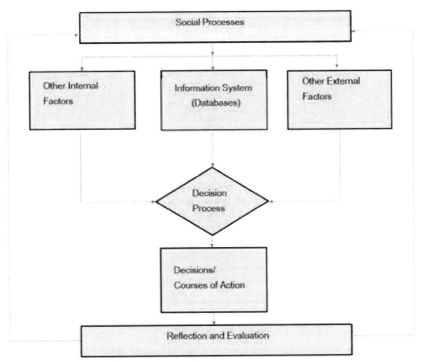

Fig. 2. The Data-Driven Decision-Making Process

Critical to the definition of analytics is the use of data to determine courses of action especially where there is a high volume of transactions. Common examples of analytics applications are examinations of Website traffic, purchases, or navigation patterns to determine which customers are more or less likely to buy particular products (i.e., books, movies) by ecommerce companies such as amazon.com or Netflix. Using these patterns, companies send personalized notifications to customers as new products become available. In higher education, analytics are beginning to be used for a number of applications that address student performance, outcomes, and persistence.

Big data concepts and analytics can be applied to a variety of higher education administrative and instructional

applications including recruitment and admissions processing, financial planning, donor tracking and student performance monitoring. This article will focus on teaching and learning, and hence will specifically examine learning analytics.

To take advantage of big data and learning analytics, it is almost a requirement that transaction processing be electronic rather than manual. Traditional face-to-face instruction can support traditional data-driven decision-making processes, however, to move into the more extensive and time-sensitive learning analytics applications, it is important that instructional transactions are collected as they occur. This would be possible within a course management/learning management system (CMS/LMS). Most CMS/LMSs provide constant monitoring of student activity whether they are responses, postings on a discussion board, accesses of reading material, completions of quizzes, or some other assessment. Using the full capabilities of a basic CMS/LMS, a robust fifteen week online course would generate thousands of transactions per student. Real-time recording and analysis of these transactions could then be used to feed a learning analytics application. Not waiting for the end of a marking period or semester to record performance measures is critical to this type of application. Monitoring student transactions on a real-time basis allows for real-time decisions. Instructors may take actions or intervene in time to alert or assist students. A CMS/LMS or something similar therefore becomes critical for

collecting and feeding this data into a "big" database for processing by a learning analytics software application. These instructional transactions should also be integrated with other resources such as student, course, and faculty data from the college information systems. Analytics software can then be used to analyze these transactions to establish patterns that are used to develop guidelines and rules for subsequent courses of action (see Figure 3). An important caveat is that the data accuracy should never be compromised in favor of timeliness of the data. Both accuracy and timeliness are required and need to be present in the learning analytics application.

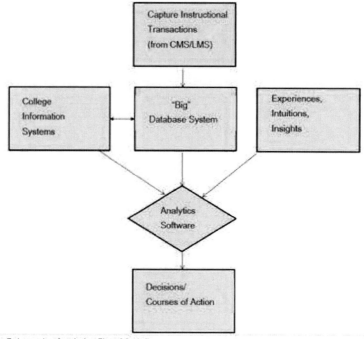

Fig. 3. Learning Analytics Flow Model

In a white paper published by IBM entitled Analytics for Achievement, eight categories of possible instructional applications utilizing analytics were described. The eight categories are as follows:

1. Monitoring individual student performance
2. Disaggregating student performance by selected characteristics such as major, year of study, ethnicity, etc.
3. Identifying outliers for early intervention
4. Predicting potential so that all students achieve optimally
5. Preventing attrition from a course or program
6. Identifying and developing effective instructional techniques
7. Analyzing standard assessment techniques and instruments (i.e. departmental and licensing exams)
8. Testing and evaluation of curricula. [14]

Of the above, monitoring individual student performance and course participation in a course is among the most popular type of learning analytics application. Anyone who has ever

taught (face-to-face or online) will monitor student participation to determine engagement with the course material. Taking attendance is a time-honored classroom activity and most instructors will become concerned about students who have too many absences. Grades on quizzes and papers are also frequently monitored. A conscientious instructor will review his/her records and meet with those students who are not meeting the standards for the course. Many colleges have instituted mid-term reviews that provide students with indicators of their progress in a course. In online courses, CMS/LMSs routinely provide course monitoring statistics and rudimentary early warning systems that allow instructors to follow up with students who are not responding on blogs or discussion boards, not accessing reading materials, or not promptly taking quizzes. These course statistics are maintained in real-time and instructors can review them as often as they wish. Students who are not as engaged as they should be can be sent emails expressing concerns about their performance. None of these interventions requires learning analytics, however, these interactions can be enhanced significantly by expanding the amount and nature of the data collected. For example, a single student response on a discussion board can be analyzed through pattern recognition to determine the depth and quality of student engagement with the course material. The pattern used in this type of analysis are uncovered by examining thousands and tens of thousands of other student responses and evaluating sentences and phrases.

Examples of well-designed learning analytics-based student monitoring systems are Rio Salado Community College's Progress and Course Engagement (PACE) system, Northern Arizona University's Grade Performance System (GPS), and Purdue University's Course Signals System.

For purposes of this article, the Course Signals System, in particular, is a good example of learning analytics software because it is one of the first to be used in blended learning environments. It combines demographic information with online student interactions and produces a red, yellow or green light to show students how well they are doing in their courses -- and also provides that information to their professors who can intervene if necessary . Developed originally at Purdue University, Course Signals was licensed to SunGard Higher Education (now Ellucian) in 2010 to make it available to other colleges and universities. Large CMS/LMS providers such as Desire2Learn and Blackboard have modeled their own retention early warning systems after Purdue's work. [15] It has won a number of awards including the Campus Technology Innovators Award, Digital Education Achievement Award, and the Lee Noel and Randi Levitz Retention Excellence Awards. Course Signals has been used in online, face-to-face, and blended learning environments. It has been particularly popular in large-section size, blended, and flipped classroom courses. [16] While there have been several studies supporting the use of learning analytics software such as Course Signals for improving student retention, more research needs to be done. [17] Michael Caulfield, director of blended and networked learning at Washington State University at Vancouver, cautioned that the early research on the effectiveness of learning analytics on retention needs further verification and review. [18] The fact is that learning analytics as a tool for retention is still in its nascent stage. The Society for Learning Analytics Research (SoLAR) is an inter-disciplinary network of leading international researchers who are exploring the role and impact of analytics on teaching, learning, training and development. This society was established in 2011 and has held four conferences to discuss issues related to learning analytics research. To provide a vehicle for documenting the research, SoLAR established The Journal of Learning Analytics, a peer-reviewed, open-access journal, for disseminating research in this field. It provides a research forum within what George Siemens, the president of SoLAR calls "the messiness of science". [19] The first edition was published in June, 2014. The articles in this first edition address issues such as scaling- up learning analytics initiatives, the relationship between LMS/VLE usage and learning performance, the role of psychometric data to predict academic achievement, and the capacity to detect boredom through user log- data. All of these, while important, are just beginning to scratch the surface of effectiveness of learning analytics with respect to student performance and retention. Furthermore, there is practically no research that does cost-benefit comparisons of the large-scale implementation of learning analytics in blended learning or face-to-face environments. In sum, there is a long road ahead for researchers in this field and much study to be done.

IV. BENEFITS AND CONCERNS

The New Horizon Report is published each year by The New Media Consortium and EDUCAUSE. It predicts six emerging technologies that are likely "to enter mainstream use" over the next five years. In the 2014 Report, the six technologies in rank order were identified as follows:

1. Growth of Social Media
2. Integration of Online, Blended and Collaborative Learning
3. Rise of Data-Driven Learning and Assessment
4. Shift from Students as Consumers to Students as Creators
5. Agile Approaches to Change
6. Evolution of Online Learning [20]

The ranking of these six technologies indicates that the first two will likely enter the mainstream in one to two years; the second two within three years; and the last two within five years or more. The Rise of Data-Driven Learning and Assessment (referring to learning analytics) was ranked third and indicates that this technology has potential and that widespread adoption is projected to be about three years away. This ranking also indicates that learning analytics need more exploration at this time and refinements before their adoption.

A. Benefits

Learning analytics can have significant benefits in monitoring student performance and progress. First, and at its most basic level, learning analytics software can mine down to the frequency with which individual students access a CMS/LMS, how much time they are spending in a course, and the number and nature of instructional interactions. These interactions can be categorized into assessments (tests, assignments, or exercises), content (articles, videos, or simulations viewed) and collaborative activities (blogs, discussion groups, or wikis).

Second, by providing detailed data on instructional interactions, learning analytics can significantly improve academic advisement related directly to teaching and learning. Learning analytics can improve the ability to identify at-risk students and intervene at the first indication of trouble. Furthermore by linking instructional activities with other student information system data (college readiness, gender, age, major), learning analytics software is able to review performance across the organizational hierarchy: from the student, to courses, to department, to the entire college. It can provide insights into individual students as well as the learning patterns of various cohorts of students.

Third, learning analytics software is able to provide longitudinal analysis that can lead to predictive behavior studies and patterns. By linking CMS/LMS databases with an institution's information system, data can be collected over time. Student and course data can be aggregated and disaggregated to analyze patterns at multiple levels of the institution. This would allow for predictive modeling that in turn, can create and establish student outcomes alert systems and intervention strategies.

In sum, learning analytics can become an important element in identifying students who are at risk and alerting advisors and faculty to take appropriate actions. Furthermore, it can do so longitudinally across the institution and can undercover patterns to improve student retention that in turn, can assist in academic planning.

B. Concerns

First, in order for big data and learning analytics applications to function well, data need to be accurate and timely. Learning analytics software works best for courses that are delivered completely electronically such as online courses. Traditional face-to-face courses that require significant data conversion time are problematic. Blended learning courses (part face-to-face and part online) likewise present data collection problems. Because blended learning courses vary so much in the nature of their delivery, learning analytics software can have significant data gaps. Instructional transactions that take place in the face-to-face environment will be lost unless the faculty member or teaching assistant is willing to manually enter them into the student information system.

The second, and perhaps the most serious concern, is that since learning analytics require massive amounts of data collected on students and integrated with other databases, colleges need to be mindful of privacy, data profiling, and the rights of students in terms of recording their individual behaviors. While college classes have always involved evaluating student performance and academic behavior, learning analytics take the recording of behavior to a whole new level and scope. As well-intentioned as learning analytics might be in terms of helping students succeed, this "big data" approach may also be seen as "big brother is watching" and, as such ,an invasion of privacy that some students would find objectionable. Precautions need be taken to ensure that the extensive data collection of student instructional transactions is not abused in ways that potentially hurt individuals. Vicky Gunn, Director of the Learning and Teaching Centre at the University of Glasgow, advises:

> "... it is clear that the growth of learning analytics needs a few up-front protocols of protection as soon as possible.. We should especially be considering…Ethical consent structures to enable students to know what is being gathered, when and how it will be used as well as

opportunities for students to opt in/out." [21]

Third, there are not yet enough individuals trained to use big data and analytics appropriately. Experienced database administrators and designers capable of warehousing and integrating data across multiple files and formats are a necessity. In addition to the expertise needed to develop databases, instructional designers working with faculty will need to understand and derive insights into the student behaviors that are pertinent to the application at hand. There is also a need for institutional researchers, or others knowledgeable about statistics, decision trees, and strategy mapping, to develop algorithms that construct predictive models. College administrators may have to invest in consultants or undertake extensive professional development of their own staffs in order to develop appropriate applications. This will take time and additional resources and may or may not be worth the return on investment. Furthermore, because of the dearth of expertise, there may be a tendency to use instructional templates that are integrated into CMS/LMSs. These, although convenient, may be overly simplistic and should be considered with caution.

Fourth, a good deal of college and university student data may end up in larger governmental databases either at the state or national level. Bennett (2011) cautions that the United States is heading to an all-inclusive national K-20 database. [21] Federal education policies as promulgated by No Child Left Behind and Race to the Top funding have pushed many states to adopt comprehensive statewide student databases that could easily be the basis for establishing a national system. Furthermore, there is a certain amount of influence being exerted on the part of the U.S. Department of Education in favor of development of common database structures. Such a system might be beneficial but may also leave individuals vulnerable to privacy, data security and theft issues. In 2013, the people of the United States were awakened to the spying activities of the National Security Agency (N.S.A.) and the intelligence arms of other governments around the world. The problem became so bad that large Internet service companies such as Google, Facebook, and Yahoo invested hundreds of millions of dollars to seal up security systems that Edward J. Snowden revealed the N.S.A. had been exploiting. After years of cooperating with the U.S federal government, the goal of many of these companies is to thwart Washington as well as Beijing and Moscow. The users of "big data" and analytics need to be careful that these mega-database systems do not become the playground of exploitative individuals and organizations. [23]

Lastly, it might be beneficial to revisit the work of Herbert Simon and his theory on the limits of rational decision making that was mentioned earlier in this article. Herbert Simon was a life-long supporter of the use of computer technology to support decision making, including the application of artificial intelligence. At Carnegie-Mellon University where he taught for decades he was active in integrating artificial intelligence software in the learning sciences to improve instruction. Instructional data-driven decision making and learning analytics parallel Simon's work in this area. In his honor, Carnegie-Mellon University established the Simon Initiative in 2013 to accelerate the use of learning science and technology to improve student learning. This initiative harnesses CMU's decades of learning data and research to improve educational outcomes for students. However, as database systems become bigger and as software such as learning analytics becomes more complex, a case can be made that the limits of rational decision making are being exceeded because of the plethora of information and data available. Simon was highly focused on the efficient use of data and is famously quoted as saying that too much information can consume its recipients and that "... a wealth of information creates a poverty of attention..." [24] Simon's quote may be a most appropriate concern in the era of big data and learning analytics. Nathan Silver, an American statistician, echoed Simon in his 2012 bestseller, The Signal and the Noise...., and cautioned that in predictive models, there is a tendency to collect a lot of meaningless data (i.e., noise) creating the danger of poor predictions. [25]

V. CONCLUSION

This article started with a reference to two scenarios, one at North-West University in South Africa and one at the City University of New York. These institutions are very different, yet are facing similar decisions with regard to investing and acquiring learning analytic software. They are also similar in that, while they have some fully online academic programs, both are presently and for the foreseeable future investing heavily in blended learning. My recommendation to both institutions was that before committing to learning analytics they do a careful analysis of the costs related to acquiring this software. These would include not only direct costs such as software licenses and maintenance contracts, but also indirect costs to hire personnel and/or consultants to design and implement learning analytics applications. It would also include the feasibility and cost of data collection in blended learning environments where faculty or other personnel would be needed to provide accurate and timely data.

Colleges and universities around the world need to meet a number of challenges related to providing greater access to higher education. However, expanding access does not necessarily lead to expanding resources. To the contrary, higher education policy makers, while calling for more access, are limiting resources and instructional technology such as online and blended learning is being seen as an important vehicle for expanding access while containing costs. In its truest sense, expanded access does not just mean getting acceptance into college programs; it also means successful completion of degrees. Student attrition in many colleges and universities is at unacceptable levels and needs to be addressed as well. Data-driven decision making and learning analytics software have the potential to assist colleges in identifying and evaluating strategies that can improve retention. At the present

time, however, these software are best suited for fully online environments, not face-to-face or blended learning environments. Nevertheless, as data-driven decision making enters the big data and learning analytics era, these new approaches, while not silver bullets, may be part of the solution. Higher education administrators would do well to consider the benefits, concerns, and costs iterated above when evaluating whether big data and learning analytics can be used in their institutions and determining the exact role they can play.

REFERENCES

[1] Allen, I. E. & Seaman, J. (2014). "Grade Change: Tracking Online Learning Education in the United States." Needham, MA: Babson Survey Research Group. http://www.onlinelearningsurvey.com/reports/gradechange.pdf

[2] Accessed June 6, 2014.

[3] Simon, H. A. (1945). Administrative Behavior. New York: Macmillan.

[4] Simon, H. A. (1957). Administrative Behavior (2nd ed.). New York: Macmillan.

[5] Simon, H. A. (1960). The New Science of Management Decision. New York: Harper & Row.

[6] Simon, H. A. (1979). Rational Decision Making in Business Organizations. American Economic Review, 69, 493–513.

[7] Simon, H. A. (1982). Models of Bounded Rationality. Cambridge, MA: MIT Press.

[8] Tyson, C. (2002). The Foundations of Imperfect Decision Making. Stanford, CA: Stanford Graduate School of Business Research Paper Series.

[9] Carlson, R. V., & Awkerman, G. (Eds.). (1991). Educational Planning: Concepts, Strategies and Practices. New York: Longman.

[10] Senge, P. M. (1990). The Fifth Discipline: The Art & Practice of the Learning Organization. New York, NY: Doubleday Currency.

[11] Dibello, A.J. & Nevis, E.C. (1998). How Organizations Learn. San Francisco: Jossey-Bass.

[12] Goldstein, P.J. & Katz, R. N. (2005). Academic Analytics: The Uses of Management Information and Technology in Higher Education. Boulder, CO: EDUCAUSE Center for Applied Research.

[13] Alias, T. (2011). Learning Analytics: Definitions, Processes, and Potential. Unpublished paper. http://learninganalytics.net/LearningAnalyticsDefinitionsProcessesPotential.pdf

[14] Kirk, J. (February 7, 2006). 'Analytics' Buzzword Needs Careful Definition. Infoworld. http://www.infoworld.com/t/data-management/analytics-buzzword-needs-careful-definition-567 Accessed: June 3, 2014.

[15] IBM Software Group (2001). Analytics for Achievement. Ottawa, Ontario. http://public.dhe.ibm.com/common/ssi/ecm/en/ytw03149caen/YTW03149CAEN.PDF. Accessed: June 10, 2014.

[16] Feldstein, M. (November 2013). Course Signals Effectiveness Data Appears to be Meaningless (and Why You Should Care). Blog posting on e-Literate Website. http://mfeldstein.com/courssignals-effectiveness-data-appears-meaningless-care/ Accessed: August 9, 2014

[17] Iten, L., Arnold, K., Pistilli, M. (March 2008). Mining Real-time Data to Improve Student Success in a Gateway Course. Paper presented at the Eleventh Annual TLT Conference. West Lafayette, IN: Purdue University. http://www.itap.purdue.edu/learning/docs/research/TLT%2008%20presentation%20summary.pdf Accessed: August 9, 2014

[18] Pistilli, M.D., Arnold, K. & Bethune, M. (November 18, 2012). Signals: Using Academic Analytics to Promote Student Success. EDUCAUSE Review http://www.educause.edu/ero/article/signals-using-academic-analytics-promote-student-success. Accessed August 8, 2014.

[19] Straumsheim, C. (November 6, 2013). Mixed Signals. Inside Higher Education.

https://www.insidehighered.com/news/2013/11/06/researchers-cast-doubt-about-early-warning-systems-effect-retention.   Accessed: August 9, 2014.

[20] Siemens, G. (June 2014).   The Journal of Learning Analytics: Supporting and Promoting Learning Analytics Research.   Journal of Learning   Analytics,   1(1). http://epress.lib.uts.edu.au/journals/index.php/JLA/article/view/3908

[21] Accessed: August 11, 2014.

[22] Johnson, L., Adams-Becker, S., and Estrada, V. & Freeman, A. (2014). The NMC Horizon Report: 2014 Higher Education Edition. Austin, Texas: The New Media Consortium.

[23] Gunn, V. (May 7, 2014).   Learning Analytics, Surveillance, and the Future of Understanding our Students.   News Blog posting of the Society   for   Research   in   the   Higher   Education. http://srheblog.com/2014/05/07/learning-analytics-surveillance-and-the-future-of-understanding-our-students/ Accessed: August 11, 2014.

[24] Bennett, E. (2011). Moving Toward a National Education Database. Unpublished paper.

[25] Sanger, D.E. & Perlroth, N. (June 6, 2014). Internet Giants Erect Barriers   to   Spy   Agencies.   New   York   Times. http://www.nytimes.com/2014/06/07/technology/internet-giants-erect-barriers-to-spy-agencies.html?_r=0.Accessed: June 15, 2014.

[26] Simon, H.A. (1971). Designing Organizations for an Information-rich World   in Martin Greenberger, Computers, Communication, and the Public Interest, Baltimore, MD: The Johns Hopkins Press.

[27] silver, N.   (2012).   The Signal and the Noise: Why So Many Predictions Fail — but Some Don't. New York: Penguin Press, Inc.

Anthony G. Picciano is a professor and executive officer in the Ph.D. Program in Urban Education at the Graduate Center of the City University of New York. He is also a member of the faculty in the graduate program in Education Leadership at Hunter College, and the doctoral certificate program in Interactive Pedagogy and Technology at the City University of New York Graduate Center. He has extensive experience in education administration and teaching, and has been involved in a number of major grants from the U.S. Department of Education, the National Science Foundation, IBM, and the Alfred P. Sloan Foundation.

## 13

Dissemination Matters: Influences of Dissemination Activities on User Types in an Online Educational Community

Min Yuan[1], Mimi Recker[1]

[1]*Utah State University*

Abstract — Emerging online educational communities provide spaces for teachers to find resources, create instructional activities, and share these activities with others. Within these online communities, individual users' activities may vary widely, and thus different user types can be identified. In addition, users' patterns of activities in online communities are dynamic, and further can be affected by dissemination activities. Through analyzing usage analytics in an online teacher community called the *Instructional Architect*, this study explores the influences of dissemination activities on the usage patterns of different user types. Results show that dissemination activities can play an important role in encouraging users' active participation, while the absence of dissemination activities can further increase participation inequality.

Keywords — Educational technology, Learning systems, Online Communities, Pattern analysis

I. INTRODUCTION

TEACHERS increasingly rely on the Internet to find online learning resources, create instructional activities using these resources, and then share these with others [1]-[4]. To help teachers in these tasks, several web-based tools, such as the *Instructional Architect*, the *Curriculum Customization Service*, and *Tapped In*, have been developed [5]-[7]. These tools are designed to help teachers' knowledge building processes, as well as to help support the development of online educational communities [8].

In an online educational community, a virtual space is provided for teachers and learners to seek information, ask questions, and interact with one and another [9]. In general, an online educational community contains the following four elements: *people* who create content and connect with each other, *computer systems* that mediate people's activities, *policies* that guide people's activities, and *purposes* that provide reasons and motivations for people to participate [10]. People participating in an online educational community typically have shared purposes, but their actual activities in the community can vary widely. For example, some teachers may actively collect resources and design instructional activities using these resources, some may willingly share their resources and teaching activities with other users, while others

may simply engage in viewing other users' activities [11], [12].

As people engage in these different activities, they can be categorized into different user types. At a high level, two main categories of users have been identified in online communities: *lurkers,* who take on more non-participatory roles and principally view other members' activities and products; and *contributors,* who take on more active roles, create new content, and share with the community [13], [14]. Prior research has also detected that the lurker-contributor ratio in communities is often skewed, with substantially more lurkers than contributors [1], [14], [15], [16].

Further, patterns of activity over time in online educational communities are dynamic, resulting in different developmental paths [17]. For example, over time, one online community may thrive and grow with more user activity, while another may shrink (or even die) with fewer users and less participation [18]. Additionally, as time passes, some lurkers may follow a trajectory toward becoming contributors in a community [19].

However, despite prior research on characterizing user typologies in online educational communities, less work has focused on understanding user activity patterns, the evolution of patterns over time, and the resulting dynamics of online educational communities. As such, in this article, we report results from applying techniques from the emerging field of learning analytics to analyze usage patterns in an online educational community for teachers, called the *Instructional Architect* (IA.usu.edu). Understanding the evolution of user activities and the dynamics of a community is complex, as the analysis revolves around mining the massive amounts of data automatically generated by the community [7], [22]. Techniques from learning analytics offer approaches for analyzing these kinds of data, such as comparing users' number of logins and visit duration, analyzing user-generated content, and examining the relationships between users [23], [24]. Outcomes of such research can provide suggestions for dissemination activities that can promote particular users' activities in order to enhance the development and sustainability of online communities [20], [21].

In particular, this article reports results of longitudinal analyses of usage data automatically collected by the IA over two full school years. During the first school-year period

(2009-10), the development team conducted extensive dissemination activities; however, these had ceased by the second school-year period (2012-13). In this way, we explored the influences of dissemination activities on different IA user types, and whether these typologies changed after dissemination activities ended. By comparing the analytics of different user types during and after dissemination, this study identified which user types and what kind of activities were most affected when dissemination activities ended, thus providing insights on the sustainability of online communities.

II. THEORETICAL CONTEXT

A. Online Educational Communities

Online educational communities have become an important part of teachers' lives, in that they can help teachers' seek instructional resources and interact with other teachers [13], [25]. Like any community, these online educational communities have different life cycles.

Researchers have provided a variety of definitions and descriptions of these life cycles. For example, [20] defined three stages in the life cycle: starting the online community, encouraging early online interaction, and moving to a self-sustaining community. [18] divided the life cycle into five stages: inception, creation, growth, maturity, and death.

Although the definitions are different, researchers have identified similar development trajectories in the evolution of online communities. For example, in the early stage of an online community, the technological components are developed and groups of users with similar purposes and needs begin to create content and/or interact with each other. At maturity or the self-sustaining stage, the community may have a large number of members and a large repository of content [18].

In addition, in analyzing the life cycles of communities, researchers have also focused on the role that dissemination plays in the development of communities. They noted that dissemination activities are important in encouraging users' early participation and interaction, in maintaining their interests over time, and in supporting the sustainability of communities [20], [18], [26].

In this vein, researchers have identified factors that can influence the development and sustainability of online community. For example, [27] listed two factors: the creation of content and the interaction between users. [9] analyzed two factors that appeared to determine the success of online communities: usability (how people can access, create, and use content), and sociability (how users can interact).

B. Users in Online Educational Communities

Research has also focused on identifying different user typologies based on users' participation practices in an online community. For example, [15] categorized users of the *Instructional Architect* based on their activity patterns using a probabilistic clustering algorithm. Results revealed three types of user groups, where each group had characteristic patterns in terms of its frequency in creating, viewing, and sharing content. Similarly, [16] investigated usage patterns in the *Curriculum Customization Service* by analyzing users' clickstream data. They found that some user types were characterized by viewing many interactive resources and shared resources, while other types were spending more time on viewing instructional materials and assessments.

By reviewing user patterns across several different online communities, [14] proposed the "90-9-1" rule. This rule divides users into three groups: 1) approximately 90% of the users are lurkers, who view other users' resources and products but do not contribute; 2) 9% of the users are intermittent contributors; and 3) 1% of the users are heavy contributors, who participate heavily and create most of the content in the community.

This "participation inequality" rate has been observed in several online communities. For example, [28] investigated the distribution of contributions made by authors in Wikipedia, and found that less than 10% of the total number of authors created more than 90% of the content. In analyzing user-generated content in nine popular websites (e.g., Amazon book review, Merlot.org, Slideshare.net), [29] found that the distribution of user-generated content similarly followed a "long-tail" distribution, thus providing further evidence of participation inequality.

This "participation inequality" phenomenon results in a skewed lurker–contributor ratio, as well as the "free riding" problem. In this phenomenon, users benefit from other users' activities without contributing anything in return [30]. If many users become "free riders" (or lurkers) in a community, participation and the number of resources created in the community will grow slowly, which may in turn negatively affect users' interest as well as the overall sustainability of the community [31].

To further examine participation inequality and the potential free riding problem, researchers have studied why lurkers may behave this way. Reasons for lurking include a desire for users to get to know the norms of a community before becoming contributors, a lack of familiarity with the community, a lack of reasons for contributing content, and technology barriers [11], [13]. In addition, by comparing lurkers and non-lurkers' activities, researchers have found that non-lurkers tend to have a desire for a greater variety of activities, such as getting answers to questions, participating in conversations, or offering expertise [11].

It is also important to note that users' activities in the communities often change over time. For example, lurkers can begin to create and share their products once they become more familiar with the functions of the online community and build trust with other users. Non-lurkers can become lurkers as they gradually lose interest or their needs are satisfied [18]. Thus, understanding how the activities of different types of users evolve over time, especially in response to changes in support or dissemination activities within the community, are needed.

III. TECHNOLOGICAL CONTEXT

The technological context for this study is the *Instructional Architect* (IA). The IA is a free, web-based tool that was first launched in 2001. Using iterative design approaches, the tool was improved several times and development stabilized in 2005, before the data were collected for the present article.

The IA enables teachers to use online educational resources to create, publish, and share instructional activities (called IA projects) within the IA online community [5], [32]. Figure 1 shows an IA project created by a teacher. This IA project, on the topic of the "Underground Railroad", provides text, maps, and links to supporting resources.

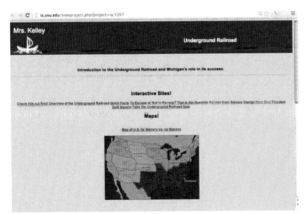

Fig. 1. A screenshot of a teacher-created IA project

Within the IA online educational community, users can engage in many different activities. Without logging in, any user can *browse* IA projects created and shared by other IA users. After logging in, a user can also *collect* online resources in his/hew own personal repository of online resources by using the 'My Resources' area of the IA to search for and save online resources from existing content repositories (e.g., the NSDL.org), or online content including web pages, pdf documents, or other public IA projects.

In the 'My Projects' area, teachers can *create* IA projects using online resources they have collected and annotate them with text. An IA project (a webpage) is then generated, which can then be used in a classroom activity. Finally, teachers can *share* IA projects by making them *public,* so that other users can easily view and copy them.

Since 2005, the IA has approximately 7,900 registered users, who have gathered over 75,600 online resources and created over 17,300 IA projects. Since August 2006, public IA projects have been viewed over 2.5 million times.

IV. RESEARCH DESIGN

A. Research Design

This study analyzed the usage log files automatically collected by the IA in order to examine the evolution of the activity patterns of different user types. Two different time periods were examined: one in which dissemination activities were ongoing, and the other in which they had ended.

Since the launch of the IA, developers and researchers have taken many approaches for disseminating the tool to teachers. These included advertising online, offering teacher professional development workshops, and presenting at conferences. [32]. For example, between 2007 and 2011, a series of teacher workshops were conducted in several U.S. states, including South Dakota, Illinois, New York, and Utah. The workshops familiarized teachers with the IA, showed them how to design IA projects, and encouraged them to integrate these IA projects in their teaching.

In addition, members of the development team presented about the IA at several conferences, including the *International Conference on Educational Data Mining, Joint Conference on Digital Library*, the *Annual Meeting of the Association for Educational Communications Technology*, and the *Annual Meeting of the American Education Research Association* [33]-[36], as well as local, teacher-oriented conferences.

To examine the influence of dissemination activities on IA users types, this study compared the activities of different IA user types during two time periods: 1) the *"active dissemination"* period (9 months between 09/01/2009 - 05/31/2010), in which developers engaged in active dissemination activities, and 2) the *"no dissemination"* period (9 months between 09/01/2012 - 05/31/2013) in which dissemination activities had ended. Note that the nine-month period corresponds to the school year of U.S. teachers, our target users. It is also noteworthy that the activities we analyzed are IA users' naturally occurring behaviors, and *not* those of users specifically recruited to participate in a research study.

Specifically, this study had two research purposes: examining 1) how the IA community evolved and changed during and after dissemination activities, and 2) more specifically, how the activities of particular subsets of IA users also changed after dissemination activities ended. To align with these purposes, different user groups and data sources were used to address two research questions (see Table 1):

1. How did the activities of **IA visitors** change between the "active dissemination" period and the "no dissemination" period?

2. How did the activities of **lurkers** and **active contributors** change between the "active dissemination" period and the "no dissemination" period?

Usage activity in the IA is automatically collected by two complementary data sources: Google Analytics (GA) and the relational database powering the IA site (IADB). As a Google service, GA records the activities of all users in the IA website (which we call *IA visitors*). In particular, GA tracks visitors to the IA website, regardless of whether they have an account. In this analysis, we used seven metrics collected by GA (see Table 2) to analyze the activities of IA visitors.

TABLE 1
RESEARCH QUESTIONS AND DATA SOURCES

Research Questions	User Group Analyzed	Data Sources
RQ1	All visitors to the IA site	Google Analytics
RQ2	Users who created an IA account, in two groups: *lurkers* (did not create IA project) and *active contributors* (created IA projects)	IA database

B. Data Sources

TABLE 2
METRICS DESCRIBING ACTIVITIES OF IA VISITORS USING GOOGLE ANALYTICS

Metric	Description
# of visits	Number of visits to the website within a date range. A visit encompasses a set of interactions within the website (e.g. multiple page views).
# of new visits	Estimated number of the first-time visits.
# of unique visitors	Number of unduplicated (counted only once) visitors to the website within a date range.
# of page views	Total number of pages viewed, including repeated views of a single page.
Pageviews per visit	The ratio of total number of page viewed to number of visits.
Average visit duration	Average duration of a visit measured in seconds.
Bounce rate	Percentage of single-page visits (users who visit only one page of the website and then leave)

Note. Descriptions provided by Google Analytics.

TABLE 3
METRICS DESCRIBING ACTIVITIES OF USERS USING THE IADB

Metric	Description
# of logins	Number of times users log into the IA website within a date range
# of IA projects created	Number of IA projects created by users within a date range.
# of IA public projects created	Number of IA projects published within a date range.
# of IA projects copied	Number of IA projects copied from others within a date range.
# of online resources used	Number of online resources added to the IA projects within a date range

In contrast, the IADB records the activities of individual users who have registered for an account in the IA website. Using this data, we defined three categories of IA users for a particular time period: *lurkers,* who did not create IA projects; *contributors,* who created but did not share IA projects; and *active contributors,* who created and shared IA projects. In this analysis, we focused on two user types – *lurkers* and *active contributors*, and analyzed five metrics collected by the IADB capturing the activities of these users (see Table 3).

Also note that based on users' activities collected by IADB and GA, we assume that *lurkers* and *active contributors* are primarily teachers, while *IA visitors* come for the general Internet user base.

V. RESULTS

A. RQ1: Influence of Dissemination Activities on IA Visitors

Using the analytics from GA, Figures 2-8 compare the activities of IA visitors during the "active dissemination" and "no dissemination" periods (averaged monthly over the time period). Table 4 compares the activities of IA visitors averaged daily over these two time periods. The comparisons are made in terms of key GA analytics: the number of visits, new visits, unique visitors, *pageviews*, and *pageviews* per visit, as well as visit duration and bounce rate.

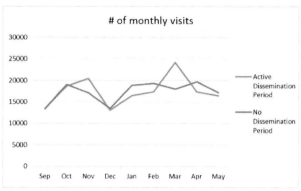

Fig. 2. Number of visits

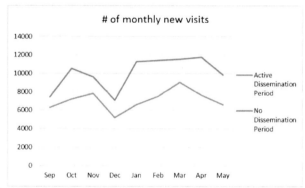

Fig. 3. Number of new visits

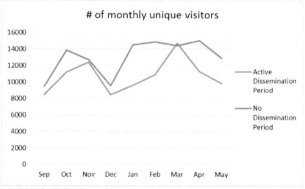

Fig. 4. Number of unique visitors

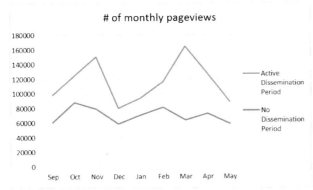

Fig. 5. Number of *pageviews*

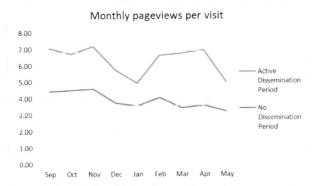

Fig. 6. Number of *pageviews* per visit

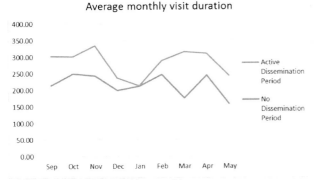

Fig. 7. Visit duration (measured in seconds)

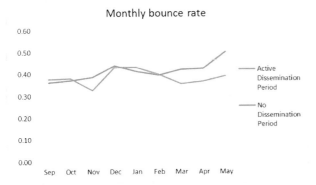

Fig. 8. Bounce rate

Due to non-normal distributions of the data, the Mann-Whitney test was used to compare whether visitors' activities between these two time periods were significantly different. As suggested by Figure 2, the overall number of visits did not differ significantly between these two time periods (U = 37129.50, p = .94). This suggests that dissemination activities had little effect on the overall number of visitors.

However, the number of new visits, the number of unique visitors, and the bounce rate all increased significantly during the subsequent "no dissemination" period (U = 24773.50, p < .001; U = 29879.00, p < .001; U = 29916.00, p < .001). In contrast, the number of *pageviews* and *pageviews* per visit, as well as average visit duration decreased significantly (U = 26917.50, p < .001; U = 12897.50, p < .001; U = 25048.00, p < .001). Taken together, these results suggest that while the overall number of visits stayed even between periods, the "active dissemination" period was characterized by more engaged visitors.

Note that one task of the IA is to help users to find useful online resources, and thus many IA projects contain links that lead users to resources outside the IA website (therefore inflating the bounce rate). It is plausible that the subsequent, "no dissemination" period was populated by more savvy users, who were quickly able to find desired resources. This would help explain the overall similar number of visits, coupled with decreased number of *pageviews*, visit duration, and higher bounce rate during this period.

TABLE 4
COMPARISON OF IA VISITORS' ACTIVITIES BETWEEN TWO TIME PERIODS

	Active dissemination			No dissemination		
	Mean	Median	SD	Mean	Median	SD
# of visits	577.70	641.00	364.73	572.48	607.00	338.52
# of new visits *	234.38	233.00	116.34	331.55	331.00	177.89
# of unique visitors *	355.03	371.00	193.73	429.33	442.00	236.35
# of *pageviews* *	3821.04	3351.00	2937.54	2321.77	2345.00	1569.38
Pageviews per visit *	6.32	5.88	2.60	3.90	3.72	1.19
Average visit duration (seconds) *	282.39	265.51	125.30	215.04	206.74	98.20
Bounce rate *	.39	.38	.09	.41	.42	.08

* Difference between the two time periods is significant (Mann-Whitney test; p < .05)

B. RQ2: Influence of Dissemination Activities on Lurkers and Active Contributors

Table 5 compares the number of lurkers and active contributors between the two time periods, using analytics from the IADB. Recall that *lurkers* are defined as users who created an IA account but did not create any IA projects during the given time period. *Active contributors* are defined as users who created and shared IA projects during the given time period.

As shown in Table 5, after the dissemination activities ended, the number of lurkers increased while the number of active contributors decreased. Note that the number of active contributors in the "active dissemination" period was about six times greater than during the "no dissemination" period, suggesting that dissemination activities may have helped encourage users' active participation. The large drop of active contributors during the "no dissemination" period may exacerbate the free riding problems, as only a very small portion of users contributed IA projects during this period. In addition, a large increase can be seen in the lurker-active contributor ratio. This suggests that ceasing dissemination activities can lead to a more skewed lurker-active contributor ratio and thus aggravate participation inequality.

TABLE 5
THE NUMBER OF USERS IN EACH CATEGORY

	Active dissemination	No dissemination
# of lurkers	3908	6201
# of active contributors	547	92
Lurker-active contributor ratio	7 : 1	66 : 1

Evolution of Lurkers

Table 6 compares lurkers' mean number of logins between the two time periods, which significantly decreased after dissemination activities ceased (U = 1.20, *p* < .001). This suggests that during the subsequent "no dissemination" period, lurkers were less likely to log in, and thus less likely to make use of features in the IA community.

As can also be seen, the number logins for lurkers was very low. Note that one function of the IA community is to facilitate teachers' browsing existing IA project, and login is not required to view IA projects. As such, the low number of logins does not necessarily mean that lurkers viewed fewer projects or became inactive – they may simply have chosen to view IA projects without logging in. Unfortunately, our analytics do not enable us to track visitors who do not log in at the individual user level.

Evolution of Active Contributors

Compared to the "active dissemination" period, all five metrics for active contributors at the aggregated level declined during the "no dissemination" period. As can be seen from Table 7, they had fewer logins, created fewer IA projects, shared fewer IA projects, copied fewer IA projects from other users, and used fewer online resources in their IA projects.

However, a closer examination of active contributors' individual activities revealed a different picture. As shown in Table 8, during the "no dissemination" period, active contributors on average had significantly fewer logins (U = 21531.00, p < .05), and used significantly fewer online resources (U = 21269.00, p < .05). However, each active contributor on average created significantly more IA projects, shared significantly more of these, but copied significantly less (U = 18826.00, p < .001; U = 16673.50, p < .001; U = 20974.50, p < .001).

TABLE 6
COMPARISON OF LURKERS' MEAN # OF LOGINS BETWEEN TWO TIME PERIODS

	Active dissemination			No dissemination		
	Mean	Median	SD	Mean	Median	SD
# of logins	.09	0	1.01	.04	0	.96

TABLE 7
COMPARISON OF ACTIVE CONTRIBUTORS' ACTIVITIES AT AGGREGATE LEVEL BETWEEN TWO TIME PERIODS

	Active dissemination	No dissemination
# of logins	3440	474
# of IA projects created	1890	399
# (%) of IA public projects created	1194 (63%)	310 (77%)
# (%) of IA projects copied	422 (22%)	18 (4%)
# of online resources used	6509	1017

TABLE 8
COMPARISON OF ACTIVE CONTRIBUTORS' ACTIVITIES **AT INDIVIDUAL LEVEL** BETWEEN TWO TIME PERIODS

	Active dissemination			No dissemination		
	Mean	Median	SD	Mean	Median	SD
# of logins *	6.29	4.00	7.60	5.15	3.00	6.59
# of IA projects created *	3.46	2.00	3.82	4.34	5.00	2.91
# of IA public projects created *	2.18	1.00	2.92	3.37	2.50	2.60
# of IA projects copied *	.77	0	1.79	.20	0	.47
# of online resources used *	11.90	8.00	16.59	11.05	12.00	8.63

* Difference between the two time periods is significant (Mann-Whitney test; p < .05)

In sum, after the dissemination activities ended, the number of active contributors significantly declined, with a corresponding decline in the number of IA projects created, shared, and copied, and resources used. However, the remaining active contributors on average increased their levels of engagement in the community by creating and sharing significantly more IA projects.

VI. DISCUSSION AND CONCLUSION

This article described a study that examined the analytics automatically collected by usage logs in order to compare user activity patterns in an online educational community during and after dissemination activities. This study first provided an overall view of the community by exploring changes in *IA visitors*' activities during the two time periods. Second, this study focused on two types of IA users – *lurkers* and *active contributors* – and compared the dynamics of their activities in the community during the two time periods.

In comparing activities of IA visitors between the "active

dissemination" and "no dissemination" period, we noted that the number of new visits and the number of unique visitors increased. This suggests that even though dissemination activities ended, the IA website attracted a growing number of new visitors and thus increased its audience size. This also suggests that users continue to find the IA online community useful for their tasks.

However, during the subsequent "no dissemination" period, the number of *pageviews, pageviews* per visit, and average visit duration decreased -- IA visitors viewed fewer IA projects and spent less time per visit. This could suggest that IA users are becoming more efficient in discovering information they desire. Alternatively, it could indicate that many IA projects were not visited, which makes content discovery a problem. Thus, the IA developers may consider user interface enhancements to recommend IA projects to users, so as to increase the number and variety of IA projects viewed by users [24].

We then compared users who have created an account in the IA in terms of two types of users: lurkers and active contributors. During the subsequent "no dissemination" period, the lurkers' number of logins decreased significantly, suggesting that they were less likely to consider themselves as members of IA community [11].

In comparing active contributors during the two time periods, we found that the number of active contributors dropped considerably during the "no dissemination" period. This resulted in an overall decrease in the amount of new content created in the community. However, on average, the remaining active contributors were much more engaged: they created more IA projects, and shared a higher percent of their IA projects. Thus while participation inequality increased after dissemination, the remaining active contributors were, plainly stated, more engaged contributors.

In sum, dissemination activities appear to play an important role in encouraging users' active participation in the IA community. With the absence of dissemination, while the overall number of visitors did not decrease, the lurker-active contributor ratio increased in the IA community. That is, participation inequality increased. Yet, those that remained active were more engaged contributors. Thus, at least for the IA community, it appears that dissemination is important in decreasing participation inequality and in increasing lurkers' sense of community, thereby contributing to the sustainability of the online community.

In conclusion, this study contributes to our understanding of how dissemination activities can influence the evolution of different user types in an online community. In addition, it shows how different kinds of analytics data can be used to help understand the dynamics of different user types. This, in turn, can help inform strategies for attracting new users, increasing the loyalty of existing users, and improving existing communities [12]. However, as this study only focused on one online educational community and contrasted user analytics during two relatively short time periods (9 months each),

future research is needed.

ACKNOWLEDGMENT

The authors would like to thank the many users of the Instructional Architect. This material is based upon work supported by the National Science Foundation under Grant No. 0937630, and Utah State University. Any opinions, findings, and conclusions or recommendations expressed in this material are those of the author(s) and do not necessarily reflect the views of the National Science Foundation. Portions of this research were previously presented at the 11th International Conference of the Learning Sciences (ICLS) in Boulder, Colorado, USA.

REFERENCES

[1] S. Abramovich, C.D. Schunn, and R. J. Correnti, "The role of evaluative metadata in an online teacher resource exchange," *Educational Technology Research and Development*, vol. 61, no. 6, pp. 863-883, 2013.

[2] D. E. Atkins, J. S. Brown, and A. L. Hammond (2007). A review of the open educational resources (OER) movement: Achievements, challenges, and new opportunities. Available: http://www.hewlett.org/Programs/Education/OER/OpenContent/Hewlett+OER+Report.htm

[3] C. L. Borgman, H. Abelson, L. Dirks, R. Johnson, K. R. Koedinger, M.C. Linn, C. A. Lynch, D. G. Oblinger, R. D. Pea, K. Salen, M. S. Smith, A. Szalay, "Fostering learning in the networked world: The cyberlearning opportunity and challenge, a 21st century agenda for the National Science Foundation". Report of the NSF Task Force on Cyberlearning. Virginia, US: NSF, 2008.

[4] M. Recker, A. Walker, S. Giersch, X. Mao, S. Halioris, B. Palmer, ... and M. B. Robertshaw, "A study of teachers' use of online learning resources to design classroom activities," *New Review of Hypermedia and Multimedia*, vol. 13, no. 2, pp. 117-134, 2007.

[5] M. Recker, "Perspectives on teachers as digital library users: Consumers, contributors, and designers," *D-Lib Magazine*, vol. 12, no. 9, 2006. Available: http://www.dlib.org/dlib/september06/recker/09recker.html

[6] T. Sumner and CCS Team, "Customizing science instruction with educational digital libraries," In *2010 Proceedings of the 10th annual joint conference on Digital libraries*, pp. 353-356.

[7] M. Schlager, U. Farooq, J. Fusco, P. Schank, and N. Dwyer, "Analyzing online social networking in professional learning communities: Cyber networks require cyber-research tools". *Journal of Teacher Education*, vol. 60, no. 1, pp. 86-100, 2009.

[8] R. J. Windle, H. Wharrad, D. McCormick, H. Laverty, and M. Taylor, (2010). Sharing and reuse in OER: experiences gained from open reusable learning objects in health. *Journal of Interactive Media in Education* [online]. 2010 (01). Available: http://jime.open.ac.uk/jime/article/viewArticle/2010-4/html

[9] J. Preece, "Sociability and usability in online communities: Determining and measuring success," *Behaviour & Information Technology*, vol. 20, no. 5, pp. 347-356, 2001.

[10] C. L. Hsu, and H. P. Lu, "Consumer behavior in online game communities: A motivational factor perspective," *Computers in Human Behavior*, vol. 23, no. 3, pp. 1642-1659, 2007.

[11] B. Nonnecke, D. Andrews, and J. Preece, "Non-public and public online community participation: Needs, attitudes and behavior," *Electronic Commerce Research*, vol. 6, no. 1, pp. 7-20, 2006.

[12] K. Panciera, R. Priedhorsky, T. Erickson, and L. Terveen, "Lurking? cyclopaths?: a quantitative lifecycle analysis of user behavior in a geowiki," In *2010 Proceedings of the SIGCHI Conference on Human Factors in Computing Systems*, pp. 1917-1926.

[13] J. Bishop, "Increasing participation in online communities: A framework for human–computer interaction", *Computers in human behavior*, vol. 23, no. 4, pp.1881-1893, 2007.

[14] J. Nielsen, (2006). Participation Inequality: Lurkers vs. Contributors in Internet Communities [online]. Available: http://www.nngroup.com/articles/participation-inequality/.

[15] B. Xu and M. Recker, "Teaching Analytics: A Clustering and Triangulation Study of Digital Library User Data", *Educational Technology & Society Journal*, vol. 15, no. 3, pp. 103-115, 2012.

[16] K. E. Maull, M. G. Saldivar, and T. Sumner, "Online Curriculum Planning Behavior of Teachers". In *2010 proceedings of EDM*, pp. 121-130.

[17] D. Maloney-Krichmar and J. Preece, "A multilevel analysis of sociability, usability, and community dynamics in an online health community," *ACM Transactions on Computer-Human Interaction (TOCHI)*, vol. 12, no. 2, pp. 201-232, 2005.

[18] A. Iriberri and G. Leroy, "A life-cycle perspective on online community success," *ACM Computing Surveys (CSUR)*, vol. 41, no. 2, pp. 11-40, 2009.

[19] B. Nonnecke and J. Preece, *Shedding light on lurkers in online communities*, Ethnographic Studies in Real and Virtual Environments: Inhabited Information Spaces and Connected Communities, Edinburgh, 1999, pp. 123-128.

[20] D. Andrews, J. Preece, and M. Turoff, M, "A conceptual framework for demographic groups resistant to online community interaction," in *2001 proceedings of the 34th Annual Hawaii International Conference on system sciences*, pp. 10-20.

[21] T. Elias, "Learning analytics: Definitions, processes and potential. Learning," *Learning*, vol. 23, pp. 134-148, 2011.

[22] G. Siemens and R. S. Baker, "Learning analytics and educational data mining: towards communication and collaboration," In *2012 proceedings of the 2nd international conference on learning analytics and knowledge*, pp. 252-254.

[23] R. Ferguson and S. B. Shum, "Social learning analytics: five approaches," In *2012 proceedings of the 2nd International Conference on Learning Analytics and Knowledge*, pp. 23-33.

[24] A. Bakharia, E. Heathcote, E., and S. Dawson, "Social networks adapting pedagogical practice: SNAPP," In: *Same Places, Different Spaces. Ascilite 2009*.

[25] J. Preece, and D. Maloney-Krichmar, "Online Communities". In J. Jacko and A. Sears, A. (Eds.) Handbook of Human-Computer Interaction, Lawrence Erlbaum Associates Inc. Publishers. Mahwah: NJ. pp. 596-620, 2003.

[26] M. Schlager, J. Fusco, and P. Schank, "Evolution of an online education community of practice". In K. A. Renninger and W. Shumar (Eds.), Building virtual communities: Learning and change in cyberspace, New York: Cambridge University Press, pp. 129-158, 2002.

[27] R. Farzan, J. M. DiMicco, and B. Brownholtz, "Spreading the honey: a system for maintaining an online community," In *2009 proceedings of the ACM 2009 international conference on Supporting group work*, pp. 31-40.

[28] F. Ortega, J. M. Gonzalez-Barahona, and G. Robles, "On the inequality of contributions to Wikipedia". In 2008 proceedings of the 41st Hawaii International Conference on System Sciences, pp. 304-304.

[29] X. Ochoa and E. Duval, "Quantitative analysis of user-generated content on the Web," In *2008 Proceedings of webevolve2008: web science workshop at WWW2008*, pp. 1-8.

[30] M. Feldman and J. Chuang, "Overcoming free-riding behavior in peer-to-peer systems," *ACM SIGecom Exchanges*, vol. 5, no. 4, pp. 41-50, 2005.

[31] L. Ramaswamy and L. Liu, "Free riding: A new challenge to peer-to-peer file sharing systems". In *2003 proceedings of the 36th Annual Hawaii International Conference on system sciences*, pp. 10-20.

[32] M. Recker, J. Dorward, D. Dawson, S. Halioris, Y. Liu, X. Mao, ... and J. Park, " You can lead a horse to water: teacher development and use of digital library resources". In *2005 Proceedings of the Joint Conference on Digital Libraries*, pp. 1–7.

[33] B. Xu and M. Recker, "Peer Production of Online Learning Resources: A Social Network Analysis," In *2010 Baker, R., Merceron, A., Pavlik, P.I. Jr. (Eds.). Proceedings of the 3rd International Conference on Educational Data Mining, pp. 315-316*.

[34] H. Leary, S. Giersch, A. Walker, and M. Recker, "Developing a Review Rubric for Learning Resources in Digital Libraries," In *2009 Proceedings of the Joint Conference on Digital Libraries, pp. 421-422.*

[35] L. Sellers, L. Ye, B. Robertshaw, M. Recker, and A. Walker, "Technology Integrated Professional Development: A Case Study of Junior High Science and Mathematics Teachers," presented at the Annual Meeting of the Associationfor Educational Communications Technology, Jacksonville, FL, Nov, 2011.

[36] A. Walker, M. Recker, B. Robertshaw, J.Olsen, L. Sellers, H. Leary, Y. Kuo, and L. Ye, "Designing For Problem Based Learning: A Comparative Study Of Technology Professional Development," presented at the Annual Meeting of the American Education Research Association, New Orleans, LA, Apr, 2011.

Min Yuan is currently pursuing her Ph.D from Utah State University, Logan, UT. Min got her bachelor's and master's degree from Nanjing Normal University, China. After that, she worked for four years at Yingtian College in China, and then started her Ph.D study at Utah State in 2011. Her research interests include teachers' evaluation of online resources, and online communities. She has several research papers in reputed international journal and conference.

Mimi Recker is Professor and Head of the Department of Instructional Technology & Learning Sciences, Utah State University, Logan, Utah. Mimi has a bachelor's degree in mathematics from the University of Pennsylvania. After a few years as a software engineer in Silicon Valley, she earned her PhD from the University of California, Berkeley. Mimi worked for two years at the Georgia Institute of Technology, and four years at Victoria University in New Zealand, then came to Utah State in 1998. Her research focuses on helping the education sector reap the benefits of cyber-learning. Her goals are to help provide teachers and learners with access to a network of high-quality, interactive and free online learning resources. Her research, largely funded by the National Science Foundation, has involved collaborations with a dynamic mix of faculty, post-doctoral students, and graduate students from Utah State University, as well as colleagues from around the world.

## 14

Model Innovation of Process Based on the Standard e-commerce International GS1

[1]Giovanny Mauricio Tarazona Bermúdez, [1]Luz Andrea Rodríguez Rojas, [2]Cristina B Pelayo,
[2]Oscar Sanjuan Martínez

[1]*Faculty of Engineering,* District University Francisco José de Caldas, Bogotá, Colombia
[2]*Computer Science Department,* University of Oviedo, Oviedo, Spain

Abstract — **This article focuses on the design and characterization of management model for MSMEs, based on e-commerce and the GS1 international e-com standard. The first part contextualizes electronic commerce and its impact on domestic industry, and briefly describes the B2B e-commerce model used in Colombia. Subsequently the first step to apply the model is presented, which corresponds to the design of a diagnostic methodology that evaluates the technological, technical, commercial and administrative aspects of the organization; after that are exposed the results of the pilot experiment performed on a MSME from Bogota, and finally will be explained the procedures for the implementation of the model.**

Keyword s— **e-commerce, Technology Management, ICT, Knowledge Management, MSMEs.**

I. INTRODUCTION

Today innovation in processes supported by technological advances are a decisive factor in the success of business organizations. [1]It is evident that the use of technology for production operations, administrative or any kind has become a tool rather than necessary, indispensable for achieving the mission of a company purposes. [2] [3]

Rapid technological progress in recent years have not only impacted the industry and production automation, but also in logistics and marketing of products, has opened the field to information technology developments in both software and hardware, [4] coupled with advances in information technology and communications are the backbone of business processes on the web, particularly electronic commerce, which has emerged as an essential tool for successful companies in a global market. [5]

The ability to sell their products to thousands or perhaps millions of people is the obsession of a business as a basic condition for sustainability, and in turn what might seem virtually unattainable for most Colombian MSMEs, given the conditions of a Latin American country with a huge digital divide and developing economy. This is why the implementation of electronic commerce as a factor for innovation in management processes in these companies is postulated as one of the alternatives that can bring major benefits to this productive sector. [6]

It is important to characterize the categories of electronic commerce (Fig. 1. Methods of Electronic Business) and to contextualize the model designed and proposed in this article, within Colombia:

Company-Company

Here are the companies that use a network as a means to make the purchase orders and receive invoices from their suppliers, and with it all other electronic documents for the purchase order cycle to be completed.

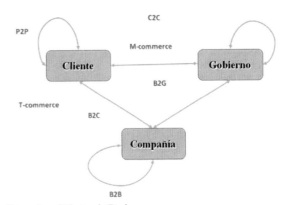

Fig. 1. Categories of Electronic Business

Company-customer

Through the network, the company offers its products to customers who accessed the quantity you need, do hereby numerous products currently marketed.

Company-Administration

Here are the transactions carried out between different companies and government organizations, such as paying taxes, even though this is true in its infancy.

Customer-Administration

Here the user would communicate with state agencies to make their tax payments or social assistance, although this is not instituted yet, it's about time it is.

Customer-Customer

It was one of the first e-business practices appeared in the early 90's web pages are little known and specialized. Your maximum evolution came with the popularization of e-bay that gives the possibility of direct sales between its users. [7]

T-commerce: The idea is to let users buy products over the Internet but through their interactive television, instead of over a phone (m-commerce) or through a PC or PDA.

B2B (business-to-business): On the Internet, also known as e-biz, is the exchange of products, services, or information between businesses rather than between businesses and consumers.

Peer to Peer. In a P2P network, the "peers" are computer systems which are connected to each other via the Internet. Files can be shared directly between systems on the network without the need of a central server. In other words, each computer on a P2P network becomes a file server as well as a client.

From this conceptual base, the project proposes applying information technologies, combined with academic concepts and skills in marketing and logistics in order to design and characterize innovative marketing processes for MSMEs producing and distribution of sweets, snacks and canned Bogotá based on the standard e-commerce GS1 International, as a means to leverage the leading commercial chain stores in the country.

II. PROCEDURE FOR PAPER SUBMISSION CHARACTERIZATION OF E-COMMERCE NATIONAL MODEL "B2B"

International GS1 is an organization of 105 institutions in over 150 countries, serving various industrial and economic sectors, by managing logistics standards to promote the efficiency of Value Networks. At home, GS1 Colombia manages the international standards of bar code (barcode), electronic commerce (e-com), synchronization of databases (GDSN) and the Electronic Product Code (EPCglobal).

Given this, it is essential that any model that seeks to facilitate the access of MSMEs to these markets is based on these standards. [8] The following will highlight the main features of the B2B model used in Colombia, approach having as standard documents that are used and their implementation within the business cycle, logistical and financial e-commerce. in the figure. 2. Logistics Cycle entitled B2B e-commerce in Colombia, sample characteristics.

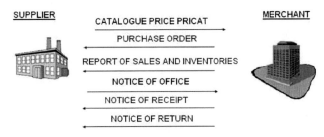

Fig. 2. Logistics Cycle B2B e-Commerce in Colombia.

The first step is to generate a *catalog business* called *PRICAT,* arising from the negotiations made between the supplier and dealer in a traditional way. In this negotiation the products are down to sell outlets where available and their sales prices are set.

PRICAT The electronic document should be based on the EDI standard, and should be sent to CABASnet it is the electronic product catalog that Colombia, Costa Rica, El Salvador, Guatemala, Honduras, Nicaragua, Paraguay and Peru, have been developed for the benefit of centralization and synchronization information to clients and suppliers use daily.[9]

Customers, suppliers, distributors and chains currently benefit from having a tool at their disposal to facilitate commercial transactions between business partners, both locally and internationally.

CABASnet who will review the structure of the catalog and sent to the e-commerce customers (chain stores, supermarkets, hypermarkets, etc.) through the interface CEN (Center for electronic business) which is operated by IBC, a group company Assenda S. Carvajal A. In Figure 3 PRICAT document processing, exemplified the expected workflow

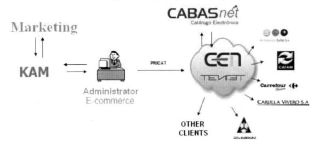

Fig. 3. Document Processing PRICAT

When a product has been coded in-store customer through the application of a PRICAT proceed from the client to generate and transmit a purchase order, the order will obey the expected demand for the product by the end customer in point of sale. The purchase order must be sent fully in the international standard GS1 EDI. [10]

After receiving the purchase order, the supplier shall dispatch in lead time, you cannot advance or delay in delivery of the order. One day before delivery at the point of sale, the producer must send a *notice of release,* electronic document which specifies the types of packaging of goods, total units shipped, the final destination of the goods, among others. Following the dispatch to print a bar code which records the information of the standard. [11]

The *notice of receipt* is an electronic document with the supermarket chains which suppliers indicate the total number of articles (products) that were received from a specific purchase order. This document is the basis for producing and sending invoices electronically from suppliers.

A key part of e-commerce model as the centerpiece of the proposal of innovative processes with large supermarket chains in the country is easy for suppliers to verify the behavior of the demand for their products. This facility provides two tools: a) purchase orders transmitted daily or as often as deemed necessary provider, or b) the sales and inventory information sent weekly supermarket chains through weekly or monthly *sales and inventory report.*

The agents involved in this innovative process serve three (3) main roles: *Manager E-Commerce* acts as the support using tools and techniques to electronic information exchange, manage and control electronic order management and physical, among others. *The commercial agent* is responsible for assembling and transmitting orders at the point of sale, track the behavior of demand and inventories, and maintain close business relationship with customers at point of sale. Finally, the *Key Account Manager* (KAM) is the one in charge of trade negotiations (products, pricing, promotions) with customers, maintain control and review of sales and inventory reports, update and ensure the availability of official price lists and catalogs to customers.

III. DIAGNOSTIC METHODOLOGY

The method of diagnosis is the initial stage of model implementation. This will determine if the company you want to apply is ready and capable to do so. The test uses the following technique is performed in the following stages: 1) Assessment of technological component and 2) Evaluation of organizational factors (technical, administrative and commercial). Assessment of the technological component is based on the model proposed by the Research Group on electronic commerce in Colombia (GICOECOL) as a diagnostic tool that will analyze the technological critical variables inherent in any company wishing to implement a model of electronic commerce

The diagnosis methodology corresponds to a classification matrix (see Figure 4), whereby a company is classified into one of four possible categories, depending on the readiness index that is the same to implement e-business models and progress in implementing these within the organization. [12]

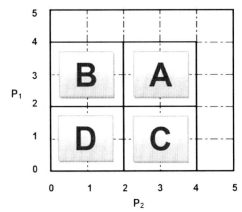

Fig. 4 Matrix diagnostic

Where P_1 represents the *readiness* of the company for the implementation of ICT and / or electronic commerce y P_2 is *the value of progress in implementation* of ICT and / or electronic commerce.

In the original methodology, the first stage evaluates the situation of the company in comparison with the economic sector in which it competes. However, for purposes of this project, modifications were made to the measurements of each of the variables, it is not necessary to compare the enterprise sector in which it competes.

In this vein, the stages for the application of the matrix, adapted to this project are:

1) Internal evaluation of the organization (Y axis).
2) Measurement of levels of implementation of e-commerce models (X axis).

Internal evaluation of the organization aims to quantify the diagnosis of the company regarding its progress in ICTs and electronic commerce. This stage is divided into four (4) steps to get a proper diagnosis quantified: Evaluation of technological resources, Web Portal Assessment, Evaluation, Human Resources and eventually final internal evaluation of the organization.

For evaluation purposes the value zero (0) is the zero impact rating, the value one (1) corresponds to the rating of low impact, impact value two (2) corresponds to the average score, and the maximum value four (4) corresponds to the highest rating. This criterion applies to all assessments.

Evaluation of technological resources (E_{RT}) is done based on the results of a questionnaire that seeks to quantify the computational resources such as computers, internet access, existence of a systems department, purchase of specific software, existence of databases, among other resources. This evaluation will yield a coefficient with value between zero (0) and four (4).

Web Portal Assessment *(EPW)* is based on a second questionnaire in which the variables of the company's Web site, such as relevant content, ease of navigation, interactivity and graphic design among others, are qualified with the degree of compliance low, medium or high. Similarly, this ratio is obtained by correcting the value on a scale from zero (0) and four (4).

For the evaluation of Human Resources *(ERH)*, there is the classification of staff competencies in three (3) categories: 1. Those who have basic computer operations; 2. Those who manage their job-specific software, and 3. Those who are competent to Web 2.0 software development capability, as well as the capabilities of category 1 and 2. From this, apply a new questionnaire to each employee of the organization to be assigned to one of these categories. For each category determines the number of employees needed to implement the model, depending on the product portfolio of the company and the number of stores in which you want to sell them. With these two facts, you get a coefficient for each category by dividing the number of employees available among the number of employees needed. Finally, average the three (3) coefficients and the average is multiplied by four (4) for the coefficient of human resources *(ERH)* with a value between zero (0) and four (4).

The final internal evaluation of the organization is calculated by averaging the evaluations of technological resources, Web portal and Human resources, so you will get the grade of zero (0) to four (4) to be called P1. See Equation (1)

$$P_1 = \frac{E_{RT} + E_{PW} + E_{RH}}{3} \qquad (1)$$

Moreover, the second stage to assess the technology component, corresponds to the evaluation of levels of implementation of e-commerce, ie, progress in the use of electronic commerce for business interaction with the different

TABLE I
CUSTOMER REQUIREMENTS OF B2B E-COMMERCE MODEL IN COLOMBIA.

Type of Activity	No	Description of requirement
Commercial	1	Presentation of the units compatible product as the chain of markets, this in order to facilitate the marketing of products focused on the end customer (consumer).
	2	Comply with legal requirements concerning net contents and labeling, it should indicate at least the following information: product name, ingredients, net contents and drained mass according to the international system of units, manufacturer's name and address, lot identification, marking date and instructions for storage, instructions for use, sanitary registration number and expiration date.
Technique	3	Evidence of a solid structure that allows production to meet minimum levels of delivery. The company must have a sufficient production capacity available to ensure an adequate level of service.
	4	Comply with the sanitary conditions laid down in legislation, including health registration for each product, which shall be in force throughout the supply relationship.
	5	Geographic coverage and capacity of local minimum to ensure continuous supply. The company must ensure compliance with the logistic distribution function, therefore must have good carrying capacity sufficient or a logistics operator offering processes of "recorded delivery".
Administrative	6	Updated financial statements. The company must demonstrate a financial capacity that allows you to fully comply with the supply contract.
	7	Legal constitution of company or corporate guiding principles and defined. The act of the company should be governed by a well-defined strategic planning.
	8	Trained and sufficient to fulfill the duties of each role involved in the model.
	9	Management of return policies and restocking of the merchandise required to cause the fulfillment of its due date or damages and damages suffered by it
	10	Clearly defined billing processes comply with all applicable laws.

agents in their environment: Government, other companies, financial sector, customers, employees and suppliers.

This measurement of a new questionnaire, which the company will get a score of thirteen (13) and sixty-five (65) points. The higher the score, the progress in implementation of e-commerce is business. As is known, the evaluation of the company in the matrix of diagnosis is based on a score of one (1) to four (4), therefore it is necessary to correct this score to finally locate the assessment index P2 the matrix.

The second part of the diagnostic assess organizational factors. Of particular interest for our analysis the technical, commercial and administrative, which are directly associated with marketing and logistics components of any company, which together with the technological component, diagnosed earlier, are central to the model. These requirements are described in Table I: Customer requirements of B2B e-commerce model in Colombia

To diagnose the organizational variables, will be based on the requirements that customers have the model in Colombia, ie, chain stores and supermarkets.

For each type of requirement applies a questionnaire, so as to assess compliance with each requirement, and you get a score between zero (0) and ten (10) for each type of activity (commercial, technical and administrative).

After obtaining the coefficients of technical activities (CAT), business (CC) and administrative activities (CAD), are weighted together with the technological coefficients P_1 y P_2, to obtain a total score consolidated company, which is between zero (0) and two hundred forty (240). Table II describes the diagnostic consolidated matrix

TABLE II
CONSOLIDATED MATRIX DIAGNOSIS

Coefficient	P_1	P_2	Total
Commercial Activities (CC)	$CC*P_1$	$CC*P_2$	Σ
Administrative activities (CAD)	$CAD*P_1$	$CAD*P_2$	Σ
Technical activity (CAT)	$CAT*P_1$	$CAT*P_2$	Σ
	Total		

In the column "Total", is located the summations of the results of the multiplications, as shown in the table, to finally get the total score will be critical for the implementation of the model, it will be the basis for categorizing the companies in three (3) categories.

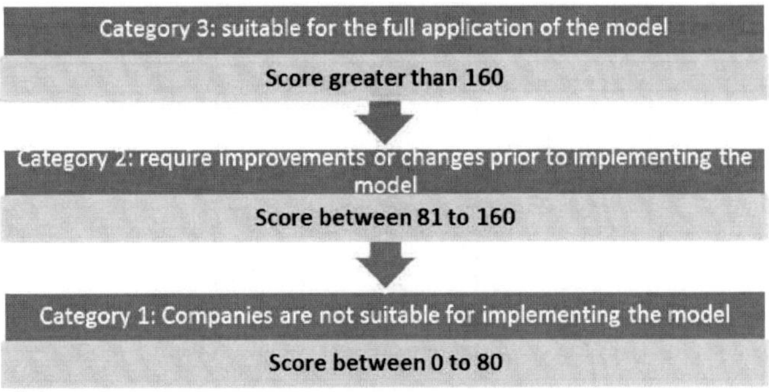

Fig. 5. Final classification of the companies evaluated

IV. PILOT TEST

A pilot test was conducted in Bogota MSMEs. The results of the evaluation of each of the coefficients technological, administrative, technical and commercial summarized below, are present en table III next.

TABLE III
RESULTS OF EVALUATION OF TECHNOLOGY COMPONENTS

Technology Assessment Results Internal Rate (P_1)	
Evaluation of technological resources (E_{RT})	0,75
Web Portal Assessment (E_{PW})	0,00
evaluation of Human Resources (E_{RH})	0,00
Average value P_1	0,25

Results Coefficient Implementation of Electronic Commerce (P₂)	
Score Electronic Commerce (PCE)	13
Final value P_2	0

TABLE IV
RESULTS OF EVALUATION OF BUSINESS

Summary of results evaluation ratio of commercial activities (CC)			
Product	Requirement 1	Requirement 5	CCi
Bocadillo veleño	10	5	7,5
Lonja de bocadillo	10	6,25	8,125
Herpo	10	8,75	9,375
Dulce de breva	0	8,75	4,375
Arequipe industrial	0	5	2,5
Glasse industrial	0	5	2,5
Bocadillo industrial	0	5	2,5
CC			5,26

In the tables (IV, V,VI and VII) are present the information obtained of pilot test

TABLE V
RESULTS OF EVALUATION OF TECHNICAL ACTIVITIES

Summary of results of technical activities evaluation ratio (CAT)	
Geographic Coverage Ratio (CCG)	0
Coefficient of Health Registry (CRS)	0
Unused capacity (CNU)	9,57
Coefficient of technical activities (CAT)	3,19

TABLE VI
EVALUATION RESULTS OF ADMINISTRATIVE

Summary of results of administrative evaluation rate (CAD)	
Requirement 2: Financial Statements	0
Requirement 7: Legal constitution of company and corporate principles	6,66666667
Requirement 8: Trained personnel and sufficient	0
Requirement 9: Handling return policies	10
Requirement 10: Billing processes defined	0
Average value Coefficient Administrative Activities (CAD)	3,3

TABLE VII
SUMMARY FINAL DIAGNOSIS

Coefficient	P_1=0,25	P_2= 0	Total
Commercial Activities (CC)	CC*P_1= 1,3169	0	1,3169
Administrative activities	CAD* P_1= 0,8333	0	0,8333
(CAD) Technical activity (CAT)	CAT*P_1= 0,7976	0	0,7976
Total			2.9472

The total weighted score for the firm diagnosis was two point ninety-four (2.94) which places him in category one (1), meaning that the company is not discussed in adequate conditions to implement the model e-commerce now.

The critical factor in obtaining this result are the poor of ICTs in that the company has, so it is recommended that initial investments in this field, also for the poor level of ownership of e-business models in the company is recommended training for employees in the use of computational tools and generate added value to the administrative processes of the company.

V. DESIGN AND IMPLEMENTATION OF THE MODEL CHARACTERIZATION

The model of innovative processes that make use of electronic commerce as tools discussed in this document requires that companies wishing to implement meet the following conditions: Register in organization dedicated to the control and monitoring the quality and safety of food and pharmaceutical products in Colombia (INVIMA) all products to market, obtaining the standard Bar Codes for the products to market, acquisition and certification of EDI mailbox E-com GS1, recruitment or training of skilled personnel for e-commerce platform, CEN Affiliation software transactional EDI transmission and acquisition of specific software to create barcode EAN 14.

Once you have met the requirements for marketing, you can implement the model. The process begins with the creation and transmission of the document PRICAT, and culminates with the delivery and return notices. The fig., 6 describes the activities proposed

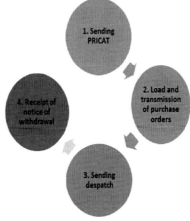

Fig. 6. Marketing process through E-com standard documents of GS1

The procedure for creating and sending the PRICAT consists of the following stages:
1) Implementation of selected software.
2) Sending a letter and attached documents.
3) Dealing with the chain (customer).
4) Development and Shipping PRICAT

Sending PRICAT´s will be necessary for the addition of new references (products), changes in existing prices or the withdrawal thereof. This will be done by the senior management of the organization and the administrator of the e-commerce platform.

After this, proceed with the preparation and transmission load of orders, the following procedure:

1) Load and transmission of purchase order.

2) Download and validation of the data associated with purchase orders.

The agents involved in this stage are the agent and manager of e-commerce platform.

The next step is to prepare and dispatch advices. For the preparation of this document should make reference to the orders received and the total quantities per order to ship. The procedure starts with the implementation of specific software for generating warnings office with a bar code to thereby generate the document itself. The software implementation is performed by the senior management and the completion and submission of dispatch by the administrator of e-commerce platform.

Finally, the procedure for receiving notice of withdrawal is as follows:

1) Receipt of notice.

2) Analysis and monitoring it.

For the preparation of this document should make reference to the orders received and the total quantities per order to ship. The agent involved in the management of refund notices are the administrator of the e-commerce platform and Key Account Manager (KAM).

VI. CONCLUSION

The government plans for the technological inclusion of micro, small and medium businesses included both in the National Development Plan, as in the plan MSMEs digital 2009, opening the possibility of obtaining the necessary funding for implementation of ICTs that support e-business models, facilitating the acquisition of software and hardware to improve the processes involved in managing the supply chain, resulting in more competitive and efficient companies.

Likewise, certification to international GS1 standards enable companies to restructure their logistics processes, thus becoming a tool to increase their ability to seek new markets and channels for marketing their products.[1*]

Critical to implementing innovative processes supported by e-business models is the appropriation of ICTs by the company and human resource training in the use of these tools, which can be checked in detail by the results obtained in the pilot test, where low scores in these areas not determined the feasibility of implementing the proposed model in the selected company.

For this reason, it is important to note that the implementation of innovative processes supported by the proposed e-commerce model, it is necessary for companies to appropriate knowledge management models that allow the previous experience in the use of technological resources and tools that facilitate the appropriation of concepts and procedures outlined in this document.

REFERENCES

[1] K. Laudon and L. Jane, Sistemas de Información Gerencial, Pearson Prentice Hall, 2004.

[2] M. Dell, Collaboration equals innovation InformationWeek, Manhasset, 2003, Jan 27.

[2] G. Tarazona and V. Medina, "Generación de Valor en la Gestión de Conocimiento," in Seventh Laccei Latin American and Caribbean Conference for Engineering and Technology, San Cristobal, Venezuela, 2009.

[4] D. Teece, "Business Models, Business Strategy and Innovation," Long Range Planning, pp. 172 - 194, 2010.

[5] T. Koupluspoulos and C. Frappaolo, Lo Fundamental y lo más efectivo de la Gerencia del Conocimiento, McGraw Hill Iteramericana S.A, 200.

[6] J.-M. Nurmilaakso, "EDI, XML and e-business frameworks: A survey," COMPUTERS IN INDUSTRY, pp. 370 - 379, 2008.

[7] F. Hayes, "The story so far: e-commerce," COMPUTERWORDL, 2002.

[8] T. Benson, PRINCIPLES OF HEALTH INTEROPERABILITY HL7 AND SNOMED Health Information Technology Standards, London: Springer, 2010.

[9] ediversa, "GUIA DE IMPLANTACIÓN PRICAT D.96A VERSION 2," EDIVERSA, Barcelona, 2006.

[10] HYPERLINK "http://web.invima.gov.co/" http://web.invima.gov.co Consultado el 26 de septiembre de 2012

[11] HYPERLINK "http://www.cabasnet.org/" http://www.cabasnet.org/ Consultado el 15 de agosto 2012

[12] D. Barrera, G. Diana and G. Tarazona, Propuesta Metodologica De Evaluación Previa A La Implementación De Modelos De Comercio Electronico, Bogota: Universidad Distrital Francisco Jose De Caldas, 2008.

Tarazona, Giovanny. Doctoral candidate in systems and computer services for internet in the Oviedo University, Asturias, Spain (2012) - diploma of advanced studies November 2007 Pontifical Salamanca University in campus Madrid Spain, Specialization in computer project (2006), Specialization in engineering software (1999). He is Industrial engineer, Francisco José de Caldas District University, Bogota, DC, (1998). He is Full Time Professor Francisco José de Caldas District University- Faculty of Engineering since July 2003. He is founding member of KAIZEN PBT GROUP Ltda, legal representative, director of several projects, Bogotá, DC, 1996 - December 2011. Director Research Group on Electronic Commerce Colombian GICOECOL Francisco José de Caldas District University, Director of several research projects.

Rodriguez, Luz Andrea: Master Engineering and website design (2012), Specialization in hygiene and occupational health (2010), Industrial Engineer, Francisco José de Caldas District University, Bogota, DC, (2008). She is Full Time Professor Foundation Liberators University (August 2011- May 2012) Area Production. She is full professor in occupational health at INPAHU (August 2010-May 2011). Director project Research "Strategies for Strengthening of Information System Tourism Health in Bogota".

Pelayo G-Bustelo, B. Cristina is a Lecturer in the Computer Science Department of the University of Oviedo. She is Ph.D. from the University of Oviedo in Computer Engineering. Her research interests include Object-Oriented Technology, Web Engineering, eGovernment, Modeling Software with BPM, DSL and MDA.

Sanjuán Martínez, Oscar is a Lecturer in the Computer Science Department of the University of Oviedo. He is Ph.D. from the Pontifical University of Salamanca in Computer Engineering. His research interests include Object-Oriented technology, Web Engineering, Software Agents, Modeling Software with BPM, DSL and MDA.

## 15

L.I.M.E. A recommendation model for informal and formal learning, engaged

Daniel Burgos

UNIR Research, International University of La Rioja. Spain

Abstract — **In current eLearning models and implementations (e.g. Learning Management Systems-LMS) there is a lack of engagement between formal and informal activities. Furthermore, the online methodology focuses on a standard set of units of learning and learning objects, along with pre-defined tests, and collateral resources like, i.e. discussion *fora* and message wall. They miss the huge potential of learning via the interlacement of social networks, LMS and external sources. Thanks to user behaviour, user interaction, and personalised counselling by a tutor, learning performance can be improved. We design and develop an adaptation eLearning model for restricted social networks, which supports this approach. In addition, we build an eLearning module that implements this conceptual model in a real application case, and present the preliminary analysis and positive results.**

Keywords — **Technology-enhanced Learning, eLearning, Personalization, Social Network, Conceptual Educational Model**

I. INTRODUCTION

Social networks focused on a specific topic or community are a powerful and precise means for user communication and interconnectivity, no matter the role they stand for. These can be learners, teachers, employees, staff, academic managers, or financial directors, who show a very determined attitude, depending on their context and their objectives. Every user can question, answer, start an activity, follow another, comment on someone else's job, score a job made by others, search onto Internet, follow a scheduled test, participate in a video-conference with a teacher, and so on. And, in all these activities, any user can be pro-active, reactive, passive, consumer, producer, dealer, and yet to show some additional facets.

To this extent, we design and develop a conceptual model, L.I.M.E. as for Learning, Interaction, Mentoring, Evaluation. These four vectors are measured and analysed as the pillars for the learning scenario, and they are depicted in various inputs which feed the model. Furthermore, we implement this model in a learning ecosystem, restricted by user access and topic. This implementation of the personalised learning model, which deals with every single input and feature aforementioned, provides the user with adaptive tutoring, thanks to a rule system. In this ecosystem, the users interact one with each other, and with the system, and they get personalised counselling.

Before and after the design and implementation of the L.I.M.E. model as a case study, we have carried out a hybrid approach mainly with qualitative studies, supported by some additional quantitative studies, with various groups of experts and end-users. Hence, we have designed and executed a Delphi study to retrieve and categorize the user requirements, as well as a number of semi-structured interviews. Furthermore, we have organized two focus groups with different experts, and one quantitative questionnaire with the students involved in the application case. In addition, we have elaborated a comprehensive state-of-the-art which combines cross-engaged topics for eLearning processes like, i.e. Education, Communication and Technology.

It is proven that the learning itinerary provided by the L.I.M.E. model is efficient and effective, and therefore, it increases the user performance. To show this approach, we have designed and implemented a learning scenario in a real class, which we have split in two groups (experimental and control) of 24 students, each. We have selected and analysed a subject of an official university online programme, during 4 weeks. This scenario engaged formal and informal activities with a comprehensive approach. The implementation shows successful results which prove the validity of the model. In addition, we have got useful recommendations and promising conclusions for further versions of the model, out of the rounds of expert and end-user consultations.

The combination of 48 learners, along 4 weeks and related milestones, the measurement of 30 inputs focused on informal and formal settings and distributed along the four main vectors, has resulted in a large dataset with sufficient information to retrieve meaningful and significant interpretation. The main outcome highlights that there is a clear and positive influence in the user performance, when the L.I.M.E. model is implemented. Furthermore, L.I.M.E. shows to be effective and efficient. This conclusion is supported by a 10,53% overall average difference between the experimental group and the control group (66,72% - 56,19%), with a peak difference between corners of 37,37% (81,41% - 44,04%). These overall results, along with the partial ones which are presented along this research, support seamlessly the online personalised learning model for thematic, restricted social networks, L.I.M.E.

II. CURRENT DEVELOPMENTS AND ADDED VALUE

In most of the e-learning environment designs, interaction and behavioral strategies have generally been neglected and therefore satisfactory uses of these strategies have rarely been realized, so that informal and formal settings are not engaged in a combined approach. Most learners are not even aware of what they have been studying (Kurt, 2007). Even when students monitor their learning, there is a broad theoretical notion that students experience illusions of competence [1], which leads to inaccurate judgment of their learning progresses and outcomes [2, 3]. For these reasons, learners need to be guided towards reflecting on their learning and improving their cognitive models of expertise. For instance, with the use of meta-cognitive expertise, which becomes crucial [4] in fostering individual's awareness of different cognitive, social, emotional, and meta-cognitive capabilities that are needed, knowledge of when and why they are useful, as well as development of regulatory skills, such as planning, monitoring, and reflecting.

Another approach makes use of recommendation settings. A recommender system is a tool that helps users to identify interesting items from a large pool of objects. It has been widely used in many commercial sites for recommending books, movies, CDs, and news articles (e.g., [5, 6]). Meanwhile, the success of these implementations has been inspiring for e-learning researchers. Multiple efforts have been made to design educational recommendation systems to recommend quality learning resources to learners to help reduce cognitive load and improve learning efficiency [7-10]. However, recommendations alone do not ensure learning performance, and how learners respond to the recommended resources defines the critical part of successful learning. Furthermore, Recommendation Systems emerge as a solution to find the right, personalized information in electronic commerce, knowledge management systems, learning management systems, social networks (open and restricted), and other fields and markets. To this extent, there are various inputs which can be used as information sources like i.e. user similarities with other users, user profile, user preferences, user behavior, user interaction, user ratings, and many other user tracking inputs [11, 12]. All these inputs provide the system and the teacher with valuable data to recommend a personalized learning itinerary and feedback.

Other sources of information are i.e. user interests, goals, and objectives, all of them more useful for educational applications. However, current educational applications lack of enough amounts of data to establish user similarities in a precise way. In this case, recommendations are based on information stored in a user model which is extended explicitly or implicitly. There are also hybrid approaches which ask some minimum information to the user and the rest is obtained in an implicit way, but none of them engage formal and informal learning in a combined model, since expressing user preferences, behavior, interaction, goals and interest with rules can be difficult, in general. Large amounts of data are required to narrow down the recommendation, although this solution comes along with an additional problem: the size and complexity of the rule-set can be unaffordable, and inconsistencies may appear.

In this paper, we design an eLearning model for personalized learning, with special focus on the combination of formal and informal settings in a combined paradigm. In doing so, we cope with the artificial difference between Learning Management Systems and specific, restricted social networks which complement the user formal activity with informal interaction.

III. DESCRIPTION OF THE LIME MODEL

The L.I.M.E. model is based on three vectors:
- What every learner does based on his/her own contribution (**L=Learning**)
- What the learner does to support interaction based and the relation with others, in addition to group interaction (**I=Interaction**)
- and what the teachers/experts value (**M=Mentoring**)
- In addition, there is a forth, transversal vector, being applied to the three previous vectors, focused on evaluation (**E=Evaluation**)
- being the final acronym **L.I.M.E., as of Learning, Interaction, Mentoring, and Evaluation**

In doing so, we take into consideration every single main role in the model (i.e. the learner -individual, group-, the teacher, the expert, and the designer), as well as the main factors for a fine adaptation, such as, i.e. the learner's performance, the group's performance, trust, and reputation. In addition, this model is based on the **knowledge structure** depicted in the beginning of this section that consists of LE (Learning Environment), LO (Learning Object), UK (Unit of Knowledge), and PLN (Personal Learning Network).

In order to define the best setting, the model designer (e.g. teacher) must design a **strategy** and (s)he should follow a step-to-step process to select a number of key elements of the model:
- **Setting**: Balance between formal and informal **settings**: the system collects specific inputs from both settings, keeping an overall balance of 100%. For instance, if the designer requires just a formal setting, the balance should be Informal:100% - Formal: 0%
- **Category**: Balance between Learning, Interaction, and Mentoring **categories**: In the L.I.M.E. model, every category is assigned with a specific weight, keeping an overall balance of 100% Watch that Evaluation is a cross-category. For instance, if individual and group actions matter alike, and there is no mentoring, the balance should be Learning: 50% - Interaction: 50% - Mentoring: 0%
- **Input**: List of specific inputs for each **category** and assigned **weight**: every input should reflect a number of diverse types of potential interaction and-or actions from the user to the community, and vice versa.

As an example, we provide a form with the following parameters:
- **Informal**: 40%. Rationale: informal activities matter, however they are not enough to pass

- **Formal**: 60%. Rationale: formal activities (e.g. exam) are key to pass, however, informal activities are required to achieve an optimum score
- **Learning**: 40%. Rationale: individual activities are key in this setting, however they are not enough to pass
- **Interaction**: 30%. Rationale: interaction itself is not enough to pass, although combined with Mentoring and-or Learning, become the key for success
- **Mentoring**: 30%. Rationale: just mentoring is not sufficient, however mentoring inputs provide they key to pass, along with learning or interaction inputs

Specific **inputs**: as listed, looking for a fine distribution between individual and groups actions; pro-active and re-active actions; personal-group-mentoring inputs; formal and informal contribution. This list is not exhaustive, but tentative, and provides a set of inputs based on the analysis of user requirements. These inputs have an assigned **weight**. These weights are shown as an example, and they should be designed and adapted by the designer based on specific requirements and objectives. For clarity's shake, in the following tables, we depict the weight in three columns, showing the **Absolute value (Abs)**, the **Relative value (Rel 100)**, taken as 100% for every Category, and the final **Relative value (Rel 40)**, related to the specific value of the Setting, Category, and Input, taken as 100% for the three Categories (L.I.M.E.). This last column shows the actual values for the final calculation. The Evaluation (E) vector is included in every other vector, and relies on their needs. For instance, in the following table, Evaluation is included in L=Learning (External examination, External continuous evaluation, External essay, External degree thesis), and M=Mentoring (Quantitative assessment, Qualitative assessment). However, these inputs (sub-vectors) might be different, based on the specific model applied to a scenario

IV. DEVELOPMENT OF THE ELEARNING PLATFORM

In order to test and evaluate the L.I.M.E. model, we have developed a software application (i-LIME) to be implemented in a learning scenario, as it will be described afterwards. This application is supported by the Learning Management System of the International University or La Rioja
 and it does not intend to be exploitable, but a prototype, since the final objective of this research is not oriented to programming but to the correct application of the model itself.

i-LIME is a learning environment (LE), built to apply the LIME model, based on Learning, Interaction, Mentoring, and Evaluation. It can be played stand-alone or integrated with another existing LE (e.g. Moodle), via web services. This platform is envisaged as a new cognitive learning concept to create, share and reuse scalable didactic content (Learning Objects, Units of Knowledge), to adapt the content to learners' individual needs, and to share with others (Personal Learning Network), according to the LIME model. In this context, the user becomes consumer and producer at the same time, the minimum unit of learning is based on a variety of resources. User education is also boosted, allowing a) more active

participation in the learning process, b) objective teaching skills assessment, and c) encouraging collaboration with other teachers and tutors and trainees with different expertise.

i-LIME combines the use of didactic contents, and knowledge and learning resources, for online teaching (OT). We develop i-LIME as a technology-enhanced learning (TEL) platform which applies the LIME model, and which will facilitate a more interactive, personalized learning process. i-LIME enhances the user's experience (e.g. teachers and tutors) using a five-pillared architecture [13]: (1) an authoring tool of Learning Objects and Units of Knowledge ; (2) a content management system that incorporates a modular and scalable system to capture, catalogue, search and retrieve multimedia content; (3) an adaptation management system which retrieves information and inputs from the users and the system and provides specific, personalized recommendations for the learning itinerary, based on the LIME model; (4) an evaluation module, which in turn is used as an additional input to the LIME model and the recommender layer [14]; and (5) a social thematic network (restricted to registered users in the same field) for collaborative learning between users, which provides input date on behaviour and interaction to the LIME model and the recommender layer. To this extent, we have installed an instance of i-LIME, fully operational with regards to user inputs, data collection and analysis, and adaptation management system (3, following the afore notation), along with generic functions for end-users.

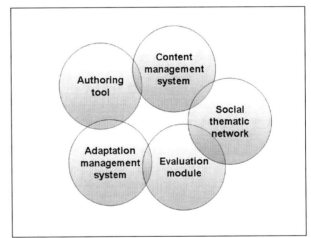

Fig. 1. i-LIME architecture

The first pillar, the **authoring tool for learning objects and units of knowledge (ATH)**, allows the building of scalable didactic content from individual users' knowledge by means of training resources (e.g. video footage) to enhance didactic information. The **content management system (CMS)** works with units of information, in the form of text, video, and audio files, or any other format required to provide useful learning objects.

Users' knowledge management is achieved within the second pillar. The **adaptation management system (AMS)** provides adaptive learning to users based on their progress (formal learning), behavior (informal learning), and other inputs, within their continuous formative path using the environment. Recommendations are given to users regarding

(1) the most suitable contents, (2) colleagues working in the same field, (3) interactions to perform, and (4) given their personal interests and progress in i-LIME, amongst other inputs. To this extent, the adaptation management system makes use of the **Recommendation Layer (Meta-Mender)**, which uses meta-rules in order to provide a new abstraction level suitable for increasing personalization and adaptation.

An important matter when developing a new training process is to develop new objective evaluation systems based on reliable and measurable data, which allow for automatic and immediate feedback and which are always available for trainees. Thus, objective evaluation is a key issue in the i-LIME environment. Thanks to the **evaluation module (EVAL)**, trainees are able to test their knowledge via closed exercises, which are immediately analyzed by the environment, and used to provide input to the **Recommendation Layer (Meta-Mender)**. Formative feedback is provided to trainees by means of corrections and future didactic content recommendations.

The final pillar in i-LIME is the **social network (SN)**, a thematic network restricted to registered members, which allows for the creation of collaborative networks of students and professionals and provides a space where users can debate and work together. In doing so, informal learning is encouraged continuously, and the social network provides feedback to the **Recommendation Layer (Meta-Mender)**, which will return a more accurate, personalized tutoring.

V. APPLICATION SCENARIO: INFORMAL AND FORMAL LEARNING, ENGAGED

The scenario consists of a Learning Environment (LE) adapted to a specific subject that compiles learning resources, tasks, and interactive activities, for future online teachers and tutors. These teachers and tutors have to get up-to-speed with techniques, processes, and strategies to foster, encourage, and facilitate actual learning and a clear methodology between the students. We integrate the i-LIME system in the Learning Environment of UNIR (UNIR LE), and hence the scenario is supported by two components: 1) the Virtual Campus at UNIR (UNIR LE), in which all the degrees lean on, and it is very much focused on daily administrative issues and scheduled events and activities (the formal component); and 2) the i-LIME component (the informal component, namely the Adaptation Management System-AMS) (Figure 2). This technical setting supports the open interaction between peers and between other target groups (i.e. learners, teachers, tutors, admin staff, et cetera). The overall system does require the following minimum software on the client side: Windows XP/7 or Mac OS X 10.x, Firefox 13.x or Explorer 8.x (both with Javascript habilitated). On the server side: the UNIR LE, Drools Engine, Microsoft Excel, PHP 5.x, Apache 2.x.

Our learning scenario (e.g. case study) was deployed from July 2nd, to July, the 29th, 2012. To this regard, we used a graduate course on "Design and management of research projects", in the Master of Science in eLearning and Social Networks, an online, official master degree at the International University of La Rioja (UNIR). This course took place between July, 2nd and July, the 26th, 2012, with 49 enrolled students. All the students but 1 took part in the experiment. Therefore, we count 48 graduate students, between 35 and 45 years old, from 2 countries (Spain -45 students-, Colombia -3 students-) and 2 continents (Europe, South America), with a gender distribution of 28 females and 20 males.

Fig. 2. Screenshot of the UNIR LE engaged with the i-LIME component

The support group consists of a teacher, an online tutor, an academic coordinator, and a master director. In addition, other cross-support departments might provide some assistant (i.e. administrative, legal, counseling, research, library, stages, et cetera). The environment is executed by every user only if the (s)he agrees with the terms described in a formal document, so that the recording of the their private date and tracking are explicitly authorized.

We have split the base group in two, equally distributed (24 members for each group). Group A (experimental) is engaged with the LIME model and receives personalized recommendation based on a number of inputs, including traditional (e.g. teacher, tutor, admin staff). Group B (control) follows the course, without the LIME model, and receives traditional support only. To make a balanced distribution of Groups A and B, on order to achieve a similar starting point, we take the previous results and evaluation. This master degree deploys the subjects in the academic program sequentially, and 9 subjects have already carried out. Therefore, there is a statistical information, quite valuable to evenly distribute members between groups (control and experimental). The final distribution is shown in Table 3 and Figure 3:

This distribution works with the individual average score after 9 subjects, out of 10-point maximum. It splits the final score of every group member in Formal (e.g. presence examination) and Informal (i.e. auto-tests, participation in online lectures, et cetera). Formal takes 60% of the final score; Formal provides 40% to the final score, based on a total of 100%. According to

TABLE 3: SAMPLE DISTRIBUTION BASED ON PREVIOUS ACADEMIC RECORDS

Group	Sample	Distribution	Formal	Informal	Total
A	24	Average Group A: Experimental	4,13	3,73	7,86
A	24	Maximum Group A	5,80	4,00	9,80
A	24	Minimum Group A	3,00	2,40	5,40
A	24	Standard Deviation Group A	0,81	0,53	1,19
B	24	Average Group B: Control	4,05	3,69	7,63
B	24	Maximum Group A	5,60	4,00	9,60
B	24	Minimum Group A	1,70	2,40	1,70
B	24	Standard Deviation Group A	0,88	0,58	1,67
Total	48	Average Total Sample	4,09	3,71	7,75
Total	48	Maximum Total Sample	5,80	4,00	9,80
Total	48	Minimum Total Sample	1,70	2,40	1,70
Total	48	Standard Deviation Total Sample	0,83	0,55	1,44

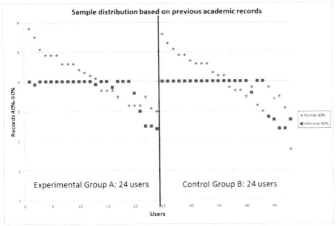

Fig. 3. Sample distribution based on previous academic records

This distribution works with the individual average score after 9 subjects, out of 10-point maximum. It splits the final score of every group member in Formal (e.g. presence examination) and Informal (i.e. auto-tests, participation in online lectures, et cetera). Formal takes 60% of the final score; Formal provides 40% to the final score, based on a total of 100%. According to the data provided in Table 3, there is a balance between Groups A and B that shows similar scores in every category, although the standard deviation is slightly different (1,19 in Group A versus 1,67 in Group B). This difference comes from a single member in Group B, who scores the minimum (1,7), while the previous one scores a total of 5,5. We can conclude that the starting point for both groups is quite similar, so that the experiment starts in the same context.

VI. LIME MODEL APPLIED TO THE LEARNING SCENARIO

With regards to the LIME model, we follow the pattern Informal50-L40-I40-M20, which the following basic rationale: "Informal and formal settings matter alike. Inputs from the user and the group make 80% of the total, being Mentoring actions taken as support and collateral ones. The Learning Environment (LE) is taken as the learning and communication platform, as well as the summative and formative resource for assessment". This model allows for an optimum adaptation to the features of the Learning Environment at UNIR, since combines formal and informal contexts, and supports self-

learning and learning from others, including mentors (i.e. teacher and tutor). In addition, this pattern encourages the use of Units of Knowledge (UK, made of Learning Objects combined with complementary information), and Personal Learning Network (PLN, made of LO and UK, along with all the interaction elicited from other users).

Based on this model, the level of integration with UNIR's Learning Environment, the learner sample, the subject, and the overall objective, we have defined a set of Inputs, which will be used as a base to write the appropriate adaptation rules that will feed the LIME model (Figure 4**Fig**):

ID	Category	Setting	Input	Weight Abs	Rel 100	Rel 40
	Learning		Input Learning Subtotal	100,00%	100,00%	40,00%
			Input Learning Informal	50,00%	50,00%	20,00%
			Input Learning Formal	50,00%	50,00%	20,00%
	L		Subtotal Learning	220,00%	100,00%	40,00%
			Subtotal Learning Informal	140,00%	50,00%	20,00%
			Subtotal Learning Formal	80,00%	50,00%	20,00%
L1	Learning	Informal	Post a message	10,00%	3,57%	1,43%
L2	Learning	Informal	Post a discussion topic	20,00%	7,14%	2,86%
L3	Learning	Informal	Meet a milestone	30,00%	10,71%	4,29%
L4	Learning	Informal	Upload a learning object	30,00%	10,71%	4,29%
L5	Learning	Informal	Enrich own learning object	40,00%	14,29%	5,71%
L6	Learning	Informal	Activity rate of recent contribution	10,00%	3,57%	1,43%
L7	Learning	Formal	EVAL: Self examination	20,00%	12,50%	5,00%
L8	Learning	Formal	EVAL: Continuous evaluation	40,00%	25,00%	10,00%
L9	Learning	Formal	EVAL: Self test	20,00%	12,50%	5,00%

ID	Category	Setting	Input	Abs	Rel 100	Rel 40
	Interaction		Input Interaction Subtotal	100,00%	100,00%	40,00%
			Input Interaction Informal	50,00%	50,00%	20,00%
			Input Interaction Formal	50,00%	50,00%	20,00%
	I		Subtotal Interaction	230,00%	100,00%	40,00%
			Subtotal Interaction Informal	205,00%	50,00%	20,00%
			Subtotal Interaction Formal	25,00%	50,00%	20,00%
I1	Interaction	Informal	Complete the profile	35,00%	8,54%	3,41%
I2	Interaction	Informal	Select topics	25,00%	6,10%	2,44%
I3	Interaction	Informal	Reply a post	20,00%	4,88%	1,95%
I4	Interaction	Informal	Rate a post	15,00%	3,66%	1,46%
I5	Interaction	Informal	Reply a discussion topic	30,00%	7,32%	2,93%
I6	Interaction	Informal	Rate a discussion topic	15,00%	3,66%	1,46%
I7	Interaction	Informal	Discussion activity	35,00%	8,54%	3,41%
I8	Interaction	Informal	Enrich other's learning object	30,00%	7,32%	2,93%
I9	Interaction	Formal	Link from-to an external subject	5,00%	10,00%	4,00%
I10	Interaction	Formal	Collaborative work rate	20,00%	40,00%	16,00%

ID	Category	Setting	Input	Abs	Rel 100	Rel 20
	Mentoring		Input Mentoring Subtotal	100,00%	100,00%	20,00%
			Input Mentoring Informal	50,00%	50,00%	10,00%
			Input Mentoring Formal	50,00%	50,00%	10,00%
	M		Subtotal Mentoring	285,00%	100,00%	20,00%
			Subtotal Mentoring Informal	105,00%	50,00%	10,00%
			Subtotal Mentoring Formal	180,00%	50,00%	10,00%
M1	Mentoring	Informal	Trust rate from a peer	25,00%	11,90%	2,38%
M2	Mentoring	Informal	Trust rate from an expert	30,00%	14,29%	2,86%
M3	Mentoring	Informal	Reputation rate from a peer	20,00%	9,52%	1,90%
M4	Mentoring	Informal	Reputation rate from an expert	30,00%	14,29%	2,86%
M5	Mentoring	Formal	EVAL: Final assessment	60,00%	16,67%	3,33%
M6	Mentoring	Formal	EVAL: Tracking assessment	60,00%	16,67%	3,33%
M7	Mentoring	Formal	Trust rate from a teacher	20,00%	5,56%	1,11%
M8	Mentoring	Formal	Reputation rate from a teacher	10,00%	2,78%	0,56%
M9	Mentoring	Formal	Interesting topic rate	10,00%	2,78%	0,56%
M10	Mentoring	Formal	Significant contribution rate	10,00%	2,78%	0,56%
M11	Mentoring	Formal	Quality of reply	10,00%	2,78%	0,56%

Strategy		Check
Cat-Setting	Weight	
Informal	50.00%	Ok
Formal	50.00%	
Learning	40.00%	Ok
Interaction	40.00%	
Mentoring	20.00%	

Fig. 4. LIME model for the application scenario. Settings, Inputs and Strategy

This set of inputs gathers most of the requirements of the LIME model, including Trust, Reputation, Assessment, Evaluation, formal activities, and informal actions. In doing so, we select a representative amount of inputs, across a variety of types, which feed (back and forth) the LIME model. We have assigned the EVAL inputs to Formal settings, since the EVAL inputs in Informal settings would have required a specific assessment model for informal learning, which is not a topic of this research, although and interesting one for the future.

The system retrieves input data and provides recommendation once a week. Since the selected subject lasts 4 weeks (from July 2nd, to July 29th), we have established four milestones in months 8, 15, 22 and 29. These milestones store the specific data for every input and user incrementally, so that we can analyze the evolution of any specific user, with and without recommendation. At the end of the period (M29), every user in Group A (experimental) has received a considerable amount of recommendations, which might or might not lead to a higher performance, and to and improvement throughout the activities and actions in the Learning Environment.

About the timeline, the recommendations are provided through the milestones M8, M15, M22 and M29. However, there is no rule defined to adapt these recommendations to the user progress. Therefore, they have to be taken in close relation to the timeline. For instance, in M8, the recommendation R9 about Evaluation (see Table 4) will be likely provided to everyone, since there is little time since the beginning to the course up to M8 to carry out the activities and actions related to the Evaluation. However, in M15, and in M22, since the course is running for a longer time, it is expected that R9 will be provided to less people, decreasingly, until the final recommendation in M29, which will show the actual performance on Evaluation of every learner. Therefore, the recommendation has to be put in context of the timeline and the user (i.e. learner, tutor, and teacher) has to achieve a contextualized, appropriate reading, in order to act accordingly. Other potential contexts might be: the user status, in relation to previous subjects; the user status, in relation to the group; the user status, in relation to other groups of the same graduation; the group status, in relation to other groups of the same graduation; the group status in relation to historic records; et cetera.

Once the experiment is finished, we analyze the overall data, in order to extract group information, behavior patterns, abnormal actions, and other relevant information which will allow for a refinement of the LIME model and, if possible, the i-LIME software development and implementation.

This stored information is processed by the recommendation rules in DROOLS (language for rules processing), which takes the raw figures, applies the LIME model, and provides a recommendation on the learning itinerary. For our research, we have implemented a rule-set, adapted to this specific learning scenario and context. This rule-set must be defined by the learning designer (e.g. teacher) and it applies the LIME model based on the collected figures, and the style that the designer wants to reach, in addition to group goals and individual

thresholds. In our case, the pseudo-code that describes the rules is as follows (Table 4):

TABLE 4: DEFINITION OF RULES

RuleID	Applied to	RulePseudoCode
R1	Input (e.g. L1 or M3)	IF any input is lower than maximum AND higher than or equal to ½ maximum THEN positive feedback about this specific input
R2	Input	IF any input is lower than ½ maximum THEN warning about this specific input
R3	Subset (Informal-Formal)	IF any subset of inputs in a category is between maximum AND ¾ of maximum THEN positive feedback about the subset
R4	Subset (Informal-Formal)	IF any subset of inputs in a category is between ½ maximum AND ¾ of maximum THEN warning about the subset to the learner and to the tutor
R5	Subset (Informal-Formal)	IF any subset of inputs in a category is lower than ½ maximum THEN warning to the learner and to the teacher, recommendation of interaction with others and the tutor and the teacher, locking of further activities in this category until the threshold (1/2 maximum) is reached
R6	Category (Learning, Interaction, Mentoring)	IF any category is between maximum AND ¾ maximum THEN positive feedback and recommendation of complementary tasks
R7	Category (Learning, Interaction, Mentoring)	IF any category is between ½ maximum AND ¾ maximum THEN warning about the category to the learner, the tutor and the teacher; request of support from other learners
R8	Category (Learning, Interaction, Mentoring)	IF any category is lower than ½ maximum THEN warning to the learner and to the teacher, recommendation of interaction with others and the tutor and the teacher, request of support from other learners, locking of further activities in this category until the threshold (1/2 maximum) is reached
R9	EVAL	IF any EVAL input is lower than ½ maximum THEN locking of activity, request of interactive session with teacher, request of resubmission of activity-action

The specific coding of every rule looks like the following one, described for R1 (Table 5):

TABLE 5: EXAMPLED-PSEUDO CODE FOR RULE R1

RuleID	Rule Coding	Recommendation provided, adapted to L1
R1	IF (L* OR I* OR M* < REL X) AND (L* OR I* OR M* >= 50%*REL X) THEN R1("Positive feedback to USER")	"Well done, when you post a message"

Technically, the raw data were stored in text files, which were translated in tables (XLS type) for easier representation, calculation, and analysis. A software application was created to analyze these files and extract the information from the XLS files. The particular scenario described here should be taken into account in order to interpret the obtained data. Each time the user executed an action foreseen in the LIME model, all the related information from that specific user was written into a log file. Every record is uniquely identified, and consists of basic ID information (i.e. date and timestamp of the event, action taken, user) and specific values provided according to the input (i.e. reputation, trust, assessment, other rates). There is an additional field with warnings, errors, and comments from the system. The information extracted from the log files was inserted into a database (XLS type) in order to organize the information and to make the information process easier. See Figure 5 for a simplified representation of the described application scenario in combination with the Adaptation Management System, which depicts the information flow from-to the end user.

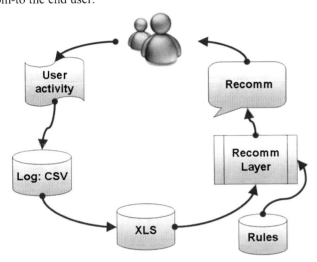

Fig. 5. Application scenario in combination with the AMS. Information flow

VII. RESULTS AND ANALYSIS OF THE APPLICATION SCENARIO

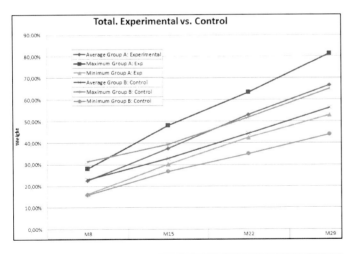

M8	M15	M22	M29
22,61%	37,47%	53,09%	66,72%
28,15%	48,07%	63,36%	81,41%
16,42%	30,12%	42,48%	52,88%
23,01%	32,83%	44,39%	56,19%
31,32%	39,28%	51,94%	65,06%
16,05%	26,88%	35,06%	44,04%

Fig. 6. Total results. Experimental group versus Control group

In Figure 6, we compare final, general results of the experimental group (A) in opposition to the control group (B). We provide data for the four milestones (M8, M15, M22, M29), and three variables per each: Maximum score,

Minimum Score, and Average Score. Therefore, we analyze a six-line web along four weeks. As expected from interviews with end users and the Delphi study, the final score is higher with the experimental group (A:66,72% vs. B:56,19%, in M29, over a 100% top). However, the crossed lines show a higher average position of the control group in M8 (A:22,61% vs. B:23,01%), before a linear increase up to M29. In addition, the maximum score in M8 is higher at the control group (A:28,15%; B:31,32%). These two higher scores at the control group at the beginning show a symptomatic progress of the impact from the recommendation system: although in the beginning A and B can be alike, or even B shows a higher rank, the systematic application of recommendations through the i-LIME environment overcomes the evolution without the LIME model

VIII. CONCLUSIONS AND FUTURE WORK

L.I.M.E. provides an optimized formula which allows for finding the balance between all the inputs related to the online learning, as in our vision. The model describes the right weight for every input, directly related to the effect to achieve along the process and every role. Based on the ground objectives, the learning scenario will define the required interaction between inputs, roles, categories and settings. The model is based on behavior, performance and the relation among the end user, himself and the peers. Furthermore, there are four main pillars or vectors: Learning, Interaction, Mentoring and Evaluation (aka L.I.M.E.). Each of them provides a key to define the relation of the user within the mode, which is translated into a set of interconnected rules. Based on what the user does in the system, and how this web is weaved, the model provides the user with personalised guidance, dynamic along the timeline, which allows for a stable tutoring support along the learning process.

In order to validate the L.I.M.E. model, we have designed and implemented a learning scenario, during 4 weeks, and counting 2 groups (experimental-A and control-B) of 24 members each. The application of the model to the described scenario shows a clear and positive progress of the users in group A, those who received recommendations by the system. The overall average of inputs, categories and students shows a final positive difference of 10,53% between the experimental group and the control group (66,72% - 56,19%), in addition to a maximum difference between corners of 37,37% (81,41% - 44,04%). These results become a tangible proof for the success of the L.I.M.E. model, based on a large number of objective measurements. They back up the conceptual design from a practical experience. Furthermore, they support the combination of inputs and categories provided by L.I.M.E., which facilitates personalized counseling to the end-user, leading to an improvement of his average performance, implemented in the context of a thematic, restricted social network, and learning scenario which engages formal and informal settings, through learning activities and user interaction.

Future work points out at an early definition phase that

should take into account every single role (i.e. student, teacher, admin, et cetera). This involvement should not come from the instructional designer only, but from actual users from every target group. In doing so, the designer builds an ecosystem which plays with every actor from inside, and not only a scenario in which the users are included from outside. In addition, the model would benefit of a more precise balance between settings, inputs and categories. The combination of these is crucial for a good use of the system. In our application case, we use a neutral approach, so that we did not influence the results because of an early selection of these elements. However, no matter what the selection is, since it always affects the result, even for being neutral. A clear definition of the implications and co-lateral effects of each configuration would better support the match between objectives and expectations from students, tutors, and instructional designers

ACKNOLEDGMENT

This paper is being supported by the EduMotion Project (grant agreement 315568), funded by the Seventh Framework Programme of the European Commission, under the Research for SMEs line (R4SME); the TELMA project (TSI-020110-2009-85) of the Spanish Ministry of Industry, Tourism and Trade; and UNIR Research , private
research initiative which supports the Research Group on eLearning and Social Networks TELSOCK at the university. Finally, we thank Prof. Dr. José Luis Rodríguez Illera and Dr. Mario Barajas, from University of Barcelona, for their support.

REFERENCES

[1]   R. A. Bjork, "Assessing our own competence: Heuristics and illusions," in *Attention and performance XVII. Cognitive regulation of performance: Interaction of theory and application*, D. Gopher and A. Koriat, Eds. Cambridge, MA: MIT Press, 1999, pp. 435-459.

[2]   V. Romero and D. Burgos, "Meta-Mender: A meta-rule based recommendation system for educational applications," presented at Proceedings of the Workshop on Recommender Systems for Technology Enhanced Learning, RecsysTEL-2010, Barcelona, Spain, 2010.

[3]   V. Romero, D. Burgos, and A. Pardo, "Meta-rule based Recommender Systems for Educational Applications," in *Educational Recommender Systems and Technologies: Practices and Challenges*, O. Santos and J. Boticario, Eds.: Information Science-Idea Group, 2011.

[4]   B. White and J. Frederiksen, "A theoretical framework and approach for fostering metacognitive development," *Educational Psychologist*, vol. 40, pp. 211–223, 2005.

[5]   G. Linden, B. Smith, and Y. J., "Amazon.com recommendations: Item-to-item collaborative filtering," *Internet Computing IEEE*, vol. 7, pp. 76-80, 2003.

[6]   B. Marlin, "Modeling user rating profiles for collaborative filtering," in *Advances in neural information processing systems*, S. Thrun, L. K. Saul, and B. Schölkopf, Eds. Cambridge, MA: MIT Press, 2003, pp. 627-634.

[7]   S. Y. Chen and G. D. Magoulas, *Adaptable and Adaptive Hypermedia Systems*. Hershey, PA: IRM Press, 2005.

[8]   K. I. Ghauth and N. A. Abdullah, "Learning materials recommendation using good learners' ratings and content-based filtering," *Education Technology Research and Development*, In press.

[9]   T. Kerkiri, A. Manitsaris, and A. Mavridou, *Reputation metadata for recommending personalized e-learning resources*. Uxbridge: IEEE Computer Society, 2007.

[10]   C. Romero, S. Ventura, P. D. De Bra, and C. D. Castro, "Discovering prediction rules in AHA! courses.," presented at 9th International User Modeling Conference, 2003.

[11]   D. Burgos, C. Tattersall, and R. Koper, "How to represent adaptation in eLearning with IMS Learning Design," *Interactive Learning Environments*, vol. 15, pp. 161-170, 2007.

[12]   J. J. Rocchio, *Relevance feedback in information retrieval, in the SMART Retrieval System. Experiments in Automatic Document Processing*. Englewood Cliffs, NJ: Prentice Hall, Inc., 1971.

[13]   P. Sánchez-Gonzáleza, I. Oropesaa, V. Romeroc, A. Fernándeza, A. Albaceted, E. Asenjoe, J. Nogueraf, F. Sánchez-Margallog, D. Burgosc, and E. J. Gómez, "TELMA: technology enhanced learning environment for Minimally Invasive Surgery," *Procedia Computer Science*, vol. 00, 2010.

[14]   Romero L, Gutiérrez M, Caliusco ML. Conceptualizing the e-Learning Assessment Domain using an Ontology Network. *International Journal of Interactive Multimedia and Artificial Intelligence*. 2012;1 (Special Issue on Intelligent Systems and Applications):20-8

## 16

Our System IDCBR-MAS: from the Modelisation by AUML to the Implementation under JADE Platform

Abdelhamid Zouhair[1], El Mokhtar En-Naimi[1], Benaissa Amami[1], Hadhoum Boukachour[2], Patrick Person[2], Cyrille Bertelle[2]

[1]*LIST Lab, The University of Abdelmalek Essaâdi, FST of Tangier, Morocco*
[2]*LITIS Lab, The University of Le Havre, France*

Abstract — **This paper presents our work in the field of Intelligent Tutoring System (ITS), in fact there is still the problem of knowing how to ensure an individualized and continuous learners follow-up during learning process, indeed among the numerous methods proposed, very few systems concentrate on a real time learners follow-up. Our work in this field develops the design and implementation of a Multi-Agents System Based on Dynamic Case Based Reasoning which can initiate learning and provide an individualized follow-up of learner. This approach involves 1) the use of Dynamic Case Based Reasoning to retrieve the past experiences that are similar to the learner's traces (traces in progress), and 2) the use of Multi-Agents System. Our Work focuses on the use of the learner traces. When interacting with the platform, every learner leaves his/her traces on the machine. The traces are stored in database, this operation enriches collective past experiences. The traces left by the learner during the learning session evolve dynamically over time; the case-based reasoning must take into account this evolution in an incremental way. In other words, we do not consider each evolution of the traces as a new target, so the use of classical cycle Case Based reasoning in this case is insufficient and inadequate. In order to solve this problem, we propose a dynamic retrieving method based on a complementary similarity measure, named Inverse Longest Common Sub-Sequence (ILCSS). Through monitoring, comparing and analyzing these traces, the system keeps a constant intelligent watch on the platform, and therefore it detects the difficulties hindering progress, and it avoids possible dropping out. The system can support any learning subject. To help and guide the learner, the system is equipped with combined virtual and human tutors.**

Keywords — **Intelligent Tutoring Systems (ITS), Multi-Agents System (MAS), Incremental Dynamic Case Based Reasoning (IDCBR), Similarity Measure, Traces.**

I. INTRODUCTION

E-LEARNING is a computer system which offers learners another means of learning. Indeed it allows learner to break free from the constraints of time and place of training. They are due to the learners' availability. In addition, the instructor is not physically present and training usually happens asynchronously. However, most E-learning platforms allow the transfer of knowledge in digital format, without integrating the latest teaching approach in the field of education (e. g. constructivism [23], ...). Consequently, in most cases distance learning systems degenerate into tools for downloading courses in different formats (pdf, word ...). These platforms also cause significant overload and cognitive disorientation for learners. Today, it is therefore necessary to design and implement a computer system (i. e. intelligent tutor) able to initiate the learning and provide an individualized monitoring of the learner, who thus becomes the pilot of training. The system will also respond to the learner's specific needs.

Solving these problems involves first, to understand the behaviour of the learner, or group of learners, who use platform to identify the causes of problems or difficulties which a learner can encounter. This can be accomplished while leaning on the traces of interactions of the learner with the platform, which include history, chronology of interactions and productions left by the learner during his/her learning process. This will allow us the reconstruction of perception elements of the activity performed by the learner.

We consider an Intelligent Tutoring System (ITS), that is able to represent, follow and analyze the evolution of a learning situation through the exploitation and the treatment of the traces left by the learner during his/her learning on the platform. This system is based, firstly on the traces to feed the system and secondly on the reconciliation between the course of the learner (traces in progress) and past courses (or past traces). The past traces are stored in a database. Our system is able to represent, follow and analyze the evolution of a learning situation through the exploitation and the treatment of the traces left by the learner during his/her learning on the platform. The analysis of the course must be executed continuously and in real time which leads us to choose a Multi-Agents architecture allowing the implementation of a dynamic case-based reasoning. Recently, several research works have been focused on the dynamic case based reasoning in order to push the limits of case based reasoning system static, reactive and responsive to users. All these works are based on the observation that the current tools are limited in capabilities, and are not able of evolving to fit the non-anticipated or emerging needs. Indeed the reuse of past experiences causes several problems, such as:

- Modeling: formalization of experience acquired (cases), indeed a few CBR systems are able to change over time the way of representing a case [6]. According Alain Mille, a case has to describe its context of use, which is very difficult to decide before any reuse and can change in time [22].
- Treatment: the use of the classic reasoning cycle is insufficient and inadequate in dynamic or emerging situations, unknown in advance.

In order to deal with this issue, we propose a Dynamic Case Based Reasoning based on a dynamic retrieve method, and we propose a dynamic retrieving method based on a complementary similarity measure, named Inverse Longest Common Sub-Sequence (ILCSS).

The rest of this paper is organized as follows: In the second section, we present a general introduction of intelligent tutoring system. In the third section we present a Multi-agents Case-Based Reasoning, and in the following part, we will propose the description of our approach in Case Based Reasoning and intelligent tutoring systems field: Incremental Dynamic Case-Based Reasoning founded on Multi-Agents System. In the next section, we present some development results of our system. Finally, we present a comparison between IDCBR-MAS system and other CBR system, and we will give the conclusion and our future work.

II. INTELLIGENT TUTORING SYSTEMS

Intelligent Tutoring Systems (ITS) are computer systems designed to assist and facilitate the task of learning for the learner. It can personalize learning for learners, providing a less expensive solution for a diverse generation of learners. They have expertise in so far as they know the domain knowledge, how to teach (pedagogical knowledge) and also how to acquire information about the learner. We note that, the general architecture of Intelligent Tutoring Systems was represented in our articles [10]. Many researches have been designed and implemented in Intelligent Tutoring System, in order to assist a learner in his/her/their learning. There are, for example, tutors or teaching agents who accompany learners by proposing remedial activities [11]. There are also the agents of support to the group collaboration in the learning [7] encouraging, the learners participation and facilitating discussion between them. Other solutions are based on Multi-Agents System that incorporate and seek to make cooperation among various Intelligent Tutoring System [5]. The Baghera platform [32] exploits the concepts and methods of Multi-Agents approach. Baghera assists learners in their work solving exercise in geometry. They can interact with other learners or teachers. The teachers can know the progress of the learners work in order to intervene if needed. These tools of distance learning do not allow an individualized, continuous

and real-time learners follow-up. They adopt a traditional pedagogical approach (behaviorist) instead of integrating the latest teaching approaches (constructivism and social constructivism [23], [30]). Finally, given the large number of learners who leave their training, the adaptation of learning according to the learners profile has become indispensable today.

Our contribution in these important areas is to design and develop an adaptable system that can ensure an automatic and a continuous monitoring of the learner. Moreover, our system is open, scalable and generic to support any learning subject.

III. MULTI-AGENTS CASE-BASED REASONING

A. Case-Based Reasoning

Case-Based Reasoning (CBR) is an artificial intelligence methodology which aims at solving new problems based on the solutions of similar past problems (past experiences) [14]. The solved problems are called source cases and are stored in a case-base (base of scenarios). The problem to be solved is called target case. A CBR is a combination of knowledge and processes to manage and re-use previous experience.

The Case-Based Reasoning cycle is composed of five steps as given at following figure (Fig. 1):

- Presentation: the current problem is identified and completed in such a way that it becomes compatible with the contents and retrieval methods of the case-base reasoning.
- Retrieve: The task of retrieve step is to find the most similar case or cases to the current problem in the case-base.
- Reuse: The goal of the reuse phase is to modify the solution of source case found in order to build a solution for the target case.
- Revise: The phase of revision is the step in which the solution suggested in the previous phase will be evaluated. If the solution is unsatisfactory, then it will be corrected.
- Retain: retaining the new experience and add it to the knowledge-base (case-base) [12], [1].

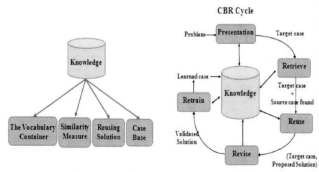

Fig. 1. The CBR components (Source [1], [12])

The systems based on the case-based reasoning can be classified into two categories [18]:

- Applications for static situation. For this type of system, the designer must have all the characteristics describing a case, in advance, in order to be able to realize its model. A data model of the field is thus refined through an expertise in the field of application which can characterize a given situation. Thus, the cases are completely structured in this data model and often represented in a list (a: attributes, v: values). For example we have the system CHIEF [13] case base planner that builds new plans out of its memory of old ones. We do not exploit this type of CBR to develop our system, because in the approach for static situation, a problem must be completely described before starting the first step. Nevertheless in our situation, the learner traces (target case) evolve dynamically over time, so we must treat a dynamic situation with some particular features.

- Applications for dynamic situation. They differ when we compare them to static cases by the fact that they deal with temporal target cases (the situation), by looking for similar cases (better cases) based on a resemblance between histories (for more details on the subject, the reader may refer to [2], [18])). Several works relate to dynamic case based reasoning such as REBECAS [18] prediction of processes from observed behaviours, application to wildfire and SAPED [2].

B. Multi-Agents Case-Based Reasoning

The Multi-Agents System based on case based reasoning are used in many applications areas [25]. We can distinguish two types of applications (Table I):

- The Multi-Agents System in which each agent uses the case based reasoning internally for their own needs (level agent case based reasoning): This type is the first model that was applied in Multi-Agents CBR Systems. For this type of system, each agent is able to find similar cases to the target case in their own case base, also able to accomplish all steps of CBR cycle. For example we have the system ProCLAIM [29], MCBR [17] for distributed systems and CBR-TEAM [26] approach that uses a set of heterogeneous cooperative agents in a parametric design task (steam-condenser component design).
- The Multi-Agents System whose approach is a case based reasoning (level Multi-Agents Case Based Reasoning) : For this types of applications, the Multi-Agents Case Based Reasoning System distribute the some/all steps of the CBR cycle (Representation, Retrieve, Reuse, Revise, Retain) among several agents. The second category might be better than the first. Indeed the individual agents experience may be limited, therefore their Knowledge and prediction, so the agents are able to cooperate with other agents for a better prediction of the situation and they can benefit from the other agents capabilities. For example we have CCBR [21], RoBoCats [20] and S-MAS [24].

To our knowledge, no dynamic CBR cycle reasoning system exists.

We propose a system called Incremental Dynamic Case Based Reasoning-Multi-Agents System (IDCBR-MAS), able to find similar cases to the target case in their own case base. Our system is founded on 1) a dynamic cycle of case-based reasoning, and 2) a dynamic retrieving method based on a complementary similarity measure, named Inverse Longest Common Sub-Sequence (ILCSS) (for more details on the subject, the reader may refer to [10, 34]).

IV. INCREMENTAL DYNAMIC CASE-BASED REASONING FOUNDED ON MULTI-AGENTS SYSTEM

A. General architecture of our approach IDCBR-MAS

Our problem is similar to the CBR for dynamic situation. Indeed, the traces left by the learner during the learning session evolve dynamically over time; the case-based reasoning must take into account this evolution in an incremental way. In other words, we do not consider each evolution of the traces as a new target. The intelligent system (IDCBR-MAS) which we propose offer important features:

- It is dynamic. Indeed we must continually acquire new knowledge to better reproduce human behaviour in each situation.
- It is incremental; this is its major feature because the trace evolves in a dynamic way for the same target case.

The main benefits of our approach are the distributed capabilities of the Multi-Agents System and the self-adaption ability to the changes that occur in each situation. The system that we propose consists of the three layers components (as indicated in Figure Fig. 2:

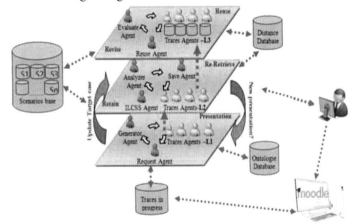

Fig. 2. General architecture of our approach

1) Presentation layer: The role of agents of this layer is to manage information arrived from the environment (the learner traces). This information feed the representation layer. The goal of this layer is to be both, a picture of the current situation being analyzed and to represent its dynamic evolution over time. The presentation layer contains the following agents:

- Request Agent: The role of this agent is to establish the link between the system and the environment. They feed the system with information from Distributed Information Systems (file traces). Also the goal of this agent is to check if there is any change in the traces file.
- Generator Agent: the role of this agent is to create and/or update the Traces Agents-L1: The Request Agent transmits the data received from environment to the Generator Agent. Two cases of figure are presented: if the Traces Agents-L1 (i) related to the learner i exist,

then this last will be updated, else the Generator Agent creates a new Traces Agents-L1 (i).

- Traces Agents-L1: For each Lerner i we have a represented Trace Agent-L1(i). These agents will encapsulate the original traces of learners.

2) Interpretation Layer and storage: A set of agents allows the comparison between the current situation and past situations stored in the memory (scenarios). The Interpretation Layer contains the following agents:

- Traces Agents- L2: These agents contain the same information and data that have in the Trace Agents-L1 of the first layer. They differ by an abstraction of the data, originally described and managed by the Trace Agents-L1, that make it comparable to the past experiences stored in the memory.

- ILCSS Agent: The role of this agent is to evaluate in a continuously way the similarity between the current situation and past experiences based on the similarity measure ILCSS. The retrieve step of our system is based on this agent. The ILCSS Agent save the distances between the current situation and past experiences in Distance Table. It is responsible for reviewing these distances every time whenever necessary.

- Analyzer Agent: The goal of this agent is to check in a dynamic way if there is any change or update in Trace Agent -L2 (with the arrival of new information and data from the environment), then the Analyzer Agent asks ILCSS Agent to update Distance Table each time they have a change in the Trace Agent -L2, if not they asks the Request Agent if there is any change in traces file.

3) Prediction and Decision Layer: The role of agents of this layer is to predict the current situation by reusing past experiences selected by second layer. The choice of similar past experiences is evaluated by this layer, so one of these scenarios will be proposed to the learner. The layer contains the following agents:

- Traces Agents-L3: At this stage of reasoning the system adds a pointer to each agent the Traces Agents-L2. So the Traces Agents-L3 is identical to Traces Agents-L2 with a small difference, in fact for each Traces Agents-L2 we associate a list of similar scenarios through a pointer to the list of similar past experiences. The advantage of a pointer is that the list is not exhaustive and it changes dynamically over time following the change of the learner traces.

- Reuse Agent: The role of this agent is to predict future events of the situation by reusing the past experiences to the current situation.

- Evaluate Agent: The role of this agent is to evaluate the solution proposed by the Reuse Agent and to ensure that the similarity between the current situation and scenarios chosen by the Prediction layer is sufficient.

- Human Tutor or Human Agent: The human tutor is solicited if the system detects a learning situation requiring his intervention (failure to find one or more similar scenarios to the current situation).

B. From static to dynamic CBR cycle

We modify the CBR cycle in order to be able to handle dynamic situations and therefore we propose changes in the order of steps and a large change in the content of the steps of this cycle. In our approach the evaluation of the similarity between the current situation and similar past situations is a process continues. The retrieve step of the CBR cycle (as indicated in figure Fig.3) must take into account the change in the current situation in a dynamic way (in real-time). Our system will be able to repeat the retrieve step following the change of the current situation or whenever necessary.

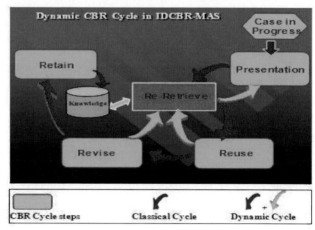

Fig. 3. Dynamic CBR Cycle in IDCBR-MAS

In addition, in our system the sequence of steps of the CBR cycle isn't important: in fact our system can stop each step in the CBR cycle and return to a previous step following the change of the current situation, and the order presentation – retrieve – reuse – revise – retain is not static or fixed, it can change and some steps can be re-run each time until the change in the situation.

Our agents are equipped with learning, communication and intelligence skills. They are able to stop the execution of the CBR cycle at a given step and time. They are able to re-run the different steps later following a change in the target situation. The highlight of our approach is that rerunning the retrieval step based our new dynamic similarity measure ILCSS. In each step CBR cycle of our approach we takes into account the previous results i.e. in time t_{i+1} we use the results in t_i. Therefore our CBR cycle takes into account the change of situation in a dynamic and incremental way.

1) Retrieval steps : Retrieval of previous case is one important step within the CBR paradigm. The success of retrieval step will depend on three factors: the case representation, case memory and similarity measure used to retrieve sources cases that are similar to the target case. There are two ways research for the sources case in dynamic situations:

- Research by evaluating similarity between the current situation and the already solved problems in a single dimension [18]. Several systems have been used this approach such as REBECAS [18] and SAPED [2].

- Research by evaluating similarity between the current problem and the already solved problems in a multiple dimension [2]. The multidimensional research, it is realized in a single step by taking into account all the parameters describing the current problem at the same time. The multidimensional research is also used in several systems, such as CASEP2 [33].

2) State of the Art on Similarity Measures: Search for similar sources cases are based on the similarity measure. In this part, we present the principles similarity measures often used in case based reasoning, for more details on the subject, the reader my refer to [2] and to our articles [10], [34].

Biological Sequences Alignment: Dynamic Programming, is an important tool, which has been used for many applications in biology. It is a way of arranging the sequences of DNA, or protein to identify regions of similarity that may be a consequence of structural or functional relationships between the sequences. They are also used in different fields, such as natural language or data mining.

Minkowski distance: The Minkowski distance is a metric on Euclidean space which can be considered as a generalization of both the Euclidean distance.

Longest Common Sub-Sequence (LCSS): the goal is to find the longest subsequence common in two or more sequences [31]. The LCSS is usually defined as: Given two sequences, find the longest subsequence present in both of them. A subsequence is a sequence that appears in the same order, but not necessarily contiguous. The main goal is to count the number of pairs of points considered similar when browsing the two compared sequences.

There are other similarity measures such as Dynamic Time Warping (DTW): The DTW algorithm is able to find the optimal alignment between two sequences. It is often used in speech recognition to determine if two waveforms represent the same spoken phrase. In addition to speech recognition, dynamic time warping has been successfully used in many other fields [2], such as robotics, data mining, and medicine.

TABLE I.
COMPARISON OF VARIOUS SIMILARITY MEASURES [2]

	Type	Dimension	Length
Biological Sequences Alignment	Symbolic	One-dimensional	Different
DTW	Digital	One-dimensional	Different
LCSS	Heterogeneous	Multidimensional	Different
Minkowski distance	Digital	One-dimensional	Same Length

3) Inverse Longest Common Sub-Sequence: The main goal of the retrieval phase in our system is to predict the behavior of the learner, by the reconciliation between the target trace and past traces or scenarios. The success of a case-based reasoning system depends primarily on the performance of the retrieval step used and, more particularly, on similarity measure used to retrieve sources cases (scenarios) that are similar to the situation (traces in progress). Several research works have

been focused on the similarity measure. Furthermore, these methods are not well suited when we compare two dynamic and heterogeneous sequences. In order to deal with this issue, we propose a complementary similarity measure entitled Inverse Longest Common Sub-Sequence an extension of the Longest Common Sub-Sequence measure.

In our system IDCBR-MAS the target case or target trace can be represented as a various actions of the learner (learner traces). It can be represented also as a collection of semantic features SF= (object, (qualification, value) +), we note object=O, qualification=Q and value=V, SF= (O,(Q,V)+), so the learner traces at time i, can be defined by the formula:

$$LT_i = \bigcup_{1 \le k \le i} SF_k$$

Where $SF_k = (O_k, (Q_{k,1}, V_1),..., (Q_{k,d}, V_d))$ is a sequence of d+1 dimension. Finally the learner traces at time i+1 is a multidimensional sequence.

Let A and B two Traces with size n x d and m x d respectively, where:

$A = ((O_{A,1}, (Q_{A,1,1}, V_{A,1,1}),..., (Q_{A,1,d}, V_{A,1,d}), (O_{A,2}, (Q_{A,2,1}, V_{A,2,1}),...,(Q_{A,2,d}, V_{A,2,d})),....., (O_{A,n}, (Q_{A,n,1}, V_{A,n,1}),..., (Q_{A,n,d}, V_{A,n,d})))$

And

$B = ((O_{B,1}, (Q_{B,1,1}, V_{B,11}),...,(Q_{B,1,d}, V_{B,1,d}), (O_{B,2}, (Q_{B,2,1}, V_{B,21}), ..., (Q_{B,2,d}, V_{B,2,d})),....., (O_{B,m}, (Q_{B,m,1}, V_{B,m,1}),...,(Q_{B,m,d}, V_{B,m,d})))$.

For a Trace A, let Tail(A) be the Trace:

$Tail(A) = (O_{A,2},(Q_{A,2,1},V_{A,2,1}),..., (Q_{A,2,d}, V_{A,2,d})),....., (O_{A,n}, (Q_{A,n,1},V_{A,n,1}),..., (Q_{A,n,d}, V_{A,n,d})))$. Tail (A) it the trace A private their first vector.

The goal is to count the number of pairs vectors considered similar when compared through the two traces. The similarity between two vectors $(V_{A,i,1}, V_{A,i,2}, ..., V_{A,i,d})$ from trace A, and $(V_{B,j,1}, V_{B,j,2}, ..., V_{B,j,d})$ from trace B it determined according to a threshold δ: if for each k $=1,...,d$ $|V_{A,i,k} - V_{B,j,k}| \le \delta$. We also define an integer N, the parameter that will be able to control the temporal variance between two vectors of each of the traces in order to consider the two traces similar.

Let A and B two Traces, and given an integer N and a real number δ, we define the similarity measures between the two traces A and B, as follows recursive process: the process is initialized by comparing the two first vectors of traces (A, B). If any of the two traces is empty then the value of the similarity measure is equal to 0, and the process stops. Else if any of the two vectors traces are similar, then the similarity measure in this case is "1" more the similarity between the two traces deprived of their first vectors. Else the similarity is equal to the maximum of the similarity between a trace and the other private its first vector.

At the instant t=ti+1 the IDCBR-MAS system recovers the traces stored in the log file of server between the two instants ti and ti+1 and we have $(A)_{t=ti+1} = Tail(A)_{t=ti+1} = A[ti,ti+1]$ see figure below.

$Tail(A)_{t=ti+1} = A_{[ti,ti+1]} = ((O_{A[ti+1,ti],1}, (Q_{A[ti+1,ti],1,1}, V_{A[ti+1,ti],1,1}),..., (Q_{A[ti+1,ti],1,d}, V_{A[ti+1,ti],1,d}), ..., (O_{A[ti+1,ti],n'},$

A_0 A_{ti} ..... A_{ti+1}

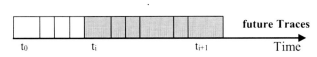

future Traces

t_0 t_i t_{i+1} Time

$(Q_{A[ti+1,ti],n,1}, V_{A[ti+1,ti],n',1}),\ldots, (Q_{A[ti+1,ti],n',d}, V_{A[ti+1,ti],n',d})))$ avec $1 <= i' <= n'$

At the instant $t=ti+1$ it only remains the block $B[j+1,m]$ of the B traces (block of the trace B have not yet been compared with the target trace), where Bj describe, the last common element between the two traces (A)t=ti and B at the instant t=ti.

B_0 B_j B_{j+1} .... B_m

$(B)_{t=ti+1} = Tail(B)_{t=ti+1} = B_{[j+1,m]}$

$Tail(B)_{t=ti+1} = B_{[j+1,m]} = ((O_{B[j+1,m],1}, (Q_{B[j+1,m],1,1}, V_{B[j+1,m],11}),\ldots,(Q_{B[j+1,m],1,d}, V_{B[j+1,m],1,d}), \ldots, (O_{B[j+1,m],m'}, (Q_{B[j+1,m],m',1}, V_{B[j+1,m],m',1}),\ldots,(Q_{B[j+1,m],m',d}, V_{B[j+1,m],m',d})))$ with $1 <= j' <= m' (m'= m-j)$

The measure between the target traces A and the source trace B at time $t = t_{i+1}$ will depend on the results instantly $t = ti$ through the following recursive formula:

$$(ILCSS_{\delta,N,ti+1}(A,B))_{t=ti+1} = (ILCSS_{\delta,N,ti}(A,B))_{t=ti} + ILCSS_{\delta,N,ti+1}(A_{[ti,ti+1]}, B_{[j+1,m]})$$

With

$$ILCSS_{\delta,N,ti+1}(A_{[ti,ti+1]}, B_{[j+1,m]}) = \begin{cases} 0 \text{ if } A_{[ti,ti+1]} \text{ or } B_{[j+1,m]} \text{ is empty.} \\ 1 + ILCSS_{\delta,N,ti+1}(A_{[ti,ti+1]}, B_{[j+1,m]}) \text{ if } O_{A[ti,ti+1],i'} = O_{B[j+1,m],j'}, Q_{A[ti,ti+1],i',k} = Q_{B[j+1,m],j',k} \\ |V_{A[ti,ti+1],i',k'} - V_{B[j+1,m],j',k'}| \leq \delta, \text{ with } 1 \leq i' \leq n', 1 \leq j' \leq m', |i'-j| \leq N \text{ et } k' = 1\ldots d. \\ \max(ILCSS_{\delta,N,ti+1}(Tail(A_{[ti,ti+1]}), B_{[j+1,m]}), ILCSS_{\delta,N,ti+1}(A_{[ti,ti+1]}, Tail(B_{[j+1,m]}))) \text{ else.} \end{cases}$$

The index of the last common element between the two traces (A)t=ti+1 and B at time $t = t_{i+1}$ is obtained using the following iterative formula.

J is initialized to 0;

And

$$\{j = j' \text{ if } O_{A[ti,ti+1],i'} = O_{B[j+1,m],j'}, Q_{A[ti,ti+1],i',k} = Q_{B[j+1,m],j',k'} |V_{A[ti,ti+1],i',k'} - V_{B[j+1,m],j',k'}| < \delta \text{ and } j' > j$$

With $1 \leq i' \leq n'$, $1 \leq j' \leq m'$, $|i'-j'| \leq N$ and $k'=1\ldots d$

We define the distance between the two Traces A and B as follow:

$$D_{\delta,N,ti}(A,B) = 1 - \frac{ILCSS_{\delta,N,ti}(A,B)}{\min(n,m)}$$

Where $D_{\delta,N,ti}(A,B)$ verify the proprieties of the distance such

as: $\begin{cases} D_{\delta,N,ti}(A,B) \geq 0 \\ D_{\delta,N,ti}(A,B) = 0 \text{ equal } A \approx B \\ D_{\delta,N,ti}(A,B) = D_{\delta,N,ti}(B,A) \end{cases}$

$A \approx B$: A and B are two similar traces.

4) *Learner's Traces and case structure*: Based on the general definition of a trace given in [19], "a trace is a thing or a succession of things left by an unspecified action and relative to a being or an object; a succession of prints or marks which the passage of a being or an object leaves; it is what one recognizes that something existed; what remains of a past thing". In ITS literature, a digital trace is an observed collection, all structured information resulting from an interaction observation temporally located [22].

In our context, a digital trace is resulting from an activity observation representing a process interactional signature. Indeed, it is composed of the objects which are respectively located the ones compared to the others when observed and registered on a support. That means that a trace is explicitly composed of the structured objects and registered compared to a time representation of the activity traces. The structuring can be sequentially explicit (each trace observed is followed and/or preceded by another) or can also come from the temporal characteristic of the objects traces [19]. Indeed, the structuring depends on the type of the time representation and the time of the activity traces. We can distinguish two types of representations:

- They can be a temporal interval determined by two dates, (start and end of observation). In this case, the observed traces may be associated with an instant or an interval of time. Then we will be able to take into account chronological relationships between observations';
- They can be a sequence of unspecified elements (for example a sub-part of the whole of the set of integers). In this case, we will focus on the succession or the precedence of the trace observed (there is no chronological time).

In the current uses of the traces for the CEHL, collected situations are contrasted: from "we take what we have in well specified formats, what is called the logs" to "we scrupulously instrument the environment to recover the observed controlled and useful for different actors (learner and tutor). The first step consists of modeling the raw data contained in the log file. It is necessary to be able to collect the traces files containing at least, the following elements: time for the start date of the action, codes action which consists in codifying the learner's actions and learner concerned.

In our system IDCBR-MAS a target case or target trace is represented by a trace learner in progress when interacting with the Moodle platform. The cases sources are previous traces learners that are stored in database. The cases sources are traces left by the learners which followed the same training on the Moodle platform. The following figure shows the target trace structure:

```xml
<?xml version="1.0" encoding="utf-8" ?>
<logs>
- <user>
    <id>5</id>
    <nom>zouhair abdelhamid</nom>
  </user>
+ <log>
- <log>
    <id>550</id>
    <cours>JADE</cours>
    <date>lun 30/9/2013 0:3</date>
    <action>launch</action>
    <ip>127.0.0.1</ip>
    <info>http://127.0.0.1/moodle/pluginfile.php/25/mod_scorm/content/1/les_protocoles_fipaquery
    <date_second>1380492184</date_second>
    <duree_second>1380492558</duree_second>
  </log>
- <log>
    <id>551</id>
    <cours>JADE</cours>
    <date>lun 30/9/2013 0:9</date>
    <action>launch</action>
    <ip>127.0.0.1</ip>
    <info>http://127.0.0.1/moodle/pluginfile.php/25/mod_scorm/content/1/la_norme_fipa.html</info>
    <date_second>1380492558</date_second>
    <duree_second>1380492758</duree_second>
  </log>
```

Fig. 4. Learner traces when interacting with the platform Moodle

The trace can be written as follows: ((OA,1, (Q A,1,1, VA,1,1),..., (QA,1,d, VA,1,d), (OA,2, (QA,2,1, VA,2,1),...,(QA,2,d, VA,2,d)),....., (OA,n, (QA,n,1, VA,n,1),..., (QA,n,d, VA,n,d)))

We developed a module in Moodle platform that can be the interface between the Moodle server and our IDCBR-MAS system. This module includes an xml file, which contains traces left by all learners in the Moodle log file and also contains the datalib file. The module uses the same Moodle database. The datalib file of Moodle platform has been modified in order to be able to record and save all traces of learners connected to the Moodle platform. The following figure shows the datalib file.

```
function insert_xml($log)
{
global $DB, $CFG;
if($log['userid']!=1 && $log['userid']!=0 && $log['userid']!=2)
{
$nomfichier=$CFG->dirroot.'\xml\user.xml';
if(file_exists($nomfichier))
{
$user=$log['userid'];
    $nomfich=$CFG->dirroot."\xml\user".$log['userid']."_xml";
    $sql_request = "SELECT u.* $ctxselect FROM {user} u WHERE u.id=".$log['userid'];
$result = $DB->get_records_sql($sql_request, null, null);
if($result != null)
foreach($result as $us)
    $user=$us->firstname."_".$us->lastname;

    $sql_request = "SELECT MAX(l.id) as max $ctxselect FROM {log} l WHERE l.userid=".$1
$result3 = $DB->get_records_sql($sql_request, null, null);
if($result3 != null)
}{

foreach($result3 as $l)
    $id=$l->max;
    }
    $sql_request = "SELECT c.* $ctxselect FROM {course} c WHERE c.id=".$log['course'];
$result2 = $DB->get_records_sql($sql_request, null, null);
if($result2 != null)
foreach($result2 as $c)
    $course=$c->fullname;
```

Fig. 5. datalib file, version IDCBR-MAS

In the next section, we present our Model based on AUML methodology. AUML or agent UML is a support notation for agent-oriented Multi-agents systems development. It consists in using the UML modeling language and extending it in order to represent agents, their behavior and interactions among them.

V. IDCBR-MAS SYSTEM MODELING

Our system IDCBR-MAS is composed of multiple interacting intelligent agents; it supports the specification, analysis, design and validation of our systems. We present the sequence diagram of the various interactions carried out between the various actors of the platform.

A. Presentation of the situation.

The presentation of the situation (learner's traces) by the platform is a task managed by several agents of the presentation layer of our system IDCBR-MAS. These agents are responsible for the update of the traces. The following sequence diagram illustrates the process of the situation presentation of the learner's traces.

Firstly the Request Agent addresses a request to server in order to retrieves the learner's traces left by the learner during the learning session and sending it to the Generator Agent, this last created/update the Traces Agents-L1: Two cases of figure are presented during the checking, if the Traces Agents-L1 (i) related to the learner i exists then the Traces Agents-L1 (i) will be updated, else the Generator Agent create a new Traces

Agents-L1 (i) able to represent the learner i. the process will be re-run each time there is a change in the learner's traces.

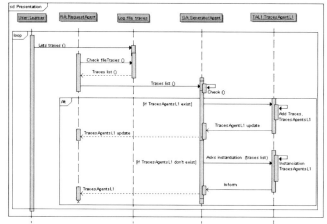

Fig. 6. The sequence diagram of the case presentation in IDCBR-MAS.

B. Interpretation of the situation

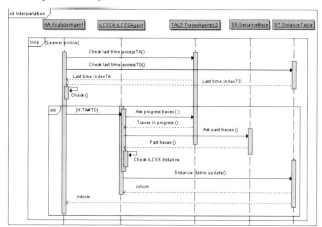

Fig. 7. The sequence diagram of the Interpretation case in IDCBR-MAS

Firstly the Analyzer Agent (AA) addresses a request to the Traces Agents-L2 and to the Distance Table in order to retrieves two chronological dates TA: the last update date in the traces file and DT: the last update date of the Distance Table. The Analyzer Agent check If TA= DT. If the two dates are not equal then the Analyzer Agent ask the ILCSS Agent to update the distance table which contains the distance between the current situation Traces Agents-L2 and the scenario stored in memory. This is based on the similarity measures ILCSS. The agent also asks periodically the Request Agent if there is any change in the learner's traces, whether the process will be re-executed.

First of all the Reuse Agent ask the Traces Agents-L3 to retrieve the current traces with the associated scenarios (the associated scenarios to the current traces are the scenarios that are very similar at learner's traces or target, based on the similarity measures ILCSS). Then the Evaluate Agent checks the Distance Table. If necessary the Reuse Agent asks the ILCSS Agent asks to check and update all distances between the current situation and scenarios stored in memory.

C. Prediction of the situation

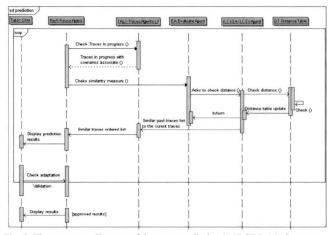

Fig. 8. The sequence diagram of the case prediction in IDCBR-MAS system

VI. IDCBR-MAS SYSTEM DEVELOPING

We developed our framework IDCBR-MAS based the JADE Agent Platform (Java Agent DEvelopment Framework). For the development of interfaces, we chose the languages Java, PHP and the tools EasyPHP, Apache, MySQL, phpMyAdmin.

A. Inter-Agent Communication in IDCBR-MAS

In order to supervise and control the communication and the IDCBR-MAS agents' behavior, we use Remote Monitoring Agent (RMA) of JADE platform. RMA is a graphical console for platform management and control. The RMA console is able to start other JADE tools. It a monitoring and debugging tool, made of a graphical user. It is able to displays the flow of interactions between agents in our IDCBR-MAS platform. The following figure shows the interactions between IDCBR-MAS agents.

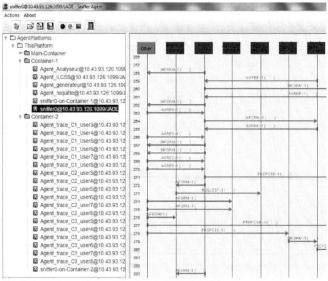

Fig. 9. Inter-Agent Communication in IDCBR-MAS

B. Monitoring the activity and communication between agents in IDCBR-MAS

This tool makes it possible to monitor the life cycle and communication of our agents: Sending and Receiving Messages by these agents. It is also possible to display the list of all the messages sent or received, completed with timestamp information in order to allow agent conversation recording and rehearsal. For example, the following figure shows the state as well as the transmitted/received messages for the ILCSS Agent of our IDCBR-MAS framework.

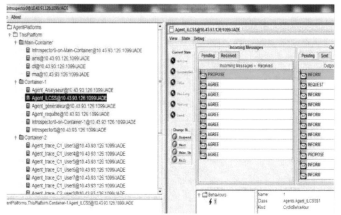

Fig. 10. Transmitted/received messages for ILCSS Agent

C. Distance between the target and previous traces

After the registration of a learner on the IDCBR-MAS platform, the learner will be able to run Moodle from our platform and subsequently launch a learning session. The tutor follows progressively the training of the learner.

The users		Target user Last access		Rachid Amernis 30/11/2013 12: 30	
Oussama Oussama		Previous users	Update target case score	Retrieve score	Adaptation score	Distance between target case and previous case
Mimoun zakhenini		Oussama Oussama	44	23	8	0.757
zouhair abdelhamid		Mimoun zakhemini	44	23	8	0.453
Hasani Ali		Zouhair abdelhamid	44	23	8	0.543
Rachid Amernis		Hasani ALi	44	23	8	0.476
said jouhane		Rachid Amernis	44	23	8	0.765
Abdelaziz Zitan		Said zouhair	44	23	8	0.124
Talibi Hamza		Abdelaziz Zitan	44	23	8	0.876
Youssra Kasmi		Talibi Hamza	44	23	8	0.945
Hajar taleb		Youssra Kasmi	44	23	8	0.344
Rachida Hadj		Hajar taleb	44	23	8	0.788
		Rachid Hadj	44	23	8	0.324

Fig. 11. Distance between the target and previous traces

All interactions, actions and productions of the learner are recorded on the log file in the Moodle database. Our system retrieves these traces through agents' interfaces permanently, and then they will be treated by the platform. In the figure we have a target case (traces left by target learner) and we have previous traces (traces left by previous learners). The update target case score present the number of update in the target case; the retrieve score present the number of re-retrieve of the previous cases very similar to target case by the agents of IDCBR-MAS platform. The distance between the target trace and past traces are calculated by the ILCSS Agent. These distances will be used as a key element in predicting of the situation achieved by the adaptation agent. The system proposes to the tutor a list of the similar traces to the target trace in order to choose the best similar traces.

D. Distances curves between the target and previous traces

The following figure displays the distances curves between the target and previous traces in order to shows the distance between them, these curves are generated in real times starting from the results of retrieval phase. These curves display also the history of these distances. For Tutor, the distances curves present very important information about the change of the distances database. The Tutor will be able to take her decision and to choose the trace most similar to the target trace.

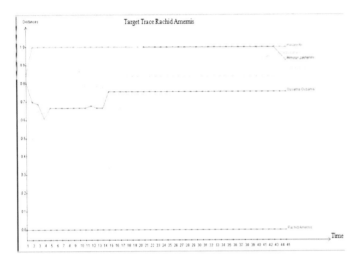

Fig. 12. Distances curves between the target traces and previous traces

VII.   IDCBR-MAS & OTHER CBR SYSTEMS

Several researchers have focused on classical versus dynamic CBR architectures where target case are static versus dynamic, but all these systems have been used static CBR cycle. Consequently, the Incremental Dynamic CBR approach has been proposed as an appropriate alternative, which have demonstrated its efficacy. For example, In our approach the evaluation of the similarity between the target case and similar past cases is a process continues and the retrieve step of the CBR cycle take into account the change in the target case in real-time. Finally our system is founded on a dynamic retrieving method. The following table (Table II) shows a summary of the CBR systems.

TABLE II.
CBR SYSTEMS CLASSIFICATION

Target case	CBR Cycle	Classical CBR Systems	CBR-MAS	CBR-Agent
Static	Static	CHEF[13], CREEK [3], CASEY [15], RADIX [8]	CCBR[21], AMAL [27]	ProCLAIM [29]
Dynamic	Static	REBECAS [18], AuRA [16] , SAPED[2], CASEP2 [33], SBR[4]	CICLMAN [28], RoBoCats [20] , S-MAS [24]	MCBR [17], CBR-TEAM[26]
Dynamic	Dynamic			IDCBR-MAS

VIII.   CONCLUSION AND FUTURE WORK

Our system allows connecting and comparing the current situation (target trace) to past situation (previous traces) that are stored in a database. The continuous analysis of information coming from the environment (learner's traces) makes it possible to suggest to various actors (learners and tutor) possible evolutions of the current situation.

The Multi-Agents architecture that we propose is based on three layers of agents with a pyramidal relation. The lower layer allows building a representation of the target case. The second layer implements a dynamic process: search for past situations similar to the current one. Finally, the prediction layer captures the responses sent by the second layer to transform them into actions proposed either by virtual tutor, or/and human tutor.

We have presented systems founded of Incremental and Dynamic Case Based Reasoning and we have also clarified that the CBR-based applications can be classified according to the study area: CBR for static situations and CBR for dynamic situations. In our situation, we have used a Dynamic system IDCBR-MAS, with a dynamic CBR cycle in order to push the limits of CBR cycle static. In fact, the current situation (target case) is a trace that evolves; the case based reasoning must take into account this evolution incrementally. In other words, it shouldn't consider each evolution of the trace as a new target case.

Our future work follows two different ways. First, we would like to use our framework in real experiment with e-learning platform of our university. Secondly, in the second part of our perspective, we will try to implement our approach in the field of Geographic Information Systems (GIS).

REFERENCES

[1]   A. Aamodt and E. Plaza, "Case-Based Reasoning : Foundational Issues, Methodological Variations, and System Approaches", AICom-Artificial Intelligence Communications, IOS Press, Vol. 7: 1, pp. 39-59, 1994.

[2]   A. Aich, Reconnaissance et prdiction de situations dynamiques : application l'assistance de personnes handicapes moteur, Thse de doctorat, Universit de Technologie de Troyes, 2007.

[3]   A. Aamodt, Knowledge-Intensive Case-Based Reasoning and Sustained Learning. Proc. of the 9th European Conference on Artificial Intelligence, ECCBR04, Lecture Notes in Artificial Intelligence, Springer, 2004.

[4]   C. Baptiste, Vers la gestion de scnarios pour la reconnaissance et l'anticipation de situations dynamiques , Universit de Technologie de Troyes, France, 2011.

[5]   P. Brusilovski, "Distributed Intelligent Tutoring on the Web". 8th World Conference of Artificial Intelligence in Education. IOS Press. pp.482-489, 1997.

[6]   A. Cordier, B. Mascret, A. Mille, Dynamic Case Based Reasoning for Contextual Reuse of Experience, Case-Based Reasoning Workshop, ICCBR 2010, Cindy Marling ed. Alessan-dria, Italy. pp. 69-78. 2010.

[7]   G. Constantino, D. Suthers and J-I. Icaza, Designing and Evaluating a Collaboration Coach: Knowledge and Reasoning, Proceedings of the Artificial Intelligence in Education, AI-ED, J.D. Moore et al (Eds). The Netherlands: IOS Press. pp. 176-187, 2001.

[8]   F. Corvaisier, Mille A., Pinon J.M., Radix 2, assistance la recherche d'information documentaire sur le web, In IC'98, Ingnierie des Connaissances, Pont--Mousson, France, INRIALORIA, Nancy, 1998.

[9]   M. Ennaji, H. Boukachour, P. Grav, Une architecture Multi-Agent pour la pedagogie de la formation distance, In: MOSIM 2006, Rabat, Maroc.

[10] E. M. En-Naimi, A. Zouhair, B. Amami, H. Boukachour, P. Person and C. Bertelle, "Intelligent Tutoring Systems Based on the Multi-Agent Systems (ITS-MAS): The Dynamic and Incremental Case Based Reasoning (DICBR) Paradigm and the Inverse Longest Common Sub-Sequence (ILCSS) in the CEHL", The IJCSI, Vol. 9, Issue 6, No 3, pp. 112-121, November 2012.

[11] C. Frasson, L. Martin, G. Gouarderes and E. Aïmeur, "A distance learning Architecture Based on Networked Cognitive Agents", 4ème International Conference on Intelligent Tutoring Systems- ITS'98, San Antonio, USA, 1998, Lecture Notes in Computer Sciences 1452, Apringer Verlag, pp. 142-151.

[12] B. Fuchs, J. Lieber, A. Mille and A. Napoli, "Une première formalisation de la phase d'élaboration du raisonnement à partir de cas", Actes du 14ième atelier du raisonnement à partir de cas, Besançon, mars, 2006. [see url : http://www.lab.cnrs.fr/RaPC2006/programme.html].

[13] K.J. Hammond, CHEF: a model of case-based planning, Proc. Of AAAI86, Morgan Kaufman, pp. 267-271, 1986.

[14] J. Kolodner, , Case-Based Reasoning, Morgan Kaufmann, San Mateo, UCA, 1993.

[15] P. Koton, Using experience in learning and problem solving, PhD Thesis, Laboratory of Computer Science, Massachusetts Instite of Technology, Cambridge Massachusetts, USA 1988.

[16] M. Likhachev, M. Kaess, and R.C. Arkin, Learning behavioral parameterization using spatiotemporal case-based reasoning, The IEEE international conference on robotics and automation (ICRA02), Washington, D.C, 2002.

[17] D. Leake and R. Sooriamurthi, When two case bases are better than one: Exploiting multiple case bases, In ICCBR, pp. 321335, 2001.

[18] S. Loriette-Rougegrez S., "Raisonnement à partir de cas pour les évolutions spatiotemporelles de processus", Revue internationale de géomatique , vol. 8, n° 1-2, 1998, p. 207-227.

[19] J-C. Marty and A. Mille, , Analyse de traces et personnalisations des environnements informatiques pour lapprentissage humain, Edition Lavoisier, 2009.

[20] C. Marling, M. Tomko, M. Gillen, D. Alexander, D. Chelberg, Case-based reasoning for planning and world modeling in the RoboCup small size league, in: Workshop on Issues in Designing Physical Agents for Dynamic Real-Time Environments: World Modeling, Planning, Learning, and Communicating (IJCAI), 2003.

[21] L. McGinty and B. smyth, Collaborative case-based reasoning: Applications in personalized route planning. In ICCBR, pp. 362–376, 2001.

[22] A. Mille, , From case-based reasoning to traces-based reasoning, Annual Reviews in Control30(2):223-232, ELSEVIER, ISSN 1367-5788. 2006.

[23] J. Piaget, Psychologie et pédagogie, Paris: Denol-Gonthier, 1969.

[24] I. Pinzón Cristian, B. Javier, F. Juan, M. Juan, B. Corchado, S-MAS: An adaptive hierarchical distributed multi-agent architecture for blocking malicious SOAP messages within Web Services environments, Expert Systems with Applications Volume 38, Issue 5, May 2011, pp. 5486-5499.

[25] E. Plaza and L. Mcginty, , Distributed case-based reasoning, The Knowledge Engineering, Review, Vol. 00:0, 14.c 2005, Cambridge University Press, 2005.

[26] M. Prassad, V. Lesser, and S. Lander, Retrieval and reasoning in distributed case bases. Technical report, UMass Computer Science Department, 1995.

[27] S. Ontañón and E. Plaza, Learning and Joint Deliberation through Argumentation in Multi-Agents Systems, in AAMAS'07 Proceedings of the 6th international joint conference on Autonomous agents and Multi-Agents systems, Honolulu, HI, USA, May 14-18, 2007.

[28] L. k. Soh and J. Luo, Combining individual and cooperative learning for multiagent negotiations, In Int. Conf. Autonomous Agents and Multiagent Systems AAMAS03, 2003.

[29] P. Tolchinsky, S. Modgil, U. Cortes, and M. Sanchez-marre, Cbr and argument schemes for collaborative decision making. In Conference on computational models of argument, COMMA-06 (Vol. 144, pp. 71–82), 2006.

[30] L-S., Vygotski, Mind in society: the development of higher psychological processes, Harvard University Press, Cambridge, MA, 1978.

[31] M. Vlachos, K. Kollios, and G. Gunopulos, Discovery similar multidimensional trajectories. The 18th International Conference on Data Engineering (ICDE02), pages 673–684, San Jose, CA, 2002.

[32] C. Webber and S. Pesty, , Emergence de diagnostic par formation de coalitions - Application au diagnostic des conceptions d'un apprenant, Journes Francophones pour l'Intelligence Artificielle Distribue et les Systmes Multi-Agents, Hermes, Lille, pp.45-57, 2002.

[33] F. Zehraoui, Systèmes d'apprentissage connexionnistes et raisonnement partir de cas pour la classification et le classement de séquences, Thèse de doctorat, Université Paris13, 2004.

[34] ZOUHAIR Abdelhamid, El Mokhtar EN-NAIMI, Benaissa AMAMI, Hadhoum BOUKACHOUR, Patrick PERSON, Cyrille BERTELLE, Intelligent Tutoring Systems Founded on The Multi-Agent Incremental Dynamic Case Based Reasoning, IEEE CIST'12, Fez, Morocco, 2012.

Abdelhamid ZOUHAIR is a PhD student in Cotutelle between the Laboratory LIST, FST of Tangier, Morocco and the Laboratory LITIS, the University of Le Havre, France, since September 2009.

El Mokhtar EN-NAIMI is a Professor in Faculty of Sciences and Technologies of Tangier, Department of Computer Science. He is a member of the Laboratory LIST (Laboratoire d'Informatique, Systèmes et Télécommunications), the University of Abdelmalek Essaâdi, FST of Tangier, Morocco. In addition, he is an associate member of the ISCN - Institute of Complex Systems in Normandy, the University of Le Havre, France.

Benaissa AMAMI is a Professor in Faculty of Sciences and Technologies of Tangier. He was an Ex-Director of the Laboratory LIST (Laboratoire d'Informatique, Systèmes et Télécommunications), the University of Abdelmalek Essaâdi, FST of Tangier, Morocco.

Hadhoum BOUKACHOUR and **Patrick PERSON** are Professors in the University of Le Havre, France. They are members in the Laboratory LITIS (Laboratoire d'Informatique, de Traitement de l'Information et Système), The University of le Havre, France.

Cyrille BERTELLE: Professor in Computer Science, Complex Systems Modelling and Simulation. Member of the Research Laboratory LITIS at the University of Le Havre, Normandy, France (RI2C Team). Co-founder of ISCN - Institute of Complex Systems in Normandy. Vice-President of Research and Development at University of Le Havre, France

## 17

Confidentiality of 2D Code using Infrared with Cell-level Error Correction

Nobuyuki Teraura[1] and Kouichi Sakurai[2]
[1] *Terrara Code Research Institute , Tokai, Japan*
[2] *Information Science and Electrical Enginerring, Kyushu University, Fukuoka, Japan*

Abstract — **Optical information media printed on paper use printing materials to absorb visible light. There is a 2D code, which may be encrypted but also can possibly be copied. Hence, we envisage an information medium that cannot possibly be copied and thereby offers high security. At the surface, the normal 2D code is printed. The inner layers consist of 2D codes printed using a variety of materials, which absorb certain distinct wavelengths, to form a multilayered 2D code. Information can be distributed among the 2D codes forming the inner layers of the multiplex. Additionally, error correction at cell level can be introduced.**

Keywords — **confidentiality, error correction, multilayer, 2D code .**

I. NTRODUCTION

THIS paper discusses the advancement of confidentiality by hiding information within an optical information medium based on a paper medium.

A. Background

In optical information media, one-dimensional codes (barcodes) and two-dimensional codes (2D codes) are used as information symbols. Since little data volume can be accommodated, a barcode is applicable when accommodating only identification numbers, such as product numbers. When accommodating comparatively many data, a 2D code is used. The same quantity of data can be printed within a smaller area, so 2D codes have found use in various fields. Moreover, a Web address can be accommodated by a 2D code, making it readable with a mobile cellular telephone. Thus, it is becoming easy for someone to read a 2D code and be guided to a Web site.

B. Motivation

The usual 2D code was developed for ease of reading, like in the abovementioned invocation of a Web site. However, the usual 2D code is not suitable for a use that requires confidentiality, like a credit card transaction. In particular, the usual 2D code is easy to copy, and the fact that the duplicate can be read instead the original is a great defect for such use.

C. Previous Work

In order to prevent reading by a third party, a 2D code that has a secret fill area has been developed [1]. Although this also has an open fill area that can be read as a normal 2D code, the secret fill area can only be read by a unit that possesses the encryption key.

For detecting a manipulation attack and forgery, inserting a digital watermark into a 2D code has been proposed [2]–[5]. Similarly, hiding input data by using steganography has been proposed [6]. Further, embedding data in the 2D code of a multi-stage barcode format by using spectrum spreading has been proposed [7]–[9].

Although a 2D code with the abovementioned secret fill area offers confidentiality and cannot be read by a third party, making a copy of the 2D code is easy. Since it is possible to make a copy that reads like the original, this remains a subject of concern in applications.

A 2D code with a digital watermark inserted can disclose a manipulation attack and forgery at the time of reading, and it can prevent data input. However, the content will probably be accessible to a third party and hence lack confidentiality.

D. Our Contribution

This paper considers improvements in confidentiality and copy protection, which are challenges faced by current optical information media. Furthermore, a basic configuration for a 2D code that solves these two problems simultaneously is proposed.

In the present research, a 2D code using ink that absorbs ordinary visible light is printed on the surface of a paper medium. Two or more 2D codes using inks that absorb different wavelengths of the infrared region are printed in a pile as the inner layers at the bottom, and so a multilayer 2D code is formed. A high degree of confidentiality is realized by distributing the information among the 2D codes forming the inner layers of the multiplex. The encoding table used for distributing information plays the role of an encryption key. The number of combinations for an encoding table is immense. In fact, decryption by a round-robin attack is impossible.

Copying a 2D code of such a configuration by using visible light is also impossible, since the inks of the inner layers are penetrated by visible light. Moreover, a third party who does not know the encoding table used for distributing the information cannot restore the original 2D code. Thus, a 2D code that simultaneously affords great confidentiality and copy protection is realizable. This enables its safe employment on theatre tickets, parking stubs, highway toll coupons, betting slips, etc.

E. Comparison with Related Work

In order to embed discriminable information visibly in a 2D code, an encoding of three bits is utilized. The encoding adds 1 bit of visual data to 2 bits of regular data and arranges these in the shape of an L character. A visual check is made of whether the data are correct [10]. An encoding table approach is proposed for encoding the module in the shape of the L character.

In the present research, the virtual 2D code that incorporates an actual data bit is distributed between two or more real 2D codes using an encoding table, and the pixels of the virtual 2D code are distributed as many small bits using an encoding table.

Whereas the related work mentioned above was aimed at the authentication of the 2D code through a visual inspection by a person, the present research is aimed at improvement of confidentiality through encryption by data variance.

F. Related Work on Identification using an Image

Information media and persons can be objects of automatic identifications using image data. As examples of information media that are identified from images there are barcodes and two-dimensional codes. The main aims of identifying a person are to maintain security and perform an authentication of the person. In the case of information media, such as a two-dimensional code, the data memorized according to the rule of the structure is read. However, the approach to identifying a person involves learning an individual characteristic beforehand and judging the degree of similarity to the person by comparing with the learned pattern. On occasions when the similarity is high, the algorithm will judge the person to be authentic. The body trait used for this identification can be a fingerprint [11], an iris [12], [13], the face [14], etc., and is put to practical use. Since these approaches use a biological feature of the person, they are called biometrics.

II. HIDING OPTICAL INFORMATION

A. Optical Information Media

Although optical information media were originally conceived for identification of alphanumeric characters, this was difficult with the processing capability in those days. Then, symbols representing characters were conceived for computing devices. Even though interpretation would be difficult for people, a symbol easily discerned by a computing device was conceivable. At a time when the microprocessor unit (MPU) had not quite been invented yet, the blue-eye code was devised. Then, the barcode as shown in Fig. 1 was invented with the advent of the MPU and the appearance of a one-dimensional linear sensor. Based on the class of data

(numbers, letters, symbols, etc.) accommodated in a barcode, various kinds of barcodes have been devised and currently are in practical use. Moreover, these follow an international standard fixed by the ISO/IEC.

Fig. 1. Examples of EAN-13 [15] and Code 39 [16].

A barcode contains information only in the transverse direction, not in the longitudinal direction. Thus, the lengthwise direction of the symbol functions to provide redundancy. When the central part cannot be read, due to dirt etc., it may be possible to read the upper or lower part instead. However, a large area was needed for printing, and there arose the problem that little data volume was contained. Although the barcode was initially put into practical use by encoding only identification, the need for memorizing a larger volume of data has gradually evolved.

The matrix type and stack type of 2D code, as shown in Figs. 2 and 3, were devised in order to meet that need. These have various characteristics, depending on the specific needs.

Fig. 2. QR code [17] and data matrix [18] as examples of the matrix type.

Fig. 3. PDF417 code [19] as an example of the stack type.

B. Security of 2D Code

The following are important for the security of a 2D code: confidentiality of data, impossibility of copying, and impossibility of forgery. The proposed scheme not only realizes confidentiality and copy protection but also prevents forgery.

C. Improvements in Confidentiality

The specifications of 2D codes, such as the QR code, are disseminated and readers are put on the market by assorted manufacturers. Nowadays, codes can also be read with a mobile cellular telephone. The 2D code provides confidentiality in comparison with characters, in that a person can see it but cannot understand it. However, for those who have a reader, the content can be read easily. In addition, the following two approaches are used to guarantee confidentiality: decryption at application level and decryption at system level.

Decryption at Application Level

The decryption at application level involves a system that performs data encryption with an application, creates a 2D code, and then performs data decryption with an application at the time of reading. Since it becomes impossible for a third party to interpret data without the decryption key, a guarantee of confidentiality is feasible. However, the facility to process both encryption and decryption is needed for every individual application, and there is the disadvantage of complexity.

Decryption at System Level

The decryption at system level involves both a system that performs data encryption with an application and a reader that performs data decryption using the encryption key chosen beforehand. A 2D code is created by the application to memorize the data encryption. This may include not only the case where all the storage areas are encryption data areas but also the case where the usual non-enciphering fill area combines with an encryption fill area. Although encryption with an application is required by this system, there is the advantage that decoding is unnecessary. Moreover, in the case of a non-enciphering fill area, reading as with a normal 2D code is possible. It can be said that decryption at system level enabled users easily to keep data secret from a third party.

D. Copy Protection

It is impossible to prevent copying of common optical information media. This is because the reading unit operates by receiving the waves reflected from the medium and a copying machine receives a reflection in the same way. Hence, for copy protection, a theoretically different system is required.

Incidentally, optical information media are very easy to reproduce. Thus, in the case of application to a credit card, the account number is not easily read by others, but uses of replicas cannot be prevented.

III. PHYSICAL PRINCIPLE

For secure optical information media, prevention of reading and protection from copying are important. Thus, an information hiding method for simultaneously realizing both objectives has been developed.

With the usual optical information media, as shown in Fig. 4, a wavelength of the visible light region is used for reading. Conversely, with multilayer optical information media, as shown in Fig. 5, there is a characteristic present so that wavelengths of the infrared light region can be used for reading. On materials that reflect infrared light (e.g., paper), a 2D code is printed using a material that absorbs infrared light as shown in Fig. 6. Therefore, a printed segment and unprinted segment that are irradiated with infrared light become possible to discriminate in a manner similar to that for black and white in visible light. Moreover, different segments can be printed using materials with different peak absorption wavelengths in the infrared light region as shown in Fig. 7. It thus becomes possible to acquire the image of a 2D code by using a luminous source that matches the absorption wavelength of each layer at the time of reading, even if the code is printed on top of a multilayer.

The 2D code is printed on the surface of the information medium in a material that transmits infrared light but absorbs visible light. Since only a superficial 2D code can be seen when this configuration is irradiated with visible light, it becomes impossible to copy a lower layer.

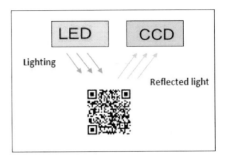

Fig. 4. Principle for reading an optical information medium.

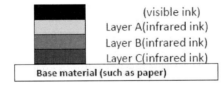

Fig. 5. Multilayer structure.

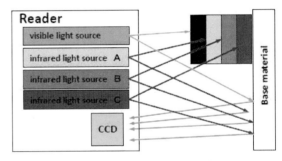

Fig. 6. Principle for reading an optical information medium.

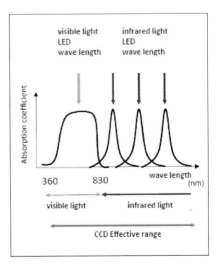

Fig. 7. Light absorption wavelengths of optical multilayer.

IV. PROPOSED SECURITY SYSTEM

As mentioned above, copy protection is realized by the hardware for the information media. In multilayer optical information media with the prescribed structure, the number of layers and the absorption wavelengths of the printing materials are used as the means of confidentiality. The information is memorized by distributing it among two or more layers. The confidentiality of the data is realized by introducing an information variance into the hardware configuration.

Various software approaches to confidentiality may be followed. Here, application of the visual secret sharing scheme is examined. With the visual secret sharing scheme the original image is disassembled into two or more images. Consequently, the image data cannot be identified through human vision unless those images are superposed.

In the decryption of a 2D code, the image (symbol) identification is done by image sensors, so the image editing and identifying capabilities of humans cannot be used. However, since the image sensing capability of an image sensor is greater than that of a human, this identification approach is employed profitably.

A. Encryption and Decoding at Cell Level

A data distribution at cell level is realized by distributing the monochrome data of the original 2D code among the 2D codes of the inner layers. For example, the case of three inner layers shown in Fig. 8 will be examined. The data distribution follows the logical table listed as Table I. Four alternative data encodings are possible for white and black, respectively. These are chosen with a random number.

Fig. 8. Distribution to each layer.

TABLE I
CODING TABLE

Coding			Decoding
W	W	W	B
W	W	B	W
W	B	W	W
W	B	B	B
B	W	W	W
B	W	B	B
B	B	W	B
B	B	B	W

W:White   B:Black

Even if a third party is able to read all three of the inner layers, decryption is impossible unless the logical table used for the encoding is known. For three inner layers, there are eight merged colors to distribute, from white-white-white to black-black-black, and four of these are chosen for black (or white). The number of encoding tables is $_8C_4$, which becomes 70.

When the number of inner layers, N, is equal to n, the number of hue combinations to distribute, D, is

$$D = 2^n. \tag{1}$$

Since the black (white) half is chosen from these combinations, the number of cell encoding tables, T_S, is

$$T_S(n) = DCD/2 = (2^n)C(2^{n-1}). \tag{2}$$

The number of encoding tables for each number of inner layers is listed in Table II. This is introduced here in order to apply several different encoding tables to each cell. The number of different encoding tables is denoted by L.

TABLE II
NUMBER OF ENCODING TABLES

N	T_S			
	L = 1	L = 2	L = 4	L = 8
1	2	4	8	16
2	6	36	12966	1.68E+08
3	70	4900	2.4E+07	5.76E+14
4	12870	1.65E+08	2.74E+16	7.53E+32
5	6.01E+08	3.61E+17	1.30E+35	1.70E+70

Since a layout is chosen with a random number, the inner layers that carry out a cell distribution may become a hue layout that is greatly inclined toward black or white. In that case, since identification of an optical cell becomes difficult, filtering to generate a uniform layout of white and black is needed. However, in the subcell distribution described below, white and black are represented by a subcell that undergoes the same number of occurrences for each, and so this polarization is corrected.

B. Encryption and Decoding at Subcell Level

A data distribution (information hiding) at subcell level is realized by dividing a cell into several squares (subcells) and distributing those bits among the subcells of the inner layers as shown in Fig. 9.

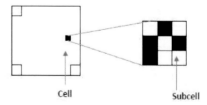

Fig. 9. Units of cell and subcell.

There exist both a horizontal manner and a vertical manner for data distribution at subcell level. For a horizontal distribution system as shown in Fig. 10, after first distributing a cell among the cells of an inner layer, the subcells of the same layer are made to redistribute the distributed cell. Conversely, for a vertical distribution system as shown in Fig. 11, after first distributing a cell among virtual subcells, the subcells of the same layer are made to redistribute the distributed subcells.

Fig. 10. Horizontal distribution.

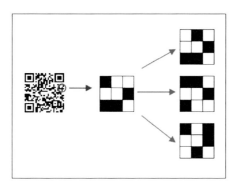

Fig. 11. Vertical distribution.

Here, we argue by using the horizontal manner of distribution for the case in which the number of inner layers is three, and so a cell is decomposed into 3 × 3 subcells. Moreover, in order to employ the same number of white and black subcells, have symmetry, and make identification of a subcell easy, a central subcell is removed from an encoding area and is always considered white. Then, the number of subcells is set to eight. The distribution to the subcells of a cell is performed using the distribution table (encoding table) listed as Table III. This is the same as the case of the previous cell distribution.

TABLE III
CODING TABLE

Coding								Decoding
B	B	B	B	W	W	W	W	B
B	B	B	W	B	W	W	W	W
B	B	B	W	W	B	W	W	W
B	B	B	W	W	W	B	W	B
B	B	B	W	W	W	W	B	W
B	B	W	B	B	W	W	W	B
...								B
W	W	W	W	B	B	B	B	W

W:White B:Black

The number of hue combinations to distribute is $_8C_4$ (i.e., 70). Since these 70 are assigned equally to black and white, the number of bit encoding tables, T_B, becomes

$$T_B = {_{75}C_{35}} \doteqdot 1.12 \times 10^{20}. \tag{3}$$

In general, the bit count to distribute is M^2. When the number M^2 is even, the number of hue combinations to distribute, D, becomes

$$D = (M^2)C(M^2/2), \tag{4}$$

Since these combinations are assigned equally to black and white, the number of bit encoding tables, T_B, becomes

$$T_B = DCD/2$$
$$= ((M^2)C(M^2/2))C((M^2)C(M^2/2) / 2). \tag{5}$$

Moreover, since a central subcell is eliminated from an encoding area when the number M^2 is odd, the number of blacks, B, becomes

$$B = M^2 - 1. \tag{6}$$

Since the black (white) half is chosen, the number of hue combinations of a subcell, D, becomes

$$D = {_BC_{B/2}}. \tag{7}$$

Since these combinations are assigned equally to black and white, the number of encoding tables, T_B, becomes

$$T_B = {_DC_{D/2}}. \tag{8}$$

For M from 1 to 3, the number of hue combinations, D, and the number of encoding tables, T_B, are listed in Table IV.

TABLE IV
NUMBER OF ENCODING TABLES

TABLE IV
NUMBER OF ENCODING TABLES

M	T_B
1	2
2	20
3	1.12E+20

C. Number of Effective Encoding Tables

When the extent of the target 2D code is small and there are few cells, the rule used for the encoding is evident in many of the encoding tables, and so the number of effective encoding tables can be considered to decrease.

If the case of $M = 3$ is examined, the hue combinations amount to 224. Thus, when the cells exceed this number, the previous argument holds. In the case of a cell size of not more than 15×15, if the number of cells is set to j, the number of effective encoding tables becomes $_jC_{j/2}$

V. VERIFICATION OF PROPOSED SECURITY SYSTEM

When the number of layers N increases, the number of combinations of cell distributions and subcell distributions (horizontal or vertical) will increase. Here, the number of combinations in the case of the encoding table is examined in the cases of from one to three layers and in the general case of n layers. When the number of inner layers is set to N and the number of subcell distributions is set to M^2, the distribution state can be expressed as $P(N, M)$. Below, the number of cases in a distribution is examined using this expression.

A. In the Case of $N = 1$

Since there is one inner layer in the case of $N = 1$, there is no distribution to the orientation of an inner layer and only a horizontal subcell variance is possible, as shown in Fig. 12.

Fig. 12. The case $N = 1$.

If the number of encoding tables for a subcell distribution is set to $T_B(M)$, the number of cases becomes

$$P(1, M) = T_B(M). \quad (9)$$

This is equal to the number of encoding tables for a subcell distribution.

B. In the Case of $N = 2$

In the case of $N = 2$ there are two kinds of distributions, as shown in Fig. 13. The first distribution is one in which a horizontal subcell distribution of each cell is carried out after performing a cell variance. The other distribution is one in which a vertical subcell distribution is carried out.

Fig. 13. The case $N = 2$.

If the number of cases at the ith subcell of a virtual cell is set to $S(k)$, the total number of cases is obtained as follows:

$$\begin{aligned} P(2, M) &= S(1) + S(2), \\ S(1) &= T_S(2) \cdot T_B(M), \quad (10) \\ S(2) &= T_B(M) \cdot T_S(2). \end{aligned}$$

Here, the encoding table of the subcell distribution is assumed identical for each layer. Hereinafter, the same is true.

C. In the Case of $N = 3$

In the case of $N = 3$ there are four kinds of distributions, as shown in Fig. 14. A characteristic is that not only the horizontal subcell distribution and vertical subcell distribution appear but also the pair in combination.

The number of cases is obtained as follows:

$$\begin{aligned} P(3, M) &= S(1) + S(2) + S(3), \\ S(1) &= T_B(M) \, T_S(3), \\ S(2) &= 2T_S(2) \, T_S(2) \, T_B(M), \quad (11) \\ S(3) &= T_S(3) \, T_B(M). \end{aligned}$$

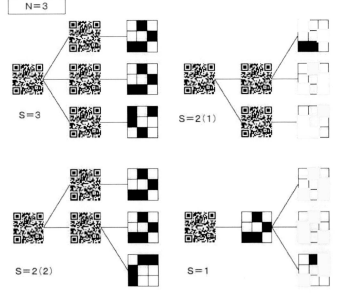

Fig. 14. The case $N = 3$.

D. In the Case of $N = n$

The general case of $N = n$ cannot be illustrated like the examples above, but it can be evaluated. If k is the number of virtual cells, the number of cases is obtained as follows:

$$P(n,M) = \Sigma\, S(k)$$
$$= \Sigma\, E(n,k) \cdot T_S(k) \cdot T_B(M). \qquad (13)$$

Here, $T_S(k)$ and $T_B(M)$ are given by (2) and (4), respectively, while $E(n,k)$ is a coefficient listed in Table V. The number of patterns is determined from the numbers for the case of one fewer layer and the case of one fewer layer with one fewer virtual cell. Therefore, the coefficient obeys the following recurrence formula:

$$E(n, k) = E(n-1, k-1) + E(n-1, k). \qquad (14)$$

TABLE V
COEFFICIENT VALUES

	E(n,k)					
n	1	2	3	4	5	6
1	1					
2	1	1				
3	1	2	1			
4	1	3	3	1		
5	1	4	6	4	1	
6	1	5	10	10	5	1

VI. CONFIDENTIALITY ESTIMATION

Based on the formula given in the preceding section, the number of calculated encoding tables is listed in Table VI. The subcell distribution table and the table in which the cell encodings differ for each number of inner layers were calculated with the same table.

TABLE VI
NUMBER OF ENCODING TABLES

N	M		
	1(L=8)	2(L=8)	3(L=1)
1	128	1280	7.17E+21
2	3.36E+08	3.36E+09	1.88E+28
3	1.15E+15	1.15E+16	6.45E+34
4	1.50E+33	1.50E+34	8.43E+52
5	3.40E+70	3.40E+71	1.90E+90

This result means that for $N = 1$, $M = 3$, and $L = 1$, or for $N = 3$, $M = 1$, and $L = 8$, the configuration is easily realized and is effective. Furthermore, the number of cases increases

with an encoding table, so the number of subcell slices, M, is large and confidentiality becomes great. However, a subcell image becomes difficult for a person to read, because its resolution falls. Thus, confidentiality and legibility form the basis of a trade-off in terms of M.

VII. INTRODUCTION OF ERROR CORRECTING CODE

The size of the subcells introduced above is comparatively small, and so the possibility of a mistaken reading as a result of dirt or other blemishes on the 2D code is larger than with a regular cell. Accordingly, we now discuss the introduction of an error-correction function for the data in the subcells.

A. Extended Hamming Code

A Hamming code corresponding to the whole number m is constituted with a code length $n = 2^m - 1$ and data length $k = n - m$. The data length is the bit count of the original data, and the code length is the bit count of the whole code that is generated. Furthermore, an extended Hamming code has a parity bit added, in order to distinguish between 1- and 2-bit errors.

In the case of $m = 3$, each eight bits consists of four data bits, three error-correction bits, and one parity bit. We now discuss performing error correction using this 8-bit extended Hamming code.

TABLE VII
EXAMPLE OF AN EXTENDED HAMMING CODE

DATA BITS				CORRE CTION			PAR ITY	DATA BITS				CORRE CTION			PAR ITY
0	0	0	0	0	0	0	0	1	0	0	0	1	0	1	1
0	0	0	1	0	1	1	1	1	0	0	1	1	1	0	0
0	0	1	0	1	1	0	1	1	0	1	0	0	1	1	0
0	0	1	1	1	0	1	0	1	0	1	1	0	0	0	1
0	1	0	0	1	1	1	0	1	1	0	0	0	1	0	1
0	1	0	1	1	0	0	1	1	1	0	1	0	0	1	0
0	1	1	0	0	0	1	1	1	1	1	0	1	0	0	0
0	1	1	1	0	1	0	0	1	1	1	1	1	1	1	1

The 3 × 3 subcell configuration has eight subcells because a central subcell is eliminated from the encoding area. We now consider layouts that correspond to the bit array of the extended Hamming code listed in Table VII, where 0 and 1 represent opposite hues. During decryption, subcells with the same hue as the cell are assigned 0 while subcells of the opposite hue are assigned 1, and the extended Hamming code is checked. In this case, on the occasions that a subcell is incorrectly identified due to dirt or blemishes on the 2D code, errors in two subcells can be detected and those in one subcell can be corrected. In addition to this error checking at the subcell level, the 2D code has an error-correction function at the cell level. Thus, correction may occur even when not possible at the subcell level.

The encoding examples shown in Table VIII correspond to the extended Hamming code shown in Table VII.

Fig. 15. Images of 2D code.

TABLE VIII
ENCODING EXAMPLES CORRESPONDING TO
AN EXTENDED HAMMING CODE

Coding								Decoding
B	B	B	W	B	W	W	W	B
B	B	W	B	W	W	B	W	W
B	B	W	W	W	B	W	B	W
B	W	B	B	W	W	W	B	B
B	W	B	W	W	B	B	W	W
B	W	W	B	B	B	W	W	B
			...					...
W	W	W	B	W	B	B	B	W

W:White B:Black

B. Number of Encoding Tables

In the full encoding list, there are 14 lines (Table VIII gives 8 examples) in which four subcells become of the opposite hue. This is adopted as an encoding bit stream. Therefore, the number of encoding patterns D is

$$D = 14. \tag{15}$$

Then, T_B becomes

$$T_B = {}_D C_{D/2} = {}_{14} C_7$$
$$\doteqdot 1.7 \times 10^7. \tag{16}$$

This value is comparatively small in order to correspond with a round-robin attack. When two encoding tables are used ($L = 2$), T_B becomes

$$T_B \doteqdot 3.0 \times 10^{14}. \tag{17}$$

This result means that for $N = 1$, $M = 3$, and $L = 2$ the configuration is suitable for introduction of error correction.

VIII. EXAMPLE OF VERTICAL DISTRIBUTION

A detailed image of the 2D code that introduces the error-correction function using the extended Hamming code is shown in Fig. 15. The left-hand side is the 2D code before a data distribution, and the right-hand side is the image after the data distribution. A random number was used when encoding each cell of the original 2D code into subcells.

IX. CONSIDERATION OF PRACTICAL DIFFICULTIES

A. Anti-copying Prerequisites

This paper has discussed the prerequisites that the following three be kept secret: the contents of the inner layers of the 2D code, an infrared wavelength, and the encoding table at the time of data distribution. Therefore, if these pieces of information are known and printing material corresponding to the infrared wavelength is prepared, then creating a replica becomes possible, even though simple copying is impossible.

B. Printing Material and LEDs

The infrared absorption properties of the printing materials now on the market are insufficient to realize multilayer information media [23]. This is because the printing materials now offered have wavelength windows that are wide for absorption of infrared light, so multilayering is not easy. Hence, the development of a marking material with a narrow wavelength window for infrared absorption is expected.

Various LEDs that emit infrared rays have been developed, put on the market, and used for lighting. However, the wavelength range of their infrared light is limited, so infrared LEDs corresponding in wavelength to printing materials still are needed for multilayering.

C. Camera Shake and Focus

In a horizontal distribution, a cell is divided into small subcells and the data are distributed. In order to identify the small subcells, the picturized data need to reveal these as either white or black. However, at the time of image capture, the adjoining subcells of the image may overlap under the effect of camera shake and a clear image may not be obtained. Moreover, identification becomes impossible when the image is not assembled in sharp focus. Camera shake and resultant blurriness that do not pose a concern a cell level may pose a concern at subcell level.

D. Image Resolution

The reading unit of the present 2D code uses about 4 million CCD pixels. Assuming that image formation is carried out with one-quarter of the imaging device, this becomes 1 million pixels or 1000 pixels in each direction. Conversely, when each of the 50×50 cells in a 2D code is divided into nine, there will be only 150 bits in each direction. Hence, 6×6 pixels will generally be assigned to each bit. According to conventional wisdom, stable identification is possible when there are

3×3 pixels in the identification of a so-called atomic unit. Thus, in the identification of the subcells mentioned above, there will be sufficient image resolution.

X. CONCLUSION

In this paper, multilayer information media using inks that absorb infrared light were introduced, and information media that cannot be copied were proposed. By distributing data among layers, information media with a high degree of confidentiality are realizable. Indeed, the confidentiality has been verified, since combinations of the number of layers and the number of bit distributions that ensure good confidentiality were ascertained.

REFERENCES

[1] M. Hara, "Method for producing 2D code reader for reading the 2D code," US patent application 20090323959, by Denso Wave Inc., Patent and Trademark Office, 2009.

[2] J.-J. Shen and P.-W. Hsu, "A fragile associative watermarking on 2D barcode for data authentication," *Int. J. Network Security*, vol. 7, no. 3, pp. 301–309, Nov. 2008.

[3] L. Li, R.-L. Wang, and C.-C. Chang, "A digital watermark algorithm for QR code," *Int. J. Intell. Inform. Process.*, vol. 2, no. 2, pp. 29–36, 2011.

[4] F. Ming, H. Ye, and L. Hong, "A method of 2D BarCode anti-counterfeit based on the digital watermark," *J. Changsha Commun. Univ.*, vol. 24, no. 2, pp. 85–89, 2008.

[5] M. Sun, J. Si, and S. Zhang, "Research on embedding and extracting methods for digital watermarks applied to QR code images," *New Zealand J. Agric. Res.*, vol. 50, pp. 861–867, 2007.

[6] W.-Y. Chen and J.-W. Wang, "Nested image steganography scheme using QR-barcode technique," *Opt. Eng.*, vol. 48, no. 5, 057004, May 2009.

[7] N. Xiamu, H. Wenjun, W. Di, and Z. Hui, "Information hiding technique based on 2D barcode," *Acta Sci. Natur. Univ. Sunyatseni*, vol. 43, pp. 21–25, 2004.

[8] L. Xue, Y. Chao, L. Liu, and X. Zhang, "Information hiding algorithm for PDF417 barcode," in *Proc. 5th Int. Conf. Natural Computation (ICNC '09)*, Tianjian, 2009, vol. 6, pp. 578–581.

[9] Z. Bo and H. Jin, "Information hiding technique based on PDF417 barcode," *Comput. Eng. Design*, vol. 19, pp. 4806–4809, 2007.

[10] C. Fang and E.-C. Chang, "Securing interactive sessions using mobile device through visual channel and visual inspection," in *Proc. 26th Annu. Computer Security Appl. Conf. (ACSAC '10)*, Austin, TX, 2010, pp. 69–78.

[11] M. Jampour, M. M. Javidi, A. S. Nejad, M. Ashourzadeh, and M. Yaghoobi, "A new technique in saving fingerprint with low volume by using chaos game and fractal theory," *Int. J. Interact. Multimed. Artif. Intell.*, vol. 1, no. 3, pp. 28–32, 2010.

[12] V. L. Hidalgo, L. M. Garcia, and M. T. Lorenzo, "Iris recognition using the JavaVis library," *Int. J. Interact. Multimed. Artif. Intell.*, vol. 1, no. 1, pp. 43–48, 2008.

[13] M. F. Hurtado, M. H. Langreo, P. M. de Miguel, and V. D. Villanueva, "Biometry, the safe key," *Int. J. Interact. Multimed. Artif. Intell.*, vol. 1, no. 3, pp. 33–37, 2010.

[14] J. A. Dargham, A. Chekima, and E. G. Moung, "Fusing facial features for face recognition," *Int. J. Interact. Multimed. Artif. Intell.*, vol. 1, no. 5, pp. 54–60, 2012.

[15] *Information technology — Automatic identification and data capture techniques — EAN/UPC bar code symbology specification*, ISO/IEC 15420:2009.

[16] *Information technology — Automatic identification and data capture techniques — Code39 bar code symbology specification*, ISO/IEC 16388:2007.

[17] *Information technology — Automatic identification and data capture techniques — QR Code 2005 bar code symbology specification*, ISO/IEC 18004:2006.

[18] *Information technology — Automatic identification and data capture techniques — Data Matrix bar code symbology specification*, ISO/IEC 16022:2006.

[19] *Information technology — Automatic identification and data capture techniques — PDF417 barcode symbology specification*, ISO/IEC 15438:2006.

[20] R. Villan, S. Voloshynovskiy, O. Koval, and T. Pum, "Multilevel 2D bar codes: Towards high-capacity storage modules for multimedia security and management," *IEEE Trans. Inf. Forens. Security*, vol. 1, no. 4, pp. 405–420, 2006.

[21] N. Degara-Quintela and F. Perez-Gonzalez, "Visible encryption: Using paper as a secure channel," in *Proc. SPIE-IS&T Electronic Imaging 2003: Security and Watermarking of Multimedia Contents V*, Santa Clara, CA, 2003, vol. 5020, pp. 413–422.

[22] S. Ono, "Fusion of interactive and non-interactive evolutionary computation for two-dimensional barcode decoration," in *Proc. 2010 IEEE Congress on Evolutionary Computation (CEC)*, Barcelona, 2010, pp. 1–8.

[23] TOSCO Co. Available: http://www.tosco-intl.co.jp/cgibin/imgchemi/general_display_sensitive.php?id=85&code=SDA5677.

## 18

Engineering Education through eLearning technology in Spain

Juan Carlos Fernández Rodríguez[1], José Javier Rainer Granados[1], Fernando Miralles Muñoz[2]

[1]*Bureau Veritas Centro Universitario, Madrid, Spain.*
[2]*Universidad San Pablo CEU, Madrid, Spain*

Abstract — **eLearning kind of education is stirring up all the disciplines in the academic circles, especially since it provides an access to educational areas that are uneasy and traditionally in-person, such as Engineering. Even though it had an outbreak in some of the most prestigious American universities, eLearning has being a reality in Spain for some years now, changing educational and teaching habits. To ensure a proper education is not an easy task with it comes to engineering fields, therefore this article shows an update on the works developed on this issue and the technologies they used. In this report it is given a perspective of the intimate relationship between the eLearning method of learning and the studies of Engineering in Spain, through the TIC development and the current educational legislation. In this regard, teaching examples are given on several subjects of different engineering studies, emphasizing the good results obtained in the abovementioned experiences. Below here is a evaluation on the results obtained in the analyzed studies.**

Keywords — **eLearning, engineering, competencies, evaluation.**

I. INTRODUCTION

ROYAL Decree 1393/2007 establishes the new regulation on official university educations. Through this decree, the Spanish university system is integrated in the European Higher Education Area (EHEA). In accordance to this new model, there has been a major swift, going from a teaching model based in the transmission of knowledge directly from the professor, to a model based on acquiring different competencies and the alumni learning process. Engineering studies, both from a grade and postgraduate point of view, have not been an exception.

Concisely, a competency, in the engineering environment, refers to the activities the engineer must be able to perform, using the information, skills and tools required to accomplish his professional practice [1]. This way, an education based on competencies is referred basically to expected and visible performances, meaning analysis, synthesis and evaluation.

The necessary learning process is not oblivious to the present technological changes, the use of TIC has lead to a big leap in evolution of distance learning, creating the eLearning method of education. eLearning provides the opportunity to create virtual learning environments focused on the student, as EHEA demands. The aim of these virtual learning environments is to move the emphasis from the teaching to the learning [2].

These scenarios are characterized by being basically interactive, efficient, distributed and easily accessible. According Khan, quoted by Boneu [3], an ELearning scenario must consider eight facts: instructional design, educational model, technology, interface development, evaluation, management, support and use ethics. The platform in which the eLearning is developed is the software server responsible for the users management, courses management and communication services. These platforms are not isolated systems, given that they can rely on tools developed by third parties or on integrations developed by the designers or administrators.

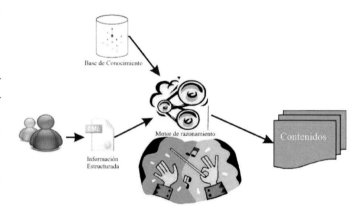

Fig.1. General Diagram of Contents Generation

eLearning can enhance some of the competencies that an engineer must develop, such as: identification, formulation and resolution of problems, the ability to design experiments or the ability to apply math, among others.

The specifications development, standard and tools regarding cognitive systems, ontologies and semantic maps are also helping in the formative systems enhacement.

In essence, the systems are based in showing some contents after receiving some request from the user. To this effect, the knowledge basis provides all the available information on this issue and some restrictions will select the definitive contents to show. Work on Intelligent Educational Systems (IESs) is traditionally divided into two main paradigms [4]: Intelligent Tutoring Systems (ITSs) [5] [6] and Adaptive Hypermedia Systems (AHSs) [7] [8].

According Caravantes and Galán [9], the essential part of the teaching-learning model is the educational domain, which is responsible for the stimuli generated toward the student to properly modify his cognitive state. All intelligent educational systems incorporate an educational domain that determines its scope and the process effectiveness. Usually the educational domain is divided into two parts: one represents the target knowledge of the learning process and is called domain model, and the other defines rules or procedures governing the process and is called the pedagogical/adaptive/operational model.

Teachers use the educational knowledge of a particular domain together with a meta-knowledge that encodes pedagogical skills for process controlling. This pedagogical knowledge represents instructional principles such as positive reinforcement, variability, action, etc., that facilitate the proper selection and sequencing of contents. It is a type of procedural knowledge based on Pedagogical Regulators (PRs) that controls the process, reading information from the emotional, characteristic and instructional domains. Common IESs implement an explicit pedagogical knowledge just as expert systems do using PRs called logical rules. However, there are other valid implicit representations such as neural networks, in which the PRs are called nodes, artificial neurons, and so on.

Learning content specifications like ADL-SCORM [10] or IMS-CC [11] are based on independent and interchangeable objects or packages that encode one or more ways to teach-learn something.

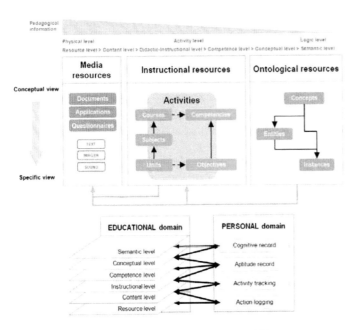

Fig.2. Levels of the educational knowledge representation [9].

Distance learning has usually made available to the student a set of continuous learning resources (documents, presentations, videos, animations and simulations) and discrete resources (texts, graphics, links and images) [12]. Resources are located at the lower material level of the educational knowledge structure to interact with the student to transfer knowledge. Educational resources are increasingly specified

by soft links [13] that allow them to be searched, filtered and selected from large and dynamic repositories using metadata such as type (exercise, questionnaire, diagram, graph, table, text...), format, language, difficulty, etc. (see IEEE-LOM).

In this article, we will go through some of the experiences performed in the engineering area from the eLearning point of view, since just from the beginning eLearning and engineering have got along very well. Due to this connection, engineering learning becomes a higher quality learning, therefore it provides engineering a wider coverage regarding its education and extension [14].

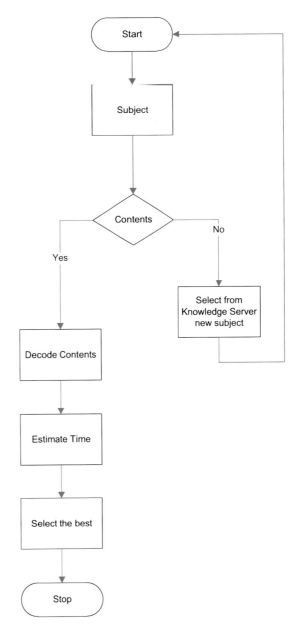

Fig. 3. General Diagram of Contents Management.

II. ELEARNING AND ENGINEERING

Engineering education has always been liked to attendance, especially because the help of a tutor easies the comprehension of the concepts and the assimilation of contents. It has been required the correct performance of the tools that integrate eLearning education in order to make sense out of engineering eLearning education. Therefore, the first works are somehow recent, as shown in some of the most important works, summarized below.

One of the first approaches in literature we can find was in 2000. In that year, there were already many American universities that would offer a wide range of courses with the eLearning teaching method [15], proving that, right from the start, eLearning was meant to become one of the strongest lines of high education.

Databases knowledge is one of the paramount subjects in the high courses of computer engineering. Back in 2006, and through the use of eLearning platforms, it was achieved not only to increase the motivations but to improve the academic results of the alumni in the Technical Engineering in Computer Managements and Systems in Gerona University [16]. The most relevant achievement of this study was the tool that auto corrects the exercises related to the subject. This tool allowed the professor to acknowledge the learning level of the students and realize their possible deficiencies. Also, there are significant gains for the students, since the passing rate increased around a 9%. This increase might be caused by a sizeable boost of students that have taken on tutorial classes on the course.

In courses like "Databases" and "Business and Commercial Management Techniques" the auto correcting system had a great acceptance both within alumni and teachers, saving the later a significant work load: having to correct several exercises [17].

A very important aspect of this learning method is all that is related with the use and development of tools that will allow us to evaluate the assignments of the students in every subject automatically. In other words, a field that refers to the application of the different information and communication technologies in order to establish learning platforms and environments to make to evaluation of the alumni easier.

This way, the Computer Based Assessment (CBA) represents one of the eLearning technologies, distinguished by the automation of every teaching/learning feature of the student, integrating advanced functions held jointly, i.e., correcting databases structure diagrams and related consults [18]. With this CBA, there is an interaction between teacher and student all along the evaluation process. In this process, the turn in of the course exercises, its correction and the feedback generated is performed by the system automatically.

Put this into practice, CBA has been used in educational subjects of the science/technical area, mainly in test or multiple choice questions, with a limited scenarios feedback. The reason of these limitations is the disaffection toward these kinds of questions, since they can be perceived as distant and only acceptable in some low cognitive leveled tasks, which require fixed answers.

With this tool (CBA), the author scored better academic results and a higher satisfaction on the environment developed in students of the Databases subject of the Technical Computer Management Engineer of the Gerona University.

One of the tools that contributes to improve the learning process in multimedia environments are the Learning Objects, which are digital resources based on the Web, whose main feature is they can be used and reused to support the learning. A Learning Object (LO) is the minimal learning unit that has sense by itself, regardless of the context. Furthermore, it is a unit with an educational content and reusable in its digital format. Since this format must be standardized, it can be reused in different platforms, ensuring its reusability and usefulness [19]. Among these digital resources you can incorporate images, videos or pre-recorded audios, small text pieces, animations, little Web apps or even entire Web sites combining texts, images and other communication media.

One good example of the reusability and usefulness of the Learning Objects is the one performed on the Industrial Engineer School of Vigo University. Through this action, it was expected to encourage and motivate the engineering learning of the alumni, even though it can be conducted in any other discipline [20]. The authors designed a learning pill (very short course the summarizes the main concepts of the subject) in order to use it as a tool the students must use before the master lectures, but due to the specific features of the learning pills, they can be reached and used at any time and any place, thanks to their free access. The learning pill was effectively used by the whole alumni and it was verified that it was used worldwide.

The incorporation of multimedia technology and eLearning education has been applied equally to the Project Direction learning [21]. These authors instituted the eLearning technology in the "Projects" subject on the Industrial Engineering degree at Escuela Politécnica Superior de Ingeniería in Gijón. In order to achieve this, in this occasion it was selected a platform different from the traditional ones, such as Moodle. In this case, Microsoft Sharepoint was used, a specific project management tool, favoring the approach of the teacher's work towards the professional environment. The experience, besides enhancing the cooperative work between students, contributed to preparing the alumni towards the analysis, evaluation and alternatives choice, leading them to an educated decision making, something of paramount importance in their future engineering works. Nowadays, the eLearning method is widely spread in Projects Direction and Management and programs exist in most of the Spanish universities.

In engineering teaching, on-line methodologies have also been applied for evaluation and formation in generic competences. In the Technical Computer Engineering School of the Universidad Politécnica de Madrid it has been developed a competence approach for the "Telecommunications History" and "Telecommunications Policy for the Information Society" subjects, which were given through the Moodle platform. It is worth mentioning that the chosen teaching method was bLearning which, unlike eLearning, it combines online contents with in-person given contents. The results, evaluated through an online survey to the alumni, were highly satisfactory, pointing out several technical aspects, mainly the simplicity in the use of the Moodle platform [22].

The eLearning app can be used in any kind of subject, being the Logic subject of Computer Engineering both a particular and relevant example of application of this educational method [23]. In the Computer Engineering degree at UOC (Universidad Abierta de Cataluña), there is this Basic Logics subject. Said subject has very low performance and very high abandon ratings and by the application of eLearning with the idea of improving these rates in mind, eLearning was implemented. The results scored may be considered as discreet, being the reduction in abandoning rate just a 5%, same as academic results improvement. It is important to point out that the measurement tools used to calculate these rates does not allow ensuring the reason of these changes is only the eLEarning based tool. The web sites of the tools have been developed using PHP for the server program, as well as HTML, CSS and Javascript. It is also worth mentioning that for the data lodging and abidance a MySQL database was used, granting an efficient session management.

The engineering laboratory practices have not been an exception on the eLearning educational method [24]. Particularly [25], the alumni were offered in their programming practices to use robots with eLearning method. In said practices, the student could book the robot for 30 minutes, and download and execute the program, being able to visualize it through an IP camera. Meanwhile, the web server was programmed to offer use statistics.

This project constantly seeks for the flexibility, therefore searches for a system design that is easily adaptable to any kind of experiment where the student used to utilize hardly reachable hardware, along making the high costs of an industrial robot profitable.

The main thing is that the learning curve is ascendant, even if it is the student who adjusts the intensity, leading to cases where the performance of the student behaves as shown in the following figure. The figure initials correspond to IN: I, initial phase of the course and E, end of the course.

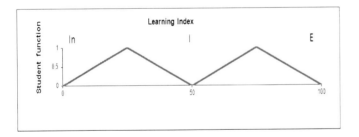

Fig. 4. Learning intensity along the course.

In a similar line [26], two traditional Systems and Automatic Engineering laboratories (three tanks control system and robot programming) of different universities have been transformed into two virtual and remote laboratories. This way, students can perform their lab exercises virtually, organized by an automatic booking system. The experience evaluation, gathered by a survey to the alumni, pointed out the achievement of an elevated satisfaction rate, existing among the students a high rate of motivation to use the technology in their learning activities.

III. CONCLUSION

In every experience analyzed in the present article is possible to detect the efficiency of the eLearning educational method in all the Engineering areas. In the abovementioned projects and their corresponding evaluations, is obvious the good results scored and the satisfaction of the students. The alumni feedback is very important for every learning method, through a satisfaction survey or test, but especially in this kind of method, since the student judges only the knowledge he has acquired, withdrawing any personal relationship he may have with his tutor, which can get even closer that in-person classes.

When it comes to eLearning education, the behavior of the system relies mainly in two factors: architecture and contents. In every cases previously analyzed, both factors are combined. The potential of these systems increases remarkably when Artificial Intelligence techniques are integrated, leading the system to a teacher-cognitive system combination that ensures not only the contents transmission but the proper choice of content within the wide knowledge database, supported by teaching techniques that permit an effective contents transmission as well as a certain knowledge acquisition.

Therefore it seems to be proof enough to state the validity of eLearning when it regards to engineering, as The American Accreditation Board for Engineering and Technology (ABET) claims [27]. Accordingly, not only the students score better results, but there is a possible chance to widely extend the education while cutting expenses, two important features when it comes to practice subjects to perform in laboratories.

However, there is a certain lack of more specific experiences, with a better educational design, and a lack of experiences that affect the paramount subjects of every engineering university title, both degree and masters. Besides, it would be convenient to expand the evaluation to teachers and apply a more severe criteria to evaluate de possible academic scores improvement, establishing the criteria required in order to ensure the students the correct acquisition of competencies.

Also it would be desirable a future research on the feelings of the student towards his presence and involvement in certain subjects and the improvements this might bring, being this an aspect where is pivotal the development and application of every multimedia technology available.

REFERENCES

[1] M. Duque, "Competencias, aprendizaje activo e indagación: un caso práctico en ingeniería". Revista de Educación en Ingeniería, 2, 2006, pp.7-18.

[2] J.E. Silva, "Diseño y moderación de entornos virtuales de aprendizaje". Barcelona: UOC, 2011.

[3] J.M. Boneu, "Plataformas abiertas de e-learning para el soporte de contenidos educativos abiertos". Revista de Universidad y Sociedad del Conocimiento (RUSC), (4) 1, 2007, pp. 36-47.

[4] A. Nicholas, B. Martin. "Merging adaptive hypermedia and intelligent tutoring systems using knowledge spaces". Adaptive Hypermedia (AH2008), 2008, pp. 426–430

[5] T. Murray. "Authoring Intelligent Tutoring Systems: An analysis of the state of the art". International Journal of Artificial Intelligence in Education, 98, 1999, pp. 98-129.

[6]   E. Wenger. "Artificial Intelligence and Tutoring Systems: Computational and Cognitive approaches to the communication of knowledge". San Francisco, USA, Morgan Kaufman, 1987.

[7]   P. Dolog. "Designing Adaptive Web Applications". In SOFSEM 2008: Theory and Practice of Computer Science, pp. 23-33.

[8]   P. Brusilovsky. "Methods and techniques of adaptative hypermedia". User Modeling and User Adapted Interaction, Special issue on adaptive hypertext and hypermedia, 6 (2-3), 1996,pp-87-129.

[9]   A. Caravantes y R. Galán. "Generic educational knowledge for adaptive and cognuitive systems". Educational Technology & Society, 14 (3), 2011, pp-252-266.

[10] ADL. "Sharable Content Object Reference Model (SCORM)". Retrieved June December, 11, 2012, from http://www.adlnet.gov/Technologies/scorm/default.aspx.2004.

[11] IMS. "Common Cartridge Specications". Retrieved December, 12, 2012, from http://www.imsglobal.org/cc. 2008.

[12] K. Verbert, E. Duval.. "Towards a Global Component Architecture for Learning Objects: A Comparative Analysis of Learning Object Content Models". World Conference on Educational Multimedia, Hypermedia and Telecommunications 2004, pp. 202–208.

[13] P Brusilovsky, N. Henze, N." Open corpus adaptive educational hypermedia. Adaptive Web 2007" (AW2007). pp. 671–696. Heidelberg: Springer.

[14] J. Bourne, D. Harris and F. Mayadas, (Janaury, 2005) "Online Engineering Education: Learning Anywhere, Anytime". Journal of Engineering Education. (94) 1, pp. 131-146 Avaible http://digitalcommons.olin.edu/facpub_2005/1.

[15] R. Ubell. "Engineers turn to e-Learning". IEEE Spectrum, 37, 2000, pp. 59-63.

[16] J. Soler, F. Prados, I. Boada and J. Pocho. "Utilización de una plataforma eLearning en la docencia de bases de datos". In Actas de las XII Jornadas de la Enseñanza Universitaria de la Informática, JENUI. Bilbao, 2006, pp. 581-586.

[17] J. Soler, I. Boada, F. Prados, J. Poch and F. Fabregat. "Experiencia docente en diseño de bases de datos con la ayuda de herramientas de eLearning" In Actas de las XII Jornadas de la Enseñanza Universitaria de la Informática, JENUI. Barcelona, pp. 63-70

[18] J. Soler. "Entorno virtual para el aprendizaje y la evaluación automática en bases de datos". Doctoral Thesis. University of Gerona, Spain, 2010.

[19] J.C. Fernández, J.J. Rainer and F. Miralles. "Aportaciones al diseño pedagógico de entornos tecnológicos eLearning". Madrid, Lulu, 2012.

[20] R.Maceiras, A. Cancela and V. Goyanes. "Aplicación de Nuevas Tecnologías en la Docencia Universitaria". Formación Universitaria (3) 1, 2010, pp. 21-26.

[21] J.M. Mesa, J.V. Álvarez, J.M. Villanueva and F.J. de Cos. "Actualización de métodos de enseñanza-aprendizaje en asignaturas de Dirección de Proyectos de Ingeniería". Formación Universitaria (1) 4, 2008, pp. 23-28.

[22] R. Herradón, J. Blanco, A. Pérez and J.A. Sánchez.). "Experiencias y metodologías "bLearning" para la formación y evaluación en competencias genéricas en Ingeniería". La Cuestión Universitaria, 3, 2009, pp. 33-45.

[23] M. Hertas, E. Mor and A. Guerrero-Roldan. "Herramienta de apoyo para el aprendizaje a distancia de la Lógica en Ingeniería Informática". Revista de Educación a Distancia, 24, 2010, pp. 1-10.

[24] L. Gomes and J. García-Zubia. "Advances on remote laboratories and eLearning experiences". Bilbao, Universidad de Deusto, 2007.

[25] Rosado, Muñoz-Marí and Magdalena. "Herramienta eLearning para la programación de robots mediante entorno web". Revista d´Innovació Educativa, 1, 2008, pp. 45-48.

[26] H. Vargas, J. Sánchez, C.A. Jara, F.A. Candelas, O. Reinoso and J.L. Díez. "Docencia en automática. Aplicación de las TIC a la realización de actividades prácticas a través de Internet". Revista Iberoamericana de Automática e Informática Industrial, (7) 1, 2010, pp. 35-45.

[27] ABET, Acreditation Board for Engineering and Technology. "Acreditation policy and procedure manual". USA, Engineering Accreditation Commission Publication, 2009.

## 19

BROA: An agent-based model to recommend relevant Learning Objects from Repository Federations adapted to learner profile

[1,2]Paula A. Rodríguez, [1,2]Valentina Tabares, [2]Néstor D. Duque, [1]Demetrio A. Ovalle, [3]Rosa M. Vicari

[1]*Departamento de Ciencias de la Computación y la Decisión*, Universidad Nacional de Colombia-Medellín, Colombia

[2]*Departamento de Informática y Computación*, Universidad Nacional de Colombia-Manizales, Colombia

[3]*Instituto de Informática*, Universidade Federal do Rio Grande do Sul, Brasil

Abstract — **Learning Objects (LOs) are distinguished from traditional educational resources for their easy and quickly availability through Web-based repositories, from which they are accessed through their metadata. In addition, having a user profile allows an educational recommender system to help the learner to find the most relevant LOs based on their needs and preferences. The aim of this paper is to propose an agent-based model so-called BROA to recommend relevant LOs recovered from Repository Federations as well as LOs adapted to learner profile. The model proposed uses both role and service models of GAIA methodology, and the analysis models of the MAS-CommonKADS methodology. A prototype was built based on this model and validated to obtain some assessing results that are finally presented.**

Keywords — **Artificial Intelligent in Education, GAIA, Learning objects repository federations, MAS–CommonKADS, Multi-agent Systems, Student-centered recommender systems**

I. INTRODUCTION

THE growth of digital information, high-speed computing, and ubiquitous networks has allowed for accessing to more information and thousands of educational re-sources. This fact has led to the design of new teaching-learning proposals, to share educational materials, and also to navigate through them [1]. Learning Objects (LOs) are distinguished from traditional educational resources for their easy and quickly availability through Web-based repository, from which they are accessed through their metadata. In order to maximize the number of LOs to which a student could have access, to support his/her teaching-learning process, digital repositories have been linked through centralized repository federations sharing in this way educational resources and accessing resources from others [2]. LOs must be tagged with metadata so that they can be located and used for educational purposes in Web-based environments [3]. Recommender systems are widely used online in order to assist users to find relevant information [4]. Having a user profile allows a recommender system to help the student to find the most

relevant LOs based on the student's needs and preferences. Intelligent agents are entities that have sufficient autonomy and intelligence to be able to handle specific tasks with little or no human supervision [5]. These agents are currently being used almost as much as traditional systems, making it a good choice to solve problems where autonomous systems are required and thus they work not only individually but also cooperate with other systems to achieve a common goal. The aim of this paper is to propose a model for LO searching, retrieving, recommendation, and evaluator modeled through the paradigm of multi-agent systems from repository federations. For doing so, the searching process needs a query string that is entered by the user and a similar relevance user profile according to the student's learning style (LS). The LO searching process is performed using local and remote repositories, or repository federations, that are accessible via web along with LO descriptive metadata. Since LO Repositories (LORs) are distributed, are different in design and structure, and not handle the same metadata standards. There is also a coordinator to be responsible for directing the search to different repositories according to their characteristics. The recommendation is made through collaborative filtering, searching for a similar profile to the user who is doing the quest to deliver a user pair LOs evaluated positively.

The rest of the paper is organized as follows: Section 2 outlines main concepts involved in this research. Section 3 describes some related works to the model pro-posed. Section 4 introduces the multi-agent model proposal based on both role and service models of GAIA methodology, and the analysis models of the MAS-CommonKADS methodology. A validation of the system's operation can be visualized is shown in Section 5. Finally, conclusions and future work are presented in Section 6.

II. BASIC CONCEPTS

A. Learning objects, repositories and federations

According to the IEEE, a LO can be defined as a digital

entity involving educational design characteristics. Each LO can be used, reused or referenced during computer-supported learning processes, aiming at generating knowledge and competences based on student's needs. LOs have functional requirements such as accessibility, reuse, and interoperability [6][7]. The concept of LO requires understanding of how people learn, since this issue directly affects the LO design in each of its three dimensions: pedagogical, didactic, and technological [7]. In addition, LOs have metadata that describe and identify the educational resources involved and facilitate their searching and retrieval. LORs, composed of thousands of LOs, can be defined as specialized digital libraries storing several types of resources heterogeneous, are currently being used in various e-learning environments and belong mainly to education-al institutions [8]. Federation of LORs serve to provide educational applications of uniform administration in order to search, retrieve, and access specific LO contents available in whatever of LOR groups [9].

B. Recommender Systems

Recommender systems are aimed to provide users with search results close to their needs, making predictions of their preferences and delivering those items that could be closer than expected [10],[11]. In the context of LOs these systems seeks to make recommendations according to the student's characteristics and its learning needs. In order to improve recommendations, recommender systems must perform feedback processes and implement mechanisms that enable them to obtain a large amount of information about users and how they use the LOs [2],[12].

C. Multi-Agent Systems

Agents are entities that have autonomy in order to perform tasks by achieving their objectives without human supervision. The desirable characteristics of the agents are as follows [13]: **Reactivity**: they respond promptly to perceived changes in their environment; **Proactivity**: agents can take initiative; **Cooperation and Coordination:** they perform tasks communicating with other agents through a common language; **Autonomy**: agents do not require direct intervention of humans to operate; **Deliberation**: they perform reasoning processes to make decisions, **Distribution of Tasks**: each agent has definite limits and identified the problems to be solved; **Mobility**: they can move from one machine to another over a network; **Adaptation:** depending on changes in their environment they can improve their performance, and **Parallelism**: agents can improve performance depending on changes in their environment.

Multi-agent Systems (MAS) are composed of a set of agents that operate and interact in an environment to solve a specific and complex problem. This paradigm provides a new way of analysis, design, and implementation of complex software systems and has been used for the development of recommender systems [14].

D. Student Profile

The student profile stores information about the learner, its characteristics and preferences, which can be used to obtain search results according to its specificity. To handle a user profile can be used to support a student or a teacher in the LO selection according to its personal characteristics and preferences [14]. Gonzalez et al. [15] include in the student profile contextual characteristics that can be seen as transient values that are associated with environmental changes during one student's learning system session along with different physical and technological variables. Duque (2009) presents a combination of VARK y FSLSM models with good results to characterize the students profile and thus, provide students with learning materials tailored to their specific learning styles [16].

III. RELATED WORKS

Morales et al. (2007) present an architecture based on the multi-agent paradigm to identify and retrieve relevant LOs using the information request supplied by the user. In addition, this proposal includes aspects related to quality of LOs which are specified within their semantic description to improve the LO selection [17]. Authors propose a multi-agent architecture to retrieve LOs, however they do not use student cognitive characteristics such as learning styles in order to make recommendations.

Gerling (2009) proposes an intelligent system to assist a user in finding appropriate LO, according to the search's subject by using the user profile which takes into account its characteristics, preferences, and LO *relative importance*. The recommender system incorporates an intelligent agent in order to retrieve educational resources on the Web, considering student's learning style [18]. However, the system's design only considers the utilization of one intelligent agent.

Duque (2009), in his doctoral thesis, proposes a multi-agent system for adaptive course generation. The system is composed of several intelligent agents: an agent for the student profile information; a domain agent, having the structure of the virtual course and the teaching material (TM); a HTN planner agent, and finally, a TM recovery agent which makes the process of TM search and retrieval [16]. This work focuses on creating customized virtual courses taking into account student's learning styles; however, it does not focus on LOs.

Prieta (2010) proposes a multi-agent architecture for the process of search and retrieval of LO in distributed repositories. An additional functionality is provided to the system is making the LORs statistics on the number of results found and response time, then make future consultations in the LORs rated [19]. This system offers neither recommendations to the user nor customized searches based on the LO metadata. Casali (2011) presents an architecture and implementation of a recommender system prototype based on intelligent agents, whose goal is to return an ordered list of the most appropriate LOs according to the parameters that characterizes the user profile, language preferences and the interaction degree that the user wants to have with the LO. The search is performed in repositories having descriptive LO metadata which involves educational characteristics [14]. The main limitation of this research is that although some student characteristics are considered into the user profile the user learning styles were not taken into account.

IV. MODEL PROPOSED

BROA (Spanish acronym for Learning Object Search, Retrieval & Recommender System) is a multi-agent system for searching, retrieving, recommendation and evaluator of LO, according to a search string entered by the user. The LOs resulting from the search are recommended based on the student's style of learning and other users' assessments. The Web-based LO search is performed over local and remote repositories, or by using LO repository federations through metadata descriptive LOs. Considering that LORs are distributed, they are different in design and structure, and hence they do not handle the same metadata standards. BROA was built under the MAS approach in order to exploit their advantages as follows: the *Parallelism of Tasks* for simultaneously searching in both local and remote LOR, the *Deliberation* ability for making decisions on which of LORs must perform the search and for performing user recommendations; *Cooperation*, *Coordination* and *Distribution* of tasks among agents by clearly identifying the problems to be solved by each agent and to define its limits. In our model each agent knows how LOs are stored and how each LO can be searched, accessed, and retrieved.

A. *Development Methodology*

There are different kinds of methodologies for modeling MAS, such as GAIA characterized for analyzing and designing agent-oriented systems. The main key concepts of GAIA are the following: roles, which are associated with responsibilities, permissions, activities, and protocols [5]. Another well-known MAS design methodology is MAS-CommonKADS proposed by Iglesias in his doctoral thesis [20] which integrates knowledge and software engineering along with object-oriented protocols. An integration of both methodologies was used in order to model the BROA system. The following is a brief description of each of these models: *Role Model* (GAIA): Allows the system designer to identify the expected functions of each of the entities that composes the system (goals, responsibilities, capabilities, and permissions). *Service Model* (GAIA): This model identifies all the services associated with each of the roles, its inputs, outputs, pre-conditions, and post-conditions. *Agent Model*: Describes the characteristics of each agent, specifying name, kind of agent, role, description, skills, services, activities, and goals. According to the GAIA methodology an agent can play several roles as shown in Figure 1, thus, a changing role diagram must be used in this case. *Task Model:* This model describes all the tasks that agents can perform along with the objectives of each task, its decomposition, and troubleshooting methods to solve each objective. Figure 2 shows the BROA's task diagram. *Expertise Model:* Describes the ontologies (knowledge and its relationships) that agents need to achieve their objectives.

Communication Model: Describes main interactions among humans and software agents along with human factors involved for the development of these interfaces. *Organization Model*: This model aims to describe the human organization in which the multi-agent system is involved along with the software agent organization structure. *Coordination Model*: Dynamic relationships among software agents are expressesed through this model. For doing so, all the conversations among agents must be described: interactions, protocols, and capabilities required. Figure 3 shows the BROA's sequence diagram that specifies main interactions among agents.

B. *BROA's Architecture*

The design phase of MAS-CommonKADS methodology takes as input all the models got from the analysis phase and transforms their specifications for implementation. In addition, the architecture of each agent and the global network architecture must be provided [20].

Figure 4 shows the multi-agent architecture of the model proposed. This architecture was used to develop the BROA

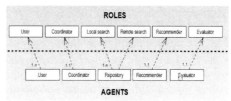

Fig. 1. Transformation of roles in agent's diagram

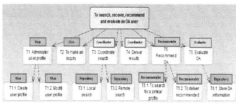

Fig. 2. Task Diagram

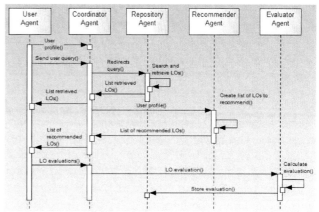

Fig. 3. Sequence diagram

system, implemented using JADE (Java Agent Development Framework) agents [21]. The next Section describes each of the agents of the BROA system along with the main interactions that exist among them.

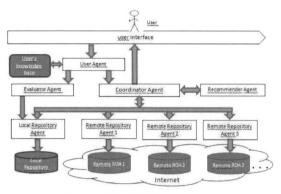

Fig. 4. BROA/SRLO's Architecture

Fig. 5. BROA/SRLO's Web-based Interface

Agent Description

User Agent: This agent communicates directly with the human user and whose role is representing him within the system along with communications with other agents (Coordinator and Evaluator). Also, the user agent manages the user's profile, enabling the creation and modification of profile's characteristics and preferences. Finally, this agent sends the query string to the coordinator agent in order to perform the LO search and the evaluation of the recommended LOs. *Coordinator Agent:* This agent is of deliberative nature since it takes care of redirectioning queries that the user makes to both the local and the remote repositories. This agent knows the repositories associated with the system and the information that each of them manages. In addition, it can access the user agent's profile to know what characteristics are useful for making a recommendation (learning style, educational level, language preference, among others). *Local and Remote Repository Agent:* Repository agents are responsible for making accurate LO searches in both local and remote repositories. This agent recognizes how LOs are stored inside the repositories, under what standard and type of metadata that manages. Also knows the type of search that can be performed within the repository and how to recover a particular LO stored. The local repository agent is also responsible for storing the LO evaluation given from an evaluator agent. Similarly, in the proposed architecture there is a repository for each LOR agent federation is local or remote. *Recommender Agent:* This agent makes two recommendations; the first stage is to find users registered in the system with similar profile to the user so having the same learning style and education level. The LOs selected by those users having a score greater or equal than 4 are shown. The second stage of recommendation

is based on LOs recovered in all different repositories, based on user's LO query. This recommendation is based on the student's learning style. It is important to highlight that in the model proposed, the recommendation is based on the metadata that describes the LO and the information of learning style, educational level, and language preference of the registered student. In order to represent the agent's knowledge production rules were used, such as the following rule:

$$LearningStyle(Visual\text{-}Global) \wedge$$
$$LearningResourceType\ (figure)\ \vee$$
$$LearningResourceType(graph) \vee$$
$$LearningResourceType(slide) \vee$$
$$LearningResourceType(table) \wedge$$
$$InteractivityLevel(medium) \vee$$
$$InteractivityLevel(high).$$

When there is a failure of similar users, the system shows only the results of the second recommendation and then stored the user profile information and evaluated LOs, within the knowledge base. *Evaluator agent:* This agent manages the evaluation performed by a user to some of the LOs that have been explored. The evaluation is made through explicit qualification that is given by the selected student who rates the specific LO from 1 to 5 according to his/her own satisfaction level.

Platform Design

The BROA's agent architecture was developed in JAVA, using JDOM for handling XML user's profiles. The local repository manager is stored in the PostgreSQL database that is characterized to be stable, with high performance, and great flexibility. The agent creation and management is made by using JADE platform using FIPA-ACL performatives [21]. The ontology creation was performed by using Protégé and finally, the Web integration was made based on the ZK framework. Figure 5 shows BROA's Web interface with the recommended and retrieved LOs. For the LO search process there was a student who had a Visual-sequential learning style and the search string used was: "computer science". Thus, a total of 196 LOs were recovered and only recommended, after a "learning style" filtering just 45 of them.

V. EXPERIMENTS AND RESULTS

BROA system provides to the human user LO lists by using its interface. The first list is the result of the search made by the user according to his criteria. The second list presents list of recommended items to the user, which correspond to those LOs that are the most adapted to his own learning style.

To validate the BROA system a test was performed based on the keyword "computer science". In addition, a comparison was made with the results given by the system concerning the LOs recommended for users with different learning styles proposed by Duque [16]: Visual-Global, Visual-sequential, Auditory-Global, Auditory-sequential, Kinesthetic-Global, Kinesthetic-sequential, Reader-Global, Reader-sequential.

Thus, virtual users with different profiles were generated and LOs from real repositories were recovered. Figure 6 shows the results got for the tests being performed. A total of 196 LOs were retrieved after the search process for students with different learning styles. Figure 5 shows the quantity of LOs for each of the different learning styles. The BROA system makes a good recommendation process since the LOs provided are well adapted to the student's learning profile.

In order to evaluate the results of recommendations given by the system the Precision measure [22] was used which purpose is to analyze the quality of the retrieval.

$$Precision = \frac{Relevant\ LOs}{Relevant\ LOs + Retrieved\ LOs}\ (1)$$

Figure 6 shows the results obtained by applying the Precision measure formula (1) to each learning style and additionally comparing values obtained with and without

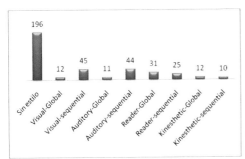

Fig. 5. LOs retrieved after search

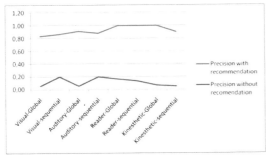

Fig. 6. Precision

recommendation when accessing LO Merlot repository.

VI. CONCLUSION AND FUTURE WORK

This paper proposes a model for learning object searching, retrieving, recommendation, and evaluation modeled through the paradigm of MAS from repository federations. The BROA (Spanish acronym for Learning Object Search, Retrieval & Recommender System) system was built using this model. There is an agent in the BROA system dedicated to each repository accessed by the system. In order to facilitate LO searches, the agent knows how the LOs are stored, how is the way of accessing and recovering them, under what standard and type of metadata the LOs are stored and handled by the specific repository. Those searches are performed in a local LOR, where the already evaluated LOs are stored, and also

performed in remote LORs associated to the system. The BROA system offers two types of recommendation; the first one is based on finding similar profiles. This first recommendation approach has not already been implemented in this prototype. The second type of recommendation is by searching the metadata of the LO, taking into account the query performed by the user, the results are presented at the right side on Figure 5. The model proposed in this paper addressed issues such as working on LOs and learning styles and making recommendations by the system to the user based on customized searches using the LO metadata. In addition, the problem modeling using a MAS technique was an excellent option, which allowed the disintegration into functional blocks, without losing the systemic point of view, which leads to distributing the solution in diverse entities that require specific knowledge, processing and communication between each other. The MAS allowed a neutral vision in the model proposed.

It is envisaged as future work to add an interface agent to make context-aware adaptations, along with the list of LOs delivered by the system considering other issues such as type of device from where the query is made, bandwidth, among others. For the evaluation process, it is intended to make templates for the user to rate its opinion about recommended LOs (explicit evaluation). The agent should analyze the results of the explicit evaluation and use logs, to assign a rating to each LO. Also it is envisaged to improve the theoretical and practical basis of the first stage of recommendations made by the system through collaborative filtering techniques. The learning style for this prototype should be selected by the user, an additional future work aims to propose a learning style test that will define which kind of learning style the user who is logged in the system has.

ACKNOWLEDGMENT

The research reported in this paper was funded in part by the COLCIENCIAS project entitled "ROAC Creación de un modelo para la Federación de OA en Colombia que permita su integración a confederaciones internacionales" Universidad Nacional de Colombia, with code 1119-521-29361.

REFERENCES

[1]	C. I. Peña, J. L. Marzo, J. L. De la Rosa, and R. Fabregat, "Un Sistema de Tutoría Inteligente Adaptativo Considerando Estilos de Aprendizaje," VI Congreso Iberoamericano de Informática Educativa, pp. 1 – 12, 2002.

[2]	J. Z. Li, "Quality, Evaluation and Recommendation for Learning Object," International Conference on Educational and Information Technology (ICEIT 2010), pp. 533–537, 2010.

[3]	A. B. Gil and F. García, "Un Sistema Multiagente de Recuperación de Objetos de Aprendizaje con Atributos de Contexto," ZOCO'07/CAEPIA, 2007.

[4]	K. Niemann, M. Scheffel, M. Friedrich, U. Kirschenmann, H.-C. Schmitz, and M. Wolpers, "Usage-based Object Similarity," Journal of Universal Computer Science, vol. 16, no. 16, pp. 2272–2290, 2010.

[5]	M. Wooldridge, N. R. Jennings, and D. Kinny, "The Gaia Methodology for Agent-Oriented Analysis and Design," Autonomous Agents and Multi-Agent Systems, vol. 3, pp. 285 – 312, 2000.

[6]   Y. Ouyang and M. Zhu, "eLORM: Learning Object Relationship Mining-based Repository," Online Information Review, vol. 32, no. 2, pp. 254–265, 2008.

[7]   D. Betancur, J. Moreno, and D. Ovalle, "Modelo para la Recomendación y Recuperación de Objetos de Aprendizaje en Entornos Virtuales de Enseñanza/Aprendizaje," Avances en Sistemas e Informática, vol. 6, no. 1, pp. 45–56, 2009.

[8]   F. De Prieta and A. B. Gil, "A Multi-agent System that Searches for Learning Objects in Heterogeneous Repositories," Advances in Intelligent and Soft Computing, vol. 71, pp. 355–362, 2010.

[9]   H. Van de Sompel, R. Chute, and P. Hochstenbach, "The aDORe Federation Architecture: Digital Repositories at Scale," International Journal on Digital Libraries, vol. 9, no. 2, pp. 83–100, 2008.

[10] F. Chesani, "Recommendation Systems," Corso di laurea in Ingegneria Informatica, pp. 1–32, 2007.

[11] K. Mizhquero and J. Barrera, "Análisis, Diseño e Implementación de un Sistema Adaptivo de Recomendación de Información Basado en Mashups," Revista Tecnológica ESPOL-RTE, 2009.

[12] O. Sanjuán, E. Torres, H. Castán, R. Gonzalez, C. Pelayo, and L. Rodriguez, "Viabilidad de la Aplicación de Sistemas de Recomendación a entornos de e-learning," 2009.

[13] N. R. Jennings, "On Agent-based Software Engineering," Artificial Intelligence, vol. 117, no. 2, pp. 277–296, Mar. 2000.

[14] A. Casali, V. Gerling, C. Deco, and C. Bender, "Sistema Inteligente para la Recomendación de Objetos de Aprendizaje," Revista Generación Digital, vol. 9, no. 1, pp. 88–95, 2011.

[15] H. González, N. Duque Méndez, and D. Ovalle C., "Técnicas Inteligentes para la Actualización Dinámica del Perfil del Usuario en un Sistema de Educación Virtual," in Tendencias en Ingeniería de Software e Inteligencia Artificial, 2009.

[16] N. Duque, "Modelo Adaptativo Multi-Agente para la Planificación y Ejecución de Cursos Virtuales Personalizados - Tesis Doctoral," Universidad Nacional de Colombia, 2009.

[17] E. Morales and A. Gil, "Arquitectura para la Recuperación de Objetos de Aprendizaje de Calidad en Repositorios Distribuidos," SCHA: Sistemas Hipermedia Colaborativos y Adaptativos. II Congreso Español de Informática CEDI 2007, vol. 1, no. 1, pp. 31 – 38, 2007.

[18] V. B. Gerling, "Un Sistema Inteligente para Asistir la Búsqueda Personalizada de Objetos de Aprendizaje," Universidad Nacional de Rosario, 2009.

[19] F. de la Prieta, A. G. González, J. M. Corchado, and E. Sanz, "Sistema Multiagente Orientado a la Búsqueda, Recuperación y Filtrado de Objetos Digitales Educativos," VIII Jornadas de Aplicaciones y Transferencia Tecnológica de la Inteligencia Artificial, pp. 65 – 74, 2010.

[20] C. Á. Iglesias Fernández, "Definición de una Metodología para el Desarrollo de Sistemas Multiagentes," Universidad Politécnica de Madrid, 1998.

[21] F. Bellifemine, A. Poggi, and G. Rimassa, "JADE – A FIPA-compliant Agent Framework," Proceedings of PAAM, 1999.

[22] G. Shani and A. Gunawardana, "Evaluating Recommendation Systems," Recommender Systems Handbook, pp. 257 – 297, 2011.

## 20

Fusing Facial Features for Face Recognition

Jamal Ahmad Dargham, Ali Chekima, Ervin Gubin Moung

Universiti Malaysia Sabah

Abstract — **Face recognition is an important biometric method because of its potential applications in many fields, such as access control, surveillance, and human-computer interaction. In this paper, a face recognition system that fuses the outputs of three face recognition systems based on Gabor jets is presented. The first system uses the magnitude, the second uses the phase, and the third uses the phase-weighted magnitude of the jets. The jets are generated from facial landmarks selected using three selection methods. It was found out that fusing the facial features gives better recognition rate than either facial feature used individually regardless of the landmark selection method.**

Keywords—**Gabor filter; face recognition; bunch graph; image processing; wavelet**

I. INTRODUCTION

Face recognition approaches can be divided into three groups [2]; global, local, and hybrid approaches. In global based methods the face image is represented as a low dimension vector by being projected into a linear subspace [1][2]. The advantages of global based methods are: their simple applicability, easy computation, and their general function. However, the limitation of global based methods is that they do not detect the differences in faces local regions and as such are not capable of extracting the local or 'topological' structures of the face. In local based approaches, the geometric features such as the position of eyes, nose, mouth, eyebrows, measurements of width of eyes, are used to represent a face [2][3][4]. There are several ways on how to select local features to represent a face, for example; manual feature selection by positioning nodes on fiducially points (e.g, eyes, and nose), and automatic feature selection. Hybrid methods are a combination of global and local approaches.

The bunch graph method is a local approach that works by first locating a landmark on a face, then convolving a sub-image around each landmark with a group of Gabor filters.

J. Dargham is with Computer Engineering Program, School of Engineering and Technology, Universiti Malaysia Sabah, Jalan UMS, 88400 Kota Kinabalu Sabah, Malaysia (e-mail: chekima@ums.edu.my).

A. Chekima is with Computer Engineering Program, School of Engineering and Technology, Universiti Malaysia Sabah, Jalan UMS, 88400 Kota Kinabalu Sabah, Malaysia (e-mail: jamalad@ums.edu.my).

E.G. Moung is with Computer Engineering Program, School of Engineering and Technology, Universiti Malaysia Sabah, Jalan UMS, 88400 Kota Kinabalu Sabah, Malaysia (e-mail: menirva.com@gmail.com).

This produces a jet from each landmark. These jets will be used for face recognition by computing and comparing similarity scores between jets of two different images. Wiskott et al. introduced a face recognition method called the Elastic Bunch Graph Method [3] and compared the EBGM with several face recognition methods on the FERET and Bochum image databases in different face poses. Their system achieved 98% recognition rate for frontal images. Bolme [4] also used Elastic Bunch Graph Method but he only used one training image per person and the jets were computed from manually selected training images landmarks. These jets were used to find new jet from new image using a displacement estimation method to locate the node on the new image. These new jets are then added to the existing jets database. By using the automatically obtained jets for recognition task an 89.8% recognition rate was reported on the FERET database. Sigari and Fathy [5] proposed a new method for optimizing the EBGM algorithm. Genetic algorithm was used to select the best wavelength of the Gabor wavelet. They had tested the proposed method on the frontal FERET face database and achieved 91% recognition rate. In this paper, a face recognition system that fuse facial features extracted using Gabor wavelet is presented. In section 2 the theory of Gabor wavelet method will be presented while in section 3 the application of bunch graph method to extract facial feature is presented. Section 4 describes the proposed system, while in section 5 the experimental results are discussed before the paper concludes in section 6.

II. GABOR WAVELET TRANSFORM

Gabor wavelet is the fundamental features extraction tool in the bunch graph method. Two dimensional Gabor wavelets shown in (1) were used to extract features from landmarks by convolving the wavelet on the landmarks of the faces. The wavelet has a real and imaginary component representing orthogonal directions. These two parts can be formed into a complex number or used individually. The magnitude and phase of the image content at a particular wavelet's frequency can be computed from the complex number given in (1)

$$g(x, y) = \exp\left(-\frac{x'^2 + \gamma^2 y'^2}{2\sigma^2}\right)\exp\left(i\left(2\pi\frac{x'}{\lambda} + \psi\right)\right) \quad (1)$$

Where $x' = x\cos\theta + y\sin\theta$, $y' = -x\sin\theta + y\cos\theta$.

λ specifies the wavelength of the cosine (or sine) wave. Wavelets with a large wavelength will respond to gradual changes in intensity in the image. Wavelets with short wavelengths will respond to sharp edges and bars.

θ specifies the orientation of the wavelet. This parameter rotates the wavelet about its centre. The orientation of the wavelets dictates the angle of the edges or bars for which the wavelet will respond.

ψ specifies the phase of the sinusoid. Typically, Gabor wavelets are based on a sine or cosine wave. Cosine wavelets are thought to be the real part of the wavelet and the sine wavelets are thought to be the imaginary part of the wavelet. Therefore, a convolution with both phases produces a complex coefficient. The mathematical foundation of the algorithm requires a complex coefficient based on two wavelets that have a phase offset of $\pi/2$.

σ specifies the radius of the Gaussian. The size of the Gaussian is sometimes referred to as the wavelet's basis of support. The Gaussian size determines the amount of the image that effects convolution. In theory, the entire image should effect the convolution; however, as the convolution moves further from the center of the Gaussian, the remaining computation becomes negligible. This parameter is usually proportional to the wavelength, such that wavelets of different size and frequency are scaled versions of each other.

γ specifies the aspect ratio of the Gaussian. Most wavelets tested with the algorithm use an aspect ratio of 1.

The value of the parameters used in this paper are the same as those used by Wiskott in [3], which give 40 Gabor wavelets with different frequencies and orientations.

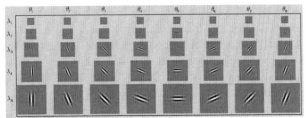

Fig. 1. The real part of the 2D Gabor wavelet mask with different wavelength and orientation.

Convolving the same landmark with many Gabor wavelet configurations produces a collection of Gabor coefficients called jets. Each Gabor coefficient has a real and imaginary component. The magnitude and phase of the image's content at a particular wavelet's frequencies can be computed from the complex number. Let J be a complex number Gabor coefficient, the magnitude. $J_{magnitude}$ and the phase angle ϕ of J are given as in (2) and (3) respectively.

$$J_{magnitude} = \sqrt{J_{real}^2 + J_{imaginary}^2} \qquad (2)$$

$$\phi = \cos^{-1}\left(\frac{J_{real}}{J_{magnitude}}\right) = \sin^{-1}\left(\frac{J_{imaginary}}{J_{magnitude}}\right) \qquad (3)$$

III. BUNCH GRAPH METHOD

A. Selecting Facial Features

A face image is represented as a bunch graph. A bunch graph is a collection of jets for an image. Fig. 2(a) shows the landmarks that were selected as point of interest to be convolved with a group of Gabor wavelets. An example of a convolution of a Gabor wavelet at the chin of a person is shown in Fig. 2(b). Face images are zero padded for the convolutions where the wavelet exceeds the image dimensions, which normally occur near the edge of the image.

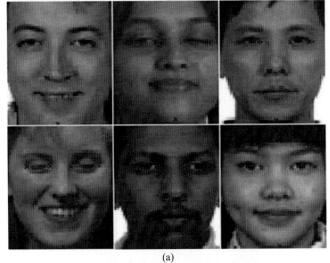

(a)

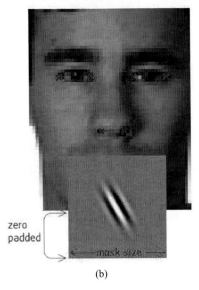

(b)

Fig. 2. (a) FERET face images with the seven landmarks selected (b) convolution of a Gabor kernel at the chin. Face images are zero padded for the convolutions where the wavelet exceeds the image dimensions.

B. Jet Extraction and Bunch Graph Creation

The convolution process produces a matrix having the same dimension as the Gabor wavelet dimension. According to [7], when the mask size of the wavelet comes closer to image size, the recognition performance increases. In this paper, the mask size was set 51 x 51 dimensions. Assuming that matrix **A** contains the complex Gabor wavelet coefficients for one landmark given by a single wavelet from a given image. All matrices **A** for a given landmark given by the 4o wavelets are concatenated into a single vector. A collection of the concatenated version of matrix **A** for one landmark is called a jet. Thus, assuming matrix **B** represent the Jet then, **B** = {A_{J1}, A_{J2}, ..., A_{J40}} contains the entire Gabor coefficient for one landmark. A bunch graph for an image is a collection of jets. Let matrix **C** represent a bunch graph, then Matrix **C** = {B_{N1}, B_{N2}, ..., B_{N7}} will be used for similarity score calculation between images.

IV. PROPOSED SYSTEM

A. Face Recognition System Block Diagram

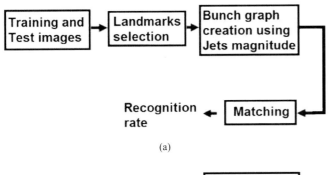

(a)

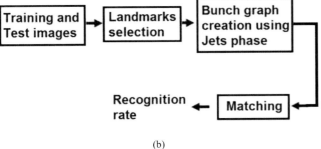

(b)

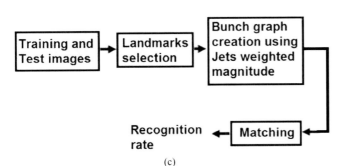

(c)

Fig. 3. Bunch graph face recognition system (a) magnitude only (b) phase only (c) weighted magnitude

Fig. 3 shows the block diagram of Gabor based face recognition system. The seven landmarks as shown in Fig.2(a) selected from face images are convolved with group of Gabor wavelets. Jets from each landmark were then collected together to create a bunch graph as face representation and will be use for the matching task. Three systems will be tested.

1) System A uses the jets magnitude information only
2) System B uses the jets phase information only
3) System C uses jets magnitude weighted by similarity of the phase between two different jets

B. Landmark Selection

The landmark selection for training images was done manually. For testing image, three method of landmark selection were conducted.

1) The first method is by manually selecting landmark on the testing image.
2) The second method is by using the mean coordinate from all training image landmark coordinates as shown in (4)

$$mean\_coord = \frac{1}{M}\sum_{i=1}^{M}\{(x,y)_{i1},(x,y)_{i2},...,(x,y)_{iN}\} \quad (4)$$

3) The third method is by using the mode coordinate from all training image landmark coordinates as in (5)

$$mode\_coord=\{mode(x,y)_1,mode(x,y)_2,...,mode(x,y)_N\} \quad (5)$$

where M = total of training image, and N = total landmark.

C. Similarity Score

For bunch graph similarity measurement, three similarity measurements are considered [4];

$$S_m(B,B') = \frac{\sum_{i=1}^{G}J_iJ'_i}{\sqrt{\sum_{i=1}^{G}J_i^2\sum_{i=1}^{G}J'^2_i}} \quad (6)$$

$$S_\phi(B,B') = \frac{\sum_{i=1}^{G}\phi_i\phi'_i}{\sqrt{\sum_{i=1}^{G}\phi_i^2\sum_{i=1}^{G}\phi'^2_i}} \quad (7)$$

$$S_p(B,B') = \frac{\sum_{i=1}^{G}J_iJ'_i\cos(\phi_i-\phi'_i)}{\sqrt{\sum_{i=1}^{G}J_i^2\sum_{i=1}^{G}J'^2_i}} \quad (8)$$

Where G is number of wavelet coefficients in a jet, J_i is the magnitude of the jet and ϕ_i is the phase angle. **B** and **B'** are the jets for two different images. Equation (6) computes jet similarity score using jet magnitude (System A), (7) computes jet similarity score using jet phase (system B), while (8) use magnitude weighted by similarity of the phase angle to compute jet similarity score (System C). To compute the similarity score between two bunch graphs, (9) was used and N is total number of landmarks.

$$S_{bunch}(C,C') = \frac{1}{N}\sum_{i=1}^{N} S(B,B') \qquad (8)$$

D. Matching

For the matching task, if the score $S_{bunch}(C,C')$ produced by (9), between the bunch graphs of a test image y and an image x in the training database is larger than a given threshold t, then images y and x are assumed to be of the same person. The scores produced by equation (8) were normalized so that $0 \le S_{bunch}(C,C') \le 1$, and the threshold t value can be tuned between 0 and 1. To measure the performance of the individual system, several performance metrics are used. These are:

i. For Recall Test
   a. **Correct Classification**. If a test image $\mathbf{y_i}$ is correctly matched to an image $\mathbf{x_i}$ of the same person in the training database.
   b. **False Acceptance.** If test image $\mathbf{y_i}$ is incorrectly matched with image $\mathbf{x_j}$, where i and j are not the same person
   c. **False Rejection.** If image $\mathbf{y_i}$ is of a person i in the training database is rejected by the system.

ii. For Reject Test
   a. **Correct Classification**. If $\mathbf{y_i}$, from the unknown test database is rejected by the system
   b. **False Acceptance**. If image $\mathbf{y_i}$ is accepted by the system.

iii. **Equal Correct Rate (ECR).** Recall correct classification is equal to reject correct classification.

E. Data Fusion

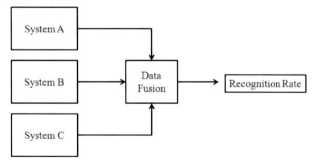

Fig. 4. Block diagram of the fusion system

Fig. 4 shows the block diagram of the fusion of systems A, B, and C, mentioned in Section 4(A). The fusion decision stage is a module that consists of several rules.

1) For Recall
   • If both systems give correct matching, then correct match is found
   • If one system give correct matching and the other system give wrong matching or not found, then correct match is found
   • If both systems give wrong matching, then the fusion system give wrong matching
   • If one system gives wrong matching and the other system give not found, then the fusion system give wrong matching
   • If both system give not found, then the fusion system give not found

2) For Reject
   • If both system correctly reject image from unknown test database, then the fusion system give correct reject
   • If one system correctly reject image from unknown test database and the other system accept unknown test image, then the fusion system give correct reject
   • If both system accept image from unknown test database, then the fusion system give false acceptance

The fusion decision rules can be summarize as an OR operator as shown in Table I, Table II, Table III, and Table IV.

TABLE I
FUSION DECISION RULES

System A	System B	Fusion System output
0	0	0
1	0	1
0	1	1
1	1	1

TABLE II
FUSION DECISION RULES

System A	System C	Fusion System output
0	0	0
1	0	1
0	1	1
1	1	1

TABLE III
FUSION DECISION RULES

System A	System B	Fusion System output
0	0	0
1	0	1
0	1	1
1	1	1

TABLE IV
FUSION DECISION RULES

System A	System B	System C	Fusion System Output
0	0	0	0
1	0	0	1
0	1	0	1
0	0	1	1
1	1	0	1
1	0	1	1
0	1	1	1
1	1	1	1

The definition of the *0* and *1* result for both Recall and Reject test are as follow;
1) Definition for Recall test
   - 0 = Match not found
   - 1 = Correct Match found
2) Definition for Reject test
   - 0 = False Acceptance
   - 1 = Correct Reject

F. Probabilistic OR Rules

A modified OR, Probabilistic OR, is proposed. The rules of this OR gate takes into account confidence score of each individual system during the fusion stage. Table V shows the summary of the Probabilistic OR Rules.

TABLE V
PROBABILISTIC OR RULES

System A	System C	Fusion System output
0	0	0
1	0	$CS_A > CS_C \rightarrow 1$
		$CS_A < CS_C \rightarrow 0$
0	1	$CS_A > CS_C \rightarrow 1$
		$CS_A < CS_C \rightarrow 0$
1	1	1

If all individual system gives no match found, then the fusion system output give no match found result. The same applies if all individual system gives match found, then the fusion system output give match found result. However, when one system gives a match is found while the other system gives a match not found, then the output will be the state of the system having the highest confidence score. The confidence score is the modulus of the similarity score between test and matched training image, minus the score threshold of the individual system as shown in (10).

$$CS = \|S - t\| \qquad (9)$$

CS is confidence score, *S* is similarity score between test image and the matched training image, and *t* is the score threshold of the individual system.

G. Face Database

A total of 500 images with frontal face of a person were selected from the FERET database. They represent 200 different individuals. 100 individuals are used for training & testing, and the other 100 different individuals are used for testing only. All the 500 selected FERET images were cropped to get only the desired face part of a person (from forehead to the chin). All images are adjusted so that both eyes coordinates of an individual are aligned in the same horizontal line and the dimension for each image is set to 60 x 60 pixels. Three images per individual will be used for training. Two testing databases were created. The first database, Known Test

Database, has 100 images of the 100 persons in the training database. This database will be used to test the Recall capability of the face recognition system. The second database, Unknown Test Database, has also 100 images of 100 different persons. This database will be used to test the Rejection capability of the system. Fig. 5 shows the example of the normalized face image and Fig. 6 shows the FERET Face database tree chart used for experiments.

Fig. 5. Examples of the selected FERET face images are cropped from forehead to chin, eyes coordinates are aligned and images are converted into gray scale format.

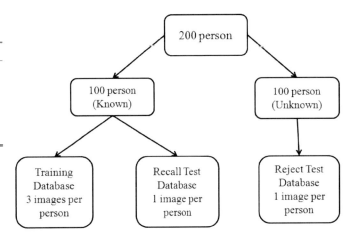

Fig. 6. FERET Face database chart used for experiments

V. RESULTS AND DISCUSSION

As stated earlier, the range of the similarity score can be between 0 and 1. The threshold also can be tuned so that the performance of the system can either have high correct recall with high false acceptance rate for application such as boarder monitoring or high correct rejection rate for unknown persons for application such as access control. For this work, the threshold tuning parameter was set so that each system has equal correct recall rate and correct rejection rate. Three landmark selection criteria were tested and three systems were considered.

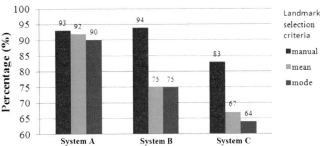

Fig. 7. Recognition rate using magnitude, phase, and magnitude with phase

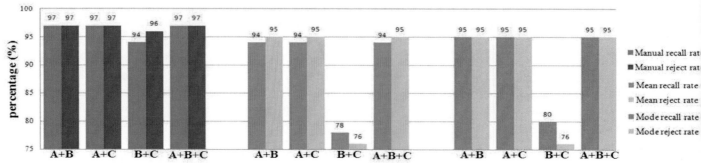

Fig. 8. Recognition rate for data fusion. The '+' sign means two or more systems were OR'ed.

Fig. 7 shows the performance of the system individually.

System A uses the jets magnitude, System B uses the jets phase, and System C uses the jets weighted magnitude. The manual landmark selection method outperforms the mean and mode selection methods for all three systems. Comparing the two automatic selection methods (mean and mode), the mean outperforms the mode selection criteria for all three systems. Comparing the performance of the individual system, system A outperforms the other systems in general except system B which gives slightly better result for the manual selection method.

Fig. 8 shows that the recognition rates for the fusion of all possible combination of two or three systems. In general, the fusion of two systems or more give better performance than a single system alone. In addition, the fusion reduces the effect of the landmark selection method. The result in Fig. 8 shows that fusion of magnitude and phase gives the best performance (system A and system B), thus only the fusion of magnitude and phase features of Gabor wavelet will be used for Probabilistic OR rules experiment.

Fig. 9 shows the result of data fusion using Probabilistic OR rules. Fusion system that uses the manual landmark selection outperforms fusion system that uses the mean and mode landmark selection by 15% approximately, while the performance between mean and mode selection more or less the same.

Comparing the Probabilistic OR rules result and the original OR rules result, the Probabilistic OR rules perform worst than the original OR rules regardless of the landmark selection method. When comparing the Probabilistic OR result with the individual system, the Probabilistic OR fusion based system outperforms all the individual system when using manual landmark selection method. However for the automatic landmark selection method (mean and mode), the Probabilistic OR fusion based system outperformed by System A, but outperform both systems B and C.

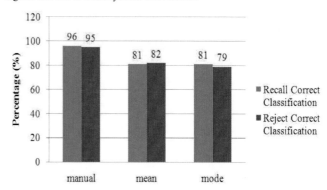

Landmark Selection Method

Fig. 9. Recognition rate for data fusion of magnitude and phase (A+B) using the Probabilistic OR rules.

The performance of our system is also compared with several methods that are based on bunch graph methods and use the same database as shown in Table VI. Our system performs better than both systems reported in [4] and [5] but lower than [3]. This may be due to the fact that [3] uses a precise jets extraction instead of just manually selecting a node on a face, thus creating a very detailed face graph with high precision as well designing the system specifically for in-class recognition task.

TABLE VI
COMPARISON OF SEVERAL EBGM-BASED FACE RECOGNITION METHODS ON FERET DATABASE.

Methods	Recognition Rate
Elastic Bunch Graph Method [3]	98%
EBGM (automatic facial feature selection) [4]	89.8%
Gabor wavelength selection based on Genetic Algorithm [5]	91%
Our proposed method (Original OR rules)	
Mean facial feature coordinate selection	94% (recall), 95% (reject)
Mode facial feature coordinate selection	95% (recall), 95% (reject)

VI. CONCLUSION

In this paper, a system that fuses the outputs of three systems is presented. These systems are based on the bunch graph method but one use magnitude of the jets only while the second one use the phase only, and last one use the magnitude weighted with phase. Three methods for selecting the landmarks where the jets are generated are used. It was found that selection method did not significantly affect the performance of the fused system. However, the manual selection gives the highest recognition rate followed by the mean and mode methods. It was also found that the output of the fusion system using the OR rules gives higher recognition rate than all system individually. We have also introduced a fusion stage based on Probabilistic OR rules. However, it was found that Probabilistic OR rules perform worst than the original OR rules.

APPENDIX

TABLE XI
GABOR WAVELET PARAMETERS, WISKOTT [3]

Parameter	Symbol	Values
Orientation	θ	$\{0, \pi/8, 2\pi/8, 3\pi/8, 4\pi/8, 5\pi/8, 6\pi/8, 7\pi/8\}$
Wavelength	λ	$\{4, 4\sqrt{2}, 8, 8\sqrt{2}, 16\}$
Phase	ϕ	$\{0, \pi/2\}$
Gaussian Radius	σ	$\sigma = \gamma$
Aspect Ratio	γ	1

VII. REFERENCES

[1] M. A. Turk and A. P. Pentland, "Face recognition using eigenfaces", *In Proc. IEEE Conf. on Computer Vision and Pattern Recognition*, pp. 586-591, 1991.

[2] Zhao, W., Chellappa, R., Phillips, P. J., Rosenfeld, A., Face recognition: A literature survey, *ACM Computing Surverys (CSUR)*, V. 35, Issue 4, pp. 399-458, 2003.

[3] L. Wiskott, J.-M. Fellous, N. Kruger and C. Von Der Malsburg, "Face Recognition by Elastic Bunch Graph Matching", *In Intelligent Biometric Techniques in Fingerprint and Face Recognition*, Chapter 11, pp. 355-396, 1999.

[4] David Bolme. *Elastic bunch graph matching*. Master's thesis, Colorado State University, Summer 2003.

[5] Mohamad Hoseyn Sigari and Mahmood Fathy, "Best wavelength selection for Gabor wavelet using GA for EBGM algorithm", *Machine Vision, ICMV 2007*, Islamabad, pp. 35 - 39. 28-29 Dec. 2007.

[6] L. Wiskott, J.M. Fellous, N. Kruger, C.V.D Malsburg. "Face Recognition by Elastic Bunch Graph Matching". *IEEE Transaction on Pattern Analysis and Machine Intelligence*, Vol. 19, No. 7, pp. 775-779. July 1997.

[7] Berk Gökberk. *Feature Based Pose Invariant Face Recognition*. Master's thesis, Bogazici University, 2001.

J. Dargham, he received his B.Sc. in Control Systems Engineering from Iraq and his M.Sc. in Control System Engineering (UMIST) from Malaysia. He received his PhD from Universiti Malaysia Sabah (UMS). He is holding senior lecture position at Universiti Malaysia Sabah (UMS) and was the head of the Computer Engineering Program from 2006 till 2011. His research interests include Pattern Recognition, Medical Imaging, Biometrics, and Artificial Intelligence. He has published more than 70 papers in refereed journals, conferences, book chapters and research reports. (E-mail: jamalad@ums.edu.my).

A.Chekima, he received his BEngg in Electronics from Ecole Nationale Polytechnique of Algiers in 1976 and his Msc and Phd both in Electrical Engineering from Rensselaer Polytechnic Institute Troy, New York, in 1979 and 1984 respectively. He joined the Electronics Department at the Ecole Nationale Polytechnique in 1984, where he was Chairman of the Scientific Committee of the Department as well as in charge of the Postgraduate Program while teaching at both graduate and undergraduate levels. He was member of several scientific committees at the national level. He has been working as an Associate Processor at the School of Engineering and Information Technology at Universiti Malaysia Sabah since October 1996. His research interests include Source Coding, Antennas, Signal Processing, Pattern Recognition, Medical Imaging, Biometrics, Data Compression, Artificial Intelligence and Data Mining. He has published more than 120 papers in refereed journals, conferences, book chapters and research reports. (E-mail: chekima@ums.edu.my).

E.G. Moung, he received the B.Sc. degree in Computer Engineering from Universiti Malaysia Sabah, Malaysia 2008. He has been working as a research assistant at Universiti Malaysia Sabah, Malaysia. His present research interests include the biometric and image processing. (E-mail: menirva.com@gmail.com).

## 21

Improved Differential Evolution Algorithm for Parameter Estimation to Improve the Production of Biochemical Pathway

Chuii Khim Chong, Mohd Saberi Mohamad , Safaai Deris, Mohd Shahir Shamsir, Yee Wen Choon, Lian En Chai

Abstract —This paper introduces an improved Differential Evolution algorithm (IDE) which aims at improving its performance in estimating the relevant parameters for metabolic pathway data to simulate glycolysis pathway for yeast. Metabolic pathway data are expected to be of significant help in the development of efficient tools in kinetic modeling and parameter estimation platforms. Many computation algorithms face obstacles due to the noisy data and difficulty of the system in estimating myriad of parameters, and require longer computational time to estimate the relevant parameters. The proposed algorithm (IDE) in this paper is a hybrid of a Differential Evolution algorithm (DE) and a Kalman Filter (KF). The outcome of IDE is proven to be superior than Genetic Algorithm (GA) and DE. The results of IDE from experiments show estimated optimal kinetic parameters values, shorter computation time and increased accuracy for simulated results compared with other estimation algorithms

Keywords— Parameter Estimation, Differential Evolution Algorithm, Kalman Filter, Simulation.

I. INTRODUCTION

The crucial step in the development of predictive models for cells or whole organisms is building dynamic models of biological systems. Such models can be regarded as the keystones of Systems Biology, ultimately providing scientific explanations of the biological phenomena [1]. Hence, one of the major challenges in the age of post-genomics is

This work is financed by Institutional Scholarship MyPhd provided by the Ministry of Higher Education of Malaysia and Universiti Teknologi Malaysia with UTM GUP research grants (vot number: QJ130000.7123.00H67 and QJ130000.7107.01H29).

C. K. Chong is with the Universiti Teknologi Malaysia, Skudai, 81310 Malaysia (e-mail: ckchong2@live.utm.my)

M. S. Mohamad is with the Universiti Teknologi Malaysia, Skudai, 81310 Malaysia (corresponding author to provide e-mail: saberi@utm.my).

S. Deris Author is with the Universiti Teknologi Malaysia, Skudai, 81310 Malaysia (e-mail: safaai@utm.my).

M. S. Shamsir is with the Universiti Teknologi Malaysia, Skudai, 81310 Malaysia (e-mail: shahir@fbb.utm.my)

Y. W. Choon is with the Universiti Teknologi Malaysia, Skudai, 81310 Malaysia (e-mail: ywchoon2@live.utm.my).

L. E. Chai is with the Universiti Teknologi Malaysia, Skudai, 81310 Malaysia (e-mail: lechai2@live.utm.my).

considered to be the understanding of dynamic metabolic behaviour of living cells [2]. Understanding of biological pathway's functions due to their complexity is difficult. Thus, not only we need to determine the components and their characteristics but also we need to focus on their continuous dynamic changes over time. One method to deal with this problem is to study the pathway as a network of biochemical reaction and subsequently model them as a system of ordinary differential equations (ODEs) [3, 4]. ODE based mathematical models can be implemented in various applications such as to simulate experiments before actual experiment is being performed, to study the phenomena that cannot be solved with experimentally, to aid in understanding the functions of a system etc. [5]. Design, analysis, optimization, and controlling of the biological system can be done with these ODEs. Different types of kinetic models such as Michaelis–Menten model or power law model are introduced with the purpose of studying the dynamic behavior of biological reaction systems [6]. Differential equations were used by scientists to simulate these dynamic changes in metabolic concentration but they require information which is related to the network structure and plethora of experimental data such as detailed kinetic rate laws, initial concentrations of metabolites and kinetic parameters [2]. Several models in metabolic networks modeling such as the threonine synthesis pathway in *Escherichia coli* have been developed by researchers [7].

The expert's proposition on dynamic model, how it is later fitted to the data, and how changes are taken into considerations if the predictions were not good enough are the process of modelling. Estimation of the parameters' value in the mathematical models for biochemical networks is typically done through minimization means [8]. Simulated result retrieved from simulation of the mathematical model with the aims to compare model results with the experimental data is called the forward problem. The inverse problem, on the other hand is the process where estimation of parameters of a mathematical model is done based on the measured observations [5]. This step is called parameter estimation and is one of the essential parts of model building. Without identifying the model parameters that define the data can cause inaccuracy in the conclusion [9]. Only some of these parameters in the model can be retrieved from experiments or from the previous works that have been done by other researchers and others have to be retrieved by comparing model results with experiments data [5]. Gathering data via experiments on genomic, proteomic, and metabolomic scales are growing generally in biological sciences. An accurate model building methods which can handle the high complexity is highly needed when the quality and the size of experimental data continue to grow rapidly [1]. Nevertheless, when the available data is noisy and sparse, i.e. widely and unevenly spaced in time, as is generally when measuring biological quantities at the cellular level makes the parameter estimation problem even more difficult to solve [10]. Noisy data can also occur when the collected results differ from each other and this is caused by the human error or apparatus limitation.

Parameter estimation (also known as model calibration) aims at finding the parameters of the parameters' value which give the best fit to a set of experimental data [1]. Biological data usually are nonlinear and dynamic. This problem is considered as a nonlinear programming (NLP) problem which generally known to be non-trivial and multimodal. Hence, traditional approach such as gradient-based or local optimization methods fail to provide optimal solutions. In order to overcome this limitation several state-of-the-art deterministic and stochastic global optimization methods are used by many researches [11]. The subsequent session is the explanation of few methods which include basic estimation approach and evolutionary algorithms.

In 1965, The Nelder-Mead algorithm (NM), also known as non-linear simplex method [12], is one of the best known algorithms for multidimensional unconstrained optimization without the need of derivatives information, which makes it appropriate for problems with non-smooth functions. NM is commonly used to solve parameter estimation problem which the function values are uncertain or in the cases where noise exists. It can also be implemented in problems with discontinuous functions which often occur in statistics and experimental mathematics. NM is very effective, particularly with a large number of parameters [13]. As a limitation of NM, where information regarding the convergence is very constrained and many of the iterations can run without a significant decrease of function values while the current results are still far from the optimal result. Besides that, the location of the initial seed for NM may affect convergence of the algorithm in the case of a function with more than one minimum.

Simulated annealing (SA) is another method which aimed at finding a better approximation to the global optimum in a large search space of a given function. SA is a generic probabilistic and metaheuristic approach and is implemented where the search space is discrete. One of the benefits of SA is its capability of not getting stuck in the local minima and the convergence is guaranteed in case of existence of large number of iterations [14, 15]. In addition, choosing the initial temperature or cooling schedule is challenging in SA. Furthermore, waste of computation time result by using too high temperature and using too low temperature would cause the reduction of quality of the search [14] and as a result, solving a complex system problem becomes very slow and uses more processor time [16]. Richard and his colleagues (2007) did use SA to estimate the relevant kinetic parameter in solving biochemical nonlinear parameter estimation problem. [17].

Genetic Algorithm (GA) is a subclass of evolutionary algorithms which is based on inheritance, mutation, selection, and crossover. Many scholars and researchers like Katera et al., 2004, and Donaldson and Gilbert (2008) used this algorithm to solve parameter estimation problem [9, 18]. The advantages of GA are its parallel search and searching efficiency [19] whereas finding local minima which may not be a true solution is considered as a disadvantage of genetic algorithm [20].

As a parallel search method, the Differential Evolution algorithm (DE) optimizes a problem by repeatedly trying to enhance a candidate solution with the goal of achieving the defined measure of quality. It is generally categorized as metaheuristic approach due to the fact that it works on no assumptions regarding the problem being optimized and can deal with substantial spaces of candidate solutions. The advantages of DE are considered to be high speed, efficiency, simplicity, and ease of use [21]. It was implemented by Moonchai Sompop *et al.* (2005) to enhance the production of bacteriocin, aspartate, beer, and cell process simulation by utilizing control and kinetic parameters [22]. DE shows to be very sensitive to control parameters: crossover constant (CR), population size (NP), and mutation factor (F) [23].

We proposed an improved Differential Evolution algorithm (IDE), a hybrid of DE and the Kalman Filter (KF), to solve the problems regarding the existence of noisy data that leads to low accuracy for estimated result and the increasing number of unidentified parameters which results in adding to the difficulties of the model in estimating the kinetic parameters. DE which is a stochastic-based approach, proved to be the best optimization algorithm out of the others. Stochastic-based approach is more appropriate to implement in the biological data in which they are usually non-convex and are easily trapped in local minimal [24]. Parameter estimation with DE is done without noisy data handling process. IDE takes advantage of KF which adds the feedback gathering feature from the noisy measurement to improve the performance of each output that was resulted by DE which provides higher accurate results. Biochemical pathways are regulatory pathway, signalling pathway, and metabolic pathway. Cell cycle pathway and aspartate biosynthesis pathway are the metabolic pathways which are the series of events that happened in a cell causing its division and duplication (replication) and synthesis aspartate, the essential amino acid. These are the symbolic pathways that are studied in this paper.

II. PROPOSED ALGORITHM

A. Experiment Setup

This paper proposes a hybrid of DE [25] and KF [26], which is an improved differential evolution algorithm (IDE). In parameter estimation, existing algorithms [22] merely implement DE whereas IDE implements a hybrid of DE and KF. Fig. 1 shows the details of the IDE. Kinetic parameters existed in the glycolysis pathway model for yeast [27] and Novak Tyson Cell Cycle in frog egg cell [28] go through IDE to estimate its optimal value. Fixed control parameter values used in this study are

     i. population size, $NP = 10$,
     ii. mutation factor, $F = 0.5$,
     iii. crossover constant, $CR = 0.9$.

SBToolbox in Matlab 2008a and Copasi are the two main software implemented in this study. The mentioned metabolic pathways were collected from online database called Biomodel which is sustained by European Bioinformatics Institute (EMBL-EBI).

B. Improved Differential Evolution Algorithm (IDE)

In IDE, we added the process of updating the population as a new step that improved the conventional DE. This is a self-adapt approach. In conventional DE, the original population which is an m x n population matrix, is generated from the first generation (Gen_1) and continues until it reaches the maximum generation (Gen_i) in initialization process. m represents the number of generations and n represents the number of identifiable parameters. In evaluation process, the fitness function, J represented as

$$J = \sum_{i=1}^{N} | f(X, X0, \theta 0) - f(Y, X0, \theta) |^2 \qquad (1)$$

is applied to evaluate the fitness of each individual. X represents the state vector for measurement system, Y represents the state vector for simulated system, $\varnothing 0$ represents a set of original parameters, $\varnothing$ represents a set of estimated parameters, $X0$ represents the initial state, N=the ending index, and i=the index variable.

In mutation process, three individuals (Ind1, Ind2 and Ind3) first being selected then treated with the formula showed in Fig 1. In the mutation section, temp_population represents the mutated population matrix, F represents the mutation factor, and Pop represents the original population matrix. The subsequent crossover process is mainly performed based on CR, which indicates crossover constant value, and Randb(i) which indicates i-th random evaluation of a uniform random number generator [0,1]. If the randb(i) value of the individual in mutated population is lower than the CR value then that individual becomes the individual for the resultant population of the crossover process and vice versa. This is followed by the updating process that is performed according to the Equation 2. This step updates the population, which is

generated by the crossover process and it is based on the Kalman gain value K, retrieved from the Equation 3. The Kalman gain value from the Equation 3 takes into account the process noise covariance and measurement noise covariance. These noisy data values were obtained from the experiment and in this study the noisy data values used are 0.1. After handling the noisy data, the updated population once again undergoes the evaluation process and the whole process is repeated till the stopping criterion is met. The stopping criteria are set via predefined maximum loop values or when the fitness functions have converged. The updating population process is highlighted with the dotted box in Fig. 1 and is carried out according to the following formula.

$$temp\_population = (temp\_population' + K)' \qquad (2)$$

$$K = P * H' * inv(H * P * H' + R) \qquad (3)$$

Table 1
Pseudocode for IDE

Algorithm: IDE
BEGIN
STEP 1: Initialize population P based on D and evaluate it.
    WHILE (k<Max)
        FOR ($i = 0$; $i < NP$; i++)
            STEP 1.1: Initialization
                Randomly select parents $P[i_1]$,
                $P[i_2]$, and $P[i_3]$ where i, i_1, i_2,
                and i_3 are different.
            STEP 1.2: Mutation
                Create initial candidate $C_1[i] =$
                $P[i_1] + F *(P[i_2] - P[i_3])$.
            STEP 1.3: Crossover
                Create final candidate $C[i]$ by
                crossing over the genes of $P[i]$
                and $C_1[i]$ as follows:
                FOR ($j = 0$; $j < NP$; j++)
                    IF ($U(0, 1) < CR$)
                      $C[i][j] = C_1[i][j]$
                  ELSE
                      $C[i][j] = P[i][j]$
            END-FOR
            STEP 1.4: Updating Population
                $C[i] = inv(inv(C[i]) + K)$
                $K = P*H'*inv(H*P*H'+R)$
            STEP 1.5: Evaluate $C[i]$
                IF ($C[i]$ is better than $P[i]$)
                  $P'[i] = C[i]$
                ELSE
                  $P'[i] = P[i]$
                END-IF
        END-FOR
        $P = P'$
    END-WHILE
END

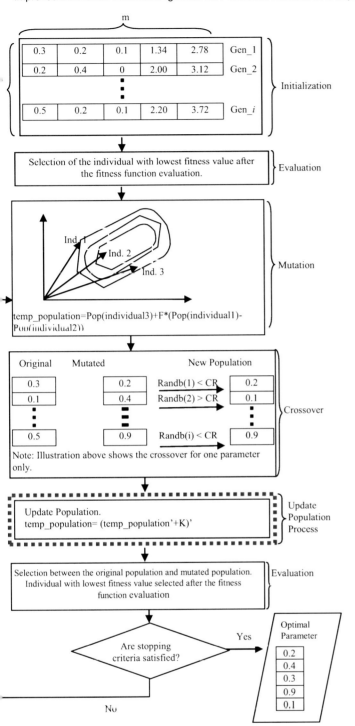

Fig. 1. Schematic Overview of IDE.

Note: Updating population process is added after the crossover process to improve DE performance and it is highlighted with the dotted box.

Where
K = Kalman gain value,
H = observation matrix,
Q = process noise covariance,
D = number of the unknown parameters,
R = measurement noise covariance,
B = covariance of the state vector estimate,
H' = inverse of matrix H,

P = population of the current generation,
P' = the population to be formed for the next generation,
$C[i]$ = the candidate solution with population index i,
$C[i][j]$ = the j'th entry in the solution vector of $C[i]$,
N = the problem dimensionality,
$U(0, 1)$ = a uniformly distributed number between 0 and 1,
k = the scaling factor,
inv = the inverse function,
Max = maximum generation.

III.   EXPERIMENTAL RESULT

Three estimation algorithms (GA, DE, and IDE) are compared in this study. Kinetic parameter values in Table 1and Table 2 are produced by the estimation algorithms and collected from literature review [27, 28]. Time series data for concentration of adenosine monophosphate (AMP) and Clycin were generated in order to evaluate the accuracy of each estimation algorithm. AMP and Clycin are significant metabolites. AMP acts as an energy regulator and sensor while Cyclin acts as a regulator for cell cycle. From the time series data, we calculate the average of error rate. The details of the accuracy measurement are discussed in this session.

Table 1.
Kinetic parameter values of IDE compared with GA and DE.

Kinetic parameters	Measurement kinetic parameter values[27]	Simulated kinetic parameter values		
		GA	DE	IDE
k9f	10	26.57	1.12	2.21
k9b	10	6.184	54.37	10.15

Note: Table shows the kinetic parameter values used in the calculation of average of error rate for metabolite AMP in Table 3.

Table 2
Kinetic parameter values of IDE compared with GA and DE.

Kinetic parameters	Measurement kinetic parameter values [28]	Simulated kinetic parameter values		
		GA	DE	IDE
k1	0.01	0.026	0.028	0.0102
k3	0.500	0.140	2.028	0.602
V2p	0.005	0	0.01	0.018
V2pp	0.250	0.069	0.658	0.347

Note: Table shows the kinetic parameter values used in the calculation of average of error rate for metabolite Cyclin in Table 4.

The simulated kinetic parameter values and measurement kinetic parameter values were replaced into the ordinary differential equations (ODEs) (Equation 4 and Equation 5) of AMP and Cyclin respectively.

$$\frac{dAMP}{dt} = -AMPflow - reaction9 \qquad (4)$$

$$\frac{dCyclin}{dt} = R1 - R2 - R3 \qquad (5)$$

Where

$reaction\_9$= compartment * (k9f * amp * atp - k9b * power(adp,2)),

$AMPflow$=compartment * amp * flow,

compartment=constant value of 1,

amp=concentration of AMP,

pyr=concentration for PYR,

adp=concentration for adenosine diphosphate,

atp=concentration of adenosine triphosphate,

$R1$=+$k1$,

$R2$=+$k2$*CYCLIN,

$R3$=$k3$* CYCLIN,

$k2$=$V2p$+apcstar*($V2pp$-$V2p$)

CYCLIN=concentration for cyclin,

apcstar=concentration of anaphase-promoting complex.

Time series data for concentration of AMP and Cyclin were ultimately produced from Equation 4 and Equation 5. The time series data contain measurement result, y, and simulated results yi for IDE, DE, and GA respectively. Error rate (e) and Average of error rate (A) are calculated according to Equation 6 and Equation 7 respectively.

$$e = \sum_{i=1}^{N} (y - yi)^2 \qquad (6)$$

$$A = \frac{e}{N} \qquad (7)$$

Table 3 and Table 4 show the average of error rate for AMP and Cyclin respectively.

Table 3.
Average of error rate for AMP.

Evaluation criteria	GA	DE	IDE
Average of error rate, A	0.000248	0.059148	0.000010

Note: Shaded column represents the best results.

Table 4.
Average of error rate for Cyclin.

Evaluation criteria	GA	DE	IDE
Average of error rate, A	1.156E-05	1.338E-05	0.001E-05

Note: Shaded column represents the best results.

For AMP (Table 3), IDE showed the lowest average of error rate with 0.000010. DE showed the worst performance with 0.059148 for the average of error rate. GA showed more moderate performance with average of error rate of 0.000248. However, for Cyclin (Table 4), IDE once again performed better than other estimation algorithms where average of error rate is 0.001E-05. The average of error rate for DE and GA are 1.338E-05 and 1.156 E-05 respectively. Lower average of error rate denotes that the simulated results are close to the measurement results and this shows the ability of Kalman filter to handle noisy data makes the IDE robust to noisy data.

Table 5 shows execution time of each estimation algorithm on a Core i5 PC with 4GB main memory. The result shows that DE required the longest time (6 minutes and 1 second and 9 minutes and 30 seconds) to find the optimal value for all kinetic parameters compared to IDE which took the shortest time (5 minutes and 35 seconds and 6 minutes 55 seconds). It is shown that IDE tends to use less computation time than DE and GA for glycolysis pathway and Novak Tyson Cell Cycle respectively.

Table 5.
Execution time of IDE compared with GA and DE.

Execution time (hh:mm:ss)	GA	DE	IDE
glycolysis pathway	00:05:42	00:06:01	00:05:35
Novak Tyson Cell Cycle	00:07:12	00:09:30	00:06:55

Note: Shaded column represents the best results.

Figure 2 shows the metabolite production graphs for the metabolites AMP and Cyclin based on the kinetic parameters that are collected from previous works [27, 28] and produced by IDE. The results showed that the kinetic parameters generated by IDE, enhanced the production rate where the dotted simulated lines (generated with the kinetics parameters that resulted by IDE) are moved to left when compared to the measurement lines (generated with the kinetics parameters that retrieved from experimental work).

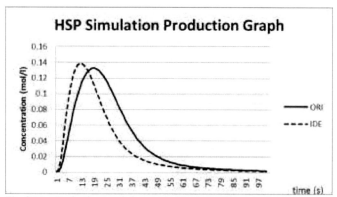

Fig. 2 (a). Production graph for metabolite HSP (ORI generated with the kinetic parameters that retrieved from experimental work and IDE generated with the kinetic parameters that was produced by IDE)

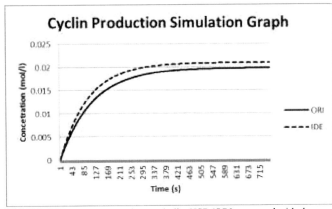

Fig. 2(b). Production graph for metabolite HSP (ORI generated with the kinetic parameters that retrieved from experimental work and IDE generated with the kinetic parameters that was produced by IDE)

Mean (*mu*) and standard deviation (STD) values are calculated according to the equation below.

$$mu = \frac{\sum_{i=1}^{N} e}{N} \tag{8}$$

$$S = \frac{\sum_{i=1}^{N} \left((y - yi)^2 - mu \right)^2}{N - 1} \tag{9}$$

Table 6 shows the mean and STD values of fitness value for glycolysis pathway, and theronine biosynthesis pathway for 50 runs respectively. Fitness function implemented in this study is to minimize the difference between measurement results and simulated results. Based on the result from the table, STD values for metabolites AMP and Cyclin are 0.0992 and 0.0182. However, the mean for metabolites AMP and Cyclin are 0.0453 and 0.0027. The standard deviation is a measure of how widely values are scattered from the average value (the mean). The mean and STD values are close to 0 and this shows that results produced by IDE are consistent with low error rate. Other than that, it can also be analyzed that in the 50 runs simulation, the differences between each run are small as the STD values showed are close to the mean values which is close to 0. This deduces that IDE is a stable and reliable algorithm.

Table 6

Mean and standard deviation (STD) values of fitness value for glycolysis pathway, and Novak Tyson Cell Cycle for 50 runs.

	AMP	Cyclin
Mean	0.0453	0.0027
STD	0.0992	0.0182

According to Lillacci and Khammash (2010), to ensure that the final estimates are guaranteed to be statistically consistent with the measurements, chi-square test (X^2 test) as a statistical test is implemented. The degrees of freedom, s and confidence coefficient, γ implemented in this paper are 1 and 0.995. Interval estimates, σ^2 formed based on s, γ, and the

formula found in Lillacci and Khammash (2010) is 0.0000393 $< \sigma^2 < 9.550$. The hypothesis made here is that the simulated results are statistically consistent with the measurement results. X^2 value for metabolite HSP is 0.028956054 and metabolite Cyclin is 0.0000563 where both are appeared to be in between σ^2. Therefore, IDE passed the X^2 test, hypothesis accepted and the simulated results are proved to be statistically consistent with the measurement results.

IDE exhibits lesser computation time and possesses a higher accuracy when compared to both GA and DE. The implementation of DE that aims to estimate the relevant kinetic parameters and the additional of Kalman gain value which targets to handle the noisy data has improved the computational time and accuracy. Hence, the IDE, a stable and reliable estimation algorithm, which is a hybrid of DE and KF minimizes the computational time and also increases the accuracy between the simulated results and measurement results.

IV. CONCLUSION

In this paper, the experiment to compare the performances of three different estimation algorithms using glycolysis pathway data in yeast [27] and Novak Tyson Cell Cycle in frog egg cell [28] showed that an improved algorithm, IDE which is a hybrid algorithm of DE and KF performed the best with the shortest execution time and the lowest average of error rate. It successfully minimizes the high difficulty of the system in estimating the relevant kinetic parameters resulting in shorter computation time. The ability to handle noisy data has contributed to an improved accuracy of the estimated results. Besides that, IDE shows that it is a stable and reliable estimation algorithm by passing the chi square test (X^2 test) and showing the mean and STD value closer to 0 with 50 runs. In conclusion, IDE, a reliable algorithm is shown to be superior compared to both GA and DE in terms of computational time and accuracy. IDE can be generalized where it can be implemented in the areas which its data consists of noisy for example electrical and electronic engineering field [29].

DE shows to be very delicate to control parameters: population size (*NP*), crossover constant (*CR*), and mutation factor (*F*) [23]. Thus, for future work, self-adapting approach to these control parameters can be implemented to enhance the performance of the IDE. Moreover, additional steps can be added to the process of generating new populations with the aim of improving the performance of IDE.

ACKNOWLEDGMENT

Here we would like to take this opportunity to express our gratitude and appreciation to all the people who have given their heart whelming full support in making this paper a magnificent experience. To God the father of all, we thank him for the strength and wisdom that keeps us standing and for the hope that keeps us believing that this work would be possible and more interesting. We also wanted to thank our family who inspired, encouraged and fully supported us for every trial that comes our way. To our colleagues who helped us ideas that needed for this work.

REFERENCES

[1] M. R. Fernandez, P. Mendes, and J. R. Banga, "A hybrid approach for efficient and robust parameter estimation in biochemical pathways," Biosystems, vol. 83, no. 2-3, 2006, pp. 248-265.

[2] R. S. Costa, D. Machado, I. Rocha, and E. C. Ferreira, "Hybrid dynamic modeling of Escherichia coli central metabolic network combining Michaelis–Menten and approximate kinetic equations," BioSystems, vol. 100, 2010, pp. 150-157.

[3] G. Koh, D. Hsu, and P. S. Thiagarajan, "Component-based construction of bio-pathway models: The parameter estimation problem," Theoretical Computer Science, vol. 412, 2011, pp. 2840-2853.

[4] P. Lecca, "Simulating the cellular passive transport of glucose using a time-dependent extension of Gillespie algorithm for stochastic π-calculus," Int. J. of Data Mining and Bioinformatics, vol. 4, 2007, pp.315-336.

[5] M. Ashyraliyev, Y. F. Nanfack, J. A. Kaandorp, and J. G. Blom, "Systems biology: parameter estimation for biochemical models," FEBS J. vol 276 no. 4, Feb 2009, pp.886-902.

[6] P. K. Liu, and F. S. Wang, "Hybrid differential evolution with geometric mean mutation in parameter estimation of bioreaction systems with large parameter search space," Computers and Chemical Engineering, Vol. 33, 200, pp. 1851–1860.

[7] C. Chassagnole, D. A. Fell, B. Rais, B. Kudla, and J. P. Mazat, "Control of the threonine-synthesis pathway in Escherichia coli: a theoretical and experimental approach," Biochem J., Vol. 356, No. 2, 2001, pp. 433-444.

[8] O. R. Gonzalez, C K, K. Jung, P. C. Naval Jr, and E. Mendoza, "Parameter estimation using Simulated Annealing for S-system models of biochemical networks," Bioinformatics, vol. 23, no. 4, 2007, pp. 480-486.

[9] S. Katare, A. Bhan, J. M. Caruthers, W. N. Delgass, and V. Venkatasubramanian, "A hybrid genetic algorithm for efficient parameter estimation of large kinetic models," Computers and Chemical Engineering, vol. 28, 2004, pp. 2569–2581.

[10] J. R. Porter, J. S. Burg, P. J. Espenshade, and P. A. Iglesias, "Identifying static nonlinear structure in a biological system using noisy, sparse data," Journal of Theoretical Biology, in press.

[11] C. G. Moles, P. Mendes, and J. R. Banga, "Parameter Estimation in Biochemical Pathways: A Comparison of Global Optimization Methods," Genome Res., vol. 13, 2006, pp. 2467-2474.

[12] J. A. Nelder, and R. Mead, "A Simplex Method for Function Minimization, " The Computer Journal, vol. 7, no. 4, 1965, pp. 308-313.

[13] J. L. M. González, Parameter Optimisation and Adjustment by the Simplex Method (Nelder-Mead). Valladolid, Spain: Universidad de Valladolid, 2001.

[14] Back, T. (2009) Simulated Annealing [online]. LIACS Natural Computing Group Leiden University.

[15] A.T. Kalai, and S. Vempala, "Simulated Annealing for Convex Optimization," Mathematics of Operations Research, vol. 31 no. 2, 2006, pp. 1–17.

[16] D. Handerson, H. S. Jacobson, and A. W. Johnson "The Theory And Practice Of Simulated Annealing," Theory and Practice, vol. 7, 2003, pp. 287–319.

[17] F. Richard, S. G. Harvey, and W. Gunter, "A Hybrid Optimization Approach to Parameter Estimation," in Proceedings of 17th European Symposium on Computer Aided Process Engineering (ESCAPE17), Bucharest, Romania, 2007, pp. 75-80.

[18] R. Donaldson, and G. David, "A Model Checking Approach to the Parameter Estimation of Biochemical Pathway," in Proceedings of 6th Conference on Computational Methods in Systems Biology (CMSB), Rostock-Warnemünde, Germany, 2008, pp. 269-287.

[19] M. J. Gao, J. Xu, J. W. Tian, and H. Wu, "Path Planning for Mobile Robot Based on Chaos Genetic Algorithm," in Proceedings of Fourth International Conference Natural Computation (ICNC), Jinan, China, 2008, pp. 409-413.

[20] S. F. Hwang, and R. S. He, "A hybrid real-parameter genetic algorithm for function optimization," Advanced Engineering Informatics, vol. 20, 2006, pp. 7–21.

[21] F. S. Wang, and J. P. Chiou, "Estimation of Monod model parameters by hybrid differential evolution," Bioprocess and Biosystems Engineering, vol. 24, 2001, pp. 109–113.

[22] S. Moonchai, W. Madlhoo, K. Jariyachavalit, H. Shimizu, S. Shioya, and S. Chauvatcharin, "Application of a mathematical model and Differential Evolution algorithm approach to optimization of bacteriocin production by Lactococcus lactis C7," Bioprocess and Biosystems Engineering, vol. 28, 2005, pp. 1–17.

[23] L. Feng, Y. F. Yang, and Y. X. Wang, "A New Approach to Adapting Control Parameters in Differential Evolution Algorithm," Lecture Notes in Computer Science, vol. 5361/2008, 2008, pp. 433-444.

[24] M. J. Dunlop, E. Franco, and R. M. Murray, "A Multi-Model Approach to Identification of Biosynthetic Pathways" in Proceedings of American Control Conference (ACC), New York, USA, 2007, pp. 1600 – 1605.

[25] R. Storn, and K. Price, "Differential Evolution – A Simple and Efficient Heuristic for Global Optimization over Continuous Spaces.," Journal of Global Optimization , vol. 11, no. 4 1997, pp. 341-359.

[26] J. A. Cetto, The Kalman Filter [online]. Institut de Robotica i Informatica Industrial, UPC-CSIC. Llorens i Artigas 4-6, Edifici U, 2a pl.   Barcelona   08028,   Spain.

[27] K. Nielson, P. G. Sorensen, F. Hynne, and H. G. Busse, "Sustained oscillations in glycolysis: an experimental and theoretical study of chaotic and complex periodic behavior and of quenching of simple oscillations," Biophysical Chemistry, vol. 72, 1998, pp. 49-62.

[28] M. T. Borisuk, and J. J. Tyson, "Bifurcation analysis of a model of mitotic control in frog eggs," J Theor Biol, vol. 195, no. 1, 1997, pp. 69-85.

[29] U. Z. Ijaz, A. K. Khambampati, J. S. Lee, S. Kim, and K. Y. Kim, "Nonstationary phase boundary estimation in electrical impedance tomography using unscented Kalman filter," Journal of Computational Physics, vol. 227, no. 15, 2008, pp. 7089-7112.

Chuii Khim Chong was born in Malaysia, on March 22, 1986. She received the BSc degrees in Computer Science from Universiti Teknologi Malaysia, in 2010. She is now a PhD student at the Artificial Intelligence and Bioinformatics Research Group, Faculty of Computer Science and Information System, Universiti Teknologi Malaysia, Malaysia. Her research interests include evolutionary algorithms, database, and programming. She has published 2 international referred publications.

Dr. Mohd Saberi Mohamad was born in Malaysia, on February 03, 1980. He received the BSc and MSc degrees in Computer Science both from Universiti Teknologi Malaysia, in 2002 and 2005, respectively. He received the PhD degree in Intelligent Systems for Bioinformatics from Osaka Prefecture University in 2010. He is now a senior lecturer at Faculty of Computer Science and Information Systems, Universiti Teknologi Malaysia, Malaysia. His journal papers in the field of bioinformatics using computational intelligence approaches have been published with the total number is more than 20 papers. He has interests in computational methods such as particle swarm optimizers, hybrid approaches, genetic algorithms, support vector machines, and neural networks.

Prof. Dr. Safaai Deris (M'98) was born in Malaysia on August 13, 1955. He is a Professor of Artificial Intelligence and Software Engineering at Faculty of Computer Science and Information Systems, Universiti Teknologi Malaysia. He received the M. E. degree in Industrial Engineering, and the Doctor of Engineering degree in Computer and System Sciences, both from Osaka Prefecture University, Japan, in 1989 and 1997, respectively. His recent academic interests include the application of intelligent techniques in scheduling and bioinformatics. He is also a reviewer for several refereed journals.

Dr. Mohd Shahir Shamsir received his PhD in Computer Science from the University of Exeter in 2005. He is currently a senior lecturer and IT Manager in Universiti Teknologi Malaysia. His research interests include Biodiversity informatics, biodiversity databases, visualisation of data and data curation for biodiversity. Using Molecular Dynamics in studying protein folding, behaviour and conformations especially those related to conformational diseases. Other interests are in the area of pedagogy used in bioinformatics education.

Yee Wen Choon is a postgraduate student at the Artificial Intelligence and Bioinformatics Research Group, Faculty of Computer Science and Information System, Universiti Teknologi Malaysia. Her research interests include evolutionary algorithms, metabolic engineering, and programming. She has published 1 international referred publication.

Chai Lian En is a postgraduate student at the Artificial Intelligence and Bioinformatics Research Group, Faculty of Computer Science and Information System, Universiti Teknologi Malaysia. His current research interests involve modelling gene networks using statistical methods, including DBN, as well as analysis of cDNA microarray gene expression data.

Integration of Multiple Data Sources for predicting the Engagement of Students in Practical Activities

Llanos Tobarra[1], Salvador Ros[1], Roberto Hernández[1], Antonio Robles-Gómez[1], Agustín C. Caminero[1], and Rafael Pastor[1]

[1]*Communication and Control System Department, from Spanish University for Distance Education (Universidad Nacional de Educación a Distancia, UNED)*

Abstract — **This work presents the integration of an automatic assessment system for virtual/remote laboratories and the institutional Learning Management System (LMS), in order to analyze the students' progress and their collaborative learning in virtual/remote laboratories. As a result of this integration, it is feasible to extract useful information for the characterization of the students' learning process and detecting the students' engagement with the practical activities of our subjects. From this integration, a dashboard has been created to graphically present to lecturers the analyzed results. Thanks to this, faculty can use the analyzed information in order to guide the learning/teaching process of each student. As an example, a subject focused on the configuration of network services has been chosen to implement our proposal.**

Keywords — **Learning Analytics (LA), Assessment and Evaluation Strategies, Virtual/Remote Laboratories, Collaborative Tools, Distance Education.**

I. INTRODUCTION

THE evaluation procedure is a key element within the process of learning. Basically, it allows faculty to check whether educative objectives are accomplished, not only by students, but also by all the participants involved in an educative program [25], such as pedagogical resources. As a consequence, lecturers are required to adapt the learning process to students' needs or preferences, reinforcing or extending it if necessary, according to the European Higher Education Area (EHEA) [27]. The importance of evaluation procedures is even greater at distance Universities since their students' learning process is different from that of face-to-face universities. In distant Universities, students must be more independent and self-demanding since there are no tight schedules, and this heavily affects the evaluation process. By means of evaluation, faculty can select the suitable learning results and adapt dynamically the subject contents to students [22].

On the other hand, adaptive hypermedia has been widely used for the development of customized Web-based courses in the field of Education [3]. Therefore, the students' learning process was guided, adapting both pedagogical resources and learning ways to specific user's features. Since lecturers adapt course materials to students' skills and usage data dynamically [15], they were able to acquire more knowledge in less time. ELM-ART [31] and TANGOW [4] are some examples of traditional educational adaptive systems. The students' interaction in these types of architectures is different from face-to-face students, as stated in [28]. In particular, students have to be able to adapt their communication way to the user interfaces of systems adapted to the students' needs [14].

It is also important to include collaborative issues taking into account the students' behavior. The most relevant research works related to adaptation in Computer Support for Collaborative Learning (CSCL) systems are COALE [9], WebDL [12], and COL-TANGOW [4]. COALE is a collaborative environment where different exercises are recommended to students. The main goal in WebDL is to facilitate user access to services. It focuses on adaptive support for navigation. COL-TANGOW is also a system that supports the dynamic generation of adaptive Web-based courses by selecting, at every step and for each student, the most suitable activities to be proposed.

Nowadays, the evolution of the Web 2.0 allows us to develop more sophisticated techniques to analyze more efficiently the students' learning process, in order to improve the learning contents and structure of a course. One of the most recent research areas is Learning Analytics (LA) [5], [7], [19] in order to discover and organize the information contained in the educational platform. Its main goal is to discover and organize the existing information in order to extract useful knowledge during the teaching/learning process.

Thus, this work is focused on a case of study in which two sources of information, AutoES (our automatic assessment system for virtual/remote laboratories) and the institutional Learning Management System (LMS), are aggregated to analyze the students' progress and their collaborative learning in virtual/remote laboratories. Guiding this process the following research questions arise:

1. Are the students engaged with the proposed practical activities or are they at risk of quitting the activities?

2. Can we create a system that helps to evaluate if the proposed activities are well-designed?

Within the context of the evaluation activities, two different learning processes have been detected. First, the practical experimentation in the virtual/remote laboratory with the virtual machines picked up by AutoES and, second, the students' knowledge creation through the discussion threats contained in the evaluation forums. Both of these learning processes are highlighted by lecturers when they are asked about how they perform the evaluation of students. So, there is a strong need to aggregate both data sources in order to answer to the aforementioned questions. In order to present these aggregated data to lecturers, a dashboard has been developed. This dashboard contains quantitative and qualitative information for lecturers about the students' experimental and collaborative progress during the evaluation procedure. These data will be validated by means of a set of learning indicators and their graphical visualization. In particular, the dashboard shows a set of evaluation events for each activity, the students' social network, the students' timeline for their activities, and some relevant metrics associated to them.

The remainder of this paper is organized as follows. Section II presents the different data sources that are aggregate in order to fulfill our research questions. After that, our proposal of the aggregated Learning Analytics dashboard, as a result of the integration of AutoES and the institutional LMS, is detailed in Section III. Section IV describes the visualization of the selected learning parameters, and Section V discusses the implications of this research work and some recommendations are given. Finally, Section V highlights our final remarks and suggests guidelines for future work.

II. DATA SOURCES

The sources used in this work come from a self-evaluation system, named AutoES (AutoEvaluation System) [21], and the institutional Learning Management System (LMS). From this information, a data aggregation process will be done.

A. AutoES

The main objective of AutoES [21] is the management of the self-evaluation of practical activities with virtual/remote laboratories and the continuous assessment of the students' progress. It is a service-oriented application, which is considered as the latest generation of Internet-based platforms [20]. Using it, students will be able to perform a self-evaluation of their activities, which they performed with remote laboratories. Additionally, AutoES can solve all the errors made in the activity or configure it completely, with a penalty in the mark for the activity.

AutoES has several main benefits for the members of the learning community, especially within the field of distance higher education. First, it minimizes the response time in correcting students' practical activities, allowing the continuous evaluation process to be performed smoothly. Furthermore, it provides a more detailed monitoring of the students' progress, thereby reducing the time spent on the assessments themselves. The importance of these benefits is really significant, since the number of students enrolled in a course with a distance methodology can become very high. Thus, lecturers can focus on other tasks, such as dynamic adaptation of new activities to students' necessities or expanding the existing ones, which in turn improves the learning process more than devoting their time to correcting the students' activities.

AutoES is made of two different parts: the lecturers 'view and the students' view. From the lecturers' view, lecturers can perform subject management tasks such as selecting the activities for the subject, creating different groups with activities adapted to the students' level, checking students' progress by means of reports, etc. This view is presented by a Web application, named *LabManager*, which is accessible by lecturers through any Internet browser. For each particular student, Lab Manager provides last, maximum, and mean qualifications for each activity. Lecturers will be able to assign a student's final qualification according to these previous ones. It also includes the groups to which he/she belongs and the corresponding activities assigned. Note that the system allows lecturers to split up the subject's students by levels or types of activities. In addition, the system provides statistics about the student's run status and run time. From the learning process point of view, lecturers have several indicators of the students' performance, among others, number of tries for each activity, number of successful evaluations per activity and student, number of failed evaluations per activity and student, and a summary of the evaluation logs. Finally, a list of recent reports is stored for each of them, which can be checked by lecturers at will.

From the students' view, AutoES can automatically configure and/or evaluate a particular activity. Every time they check an activity, a report is created that summarizes the results of this checking. This report is presented each time the student checks an activity as a console message. So, students find out which parts of a particular activity are wrong and, additionally, AutoES can help them when they are not able to do a part of the activity. All this information will be automatically updated on the server side so that it can be used by lecturers to improve the learning process and to decide on the students' marks.

The architecture of AutoES is shown in Figure 1, including the interaction between its main elements, which are Web Client, Lab Manager, and Web Server.

Apart from the learning indicators that will be detailed in the next section, AutoES offers a set of parameters for each proposed activity and student:

1) Start date and time.
2) Finish date and time.
3) Number of successfully evaluations for that activity.
4) Number of failed evaluations for that activity.
5) Logs of errors.

These parameters are included in the aggregation data and

in the dashboard.

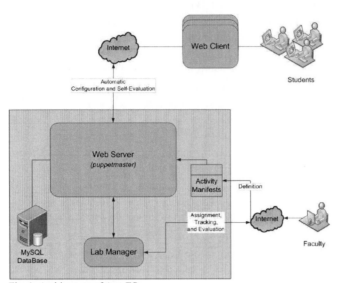

Fig. 1. Architecture of AutoES.

B. The Institutional LMS

The LA process is focused on all the information gathered from all the activities that are crucial for the lecturer's daily-work, especially when applying to a distance methodology. For this reason, a clear necessity of processing all this information appears in order to allow lecturers to extract interesting conclusions for the dynamic adaptation of the learning process to students. It is clear that the information provided by AutoES allows lecturers to have a partial view of the learning process, and it must be combined with the data contained within the LMS.

Therefore, there is a need to enrich the lecturer knowledge of the learning process through the information gathered by both AutoES and the LMS. After the revision of all the relevant educational tools inside the LMS, the forums have been pointed out as the most relevant information source for collaborative evaluation. The use of asynchronous on-line discussion forums is thought to be essential for the negotiation and exchange of ideas, as well as the development of critical thinking skills, all of which are important components of the collaborative learning process [10], [11], [16]. Furthermore, several studies have demonstrated a high correlation of students' participation levels in discussion forums with positive learning outcomes and knowledge constructions [23], [24].

In this sense, as a result of the integration of both learning environments, the aggregation dashboard can graphically show the students' progress both in an experimental and collaborative way at the same time. Therefore, lecturers can guide each student through the learning process based on his/her particular level of proficiency and grade her/him at the end of the term. In particular, the data aggregation, the computation of learning parameters, and their visualization are detailed below.

C. Data Aggregation

As explained before, within the context of the evaluation activities, we have found two learning processes. First, the practical experimentation with the virtual machines picked up by AutoES, and second, the students' knowledge creation through the discussion in the evaluation forums. These learning processes are highlighted by lecturers when they are questioned about how they perform the evaluation of students. Therefore, if we want to represent the learning process into our analysis, at least these two sources of information should be merged: AutoES' events and forums' evaluation messages.

There are other data sources that provide relevant data for the learning process. On one hand, we cannot extract further data from AutoES without changing the basis of the system. Nevertheless, the LMS can offer additional information, such as quizzes scores, activities' deadlines, time spent in the platform, and so on. As this work is a starting point of our research, we only consider the most relevant data sources, but in the future additional data should be aggregated in order to capture all the possible factors. According to this, there are several factors that cannot be obtained neither AutoES nor the LMS, such as personal conditions of students (social environment, health status…), and they may affect the learning process.

Because of the fact that both systems, AutoES and the LMS, have their own data representation, a database merging process is defined. So, in order to have the same representation for both databases, a generic register is created. Afterwards, the data from AutoES and forums are stored in the same database thus further computations are easier.

Each student's interaction is represented by a register within this "merging" process. A register is a structured data generated every time that a student performs an activity which happens at a particular time, and it could produce an output result. Each register contains the following data:

1) A register identifier.
2) The identifier of the user that generates the event.
3) The course to which the students belongs.
4) The type of activity that is represented by the register.
5) An associated report about the activity.
6) The practice associated with the activity.
7) The date and time when the activity takes place.

Thus, a student can produce a set of types of activities inside our learning context, namely:

1) Creation of a user at AutoES (called *created event*). Students enroll themselves dynamically, thus a register is created in this case. In this case, the report field is empty.
2) When a user starts AutoES tool (called *unchanged event*). The report field is empty.
3) A successful evaluation that produces a report as an output result (called *success event*). In this case, the report field contains a brief text that reports about the evaluation.
4) A failed evaluation that produces a report as an output

result (called *fail event*). In this case, the report field contains a brief summary about the errors that are found.

5) Publication of a new thread message inside the evaluation forum, where the message is the output result (called *init message event*). In this case, the report contains the posted message.

6) Response to a previous message inside the evaluation forum, where the message is the result (called *response to event*). In this case, the report contains the posted message.

7) Initiates a new activity, and the previous activity is finished (called *added to event*). The report field contains a reference to the finished activity and the activity field contains the identifier of the just started activity.

8) When a user gives up the AutoES tool (called *removed event*). The report field is empty in this type of register.

For this analysis, not all messages located at the forums are interesting. In this sense, previously to the merging process, the messages have been classified in several topic categories by using the cluster k- means algorithm and a bag-of-words approach. So, messages can be correlated with the evaluation activities due to their content and, additionally, filter which messages are relevant for the learning/evaluation process. Messages not related to the evaluation activities or whose contents are not relevant, are dropped from our study.

III. DESCRIPTION OF LEARNING INDICATORS

Lecturers should evaluate not only the results, but also the experimental process conducted in the student's virtual/remote laboratory. During the learning process, it is very relevant to detect students at risk of quitting the activities and help them, because if nothing is done, they will not acquire the required learning skills. So, the main objective of this work is answering the following questions using the aggregation of the information of the previously described data sources.

1. Are the students engaged with the proposed practical activities or are they at risk of quitting the activities?
2. Can we create a system that helps to evaluate if the proposed activities are well-designed?

For that purpose, we have computed three indicators that represent their learning outcomes from the activities and four indicators correlated with the behavior of the student in the forums. All the indicators are graphically represented in the aggregation dashboard so lecturers can easily get an overview of the learning progress of each student.

The "*On time*" indicator is focused on the time spent on the realization of the evaluation activity. For the whole population, the average time to solve each activity is computed. Each student's time is compared to this average result by computing the student's corresponding z-score. A higher z-score means that the student is delayed with regard to his/her group and he/she is at risk of quitting. As oppose to this, a lower value

means that he/she is solving the activities quickly. This indicator is usually higher at the beginning of the course, and it should decrease as the course goes by and the student is achieving the subject's objectives.

In a similar way, the second parameter called "*Failure rate*", is devoted to analyzing the number of failed evaluations for each student. The number of failed evaluations per activity, the time between failed evaluations, and the student's z-score, calculated by comparing each students' statistics with the average of all the students', are also calculated. A high z-score value means that the student has problems to solve the activity, so the lecturer should offer some additional help. It is also a source of frustration for the student and he/she may decide to quit. A lower value of this indicator means that the student has solved the activity with fewer problems than his/her classmates.

Finally, the third parameter called "*Success rate*" is correlated to successful evaluations. It is computed similarly to the failed evaluation parameter. The number of success evaluations per activity, the time between success evaluations, and the student's z-score, calculated by comparing each student's statistics with the average of all the students', are also calculated. A high z-score value means that the student has not problems to solve the activity. On the other hand, a low value for "*Success rate*" indicator in combination with a high value of "*Failure rate*" indicator could mean that the student is having trouble to solve the activities.

On the other hand, Social Network Analysis (SNA) provides a powerful mechanism for understanding how human relationships are created and developed, as well as detecting communication patterns and structures that should appear from these interactions [13], [26]. In [18], it is proved that there is a correlation between forum interactions and the students' performance. This correlation is also explored by the tool SNAPP [6] and Vercellone-Smith et al. [29] by means of social networks analysis. According to this, a Social Network (SN) can be represented as a directed graph in which nodes are individual or grouped users and links are the relationships among people. Nodes are also used to represent concepts, events, ideas, and other learning elements. These networks are usually built upon gathering and processing the information obtained from the LMS, where interactions among nodes are established in order to acquire new knowledge within a social community.

In our particular case, the creation of a SN graph for the analysis of educational communities is based on the messages published in discussion forums. More in detail, links between two nodes, where each node represents a particular student, are weighted with the amount of messages exchanged [6]. Thus, the analysis performed of the resulting social network allows lecturers to analyze the interest propagation of their group of students, as observed in Figure 3.

We have computed four basic indicators inside the social network that help lecturers analyze the student's progress and their level of proficiency.

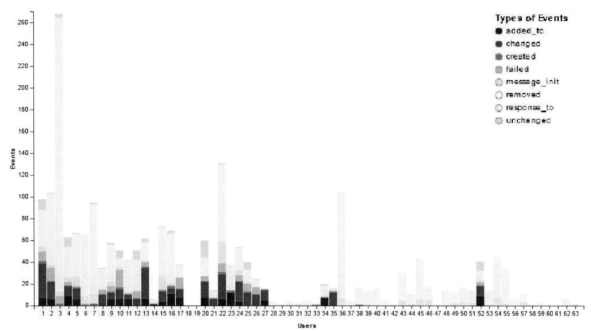

Fig. 2. Events per User by Including Students' Forums Interactions.

There are a variety of different measures to evaluate the importance, popularity, or social capital of a node within a social network:

1) *Degree centrality (interactivity)* focuses on individual nodes, it counts the number of edges that a node has. This value represents the interactivity level of the student; that is, how often the student posts in forums. This indicator could have several meanings that are qualified with the rest of learning indicators.

2) *Betweenness centrality (broker/hub)* of a node is the sum of the fraction of all-pairs shortest paths that pass through that node. Nodes that occur on many shortest paths between other nodes in the graph have a high betweenness centrality score and are more likely to behave as a hub or broker in the network. In this context, students tend to group into communities at forums. The students that behave as hubs or brokers in the social networks allow the exchange of ideas among communities due to the fact that they take part in several of them.

3) *Eigenvector centrality (neighborhood)* of a node, which is proportional to the sum of the centrality scores of its neighbors. A node is important if it is connected to other important nodes. A node with a small number of influential contacts may outrank one with a larger number of non-popular contacts. Thus, this parameter measures the relevance of the neighbors of a student. A better group of neighbors will help a student to create a better collaborative knowledge and it will encourage him to do the activities.

In addition to popularity measures, we pay attention to the *clustering coefficient (integration)* for each student. The bachelorhood of a node that represents a student is a set of nodes connected to it by an edge, not including itself inside the social network. The clustering coefficient of a node is the fraction of pairs of its neighbors that have edges between one another. Locally, this indicates how concentrated the neighborhood of a node is. A higher clustering coefficient means that the student has been exchanging messages with a high portion of the classroom.

The combination of these learning indicators allows lecturers to answer our research questions. According to the first question related to the *student's engagement with the activities*, an interactive student that presents a high degree centrality value with also a high value for "*Success rate*" indicator and a low value for "*Failure rate*" indicator means that the student is helping other students with the activities sharing his/her knowledge. It is common that each community is created with at least one student with these parameters. A particular case is if this student could have a high value as *betweennes centralities* because his/her answers are popular and he/she becomes member of more than one community. And it is also very frequent that the *eigenvector centrality value* of the student is as high as the clustering coefficient. So, this student is going to successfully pass the activities with high scores.

On the other hand, a very interactive student with a high value for "*On time*" indicator and a high value for indicator "*Failure rate*" could have serious problems in order to solve the activity and he/she is searching for help among his/her peers. Lecturers in this case must pay attention to the student and they should offer additional learning resources because he/she is at risk of quitting the activities. Students at risk could also have a low value of *betweenness centrality* and a low value of *eigenvector centrality* because he/she is not posting solutions of problems, which are popular messages.

Our second research question is easily answered starting from the previous results. If during the period of an activity, the number of students at risk of quitting computed with learning indicators has increased substantially, while during other activities the same students have a more successful performance, maybe lecturers should consider redesign the activity. That activity could be too complex or the resources for the development of the activity are not clear. This type of situation is often accompanied by an increase of the number of exchanged messages at the forums under the label of that activity. So, lecturers must be aware of the evolution of the performance of the students during the course. Further analysis over the interrelation of these parameters could help to detect automatically an activity, whose design is not correct by describing some threshold values. But, lecturers should supervise this classification. In addition, these value thresholds could be correlated to the learning context (subject, course…), thus it is a difficult task for automation.

IV. VISUALIZATION OF LEARNING PARAMETERS

In order to allow faculty to easily see these indicators and use them to guide the learning/teaching process of students, a dashboard with a Graphical User Interface (GUI) has been developed. Figures 3 and 4 show the most relevant lecturers' interfaces of our proposed LA dashboard.

When a faculty starts browsing in the home view of our LA dashboard, he/she can visualize several graphs, such as the one depicted at Figure 2, which summarize all the events. In addition to offering a global view of what happens in AutoES and evaluation forums at the same time, the lecturer can also observe (as a colored calendar) the set of events generated by each student, as presented in Figure 4(b). This way, a lecturer can easily verify the generated events, and why they are produced. An improvement will be that students and lecturers can compare this activity with the average activity of the course. So, students can be aware of their performance and adapt it in order to improve their learning outcomes.

As we mentioned above, we offer lecturers the possibility of examining the social network generated in the course. The size of students' node is directly proportional to his/her network degree. Additionally, the virtual students' communities represented by the social network are computed by following the Louvain method [2]. Students in the same community are colored with the same color. This visualization is represented at Figure 3.

Finally, we include a graphical visualization for the previously explained indicators; see Figure 4(a). There is a matrix with a cell for each pair <student, indicator>. If a student has a poor performance in an indicator, the cell representing it is colored in a darker red. On the other hand, if the performance of the student for an indicator is good, the indicator cell is colored with a dark blue color. So, lecturers can easily interpret the combined indicators through this graphical representation.

V. DISCUSSION

This section discusses the implications of this research work

by taking into account our current learning context.

A. Learning Context

In order to focus this work, AutoES will only use activities related to the configuration of network services. Its scope is much broader, since this system has been designed and implemented as a modular system, which is independent of the design and implementation of specific activities with remote laboratories. In this regard, we focus on the "Network Services Management in Operating Systems" (NetServicesOS) course belonging to the "Communications, Networks, and Content Management" post-graduate program at Spanish University for Distance Education (in Spanish, Universidad Nacional de Educación a Distancia – UNED). The duration of the subject is 15 weeks in the first semester of the academic year. The main goals of the NetServicesOS are the deployment and configuration of several network services for Windows and Linux operating systems, such as DNS, DHCP, FTP, Web, etc., using virtual machines (VMs).

Thanks to the use of AutoES, lecturers can track the progress of a large number of students and adapt dynamically the learning/teaching process. Students can also receive timely feedback on their activities – which was totally impossible with our traditional evaluation system based on explanation reports for each activity.

Since the UNED University follows a distance methodology, the main element of interaction among participants in the learning/teaching process (students and lecturers) are forums, which motivate the learning/teaching process of the subject and allow the formation of virtual social communities. Lecturers play a vital role in promoting a suitable learning space that motivates the interaction among students. In our particular case, lecturers provide students with a set of practical activities which require a great interaction among students to solve them. Lecturers have created a dedicated forum related to the activities for these purposes. The interactions in forums are also taken into account by lecturers when calculating students' final grades.

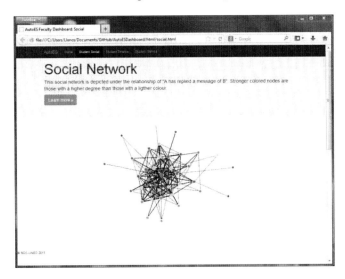

Fig. 3. Representation of the Social Network into the Dashboard.

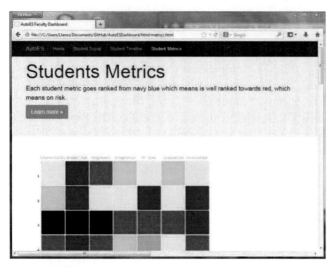

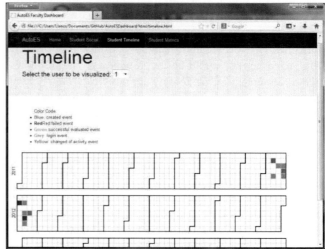

(a) Table Summary of the Student's Metrics in the Dashboard.

(b) Calendar Interface by Representing Each Student's Event.

Fig. 4. Lecturers' Visualizations in our Proposed LA dashboard (Metrics and Calendar).

B. Results

After the cleaning phase previous to the data aggregation phase, an 83% percentage of messages are relevant to the analysis. The discarded messages are not related to the subject development. Instead, they are Christmas greetings, the place where students can buy/find the bibliography, or students introductions. These topics have a very low correlation with any subject topic, but they are very correlated to an external event. They are initially inactive, although they become very active within a particular time sub-window. After that, they become again inactive. Topic characterization and its impact in the learning outcomes have been widely studied at several works, such as [7], [29], and [30].

As a result of this merging process, there are 2179 events located in the final database, where 1583 are forum's events; this result is depicted in Figure 2. As stated above, there is a high percentage of information related to the student's learning process within the LMS. Therefore, it can be seen that the aggregation of the LMS data provides a large amount of information of great interest in order to guide our learning/teaching process. An initial approach of the statistical analysis of these events shows some relevant results, which are reflected in Figure 2. Each practice takes eleven days to be completed by a student in average.

If we pay attention to the correlation of messages and evaluation activities, we have found that most of the failed evaluations are followed by a message event; almost the 73% (see Figure 5). The visualization of Figure 5 shows the number of events per day. Each circle represents the amount of events. Thus, as the number of events is bigger, the circle is redder and its size is bigger. As we can see at day 4, as example, after the first occurrence of Failed events (which means that students fails the evaluation test), the number of events of "New threads" (which means a student has initiated a new thread in the forum) is increased. The following days the

number of events of type "Responses", which mean that students are replying messages at the forums, is higher. This frequency analysis has been completed with a topic detection analysis in order to correlate forum messages and failure events.

Also, at least the 80% of students have posted a correlated message when they are moving from one activity to other. And 68% students who did not use AutoES have replied to the doubts of the AutoES students. This means that the doubts are more related to the development of the experiment itself than to the use of AutoES.

From the Social Network graph, depicted at Figure 3, three communities are detected: blue nodes, green nodes and orange nodes. Most of the students belong to the blue cluster, while the other two are smaller. Each node represents a student, and an arc between two students represents a message exchange. The size of the representation of the node indicates the popularity of the student. There is a clear big blue node in the center of the social network that is the lecturer, who plays a relevant role in the bigger community. In the same figure, we can clearly see that there are several students which have exchanged a very few messages. These students could be at risk and the lecturer should pay attention to the other learning indicators.

There are 36 students in the classroom who decided to work with AutoES. It is also relevant that students execute more than once the evaluation of each practice if he/she has obtained a successful evaluation. This fact can be easily detected with the timeline representation (see Figure 4(b)). As an example, the first activity, when a user is successfully evaluated, he/she is evaluated nine times in average. This situation occurs more often at the beginning of the use of AutoES rather than in the last part. So, students need a period of time for learn how to use the AutoES tool. Also, AutoES output must be improved in order to help students with this

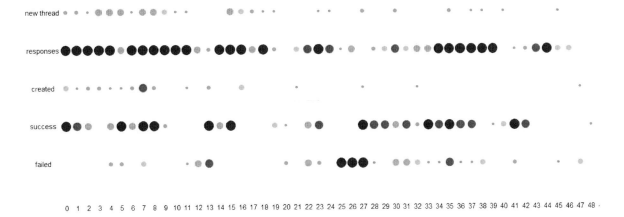

Fig. 5. Graph related to the Evolution of the Activity during the Course.

regard. Another relevant result is that failed evaluations are more common at the first activities rather than the last ones. While the average of failed evaluations of first practice is three by student; the average of failed evaluations of the last activity is 0.47.

There is high percentage of quitting the platform. At least 12 students stopped using the platform at the end of the course. Half of them have quitted the platform during the first activity. This fact is reflected at the dashboard Student Metrics (see Figure 4(a)), such as the learning indicators of the student 3 at Figure 4(a). This student has red values in the "On time", "Successful rate", "Failure rate" and clustering coefficient indicators. On the other hand, he has blue values degree centrality, betweenness centrality and eigenvector centrality. This student belongs to the orange community detected in the social network. It seems that he/she has sought for advice at the forum but he/she could not solve the activity. Finally, this student has stopped using AutoES.

On the other hand, at the same Figure 4(a), although student 1 has a red colored value for betweenness centrality and a pale value for eigenvector centrality, he/she has light green values for the rest of the learning indicators, which means he/she is successfully completing the activities with the help of forums. In fact, this student achieved a high ranking at the course

The activity of students at risk is in some cases average, with pale red values for "On time", "Successful rate" and "Failure rate" indicators, although most of them have strong red values. Out of the 12 students who quitted using AutoES, three of them, as the student 3 of our example, have blue values for degree centrality, betweenness centrality and eigenvector centrality. This means that students were searching for advice at the forums before quitting the activity. The rest of them also have pale red values for the seven learning indicators. Lecturers must detect these students and should offer them additional help to prevent their desertion from the platform.

The number of students that have stopped using the tool is around 30% of the total. On this fact, students were requested to fill in a survey about the tool. According to this, most of the students found AutoES useful and easy to use, as detailed in

[21]. From the obtained feedback, the main drawback of AutoES was that students were not confident with the automated evaluation of the tool. This topic has also arisen in the forum messages. Thus, the activities design seems correct. But, it looks like the supporting documentation must be increased.

The obtained results from the research questions presented in this section have been validated with the real lecturers during the courses. There is a correlation among the score of the activities and the information obtained from the proposed system.

The proposed dashboard is useful with this regard. Moreover, students should have a reporting tool, such as a dashboard, that allows them to keep track of their learning process. Lecturers should periodically supervise the results of this dashboard in terms of the design of the activities.

VI. CONCLUSIONS AND FUTURE WORK

This work integrates the information gathered from AutoES, a Learning Analytics (LA) system, and the most relevant tools of our institutional LMS. Therefore, lecturers are able to acquire new useful knowledge in order to improve the learning/teaching process of our subjects. As an example, a subject focused on the configuration of network services has been chosen to implement our approach. In particular, a graphical dashboard has been built from this integration and a set of learning parameters has been analyzed, so that lecturers can guide each student through the learning process based on his/her particular knowledge-level and grade her/him at the end of the term.

As a future work, we plan to improve the functionality of the system by developing alternative indicators for the analysis of the aggregated data from AutoES and forums' messages, this way improving the adaptation of the evaluation resources to achieve more intelligent curricula [17]. Additionally, we will also aggregate other information sources that can improve the vision of the learning process. Finally, different frameworks or contexts from EHEA, as the ones proposed by the ASEE Educational Research Methods (ERM) Division [1], could be explored in order to analyze if the results obtained are similar and/or there is a need of making some changes.

ACKNOWLEGDEMENTS

Authors would like to acknowledge the support of the following European Union projects: RIPLECS (517836- LLP-1-2011-1-ES-ERASMUS-ESMO), PAC (517742-LLP-1-2011-1-BG-ERASMUS-ECUE), EMTM (2011-1-PL1-LEO05-19883), and MUREE (530332-TEMPUS-1-2012-1-JO-TEMPUS-JPCR). Furthermore, we also thank the Community of Madrid for the support of E-Madrid Network of Excellence (S2009/TIC-1650).

REFERENCES

[1] American Society for Engineering Education Educational Research and Methods Division. Web page at http://erm.asee.org/. Date of last access: June 25, 2014.

[2] V. Blondel, J. Guillaume, R. Lambiotte, and E. Mech. Fast unfolding of communities in large networks. J. Stat. Mech, 2008.

[3] P. Brusilovsky and E. Millán. User models for adaptive hypermedia and adaptive educational systems. In P. Brusilovsky, A. Kobsa, and W. Nejdl, editors, The Adaptive Web: Methods and Strategies of Web Personalization, Lecture Notes in Computer Science, pages 3–53. Springer Berlin Heidelberg, 2007.

[4] R. M. Carro, A. Ortigosa, E. Martín, and J. H. Schlichter. Dynamic generation of adaptive web-based collaborative courses. In CRIWG, pages 191–198, 2003.

[5] T. N. M. Consortium. The horizon report (2011 edition). On-Line, 2011. Date of last access: June 25, 2014.

[6] S. Dawson, L. Lockyer, A. Bakharia, E. Heathcote, L. Macfadyen, P. Long, R. Phillips, and P. Poronnik. SNAPP. On-Line, 2011. Date of last access: June 25, 2014.

[7] L. P. Dringus and T. Ellis. Temporal transitions in participation flow in an asynchronous discussion forum. Computers and Education, 54(2):340–349, 2010.

[8] T. Elias. Learning analytics: Definitions, processes and potential. On-Line, 2011. Date of last access: June 25, 2014.

[9] N. Furugori, H. Sato, H. Ogata, Y. Ochi, and Y. Yano. COALE: Collaborative and adaptive learning environment. In Proceedings of CSCL 2002, pages 493–494, 2002.

[10] D. R. Garrison, T. Anderson, and W. Archer. Critical thinking, cognitive presence, and computer conferencing in distance education. American Journal of Distance Education, 15(1):7–23, 2001.

[11] D. R. Garrison and M. Cleveland-Innes. Facilitating cognitive presence in online learning: Interaction is not enough. American Journal of Distance Education, 19(3):133–148, 2005.

[12] E. Gaudioso and J. Boticario. Supporting personalization in virtual communities in distance education. World Scientific Publishing Company, 2002.

[13] R. Hanneman and M. Riddle. Introduction to social network methods (online textbook). On-Line, 2005. Date of last access: June 25, 2014.

[14] I.-H. Hsiao and P. Brusilovsky. The role of community feedback in the student example authoring process: An evaluation of annotex. British Journal of Educational Technology, 42(3):482–499, 2011.

[15] A. Kobsa, J. Koenemann, and W. Pohl. Personalized hypermedia presentation techniques for improving online customer relationships. The Knowledge Engineering Review, 16:111–155, 2001.

[16] J. B. Pena-Shaff and C. Nicholls. Analyzing student interactions and meaning construction in computer bulletin board discussions. Computers and Education, 42(3):243–265, 2004.

[17] A. Robles-Gómez, S. Ros, R. Hernández, L. Tobarra, A. C. Caminero, R. Pastor, M. Rodríguez-Artacho, M. Castro, E. SanCristóbal, and M. Tawfik. Towards an adaptive system for the evaluation of network services. In 2013 Frontiers in Education Conference - Energizing the Future, 2013. FIE'13. 43rd Annual, pages 1–7. IEEE, 2013.

[18] C. Romero, M. I. López, J. M. Luna, and S. Ventura. Predicting students' final performance from participation in on-line discussion forums. Computers and Education, 68:458–472, 2013.

[19] Pardo, D. Burgos, and C. D. Kloos. Monitoring student progress using virtual appliances: A case study. Computers and Education, 58(4):1058–1067, 2012.

[20] S. Ros, R. Hernández, A. Robles-Gomez, A. C. Caminero, Ll. Tobarra, and E. SanCristobal. Open service-oriented platforms for personal learning environments. IEEE Internet Computing, 17(4):26–31, 2013.

[21] S. Ros, A. Robles-Gómez, R. Hernández, A. Caminero, and R. Pastor. Using virtualization and automatic evaluation: Adapting network services management courses to the EHEA. IEEE Transactions on Education, 55(2):196–202, 2012.

[22] C. Saul and H.-D. Wuttke. Towards a high-level integration of interactive tools with e-assessments. In Proceeding of IEEE International Conference on Advanced Learning Technologies (ICALT), 2012.

[23] T. Schellens and M. Valcke. Fostering knowledge construction in university students through asynchronous discussion groups. Computer and Education, 46(4):349–370, 2006.

[24] T. Schellens, H. van Keer, M. Valcke, and B. de Wever. Learning in asynchronous discussion groups: a multilevel approach to study the influence of student, group and task characteristics. Behavior and Information Technology, 26(1):55–71, 2007.

[25] L. Schrum, M. D. Burbank, and R. Capps. Preparing future teachers for diverse schools in an online learning community: Perceptions and practice. The Internet and Higher Education, 10(3):204–211, 2007.

[26] J. P. Scott. Social Network Analysis: A Handbook. SAGE Publications, 2000.

[27] Spanish Government. Ministry of Education, Culture and Sports. What is bologna? (In Spanish). On-Line, 2009. Date of last access: June 25, 2014.

[28] Ll. Tobarra, A. Robles-Gómez, S. Ros, R. Hernández, and A. C. Caminero. Analyzing the students' behavior and relevant topics in virtual learning communities. Computers in Human Behavior, 31(2):659–669, 2014.

[29] P. Vercellone-Smith, K. Jablokow, and C. Friede. Characterizing communication networks in a web-based classroom: Cognitive styles and linguistic behavior of self-organizing groups in online discussions. Computers and Education, 59(2):222–235, 2012.

[30] E. Webb, A. Jones, P. Barker, and P. van Schaik. Using e-learning dialogues in higher education. Innovations in Education and Teaching International, 41(1): 93–103, 2004.

[31] G. Weber and P. Brusilovsky. ELM-ART: An adaptive versatile system for web-based instruction. International Journal of Artificial Intelligence in Education, 12:351–384, 2001.

Llanos Tobarra received her M.Sc. degree in Computer Science in 2004 and his Ph.D. in Computer Science in 2009, both from the University of Castilla-La Mancha, Albacete, Spain. She is currently a Lecturer at the Control and Communication Systems Department at the Spanish University for Distance Education, UNED. Her interests include security support in distributed systems and the analysis of social networks and remote labs for e-learning. She has co-authored more than 30 publications in international journals and conferences on these topics.

Salvador Ros (SM'07) received his M.Sc. degree in Physics, specialized in Control and Automatic Systems, in 1991 at Complutense University, Madrid, Spain, and his Ph.D. in Computer Science in 2012 at the Spanish University for Distance Education, UNED. He is Associate Professor at the Control and Communication Systems Department at UNED. For five years (May 2004-June 2009), he has been an Educational Technologies Manager at UNED. He managed the Virtual Campus and Multimedia Production at UNED. He has also been a Technological Projects Evaluator for the Scientific Investigation, Development and Technological Innovation, Spanish National Program. He is currently a Vice Dean of Technologies at School of Computer Science at UNED. He is a senior member of IEEE.

Roberto Hernández (SM'07) received his M.Sc. degree in Physics, specialized in Electronics, in 1989 at Complutense University, Madrid, Spain. He also received his Ph.D. in Sciences in 1994 at Spanish University for Distance Education, UNED, and Madrid, Spain. He is Associate Professor at the Control and Communication Systems Department at UNED. He was the Dean of Technologies at School of Computer Science at UNED from 2005 to 2013. His research interests include quality of service support in distributed systems and development of infrastructures for e-learning. He has co-authored more than 60 publications in international journals and conferences on these topics. He is a senior member of IEEE.

Antonio Robles-Gómez (M'10) received his M.Sc. degree in Computer Science in 2004 and his Ph.D. in Computer Science in 2008, both from the University of Castilla-La Mancha, Albacete, Spain. He is an Assistant Professor at the Control and Communication Systems Department at the Spanish University for Distance Education, UNED. He teaches graduate and postgraduate courses related to the network interconnection and security domains. His research interests include quality of service support in distributed systems and development of infrastructures for e-learning. He has co-authored more than 35 publications in international journals and conferences on these topics. He is a member of IEEE.

Agustín C. Caminero (M'10) received his M.Sc. and Ph.D. degrees in Computer Science in 2004 and 2009 respectively, both from the University of Castilla-La Mancha, Albacete, Spain. After that, he was awarded with a Post-doctoral grant at Complutense University, Madrid, Spain. He is an Assistant Professor at the Control and Communication Systems Department at the Spanish University for Distance Education, UNED. His interests include quality of service support in parallel distributed computing systems, and development of infrastructures for e-learning. He has co-authored more than 35 publications in international journals and conferences on these topics. He is a member of IEEE.

Rafael Pastor (M'06) received his M.Sc. degree in Physics in 1994 at Complutense University, Madrid, Spain. He also received his Ph.D in 2006 at Spanish University for Distance Education, UNED, Madrid, Spain. He is an Associate Professor at the Control and Communication Systems Department at UNED. From 1994 to 2009, he worked at the UNED Computer Sciences Faculty, and as Innovation Manager of the Innovation and Development Centre of UNED. Since then he has been a General Manager, adding innovative services in the learning model of UNED. He is a member of the IEEE, Spanish Education Society, and .LRN Board Consortium.

## 23

A multi-agent system model to integrate Virtual Learning Environments and Intelligent Tutoring Systems

Giuffra P., Cecilia E., Silveira Ricardo A.
Departament of Informatic and Statistics
Federal University of Santa Catarina, Brasil

Abstract — **Virtual learning environments (VLEs) are used in distance learning and classroom teaching as teachers and students support tools in the teaching–learning process, where teachers can provide material, activities and assessments for students. However, this process is done in the same way for all the students, regardless of their differences in performance and behavior in the environment. The purpose of this work is to develop an agent-based intelligent learning environment model inspired by intelligent tutoring to provide adaptability to distributed VLEs, using Moodle as a case study and taking into account students' performance on tasks and activities proposed by the teacher, as well as monitoring his/her study material access.**

Keywords — **Agents, Intelligent Tutoring Systems, Multi-Agent System, Virtual Learning Environments.**

I. INTRODUCTION

THE number of students with computer access has increased substantially in recent years. A qualitative change in the teaching–learning process happens when we can integrate within an innovative view all technologies, including telematics, audiovisual, textual, oral and physical [11]. The fact of students seeking information on the computer converts them into more active students. "There are activities that can be performed with the computer, forcing the student to seek information, process it and use it to solve problems, allowing the understanding of what makes and the construction of their own knowledge" [18].

Virtual learning usually offer the same learning experience, during the course, for all students, without considering their specific needs. The problem is that the students are treated as if they always had the same profile, the same goals and the same knowledge [12].

In order to provide adaptability to learning environments, according to student characteristics, and to allow a greater interactivity degree between the learning environment and the users, the research points to the use of resources provided by artificial intelligence (AI) and in particular the use of multi-agent system-based architectures [15].

In agreement with this emerges the motivation of this research: to enhance the teaching–learning process in virtual learning environments using artificial intelligence techniques to make the environments more adaptive and more interactive. This paper proposes the use of agent-based intelligent tutoring systems architectures to get personalized teaching strategies, taking into account the student profile and his/her performance, exploring their skills as best as possible, in order to have better and more effective learning in an intelligent learning environment.

This paper is structured as follows: the second section presents the theoretical reference and related works, the third section presents the definition of the model, the fourth section presents an explanation about the model implementation and the last section presents the conclusions.

II. BACKGROUND

Virtual learning environments are technological tools and resources using cyberspace to lead content and enable pedagogical mediation through the interaction between the educational process actors [14]. The use of these environments has increased significantly by the strong possibility of interaction between student and teacher that they offer, and by easy access anywhere and anytime. The virtual learning environments provide tools for interaction, such as forums and chats, and enable the provision of materials by teachers about the content of the course.

For Dillenbourg [6], virtual learning environments are not only restricted to distance learning. Web-based education is often associated with distance learning; however, in practice it is also widely used to support classroom learning. The author also comments that the difference between these two types of education is disappearing. Many students in distance courses do not live far from school, but have time constraints. Often they work. In addition, there are courses that combine distance and presence, which makes for more robust learning environments.

Virtual learning environments, at first, were used primarily in distance learning; now they also serve as support in classroom courses, as a teacher's tool to provide materials, to review tasks, to keep track of the students on course (activity logs) and also to evaluate them. For students, the environment facilitates the delivery of tasks, the obtaining of materials for the course and the monitoring of their evaluation.

Virtual learning environments can be enhanced with artificial intelligence techniques, using intelligent agents, having intelligent learning environments as result. An agent is an abstraction of something that can perceive its environment through sensors and can act upon that environment through actuators [16]. Intelligent agents are those that have at least the following characteristics: autonomy, reactivity, proactivity and social ability[21].

In practice, systems with only one agent are not common. The most common are the cases of agents that inhabit an environment containing other agents. There are two major types of multi-agent systems: reactive and cognitive. The reactive acts under a stimulus-response scheme; the cognitive has, in general, few agents because each agent is a complex and computationally heavy system[4].

A rational agent is one who chooses his/her actions according to their own interests, given the belief that he/she has about the world. The Belief, Desire, Intention (BDI) model recognizes the importance of beliefs, desires and intentions in rational actions [20].

The BDI model represents a cognitive architecture based on mental states, and has its origin in the human practical reasoning model. An architecture based on the BDI model represents its internal processes through the mental states: belief, desire and intention, and defines a control mechanism that selects in a rational way the course of actions [7].

In the context of this work, an agent is considered as an autonomous entity, able to make decisions, respond in a timely manner, pursue goals, interact with other agents, and has reasoning and character. This agent is a of type BDI, with beliefs, desires and intentions, and operates in a virtual learning environment as an intelligent tutor.

Intelligent tutoring systems (ITS) are complex systems involving several different types of expertise: subject knowledge, knowledge of the student's knowledge, and pedagogical knowledge, among others. According to Santos et al. [17], an ITS is characterized for incorporating AI techniques into a development project and acts as a helper in the teaching–learning process.

According to Conati [5], intelligent tutoring systems are an interdisciplinary field that investigates how elaborate educational systems provide adapted instructions to the needs of students, as many teachers do.

ITS research has been investigating how to make computer-based tutors more flexible, autonomous and adaptive to the needs of each student by giving them explicit knowledge of the relevant components of the teaching process and reasoning skills to convert this knowledge into intelligent behavior.

To Giraffa and Viccari [9], ITS developments consider a cooperative approach between student and system. The goal of ITS is to complement or replace a human tutor, with the advantage of monitoring the student in each learning step [13].

Research in intelligent tutoring systems is concerned about the construction of environments that enable more efficient learning. [8].

Intelligent tutoring systems offer flexibility in the presentation of material and have the major ability to respond to students' needs. They seek, in addition to teaching, learning relevant information about the student, providing an individualized learning. Intelligent tutoring systems have been shown to be highly effective in improving performance and motivation of students [10].

Intelligent tutoring systems in virtual learning environments potentiate the teaching–learning process, making the virtual environment into an intelligent learning environment. Intelligent learning environments use AI techniques to respond to students' needs, making that learning personalized [10].

According [15], the intelligent learning environment must build and update the student model in terms of what he/she already knows, which can vary significantly from one student to another.

Related Works

In order to know the current status of recent research about virtual learning environments and the use of intelligent agents as tutors in these environments, we performed a systematic literature review. Among them, there were three items which were most closely related to the purpose of this study.

"Approach to an Adaptive and Intelligent Learning Environment" [1], which proposes an agent-oriented approach for the design and implementation of an adaptive and smart component for a virtual learning environment. The adaptivity in the model is defined as a system's ability to create and, during the learning process, uniformly upgrade the curriculum that satisfies the student's needs. The proposed model has three parts that describe the main features of intelligent and adaptive component. First, the student chooses the courses based on his/her needs, the level of excellence that he/she wants to achieve, and his/her preference concerning the type of study material. Second, the system will decide how to act – for example, show the material to the student, based on the belief (student model) that the system has about it. In the last part it is decided when to propose an evaluation test for the student or any other activity that can evaluate any specific knowledge in relation to the curriculum. After completing the evaluation, the belief about the student is updated.

"Cluster Analysis in Personalized E-Learning" [22]: this is a proposed system architecture in which teaching techniques and appropriate layouts are set to groups of students with similar preferences, created by applying clustering techniques. Teaching materials and content can be adapted to the needs of each group and different learning paths can be created. New students fill out a questionnaire to determine their learning style and their choices of usability and, according to this, the appropriate group is chosen for them. The idea of the proposed solution is to divide the process into two steps: first, to look for groups of students with a great similarity and detect those isolates. In the second step the groups are mixed in larger groups if necessary and the isolates are indicated. The objective of the experiment was to examine the performance of the proposed clustering technique for different student's data sets, depending on the choice of parameters.

"Supporting Cognitive Competence Development in Virtual Classrooms" [19]. The approach described in this article implements a mechanism to adaptively create self-assessment questionnaires in a Moodle environment. The Learning Management System (LMS) is capable of saving all online activities of the students in log files. This information can be used also to automatically generate intelligent feedback to the student. The questions are derived from an ontology of skills that is also used for indexing learning materials. The student traces through the learning materials used to determine the current state of "expected knowledge" or skills. The system includes two main agents: the goals manager agent, which guides the student in planning activities; and the content manager agent, which guides the student during the resources review. In this paper, an extension of the Moodle LMS – in which ontologies are used to structure the learning process by providing resources and generating questionnaires automatically for self-assessment of the students – is presented.

In the conducted research to analyze the state of the art, papers were found dealing with adaptability in virtual learning environments, taking into account the students' needs, learning styles, usability preferences and their activities report (log).

In the first related paper, adaptability is based on the preferences of students regarding the study material, where the agent provides this material according to the information that he/she has about the student's preferences. In the second paper, the proposal is to provide different layouts to the students, taking into consideration similar preferences with regard to learning styles and usability choices. In the last related paper, self-assessment questionnaires are used, adaptively created in the virtual learning environment Moodle, and ontologies are used to index the learning materials. This paper proposes to join data that can be obtained from the database (information of student performance and logs) that most virtual learning environments widely used usually have, in order to set the discipline in a personalized way for each student, with regards to the available material for the student as the activities proposed to him/her, exploring his/her skills and bypassing disabilities, always having a baseline with material and compulsory activities, and activities outside of this line divided into different levels of difficulty.

III. Definition of the Model

The aim of this work is to create an agent architecture and a knowledge base of these agents that compose an intelligent tutoring system with information obtained from the database of a teaching–learning virtual environment. For this, a case study is done based on the Moodle platform architecture, chosen because it is a platform widely used today, in addition to being consolidated from the standpoint of operation, and also to be

formally used in the institution where the research is performed.

The classical model of ITS contains the pedagogical model, the student model, the domain base and the control. In the proposed model, two types of agents, called "Bedel" and "tutor" are used. The Bedel Agent and all their knowledge and interaction structure corresponds in the classical model of intelligent tutoring to the Pedagogical Model. The Tutor Agent and all their structure corresponds in the model of intelligent tutors to the Student Model. The content of the discipline, in turn, may be associated with the abstraction of the Domain Base (Fig. 1).

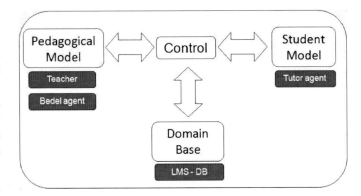

Fig. 1 Classical model with proposed model

The model of agents "Bedel" (agent of the discipline) and "Tutor" (agent of the student) is defined; they are connected with the learning virtual environment through the database. The interface in which the teacher sets the priority and levels of the resources and tasks in the environment is developed. The database is adapted with the creation of the table of grade profiles of the students and the table of dependencies of resources and activities, configured by the teacher by means of a Moodle block into his discipline, and is made the integration of the actions of agents with the virtual learning environment Moodle. The agents model (Fig. 2) shows the agents "Tutor" and "Bedel" their actions, messages and perceptions, as well as their connection to the database. The actor "teacher" is the figure of the discipline teacher who inserts the resources and activities into the learning environment, sets the type of profile and sequence, and this information is stored in the database, so the agent "Bedel" knows how to show them to students.

The database has information concerning the student, such as personal data, performance data and data from student interaction in the system. Every student interaction in the environment is saved in the base in the form of a log. Similarly, the student's performance in each of the activities and tasks is stored in the database and updated constantly every access and interaction of the student, providing rich material for the agent's performance. The agents share the information from the database. The "Tutor" updates the student profile and, if necessary, shows a message to him/her about his/her performance. The "Bedel" obtains from the database the configuration of resources and activities in the discipline made by the teacher; it sets their preview and verifies if tasks were evaluated to send a message to the "Tutor" who, upon receiving the message, updates the data of the student profile.

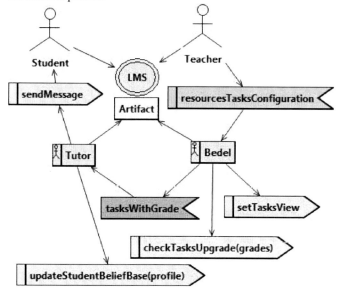

Fig. 2. Agent System Model

The model works as follows:

1) The teacher inserts the resources and creates tasks in the Moodle environment as usual. After that, he/she adds the tutor block in his/her discipline and configures the Bedel setting the first resource and activity (Fig. 3), the dependencies (Fig. 4) of activities and resources, and their level (basic, intermediate and advanced), also by means of the Moodle environment. In addition, the teacher has the option to choose resources that must be shown to all students in a general way. The first reading (resource) and the first activity are shown for all students; therefore the teacher needs to indicate which they are. This information is stored in the database, where some tables which are necessary for the model are added. With this information, the "Bedel" knows about resources and activities of the discipline and knows how the course should be developed for each type of student.

2) In the environment's database the grade_profile table (Fig. 5) is also added, which contains a numeric value, calculated with the grades of the activities performed by students and the access made by them in different files provided by the teacher. This table is updated each time a teacher updates the worksheet with the grades of some of the tasks that he/she provides to students.

3) The grade_profile average of all students is computed and students are separated by profile into groups – basic, intermediate or advanced – according to their grade_profile. Whoever has average grades is in the average profile, whoever has grades below average is in the basic profile, and those who have grades above average are in the advanced profile.

4) Tasks are provided independently for each student,

according to their performance in the previous tasks, and their access to previous reading material. The availability of tasks and resources is made by the "Bedel" using the conditional access resource of Moodle.

5) Each time the Bedel calculates the grade_profile it updates the belief base of the current profile of the student, which can go from basic to intermediate or advanced and vice-versa during the time that the course is offered.

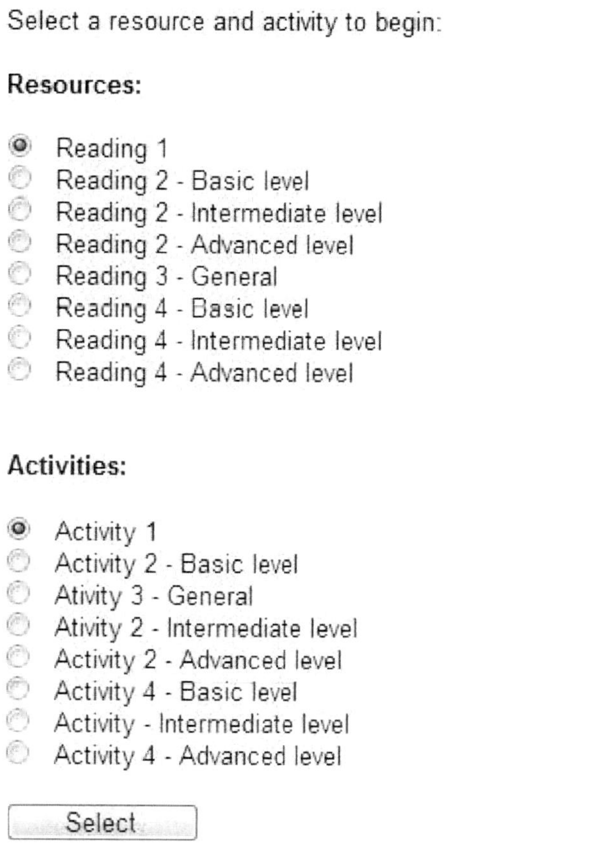

Select a resource and activity to begin:

Resources:

⊙ Reading 1
○ Reading 2 - Basic level
○ Reading 2 - Intermediate level
○ Reading 2 - Advanced level
○ Reading 3 - General
○ Reading 4 - Basic level
○ Reading 4 - Intermediate level
○ Reading 4 - Advanced level

Activities:

⊙ Activity 1
○ Activity 2 - Basic level
○ Ativity 3 - General
○ Ativity 2 - Intermediate level
○ Activity 2 - Advanced level
○ Activity 4 - Basic level
○ Activity - Intermediate level
○ Activity 4 - Advanced level

[Select]

Fig. 3 First resource and activity

The calculation of grade_profile is done as follows: The student grade of the last activity assessed by the teacher and the grade of the student access on reading that is a pre-requisite for activity are summed. If the student accesses the reading, two points in the activity grade are added. If he/she does not access, four points are added. This difference is given for increasing the possibility to the student who does not access the reading, to have a higher grade_profile and then go to a higher level task than the profile that he/she would belong to if he/she had a lower grade, stimulating him/her to read before accomplishing future activities.

After this, the average value of the grade_profile field is computed for all students. The lowest value considered for the profile average is 6; if the profile average is lower, it automatically becomes 6. For the student to be at an average profile, his/her grade_profile must be between 5.5 and 6.5; if the student has a grade_profile less than 5.5 he/she is on a basic profile and if he/she has grade_profile greater than 6.5

he/she is on an advanced profile.

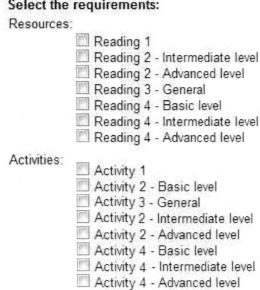

Fig. 4 Dependencies configuration

The maximum value considered for the profile average is 8. If the average profile is greater than that, it automatically becomes 8. For the student to be at average profile, his/her grade_profile must be between 7.5 and 8.5, if the student has a grade_profile less than 7.5 he/she is on the basic profile and if he/she has a grade_profile greater than 8.5 he/she is on the advanced profile.

The student belongs to the average profile if his/her grade_profile is 0.5 less or more than the average grade_profile in his/her class; for example, if the grade_profile average is 7.5, he/she will be in the intermediate profile if he/she has a grade_profile between 7 and 8. The student who has a higher grade with more than 0.5 of diference with the average will be in the advanced profile and the student who has a lower grade with more than 0.5 of diference will be in the basic profile.

The student will have access to the material of their profile (basic, intermediate, advanced), according the configuration of resources and tasks made by the teacher.

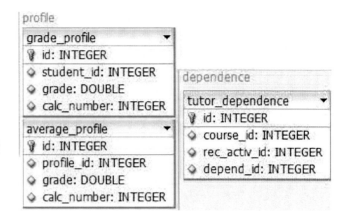

Fig. 5. Profile and dependence tables

IV. IMPLEMENTATION OF THE MODEL

The model integrates concepts of intelligent tutoring systems architectures with VLE's that have their use consolidated as Moodle, which are not adaptive for itself only, and can be potentiated with artificial intelligence techniques, resulting in intelligent learning environments which are shown to be adaptive and more suitable to the implementation of teaching defiant methodologies for the student.

The use of agents in the implementation of this model is important because of the agent's ability to adapt to environment changes, showing resources and activities to students in a personalized way, according to their performance in the discipline, and taking into account the teacher's initial settings.

For the agent implementation the Jason tool was used, which is an interpreter for an extended version of AgentSpeak, oriented agent programming language, implemented in Java. The basic idea of AgentSpeak is to define the know-how (knowledge about how to do things) of a program in the form of plans [3].

One of the most interesting aspects of AgentSpeak is that it is inspired by and based on a model of human behavior that was developed by philosophers. This model is called the Belief Desire Intention (BDI) model. The language interpreted by Jason is an extension of AgentSpeak, based on BDI architecture. A component of the agent architecture is a beliefs base and an example of what the interpreter does constantly, without being specifically programmed, is to perceive the environment and update the beliefs base accordingly with this [3].

The teaching–learning virtual environments are designed to enable the knowledge-building process. Different to conventional software, which seeks to facilitate the tasks achievement by user, learning environments incorporate the complexity to more flexible different forms of users (students), relations, to learn and to practice content, and to collaborate. These environments are used by students of various cognitive profiles [2].

The version of virtual learning environment Moodle used for this work is 2.2, where the task condition resource is available, which allows the provision of content and activities with a restriction. This feature must be activated by the administrator of Moodle in the environment advanced settings, enabling the option "Enable tracking of completion" and "Enable conditional access." Moreover, in course settings, in "student progress" topic, the teacher must enable the completion tracking option.

With this feature enabled, tasks can be made available only to students who perform the pre-requisites set, which can be: a grade on a specific activity; the viewing of a resource; or his/her grade.

In this work, the availability of resources and activities is done taking into account the student's performance and his/her access in the system and is made available to the student depending on his/her grade_profile, computed according to his/her performance and participation in the discipline. The information between the agent system and the virtual learning environment are exchanged through the database of the learning environment which contains information about the pre-requisites and profiles of tasks and resources, defined by the teacher at a time to configure the Bedel. The development was made in 4 steps. On Fig. 6 we can see the Bedel sequence diagram, with the Artifact working like an interface between the database and the Bedel Agent.

on database. The Bedel Agent access the database trough the Artifact and execute the plans it has for calculating this profile. Then, the Bedel Agent calculate the profile average of all the students and separate them into profiles (basic, intermediate and advanced).

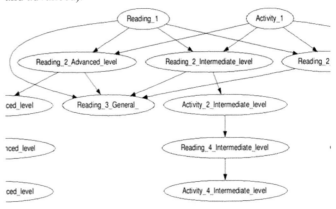

Fig. 7 Dependency graph

The Bedel Agent implementation has a definition file, where is specified the infrastructure, the Cartago environment used to program the artifacts (Fig. 8) and the Tutor and Bedel Agents.

C. Development of the code to display resources and activities

For the availability of resources and activities according to the student profile was created the tutor_profile_availability table in the database, to store the information of the minimum and maximum grades of the intermediate profile. Verifying this information the resources and activities can be provided, according to the students profile.

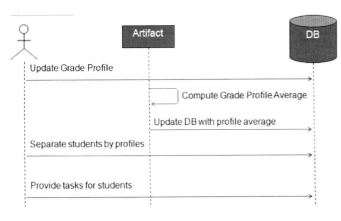

Fig. 6 Bedel Sequence Diagram

A. Development of the tutorblock in Moodle LMS.

It was developed a moodle block for the teacher to configure the agent. This block was created following the Moodle standard programming for creating blocks. The name was defined as "Tutor Block". This block have to be added by the teacher and is used by him/her to set the Bedel Agent, after the insertion of resources and activities in the environment.

After the teacher configures the agent through the block, he/she can see the dependency graph (Fig. 7) generated after setting all prerequisites. This graph shows the relations between the resources and activities setting by the teacher.

B. Development of the Bedel Agent. Programming student profile

In this step was implemented the code for the Bedel Agent to calculate de student profile, using the information available

```
package artifact;

import java.sql.Connection;

//import cartago.OpFeedbackParam;

public class BD_Artifact extends Artifact {

    Connection conn;
    int idCourse = 2;
    String contextid;
    boolean counting;
    final static long TICK_TIME = 5000;//86400000; //24 horas em milisegundos
    ArrayList<String> id_grade_item_Tarefas_entregues;
    ArrayList<String> lista_tarefas_avaliadas;

    void init(int initialValue) {
        counting = false;
        // defineObsProperty("idCourse", 2);
    }

    ResultSet select(String string) throws SQLException, ClassNotFoundException {
        ResultSet result = null;
        try {
            Statement stm = conn.createStatement();
            result = stm.executeQuery(string);
        } catch (Exception e) {
            System.out.println(e);
        }
        return result;
    }
}
```

Fig. 8 Artifact Source Code

D. Development of the Tutor Agent to send messages to the students

It was implemented the Tutor Agent, that is responsible for

sending messages of encouragement to the student, taking into account his/her performance. This agent receives the student profile information from the Bedel Agent, updates the belief it has about this student and sends some message to him/her according to the student situation. If the student had a better performance than in the previous activity the Tutor Agent send a congratulation message (Fig. 9), if not, it sends a message to encourage him to be better the next time.

At this stage, also, the Bedel Agent is updated, inserting methods that enable communication between it and the Tutor Agent. Sending the student information to the Tutor Agent.

Fig. 9 Congratulation message (in Portuguese)

V. CONCLUSIONS

In this study is proposed a solution for virtual learning environments to assist teachers to provide activities and resources in a personalized way depending on the student's performance and his/her behavior in the discipline.

Students are assessed by their interaction in the discipline and the grades obtained in tasks, creating different profiles for groups of students with the same behavior. More advanced tasks are available for students who have improved performance, enabling more efficient learning, exploring students' skills, and maintaining a basic level for learning the discipline content.

Works related to virtual learning environments and adaptivity in general differentiate students by learning style – for example, a student who learns better with pictures than with reading lots of text. In this work students are distinguished by their performance, taking into account the grades obtained, and their participation (access) in the various resources available in the discipline, creating an adaptive environment that constantly updates the profile of students, and therefore, a student with a basic profile, at the end of the course may have an average profile. These profile changes can be studied and displayed to the teacher, in an extension of this model.

REFERENCES

[1] Baziukaité, D.: Approach to an Adaptive and Intelligent Learning Environment. In: Elleithy, K., Sobh, T., Mahmood, A., Iskander, M., Karim, M. Advances in Computer, Information, And Systems Sciences, And Engineering, pp. 399–406. Springer Netherlands (2006)

[2] Boff, E.: Collaboration in Learning Intelligent Environments mediated by a Social Agent Probabilistic. In: Thesis (Ph.D.) Computer Science Course. Federal University of Rio Grande do Sul, Porto Alegre. (2008) (in Portuguese)

[3] Bordini, R.H., Hubner, J.F., Wooldridge, M.: Programming Multi-Agent Systems in AgentSpeak using Jason. Editora Wiley. England (2007)

[4] Bordini, R., Vieira, R., Moreira, A.F.: Fundamentos de Sistemas Multiagentes. In: Ferreira, C. E. (ed.). Jornada de Atualização em Informática (JAI'01), vol. 2, pp. 3–44. SBC, Fortaleza, Brasil (2001)

[5] Conati, C.: Intelligent Tutoring Systems: New Challenges and Directions. Paper Presented at the Proceedings of the 21st International Joint Conference on Artificial intelligence (2009)

[6] Dillenbourg, P.: Virtual Learning Environment . EUN Conference 2000. Workshop on Virtual Learning Environment (2000). Available in: http://tecfa.unige.ch/tecfa/publicat/dil-papers-2/Dil.7.5.18.pdf

[7] Fagundes, M.: An environment for development of BDI agents. Course Completion Work. Federal University of Pelotas (2004) Available in: http://www.inf.ufsc.br/~silveira/INE602200/Artigos/TCC_Moser.pdf. (in Portuguese)

[8] Frigo, L. B., Pozzebon, E., Bittencourt, G.. The Role of Intelligent Agents in Intelligent Tutoring Systems. In: Proceedings of the WCETE - World Congress on Engineering and Technology Education, São Paulo, Brasil, pp. 667-671. (2004). (in Portuguese)

[9] Giraffa, L.M.M., Viccari, R.M.: The Use of Agents Techniques on Intelligent Tutoring Systems. In: Computer Science SCCC '98. XVIII International Conference of the Chilean Society, pp. 76-83. IEEE Computer Society Washington, DC, USA (1998).

[10] Lima R.D., Rosatelli, M.C.: An intelligent tutoring system to a virtual environment for teaching and learning. In: IX Workshop de Informática na Escola, Campinas. Anais do XXIII Congresso da Sociedade Brasileira de Computação. (2003). (in Portuguese)

[11] Moran, J.M.: Computers in Education: Theory & Practice. Porto Alegre, vol. 3, n.1. UFRGS. Postgraduate Program in Computer oin Education, pp. 137–144 (2000). (in Portuguese)

[12] Mozzaquatro, P.M., Franciscato, F., Ribeiro, P.S., Medina, R.D.: Modeling a Framework for adaptation of Virtual Learning Environments Mobiles to different cognitive styles. vol 7, n 3, pp. 253-263. Renote - New Technologies in Education Journal. ISSN 1679-1916 (2009). (in Portuguese)

[13] Oliveira, C.L.V.: AutoExplC: intelligent tutoring system to aid the teaching of "C" languagebased on learning by self-explanation of examples. PUC, Campinas (2005). (in Portuguese)

[14] Pereira, A.T.C., Schmitt, V., Álvares, M.R.C.: Virtual Learing Environments. Culture Bookstore. (2007). Available in: http://www.livrariacultura.com.br/imagem/capitulo/2259532.pdf. (in Portuguese)

[15] Silveira, R. A. Ambientes inteligentes distribuídos de aprendizagem. Porto Alegre: CPGCC da UFRGS, (1998)

[16] Russell, S., Norvig, P.: Artificial Intelligence: A Modern Approach. Prentice-Hall, Inc. New Jersey (2002)

[17] Santos, C.T., Frozza, R., Dahmer, A., Gaspary, L.P.: Doris - Pedagogical Agent in Intelligent Tutoring Systems. In: Cerri, S., Gouardères, G., Paraguaçu, F. Intelligent Tutoring Systems, pp. 91-104. Springer Berlin, Heidelberg (2002)

[18] Valente, J.A.: Computers in Education: conform or transform the school, pp. 42. (2009).

[19] Weinbrenner, S., Ulrich, H., Leal L., Montenegro, M., Vargas, W., Maldonado, L.: Supporting Cognitive Competence Development in Virtual Classroom In: 10th International Conference on Advanced Learning Technologies. IEEE Computer Society (2010)

[20] Wooldridge, M.: Reasoning about Rational Agents. The MIT Press. Cambridge, Massachussetts. London, England. (2000)

[21] Wooldridge, M.: An Introduction to Multiagent Systems, 2nd edition. John Wiley & Sons Ltd in Hoboken, NJ (2009)

[22] Zakrzewska, D.: Cluster Analysis in Personalized E-Learning Systems. Springer-Verlag, Berlin Heidelberg (2009)

Ms. Cecilia E. Giuffra P. Doctoral student of the postgraduate course in Engineering and Knowledge Management from the Federal University of Santa Catarina (UFSC). Master's (2013) and Bachelor's (2009) at Computer Science from the same University. Has experience in Computer Science, focusing on the following subjects: Artificial Intelligence, Learning Management Systems, Multiagent Systems, Computers in Education, Repositories, and Learning Objects. Has knowledge of the Moodle platform and had participation in teacher training and EaD staff.

Dr. Ricardo A. Silveira, PhD in Computer Science from Universidade Federal do Rio Grande do Sul (2001). Master's at Education from the Pontifical Catholic University of Rio Grande do Sul – PUC-RS (1992). Graduate at Electronic Engineering from PUC-RS from Departamento de Engenharia Elétrica (1980). Associate Professor of the Department of Informatic and Statistics (INE) on Federal University of Santa Catarina (UFSC). Has experience in Computer Science, focusing on Formal Languages and Automata, acting on the following subjects: Artificia Intelligence, Multiagent Systems, Computer in Education, Pedagogical Agents and Learning Objects.

## 24

Improving Web Learning through model Optimization using Bootstrap for a Tour-Guide Robot

Rafael León, J. Javier Rainer, José Manuel Rojo and Ramón Galán.

Centre for Automation and Robotics UPM - CSIC

Universidad Politécnica de Madrid, Spain

Abstract —We perform a review of Web Mining techniques and we describe a Bootstrap Statistics methodology applied to pattern model classifier optimization and verification for Supervised Learning for Tour-Guide Robot knowledge repository management. It is virtually impossible to test thoroughly Web Page Classifiers and many other Internet Applications with pure empirical data, due to the need for human intervention to generate training sets and test sets. We propose using the computer-based Bootstrap paradigm to design a test environment where they are checked with better reliability.

Keywords —Web Mining, Supervised Learning, Bootstrap, Patterns Mining, Web Classifiers, Knowledge Management.

I. INTRODUCTION

THE Internet is an enormous information repository with spectacular growth and a high degree of updating. Using this exceptional database in an automatic way is a challenging field of research. Data mining has been extensively used by many organizations, large amount of data are processed to extract relevant information; applying these technologies to the Web it is possible to build systems that considerably improve the process of information gathering from the Internet. Web Mining has peculiarities that made it a subject of research in its own right. It can be applied to several aspects of the network like page content, user click stream, link structure of the web or social community opinion. Internet mining is performed in several steps: web pages covering a particular matter or belonging to a social community are searched and classified. Then, they are processed to remove all the words and tags that have no influence in the meaning of text and a mining algorithm is applied to harvest useful information from the pages. This knowledge can be used in several manners: analysis to study behavior patterns, social community opinions and product success or it can be incorporated into a knowledge repository that is the application for our robot.

In this article, we have dedicated our efforts to pattern classifiers that allow a binary classification of Web pages. Classification models that use patterns to define features or rules have been built for a long time. These models can be either more accurate or less precise, but they achieve more understandable results for humans. A lot of work has been performed on pattern finding and selection, algorithms and model building, but there is scarce work on model verification and comparison as stated in [1] by B. Bringmann. We have developed a test environment that implements Bootstrap resample strategy allowing to determine with more confidence how the model performs, so criteria can be clearly defined to compare between models performance, thus improving the whole learning process.

Bootstrap is a computer approach to get statistical accuracy. It is applied to a wide variety of statistical procedures like non parametric regressions, classification trees or density estimation. This technique requires fewer assumptions and offers greater accuracy and insight than other standard methods for many problems. Bootstrapping is an analogy in which the observed data assume the role of an underlying population: variances, distributions and confidence intervals are obtained by drawing samples from the empirical sample, as R. Stinewrotein [2]. A typical problem in applied statistics involves the estimation of an unknown parameter. The two main questions are: what estimator should be used? and having chosen a particular one, how accurate is the estimator? Bootstrap is a general methodology to answer the second question, as stated by Efron and Tibshiraniin [3].

This work is framed within the Intelligent Control Group, Universidad Politécnica de Madrid, whose members are carrying out research into robotics and intelligent control systems. Three robots have already been built which are designed to show visitors round museums and fairs described by Rodriguez-Losada in [4]. Research covers a wide number of areas: path finding, navigation, speaking, facial expression, mood and knowledge management.

II. SOFTWARE ARCHITECTURE FOR BASED ON INTELLIGENT AGENTS

We have developed our own interactive mobile robot called Urbano specially designed to be a tour guide in exhibitions. Urbano is a B21r platform from iRobot, equipped with a four wheeled synchrodrive locomotion system, a SICK LMS200 laser scanner mounted horizontally on the top used for navigationas well as a mechatronic face and a robotic arm used to express emotions such as happiness, sadness, surprise or anger. The robot is also equipped with two sonar rings and one infrared ring, which allows detecting obstacles at different heights that can be used for obstruction avoidance and safety. The platform also has two onboard PCs and one touch screen, as explained by J. Rainer in [5].

The software is structured in several executable modules to allow a decoupled development by several teams of programmers, and they are connected via TCP/IP and CORBA. Most of these programs are conceived as servers or service providers, as the face control, the arm control, the navigation systems voice synthesis and recognition, and the web server. The client-server paradigm is used, the only client being a central module that we call the Urbano Kernel. This kernel is responsible for managing the whole system, as illustrated in [4].

Modules with a more advanced implementation are: Decision Making, Knowledge Server, Automatic Presentation Generator and Acquisition of Information, as can be seen at Fig. 1.

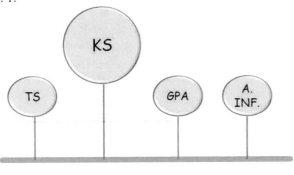

CORBA

Fig. 1. Modular Architecture based on Intelligent Agents: TS, Decision Making, KS, Knowledge Server, GPA, Automatic Presentation Generator, and A. Inf., Acquisition of Information

We have built the Acquisition of Information Agent which aims to automate as much as possible the incorporation of information to the Knowledge Server, using the Internet the as primary source of Information.

A. KS: Knowledge Server, Urbano Ontology Implementation

Knowledge Server is at the center of the architecture, providing data and intelligence to the behavior of the rest of the components. It incorporates cognitive inspired ontologies that store the information and concepts. Feeding these ontologies in an automated way is a challenge. URBANOntology consists of a foundational ontology (DOLCE) plus different domain specific ontologies, like art, history etc. The robot is able to give presentations about different topics as domain ontologies that are mapped to

DOLCE as described in [6]-[8]. It is not only a classification; it also provides the tools needed to conceptualize the world and describes how the different objects relate to each other. DOLCE is made up of categories based on perception and human common sense, cultural details and social conventions.

Using DOLCE as a fundamental ontology, we are setting out a general framework that can be tailored to any specific domain; in this way the URBANOntology can serve as a reliable tool to potentially generate presentations in all possible areas. Every component in the Museum Ontology must be mapped to its respective fundamental concept in DOLCE. The use of a knowledge server means having a useful tool with which to meet the needs of handling the knowledge. By abstraction of knowledge we understand a learning process that involves the formation of new concepts or categories based on information available about the world. The knowledge server consists of a Java application developed using the libraries of Protégé-OWL API. In [5], J. Rainer y R. Galán explain it with more detail.

The robot changes between museums and exhibition fairs makes it necessary to update its knowledge database for each location. We have optimized the information gathering process, including the option of Web Mining from the Internet, as shown in Fig. 2.

Web Learning is performed in several steps, in this paper we suggest an improvement for the Page Selection phase, proposing a test environment that increases the reliability of

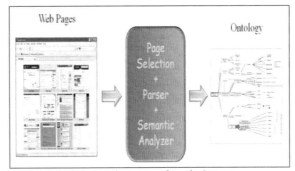

Fig. 2. Information extraction process from the Internet

the results obtained by the Selection Models. The robot's environment has been enriched with the application of these techniques.

III. A REVIEW ON MINING TECHNIQUES APPLIED TO WEB LEARNING

We present in this section a review of mining techniques that have been developed and theoretical support for Web Mining. Many approaches have been proposed to extract information from raw data, ranging from those involving more human intervention, supervised methods, to more unattended systems, unsupervised ones. The selection depends on several factors like the type, heterogeneity and volume of data.

Supervised learning is also known as classification or inductive learning. It is similar to the human behavior of learning from past experiences thus gaining new knowledge and abilities. The experiences are represented as past data, so there are the following sets of data: training data, that allow model training, test data, that allow the verification of the classification and the real data that are processed by the model. The Accuracy of the classifier is evaluated in terms of the number of correct classifications versus the total number of cases. Decision tree is one of the most popular methods of classification; it is efficient and can compete with other classification techniques, like Bayesian Classification, D. Hand in [9], or Support Vector Machines, V. Vapnik in [10].

Another approach is Unsupervised Learning that discovers patterns in the attributes of the data, that are used to predict the value of class attribute of future instances. The classes are used to classify items, for example decide if a web text is a social science article or if it is about microelectronics. When the data have no class attributes, clustering techniques are applied to find similarity groups. Clustering makes partitions of data or can have a hierarchical approach. A distance function is chosen between data points, and a set of centroids are calculated and recalculated recursively until similar groups are found. K-means Algorithm is an example of this strategy, as explained by MacQueen in [11].

There is an intermediate approach that is Partially Supervised Learning. Supervised Learning requires a lot of human effort and a large set of labeled data, therefore an alternative was proposed. To minimize the tedious task of labeling data, the model is trained with labeled and unlabeled examples, also known as LU learning, an example of the algorithm used is EM, Expectation and Maximization, A. Dempster in [12]. There is a lot of classified data and a large set of unlabelled data that are used to improve learning of the model. Subsequently the learning process uses positive and unlabeled data, PU learning, assuming a two classes set of data. This method can be applied successfully for classification of web pages.

In this section a number of general mining techniques have been described. As stated before, we have focused our efforts on mining patterns for Supervised Learning and their use to build a Web page classifier.

A. Peculiarities of Web Mining

Web mining is an activity that discovers useful information from the Web. It can target data or hyperlinks and can be classified into three kinds: Web Structure Mining, Web Content Mining and Web Usage Mining. Web Structure Mining discovers useful knowledge from hyperlinks structure. It is used to find important sites and communities and gives an image of the structure of the Internet itself. Web Content Mining extracts useful information from page contents. Web Usage Mining discovers how the users make use of a Web Server. Analyzing the Web logs it is possible to review the click stream and determine the user behavior and what he likes and what he dislikes, as stated by Bing Liu in [13].

One key step for Web mining is the pre-processing of the

Web pages. To begin with HTML information is identified to classify the importance of the different paragraphs of the page. HTML codes allow recognizing titles, main content blocks or anchor text; this information can be used to speed up the identification and processing of the page.

Subsequently HTML tags are removed in order to extract the information in a more efficient way. When the page text has no tags it is clean from words that form syntactic constructions that have little influence on the meaning of the phrases, stop words like prepositions, conjunctions and articles are removed. The rest of the words are converted to their roots in a procedure called stemming. Verbs are transformed to the infinitive form and suffixes are stripped from words to get the roots which are easier to recall. A good example of stemming algorithm is from M. Porter in [14]. After the page is pre-processed a better precision for classification is obtained, getting improved results using distance functions like cosine similarity.

Parts of Speech, POS, can be used at a later stage in order to get the sentiments and semantic meaning attached to the text. With these techniques a word is identified in its category: noun, verb, adjective, adverb, pronoun, etc. Knowing the type of word it is possible for a machine to perform further processing to extract information from a text, being able to identify pictures by a painter, dates of birth or companies working in a particular sector. An algorithm implementing this approach was proposed by P. Turney in [15]. Using methodologies like Latent Semantic Analysis, was proposed by S. Dreewester [16], it is possible to apply statistical analysis to find the Singular Value Decomposition of a Web page, discerning when several texts have the same semantic meaning expressed with different words.

IV. USING STATISTICAL TECHNIQUES TO TEST AND DEVELOP

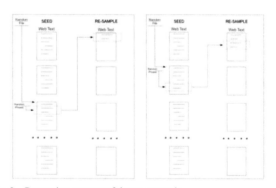

Fig. 3. Generation process of the new sample

SUPERVISED LEARNING MODELS

One of the main challenges of Supervised Learning Models like classifiers for Web Pages is the sheer number of pages that has to be processed, but the training and test pages set have a limited size due to the need for a human operator that classifies pages manually. There is a plethora of algorithms and literature about pattern classifiers, but fewer studies have been carried out so far on verification and comparison between models. To solve this problem, we have developed a methodology based on the statistical paradigm called Bootstrap that allows one to synthesize re-samples automatically with replacement therefore greatly improving the accuracy of the verification and refining phase of the models, strengthening the reliability of their results and giving a clear idea about their optimum working conditions. Bootstrap is a computer approach to get statistical accuracy. It is applied to a wide variety of statistical procedures like non parametric regressions, classification trees or density estimation. We go a little further, iteratively varying the attributes of the population and applying Bootstrap for each situation.

A. The Bootstrap estimate

In our case we used Bootstrap to estimate parameters for a classifier. From an equally distributed empirical population, a collection of samples are constructed replacing randomly the original dataset. Given a set of independent and identically distributed observations, web pages in our case:

$$x_i, \; i = 1,2,\dots,n$$
(1)

from an unknown probability distribution F has been observed. To estimate a parameter of interest $\theta = t(F)$ on the basis of x. For this purpose we calculate estimate $\hat{\theta} = s(x)$ from x. To know how accurate $\hat{\theta}$ is, Bootstrap was introduced as a computer based method. It is completely automatic no matter how complicated the estimator is from a mathematical point of view. Let $\hat{F}$ be the empirical distribution with a probability of 1/n on each of the observed values:

$$x^*(x_1^*, x_2^*, \dots, x_n^*)$$
(2)

A bootstrap sample is defined as a random sample of size n drawn from $\hat{F}$, say

$$x^* = (x_1^*, x_2^*, \dots, x_n^*)$$
(3)

$$\hat{F} \to x^* = (x_1^*, x_2^*, \dots, x_n^*)$$
(4)

Corresponding to bootstrap dataset x^*, the sample of pages that are generated, is a Bootstrap replication of $\hat{\theta}$:

$$\hat{\theta} = s(x^*)$$
(5)

It is necessary to evaluate the bootstrap replication corresponding to each bootstrap sample:

$$\hat{\theta} = s(x^{*b})_{b=1,2,\dots,B}$$
(6)

As an example, to estimate an estimator as the standard error:

$$se_F = (\hat{\theta})$$
(7)

The sample standard deviation of the B replications:

$$\widehat{se}_B = \left\{ \sum_{b=1}^{B} [\hat{\theta}^*(b) - \hat{\theta}^*(.)]^2 / (B-1) \right\}^{1/2}$$
(8)

Where:

$$\hat{\theta}^*(.) = \sum_{b=1}^{B} \hat{\theta}^*(b)/B$$
(9)

As stated by Efron and Tibshiraniin [17].

V. TEST ENVIRONMENT

As explained above, the test environment is based on Bootstrap statistical estimation and it is applied to evaluate pattern classifier models and how they perform when some features of the pages change. The generation of Web page re-samples with replacement is as follows: from a set of thoroughly classified web pages used as seeds, a page is selected at random and inside this page, a phrase is randomly chosen and is written in the new sample, as can be seen in Fig. 3.

Bootstrap demonstrates that the new sample has the same underlying conditions than the original. We create two sets of pages: one from pages referring to Francisco de Goya as a painter and other one from pages that have to be discarded by the model. The two sets are evaluated and the confusion matrix is built:

		Actual value	
		p	N
PredictedValue	p'	A	B
	n'	C	D

Then we calculate the statistical tests Sensibility and Specificity for the model according to the following equations:

$$sensibility^* = \frac{A}{A+C}$$
(10)

$$sensibility^* = \frac{D}{B+D}$$
(11)

We greatly improve the accuracy of the verification and refining phase of the models, strengthening the confidence in their results and giving a clear idea about their optimum working conditions. With this information for example, we are able to adjust the models more precisely, improving their performance and enabling the building of dynamic strategies that obtain better results.

In our case we have tested how the models are affected by the size of the pages. The sample generation process can be easily modified to configure different page sizes for the generated sample. It is very difficult to implement this test with pure empirical data, selecting a big enough set of pages manually according to size and accuracy.

We have implemented classifiers based on text patterns that recognize if a Web page is about the Spanish painter Francisco de Goya, discarding pages about Goya Street, Goya Awards, Goya Train, etc. Search engines return links to a collection of Web pages that have to be filtered. In a mining process of information about Goya, is necessary to discard all the pages that, while referring to the painter's name, are about other matters. To perform the page filtering, models implement a variety of approaches: from a simple static configuration to more advanced and dynamic methods.

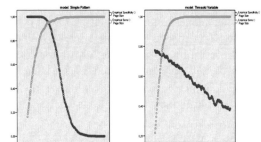

Fig. 4 and 5. Sensibility and Specificity of Model 1 and Model 2

A. Implementation details

The implementation is written in Python language and is modular, using a collection of classes that provide a flexible test environment to analyze new models. These classes are:
The control program: that implements the global loop, and

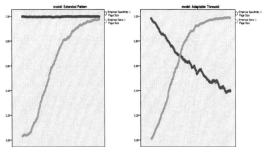

Fig. 6 and 7. Sensibility and Specificity of Model 3 and Model 4

calls the other classes.
The extraction class: that extracts text from web pages. Dynamic content adds noise to the text data of web pages and is hard to remove completely. Fortunately, this noise has very little effect on pattern mining that precisely is a good tool to filter it.
The generation class: that is responsible for generating the samples. It uses a method that generates the pages and another that is responsible for cleaning the samples in preparation for the next iteration.

The model classes: they implement a collection of models. In addition they use two of methods: one to calculate the sensibility and the other the specificity.

A random set of 200 files of re-sampled pages are created, increasing the page size with one phrase at each iteration. They are built from positive and negative seeds and placed in a directory where the model being assessed is applied. Then, the corresponding sensitivity and specificity are calculated. The results are rendered in the next section.

VI. RESULTS ANALYSIS

As described above, we have run our models over samples of 200 correct pages and 200 bad pages, with increasing size from 10 to 300 phrases. We have chosen to test the influence of the size of the page on the performance of the classifier.

We were able to verify that the size of the pages is strongly

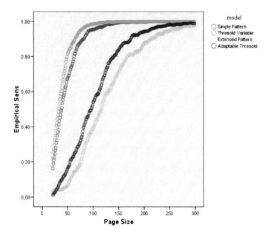

Fig. 8. Sensibility comparison for all Models

related to the performance of the models. As can be seen on the graphics, when the pages are small, models have low Sensibility: a lot of good pages are classified as bad pages. But when the pages are larger, the classifiers fail to recognize bad pages, so the Specificity decreases.

The result obtained Model 1 is shown in Fig. 4. It is the simplest approach, being static and using a short set of patterns. It has its best performance with pages of around 90 phrases where sensibility and specificity curves crossover.

We can see in Fig. 5 the results for Model 2, it has a similar pattern set to Model 1, but dynamically adjusted to the size of the page. Its performance is better than Model 1, having linear decrease of its specificity.

Model 3 and Model 4 use a larger set of patterns and both are dynamic but with different thresholds. We can see in Fig. 6 and 7 that their results are better than Models 1 and 2.

In Fig. 8 we can see the comparison of sensibilities of all the models and in Fig. 9 we see the comparison of specificities.

As we have stated, our test environment provides us with a clear comparison between models and how they perform with respect to the feature that we are analyzing. With this information, we can adapt the models and we can determine the best working conditions for them or design a strategy where models are dynamically selected based on the size of the page.

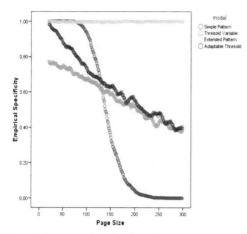

Fig. 9. Specificity comparison for all Models

VII. CONCLUSIONS

It is possible to improve the Web Learning process by refining page selection using Bootstrap technique to evaluate, refine and compare models based on patterns implemented for binary classification. A pure empirical sample for training and testing is limited, because the need for human intervention and the difficulty in finding pages with the desired qualities. Bootstrap provides a computer-based methodology that helps to have a wider dataset, where specific page features can be tested to determine how they really affect model performance and its outcome when real data are processed. We go further, by varying the characteristics of the sample and applying Bootstrap for each case analyzing model performance.

In our case, we were able to test how a pattern classifier is affected by the size of the page. We observed that if the page size was too small, the number of false negatives was excessively high and if the page size was big enough, the model performed better. This is an intrinsic problem for pattern models. Bootstrap technique provides excellent support for building dynamic models and their evaluation.

In addition, Bootstrap technique is a powerful tool for all related works with the Internet. It allows creating test environments that can simulate real conditions involving less human effort. Further work can be accomplished including new page and model features on the test environment as well as more advanced statistical techniques related with Bootstrap.

Web Learning improvement is used in the Urbano Robot environment. Information management is a key aspect of the robot software architecture; it allows a higher level of control providing intelligence to all the agents that comprise the system.

REFERENCES

[1] Bringmann, B., Nijssen, S., & Zimmermann, A. Pattern-Based classification: a Unifying perspective. 2009.ISSN 0718-3305

[2] Stine, R. An Introduction to Bootstrap. Sociological Methods and Research, Vol. 18, Nos. 2&3, November 1989/February 1990 243-291. 1990.ISSN: 1552-8294

[3] Efron, B., &Tibshirani, R. J..Bootstrap Methods for Standard Errors, Confidence Intervals, and Other Measures of Statistical Accuracy. Statistical Science, 1986, Vol. 1, 54-77. 1986.ISSN 1726-3328

[4] Rodriguez-Losada, D., Matia, F., Galán, R. Hernando, M., Montero, J.M., & Lucas, M. .Service Robotics. Urbano, an Iteractive Mobile Tour-Gide Robot. pp. 229-252. I-Tech Education and Publishing Alekasandar Lazinica, Viena, Austria. 2008.ISBN978-3-902613-24-0

[5] Rainer, J.J, Gómez, J., &Galán, R.An automatic Generator of Presentations for Gide-Tour Robot.Mathware&Soft Computing. Vol. 16, No 2. 2009.ISSN 1134-5632

[6] Gruber, T.R..Ontolingua: a mechanism to support portable ontologies, KSL-91-66, Knowledge System Laboratory, Stanford University, Stanford, CA, USA, 1991.

[7] Guarino, N..Understanding building and using ontologies, Int. J. Human–Computer Stud. 46 (2/3) 293–310, 1997. ISSN 1095-9300.

[8] Sowa J.F..Ontology, metadata, and semiotics, Lecture Notes in Artificial Intelligence, Vol. 1867, pp. 56–83 Springer, Berlin, 2000.ISSN 0302-9743.

[9] Hand, D. J., and Yu, Y. . Idiots Bayes - not so stupid after all? International Statistical Review 69:385–389. 2001.

[10] Vapnik, V. The Nature of Statistical Learning Theory. Heidelberg, Germany. Springer.1995. ISBN 0-387-98780-0

[11] MacQueen, J. B.. Some Methods for classification and Analysis of Multivariate Observations, Proceedings of 5-th Berkeley Symposium on Mathematical Statistics and Probability, Berkeley, University of California Press, 1:281-297. 1967.ISSN 0097-0433

[12] Dempster, A. P., Laird, N. M., & Rubin, D. R. . Maximum Likelihood from Incomplete Data via the EM algorithm. Journal of the Royal Satistical Society, Series B, 39 (1). pp. 1-38. 1997. ISSN 1467-985X

[13] Liu, B. . Web Data Mining. Berlin, Heidelberg, Germany. Springer-Verlag. 2007. ISBN10 3-540-37881-2

[14] Porter, M. F. . An Algorithm for Suffix Stripping. Program, 14(3), pp. 130-137. 1980.ISBN:1-55860-454-5

[15] Turney, P..Thumbs Up or Thumbs Down? Semantic Orientation Applied to Unsupervised Classification of Reviews. In Proc. of the Meeting of Association for computational Linguistics (ACL 02), pp. 417-424. 2002.DOI 10.3115/1073083.1073153

[16] Dreewester, S., Dumais, S. T., Furnas, G. W., Launderer, T. K., &Harshman. Indexing by Latent Semantic Analysis. Journal of the American Society for Information Science. 41, pp. 391-407. 1990.ISSN: 1532-2890

[17] Efron, B., &Tibshirani, R. J..An Introduction to the Bootstrap, Chapman & Hall, Boca Ratón. 1993.ISBN 0-412-04231-2

## 25

A Grammatical Approach to the Modeling of an Autonomous Robot

Gabriel López-García, A. Javier Gallego-Sánchez, J. Luis Dalmau-Espert, Rafael Molina-Carmona
and Patricia Compañ-Rosique

Abstract — **Virtual Worlds Generator is a grammatical model that is proposed to define virtual worlds. It integrates the diversity of sensors and interaction devices, multimodality and a virtual simulation system. Its grammar allows the definition and abstraction in symbols strings of the scenes of the virtual world, independently of the hardware that is used to represent the world or to interact with it. A case study is presented to explain how to use the proposed model to formalize a robot navigation system with multimodal perception and a hybrid control scheme of the robot. The result is an instance of the model grammar that implements the robotic system and is independent of the sensing devices used for perception and interaction. As a conclusion the Virtual Worlds Generator adds value in the simulation of virtual worlds since the definition can be done formally and independently of the peculiarities of the supporting devices.**

Keywords — **Autonomous robots, virtual worlds, grammatical models, multimodal perception.**

I. INTRODUCTION

Autonomous robots are physical agents that perform tasks by navigating in an environment and by manipulating objects in it. To perform these tasks, they are equipped with effectors to act on the environment (wheels, joints, grippers...) and with sensors that can perceive it (cameras, sonars, lasers, gyroscopes...). It should be notice that, in general, the environment in which a robot operates may be inaccessible (it is not always possible to obtain all the information necessary for decision-making in every moment) non-deterministic (the effect of the action taken by the robot in the environment cannot be guaranteed), non-episodic (the action to be performed by the robot depends on the current perceptions and on the previous decisions), dynamic (the robot and the other elements in the environment may be constantly changing) and continuous (the location of the robot and the moving obstacles change in a continuous range of time and space) [8].

The growing disparity of available sensors adds complexity to systems, but it also allows the control of robots to be more accurate. There are several reasons that support the use of a combination of different sensors to make a decision. For example, humans and other animals integrate multiple senses.

Gabriel López-García, A. Javier Gallego-Sánchez (corresponding author), J. Luis Dalmau-Espert, Rafael Molina-Carmona and Patricia Compañ-Rosique are in the Group of Industrial Computing and Artificial Intelligence, University of Alicante, Ap. 99, 03080 Alicante, Spain (e-mail: [glopez, ajgallego, jldalmau, rmolina, patricia]@dccia.ua.es).

Various biological studies have shown that when the signals reach the superior colliculus converge to the same target area [9], which also receives signals from the cerebral cortex and causes the resulting behavior. A large majority of superior colliculus neurons are multisensory. There are other reasons of mathematical nature: combining multiple observations from the same source provides statistical advantages because some redundant observations are obtained for the same estimation.

The concepts from biology can be extrapolated to the field of robotics. In fact, one of the current research fields that arouses most interest is the management of several inputs from different types, the so called multimodal data.

Combining data from different sensors is an open field of research. In this sense, there are several concepts related to this subject that deals with the concept of multimodality from different points of view. Signhal and Brown [10] consider that two main processes may be performed from several multimodal inputs: multisensor fusion and multisensor integration. Multisensor integration refers to the synergistic use of the information provided by multiple sensory devices to assist in the accomplishment of a task by a system. Multisensor fusion refers to any stage in the integration process where there is actual combination (fusion) of different sources of sensory information into one representation format. Other authors describe the evidence that humans combine information following two general strategies: The first one is to maximize information delivered from the different sensory modalities (sensory combination). The second strategy is to reduce the variance in the sensory estimate to increase its reliability (sensory integration) [3]. Another example is set in [11]. They consider that, in general, multimodal integration is done for two reasons: sensory combination and sensory integration. Sensory combination describes interactions between sensory signals that are not redundant. That means crossmodal integration leads to increased information compared to single modalities. By contrast, sensory integration describes interactions between redundant signals. This leads to enhanced robustness and reliability of the derived information.

In this paper we deal with the integration of multimodal inputs in the sense stated by Signhal and Brown [10], that is, the use of data of different nature for decision-making in high-level tasks performed by a robot. However, the proposed system can also deal with the concept of fusion, defined as the combination of low-level redundant inputs for the cooperative construction of the complete information of the environment, reducing, as a consequence, the levels of uncertainty.

Different architectures have been described for defining the behavior of a robot and the combination of sensory information. A robotic control architecture should have the following properties: programmability, autonomy and adaptability, reactivity, consistent behavior, robustness and extensibility [4].

To achieve those requirements, most robot architectures try to combine reactive control and deliberative control. The reactive control is guided by sensors and it is suitable for low-level decisions in real time. The deliberative control belongs to a higher level, so that global solutions can be obtained from the data collected by the sensors but also from information from an a priori model. They are, therefore, hybrid architectures.

Hybrid architectures arise due to the problems and inconveniences of pure reactive approaches, such as the lack of planning, and of pure deliberative approaches, such as the slow reactions. An example of hybrid architecture is the PRS (Procedural Reasoning System). When the hybrid architectures face a problem, the deliberative mechanisms are used to design a plan to achieve an objective, while the reactive mechanisms are used to carry out the plan. The communications framework is the base that enables the necessary interaction between reactive and deliberative levels, by sending distributed sensory information to tasks at both levels and sending actions to actuators. Deliberative and reactive tasks can be structured in a natural way by means of independent software components [6].

An example of implementation is the model SWE (Sensor Web Enablement), which is applied to systems that are based on the use of sensors to obtain the information that is processed later [1]. In [7] an architecture based on models SWE and DDS (Data Distribution Service) is proposed. DDS is a general-purpose middleware standard designed specifically to satisfy the performance and Quality of Service (QoS) requirements of real-time systems.

The Virtual Worlds Generator (VWG), our proposal, is a grammatical model, which integrates the diversity of interaction and sensing devices and the modules that make up a Graphics System (Graphics, Physics and AI engines). The scene definition is separated from the hardware-dependent characteristics of the system devices. It uses a grammar definition, which integrates activities, visualization and interaction with users. The hypothesis is that it can be used as a formal framework to model a robot navigation system, including several multimodal inputs, sensor fusion and integration, and behavior strategies.

In section 2, the formal model for the VWG is presented. In section 3, the formal model is applied to construct a robotic system. Finally, some conclusions are presented in the last section.

II. MODEL FOR VIRTUAL WORLDS GENERATION

In the VWG model, a virtual world is described as an ordered sequence of primitives, transformations and actors. A primitive is the description of an object in a given representation system (typically, they are graphical primitives but they could also be sounds or any other primitive in a representation space). Transformations modify the behavior of primitives, and actors are the components that define the activities of the system in the virtual world. The actors may be finally displayed through primitives and transformations. To model the different actor's activities, the concept of an event is used. Events cause the activation of a certain activity that can be processed by one or more actors.

Each element in the scene is represented by a symbol from the *set of symbols of the scene*. The symbols make up strings that describe the scenes, in accordance with a language syntax, which is presented as a grammar [2].

A. Syntax

A grammar M is a tuple $M = <\Sigma, N, R, s>$, where Σ is the finite set of terminal symbols, N is the finite set of non-terminal symbols, R is the finite set of syntactic rules (a syntactic rule is an application $r: N \rightarrow W^*$, where $W = \Sigma \cup N$) and $s \in N$ is the initial symbol of the grammar. In our case, M is defined as:

- $\Sigma = P \cup T \cup O \cup A^D_{ATTR}$, where:
    - P: set of symbols for primitives.
    - T: set of symbols for transformations.
    - $O = \{\cdot \ ()\}$: symbols for indicating the scope () and the concatenation $\cdot$.
    - A^D_{ATTR}: set of symbols for actors, where D is the set of all the types of events generated by the system and $ATTR$ is the set of all the attributes of actors, which define all the possible states. For example, the actor a^H_{attr} will carry out its activity when it receives an event e^h, where $h \in H$, $H \subseteq D$ and $attr \in ATTR$ is its current state.
- N = {WORLD, OBJECTS, OBJECT, ACTOR, TRANSFORM, FIGURE}.
- Grammar rules R are defined as:
    - Rule 1. **WORLD** →OBJECTS
    - Rule 2. **OBJECTS** → OBJECT | OBJECT · OBJECTS
    - Rule 3. **OBJECT**→ FIGURE | TRANSFORMATION | ACTOR
    - Rule 4. **ACTOR**→ a^H_{attr} , $a^H_{attr} \in \mathbf{A}^D_{ATTR}, H \subseteq D$
    - Rule 5. **TRANSFORMATION** → t(OBJECTS), $t \in T$
    - Rule 6. **FIGURE**→ $p+, p \in P$
- s = WORLD is the initial symbol of the grammar.

M is a context-free grammar. $L(M)$ is the language generated by the grammar M: $L(M) = \{w \in \Sigma^* \mid WORLD \rightarrow^* w\}$.

B. Semantics

Apart from the language syntax, it is necessary to define the semantics of $L(M)$. It will be defined with a denotational method, that is, through mathematical functions.

1) Semantic Function of Primitives (Rule 6)

Rule 6 defines a figure as a sequence of primitives. Primitive's semantics is defined as a function α, as follows:

$$\alpha = P \rightarrow G \tag{1}$$

Each symbol in the set P carries out a primitive on a given geometric system G. So, depending on the definition of the function α and on the geometry of G, the result of the system may be different. G represents the actions to be run on a specific visual or non-visual geometric system (e.g. the actions on OpenGL or on the system of a robot). The function α provides the abstraction needed to homogenize the different implementations of a rendering system. Therefore, only a descriptive string is needed to run the same scene on different systems.

2) Semantic Functions of Transformations (Rule 5)

In Rule 5, two functions are used to describe the semantics of a transformation, whose scope is limited by the symbols "()":

$$\beta : T \rightarrow G$$
$$\delta : T \rightarrow G \tag{2}$$

β represents the beginning of the transformation. It is carried out when the symbol "(" is processed. Function δ defines the end of the transformation which has previously been activated by the function β. It is run when the symbol ")" is found. These two functions have the same features that the function α, but they are applied to the set of transformations T, using the same geometric system G.

3) Semantic Functions of Actors (Rule 4)

Rule 4 refers to actors, which are the dynamic part of the system. The semantics of the actor is a function that defines its evolution in time. For this reason, the semantic function is called *evolution function λ* and it is defined as

$$\lambda : A^D_{ATTR} \times E^D \rightarrow L(M) \tag{3}$$

where E^D is the set of events for the set of all event types D. Some deeper aspects about events will be discussed later.

The function λ has a different expression depending on its evolution. However, a general expression can be defined. Let $H = \{h_0, \ldots, h_n\} \subseteq D$ be the subset of event types which the actor a^H_{ATTR} is prepared to respond to. The general expression for λ is:

$$\lambda\left(a^H_{ATTR}, e^h\right) = \begin{cases} u_0 \in L(M) & if\ h = h_0 \\ \cdots & \\ u_n \in L(M) & if\ h = h_n \\ a^H_{ATTR} & if\ h \notin H \end{cases} \tag{4}$$

where $u_0, \ldots, u_n$ are strings of $L(M)$. This equation means that an actor a^H_{ATTR} can evolve, that is, it is transformed into

another string u_i when it responds to an event e^h which the actor is prepared to respond to. However, the actor remains unchanged when it is not prepared to respond.

As well as dynamic elements, actors can also have a representation in the geometric space G. To be displayed, an actor must be converted to a string of primitives and transformations. This visualization function is defined as:

$$\theta : A^D_{ATTR} \times E^V \rightarrow L(M') \tag{5}$$

where $V \subseteq D$, $E^V \subseteq E^D$ are events created in the visualization process, and $L(M')$ is a subset of the language $L(M)$, made up of the strings with no actors. Let $H \cap V = \{v_0, \ldots, v_n\} \subseteq D$ be the subset of visual event types which the actor a^H_{ATTR} is prepared to respond to. The expression of Θ is defined as:

$$\theta\left(a^H_{ATTR}, e^v\right) = \begin{cases} z_0 \in L(M') & if\ v = v_0 \\ \cdots & \\ z_n \in L(M') & if\ v = v_n \\ \varepsilon & if\ v \notin H \cap V \end{cases} \tag{6}$$

4) Semantic Functions of OBJECT, OBJECTS and WORLD (Rules 1, 2 and 3)

The semantic function of Rules 1, 2, and 3 breaks down the strings and converts them into substrings, executing the so called *algorithm of the system*, which performs the complete evolution of the system and displays it in the current geometric system. It performs several actions, which are described in the following paragraphs.

To display the scene on the geometric system G, the function φ is defined, for the set of symbols that can directly be displayed: primitives and transformations. Given a string $w \in L(M)$ and using only symbols of P and T, φ is defined as:

$$\varphi(w) = \begin{cases} \alpha(w) & if\ w \in P \\ \beta(t); \varphi(v); \delta(t) & if\ w = t(v) \wedge v \in L(M) \wedge t \in T \\ \varphi(u); \varphi(v) & if\ w = u \cdot v \wedge u, v \in L(M) \end{cases} \tag{7}$$

In the case of strings including both displayable elements, and actors, two functions must be defined. The first one is the so called *function of the system evolution η*, which requires a sequence of sorted events $S = e^1 \cdot e^2 \ldots .e^n$, where every $e^i \in E^D$ and a string of $L(M)$ including actors, and implements a set of recursive calls to the function λ to perform the evolution of all the actors in the system at a given frame:

$$\eta(w, S) = \begin{cases} w & if\ w \in P \\ t(\eta(v, S)) & if\ w = t(v) \\ \prod_{e^i \in S} \lambda(a^H_{attr}, e^i) & if\ w = a^H_{attr} \\ \eta(u, S) \cdot \eta(v, S) & if\ w = u \cdot v \end{cases} \tag{8}$$

The operator $\prod_{e_i \in S} \lambda\ (a^H_{attr}, e_i)$ concatenates the strings of the function λ.

The actors to be displayed in the system must be converted to displayable elements, that is, primitives and transformations. The second function, returns a string of the language $L(M')$ given a string $w \in L(M)$ and a sequence of ordered visualization events $S' = e^1 \cdot e^2 \ldots e^n$, where every $e^i \in E^V$ and $S' \subseteq S$. This function is called *function of system visualization* π and it is defined as:

$$\pi(w,S) = \begin{cases} w & \text{if } w \in P \\ t(\eta(v,S')) & \text{if } w = t(v) \\ \prod_{e^i \in S} \theta(a_{ATTR}^H, e^i) & \text{if } w = a_{ATTR}^H \\ \pi(u,S') \cdot \pi(v,S') & \text{if } w = u \cdot v \end{cases} \quad (9)$$

C. Events and Generators

The events are the mechanism to model the activity in the system. The actors' activity is carried out when a certain type of event is produced. The following event definition is established: e^d_c is defined as an event of type $d \in D$ with data c.

A new function called *event generator* is defined as: Let $C^d(t)$ be a function which creates a sequence of ordered events of type d at the time instant t, where $d \in D$ and D is the set of event types which can be generated by the system. This function is:

$$C^d : Time \rightarrow (E^D)^* \quad (10)$$

In the previous definition, it should be noticed that events are generated in the time instant t. It is due to synchronization purpose. The event generator can generate several or no events at a given moment.

Different event generators can create the same type of events. So, a priority order among event generators must be established to avoid ambiguities. Given two generators C_i and C_j which create the same event, if $i < j$, then the events generated by C_i will have a higher priority.

D. System Algorithm

Once all the elements involved in the model have been defined, the *System Algorithm* can be established. It defines the system evolution and its visualization at every time instant t or frame:

    1) $w = w_0$; $t = 0$
    2) while $w \neq \varepsilon$ do
        - S = collect events from generators C^* in order of priority.
        - Z = extract visual events from S.
        - $w_{next} = \eta(w, S)$
        - $v = \pi(w, Z)$; $g = \varphi(v)$
        - $w = w_{next}$; $t = t + 1$
    3) end while

where w_0 is the initial string, $C^* = \{$All the event generators which generate events of type $D\}$, $D = \{$Set of all the types of possible events in the system$\}$, g is the output device, S is a sequence of all the events generated by the system at instant t, Z is a subsequence of S, and it includes all the events from visual devices. These events are the input of the visual algorithm π.

A diagram of the virtual world generation algorithm is shown in Fig. 1.

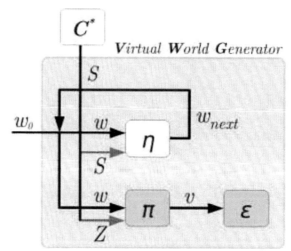

Fig. 1. Virtual world generator algorithm.

This formalization of the system has two main consequences. First, the scene definition is separated from the hardware-dependent characteristics of components. The functions α, β and δ provide the independence from the visualization system, and the event generators provide the independence from the hardware input devices. Secondly, due to the fact that there is a specific scheme to define the features of a system, the different system elements can be reused easily in other areas of application.

III. CASE STUDY

A. Description

Let us consider a robot with several sensors that provide information about the environment. It is programmed to autonomously navigate in a known environment, and to transport objects from one place to another. The input data are: the data from a range sensor (e.g. a laser to detect obstacles and distances), the image from a camera to identify objects and places using markers, an internal representation of the environment (a map) and a human supervisor who is controlling the robot (he can give some high level instructions, such as interrupt the current task or begin a new task). The information is combined using a multimodal algorithm based on priorities, so that the robot can attend to the users' request, select the best way to follow to the destination and use the sensors to detect and avoid obstacles, as well as to identify the objects and the places.

A system like this can be modeled using a classical hybrid scheme (Fig. 2), based on the combination of a reactive system and a proactive system. This hybrid scheme can be adapted using the VWG introduced in the previous section.

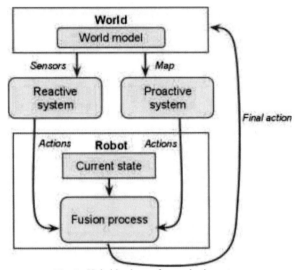

Fig. 2. Hybrid scheme for a robotic system.

In this picture the world is the real environment. The world model is a map containing the static elements of the environment. The reactive system is made of several generators, for the sensors and for the user's orders. The proactive system is the AI of the robot. The robot is the only actor in the system. The current state is the set of robot attributes. The multisensorial integration process is the evolution function of the robot. The final action is the result of the process of sensor integration and the final action carried out by the robot.

B. Primitives and Transformations

As it was stated in section 2, primitives are the description of objects in the space of representation, and transformations are used to modify primitives. In our robotic system, only one primitive is needed, the robot, and it is modified by two possible transformations: move and rotate (table I). When the system is executed in a real environment, the robot primitive represents the real robot and the transformations correspond to the actual operations performed by the robot. If it is executed in a simulator, the primitive and the transformations will represent the operations carried out in the simulated robot, that is, the operations in the graphics system (GS). The operations are performed by the semantic functions α for the primitives and β and δ for the transformations.

TABLE I
PRIMITIVES AND TRANSFORMATIONS OF THE ROBOTIC SYSTEM

	Real Environment	Simulator
PRobot	No action	Draw the robot in the GS
TMove<dist>	Move a distance dist	Move a distance dist in the GS
TRotate<angle>	Rotate an angle angle	Rotate an angle angle in the GS

C. Events and Generators

Events are used to define the activity in the system. Each event is defined by its identifier and some attributes. They produce changes on the actors through their evolution functions. These events are produced by generators. There is a generator for each event type. In the robotic system, five generators are needed:

- *gLaser*: It generates an *eLaser* event when the laser detects an obstacle, by obtaining the laser data and processing them to find the possible obstacles.
- *gCamera*: It generates an *eCamera* event when a marker is detected in the camera image. Markers are used to identify the rooms in the environment.
- *gDecide*: It generates an *eDecide* event each frame to indicate to the robot to make a decision.
- *gExecute*: It generates an *eExecute* event to indicate the system to execute the robot actions in the current representation space. If the representation space is the real environment, the real operations will take place (move the robot, rotate the robot...). If the current space is the simulator, the operations will take place in the graphics system.
- *gObjective*: It generates an *eObjective* event to set a new objective marker. This generator is connected to the users' orders. Users can specify a new target room simply by selecting its associated marker.

The generators in our system and their associated events are shown in table II.

TABLE II
GENERATORS AND EVENTS OF THE ROBOTIC SYSTEM

Generator and Events	Description	Associated data
gLaser = eLaser<dist,angle> if obstacle	Event produced when the laser detects an obstacle	dist: disntace to the obstacle angle: angle to the obstacle
gCamera = eCamera<marker> if marker	Event produced when the camera detects a marker	marker: detected marker
gDecide = eDecide each frame	Event generated each frame to indicate to the robot to make a decision	No data
gExecute = eExecute each frame	It runs the robot action in the real environment or in the simulator	No data
gObjective = eObjective<marker> if user order	Event produced by the user to set the objective marker	marker: objective marker

An order relation must be defined to establish an execution priority among generators. In the robotic system, the order relation is: *gLaser, gCamera, gObjective, gDecide, gExecute*. Therefore, events related with the acquisition of data have the highest priority, compared with the events of decision and execution.

D. Actors

The only actor in our robotic system is the robot, which is defined as:

$$ARobot_{<grid,row,column,angle,objective,action>}^{eLaser,eCamera,eDecide,eExecute,eObjective} \qquad (11)$$

where the superscript are the events which it is prepared to respond to, and the subscript are the attributes, whose meanings are: the *grid* represents the environment where the robot moves in. Each cell stores the registered data obtained from the sensors (the detected obstacles and markers). *Row* and *column* are the position occupied by the robot in the grid. *Angle* is the robot orientation. *Objective* is the objective room, represented by its marker. And *action* is the string of primitives and transformations that indicates the next command to be executed by the robot. To simplify, in the following equations this actor will be referred as $ARobot_{<g,r,c,an,o,ac>}^{E}$.

The evolution function is, probably, the most important element in the system, as it defines the way the robot behaves in the environment, that is, it defines the artificial intelligence of the robotic system. Let *e* be an event that is received by the actor, the evolution function is defined as:

$$\lambda(ARobot_{<g,r,c,an,o,ac>}^{E}, e) =$$

$$= \begin{cases} ARobot_{<g',r,c,an,o,ac>}^{E} & if\ e = eLaser_{<dist,angle>} \\ ARobot_{<g',r,c,an,o,ac>}^{E} & if\ e = eCamera_{<marker>} \\ ARobot_{<g,r',c',an',o,ac'>}^{E} & if\ e = eDecide \\ \alpha(ARobot_{<g,r,c,an,o,ac>}^{E}) & if\ e = eExecute \\ ARobot_{<g,r,c,an,o',ac>}^{E} & if\ e = eObjective_{<marker>} \\ ARobot_{<g,r,c,an,o,ac>}^{E} & otherwise \end{cases} \qquad (12)$$

where the symbol apostrophe (') on an attribute indicates that it has changed as a consequence of the received event. The way the attributes change is the following:

- If $e = eLaser_{<dist,angle>}$, the grid (*g*) must be updated to indicate that an obstacle has been detected. The cell to mark is the one in position ($r + dist\ cos(ang + angle)$, $c + dist\ sin(ang + angle)$).
- If $e = eCamera_{<marker>}$, the grid (*g*) must be updated to indicate that a marker has been detected. The cell to mark is ($r + dist\ cos(ang)$, $c + dist\ sin(ang)$).
- If $e = eDecide$, the current position and orientation of the robot (row *r*, column *c* and angle *ang*), must be updated, as well as the actions to be executed. This function is very important, as it provides the behavior of the robot. In the following section, the way to introduce intelligent behaviors will be shown.
- If $e = eExecute$, the actions of the robot must be executed in the representation space, through the use of the α function.
- If $e = eObjective_{<marker>}$, a new objective has been set by the user, so the objective (*o*) must be changed to the new one (*marker*).

- In any other case, the actor must remain unchanged.

E. Initial string

The initial string in our systems defined as:

$$ARobot_{<grid,row,column,angle,\varepsilon,\varepsilon>}^{eLaser,eCamera,eDecide,eExecute,eObjective} \qquad (13)$$

where the attribute *grid* is initialized to a set of empty cells, the attributes *row*, *column* and *angle* are the initial position and orientation, and the *objective* and the *action* are empty.

F. Analysis

A set of tests has been designed to prove the features of our model. Specifically, five tests have been carried out.

1) Test of the evolution function

As it was stated before, the evolution function is the way of introducing intelligent behaviors in an actor. Therefore, the aim of this test is to prove the suitability of the evolution function to introduce new AI algorithms. This test is not to obtain the best AI algorithm to achieve the goal, but to prove that a new intelligent behavior can be introduced by just changing the evolution function. An important question is guaranteeing the same conditions for all the experiments, so the AI algorithms are introduced with no other modification in other parts of the system.

Two simple decision algorithms have been used to decide how the robot should move in the world. The first algorithm makes decisions randomly to find the target position. The second one is the A* algorithm [5], considering the Euclidean distance to the goal as the weights. If there is an obstacle the distance is defined as infinite.

2) Test of device independence

One of the main features of our model is that the system definition is independent from the input devices. The aim of this test is to prove that the input devices can be replaced without changing the definition of the string representing the system.

In our original system, a laser range sensor was used to detect obstacles. In this test, a Kinect device is introduced. To add this new device, we have just designed a new event generator (*gKinect*) that creates events of the same type that the ones generated by the laser generator. That is, it provides the same information: the angle and the distance to the obstacle. The new device is then introduced with no other modification in the system. The Kinect is then used to replace the laser device or to obtain redundant information for the detection of obstacles.

3) Test to validate the simulation

The most important achievement in the proposed model is the fact that the description for the simulation and for the real robot is exactly the same. That is, the command execution for the simulated robot can be directly used for the real robot with no change in the string that represents the system.

To achieve this goal, two generators for the execution of the robot commands have been implemented: one for the real robot and one for the robot simulation. This way, the commands are transparently executed no matter whether the robot is real or simulated, just using the appropriate generator. As a result, the navigation would be exactly the same for the simulated robot and for the real one, if there were not odometry errors. A good way to improve the simulation is introducing some odometry errors in the motors and in the sensor signals, accordingly with the features of the real robot.

4) Test of the system extensibility

The proposed model is, by definition, easily extensible. The updating of the definition string supposes the extension of the model and the addition of new features. Moreover, most elements can be reused in new definition strings to obtain new behaviors with little effort.

In our case, new instances of the actor symbols (representing robots) have been added to the definition string to extend the system in an almost immediate way and to create a multi-robot system.

5) Test of changes in the environment

A desired capability in a robot navigation system is, obviously, to be flexible enough to work under very different conditions. To prove this feature, the system has been tested with different maps (Fig. 3, 4 and 5), in the case of the simulated robot, and in different real environments, in the case of the real robot.

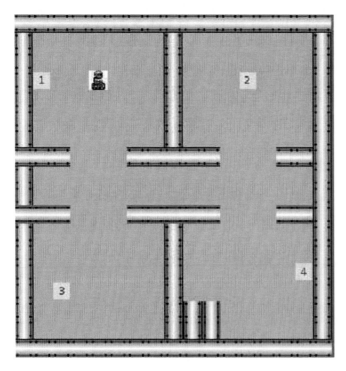

Fig. 3. Example map in 2D.

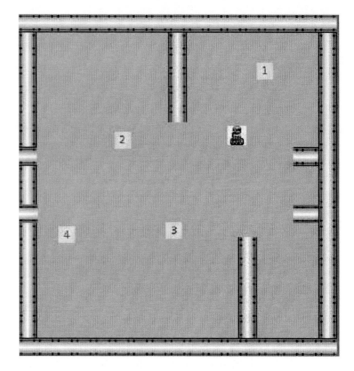

Fig. 4. Example map in 2D.

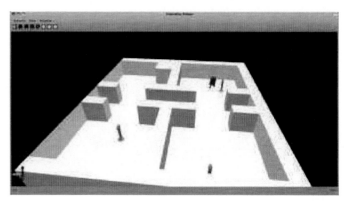

Fig. 5. Example map in 3D

IV. CONCLUSIONS

A new model to formally define virtual worlds, independently from the underlying physical layer, has been presented. Is has been used to model the control of a mobile robot, navigating in a given environment, and using a set of multimodal inputs from different types of sensors.

The model is based on a grammar which consists, on the one hand, of symbols to abstract and represent the elements of the system (primitives, actors, and so on) and, on the other hand, of a set of evolution functions so that all these elements can be combined in different ways leading to an infinite set of possible strings belonging to the grammar. By definition, each string has the ability to represent the interaction between the elements (symbols) of the system and their state at any given instant. By extension, these strings can also synthesize and formally define the system state.

As in other systems for modeling virtual worlds, the event and, in particular, the occurrence thereof, can bring about a change in the state of a particular element and, in general, a change in the state of the system. Within the model, the event generators are responsible for managing all the possible events associated with the elements of the system.

The result of the events, namely the transition between states, involves an evolution of the original string of the system to another evolved string, which is obtained from the application of certain rules on the first string. These rules are defined within the actors, which contain the logic of how to act and deal with an event if it is activated. The main restriction to design the rules is that they should be able to translate the consequence of the events into grammar rules. The grammar rules must be applicable to the symbols of the state string and the outcome of the rules application must return a consistent string, syntactically and semantically possible.

The evolution function of the actors can be as complex as needed. In fact, this function is the vehicle to introduce intelligent behaviors in the system. This way, artificial intelligence algorithms can be introduced into the evolution function of the actor to provide it with the needed behavior.

Taking into account the diversity of virtual worlds systems available nowadays and the wide variety of devices, this model seems to be able to provide interesting features. Firstly, it is a formal model based on a grammar that allows abstracting and representing the states of the system in a general way by avoiding the specific features of other existing systems. The use of strings facilitates the parallelization and optimization of the system processes. It is also a device-independent model, therefore, is not linked to the implementation of the system with a given set of devices. It also allows the replacement of physical devices by simulated ones, and the easy addition of new ones. For instance, in the case of our robotic system, the definition string of the system is exactly the same for the simulator and for the real robot. Finally, it is a flexible model since it contemplates the possibility of reinterpreting the outputs of the actions.

In conclusion, it has been achieved the main objective of defining a new formal and generic model that is able to model general virtual worlds systems by avoiding the specific peculiarities of other models existing today.

REFERENCES

[1]   Botts, M.; Percivall, G.; Reed, C. and Davidson, J.: OGC Sensor Web Enablement: Overview And High Level Architecture. OGC White Paper. Open Geospatial Consortium Inc., 2006.

[2]   Davis, Martin; Sigal, Ron and Weyuker, Elaine J.: Computability, Complexity, and Languages, Fundamentals of Theoretical Computer Science, 2nd ed. San Diego: Elsevier Science, 1994.

[3]   Ernst, Marc O. and Bülthoff, Heinrich H.: Merging the senses into a robust percept. TRENDS in Cognitive Sciences, vol.8, no.4, 2004.

[4]   Ingrand, F.; Chatila, R. and Alami, R.: An Architecture for Dependable Autonomous Robots. IARP-IEEE RAS Workshop on Dependable Robotics, 2001.

[5]   Luo, Ren; Lin, Yu-Chih; Kao, Ching-Chung: Autonomous mobile robot navigation and localization based on floor paln map information and sensory fusion approach. IEEE MFI, 2010.

[6]   Posadas, J.L.; Poza, J.L., Simó, J.E.; Benet, G.; Blanes, F.: Agent-based distributed architecture for mobile robot control. Engineering Applications of Artificial Intelligence, pp. 805-823, 2008.

[7]   Poza, L.; Posadas, J.; Simó, J.; Benet, G.: Arquitecturas de control jeraárquico inteligente con soporte a la calidad de servicio. XXIX Jornadas de Automática, 2008.

[8]   Russell, Stuart Jonathan and Norvig, Peter: Artificial intelligence: a modern approach. Prentice Hall. ISBN: 0136042597, 2010.

[9]   Sharma, R.; Pavlovic, V. I.; Huang, T. S.: Toward Multimodal Humar-Computer Interface. Proceedings of the IEEE, vol. 86(5), pp. 853-869, 1998.

[10] Singhal, A.; Brown, C.: Dynamic bayes net approach to multimodal sensor fusion. SPIE, 1997.

[11] Weser, Martin; Jockel, Sascha and Zhang, Jianwei: Fuzzy Multisensor Fusion for Autonomous Proactive Robot Perception IEEE International Conference on Fuzzy Systems (FUZZ), 2263-2267, 2008.

## 26

Mining Social and Affective Data for Recommendation of Student Tutors

Elisa Boff[1] and Eliseo Berni Reategui[2]
[1]*Universidade de Caxias do Sul (UCS) – Brazil*
[2]*Universidade Federal do Rio Grande do Sul (UFRGS) – Brazil*

Abstract — **This paper presents a learning environment where a mining algorithm is used to learn patterns of interaction with the user and to represent these patterns in a scheme called item descriptors. The learning environment keeps theoretical information about subjects, as well as tools and exercises where the student can put into practice the knowledge gained. One of the main purposes of the project is to stimulate collaborative learning through the interaction of students with different levels of knowledge. The students' actions, as well as their interactions, are monitored by the system and used to find patterns that can guide the search for students that may play the role of a tutor. Such patterns are found with a particular learning algorithm and represented in item descriptors. The paper presents the educational environment, the representation mechanism and learning algorithm used to mine social-affective data in order to create a recommendation model of tutors.**

Ketwords — **Collaboration, Learning Environment, Recommender Systems, Social-Affective Data.**

I. INTRODUCTION

MINING data in educational environments is often used with two main purposes:

(1) to give educators a better understanding of how users learn with the system;

(2) to define different paths of study according to students' profiles learned from data.

The first goal may be achieved by using mining algorithms to identify patterns and represent them in a scheme that is easy to understand. The second goal can be pursued by employing a mechanism capable of using the patterns found to suggest topics related to the subjects being studied.

We used mining algorithms here in order to accomplish both purposes (1 and 2), and also to identify suitable student tutors that may help other students needing assistance. The use of data mining in Education has expanded considerably in the last decade mostly because of the growing number of systems that store large databases about students, their accesses to material available, their assignments and grades. Such expansion in the field yielded the establishment of a community concerned mostly with the development of methods for exploring data coming from educational settings, and employing those methods to better understand students and learning processes [4].

Current research has shown the potentiality of cooperative learning, demonstrating that group work is fundamental for the cognitive development of the student [7] [8]. It is known that knowledge composition occurs on an individual basis, but cooperation (subjects acting together over the same topic, with common goals, interacting and exchanging ideas) is capable of involving all participants in learning [18]. In this perspective, motivating the students to interact can lead to an effective learning practice.

The recommendation service of tutors works in the sense of motivating group formation among the students. According to Andrade [1], a group can be formed due to similarity and empathy of its members or to the necessity of support for the accomplishment of some task. The latter can be motivated by prestige or status, economic benefits or the necessity and desire of contribution. [1] also says that the affective states of the individuals have significant importance in the interaction process. The author complements affirming that some dimensions of the personality seem to have certain connections with the social performance in the interaction, but establishing an accurate relationship between them seems to be a complex task.

Our tutor recommendation service explores the social-affective dimension through the analysis of emotional states and social behavior of the users. A recommender system analyses students' interactions and finds suitable tutors among them as well as contents to be recommended. A specific algorithm was built to identify behavioral patterns in the students interaction, and to store this knowledge in structures called item descriptors [19]. The method proposed shows a good performance with respect to processing time and accuracy, and has an advantage over other techniques when it comes to understanding the knowledge elicited and letting users modify it. The first section of the paper gives an overview of the types of data collected from the interaction with the users. Then, the mechanism employed to represent knowledge is explained, in addition to its learning algorithm and recommendation process. Finally, preliminary results are discussed, as well as conceptual advantages and drawbacks of the approach. The last section of the paper offers conclusions and directions for future work.

II. COLLECTING INTERACTION DATA

When students navigate in our learning environment (Fig.2), different types of data are collected from their interaction. By keeping the navigation history of every student, for example, we are able to identify navigation patterns and to use them in real-time recommendation of contents. For the recommendation of tutor colleagues, six other types of data are collected: Social Profile; Acceptance Degree; Sociability Degree; Mood State; Tutorial Degree and Performance.

The Social Profile (SP) is built during the communication process among students. The following information is collected during the interaction of the students through an instant message service:

• *Initiatives of communication*: number of times that the student had the initiative to talk with other pupils.

• *Answers to initial communications*: in an initial communication, number of times that the student answered.

• *Interaction history*: individuals with whom the student interacts or has interacted, and number of interactions.

• *Friends Group*: individuals with which the student interacts regularly, and number interactions.

Based on Maturana [15] we defined the Acceptance Degree (AD), which measures the acceptance a student has for another one. Such data is collected through a graphical interface that enables each student to indicate his/her acceptance degree for other students. This measure may also be considered from a point of view of Social Networks, which constitutes one of the most popular approaches for the analysis of human interactions. The most important concept in this approach is centrality. If an individual is central in a group, he/she is popular and gets a great amount of attention from the group members. As the AD is indicated by the students themselves based on their affective structures, the measurement can indicate diverse emotions, such as love, envy, hatred, etc. The average of all AD received by a student influences his/her Sociability Degree (SD).

The Mood State (MS) represents our belief in the capability of a student to play the role of a tutor if he/she is not in a positive mood state (although the student may have all the technical and social requirements to be a tutor). We consider three values for the MS: "bad mood", "regular mood" and "good mood". These states are indicated by the students in a graphical interface through corresponding clip-arts.

After a helping session, a small questionnaire is submitted to the student who got assistance. The goal of this questionnaire is to collect information about the performance of the tutor. The questions made are based on concepts from Social Networks and Sociometry, and may be answered by four qualitative values: "excellent", "good", "regular", and "bad". They are:

• *How do you classify the sociability of your class fellow?*

• *How do you classify the help given by your class fellow?*

The answer to the first question together with the average of the ADs of a student, form his/her Sociability Degree (SD). This measure indicates how other individuals see the social capability of this student.

The Tutorial Degree (TD) measures a student's pedagogical capacity to help, to explain and teach. This value is obtained from the answers given for the second question of the questionnaire above and from the marks the tutor got when he/she studied the contents for which he/she was asked for help. These marks were called Performance (P) and were used in the computation of the TD because when a tutor is not able to help another student it does not necessarily mean that the student is a bad tutor. He/she may simply not know very well the content for which his/her help was requested. Therefore, the answers of the students have to be "weighted".

A mining process determines relationships among these factors, and represents such relationships in item descriptors, which are later used for recommendation purposes.

III. THE ITEM DESCRIPTORS

An item descriptor represents knowledge about when to recommend a particular item (a topic of study, an exercise, or a tutor) by listing other items found to be related to it. Users have features that may be classified as:

• *demographic*: data describing an individual, such as age, gender, occupation, address;

• *behavioral*: data describing tutoring and social capacity, navigation and study patterns.

It has been shown that both types of data are important when building a user profile [13] and inferring user's needs [5] [6]. Demographic material is represented here in attribute-value pairs. Behavioral information is represented by actions carried out by the user, such as the selection of a topic for reading. Emotional states and social behavior can either be inferred or collected explicitly in questionnaires.

While attributes used to define demographic features are typically single-valued, behavioral data is usually multi-valued. For instance, a person can only belong to one age group (demographic), but he/she may be friendly and patient at the same time (behavioral). Nevertheless, both types of information are represented in our model in a similar way. Let us examine an example of an item descriptor and its related items (Table 1).

TABLE I
ITEM DESCRIPTOR AND RELATED ITEMS

DESCRIPTOR D_N	
Correlated terms	**Confidence**
t_a	0.92
t_e	0.87
t_c	0.85
t_d	0.84
t_b	0.77

The descriptor has a *target* (d_n), i.e. an item that may be recommended in the presence of some of its correlated terms. Each term's class and *confidence* (the strength with which the term is correlated with the target item) is displayed next to its identification.

We use *confidence* as a correlation factor in order to determine how relevant a piece of information is to the recommendation of a given item. This is the same as computing the conditional probability $P(d_j|e)$, i.e. the probability that the item represented by descriptor d_j is rated positively by a user given evidence e. Therefore, the descriptors can be learned through the analysis of actual users' records. For each item for which we want to define a recommendation strategy, a descriptor is created with the item defined as its target. Then, the confidence between the target and other existing demographic features and behavioral data is computed. This process continues until all descriptors have been created. For the recommendation of tutors, descriptors are built indicating the features of good and bad instructors.

IV. THE RECOMMENDATION OF TUTORS

Collaborative Filtering, one of the most popular technologies in recommender systems [15], has been used in the past in several research projects, such as Tapestry [13], GroupLens [27], and more recently in related research focusing on the extraction of information from social networks [9][21]. The technique is based on the idea that the active user is more likely to prefer items that like-minded people prefer [28]. To support this, similarity scores between the active user and every other user are calculated. Predictions are generated by selecting items rated by the users with the highest degrees of similarity.

Here, a different approach has been followed, as the main idea in the project was not to keep track of users' interests, but to evaluate their willingness to collaborate. This task, called here recommendation of tutors, is explained below.

Given a list of possible tutors $U=\{u_1, u_2,..., u_m\}$, the recommendation process starts with the gathering of demographic and behavioral information about each of them. Next, the data collected for each user is matched against a descriptor d_j which lists the most important features of good instructors, according to the terms $T=\{t_1,t_2,...,t_k\}$ stored in the descriptor. The system computes a score for each student that ranges from not similar (0) to very similar (1), according to the formula:

$$Score\ (d_j) = 1 - \prod (Noise\ (t_p))_{kji}$$

where $Score(d_j)$ is the final score of the descriptor d_j; $Noise(t_p)$ is the value of the noise parameter of term t_p, a concept used in noisy-OR probability models (Pradhan et al., 1994) and computed as $1 - P(d_j \mid t_p)$. The individual with the highest score is selected to assist the student needing assistance.

That expression contains an assumption of independence of the various t_p - which the designer of a practical system should be trying to achieve in the choice of terms. Ultimately the test of the assumption is in the users' perception of the quality of a system's recommendations: if the perception is that the outputs are fully satisfactory, this is circumstantial evidence for the soundness of the underlying design choices. The situation here is the same as in numerical taxonomy [21], where distances between topics id in a multidimensional space of attributes are given by metric functions where the choice of distinct dimensions should obviously aim to avoid terms that have mutual dependences. If the aim fails, the metric cannot - except occasionally by accident - produce taxonomic clusters C (analogous to sets of topics offered by a recommender system once a user has selected one member of C) that satisfy the users. This method is based on the assumption that any term matching the user's terms should increase the confidence that the descriptor holds the most appropriate recommendation. In a real-life example, let us suppose that we have a certain degree of confidence that a student who has shown a good ability in answering factorial exercises is our best bet to help another student who is having problem with the subject. Knowing that that same student is friendly and is in a good mood should increase the total confidence on his recommendation as a tutor, subject to not exceeding the maximum value of 1.

The Virtual Character is the interface element that delivers to student the result of recommendation process in natural language (Fig.1).

The knowledge base of the Virtual Character stores knowledge about Algorithms, enabling the character to assist students mainly in theoretical questions. The Artificial Intelligence Markup Language (AIML) is used to represent the character's conversational knowledge [30], employing a mechanism of stimulus-response. The stimuli (sentences and fragments which may be used to question the agent) are stored and used to search for pre-defined replies. The most important AIML tags are:

- **<aiml>**: indicates the beginning of a document.
- **<category>**: the simplest knowledge unit in AIML. Each category consists of an input question, an output answer and an optional context. The question, or stimulus, is called the pattern, while the answer is called the template.
- **<pattern>**: keeps a set of words which is searched for in sentences which the user may enter to communicate with the virtual character. The language that may be used to form the patterns includes words, spaces, and the wildcard symbols _ and *;
- **<template>**: when a given pattern is found in the input sentence, the corresponding template is returned and presented to the user. In its simplest form, a pattern is a word and the template consists of plain text. However, the tags may also force the conversion of the reply into a procedure which may activate other programs and recursively call the

pattern matcher to insert the responses from other categories.

The optional context of a category enables the character to remember a previous statement. This feature, together with the possibility of launching particular programs when a certain pattern is found, makes the AIML communication mechanism very distinct from a simple retrieval of questions and answers from a database.

Fig. 1. Recommendation example.

The user's affective state is also considered in order to choose the type of language the character uses to talk at a given moment. The affective state is entered as a pattern which has to be matched for the selection of a given sentence. For instance, the pattern *RECURSION* is modified into *RECURSION CHEERFUL* if the user is in a cheerful mood.

In addition to the existing AIML tags, new ones were created to manage the agents' emotional appearance. For instance, we created the tag *<humor>* to control the image changes reflecting different moods of the virtual character (happy, receptive, annoyed, etc).

Therefore, when the user poses a question (stimulus), the character starts the AIML Retrieval Mechanism in order to build an appropriate reply using the information, patterns and templates from the AIML database. A suitable picture of the character is picked from the Image Database to match the sentence retrieved according to the humor tag.

In addition to being able to answer questions in natural language, our character is also able to monitor the actions of each student and notice, for instance, that a particular topic is related to a given exercise. Such a behavior is achieved through the use of the template tag to launch the recommender

system, which looks for appropriate activities and contents to each student.

V. VALIDATION AND DISCUSSION

An Environment for the Learning of Algorithms (A3), Fig. 1, has been developed at the Department of Computer Science of the University of Caxias do Sul with the main goal of making the courses more dynamic, increasing the interest and participation of the students and providing an environment where students may interact in order to improve their knowledge. The environment presents students with the regular contents of algorithms (central area of Fig.2), it proposes exercises, provides a forum for discussion and a tool for the testing and running of algorithms. All website functions can be accessed by the left menu on the detail 3 of Fig.2. Having been developed as a dynamic website, the system enables teachers and administrators to modify contents easily. Online users are shown in the interface (detail 2 of Fig.2). And most importantly, the system promotes the communication among students by suggesting individuals that may help others showing difficulty in learning a given topic. The recommendation is present in the detail 4 of Fig.2, below the image of Virtual Character.

Fig. 2. Environment for the Learning of Algorithms (A3).

The Affective States of students describe social-affective data which is used to recommend students tutors. The system does not try to infer social-affective states, but the user deliberately informs it about how he/she feels at login time (detail 1 in Fig.2). This information is used to define the type of language and stimuli that our Virtual Character has to show in order to communicate better with the user.

The A3 environment started to be tested in 2 courses at the Department. Descriptors were built manually in order to get the system to recommend contents and tutors. The data collected so far has not been sufficient for us to carry out conclusive experiments as to whether the system is making tutoring recommendations appropriately. However, initial experiments carried out and reported in Reategui [19] show that the item descriptors have a good performance in terms of processing time and accuracy, when compared with collaborative filtering, one of the most popular approaches in recommender systems.

For the MovieLens database[1], for example, storing anonymous ratings of 3900 movies assigned by 6040 users, the item descriptors show an accuracy rate that is 6 points higher than that of the k-nearest neighbor algorithm. The Table 2 summarizes the results obtained.

The experiments were carried out considering neighborhoods with sizes 1, 20 and 40 (we did not observe any significant improvement in accuracy for the nearest-neighbor algorithm with neighborhoods larger than 40). The topic descriptors performed better than the k-nearest-neighbor algorithm, no matter what size of the neighborhoods was chosen.

Sarwar [20] have carried out a series of experiments with the same data set, employing the Mean Absolute Error (MAE) method to measure the accuracy of item-based recommendation algorithms. The results reported could not be compared directly with our own as the authors computed their system's accuracy using the MAE and considering integer ratings ranging from 1 to 5 (reaching values around 75%). In our experiment, we only took into account whether a user rated (1) or did not rate (0) a topic.

TABLE II
SCORING RESULTS FOR THE MOVIELENS DATA SET

Method	Scoring
Item Descriptors	65,7
k-nearest-neighbor (k=1)	39,3
k-nearest-neighbor (k=20)	54,9
k-nearest-neighbor (k=40)	59,7

In order to evaluate the system's performance, we monitored how much time was spent by the system in order to recommend the 2114 topics in the test data set[2]. For k=1, the nearest-neighbor approach needed less time than the topic descriptors to perform the tests, though showing a lower rate of accuracy. However, for larger values of k (or simply larger numbers of users) the performance of the nearest-neighbor algorithm degrades, while that of the topic descriptors remains stable. Table 3 summarizes the results of the experiment.

In more realistic situations where the nearest-neighbor algorithm may have to access a database containing actual users' transactions, the nearest-neighbor approach may become impractical. For the same experiment described above, we tested the nearest-neighbor through access to an actual database, using k=10. A few hours was needed for the system to make the whole set of recommendations. Further validation results may be found in Reategui [19].

Another popular approach applied to recommender systems is association rules [14] (Mombasher, 2001). This technique use well-known inductive learning algorithms, such as *a priori* [2], to extract knowledge and represent them in "if ... then ..." rules format. The main advantage of such learning method relies on the robustness and stability of the algorithms available. Although being successfully applied in innumerable application areas, association rules are hard to modify while keeping the rule base consistent (e.g. adding new rules without

TABLE III
PERFORMANCE RESULTS FOR THE MOVIELENS DATA SET

Method	Time spent in secs.
Topic Descriptors	32
k-nearest-neighbor (k=1)	14
k-nearest-neighbor (k=20)	43
k-nearest-neighbor (k=40)	86

contradicting existing ones). Keeping track of and trying to understand the large number of generated rules for each topic is another difficulty of this approach.

The item descriptor approach is different in that it represents knowledge in the form of descriptors and correlation factors. When compared with the other approaches in this respect, descriptors are interesting because they make it easy for users to understand as well as modify the knowledge represented. This is particularly important when the user wants to make the system respond in a certain way in given circumstances, e.g. if the teacher wants the system to recommend a certain reading when the student is viewing a particular topic.

The learning mechanism used on the item descriptors also exploits well-known methods to compute correlation factors and define the strength of the relationships among features and topics. The option to use term confidence instead of conditional probability to describe the model comes from the fact that other correlation factors that are not supported by probability theory are computed by the system, such as interest and conviction [4]. However, at present these are provided only to let the user analyze and validate the knowledge extracted from the database. We are currently testing different variations on the combination of these factors in the reasoning process.

Although the system learns and updates its descriptors in an offline process (therefore not critical for the application to recommend topics in real time), our learning algorithm is fairly simple and fast. Above all, it is faster than algorithms that group evidence and try to compute the relevance of each topic and then of each group of evidence.

Our model may also be compared with Hidden Markov Models (HMM), employed in tasks such as the inference of grammars of simple language [10], or the discovery of patterns in DNA sequences [3]. The two models are similar in that both

---

[1] MovieLens is a project developed in the Department of Computer Science and Engineering at the University of Minnesota (http://movielens.umn.edu).

[2] The tests were performed on a PIII 500MHZ PC with 128Mb of RAM.

use probability theory to determine the likelihood that a given event takes place. However, the actual methods used to compute probabilities of events are different: while HMM considers the product of the probabilities of individual events, we consider the product of noise parameters. Both models are based on the assumption that an output is statistically independent of previous outputs. This assumption may be limiting in given circumstances, but for the type of application we have chosen, we do not believe this to be a serious problem (e.g. as we have remarked above in our comments on independence). To take one practical example, the probability that a user studies topic C is very rarely dependent on the order in which users have read other topics (e.g. B before A, or A before B).

The recommendation method we use has the peculiarity of computing the correlation of individual terms initially, and then combining them in real time. This is analogous to finding first a set of rules with only one left-side term, followed at run time by finding associations between the rules. This is a good technique to avoid computing the relevance of all possible associations among terms in the learning phase.

Gomes [11] proposes a different recommendation strategy to identify tutors based on the computation of a utility function. Their strategy combines features in a mathematical expression to determine how effective a student can be for a given tutoring task. Compared to this approach, our mining and recommendation mechanism is more interesting in that it uses learning algorithms to learn a model from the available data automatically, identifying the importance of each utility function variable.

VI. CONCLUSION

One important contribution of this work has been the definition of the types of data to be used in the mining and in the recommendation process of student tutors. Using the descriptors to calculate the relevance of terms individually, and then combining them at recommendation time through the use of the noisy-OR is also a novel approach. A similar use of the function can be found in research on expert systems [9], but not in applications for recommender systems. Initial results have shown that the approach can be very effective in large-scale practice for personalization purposes.

The use of social-affective information to promote the communication and collaborative learning among students is starting to be tested in the environment A3. The results obtained so far show that the use of Social Profile, Mood State, Performance Acceptance, Sociability and Tutorial Degree in tutor recommendation, is a promising alternative.

Although the data collected from students' interactions so far are not sufficient for us to draw assertive conclusions about the use of item descriptors to recommend tutors, other experiments have shown the adequacy of the approach in item recommendation.

The possibility to represent different types of information (demographic or behavioral) in a similar way seems to be advantageous when it comes to practical implementation issues. Previous work in the field has shown the importance of dealing with and combining such types of knowledge in recommender systems [17]. Current research on the identification of implicit user information also shows that recommender systems will have to manipulate different sorts of data in order to infer users' preferences [6].

One of our biggest challenges now concerns the automatic inference of students' affective states. At present we are using questionnaires and graphic interface controls to let the users indicate such states. Thus, little is done to automatically infer the social-affective information necessary for tutor recommendation. This will be one of our main research efforts in the near future.

This project should also be integrated with the JADE/MAIDE platform [11] [22] and have its knowledge used in the MACE platform [1].

REFERENCES

[1] Andrade, A.; Jaques, P.; Viccari, R.; Bordini, R. and Jung, J. 2001. A Computational Model of Distance Learning Based on Vygotsky's Socio-Cultural Approach. In Proceedings of Multi-Agent Based Learning Environments Workshop. International Conference on Artificial Intelligence on Education. Antonio, Texas, May 19-23.

[2] Agrawal, R. and Srikant, R. 1994. Fast Algorithms for Mining Association Rules. In Proceedings of the 20th International Conference on Very Large Databases, Santiago, Chile.

[3] Allison, L.; Stern, L.; Edgoose, T. and Dix, T. I. 2000. Sequence Complexity for Biological Sequence Analysis. Computers and Chemistry 24(1):43-55.

[4] Baker, R. S. J. D., Yacef, K. 2009. The State of Educational Data Mining in 2009: A Review and Future Visions, Journal of Educational Data Mining, 1(1): 3-17.

[5] Brin, S.; Motwani, R.; Ullman, J. D.; and Tsur, S. 1997. Dynamic topicset counting and implication rules for market basket data. SIGMOD Record (ACM Special Interest Group on Management of Data), 26(2):255.

[6] Buchner A. and Mulvenna, M. 1998. Discovering Behavioural Patterns in internet files. Proceedings of Intelligent Tutoring Systems '98, San Antonio, Texas, USA. 16-19. Lecture Notes in Computer Science, 1452.

[7] Claypool, M.; Brown, D.; Le, P.; and Waseda, M. 2001. Inferring User Interest. IEEE Internet Computing, 5(6):32-39.

[8] Echeita, G., Martin, E. 1995. Interação Social e Aprendizagem. Porto Alegre: Artes Médicas.

[9] Finkelstein, A., Lim, S. L. 2012. Using Social Networks and Collaborative Filtering for Large-Scale Requirements Elicitation. IEEE Transactions on Software Engineering, 38(3): 707-735.

[10] Gallant, S. 1988. Connectionist Expert Systems. Communications of the ACM, Vol. 31, Issue 2.

[11] Georgeff, M. P. and Wallace, C. S. 1984. A General Selection Criterion for Inductive Inference. European Conference on Artificial Intelligence – ECAI 84, Pisa, 473-482.

[12] Gomes, E. R; Boff, E. and Viccari, R. 2004. Social, Affective and Pedagogical Agents for the Recommendation of Student Tutors. Proceedings of The Seventh Intelligent Tutoring Systems, Workshop on Social and Emotional Intelligence on Learning Environments, Maceió, Brazil, August, 31.

[13] Goldberg, D., Nichols, D., Oki, B. M. & Terry, D. 1992. Using collaborative filtering to weave an information tapestry. Communications of the ACM, 35(12).

[14] Gomes, E. R.; Silveira, R. A. and Viccari, R. M. 2003. Utilização de agentes FIPA em ambientes para Ensino a Distância. In: XI Congresso Iberoamericano de Educação Superior em Computação (CIESC), Bolívia.

[15] Herlocker, J., Konstan, J. & Riedl, J. 2000. Explaining Collaborative Filtering Recommendations. In Proceedings of ACM Conference on

Computer Supported Cooperative Work. Philadelphia, Pennsylvania, USA.

[16] Krulwich, B. 1997. Lifestyle Finder: Intelligent User Profiling Using Large-Scale Demographic Data, Artificial Intelligence Magazine 18(2). 37-45.

[17] Lin, W.; Alvarez, S. A.; and Ruiz, C. 2000. Collaborative Recommendation via Adaptive Association Rule Mining. KDD-2000 Workshop on Web Mining for E-Commerce, Boston, MA, USA.

[18] Maturana, H. 1998. Emoções e Linguagem na Educação e na Política. Belo Horizonte: Ed. UFMG.

[19] Mobasher, B., Dai, H., Luo, T. and Nakagawa, M. 2001. Effective Personalization Based on Association Rule Discovery from Web Usage Data. Proceedings of the ACM Workshop on Web Information and Data Management. Atlanta, Georgia, USA.

[20] Nitzke, J., Carneiro, M. L., Franco, S. 2002. Ambientes de Aprendizagem Cooperativa Apoiada pelo Computador e sua Epistemologia. Informatica na educação: Teoria & Prática. Porto Alegre, v.5, n.1, p.13-23.

[21] Noel, J., Sanner, S., Khoi-Nguyen, T., Christen, P., Xie, L. Bonilla, E., Abbasnejad, E., Penna, N. D. 2012. New Objective Functions for Social Collaborative Filtering. ACM International World Wide Web, Lyon, France, 859-868.

[22] Pazzani, M. 1999. A Framework for Collaborative, Content-Based and Demographic Filtering. Artificial Intelligence Review. 13(5-6): 393-408.

[23] Piaget, J. 1973. Estudos Sociológicos. Rio de Janeiro: Companhia Editora Forense.

[24] Pradhan, M., Provan, G. M., Middleton, B., and Henrion, M. 1994. Knowledge engineering for large belief networks. In Proceedings of Uncertainty in Artificial Intelligence, Seattle, Washington. Morgan Kaufmann.

[25] Reategui, E.; Campbell, J. A. and Torres, R. 2004. AAAI - The Nineteenth National Conference on Artificial Intelligence, Workshop on Semantic Web Personalization, San Jose, USA, July.

[26] Sarwar, B. M.; Karypis, G.; Konstan, J. A. and Riedl, J. 2001. Topic-based collaborative filtering recommendation algorithms. In Proceedings of the 10th International World Wide Web Conference - WWW10, Hong Kong.

[27] Sarwar, B., Konstan, J., Borchers, A., Herlocker, J., Miller, B. & Riedl, J. 1998. Using Filtering Agents to Improve Prediction Quality in the GroupLens Research Collaborative Filtering System. Proceedings of the Conference on Computer Supported Cooperative Work. Seattle, USA, 345-354.

[28] Shardanand, U. & Maes, P. 1995. Social information filtering: Algorithms for automating "word of mouth". In Proceedings of Human Factors in Computing Systems - CHI, Denver, Colorado, USA. 210-217.

[29] Sneath, P. A. and Sokal, R. R. 1973. Numerical Taxonomy: The Theory and Practice of Numerical Classification. San Francisco, CA: Freeman.

[30] Wallace, R. The Elements of AIML Style, ALICE A. I. Foundation. 2003.

## 27

Comparative Study on Feature Selection and Fusion Schemes for Emotion Recognition from Speech

Santiago Planet and Ignasi Iriondo
La Salle – Universitat Ramon Llull

Abstract — **The automatic analysis of speech to detect affective states may improve the way users interact with electronic devices. However, the analysis only at the acoustic level could be not enough to determine the emotion of a user in a realistic scenario. In this paper we analyzed the spontaneous speech recordings of the FAU Aibo Corpus at the acoustic and linguistic levels to extract two sets of features. The acoustic set was reduced by a greedy procedure selecting the most relevant features to optimize the learning stage. We compared two versions of this greedy selection algorithm by performing the search of the relevant features forwards and backwards. We experimented with three classification approaches: Naïve-Bayes, a support vector machine and a logistic model tree, and two fusion schemes: decision-level fusion, merging the hard-decisions of the acoustic and linguistic classifiers by means of a decision tree; and feature-level fusion, concatenating both sets of features before the learning stage. Despite the low performance achieved by the linguistic data, a dramatic improvement was achieved after its combination with the acoustic information, improving the results achieved by this second modality on its own. The results achieved by the classifiers using the parameters merged at feature level outperformed the classification results of the decision-level fusion scheme, despite the simplicity of the scheme. Moreover, the extremely reduced set of acoustic features obtained by the greedy forward search selection algorithm improved the results provided by the full set.**

Keywords — **Acoustic and linguistic features, decision-level and future-level fusion, emotion recognition, spontaneous speech**

I. INTRODUCTION

ONE of the goals of human-computer interaction (HCI) is the improvement of the user experience, trying to make this interaction closer to human-human communication. Inclusion of speech recognition was one of the key points to include "perception" to multimedia devices. This improved their user interfaces [1]. However, the analysis of affective states by the study of the implicit channel of communication (i.e. the recognition of not only what is said but also how it is said) may improve HCI making these applications more usable and friendly. This is because, in general, inclusion of skills of emotional intelligence to machine intelligence makes HCI more similar to human-human interaction [2]. There is a wide range of contexts where the analysis of speech and

emotion in the input of the systems –and also the synthesis of emotional speech at the output– can be applied to, including automatic generation of audio-visual content, virtual meetings, automatic dialogue systems, tutoring, entertainment or serious games

There are many studies related to emotion recognition based on different approaches. However, a big amount of these works are based on corpora consisting of utterances recorded by actors under supervised conditions. Nowadays this is not the current trend because of the lack of realism of these data [3].

The first study where authors attempted to work with a corpus of spontaneous speech seems to be [4], collecting utterances from infant directed speech. Many other works tried to deal with realistic data, such as [5] and [6]. Nevertheless, it is difficult to compare the results of these approaches when they are using different data and different evaluation methods. A framework to generalise the research on this topic was proposed by [7]. This framework was based on a corpus of spontaneous speech where two different subsets were defined in order to allow speaker-independence during the analysis. Speech was non-acted and, for this reason, utterances were characterised by being non-prototypical and having low emotional intensity. Results obtained within this framework [8] give an idea of the complexity of the task. The combination of 7 classification approaches considering different sets of features achieved 44.00% of unweighted average recall (UAR). We worked under the same naturalistic conditions in this article.

The task of emotion recognition from speech can be tackled from different perspectives [3]. We considered the analysis of two modalities: the acoustic (referred to the implicit message) and the linguistic (referred to the explicit message), extracting acoustic parameters from the speech signal and linguistic features from the transcriptions of the utterances of the corpus. Because in a realistic scenario the analysis of acoustic information could be not enough to carry out the task of emotion recognition from speech [9] the linguistic modality could improve an only-acoustic study. In this article, both modalities were combined at the decision level and at the feature level to compare the performance of different classification approaches using both procedures. To improve the performance of the classifiers and optimize the experiment we reduced the acoustic set of features (the largest one) by selecting the most relevant parameters by a greedy algorithm before starting the learning stage. Also, for this feature selection stage, we compared two search methods (forwards and backwards) through the space of feature subsets.

This paper is structured as follows: Section II describes the corpus and details its acoustic and linguistic parameterization. Section III defines the methodology of the experiment, describes the feature selection algorithms used to optimize the acoustic set of data and details the two fusion schemes proposed. Section IV summarises the results. Conclusions are detailed in Section V.

II. Corpus

This work was based on the FAU Aibo Corpus [10] as it was defined in [7]. In this Section we describe this corpus and its acoustic and linguistic parameterization.

A. Corpus Description

The FAU Aibo Corpus consisted of 8.9 hours of audio recordings of German speech from the interaction of children from two schools playing with the Sony's Aibo robot in a *Wizard of Oz* (WOZ) scenario. These audio recordings were divided into 18,216 chunks. A chunk is each one of the segmentations of the audio recordings of the corpus into syntactically and semantically meaningful small parts. These parts were defined manually following syntactic and prosodic criteria [10]. The chunks of the two schools were divided into two independent folds (fold 1 and fold 2) to guarantee speaker-independence. Thus, each fold contained speech recordings from different children. Each chunk, after parameterization, was considered an instance of the datasets used to train and test the classification schemes. The number of resulting instances was 9,959 for the fold 1 and 8,257 instances for the fold 2. The emotions considered to label the corpus were defined by these five category labels: Anger (A), including angry (annoyed), touchy (irritated as a previous step of anger) and reprimanding (reproachful); Emphatic (E) (accentuated and often hyper-articulated speech but without sentiment); Neutral (N); Positive (P), which included motherese (similar to infant-directed speech but from the child to the robot) and joyful states; and Rest (R), a garbage class collecting three affective states: surprise (in a positive sense), boredom (with a lack of interest in the interaction with the robot) and helpless (doubtful, speaking using disfluencies and pauses).

Because of the use of a WOZ scenario to record the affective states of the children, the corpus collected spontaneous utterances of naturalistic emotional speech in a real application environment. For this reason, it included non-prototypical emotions of low intensity. Moreover, the distribution of the emotion labels was very unbalanced. For example, the majority class (N) consists of 10,967 utterances (60.21% of the whole corpus) while the minority class (P)

consists of only 889 utterances (4.88% of the whole corpus). For a full description of this corpus cf. [7].

B. Acoustic Parameterization

The acoustic analysis of the corpus consisted on calculating 16 low-level descriptors (LLDs). These LLDs were: the zero-crossing rate (ZCR) analysed in the time signal, the root mean square (RMS) frame energy, the fundamental frequency (F0) normalised to 500 Hz, the harmonics-to-noise ratio (HNR) and 12 mel-frequency cepstral coefficients (MFCC). We also computed the derivative of these LLDs.

We calculated 12 functionals from these LLDs and, also, from their derivatives. These functionals were: the mean, the standard deviation, the kurtosis and the skewness, the value and range and position of the extremes, and the range and two linear regression coefficients with their mean square errors (MSE).

To perform this parameterization we used the openSMILE software included in the openEAR toolkit release [11], obtaining $16 \times 2 \times 12 = 384$ features per instance.

C. Linguistic Parameterization

The linguistic parameterization was based on the transcriptions of the corpus. These transcriptions defined the words that children used to communicate with the robot Aibo. We used the concept of emotional salience proposed by [12] to translate the words of a chunk into 5 emotion-related features. Assuming independence between the words of a chunk, the salience of a word is defined as the mutual information between a specific word and an emotion class. Therefore, an emotionally salient word is a word that appears more often in that emotion than in the other categories. Considering this definition, let $W = \{v_1, v_2, ..., v_n\}$ be the n words of a chunk and let $E = \{e_1, e_2, ..., e_k\}$ be the emotional space defined by a set of k emotion classes. Mutual information between the word v_m and the emotion class e_j is defined by (1).

$$i(v_m, e_j) = \log \frac{P(e_j \mid v_m)}{P(e_j)} \qquad (1)$$

where $P(e_j|v_m)$ is the posterior probability that a chunk containing the word v_m implies the emotion class e_j and $P(e_j)$ is the a priori probability of the emotion e_j.

The emotional salience of the word v_m related to the emotional space E is defined by (2).

$$sal(v_m) = \sum_{j=1}^{k} P(e_j \mid v_m) i(v_m, e_j) \qquad (2)$$

We calculated the emotional salience of all the words of the training dataset retaining only those with a value greater than a threshold empirically chosen at 0.3. This resulted in a list of emotionally salient words. Next, we calculated 5 linguistic features for each chunk. These features, called activations and denoted by a_j, were calculated following (3) [12].

$$a_j = \sum_{m=1}^{n} I_m i(v_m, e_j) + \log P(e_j) \qquad (3)$$

where I_m is 1 if the word matches the list of salient words or 0 otherwise.

To guarantee the independence of the two folds during the parameterization stage, the list of emotionally salient words was created considering only the fold used for training. Next, we calculated the activation features for both folds but using only the emotional salience values and the a priori probabilities from the training fold. By following this procedure the test data remained unseen during the analysis of the training data to extract the information about the emotional salience of the words of the corpus.

III. EXPERIMENTATION

In this Section we explain the methodology of the experiment, the feature selection algorithms used to reduce the acoustic set of features and the two procedures to fusion the acoustic and linguistic modalities.

A. Methodology

The acoustic feature vector contained a big amount of information (384 features), being much larger than the vector of linguistic parameters (5 features). The inclusion of irrelevant features in the space of parameters could deteriorate the performance of the classifiers used in the learning stage [13]. Moreover, if these data were merged with the linguistic features without any previous processing then the resulting vectors would be very unbalanced because they would contain many more features related to the acoustic information than features related to the linguistic information.

Feature selection techniques are designed to create subsets of features without redundant data by discarding irrelevant input variables with little predictive information. These reduced subsets could improve the performance of the classifiers and obtain a more generalizable classification model [14]. We used a wrapper method [15] to evaluate the candidate subsets created by a search algorithm and two ways of searching the feature space to create these subsets, as it is explained in detail in Section III.B.

In the classification stage, we considered two procedures to fusion the acoustic and the linguistic data. On the one hand, we performed a decision-level fusion of these modalities classifying the acoustic and the linguistic data independently and merging the classification results by a third classifier. On the other hand, we used a feature-level fusion procedure merging the acoustic and the linguistic parameters before the classification stage. These procedures are detailed in Section III.D and Section III.E, respectively.

We evaluated the classifier schemes in a 2-fold cross-validation manner. We used one fold for training and the other fold for testing and vice versa. This allowed us to guarantee

speaker-independence in the experiment. The mean value of the performances of both folds was also calculated.

We considered three learning algorithms in this experiment using the implementations provided by the WEKA data mining toolkit [13]. The first learning algorithm was a Naïve-Bayes (NB) classifier. This algorithm was found to be the most relevant in [16] despite its simplicity. For this reason it was used as the baseline in this experiment. To improve the performance of this classifier we applied, prior to the training stage, a supervised discretisation process based on the Fayyad and Irani's Minimum Description Length (MDL) method [17]. The second classification approach was a support vector machine (SVM) classifier. For this work, we chose a SVM with a linear kernel using sequential minimal optimisation learning [18]. To allow the algorithm to deal with a problem of five classes we used pairwise multi-class discrimination [19]. Finally, the third classifier was a logistic model tree as described in [20]. This is a model tree using logistic regression at the leaves instead of linear regression. This is named Simple Logistic (SL) in WEKA.

We used the UAR measure to compare the performances of the classification approaches because the distribution of the classes in the FAU Aibo Corpus was very unbalanced. Comparing the UAR of the classifiers, instead of the weighted-average recall (WAR) measure, the most even class-wise performance was intended. Thus, the same importance was given to the majority and the minority classes of the corpus because we considered the detection of the interactions with emotional content as important as the detection of the neutral interactions. However, in most of other studies of emotion recognition the WAR measure was used because the distribution of the classes of their corpora was usually quite balanced. Equation (4) shows that the recall for one class c is calculated as the proportion of correctly classified cases (True Positives) with respect to the corresponding number of instances (True Positives and False Negatives) of this class. Equation (5) shows the computation of UAR performance of a classifier considering the recalls of each class c.

$$recall_c = \frac{TP_c}{TP_c + FN_c} \qquad (4)$$

$$UAR = \frac{\sum_{c=1}^{|C|} recall_c}{|C|} \qquad (5)$$

where TP stands for True Positives, FN stands for False Negatives and $|C|$ represents the number of classes.

B. Feature Selection Process

To reduce the set of acoustic features we chose a wrapper method. A wrapper method uses a learning algorithm to evaluate the subsets created by a search algorithm. These subsets are the candidates to be the optimal ones. We considered the Naïve-Bayes classifier to assess the goodness-of-fit of the candidate subsets. We searched the space of features by means of two greedy procedures to automatically create these subsets:

- Greedy forward (FW) search. This algorithm carried out an iterative exhaustive search through the feature space creating subsets starting with no features and adding one parameter at each iteration.

- Greedy backward (BW) search. In this case, the iterative exhaustive search consisted on creating subsets starting with all the features and discarding one at each iteration.

Before starting the feature selection stage we resampled the fold 1 reducing it by half to speed up the process and biased it to a uniform distribution. To guarantee independence between both datasets, we used only the fold 1 to select the candidate subsets of features and evaluated them on all the instances of this fold.

In the case of the FW search, the acoustic dataset was reduced from 384 features to 28 features: 21 related to the MFCC parameters, 3 related to the RMS frame energy, 2 related to the F0, 1 related to the HNR and 1 related to the ZCR. The BW search was a more conservative approach and created a set of 305 features.

A comparison of the performances of the classifiers using the full set of acoustic features and the reduced sets is shown in Fig. 1. For each algorithm we show three results: the Fold 1 column indicates the results obtained when training the classifiers with the fold 1 and testing with the fold 2, the Fold 2 column is the opposite and the Mean column is the mean of the previous results. As it can be observed, focusing on the mean values of the Fold 1 and Fold 2 experiments and except the case of the Naïve-Bayes classifier, UAR values were slightly better for the reduced sets than for the full set of features. In the case of the Naïve-Bayes classifier, the dataset created by the FW search degraded dramatically the

performance of this classifier. Nevertheless, the performance was slightly improved using the dataset created by the BW search. Thus, we chose the reduced sets for this experiment decreasing the computational cost of the classification algorithms.

C. Dataset Pre-processing

To optimize the performance of the classifiers we pre-processed the datasets used to train them. Datasets were biased to a uniform class distribution by means of a resampling with replacement technique and duplicating the total number of instances. We did not bias the distribution of classes in the case of the Naïve-Bayes algorithm because this process degraded its performance. In the case of the SVM, data was also normalised by the Euclidean norm.

D. Decision-Level Fusion

Decision-level fusion is based on the processing of the classification results of prior classification stages. The main goal of this procedure is to take advantage of the redundancy of a set of independent classifiers to achieve higher robustness by combining their results [21].

In this experiment, decision-level fusion was performed by combining hard decisions from the classifiers that were trained and tested by the acoustic and linguistic features independently. Although soft decisions could also be used, hard decision classifiers provide the least amount of information to make their combinations [22]. We followed the stacked generalization strategy introduced by [23] and used a decision tree to merge the classifications obtained by the two classifiers. This stacking approach proved to be useful in the field of emotion recognition in previous works like those by [24] and [25]. The decision tree used to merge the hard decisions of the classifiers was a J4.8 classifier. This is the WEKA implementation of the C4.5 Revision 8 algorithm [13], a slightly improved version of the C4.5, based on entropy

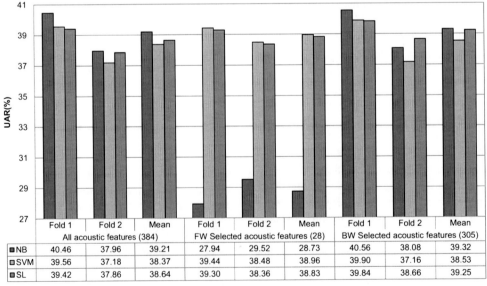

	Fold 1	Fold 2	Mean	Fold 1	Fold 2	Mean	Fold 1	Fold 2	Mean
	All acoustic features (384)			FW Selected acoustic features (28)			BW Selected acoustic features (305)		
■ NB	40.46	37.96	39.21	27.94	29.52	28.73	40.56	38.08	39.32
▫ SVM	39.56	37.18	38.37	39.44	38.48	38.96	39.90	37.16	38.53
■ SL	39.42	37.86	38.64	39.30	38.36	38.83	39.84	38.66	39.25

Fig. 1. Unweighted average recall of the classifiers using the full dataset of 384 acoustic features and using the reduced sets of the 28 and 305 acoustic features selected by the greedy forward search and greedy backward search selection algorithms, respectively. NB stands for Naïve-Bayes, SVM stands for Suport Vector Machine and SL stands for Simple Logistic. FW and BW stands for the greedy forward search and greedy backward search selection algorithms, respectively.

information [26].

To train the J4.8 algorithm we trained and tested each one of the three classifiers with the full training sets, both the acoustic and the linguistic. Next, we created a dataset merging the hard decisions of each classifier for both sets of features. This dataset was used to train the J4.8 learning scheme after biasing it to a uniform distribution and duplicating the number of instances. Once more, and as in other stages of this experiment, test data remained unseen during the training process. When the J4.8 classifier was trained, we evaluated the hard decisions of the classifiers tested with the test data, measuring the performance of the full scheme at the end.

E. Feature-Level Fusion

A feature-level fusion scheme integrates unimodal features before learning concepts, as it is described in [27]. The main advantage of a feature-level fusion scheme is the use of only one learning stage. Moreover, this fusion scheme allows

taking advantage of mutual information from data. We used concatenation of the reduced set of acoustic features and the linguistic set to create a multimodal representation of each instance. Thus, the amount of features for the merged dataset was of 33 elements per instance.

IV. RESULTS

Results of this experiment are shown in Fig. 2. Like in Fig. 1, for each algorithm we show three results: the Fold 1 column indicates the results obtained when training the classifiers with the fold 1 and testing with the fold 2, the Fold 2 column is the opposite and the third result is the mean of the previous results. The results obtained by the dataset created by the FW search procedure are shown at the top and the results achieved by the BW search dataset are shown at the bottom.

Focusing on the mean value of the two folds, it can be observed that the performance of the classifiers that only used

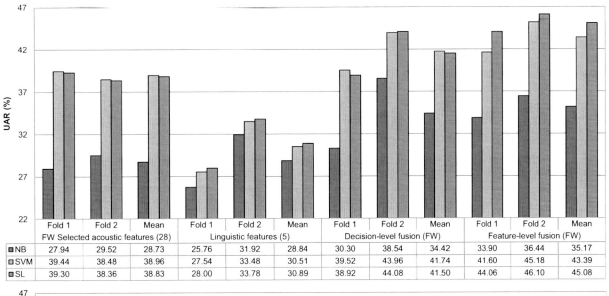

	Fold 1	Fold 2	Mean	Fold 1	Fold 2	Mean	Fold 1	Fold 2	Mean	Fold 1	Fold 2	Mean
	FW Selected acoustic features (28)			Linguistic features (5)			Decision-level fusion (FW)			Feature-level fusion (FW)		
NB	27.94	29.52	28.73	25.76	31.92	28.84	30.30	38.54	34.42	33.90	36.44	35.17
SVM	39.44	38.48	38.96	27.54	33.48	30.51	39.52	43.96	41.74	41.60	45.18	43.39
SL	39.30	38.36	38.83	28.00	33.78	30.89	38.92	44.08	41.50	44.06	46.10	45.08

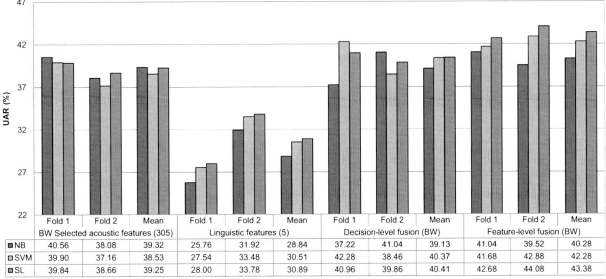

	Fold 1	Fold 2	Mean	Fold 1	Fold 2	Mean	Fold 1	Fold 2	Mean	Fold 1	Fold 2	Mean
	BW Selected acoustic features (305)			Linguistic features (5)			Decision-level fusion (BW)			Feature-level fusion (BW)		
NB	40.56	38.08	39.32	25.76	31.92	28.84	37.22	41.04	39.13	41.04	39.52	40.28
SVM	39.90	37.16	38.53	27.54	33.48	30.51	42.28	38.46	40.37	41.68	42.88	42.28
SL	39.84	38.66	39.25	28.00	33.78	30.89	40.96	39.86	40.41	42.68	44.08	43.38

Fig. 2. Unweighted average recall of the classifiers using the selected set of acoustic features (28 features selected by the greedy forward search selection algorithm (top) and 305 features selected by the greedy backward search selection algorithm (bottom)), the set of 5 linguistic features, the decision-level fusion scheme and the feature-level fusion scheme.

the 28 acoustic features selected by the FW search was better, in general, than the performance of the classifiers that only used the 5 linguistic parameters. In the case of the SVM classifier, the use of the acoustic features improved the performance of the linguistic parameters by 8.45% absolute (27.70% relative). In the case of the Simple Logistic performance was improved by 7.94% absolute (25.70% relative). Only the Naïve-Bayes got its performance improved (by only 0.11% absolute, 0.38% relative) using the linguistic features instead of the acoustic parameters. In the case of the set of features selected by the BW search, the performance of the classifiers using the 305 features was better, in all cases, than using the 5 linguistic parameters. The improvement in the case of the Naïve-Bayes, the SVM and the Simple Logistic classifiers was 10.48% absolute (36.34% relative), 8.02% absolute (26.29% relative) and 8.36% absolute (27.06% relative), respectively.

However, the combination of the linguistic and the acoustic features at the decision and at the feature levels improved the performance of the classifiers that considered both modalities independently. For the FW search, the decision-level fusion results improved the mean of the performances achieved by the acoustic and the linguistic sets in the case of the Naïve-Bayes, the SVM and the Simple Logistic classifiers by 5.63% absolute (19.56% relative), 7.00% absolute (20.15% relative) and 6.64% absolute (19.05% relative), respectively. The improvement in the case of the feature-level fusion scheme was 6.38% absolute (22.16% relative), 8.65% absolute (24.90% relative) and 10.22% absolute (29.32% relative), respectively. Considering the BW search, the decision-level fusion results improved the mean of the performances achieved by the acoustic and the linguistic sets in the case of the Naïve-Bayes, the SVM and the Simple Logistic classifiers by 5.85% absolute (16.95% relative) and 5.34% absolute (15.23% relative), respectively. In the case of the Naïve-Bayes classifier, performance was slightly degraded. The improvement in the case of the feature-level fusion scheme was 6.20% absolute (18.19% relative) for the Naïve-Bayes, 7.76% absolute (22.48% relative) for the SVM and 8.31% absolute (23.70% relative) for the Simple Logistic classifier. As it can be observed, the improvement achieved by the fusion of the acoustic and the linguistic parameters (regardless the classifier considered) is more significant in the case of the acoustic FW search selected features than in the case of the acoustic BW search selected features.

In all the cases, the fusion of both modalities at the feature level outperformed the results of the fusion at the decision level. Considering the FW search selected features, for the Naïve-Bayes, the SVM and the Simple Logistic classifiers, the feature-level fusion scheme improved the performance of the decision-level scheme by 0.75% absolute (2.18% relative), 1.65% absolute (3.95% relative) and 3.58% absolute (8.63% relative), respectively. In the case of the BW search selected features, the feature-level fusion scheme considering the Naïve-Bayes, the SVM and the Simple Logistic improved the

performance of the decision-level scheme by 1.15% absolute (2.94% relative), 1.91% absolute (4.73% relative) and 2.97% absolute (7.35% relative), respectively.

Although the Naïve-Bayes classifier performed well in a prior study [16], in the case of the FW search selected features its performance was below the other two classifiers. The main reason can be found in the fact that the feature selection algorithm used in Section III.B was not designed to avoid dependencies among the chosen parameters, being independence of features one of the requirements of this classification algorithm [28]. This degradation was not observed analysing the features selected by the BW search because it contains a larger number of parameters.

Only the Fold 1 columns of Fig. 2 must be taken into account to compare these results with the experiments carried out by other authors in the same scenario. This column shows the performance of the classification algorithms when using fold 1 for training and fold 2 for testing, i.e. the two different schools independently, as detailed in [7]. Reference [8] compiled a list of results achieved by several authors working in the same conditions and their fusion by a majority voting scheme. The fusion of the best 7 results achieved a performance of 44.00% UAR, considering different learning schemes and datasets. The best result obtained in this paper by means of the Simple Logistic classifier and the feature-level fusion scheme considering the acoustic FW search selected features (i.e. using 33 features) improved this result by 0.06% absolute (0.14% relative). Although both results were quite similar, it is noteworthy that the number of features involved in our study was dramatically lower and also the complexity of the learning scheme.

V. CONCLUSION

In this paper we presented a comparison between decision-level and feature-level fusion to merge the acoustic and the linguistic modalities in a real-life non-prototypical emotion recognition from speech scenario. Also, we compared two procedures to select the most relevant features from the large set of acoustic parameters.

We parameterized the audio recordings of a naturalistic speech corpus obtaining 384 acoustic and 5 linguistic features. To reduce the amount of acoustic features we compared two greedy search procedures for feature selection analysing the full set of features forwards and backwards, obtaining 28 and 305 relevant parameters, respectively. The performance of the classifiers with these reduced datasets was, except for the case of the Naïve-Bayes algorithm with the FW search selected features, slightly better than using the full dataset. Using fewer features we were able to speed up the emotion recognition process because we simplified the parameterization stage and the small datasets reduced the computational cost of the classification stage.

Linguistic information, by themselves, did not create a good dataset for the classifiers of this experiment and their performance was even below the performance achieved by using only the acoustic dataset. However, the combination of these modalities by means of any of the two fusion procedures outperformed the results achieved by both modalities on their own. It is remarkable, then, the importance of analysing the acoustic modality (how things are said) and the linguistic modality (what things are said) to achieve the best results in an automatic emotion recognition experiment, in a similar way as we do in the human communication. This outperformance is more significant in the case of the fusion of the linguistic parameters and the acoustic FW search selected features than in the case of the fusion of the linguistic parameters and the acoustic BW search selected features. Moreover, in general, results from the FW scheme are better than in the BW scheme, except for the case of the Naïve-Bayes algorithm.

Feature-level fusion revealed as the best scheme to merge the acoustic and the linguistic information. Moreover, this kind of fusion is simpler than decision-level fusion, which reduces the complexity of the analysis of the speech recordings. In this feature-level fusion scheme we used only one classifier to analyse a reduced set of acoustic and linguistic parameters merged by simple concatenation of vectors. The performance of this scheme was better than the decision-level scheme consisting of three classifiers: two for each modality and one to merge their results.

The best classifier in this experiment was the Simple Logistic algorithm. Although the Naïve-Bayes is a simple classifier able to achieve good results, its performance was degraded when working with the smallest set of acoustic features (those selected by the FW search procedure). One of the requirements of this classifier is the use of independent parameters but our feature selection procedure was not intended to achieve it. For this reason, in future work, we will experiment with other methods to select relevant feature subsets but also eliminating the redundancy of the data, like [29].

Future work will be related to the enhancement of the linguistic parameterization by considering not only individual words but also groups of them in the form of n-grams. With these n-grams we will be able to study the relation of more complex linguistic structures and the relations between words. Also, we will include an automatic speech recogniser module to work in a more real scenario.

REFERENCES

[1] J. Canny, "The future of human-computer interaction," Queue, vol. 4, no. 6, pp. 24–32, July 2006.

[2] R. W. Picard, E. Vyzas, and J. Healey, "Toward machine emotional intelligence: analysis of affective physiological state," IEEE Transactions on Pattern Analysis and Machine Intelligence, vol. 23, no. 10, pp. 1175–1191, October 2001.

[3] Z. Zeng, M. Pantic, G. I. Roisman, and T. S. Huang, "A survey of affect recognition methods: audio, visual, and spontaneous expressions," IEEE Transactions on Pattern Analysis and Machine Intelligence, vol. 31, no. 1, pp. 39–58, January 2009.

[4] M. Slaney and G. McRoberts, "Baby Ears: a recognition system for affective vocalizations," in Proceedings of 1998 International Conference on Acoustics, Speech and Signal Processing, vol. 2, Seattle, WA, pp. 985–988, 1998.

[5] M. Chetouani, A. Mahdhaoui, and F. Ringeval, "Time-scale feature extractions for emotional speech characterization," Cognitive Computation, vol. 1, no. 2, pp. 194–201, 2009.

[6] M. Wöllmer, F. Eyben, B. Schuller, E. Douglas-Cowie, R. Cowie, "Data-driven clustering in emotional space for affect recognition using discriminatively trained LSTM networks," in 10th Annual Conference of the International Speech Communication Association, pp. 1595–1598, 2009.

[7] B. Schuller, S. Steidl, and A. Batliner, "The Interspeech 2009 Emotion Challenge," in Proceedings of the 10th Annual Conference of the International Speech Communication Association (Interspeech 2009). Brighton, UK, pp. 312–315, September 2009.

[8] B. Schuller, A. Batliner, S. Steidl, and D. Seppi, "Recognising realistic emotions and affect in speech: State of the art and lessons learnt from the first challenge," Speech Communication, Special Issue: Sensing Emotion and Affect – Facing Realism in Speech Processing, vol. 53, no. 9-10, pp. 1062–1087, November 2011.

[9] A. Batliner, K. Fischer, R. Hubera, J. Spilkera J, and E. Noth, "How to find trouble in communication," Speech Communication, vol. 40, pp. 117–143, 2003.

[10] S. Steidl, Automatic classification of emotion-related user states in spontaneous children's speech. Logos Verlag, 2009.

[11] F. Eyben, M. Wöllmer, and B. Schuller, "openEAR - Introducing the Munich open-source emotion and affect recognition toolkit," in Proceedings of th 4th International HUMAINE Association Conference on Affective Computing and Intelligent Interaction, pp. 576–581, 2009.

[12] C. M. Lee, S. S. Narayanan, "Towards detecting emotions in spoken dialogs," IEEE Transactions on Speech and Audio Processing, vol. 13, no. 2, pp. 293–303, March 2005.

[13] I. H. Witten and E. Frank, Data mining: Practical machine learning tools and techniques. 2nd Edition. San Francisco, CA: Morgan Kaufmann, June 2005.

[14] Y. Kim, N. Street, and F. Menczer, "Feature selection in data mining," in J. Wang (ed.) Data mining: Opportunities and challenges, pp. 80–105. Idea Group Publishing, 2003.

[15] I. Guyon and A. Elisseeff, "An introduction to variable and feature selection," Journal of Machine Learning Research, vol.3, pp. 1157–1182, 2003.

[16] S. Planet, I. Iriondo, J. C. Socoró, C. Monzo, and J. Adell, "GTM-URL contribution to the Interspeech 2009 Emotion Challenge," in Proceedings of the 10th Annual Conference of the International Speech Communication Association (Interspeech 2009). Brighton, UK, pp. 316–319, September 2009.

[17] U. M. Fayyad and K. B. Irani, "Multi-interval discretization of continuous-valued attributes for classification learning," in Proceedings of the 13th International Joint Conference on Artificial Intelligence. pp. 1022–1029, 1993.

[18] J. Platt, "Machines using sequential minimal optimization," in B. Schoelkopf, C. Burges, and A. Smola (eds.) Advances in Kernel Methods: Support Vector Learning, MIT Press, 1998.

[19] T. Hastie and R. Tibshirani, "Classification by pairwise coupling", Annals of Statistics, vol. 26, no. 2, pp. 451–471, 1998.

[20] N. Landwehr, M. Hall, and E. Frank, "Logistic model trees". Machine Learning, vol. 59, no. 1–2, pp. 161–205, 2005.

[21] J. C. Bezdek, J. M. Keller, R. Krishnapuram, and N. R. Pal, Fuzzy models and algorithms for pattern recognition and image processing. Norwell, MA: Kluwer Academic Publishers, 1999.

[22] D. Ruta and B. Gabrys, "An overview of classifier fusion methods," in Computing and Information Systems, vol. 7, no. 1, pp. 1–10, 2000.

[23] D. H. Wolpert, "Stacked generalization," Neural Networks, vol. 5, pp. 241–259, 1992.

[24] D. Morrison, R. Wang, and L. C. D. Silva, "Ensemble methods for spoken emotion recognition in call-centres," Speech Communication vol. 49, no. 2, pp. 98–112, 2007.

[25] I. Iriondo, S. Planet, J.-C. Socoró, E. Martínez, F. Alías, and C. Monzo, "Automatic refinement of an expressive speech corpus assembling subjective perception and automatic classification," Speech Communication, vol. 51, no. 9, pp. 744–758, 2009.

[26] J. R. Quinlan, C4.5: Programs for machine learning. 1st Edition. Morgan Kaufmann, January 1993.

[27] C. G. M. Snoek, M. Worring, and A. W. M. Smeulders, "Early versus late fusion in semantic video analysis," in 13th Annual ACM International Conference on Multimedia, pp. 399–402, 2005.

[28] G. H. John and P. Langley, "Estimating continuous distributions in bayesian classifiers," in Proceedings of the 11th Conference on Uncertainty in Artificial Intelligence, pp. 338–345, 1995.

[29] M. A. Hall, Correlation-based feature subset selection for machine learning. Hamilton, New Zealand, 1998.

## 28

Conceptualizing the e-Learning Assessment Domain using an Ontology Network

Lucía Romero, *Universidad Nacional del Litoral (UNL)*
Milagros Gutiérrez, *Facultad Regional Santa Fe, Universidad Tecnológica Nacional*
María Laura Caliusco, *Facultad Regional Santa Fe, Universidad Tecnológica Nacional*

Abstract —During the last year, approaches that use ontologies, the backbone of the Semantic Web technologies, for different purposes in the assessment domain of e-Learning have emerged. One of these purposes is the use of ontologies as a mean of providing a structure to guide the automated design of assessments. The most of the approaches that deal with this problem have proposed individual ontologies that model only a part of the assessment domain. The main contribution of this paper is an ontology network, called AONet, that conceptualizes the e-assessment domain with the aim of supporting the semi-automatic generation of it. The main advantage of this network is that it is enriched with rules for considering not only technical aspects of an assessment but also pedagogic.

Keywords —e-assessment, ontology network, e-learning

I. INTRODUCTION

IN the last decade use of the Semantic Web technologies as tools for generating, organizing and personalizing e-learning content including e-assessment has attracted a great deal of attention [1], [2], [3], [4]. Within the applications related to assessment, these technologies could be used for different purposes [5]: (1) to capture the structure of a domain, (2) to capture experts representation of a domain, (3) to encode and bind content to a domain structure, (4) to score knowledge map, (5) to package and deliver content at different grain sizes, (6) to be part of a recommender system, and (7) to provide a structure to guide the automated design of assessment.

In literature, different approaches that define an ontology as an structure to guide the automated design of assessment can be found [5], [6], [7]. In [5] the authors have defined an ontology for supporting open questions generation whereas in [6] the authors only model simple choice questions. In [7], ontologies are used to generate individual problems examples for students that consist of a question and its solution. In spite of the advances done in this area, previous approaches have defined lightweight ontologies that only model the assessment domain from a technical viewpoint.

In order to e-Assessment be accepted by educators, a tool for supporting devising of valid and reliable assessments, from a pedagogical perspective, is needed. That means, it is required to establish an alignment of teaching, learning and assessment, and to define a mechanism for validating if the assessment covers all the learning objectives of a course and satisfies certain pedagogical principles [8]. With the aim of solving this problem, two main challenges have to be addressed. On the one hand, it is necessary to link the different knowledge sources involved in e-Assessment: the subject domain, the assessment domain and the learning objects in which the assessment has to be based. On the other hand, a set of rules that model the pedagogical principles that an e-Assessment has to fulfill is needed.

The main contribution of this paper is an ontology network, called AONet, that formalizes the conceptualization of the knowledge related to assessments in e-learning environments considering technical and pedagogical aspects. The use of networked ontologies in the context of e-Learning has been addressed by other authors. In [9] the authors address the problem of specifying the semantics relationships between networked ontologies by defining an specification of these semantic relationships for the conceptualization of a Educational Recommender Systems. In contrast to this work, the contribution of this paper is the conceptualization of the assessment in e-Learning.

The present paper is organized as follow. Section 2 defines the main concepts around the approach of this paper. Section 3 presents the main components of the AONet ontology network. Section 4 discusses an example of the AONet population. Finally, Section 5 is devoted to the conclusions and future work.

II. BACKGROUND

A. Ontology Definition

An ontology gives an explicit definition of the shared conceptualization of a certain domain [10]. Since ontology were used for different purposes in different discipline, several definition were built. Then, it is necessary to clarify what we have in mind when we talk about ontology. The definition used in this paper is based on [11].

From a pragmatic perspective, an ontology can be defined as a representational artifact based on four kinds of modeling components: concepts, roles, restrictions and individuals. *Concept* represents classes of objects. *Roles* describe binary relations among concepts; hence they also allow the description of properties of concepts. *Restrictions* are used to express properties of roles, i.e. cardinality. *Individuals* represent instances of classes, i.e. objects. Additionally, it is possible to use axioms and rules to infer new information. *Axioms* are logical sentences always true that express the properties of model paradigm. *Rules* are logical sentences that express characteristics of the domain, i.e. business rules. Formally,

Definition 1. *An ontology is a 6-tuple O:= {C, R, H, rel, A, Ru} where:*
- *Two disjoint sets, C(concepts) and R (relations).*
- *A concept hierarchy, a directed relation H → C x C which is called concept hierarchy or taxonomy. So, H(C1, C2) means C1 is a subconcept of C2.*
- *A function rel: R → C x C that relates the concepts non taxonomically.*
- *A set of axioms A expressed in an appropriate logical language.*
- *A set of rules Ru expressed in an appropriate logical language.*

In ontological community, ontologies can be classified as lightweight or heavyweight. A lightweight ontology is an ontology simply based on a hierarchy of concepts and a hierarchy of relations whereas a heavyweight ontology is a lightweight ontology enriched with rules used to fix the semantic interpretation of concepts and relations [10].

The component that differentiates an ontology is the set of rules. This set has to be expressed in an appropriate logical language. Considering that the OWL language is the standard for implementing an ontology and this is not always enough to do some deduction, then it is needed to combine OWL with other representation formalism as rules. One of the integration approaches is the Semantic Web Rule Language (SWRL), which provides the ability to express Horn-like rules in terms of OWL concepts [12].

In order to extract information from OWL ontologies a query language is needed. The most powerful language is SQWRL, which is based on the SWRL rule language and uses SWRL's strong semantic foundation as its formal underpinning. It also contains novel set operators that can be used to perform closure operations to allow limited forms of negation as fail-true, counting, and aggregation [13].

B. Ontology Network

An ontology network is a set of ontologies related together via a variety of different relationships such as mapping, modularization, version, and dependency. The elements of this set are called Networked Ontologies [14].

An ontology network differs from a set of interconnected individual ontologies in the relations among ontologies since in a ontology network the meta-relationships among the networked ontologies are explicitly expressed [9]. There are some models that cover both the syntactic and semantic aspects of dealing with ontology relationships in networked

ontologies. In the DOOR (Descriptive Ontology of Ontology Relations) ontology, general relations between ontologies, such as includedIn, equivalentTo, similarTo, and versioning were defined by using ontological primitives and rules [14].

Concerning a support for implementing and management ontology networks, the NeOn Project can be mentioned (http://www.neon-project.org). NeOn has developed an open service-centered reference architecture for managing the complete life cycle of networked ontologies and metadata. This architecture is realized through the NeOn Toolkit and complemented by the NeOn methodology, which is a scenario-based methodology that supports the collaborative aspects of ontology development and reuse [15].

From a model integration point of view, within an ontology network each ontology conceptualizes a specific domain and plays a particular role. Then, the main advantage of using an ontology network is the conceptualization of a given domain in a modular way. The networked ontology is small enough to be understandable by any person and its maintenance is easy. In addition, several ontology designers could work on different networked ontologies concurrently.

C. The Assessment Domain

Assessment is an indispensable part of teaching and learning. Essentially, it is assessment that reinforces the learning approach a student adopts. If a student is often tested on higher-order thinking skills, they are likely to adopt the desirable deep holistic approach to e-Learning. On the contrary, if students are tested on lower-order thinking skills, they would probably be encouraged to practice the undesirable surface atomistic approach to learning [16]. An assessment can be considered as difficult to be realized within a distance learning phase.

Assessment can be classified in formal, informal and semi-formal assessment, depending on the formality and structure of assessment instruments [17]. Thereby the formal assessments are structured: there is a place and a time setting where they are carried out. There are different types of formal assessment: simple choice, multiple choice, correspondence, conceptual maps and performance evaluation among others. The semi-formal assessments are homework and tasks that the student makes during lesson day and continue out of it. These types of assessments are for example reading comprehension, mathematical problems, trials, projects development, programming, conclusion development, outcome analysis among other. The informal assessments are not structured at all. They consist of quizzes and activities observations that the teacher makes during class and consume a few minutes. Some instruments that are used for systematize these types of assessments are: class daily (class journal), control list, anecdotic annotations among other.

It is considered that an assessment is composed of

reactive. When teacher elaborates a reactive in order to make an assessment, uses the Bloom taxonomy [18]. This taxonomy is used to classify the course or programs goals as function of six level of complexity:

--First, click on the View menu and choose Print Layout.Knowledge: in this level teacher wants to evaluate the concept memorized by students, for example question about concepts.

--Comprehension: teacher wants to evaluate if the student understands the semantic relation of information taught. For example, conceptual maps.

--Application: teacher wants to evaluate if student can use the information taught to solve practical problems, for example mathematic problem.

--Analysis: teacher wants to evaluate the structure of knowledge, for example, outcome analysis.

--Synthesis: teacher wants to evaluate if student can elaborate original approaches base on concepts taught, for example trial.

--Evaluation: teacher wants to evaluate if the student can make a value judgment on topics taught, for example, conclusion development.

III. THE AONET ONTOLOGY NETWORK

With the aim of developing the AONet ontology network (Figure 1), the guidelines defined by NeOn Methodology were followed [15]. All of the ontologies defined in the AONet are implemented in OWL DL 1.0. Following, each of the ontology that composes the AONet is described

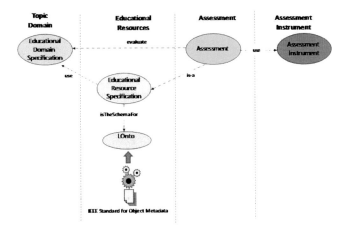

Fig. 1.   The AONet ontology network

The *Educational Domain Specification* Ontology comprises concepts and relations defined in the knowledge domain that is evaluated. As can be noted, its structure and content depends on each particular domain.

The *Educational Resource Specification* Ontology comprises the educational resources used by educator in the teaching-learning process (TL). Some standards emerge to overcome the formalization of educational resources which

are constantly evolving. In most cases, the use of learning object (LO) definition and its description by LOM [19] is the common denominator. In this way, it is possible to optimize the educational resource development process. This ontology is related with *Educational Domain Specification* ontology throughout *use* relationship. This relation identifies the connection between educational resources and concepts belonging to the specific domain. That is to say, an educational resource is developed in order to overcome different concepts, relations and definitions about to a domain topic. A LO metadata instance describes relevant characteristics of an educational resource, with the aims of facilitate the search, acquisition, interchange and evaluation of a resource by teacher, students and software systems. For this reason, we add to the ontology network the *LOnto* ontology built by Romero and Godoy (2010), which conceptualizes the semantic definition of LO based on *LOM* IEEE 1484.12.1 standard [18]. Then, the Educational Resource Specification ontology is related with LOnto through *isSchemaFor* relationship. The LOnto ontology is described in the next sub-section.

Assessments are part of the educational resources involved in the TL process when teacher wants to evaluate the concepts and skills acquired by students. In this context, the ontology network has the *Assessment* ontology which is related with *Educational Resource Specification* ontology through *is-a* relationship. In the same way, this ontology is related with *Educational Domain Specification* ontology through the *evaluate* relationship. These relations describe that an assessment is used to evaluate the results of the TL process about the Knowledge Domain.

There are different instruments to evaluate, which are modeled by the *Assessment Instrument* ontology. These instruments are used by teacher to generate an assessment. For instance an instrument is a True/False question, a conceptual map, an exercise, an essay activity among other. Then, the *Assessment* ontology has the *use* relationship with *Assessment Instrument* ontology.

The next sub-sections describe in detail the networked ontologies proposed in this paper.

A. The Assessment Ontology

The *Assessment* ontology (Figure 2) is the core of the AONet ontology network. This ontology conceptualizes the fact that an *Assessment* is an *Educational Resource* that is described by the LOM metadata (defined in the *LOnto* ontology). Each Assessment is composed by *Activity*. An *Activity* is a motto or exercise that evaluates a particular domain topic and it is composed by one or more *Reactive* which is an item that uses an *Instrument* (defined in the *AssessmentInstrument* ontology).

The objective of an assessment is to show that the learner has achieved competency in the topics of the unit or course being evaluated. These topics are conceptualizes in the

Educational Domain Specification ontology. This ontology is dependant of the course and how it could be built is out of the scope of this paper.

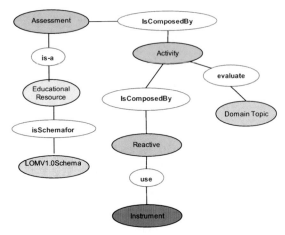

Fig. 2.   The Assesment Ontology.

B. LOnto Ontology

The *LOnto* ontology is based on the IEEE Standard for Object Metadata LOM. This ontology was built by performing the activities defined in the Methontology methody. A deeper description of the *LOnto* ontology can be found in [2].

The *LOnto* ontology is defined around the concept of *LOMv1.0schema* which is the superclass of all the elements and data types of the LOM schema. In the upper level LOM has nine metadata categories:

--General: general information to describe LO as for instance title, keywords, abstract among other.
--Lifecycle: life cycle characteristics of a LO and revision.
--Meta-Metadata: information about the metadata instances.
--Technical: characteristics and technical requirement of a LO.
--Educational: characteristics of the LO relevant to the TL process.
--Rights: copy rights properties
--Relation: characteristics that relate the LO described and other instances.
--Annotation: comments about LO in educational environments, and information about when and who develop its content.
--Classification: describes a LO related to a particular classification system (taxonomy).

For each metadata category above mentioned it has been defined in the *LOnto* ontology a class that extends *LOMv1.0schema* depicting the aim of the metadata in this category. Classes are specialized in subclasses representing each particular element. Figure 3 shows a part of the LOnto ontology. As can be seen, there are nine subclasses of

LOMv1.0schema: *Technical_Metadata, Lifecycle, Meta-Metadata, Educational, Right, Annotation* and *General_*Metadata. So, *General_Metadata* has two subclasses *Title* and *General*. Note that standard LOM describes a taxonomy of metadata for LO while LOnto not only takes into account this taxonomy but also add relation among elements and restriction rules.

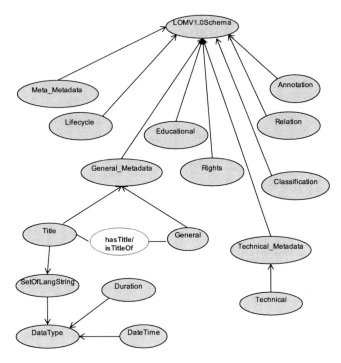

Fig. 3.   An excerpt of the ontologies that compose the network.

C. AssessmentInstrument Ontology

The *Assessmentinstrument* ontology models different instruments that could be used in an assessment depending on the evaluation technique implemented. An assessment instrument is the physical support that is used to collect the information about the expected learning of students. This ontology is shown in Figure 4. The main concept is I*nstrument*. There are two types of instruments: *FormalInstrument* and S*emiformalInstrument* representing formal and semiformal techniques respectively. As *semiformalInstrument*, we have considered two type of it: *SimpleInstrument* such as *Exercises, ConceptualMap* and *Essays*, and *CompositeInstrument* as *portfolios* that consist of a collection of *SimpleInstrument* elements that help recording learning process and students' progress.

As *FormalInstrument* we considered two classifications: *EssayActivity,* where students have to elaborate the answer and *ObjectiveActivity,* where students have to identify the correct answer. *EssayActivity*, is specialized in two sub-concepts: *RestrictedEssay* and *UnrestrictedEssay*. *ObjectiveActivity* is one of the most used by professor because it eliminates the subjectivity in the rating, even when it has an additional complexity to develop it. *Objective Activity* has three sub-concepts: *Choice, Correspondence* and *Completition. Choice* has *Option* associated. The concept *Option* is specialized in two sub-concepts: *Distractor* and *TrueOption. Distractor* are items that are not correct and *TrueOption* is the correct item. The concept *Choice* is specialized in: *SimpleChoice* contains only one correct option and *MultipleChoice* can have more than one correct option. In both cases, *Option* can only have Boolean answer associated. Finally the concept *Answer* can be of different types: *TrueFalse, Numeric, Text* and *Relation.*

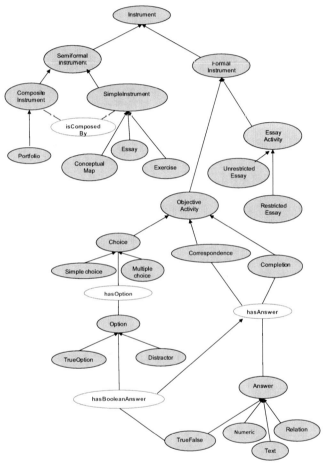

Fig. 4.   Assessment Instrument Ontology

D. Rules for determining the assessment quality.

According with [19] there are some pedagogical recommendations that teachers need to take into account in the development of assessment. If these guides are followed by teachers, we can say that the assessment is valid in a pedagogical sense. In this work, these recommendations were used in order to define rules to express the restrictions in the generation of valid assessment.

Considering that Multiple and Simple Choice are the most used instruments, we use them in this paper to illustrate the rules. From a pedagogical perspective, it is recommended that there is always a right option. It is recommended also

that this type of activities do not include options such as "none of them" or "all of them". In general, items should be belonging to the context of content area being assessed in a clear and simple way and preferably written in the affirmative mode. The *distractors* should appear as attractive as possible to the uninformed student.

Table I shows the pedagogical rules that have been taken into account. The first column describes the rule in a colloquial language. Second column shows the fist-order logic description of such rules. Note that in using First-order logic we consider reification of concepts such as:

Simple choice ∈ simpleChoices
Multiple choice ∈ multipleChoices
Option ∈ Options
trueOption ∈ TrueOptions
attribute ∈ attributes

TABLE I
PEDAGOGICAL RULES FOR SIMPLE AND MULTIPLE CHOICES EXPRESSED IN
FIRST-ORDER LOGIC

Description	First-Order Logic
Simple choice	
1. A simple choice activity must have at least four options	$\Im \models \forall x \in$ simpleChoices ($\exists$ y, z, w, r $\in$ Options (hasOption(x,y)∧hasOption(x,z) ∧hasOption(x,w) ∧hasOption(x,r) ∧y≠z≠w≠r ∧z≠w≠r ∧w≠r)
2. A simple choice activity must have only one true option	$\Im \models \forall$ x∈simpleChoices ($\exists$!y $\in$ TrueOptions hasOption(x,y))
Multiple choice	
3. A multiple choice activity must have more than one true option.	$\Im \models \forall$ x∈multipleChoices ($\exists$ y, z $\in$ TrueOptions hasOption(x,y) ∧hasOption(x,z) ∧y≠z)
4. A multiple choice activity must have more than four options.	$\Im \models \forall x \in$ multipleChoices ($\exists$ y, z, w, r $\in$ Options (hasOption(x,y)∧hasOption(x,z) ∧hasOption(x,w) ∧hasOption(x,r) ∧y≠z≠w≠r ∧z≠w≠r ∧w≠r)
5. A multiple choice activity cannot have option like: "all of them" or "none of them"	$\Im \models \forall$x∈multipleChoices ($\exists$ y $\in$ Options ((hasOption(x,y) ∧ $\exists$ z $\in$ attributes (hasAttribute(y, z) ∧ value(z,w) ∧ (w ≠ "all of them" ∨ w≠ "none of them")))

We have defined logical rules for representing each restriction above mentioned. Then, these rules were implemented in SWRL and SQWRL as shown next.

The first rule validates if a simple choice has the correct quantity of options (restriction 1) as follow:

SimpleChoice(?sc) ∧ hasOption(?sc, ?o) ∧
sqwrl:makeSet(?os, ?o) ∧ sqwrl:groupBy(?os, ?sc) ∧   (1)
sqwrl:size(?t,?os) ∧ sqwrl:greaterThanOrEqual(?t,4) →

optionQuantityValid(?sc)

In the same way, the restriction b) is validated with the following rule:

$$SimpleChoice(?sc) \wedge trueOption(?d) \wedge \\ sqwrl:makeSet(?s1,?d) \wedge sqwrl:groupBy(?s1, ?sc) \wedge \quad (2) \\ sqwrl:size(?t, ?s1) \wedge sqwrl:equal(?t,1) \rightarrow$$

$$answerQuantityValid(?sc)$$

For multiple choices we have three restrictions (3, 4 and 5 from table I). Restriction 3 and 4 from table I are represented with rules (3), (4) respectively. Restriction 5 from table I is represented with rules (5) and (6):

$$MultipleChoice(?mc) \wedge hasOption(?mc, ?d) \wedge \\ trueOption(?d) \wedge sqwrl:makeSet(?s1, ?d) \wedge \quad (3) \\ sqwrl:groupBy(?s1, ?mc) \wedge sqwrl:greaterThan(?t,1) \rightarrow$$

$$answerQuantityValid(?mc)$$

$$MultipleChoice(?mc) \wedge hasOption(?mc, ?o) \wedge \\ sqwrl:makeSet(?os, ?o) \wedge sqwrl:groupBy(?os, ?mc) \wedge \quad (4) \\ sqwrl:size(?t, ?os) \wedge sqwrl:greaterThanOrEqual(?t,4) \rightarrow$$

$$optionQuantityValid(?mc)$$

$$MultipleChoice(?mc) \wedge hasOption(?mc, ?o) \wedge label(?o, \\ ?l) \wedge sqwrl:normalizeSpace(?n,?l) \quad (5) \\ \wedge sqwrl:stringEqualIgnoreCase(?n, \text{"all of them"}) \\ \wedge sqwrl:size(?t, ?n) \wedge sqwrl:Equal(?t,0) \rightarrow$$

$$whithoutAll(?mc)$$

$$multipleChoice(?mc) \wedge \\ hasOption(?mc, ?o) \wedge lavel(?o, ?l) \wedge \quad (6) \\ sqwrl:normalizeSpace(?n,?l) \wedge \\ sqwrl:stringEqualIgnoreCase(?n, \text{"none of them"}) \wedge \\ sqwrl:size(?t, ?n) \wedge sqwrl:Equal(?t,0) \rightarrow$$

$$withoutNon(?mc)$$

Finally if a simple choice meets the restriction (1) and (2) we can say that this simple choice is valid. This statement is represented with the following rule:

$$SimpleChoice(?sc) \quad \wedge \quad optionQuantityValid(?sc) \quad \wedge \quad (7) \\ answerQuantityValid(?sc) \rightarrow valid(?sc)$$

In the same way, if a multiple choices meets the restriction (3), (4), (5) and (6) is a valid multiple choices:

$$multipleChoice(?mc) \wedge whithoutAll(?mc) \wedge \quad (8)$$

$$whithoutNon(?mc) \wedge optionQuantityValid(?mc) \wedge \\ answerQuantityValid(?mc) \rightarrow valid(?mc)$$

IV.   EXPERIMENTS AND DISCUSSIONS

As an example we consider final exam related to an Artificial Intelligence course, shown in figure 5. This exam has two activities. The first activity is about search domain topic and has two reactive. The latter is about Machine learning domain topic and has one reactive corresponding to a multiple choice.

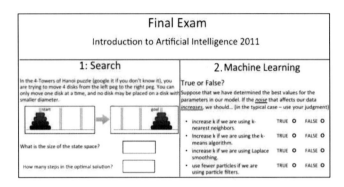

Fig. 5. The Artificial Intelligence Assessment. www.ai-class

Figure 6 shows the result to instantiate the ontology network in order to represent the artificial intelligence assessment. Note that instances have a prefix that identifies the ontology they belong. The asse:ExamIntroductionToAI instance represents the assessment, it has two activities: asse:SearchActivity   and   asse:MachingLearningActivity instances and it has   lonto:IntroductionToAITitle instance associated by the isSchemaFor relationship. Each activity evaluate a domain topic as it is shown with the relations between asse:SearchActivity and dom:Search instances and between   asse:MachingLearningActivity   and dom:MatchinLearning instances.

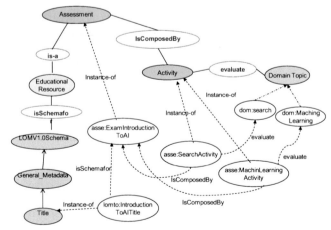

Fig. 6. Assessment instance

As can be seen in Figure 7, the *asse:SearchActivity* instance has in turn two instances of reactive associated through the link *isComposedBy*: *asse:Item1*, and *asse:Item2* instances. Both reactive instances use instruments represented by the instances: *inst:StateSpace* and *inst:OptimalSolution*. Both instances of *Completion* have answers associated represented by the instances *inst:SpaceStateNum* and *inst:OptimalSolutionNum* respectively.

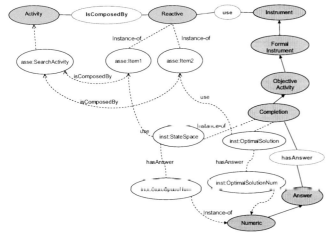

Fig. 7. Search activity decomposition

In the same way figure 8 shows the instantiation of Machine learning activity. The *asse:MachinLearningActivity* instance has *asse:Item1* instance associated. The *asse:Item1* uses as instrument the *inst:MultipleChoiceML*, which is an instance of *Multiple Choice* instrument. In turn it has two instances of *Distractor*

associated: *inst:Op3* and *inst:Op4* and two instances of *TrueOption*: inst:Op1 and *inst:Op2*. Both *inst:Op3* and *inst:Op4* have *inst:False* associated, which is in turn an instance of *TrueFalse*. Both *inst:Op1* and *inst:Op2* have *inst:True* instance associated as answer.

Taking into account the rules (3), (4), (5), (6) and (8) defined in Section III.C, it can be said that the multiple choice is well defined from a pedagogical point of view.

V. CONCLUSIONS AND FUTURE WORK

This work has shown a preliminary ontology network which purpose is to conceptualize the assessment domain in a TL process. The modularization that this network provides allows us concentrate the attention on a particular domain and incrementally build a more general model relating different ontologies. The concepts related with assessment domain were presented. Mainly, this work focused on describing the ontology network that models the different areas related to assessment in an educational context taking into account not only technical aspects but also pedagogical one.

The LOnto ontology conceptualizes not only the metadata proposed by IEEE standard but also the relations and restriction among metadata that are not present in the standard, giving as result an improvement in the use of such standard.

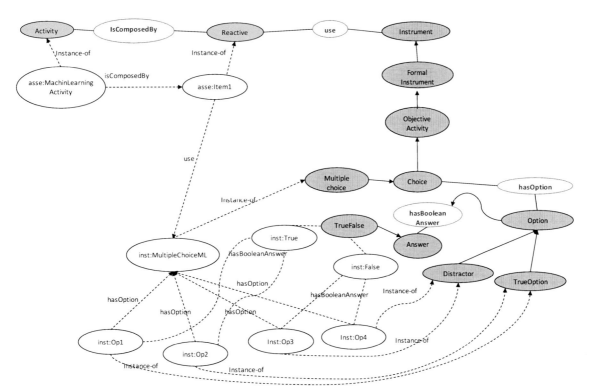

Fig. 8. Maching Learning activity instantiation

The *Assessment* ontology represents the main concepts found in an assessment domain, giving in a different ontology the instruments used to develop an assessment. In this way, we can consider on the one hand, the way in which to develop an assessment and on the other hand, the relation that this assessment has with students, teachers and educational program. Through ontology network it is possible to add new ontology and relates it with the existing one. The SWRL rules to determine the validity of a given assessment were presented. These rules are based on pedagogical criteria enabling assessment to be considered by educators in an e-learning process. In this first approach, we focus on multiple and simple choice activities due to they are the most popular activities used by educators in e-learning.

Finally, an example of the ontology network population by using an Artificial Intelligence assessment was discussed. In the future, we intend to acquire additional validation assessments for a broad evaluation and refinement of the ontology.

We are working on improvement of the ontology network adding new concepts and relation. In turn, we are developing test using different assessments provided from different knowledge domain. In addition, we are working on developing a tool for supporting an assessment generation by using the ontology network presented in this paper.

REFERENCES

[1] C. Knight, D. Gašević, and G. Richards, "An Ontology-Based Framework for Bridging Learning Design and Learning Content," *Educational Technology & Society*, 9 (1), 2006, pp. 23-37.

[2] L. Romero, and J. Godoy, "An Ontology for Semantic definition of Learning Objects" in *Proc. 5th Conferencia Ibérica de Sistemas y tecnologías de Información*. Santiago de Compostela, España. Junio 2010, pp. 420-426.

[3] M. Panteleyev, D. Puzankov, P. Sazykin, and D. Sergeyev, "Intelligent Educational Environments Based on the Semantic Web Technologies," in *Proc. of the IEEE International Conference on Artificial Intelligence Systems*, Russia, 2002, pp. 457-462.

[4] D. McMullen, "Using ontology technology to support content generation and run time adaptivity in E-learning environments," M.Sc. Dissertation, School of Computing, Dublin City University, 2007.

[5] D. Castellanos-Nieves, J. Fernandez-Breis, R. Valencia-Garcia, R. Martinez-Bjar, M. Iniesta-Moreno, "Semantic web technologies for supporting learning assessment," *Information Sciences*, vol. 2, 2011, pp.68–73.

[6] M. Cubric, and M. Tosic, "Towards automatic generation of eAssessment using semantic web technologies," in *Proc. International Computer Assisted Assessment Conference*, 2010, Springer.

[7] E. Holohan, M. Melia, D. McMullen, and C. Pahl, "The Generation of e-Learning Excercises Problems from Subject Ontologies," in *Proc. 6th International Conferenced on Advanced Learning Technologies*, 2006.

[8] H. Ashton, C. Beevers, and R. Thomas, "Can e-Assessment become Mainstream?," in *Proc. 12th Internacional Computer Assisted Assessment Conference*. 8th & 9th July 2008 at Loughborough University (United Kingdom), pp 13-24, 2008.

[9] A. Díaz, R. Motz, E. Rohrer, and L. Tansini, "An Ontology Network for Educational Recommender Systems". in *Educational recomender systems and technologies. Practics and chalenges*. IGI Global, 2012, pp. 67-93, ch 4.

[10] A. Gómez-Pérez, M. Fernandez-Lopez, and O. Corcho, *Ontological Engineering*, Springer, Heidelberg. 2004.

[11] A. Maedche, *Ontology Learning for the Sematic Web*, Kluwer Academic Publishers (2002)

[12] M. O'Connor, H. Knublauch, S. Tu, and M. Musen, "Writing rules for the semantic web using SWRL and Jess," in *Proceedings in the 8th International Protégé Conference, Protégé with rules Workshop*, 2005.

[13] M. O'Connor, and A. Das, "SQWRL: a query language for OWL," in *Proc. 6th workshop OWL: experiences and directions*, 2009.

[14] C. Allocca, M. D'aquin, and E. Motta, "DOOR-towards a formalization of ontology relations," in *Proc. Int. Conference on Knowledge Engineering and Ontology Development*, 2009, pp 13-20.

[15] M. C. Suárez-Figueroa, "NeOn Methodology for Building Ontology Networks: Specification, Scheduling and Reuse ". Thesis Doctoral, Facultad de Informática - Universidad Politécnica de Madrid. 2010.

[16] T. Govindasamy, "Successful implementation of e-Learning: Pedagogical considerations," *The Internet and Higher Education*, Vol. 4, Issues 3–4, 2001, pp. 287–299.

[17] D. Berliner, "In Pursuit of the expert pedagogue," *Educational research*, 15(7), 1986, pp. 5-13.

[18] B. Bloom, and D. Krathwohl, *"Taxonomy of educational objectives. The classification of educational goals by a committee of college and university examiners"*. Handbook 1. Cognitive domain. New York: Addison-Wesley, 1956.

[19] IEEE Standard for Learning Object Metadata. Learning Technology Standards Comittee of the IEEE Computer Society. 1484.12.1-2002

[20] C. Bolivar. "Pruebas de rendimiento académico" Technical report. Programa interinstitucional doctorado en educación. 2011

## 29

DEVELOP-FPS: a First Person Shooter Development Tool for Rule-based Scripts

Bruno Correia, Paulo Urbano and Luís Moniz,
Computer Science Department, Universidad de Lisboa

Abstract —We present DEVELOP-FPS, a software tool specially designed for the development of First Person Shooter (FPS) players controlled by Rule Based Scripts. DEVELOP-FPS may be used by FPS developers to create, debug, maintain and compare rule base player behaviours, providing a set of useful functionalities: i) for an easy preparation of the right scenarios for game debugging and testing; ii) for controlling the game execution: users can stop and resume the game execution at any instant, monitoring and controlling every player in the game, monitoring the state of each player, their rule base activation, being able to issue commands to control their behaviour; and iii) to automatically run a certain number of game executions and collect data in order to evaluate and compare the players performance along a sufficient number of similar experiments.

Keywords —Intelligent Game Characters, Behaviour Control and Monitoring, Rule Based Scripts, Development Software Tool.

I. INTRODUCTION

IN the recent years artificial intelligence become a key feature to the success of a computer game. The hard-core gamer no longer accepts "space invaders" kind of behaviour with easily identifiable patterns, he expects the game to deliver a convincing challenge always different and interesting. To the game publisher the increase of a game lifespan is also a strategic decision to make; the player capability of defining new scenarios and adversaries allows him to define his own challenges and opponents expanding the longevity of the game.

The development of game oriented platforms, consoles or special tuned computers, provided new spaces to developed and apply new AI technics in commercial games. Game development toolkits are starting to provide support to design of non-player characters' behaviour (NPCs), mainly through the use of copyrighted languages (UnrealScript on UnrealEngine [1]), open-source or free languages (Lua on World of Warcraft [2]) or libraries of behaviours (PandAI on Panda3D engine [3]). Although some commercial games include game editors, these are usually centred on terrain or level construction, giving a limited support to the artificial intelligence aspects. The high-end game developments of tools support the design and deploy intelligent NPC through limited and proprietary solutions. Most of the game companies had its own tools and development kits, which are not made available to the game community. The low-cost, open source and shareware alternatives put most of their effort in supporting the game engine and graphical design, solving problems like physical simulation, collisions detection and character animation, the tools to assist the design and development of NPCs' behaviour are usually omitted.

The existence of a debugging tool to validate the behaviour of a NPC is still a dream in the designer's mind. As the behaviour complexity of NPCs increases, also growths the need for a tool that provides a set of functionalities like: breakpoints that can stop a behaviour script at any point; recreate situations to test snippets of code; monitor variables, functions and NPCs knowledge; force the behaviour or remotely control a character. Most of the scripting languages used in the development of AI components are interpreted (directly or in byte-code), and the common tool available to construct those scripts is a text editor with colour syntax (although some languages provide plugins for standards IDE only for write the code). When some execution bug occurs, the common procedure is stopping the script, in some situations the interpreter will also crash. Some better interpreters will provide an error message identifying the type of error and its location in the code. With no tools to deploy, test and monitor the components, it is up to the programmer to perform the debug and test cycle of his own code. For instance, the Unity game development tool [4,5] provides a debug mechanism based on log messages produced in the script. The existence of mature tools providing a professional environment to support all the development process would dramatically reduce the time spend in this cycle, liberating the programmer to produce better code.

If we want that a game became a professional product, we have to provide tools that allow extensive and professional test of the code, guaranteeing the quality of the final delivery. Scripting languages without tool support can rapidly degenerate in spaghetti code with lots of tweaks and artifices that disallow any future changes or reuse of the program.

We propose a generic architecture to support the process of development and test of autonomous characters behaviour in a computer game environment. Based on this architecture we create a software tool (DEVELOP-FPS), which support the development, debug and execution of NPCs behaviours in a FPS like game. The tool is supported on the Unreal Tourment 2004 engine and uses the Pogamut API library [6] to access the environment sensor information and control of the avatar. Our tool provides the developer with a set of functionalities that allow monitor and control an individual character, define and deploy specific scenario situations, gather data and statistics of running experiments, and get different perspectives of the scenario.

In the next section we detail our generic architecture in a global perspective. In section 3 we present our application and the options made. Finally in section 4 we make some conclusions and provide future development directions.

II. GENERIC ARCHITECTURE

Our generic architecture is composed by four main components: The NPC behaviour definition script; the individual control console; the global control console; and the game engine server. These components were substantiated using the Jess Rule Based Language [7] to define the characters behaviour and the Unreal Engine as the game server. This architecture is outlined in figure 1.

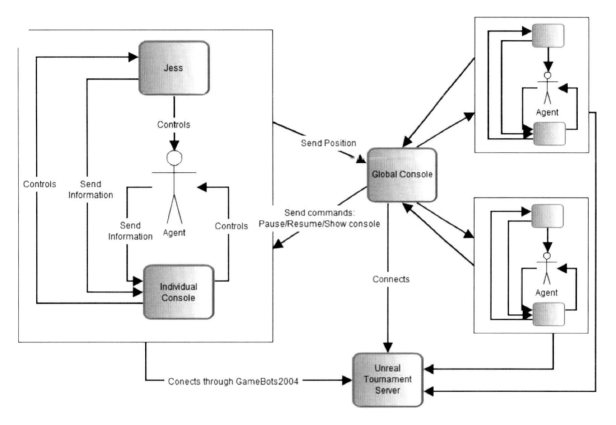

Fig. 1. Generic architecture: the Unreal Tournament Server, The Global Console and the individual Non Player Character Agents with the Jess scripts.

We can split this architecture in two main component classes: individual character management, and global management. The first group comprise the tools to access, monitor and control and individual character. Through those tools the developer can issue commands to the agents, using the individual console, which can cause a wide range of effects, from alterations in the character internal representations to consequences in the game environment. In order to maintain a certain degree on independence from the specific game environment, all the control of the NPC avatar in the environment is actuated through a middleware interface (Pogamut), that provide an intermediate abstraction over the game engine. The NPC behaviour script can be debugged and executed using the console, the developer can directly control the interpreter, issuing commands, stopping execution, testing alternatives, and monitoring execution.

The second group comprise the simulated environment where all the characters actuate, and a global management

tool. The simulated environment provides a game world with a physical engine, graphical representations of the environment from different points of view, and functionalities to interact with the scenario – actions an NPC can perform and information it can perceive. As stated before the actions and perceptions are made available through the middleware interface.

The global console offers a set of functionalities to manage the characters as group, issuing commands that all of then must accomplish.

One of our objectives with this generic architecture was to provide a relative independence between what are the tools made available to the development, debugging and execution of characters behaviour and the specifics of the game engine. This architecture is an evolution of earlier work presented originally in [8].

III. THE SOFTWARE TOOL DEVELOP-FPS

DEVELOP-FPS is a software tool written in JAVA, specially designed for the development of First Person Shooter (FPS) players controlled by Rule Based Scripts in Jess. DEVELOP-FPS may be very powerful if used by FPS developers to create, debug, maintain and compare rule base player behaviours along a number of repeated experiments. It was designed for developing scripts for the *Game Unreal Tournament* but it can easily be adapted to other game platforms.

In figure 2 we may see an example of DEVELOP-FPS in action: In the centre two NPCs are fighting, on the right the Global Console is displayed and on the top and left we can see the individual console of one the players and the 2D-map as seen from the that player perspective.

Fig. 2. A screenshot of the game control with four windows displaying a graphical view of the environment, two 2D maps representing a global situation an individual position, an individual control console.

We will now proceed to detail the tool architecture and their main components and respective functionalities.

A. Global Terminal

The global console role functions are: 1) to offer a bird eye view of the world, providing a 2D map of the game world and displaying the waypoints and character positions; 2) launching an individual console for each character giving the user the possibility to monitor and control each NPC; 3) the possibility to stop and resume the game execution; and 4) to automatically run a certain number of game executions and collect data in order to evaluate and compare the characters performance along a sufficient number of similar experiments. In Figure 3, we see a snapshot of the global console in a game played by 2 NPCs with IDs 218 and 219.

AS we said above, the global console 2D map will represent an updated bird eye view of the NPCs positions (large circular icons), with a different colour for each NPC, and also the waypoints: the reference locations in the environment defined by the user, for navigation purposes. The information is obtained from each NPC trough Sockets: each NPC sends its position to the Global Console every 0.5 seconds.

In the top of the console we see the IDs of the connected clients (the individual identification of each game character), and the one selected will have its respective console displayed, the others will be hidden—only one of the individual consoles can be displayed at any moment. In the bottom we may see two buttons that are used to stop the game execution of every character ("Stop All") and to resume their execution ("Resume All"). This is an important feature for developing behaviours for game characters, due to the frequent necessity to stop the game execution for debugging and testing behaviours.

There are three parameters for the repetition of a set of similar experiments: 1) The duration of each run; 2) the number of experiments and 3) the number of agents. Note that each game can end because there is only one player left or because the duration has reached the defined limit.

The Global Console is responsible for start up the NPCs, run the game until it finishes, collect the game reports and destroy the NPCs, repeating this procedure the right number of runs.

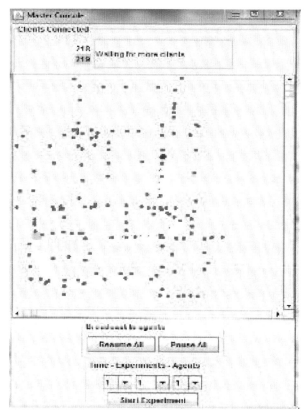

Fig. 3. The display of the Global Console: the 2D world map where we see a set of waypoints and two characters. In the bottom of the console we see the Pause All and Resume All buttons and the three important parameters to repeat a set of experiments.

At the moment, we do not provide an interface for specifying which settings the user wants varied, and what values he wants them to take for, neither for specifying what data to collect from each run. It is up to the NPC developer to program all this information directly in the JAVA code. For example, he may want to vary the set of world maps to use and he may want the report of the NPC winner, the number of survivors, the energy of NPCs in the end of the game. The repeated experiments report will be written on a file (in csv format).

B. NPC Terminals

Each Non Player Character (NPC) has its own private console (Fig. 4), which may be hided or visible and when is displayed it can be used for monitoring and controlling the game character. It displays the NPC position, orientation coordinates and sensory information, along with information regarding the rule base execution. There is the possibility to display a world map with an icon representing the Terminal Player, which can be used to tell the NPC to go to a certain position on the map. Below there is a mini-command center. The jess code entered in this command center is executed only by this NPC and the output can be visualized above the command center in a window. This jess code can be used for additional NPC behaviour monitoring and controlling. On the left, we find three manual buttons for controlling the NPC movements and on the bottom a line of buttons useful for stopping and resuming execution besides other functionalities.

In the presence of the Global Terminal only one NPC is allowed for display, as we do not want to fill the screen with terminal windows. If we want to monitor or control different agents, we have to activate the display of one after another sequentially. In order to choose to be displayed a different NPC filling a specific slot in the Global Terminal with the NPC ID.

In case the Global Console is switched off, something different happens: every time a created NPC does not detect the Global Terminal, it launches its individual terminal. Therefore, if there are 10 NPCs created from the same computer, there will be 10 individual terminals displayed in the computer monitor, visually overcharging it.

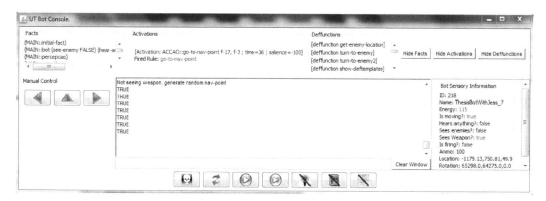

Fig. 4. Example of a NPC terminal. On the top section the Jess data, which can be totally or partially hiden. On the left, three manual movement and orientation button controls. On the right, the agent state may be displayed, and on the center, we see the command window.

1) Control Buttons Line

In the bottom of the NPC terminal we see a line of control buttons (see Fig. 5).

Fig. 5. The NPC control interface. From left to right, Kill agent, Reload logic, Play/Pause agent, Show/Hide agent state,

Show/Hide Jess state, Show/Hide map. In the Figure, the agent state is hided and the same happens with the Jess state.

We will describe each button function from left to right.

Kill agent button: The NPC is killed and disappears from the game.

Reload Logic: If we change the NPC script, by activating this button, the agent behaviour will be controlled by the most recent script version. It will be updated in the agent without being forced to close the application and reinitialize the game.

Play/Pause: The NPC execution is paused and can be resumed. This way we can stop a certain player in order to monitor its behaviour with more detail. We can resume the behaviour at any time.

Step: Behaviour is executed one step forward. Time is divided in steps and behaviour can be followed step by step.

Show/Hide Agent State: The agent state, which appears on the right section of the terminal window, may be hided or displayed.

Show/Hide Jess State: The agent information regarding the Jess rule based script execution may be hided or displayed.

Show/Hide Map: The NPC map can be hided or displayed.

2) NPC Sensory Information

In order to monitor the behaviour execution of an NPC, it is useful to access to its most important internal data, like the energy level, the position and rotation and also other relevant information like if it is moving or if it is seeing or hearing anything. What about the enemies? Is it seeing any of them? It is seeing any weapon and what about the number of ammunition that it is currently possessing? All that information can be displayed on the individual terminal window, along with the NPC ID and name (see Fig. 6).

At this point, we have considered the referred data as the most important to be displayed. As we will explain later there are other ways to monitor other aspects of the agent, by using the powerful command window tool.

3) Manual Controls

On the left we may see three manual control buttons that allow us to control manually the movement of an NPC. By clicking the right or left arrow buttons, the NPC will make a respectively clockwise or anti-clockwise 45° rotation; by clicking the north arrow, it will advance forward a certain small distance, if possible. This buttons can be very useful if we want to manually position the NPC so that it will end with a certain position and orientation.

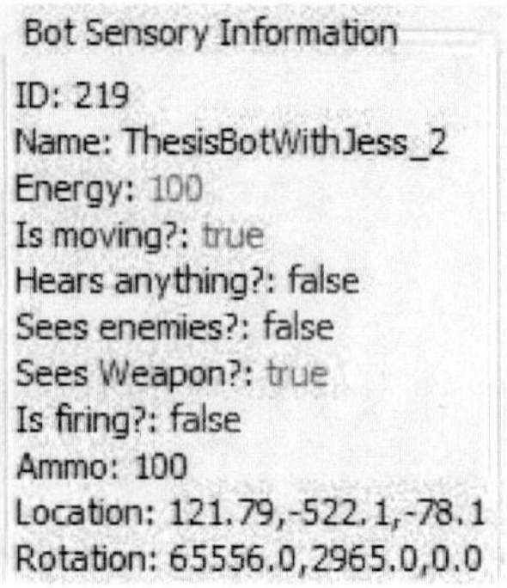

Bot Sensory Information

ID: 219
Name: ThesisBotWithJess_2
Energy: 100
Is moving?: true
Hears anything?: false
Sees enemies?: false
Sees Weapon?: true
Is firing?: false
Ammo: 100
Location: 121.79,-522.1,-78.1
Rotation: 65556.0,2965.0,0.0

Fig. 6. The displayed sensory information in a NPC console.

4) Individual 2D Map

We can visualize a world map with the position of every NPC in the game but where the position of the currently monitored NPC is highlighted (see Fig. 7).

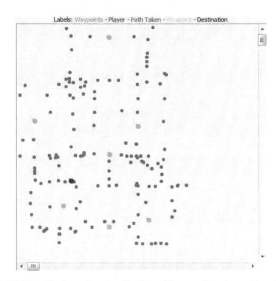

Fig. 7. 2D Map. It allows the visualization of the monitored agent in relation to the others and the world. On the top we see information regarding the colour legends.

The map may be used as an interface for controlling the position of the NPC. The user can click in any waypoint on the map, and if it is possible, the NPC goes directly to the chosen waypoint.

5) Jess Monitoring

In order to develop and maintain a rule based script it is very useful to be able to monitor the list of facts from the Jess working memory, the agenda or rule activations, the selected and fired rule and also the available user defined Jess functions along with some useful built-in ones (see Fig. 8). All this information may be displayed in the individual terminal window.

Fig. 8. Jess monitoring information: the working memory facts list, the rule activations and fired rule and also the user defined functions along with other useful built-in functions.

After stopping a NPC, it will be easy to test the script rules, monitoring their activation in a certain situation. We can follow the rule-based behaviour of a NPC using the step control button and observing the Jess information on the individual terminal window.

The user defined functions visualization was introduced with the goal of helping the user just in case he wants to execute a particular function using the command window. It will certainly be useful for him to look up for the right function name.

On the right of the terminal window, depicted in Fig. 5, we see three buttons that allow us to hide any of these three Jess information types.

6) Command Window

For a full agent monitoring and control, in the individual terminal is offered a command window, which is an interface where the game developer has the possibility to execute any Jess command and behaviour or perception functions and observe their output. This is an important tool for script exploration and debugging besides being very useful for setting up test situations.

The user can fire rules step by step tracing the NPC behaviour, following the evolution of the NPC state and facts list as well as the rules activation and selection. Or he can execute some specific Jess function that extends the NPC state besides the standard information given on the right and referred on III.B.2. The user can even create a function in real-time and execute it, and as Jess is written in Java, he can have full access to the Java API.

As an example, consider that we want to test the script when the user is facing the enemy. We would run the game until our NPC sees its enemy and that after pausing the game, we would pick up the right user defined Jess function: *(turn-to- enemy)*, and execute it in the command prompt. Afterwards we would see the ordered list of rule activations in the window terminal by executing the *(agenda)* command, so that we could check if the rules script were behaving as expected.

C. The Execution Step: the interface between JAVA and JESS

The game execution is divided in steps, but the script developer is responsible for the definition of what is a step, although there are some restrictions. The JAVA NPC controller will always put two special Jess modules in the focus stack: the PERCEPTION and BEHAVIOR, and will issue a (run) command for execution of the PERCEPTION rules followed by the BEHAVIOR ones.

Thus, it is convenient that the script developer separates the Jess rules in two modules: one specialized in gathering information like, for example, the nearest enemy location, and the other specialized in actions, like moving or shooting. In each module more than one rule can fire—each module is executed only when no more rules fire. Therefore, the script must carefully manage the return of the control to JAVA so that Jess rules in any of the two modules do not fire forever.

TABLE I
A JESS SCRIPT TO ILLUSTRATE A SIMPLE NPC BEHAVIOUR DEFINITION
USING A PERCEPTION/ACTION CYCLE.

```
;An example of Deftemplate
;to store all about the agent

(deftemplate bot
  (slot see-enemy)
  (slot hear-anything)
  (slot moving)
  (slot nav-target)
  (slot enemy-target))

;Setup
(deffacts SETUP
  (perception)
  (action)
  (bot (see-enemy FALSE)
       (nav-target nil)))

(defmodule PERCEPTION)

;Rule to collect info about the agent
(defrule perception
  ?f <- (perception)
  ?x <- (bot (nav-target ?target))
  =>
  (retract ?f)
  (assert (perception))
  (modify ?x (see-enemy
              (see-enemy-func))
              (enemy-target
              (get-enemy-location)))
  (return))

(defmodule ACTION)

;Rule to pursuit and fire at the enemy he sees
(defrule fires-and-pursuit-enemy
  (declare (salience 100))
  ?a <- (action)
  ?bot <- (bot (see-enemy TRUE)
  (enemy-target ?t&~nil))
  =>
  (retract ?a)
  (assert (accao))
  (go-to-enemy ?t)
  (shoot ?t)
  (return))
```

We show in Table I an example of a toy Jess script, only for illustration. The (return) command assures that control no more rules are executed inside the respective module: after a (return) in a PERCEPTION rule, control is given to the ACTION module, and after a (return) in an ACTION rule, control is given back to JAVA, putting an ending in the step. We can see several perception and action functions: *(see-enemy-func)* returns a boolean and *(get-enemy-location)* returns the enemy position coordinates; *(goto-enemy)* means that the MPC goes towards a position near the enemy and *(shoot)* means the NPC turns towards the enemy position and shoots.

Note that while in the JESS command window we can execute a rule after another monitoring behaviour in a thinner scale than a step. In the example given there is only one rule in each module and so a step execution will fire 2 rules in case they are both activated.

At table II we present another short example of the Jess code to control the character movement in a formation controlled by the group leader. As the previous example the behavior is controlled by a cycle of perception/action activated be a message from the squad leader. This message indicates to the character is new position on the formation and the direction it should be facing. When a new message is received, the PERCEPTION module stores the information of the character new objectives. This information is used to activate the module ACTION and execute the appropriated actions to achieve those goals.

TABLE II
AN EXEMPLE OF A PICE OF CODE THAT CONTROL THE MOVEMENT OF A CHARACTER IN A FORMATION

```
(defmodule PERCEPTION)

(defrule perception
    ?f <- (perception)
    ?x <- (bot) ; representation of BOT current attributes
    =>
    (retract ?f)
    ;If received a message to move in formation (id 9)
    (if (and (eq (get-receiver-team-id-from-message) 9))
       then (bind ?var (select-place-on-diamond-formation
                        (get-location-from-message)
                        (get-rotation-from-message)))
             ;setup destination
             (modify ?x (nav-target ?var))
             ;setup bot rotation
             (modify ?x (rot-target
                 (select-rotation-on-diamond-formation ?var)))
    )
    (assert (perception))
    (store RuleFired perception)
    (return)
)

...

(defmodule ACTION)

(defrule go-to-destination
    ?a <- (action)
    ;If there is a destination and a rotation
    (bot (nav-target ?target&~nil)(rot-target ?rot))
    =>
    (retract ?a)
    (assert (action))
    ;move bot
    (go-to-target ?target ?rot))
    (store "RuleFired" go-to-destination)
    (return)
)
...
```

This rules and modules can be combined in more complex behaviours, taking advantage of the capability of the tool environment to make extensive tests to each component.

Although the integration of different pieces of code is not entirely error free, these characteristics provide us with a significant enhancement over the current accessible tools.

IV. CONCLUSIONS AND FUTURE WORK

In this paper we presented a generic architecture to support the development of tools to assist the design, debug and execution of artificial intelligent non-player characters in a game simulated environment. We build the application DEVELOP-FPS as a concrete example of the implementation of the architecture, and introduce some of its core functionalities and capabilities. This tool allows the management of the NPCs from different levels, individually monitoring and controlling their behavior or act in a global perspective.

We have designed several experiments using this tool, from simple behaviours that only follow a fixed path to advanced cooperative team behavior which include collision avoidance and split and regroup capabilities. Our tool was fundamental in the debugging process and testing of the developed behaviours. The advantages of forcing situations when a specific behavior characteristic was triggered and follow the execution trace of the agent rules were an improvement in the character creation.

We believe that this kind of tools is fundamental in the process of constructing and deploying artificial intelligence components. Although commercial games companies had their own proprietary tools, these are not made available to the general public. The use of a text editor and a trial and error approach hardly is viable when the project grows beyond a certain dimension. The development of these tools is a something that in a close future had to taken into account when a new game project is initiated.

By now we are already extending the game developer tool in order to have different agent teams controlled by the Global Console. Another useful extension can be the addition of a command window into the Global Console so that we can broadcast Jess commands and functions to every Non Character Player or just to a specific team, which may help setting up test scenarios. The definition of teams and the definition of coordinated actions and group tactics is currently work in progress. We expect that our tool will improve and facilitate the designer tasks.

REFERENCES

[1] UnrealEngine and UnrealScript official web page (http://www.unrealengine.com/).

[2] Whitehead II, J., Roe, R.: World of Warcraft Programming: A Guide and Reference for Creating WoW Addons. Wiley; (2010).

[3] Lang, Christoph: Panda3D 1.7 Game Developer's Cookbook. Packt Publishing (2011).

[4] Goldstone, Will. Unity Game Development Essentials. Packt Publishing; (2009).

[5] Unity game development tool official web page (http://unity3d.com).

[6] Pogamut official web page (http://pogamut.cuni.cz).

[7] Friedman-Hill, Ernest. Jess in Action: Java Rule-Based Systems. Manning Publications (2003).

[8] Moniz, L., Urbano, P., Coelho, H.: AGLIPS: An educational environment to construct behaviour based robots. In Proc. of the International Conference on Computational Intelligence for Modelling, Control and Automation – CIMCA (2003).

[9] Millington, Ian: Artificial Inteligence for Games. Morgan Kaufmann (2009)

## 30

An Agent-Based Approach
for Evaluating Basic Design Options
of Management Accounting Systems

Friederike Wall, *Alpen-Adria-Universität Klagenfurt, Austria*

Abstract — **This paper investigates the effectiveness of reducing errors in management accounting systems with respect to organizational performance. In particular, different basic design options of management accounting systems of how to improve the information base by measurements of actual values are analyzed in different organizational contexts. The paper applies an agent-based simulation based on the idea of NK fitness landscapes. The results provide broad, but no universal support for conventional wisdom that lower inaccuracies of accounting information lead to more effective adaptation processes. Furthermore, results indicate that the effectiveness of improving the management accounting system subtly interferes with the complexity of the interactions within the organization and the coordination mode applied.**

Keywords — **Agent-based Simulation; Complexity; Coordination; Learning; Management Accounting Systems**

I. INTRODUCTION

MANAGEMENT ACCOUNTING is intended to provide decision-makers with judgmental information for evaluating options and to produce information for assessing managerial performance [1], [2].. For deciding whether, or not, to change the status quo in favor of an alternative option, a decision-maker requires information on the pay-offs of both options. Information related to the status quo may result from measurements of actual values (i.e., "weighting", "counting" and valuing) within accounting systems; and unfortunately, it cannot be taken for granted that these measurements perfectly reflect reality [3]. The alternative options, in principle, are subject to ex ante-evaluations by decision-makers who, according to Simon [4] may suffer from cognitive limitations. However, also ex ante-evaluations might be based on measurements, i.e., actual values received on basis of decisions made in former periods and used to "learn" for future decisions. For instance, plan cost accounting often relies on cost functions which are built from actual costs realized in former periods [5] - or as Christensen} [3] puts it: "[o]nly autocorrelation makes historical accounting relevant for decision purposes" (p. 1827).

Moreover, management accounting systems are embedded in an organizational structure and the organizational structure affects imperfections of judgmental information. In particular, in organizations the overall decision problem is segmented into partial decisions which are delegated to decentral decision-makers (e.g., [6]-[8]). With delegation further difficulties occur: partial decisions may be interdependent, decision-makers likely have different information and pursue their own objectives opportunistically. To avoid losses with respect to the organization's performance, coordination is required, though, according to Ackoff [9], more intense coordination not necessarily increases organizational performance.

Against this background the paper investigates the following research question: *In which settings of organizational structure and basic design options of the management accounting system it is effective to use measured actual values by management accounting systems for improving judgmental information?*

Hence, the paper focuses on *imperfect knowledge of pay-off functions* in organizations. The paper does not address decision-making under uncertainty due to imperfectly known future events [10]. Furthermore, the paper does not consider the diverse biases and heuristics that individuals suffer from in case of uncertainty [11]. We regard accounting errors in terms of *noise as the difference between estimated and correct values* [12]. [13]; however, the paper does not relate to biases in accounting in terms of the application of accounting principles that is not in line with the accounting principles.

For investigating the research question, a method is required that allows controlling a multitude of issues in interaction with each other like interdependent decisions, coordination mechanisms, inaccuracies of judgmental information and related adjustments due to measurement of actual values by accounting. Obviously, these interrelated issues would be particularly difficult to control in empirical research and would induce intractable dimensions in formal modeling. In contrast, simulation methods allow dealing with manifold interdependent issues [14]. Since the research question focuses on collaborative decision-making an agent-based simulation appears appropriate.

The paper contributes to research since, to the best of the author's knowledge, for the first time different settings of memorizing actual values and dynamic adjustments through actual values in management accounting are investigated in interaction with major organizational design variables. Moreover, using an agent-based method is a relatively new approach in the area of management accounting ([15]-[18]).

The remainder of this article is organized as follows: Section II places the research question within the context of related literature. In the third chapter we introduce the simulation model and in Section IV we present and discuss results of the simulations.

II. RELATED LITERATURE IN ACCOUNTING AND ORGANIZATION SCIENCE

The research question of this article obviously refers to the body of research on errors in accounting. However, our study might also be seen in the context of research on a more general question: how does organizational design influence the overall outcome of an organization with decision-makers imperfectly informed about the outcome of alternatives? Subsequently, we outline these streams of research with respect to the research question addressed in this paper.

A. Errors in Accounting

Christensen [3] gives a recent overview and discussion on errors in accounting. Stating that errors in accounting are "often neglected when the design of accounting systems is evaluated" (p. 1836) he elaborates three dimensions of this subject. Firstly, accounting information serves to update expectations of future events of the firm (e.g., future costs, cash flows). In this sense accounting is a source of learning and, in particular, allows updating beliefs. Thus, the main question is whether the accuracy of information known beforehand and the accounting information leads to more reliable expectations about future events.

Secondly, Christensen [3] points out that particularly cost accounting in various contexts is based on linear cost functions and that linearity does not necessarily reflect reality perfectly. Thus, the accounting system suffers from an endogenous error. This line of argumentation also relates to the findings of Datar and Gupta [19] who analyze the effects of erroneous choices of cost drivers in product costing and to the findings of Labro and Vanhoucke [20] related to the interactions among errors in activity based costing. Recently, Leitner [16], [17] investigates interactions among errors and biases in traditional costing systems.

Thirdly, Christensen [3] states that accounting information not necessarily is the best sort of information for a certain purpose and that, for example, the price mechanism might reveal better condensed information. In this sense, applying accounting systems rather than, for example, the market mechanism is the erroneous choice.

B. Imperfect Information on Pay-Off in Organizations

The seminal work of Sah and Stiglitz [21]-[23] may be regarded as the starting point of the stream of research which investigates the robustness of different organizational structures against so-called type I and type II errors: In analogy to statistical inference, imperfect information used in decision-making basically can lead to two different types of errors: in case of "type I errors" an option that, in fact, is superior compared to the status quo is rejected due to a false negative ex ante-evaluation. In contrary, with "type II errors" a false positive option is chosen since it is perceived to be superior to the status quo, whereas, in fact, it is inferior.

In their 1986 paper Sah and Stiglitz [22] introduce a project-selection-framework: An organization consists of several decision-making units which receive knowledge of feasible projects. Imperfect ex ante-evaluations could occur in case that a "good'" project which, in fact, would increase organizational performance is rejected (type I error) or if a "bad" project which, in fact, reduces organizational performance is accepted (type II error). Each decision-making unit is characterized by a screening function. The screening function gives the probability that a project is accepted as a function of the project's quality, i.e., the project's contribution to performance.

Sah and Stiglitz [22] distinguish two "architectures" of the decision-making organization: polyarchy and hierarchy. In the polyarchy, each decision-maker can decide in favor of a project independent from other decision-makers. In the hierarchy, in case that a decision-maker on a lower level positively evaluates a project, the project proposal has to be forwarded to a decision-making unit of a higher level. Thus, for acceptance in a two-level hierarchy, a project has to be positively evaluated twice. Sah and Stiglitz [22] show that the hierarchy reduces the likelihood that projects are accepted which better should have been rejected, i.e., hierarchies reduce type II errors; in contrary, in a polyarchic structure the tendency to falsely reject "good" projects, i.e., the occurrence of type I errors, is reduced.

The works of Sah and Stiglitz initiated further research on the decision-making properties of hierarchical versus polyarchic organizations. For example, Koh [24], [25] introduces costs for information gathering and processing on the decision-makers site and information asymmetries related to the decision-makers actions into the project-selection-framework. In the study of Visser [26] the decision-making units do not suffer from errors in their judgments but rather from obstacles to fully communicate the information they have to other decision-making units. Christensen and Knudsen [27] extend the work of Sah and Stiglitz [21]-[23] by investigating the range of organizational structures between polyarchy and hierarchy and provide a general framework for designing decision-making structures that most effectively reduce type-I and type-II errors.

It is worth mentioning that some aspects of complex decentralized decision-making systems might differ from the project-selection-framework of Sah and Stiglitz: the projects under evaluation are independent from each other, i.e., no interactions between the single project options (or decisions) exist. However, there are also decision problems which cannot be segmented without inducing interactions among partial decisions and, to some extent, interactions are a consequence of specialization. The approach presented subsequently takes segmented decisions with interactions among partial decisions into account.

III. SIMULATION MODEL

The simulation model is based on the NK model introduced by Kauffman [28], [29] of evolutionary biology and successfully applied in management research (e.g. [30]-[32], for an overview [33]). The NK model allows representing a multi-dimensional decision problem where N denotes the number of dimensions and K the level of interactions among these dimensions. However, so far the NK model has rarely been employed to analyze decision-making with imperfect judgmental information [15], [18], [34].

We adopt an advanced version of the NK model with noisy fitness landscapes, as introduced by Levitan and Kauffman [34]. In particular, to analyze our research question the model consists of three components which are presented in the subsequent sections: (1) the organizational structure which is mapped similar to Siggelkow and Rivkin [31]; (2) a representation of imperfect judgmental information that corresponds to organizational segmentation and specialization; (3) alternative modes of how inaccuracies in judgmental information might be reduced in the course of the adaptive walks by measurements by the management accounting system. Thus, the components (2) und (3) are regarded to be the distinctive features of the model.

A. Organizational Structure

In each time step t of the overall observation period T the artificial organizations face an N-dimensional binary decision problem $\mathbf{d}_t = (d_{t,1}, ... d_{t,N})$, i.e., they have to make decisions $d_{t,i} \in \{0, 1\}$ and $i = 1, ... N$. Each single state of decision $d_{t,i}$ provides a contribution $C_{t,i}$ with $0 \leq C_{t,i} \leq 1$ to organizational performance $V(\mathbf{d}_t)$. A decision $d_{t,i}$ might interact with K other decisions (for simplicity K assumed to be stable over time). Hence, K can take values from 0 (no interactions) to $N-1$ (maximum interactions). Thus, performance contribution $C_{t,i}$ may not only depend on the single decision $d_{t,i}$ but also on K other decisions so that

$$C_{t,i} = f_i(d_{t,i}, d_{t,i}^1, ..., d_{t,i}^K) \qquad (1)$$

In line with the NK model, we assume that for each possible vector $d_{t,i}, d_{t,i}^1, ..., d_{t,i}^K$ the value of $C_{t,i}$ is randomly drawn from a uniform distribution over the unit interval, i.e., U[0,1]. Hence, given equation 1, whenever one of the states $d_{t,i}, d_{t,i}^1, ..., d_{t,i}^K$ of the single decisions is altered, another (randomly chosen) performance contribution $C_{t,i}$ becomes effective. The overall performance $V(\mathbf{d}_t)$ is given as normalized sum of performance contributions $C_{t,i}$ with

$$V(\mathbf{d}_t) = \frac{1}{N} \sum_{i=1}^{N} C_{t,i} = \frac{1}{N} \sum_{i=1}^{N} f_i(d_{t,i}, d_{t,i}^1, ..., d_{t,i}^K) \qquad (2)$$

Our organizations consist of a main office and R departments subscripted by r. Each department has a department head. Our organizations segment their N-dimensional decision problem $\mathbf{d}$ into R disjoint partial problems and delegate each partial problem to one of the R departments. Hence, each department has primary control over a subset of the N single decisions $d_{t,i}$ (e.g., in case of $N = 10$ and $R = 3$ department 1 over decisions 1 to 3, department 2 over decisions 4 to 7 and department 3 over decisions 8 to 10), and from the perspective of a certain department r the organizational decision problem is partitioned into a partial decision vector $\mathbf{d}_{t,r}^{own}$ related to those single decisions which are in the "own" responsibility and into $\mathbf{d}_{t,r}^{res}$ for the "residual" decisions that other departments are in charge of. However, in case of cross-departmental interactions, choices of a certain department may affect the contributions of decisions other departments are in charge of and vice versa.

In each period t of the adaptive walk a department head seeks to identify the best configuration for the "own" subset of choices assuming that the other departments $q = 1, ... R$ and $q \neq r$ do not alter their prior subsets $\mathbf{d}_{t-1,q}^{*own}$ of decisions. In each time period a department head randomly discovers two alternative partial configurations of those binary decisions that he/she is in charge of: an alternative configuration $\mathbf{d}_{t,r}^{a1}$ that differs in one decision (a1) and another alternative $\mathbf{d}_{t,r}^{a2}$ which differs in two decisions (a2) compared to the status quo, i.e., $\mathbf{d}_{t-1,r}^{*own}$. In each time period department head has three options to choose from, i.e., keeping the status quo $\mathbf{d}_{t-1,r}^{*own}$ and the two alternatives $\mathbf{d}_{t,r}^{a1}$, $\mathbf{d}_{t,r}^{a2}$. According to economic literature, a department head favors that option which he/she perceives to promise the highest value base for compensation. In our model department heads are compensated on basis of the *overall* performance of the organization according to a linear incentive scheme so that we can ignore conflicts of interests between the organizational and departmental objectives.

However, due to specialization our department heads have different knowledge about the organization's decision problem $\mathbf{d}_t$ (we return to that point in the section III.B). In consequence, even though in our model no conflicts of interests occur, departments can have different preferences which might evoke a need for coordination. We analyze two different modes of coordination (for these and other modes [31], [36]):

– In the "decentral" mode, in fact, there is no coordination: each department autonomously makes the "own" partial decisions $\mathbf{d}_{t,r}^{own}$ and the overall configuration $\mathbf{d}_t$ of decisions results as a combination of these departmental choices without any central intervention. Hence, the function of the main office is limited to (perhaps inaccurately) observing the overall performance achieved.

– In a mode named "proposal" each department proposes two alternative configurations $\mathbf{d}_t$ to the main office and, among all proposals received, the main office finally chooses the one that promises the highest overall performance. Hence, by their proposals the departments shape the search space of the main office.

B. Informational Structure

Our agents identify superior solutions of the decisional problem according to the *perceived* contributions of the choices to their compensation or to overall performance, respectively. To represent inaccurate judgmental information - which might be improved due the management accounting system in the course of the adaptive walk (Section III.C) - we add noise on the contributions of decisions to performance. Furthermore, in order to represent expertise related to segmentation and specialization we differentiate noise according to the information quality different decision-makers in an organization reasonably have. A common idea of many organizational theories is that decision-makers in organizations dispose of information with different levels of imperfections (e.g. [7], [8]). For example, departmental decision-makers are assumed to have relatively precise information about their own area of competence, but limited cross-departmental knowledge whereas the main office might have rather coarse-grained, but organization-wide information.

We assume that departments decide on basis of the perceived value base for compensation, i.e., the perceived overall performance rather than the actual. Therefore, we "distort" the actual performance contributions according to the expertise of each single department. In particular, the perceived value base for compensation, i.e., the overall performance $\widetilde{V}_{t,r}(\mathbf{d}_t)$ department r perceives, is computed as normalized sum of the actual own performance and actual residual performance, each distorted with an error term

$$\widetilde{V}_{t,r}(\mathbf{d}_t) = [\widetilde{V}_{t,r}^{own}(\mathbf{d}_{t,r}^{own}) + \widetilde{V}_{t,r}^{res}(\mathbf{d}_{t,r}^{res})]/N \qquad (3)$$

where

$$\widetilde{V}_{t,r}^{own}(\mathbf{d}_{t,r}^{own}) = V_{t,r}^{own}(\mathbf{d}_{t,r}^{own}) + e_r^{own}(\mathbf{d}_{t,r}^{own})$$

$$\text{and } \widetilde{V}_{t,r}^{res}(\mathbf{d}_{t,r}^{res}) = V_{t,r}^{res}(\mathbf{d}_{t,r}^{res}) + e_r^{res}(\mathbf{d}_{t,r}^{res}) \qquad (4)$$

Likewise, in the coordination mode "proposal" the main office makes a choice from the proposals on basis of the *perceived* overall performance $\widetilde{V}_t(\mathbf{d}_t)$ computed as the sum of the true overall performance $V_t(\mathbf{d}_t)$ and an error term $e_{main}(\mathbf{d}_t)$.

At least with respect to accounting systems [20], it is reasonable to assume that high (low) true values of performance come along with high (low) distortions. Hence, we reflect distortions as *relative errors* imputed to the true performance (for other functions [35]). , and, for simplicity, the error terms follow a Gaussian distribution $N(\mu;\sigma)$ with expected value $\mu = 0$ and standard deviations σ_r^{own}, σ_r^{res} and σ_{main}. For example, department r perceives the "own" performance as

$$\widetilde{V}_{t,r}^{own}(\mathbf{d}_{t,r}^{own}) = V_{t,r}^{own}(\mathbf{d}_{t,r}^{own}) \cdot (1 + N(0; \sigma_r^{own}(\mathbf{d}_{t,r}^{own}))) \qquad (4^*)$$

We differentiate the standard deviations according to specialization of departments and the main office as mentioned above (see notes on parameter settings in Table 2).

C. Basic Design Options of the Management Accounting Systems

As argued in the introduction, within the search for higher levels of performance ex ante-evaluations might suffer from two deficiencies: The performance of the status quo option is misestimated and/or the performances of alternative options are inaccurately evaluated. This paper is particularly interested in the potentially beneficial role that measurements of the status quo by accounting systems can play for organizational performance. In our model, we therefore distinguish five settings of measurement and usage of actual values in the adaptive walk (summarized in Table 2) which may be regarded as basic design options of the management accounting system:

TABLE I
SETTINGS OF MEASUREMENT AND USAGE OF ACTUALS IN THE ADAPTIVE WALKS

Name of Setting	Measurement of Actuals for Status Quo	Adjustment of Inaccuracies in Adaptive Walk
(1) No measurement	no	no
(2) Measurement only	yes	no
(3) Stepwise refinement	yes	stepwise
(4) Immediate adjustment	yes	immediately at once
(5) Perfect evaluation	yes	(not necessary)

1) In case that "no measurement" is used the evaluation of the status quo configuration (i.e., the choice $\mathbf{d}_{i-1}^*$ made in period t-1) cannot be based on the measurement of the actual values achieved in the previous period. In a way, this reflects an organization which does not have any accounting system at all.

2) In a setting we call "measurement only" our departments use accounting systems which allow them to perfectly determine the performance that was achieved with the status quo configuration $\mathbf{d}_{i-1}^*$ of the decisional vector. Hence, throughout each adaptive walk, when department heads decide they perfectly get informed about the status quo by the accounting system. However, they suffer from inaccurate knowledge of the performance contributions of the alternative options $\mathbf{d}_{t,r}^{a1}$ and $\mathbf{d}_{t,r}^{a2}$, that they consider, i.e., the accounting system does not provide any refined information on the alternatives regardless of whether they have been implemented in the past or not. Thus, the accounting system does not provide any tracking or memory about the configurations that have been realized

or any information for updating of beliefs (s. section II.A) on the alternative options.

3) A setting we name "stepwise refinement" goes a step further. Like in the previously described setting the decision-makers get perfect information about the performance of the status quo $\mathbf{d}_{i-1}^{*}$, and, *additionally*, the measured actual values are used for some kind of "learning". Hence, the management accounting system is used for updating of beliefs on alternative options according to [3]. For simplicity the stepwise refinement is represented in a relatively "mechanistic" form of noise reduction: whenever a certain configuration $\mathbf{d}$ of decisions has been implemented, decision-makers receive information about the related contributions to performance measures. This information will be partially memorized in future periods, and, in particular, will then lead to a refined estimation of performance of that configuration. This situation, for example, reflects a situation where cost functions applied for cost planning might be (even automatically) adjusted with each measurement of the performance that a certain configuration of cost drivers provides: with each determined combination of cost drivers and cost measures the statistical basis is broadened from which a cost function could be derived (for example by regression analysis). For each of the $n = 2^{N}$ configurations $\mathbf{d} = (d_{1}, \dots d_{N})$ in the solution space (due to $d_{i} \in \{0, 1\}$ and $i = 1, \dots N$) a counter $count^{n}$ is introduced. Whenever a certain configuration $\mathbf{d}^{*}$ is chosen/implemented during the observation period T the related counter $count^{d^{*}}$ of configuration $\mathbf{d}^{*}$ is incremented by 1. Hence, if the performance contributions of this configuration $\mathbf{d}^{*}$ are evaluated again in a later period the corresponding errors e_{r}^{own}, e_{r}^{res} and e_{main} are divided by $count^{d^{*}}$. Thus, for example, when under coordination mode "proposal" the main office again evaluates configuration $\mathbf{d}_{t}$ the main office perceives the overall performance as

$$\widetilde{V}(\mathbf{d}_{t}) = V(\mathbf{d}_{t}) \cdot (1 + \frac{1}{count^{d_{t}}} \cdot e_{main}(\mathbf{d}_{t})) \qquad (5)$$

4) The case "immediate adjustment" slightly differs from the "stepwise refinement" setting as the accounting systems provide perfect memorizing and immediate correction of ex ante-evaluations due to measured actual values for a configuration $\mathbf{d}^{*}$ that has been implemented. Hence, whenever in the adaptive walk a configuration is considered, which has already been implemented, at least once, during the walk, the decision-makers get perfect information about the level of performance as measured by the accounting system. For example, the main office evaluates the overall performance of a configuration $\mathbf{d}_{t}$ as

$$\widetilde{V}(\mathbf{d}_{t}) = V(\mathbf{d}_{t}) \cdot (1 + e_{main}(\mathbf{d}_{t})) \text{ for } count^{d_{t}} = 1$$
$$\widetilde{V}(\mathbf{d}_{t}) = V(\mathbf{d}_{t}) \text{ for } count^{d_{t}} \geq 2 \qquad (6)$$

5) Perfect evaluations in our simulations serve as a "benchmark" so that performance differences due to imperfect evaluations can be determined. Here neither the evaluations of the status quo $\mathbf{d}_{i-1}^{*}$ nor of the alternative options $\mathbf{d}_{t,r}^{a1}$ or $\mathbf{d}_{t,r}^{a2}$ suffer from any noise, i.e., all error terms are set to zero.

IV. RESULTS AND INTERPRETATION

A. Parameter Settings in the Simulation Experiments and Measures for Effectiveness

For simulating an adaptive walk, after a "true" fitness landscape is generated, distortions are added which follow the informational imperfections in the organization as described in section III.B. Then the organizations are placed randomly in the fitness landscape and observed for 300 periods while searching for higher levels of organizational performance under the regime of various settings of management accounting systems as introduced in section III.C. As is familiar for adaptive walks we use a hill-climbing algorithm. In particular, each decision maker evaluates the options he/she knows (i.e., status quo and alternatives) and an alteration is preferred in favor of that option which promises the steepest ascent.

The results were conducted for two interaction structures of decisions (i.e., coordination needs) which, in a way, represent two extremes (for these and other interaction structures see [32]): in the low complexity case intra-departmental interactions among decisions are maximal intense while no cross-departmental interdependencies exist. This type of interactions corresponds to a "self-contained" organization structure [7] and comes close to a pooled interdependence [37], [38]. In contrast, in the high complexity case all decisions affect the performance contributions of all other decisions, i.e., the complexity of interactions and the coordination need is raised to maximum. This situation comes closest to a reciprocal interdependence [37], [38].

Empirical findings report errors of judgmental information between 5 up to 30 percent [39], [40]. Results presented in this paper relate to errors around 10 percent though differentiated due to specialization as described in section III.B and as explicated in the note to Table 2. (It is worth mentioning, that results were subject to robustness analyses, especially with respect to the magnitude of errors and the spread between knowledge about the "own" area of competence and the rest of the organization. We found that the results appear robust in a range up to a magnitude of overall error around 22 percent and with several levels of spread according to specialization of decision-makers.)

For investigating the effectiveness of the adaptive walks we rely on three measures as displayed in Table 2: "Speed $(V_{5}-V_{1})$" reports the performance enhancements achieved in the first 5 periods within the adaptive walks. This measure appears interesting because in the first periods most purely the

TABLE II
CONDENSED RESULTS

Name of Setting	Low Complexity			High Complexity		
	Speed $(V_5\text{-}V_1)$	Final Performance (V_{300})	Frequency of Global Maximum in $t = 300$	Speed $(V_5\text{-}V_1)$	Final Performance (V_{300})	Frequency of Global Maximum in $t = 300$
Decentral Mode						
(1) No measurement	0.04419	0.83689	1.66 %	0.12479	0.84374	1.94 %
(2) Measurement only	0.05211	0.85251	1.94 %	0.12488	0.86941	3.16 %
(3) Stepwise refinement	0.05734	0.89748	8.24 %	0.12818	0.86738	3.00 %
(4) Immediate adjustment	0.05771	0.89381	7.76 %	0.12121	0.86519	3.46 %
(5) Perfect evaluation	0.07321	0.89730	10.16 %	0.14536	0.86466	2.44 %
Proposal Mode						
(1) No measurement	0.06878	0.83506	1.46 %	0.05739	0.83541	1.76 %
(2) Measurement only	0.07277	0.85222	2.52 %	0.05754	0.83665	1.90 %
(3) Stepwise refinement	0.08473	0.87681	4.84 %	0.06387	0.85041	2.30 %
(4) Immediate adjustment	0.08601	0.87724	4.56 %	0.06742	0.84803	1.78 %
(5) Perfect evaluation	0.09781	0.89518	9.54 %	0.06510	0.86716	2.40 %

Notes: Each entry represents results of 5,000 adaptive walks: 1,000 distinct fitness landscapes with 5 adaptive walks on each over 300 periods. Confidence intervals for V_{300} at a confidence level of 0.001 range between ±0.003 and ±0.004. Common parameters in settings (1) to (4): $\sigma_r^{own} = 0.05$, $\sigma_r^{res} = 0.15$ and $\sigma_{main} = 0.1$ (in (5) all set to 0); all errors with expected value $\mu = 0$.

effects of refinements (settings 3 and 4) can be observed. The performance in the last observation period V_{300} can serve as an indicator for the effectiveness of the search process as well as the frequency of how often the global maximum in the performance landscape is achieved in the last period observed.

Furthermore, Fig. 1 and Fig. 2 reflect the performance differences in the course of the adaptive walks of the noisy against the perfect evaluations for low and high complexity of cross-departmental interactions.

We discuss results in two steps. Firstly, we focus on comparing the different settings of measuring and using actuals against each other (Section IV.B) and afterwards we discuss the moderating effects of complexity and coordination (Section IV.C).

B. Effectiveness of Various Settings of Management Accounting Systems

Obviously, evaluating alternative options with imperfect information can result in a choice which *appears* favorable, whereas, in fact, it reduces performance compared to the status quo ("false positive" decision) [35]. Underestimating the status quo level of performance due to missing or imperfect measurement of actuals might foster the false estimation. Vice versa, with "false negative" decisions an alternative is rejected because its marginal contribution to performance compared to the status quo appears worse than it actually is and, thus, the status quo is perpetuated [35]. This situation may be fostered by an overestimation of the status quo level of performance. These considerations let us hypothesize the following:

With increasing levels of measurement and usage of actual values for improving judgmental information (1) the speed of performance enhancements increases and (2) higher levels of organizational performance are achieved.

The five settings of management accounting systems in

terms of measuring actual values and using these numbers for judgments as displayed in table 1 incorporate an order of increasing information accuracy. We find that the speed measure $(V_5\text{-}V_1)$ in Table 2 in most cases is increasing with the more advanced settings of accounting systems. Furthermore, as Fig. 1 and Fig. 2 show at a glance, the more advanced settings of management accounting systems tend to have lower performance losses against the perfect system. However, the results provide broad, but no universal support for the hypothesis stated above and some of the results deserve a closer analysis.

First of all, it is worth mentioning that under setting (1) where no actual numbers are available at all, the performance achieved is lowest in all of the four scenarios of coordination need and mode -- in three scenarios with remarkable performance losses even to the "measurement only" setting (we discuss the "high complexity-proposal mode"-scenario below more into detail). Apparently, over- or underestimating the status quo leads to severe losses of speed and level of performance enhancements. *Hence, this indicates that using an accounting system, at least, to track the status quo (e.g., an actual cost system) is effective.*

Secondly, the results for the "stepwise refinement" and the "immediate adjustment" are rather similar for all scenarios under investigation. An obvious reason is that the "stepwise refinement" setting is modeled in a way that the decision-makers get better knowledge of the fitness landscape relatively fast. The simulation of a slower learning curve might yield other results.

Thirdly, "stepwise refinement" and "immediate adjustment" of knowledge about the fitness landscape bring performance to levels higher than achieved with "measurement only" -- except for the case of high complexity and decentral coordination which is discussed in section IV.C. Obviously, it is less likely

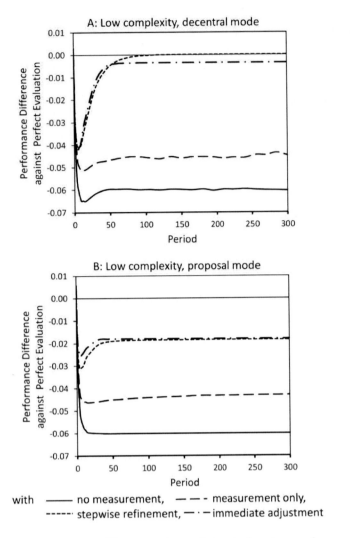

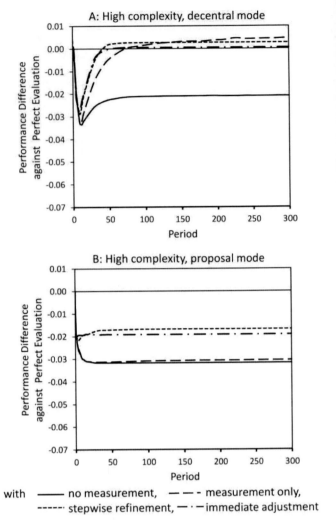

with ——— no measurement, — — - measurement only,
----- stepwise refinement, — · — immediate adjustment

Fig. 1. Performance differences against perfect evaluations in case of no cross-departmental interactions
Notes: The horizontal line at level 0 of the y-axis reflects the perfect evaluation and the other lines represent the performance differences in the course of the adaptive walks against the perfect management accounting system. Each line represents results of 5,000 adaptive walks: 1,000 distinct fitness landscapes with 5 adaptive walks on each over 300 periods. For parameter settings see Table 1 and notes to Table 2.

with ——— no measurement, — — - measurement only,
----- stepwise refinement, — · — immediate adjustment

Fig. 2. Performance differences against perfect evaluations in case of maximum cross-departmental interactions
Notes: The horizontal line at level 0 of the y-axis reflects the perfect evaluation and the other lines represent the performance differences in the course of the adaptive walks against the perfect management accounting system. Each line represents results of 5,000 adaptive walks: 1,000 distinct fitness landscapes with 5 adaptive walks on each over 300 periods. For parameter settings see Table 1 and notes to Table 2.

to opt for a false positive or false negative alternative within the adaptive walks in case of the immediate or stepwise improvement of judgmental information by actuals. *This indicates that accounting systems which allow memorizing actual values contribute to higher performance levels.*

C. Effects of complexity and coordination mode

The results provide broad support for intuition that increasing accuracy of the management accounting systems captured in settings 1 to 5 leads to faster performance enhancements und higher levels of final performance. However, some results run contrary to intuition. In particular, the complexity of the interactions structure (i.e., coordination need) and the coordination mode applied apparently interfere with the information accuracy provided by the management accounting system.

We start the discussion of the effects of coordination need and mode with the scenario of "low complexity-decentral

mode" (Fig. 1A). In this case no cross-departmental interactions exist. Therefore, no cross-departmental coordination is required: with imperfect judgmental information departments might decide in favor of a suboptimal partial option (false positive or false negative), but there are no external effects in the sense that this would reduce the performance of the other departments' decisions. The accounting systems 3 and 4, after around 75 periods in average reach the level of perfect information while systems 1 and 2 induce a rather high, nearly constant distance to perfect evaluations.

To a certain extent, things seem to change for highly intense cross-departmental interactions among decisions (Fig. 2A). In particular, with decentral coordination for high complexity even the "measurement only" setting leads to performance levels *beyond* that achieved with perfect evaluations. Fig. 2A indicates that after around 50 to 75 periods the noisy accounting systems with measurements of actuals (i.e. settings (2), (3) and (4) in table 1) *exceed* the performance achieved with perfect evaluations.

In order to provide an explanation for this "beneficial" effect of noise we refer to "false positive" evaluations. Of course, with "false positives" an organization goes a "wrong way" for a short term, but with the chance to discover superior configurations in a longer term [15], [34]. In particular, imperfect knowledge may afford the opportunity to leave a local peak in the fitness landscape. We argue that this effect is the more likely the more interactions among decisions exist: as is well investigated for the NK model in literature (e.g. [29], [30]), with higher levels of complexity the more rugged is the fitness landscapes and the more local maxima exist, and, hence, the search process is more likely to stick to a local maximum. Inaccuracies induce diversity in the search process, and "false positive" alterations, though short-term harmful, provide the chance to discover superior levels of performance and, eventually, the global maximum in the long-term. The results provide support for this intuition: In the "high complexity-decentral mode" scenario the relative frequency of how often the global maximum is found is lower with perfect evaluations than with noisy accounting systems as far as they measure the status quo.

In the next step we analyze the role of the *coordination mode*. Firstly, results indicate that with the proposal mode (i.e., with involving the main office in decision-making) the range of differences in speed and level of performance among the various forms of management accounting systems. Hence, in a way, *with introducing the information-processing power of the main office the relevance of the setting of the accounting system tends to be reduced*.

Secondly, our results (Fig. 1A versus 1B and Fig. 2A versus 2B) also suggest that with inaccurate judgmental information in the proposal mode organizations miss the chance to achieve those performance levels that can be reached with perfect evaluations. In order to provide an explanation we find it helpful to remember that in the proposal mode the status quo only is abandoned if two conditions are met. First, at least, one department has to discover a partial vector that promises a higher compensation to the respective department head (otherwise he/she would not propose the alteration); second, the main office has to accept the proposal. Hence, for being implemented each proposal has to pass an additional instance and, hence, it is less likely that false positive evaluations on the departments' site affect final decisions since the main office may detect the false positive evaluations [22].

However, by that, the "false positives" are less likely to do their beneficial work as discussed above. Furthermore, "false negative" evaluations by the main office might occur and the organization is more likely to suffer from inertia compared to the decentral mode. With more inertia the fitness landscape is less likely to be "explored" and this reduces benefits of the "stepwise refinement" and "immediate adjustment" accounting systems: To enfold the full potential of "learning" management

accounting systems (settings 3 and 4) a certain exploration of the decisional space is required, which apparently might not be given in the proposal mode.

V. CONCLUSION

The results provide broad support for the intuition that improving judgmental information by measurements of actual values in management accounting systems leads to more effective adaptive search processes for higher levels of organizational performance.

However, the results might throw some new light on basic design choices of management accounting systems: apparently, the contribution of improving information accuracy in management accounting systems subtly interferes with coordination need and mode. In particular, results do not universally support conventional wisdom that better accounting systems are more beneficial when decision-problems are highly complex. Furthermore, our results suggest that inaccuracies might have their positive sides compared to perfect information for complex decisions - given that inaccuracies are accompanied by decentral coordination.

Moreover, it appears that with more central coordination the relevance of improving information quality in the management accounting system decreased. In short, to a certain extent management accounting systems and central coordination power seem to serve as substitutes. Hence, taking into account that improvements of management accounting systems usually are not costless, these findings put claims for investments in perspective.

At the same time, our analysis is subject to several limitations which should be overcome in further research. First of all, it should be mentioned that in our model the contributions of management accounting systems to ex ante-evaluations of alternatives is represented in a rather coarse way. Of course, more sophisticated learning and forecasting methods could be integrated (i.e., methods applied in plan cost accounting systems). Moreover, the ex ante-evaluations of our decision-makers suffer from imperfect knowledge about the "production functions" (in terms of the relation between choice and organizational outcome), but the model presented does neither reflect conflicts of interests nor decision-making under uncertainty. Obvious extensions of the model could overcome these shortages, especially in order to address the function of management accounting systems to update beliefs of decision-makers as elaborated by Christensen [3].

Furthermore, organizations apply various strategies and coordination modes to deal with imperfectly known "production functions". In further extensions these strategies could be reflected in the model as well as the decision-making biases (e.g., status-quo bias) that decision-makers suffer from [11]. Including these aspects could reveal further insights into the relative benefits of basic design options of management accounting systems.

References

[1] J. S. Demski, and G. A. Feltham, *Cost Determination: A Conceptual Approach*. Ames: Iowa State Univ. Press, 1976.

[2] C. T. Horngren, S. M. Datar, G. Foster, M. Rajan, and C. Ittner, *Cost Accounting: A Managerial Emphasis*. New York: Prentice Hall, 2005.

[3] J. Christensen, "Accounting Errors and Errors of Accounting," *The Accounting Review*, vol. 85, no. 6, pp. 1827–1838, 2010.

[4] H. A. Simon, "A Behavioral Model of Rational Choice," *Quarterly Journal of Economics*, vol. 69, no. 1, pp. 99–118, Feb. 1955.

[5] C. T. Horngren, A. Bhimani, S. M. Datar, and G. Foster, *Management and Cost Accounting*. 3. ed., Essex: Pearson, 2005.

[6] J. Marschak, "Towards an Economic Theory of Organization and Information." in *Decision Processes*, R. M. Thrall, C. Coombs, and R.L. Davis, Eds. New York: Wiley, 1954, pp. 187--220.

[7] J. Galbraith, *Designing Complex Organisations*. Reading: Addison-Wesley, 1973.

[8] M. J. Ginzberg, "An Organizational Contingencies View of Accounting and Information Systems Implementation," *Accounting, Organizations and Society*, vol. 5, pp. 369–382, 1980.

[9] R. L. Ackoff, "Management Misinformation Systems," *Management Science*, vol. 14, no. 4, B-147–B-156, 1967.

[10] R. L. Keeney, "Decision Analysis," *Operations Research*, vol. 30, no. 5, pp. 803–838, 1982.

[11] A. Tversky, and D. Kahneman, "Judgment under Uncertainty: Heuristics and Biases," *Science,* vol. 185, no. 4157, pp. 1124–1131, Sept. 1974.

[12] R. M. Bushman, and R. J. Indjejikian, "Aggregate Performance Measures in Business Unit Manager Compensation: The Role of Intrafirm Interdependencies," *Journal of Accounting Research*, vol. 33, supplement, pp. 101-129, 1995.

[13] R. P. Brief, "Accounting Error as a Factor in Business History," *Accounting, Business and Financial History,* vol. 1, pp. 7–21, 1990.

[14] J. P. Davis, K. M. Eisenhardt, and C. B. Bingham, "Developing theory through simulation methods," *Academy of Management Review*, vol. 32, no. 2, pp. 480–499, 2007.

[15] F. Wall, "The (Beneficial) Role of Informational Imperfections in Enhancing Organisational Performance," in *Progress in Artificial Economics*, M. LiCalzi, L. Milone, and P. Pellizzari, Eds. Berlin: Springer-Verlag, 2010, pp. 115–126.

[16] S. Leitner, "Interactions among Biases in Costing Systems: A Simulation Approach," in *Managing Market Complexity. The Approach for Artificial Economics.* S. Alfarano, A. Teglio, E. Camacho-Cuena, and M. Ginés-Vilar, Eds., Heidelberg: Springer-Verlag, 2012, pp. 209–220.

[17] S. Leitner, "*A Simulation Analysis of Interactions among Intended Biases in Costing Systems and their Effects on the Accuracy of Decision-Influencing Information* (Accepted for publication)," *Central European Journal of Operations Research*, DOI: 10.1007/s10100-012-0275-2, online-first since Nov. 2012.

[18] F. Wall, "Comparing Basic Design Options for Management Accounting Systems with an Agent-Based Simulation," in *Distributed Computing and Artificial Intelligence* , S. Omatu, J. Neves, J. M. C. Rodriguez, J.F. Paz Santana, and S.R. Gonzalez, Eds. Heidelberg: Springer-Verlag, 2013, pp. 409–418.

[19] S. Datar, and M. Gupta, "Aggregation, Specification and Measurement Error in Product Costing," *The Accounting Review*, vol. 69, no. 4, pp. 567–591, Oct. 1994.

[20] E. Labro, and M. Vanhoucke, "A Simulation Analysis of Interactions among Errors in Costing Systems," *The Accounting Review*, vol. 82, no. 4, pp. 939–962, July 2007.

[21] R. K. Sah, and J. E. Stiglitz, "Human Fallibility and Economic Organization," *American Economic Review*, vol. 75, no. 2, pp. 292–297, 1985.

[22] R. K. Sah, and J. E. Stiglitz, "The Architecture of Economic Systems: Hierarchies and Polyarchies," *American Economic Review,* vol. 76, no. 4, pp. 716–727, 1986.

[23] R. K. Sah, and J. E. Stiglitz, "Committees, Hierarchies and Polyarchies," *The Economic Journal*, vol. 98, pp. 451–470, June 1988.

[24] W. T. H. Koh, "Human Fallibility and Sequential Decision Making: Hierarchy versus Polyarchy" *Journal of Economic Behavior and Organization,* vol. 18, no. 3, pp. 317–345, 1992.

[25] W. T. H. Koh," Making Decisions in Committees: A Human Fallibility Approach," *Journal of Economic Behavior and Organization*, vol. 23, no. 2, pp. 195–214, 1994.

[26] B. Visser, "Organizational communication structure and performance," *Journal of Economic Behavior and Organization*, vol. 42, no. 2, pp. 231–252, 2000.

[27] M. Christensen, and T. Knudsen, "Design of decision-making organizations," *Management Science*, vol. 56, no. 1, pp. 71–89, Jan. 2010.

[28] S. A. Kauffman, *The Origins of Order: Self-Organization and Selection in Evolution*. Oxford: Oxford Univ. Press, 1993.

[29] S. A. Kauffman, and S. Levin, "Towards a General Theory of Adaptive Walks on Rugged Landscapes," *Journal of Theoretical Biology*, vol. 128, no. 1, pp. 11–45, Sept. 1987.

[30] J. W. Rivkin, and N. Siggelkow, "Balancing Search and Stability: Interdependencies among Elements of Organizational Design," *Management Science*, vol. 49, no. 3, pp. 290–311, March 2003.

[31] N. Siggelkow, and J. W. Rivkin, "Speed and Search: Designing Organizations for Turbulence and Complexity," *Organization Science*, vol. 16, no. 2, pp. 101–122, March-April 2005.

[32] Rivkin, J.W., Siggelkow, N.: Patterned Interactions in Complex Systems: Implications for Exploration. Management Science 53, 1068–1085 (2007)

[33] M. Chang, and J. E. Harrington, "Agent-Based Models of Organizations" in *Handbook of Computational Economics*, vol. 2, L. Tesfatsion, and K. L. Judd, Eds. Amsterdam: Elsevier 2005, pp. 1273–1337.

[34] T. Knudsen, and D. A. Levinthal, "Two Faces of Search: Alternative Generation and Alternative Evaluation," *Organization Science*, vol. 18, no. 1, pp. 39–54, Jan.-Feb. 2007.

[35] B. Levitan, and S. A. Kauffman, "Adaptive Walks with Noisy Fitness Measurements," *Molecular Diversity*, vol. 1, no. 1, pp. 53–68, Sept. 1995.

[36] G. Dosi, D. Levinthal, and L. Marengo. L, "Bridging Contested Terrain: Linking Incentive-based and Learning Perspectives on Organizational Evolution," *Industrial and Corporate Change*, vol. 12, no. 2, pp. 413–436, 2003.

[37] T. W. Malone, and K. Crowstone, "*The interdisciplinary study of coordination*," ACM Computing Surveys, vol. 26, no. 1, pp. 87–119, 1994.

[38] J. D. Thompson. *Organizations in action. Social science bases of administrative theory*. New York: McGraw-Hill 1967.

[39] S. W. Tee, and P. L. Bowen, P. Doyle, and F. H. Rohde, "Factors Influencing Organizations to Improve Data Quality in their Information Systems," *Accounting and Finance*, vol. 47, no. 2, pp. 335–355, 2007.

[40] T. C. Redman, *Data Quality for the Information Age*. Boston/London: Artech House, 1996.

Friederike Wall earned her Diploma for Business Economics in 1988 and her Doctoral degree in 1991, both at the Georg-August-Univesität Göttingen, Germany. In 1996 she received the "venia legendi" (Habilitation for Business Economics) from the Universität Hamburg, Germany. After being a scientific Project Referent for Accounting in the context of the implementation of SAP R/3 at Max-Planck Society, Munich, Germany she became Full Professor of Business Administration, esp. Controlling and Information Management at the Universität Witten/Herdecke, Germany. Since 2009 she is Full Professor and Head of the Department of Controlling and Strategic Management at the Alpen-Adria-Universität Klagenfurt, Austria. Prof. Wall's scientific work is focused on management accounting systems and the quality of the information provided by these systems. Her main research approach is defined by agent-based simulation methods and agent-based technologies.

## 31

Review of current student-monitoring techniques used in elearning-focused recommender systems and learning analytics. The Experience API & LIME model case study

Alberto Corbi, Daniel Burgos

UNIR Research,Universidad Internacional de La Rioja - UNIR

Abstract — **Recommender systems require input information in order to properly operate and deliver content or behaviour suggestions to end users. eLearning scenarios are no exception. Users are current students and recommendations can be built upon paths (both formal and informal), relationships, behaviours, friends, followers, actions, grades, tutor interaction, etc. A recommender system must somehow retrieve, categorize and work with all these details. There are several ways to do so: from raw and inelegant database access to more curated web APIs or even via HTML scrapping. New server-centric user-action logging and monitoring standard technologies have been presented in past years by several groups, organizations and standard bodies. The Experience API (xAPI), detailed in this article, is one of these. In the first part of this paper we analyse current learner-monitoring techniques as an initialization phase for eLearning recommender systems. We next review standardization efforts in this area; finally, we focus on xAPI and the potential interaction with the LIME model, which will be also summarized below.**

Keywords — **LIME model, eLearning, Conceptual Educational Model, Rule-based recommender system, Informal learning, Social interaction, Learning Tool Interoperability, User monitoring**

I. INTRODUCTION: REVIEW OF RECOMMENDER ENGINES, ELEARNING AND NEED FOR USER INPUT DATA

RECOMMENDER engines deliver suggestions based on collected information on preferences, general user behaviour and even items bought or content searched. Trendy online stores and services massively apply this approach ([HYPERLINK \l "1167344" 1]). The information can be obtained explicitly (by processing users' manual tiering) or implicitly, typically by monitoring users' behaviour, such as songs downloaded, applications launched, chat transcriptions, web sites visited, PDFs read, or ebooks transmitted to ePub readers (2]).

Recommenders can also make use of demographic info and social information (e.g., followers, e-friends, posts, replies, chat rooms, and others), as well as geographical location data or even health signals (e.g., pedometers, blood pressure).

Collaborative filters ([HYPERLINK \l "marlinmodeling" 3]) are very often used by recommender systems along with content-, knowledge- and social-based filters. Implementation of these filters has grown as access to the Internet has become more widespread in recent years. They can be used for any type of reachable media (e.g., movies, music, television, and books) and in many different scenarios, such as eLearning, e-commerce, mobile applications, search, dating, etc. These filters need to access as much of a user's navigation and behaviour history as possible in order to offer fine-tuned purchase options or action tips.

Memory-based methods use similarities and ratings from all users who have manually expressed their preferences/level of satisfaction on a given object/issue. These similarities represent the distance between two users and their tiered records. Model-based methods establish first the sets of similar users by using Bayesian classifiers, neural networks and fuzzy systems. Generally, commercial recommender engines use memory-based methods. On the other hand, model-based methods are usually associated with research environments, including eLearning. Hybrid techniques can also be applied and have been demonstrated to be of much importance to assist and guide users through systems. Hybrid recommenders merge different types of techniques in order to get the most out of each of them. Finally, we have rule-based recommenders, like LIME, which will be analysed below. In rule-based systems, a set of conditional filters are manually defined and triggered when necessary in order to deliver the appropriate recommendation to the user/learner.

The increase in the attention paid by the research community to recommender systems is striking, as has already been pointed out in 4]. Figure 1 shows, on the Y-axis, the number of cited papers from each year as of 2013. The size of each bubble corresponds to the number of proceeding articles for that given year. It can be noted that there is a peak of interest around 2009.

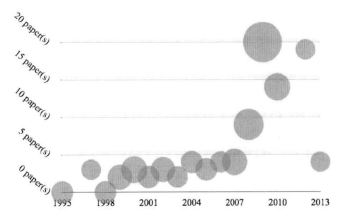

Fig. 1. # of papers and workshops related to subject *recommendation*

With the development of sophisticated eLearning environments and Learning Management Systems (LMS) ([HYPERLINK \l "abedour" 5]), *personalization* is also becoming an important feature. Personalized learning occurs when eLearning platforms are designed according to educational experiences that fit the needs, goals, and interests of each individual learner. Personalization can be achieved using different recommendation techniques, very similar to those just summarized. Ideally, recommender systems in eLearning environments should assist students in finding relevant learning actions and materials that perfectly match their profile and the best way towards self-education. The right time, the right context, and the right way are also critical. Recommenders should also keep learners motivated and enable them to complete their academic activities in an effective and efficient way. Personalization should take place, not only on enrolment-limited online campuses or *Small Private Online Courses* (site courses, college classes, student groups, etc.), but also on the now trendy MOOCs: *Massive Open Online Courses* environments (6], [HYPERLINK \l "mooeurope" 7]), where enrolment rate can be up to a few thousand students. In other words, a recommender system should have the ability to efficiently scale up or down independently of the number of students and without losing sight of the goal of improving individualized education.

Recommender systems (especially in eLearning) can also suffer from the *cold-start* problem. Cold start occurs when there is an initial lack of input data (ratings, logged actions from users, etc.) to trigger or initialize the appropriate algorithm. We can distinguish two main kinds of cold-start variants: *new item* and *new user* ([4]). The new-item problem arises because new items entered do not have initial ratings/inputs from users. Also, a priori, *new users* in a system might not yet have provided any input info, and therefore cannot receive any personalized recommendations.

Independently of the algorithm used, the identifiable potential issues (like cold start) and the scenario of application, recommender systems require input data in order to behave properly (8]). This data can be manually entered ([HYPERLINK \l "Bobadilla20111310" 9]) by the user (ratings, explicit opinions, etc.) or implicitly obtained by

monitoring software. In an eLearning environment, the latter approach is more likely to be the chosen one.

We now list the most common techniques used for monitoring learners' actions in an LMS. The next sections will present the Experience API and other standardization efforts as new and modern ways of logging learner actions, chosen materials, student paths, etc., and serving them to recommender systems. Finally, we introduce the rule-based LIME model and discuss how can it be fed from an Experience API Learning Record Store repository (which we will also discuss) in order to properly operate and deliver rule-based recommendations to students.

II. BASIC SYSTEM-DEPENDENT MONITORING TECHNIQUES

There exist three main different non-standard ways of interacting with Learning Management Systems (and electronic systems in general) and extracting user/learner data (also summarized in Figure 2):

A. Web Services

The first and most immediate way to obtain learner input data is through LMS-dependent web services and API calls. Modern LMS (10]) do usually offer simple, elegant, industry-standard and compelling ways (WSDL, SOAP, RPC and REST) of accessing their internal information and retrieving needed data. This approach has one main drawback: not every service needed is implemented and/or enabled by default. This could be easily tackled if we are granted access to the LMS infrastructure in order to add these missing *sockets* or activate existing *disabled-by-default* ones. However, this is not always possible in many scenarios (e.g., proprietary cloud-based campus environments). Another clear disadvantage is that developed web services are very unlikely to be compatible between two distinct LMS, making it necessary to re-code each of them for every platform and software version.

B. Scrapping

Web scrapping consists of, on the one hand, running automated HTTP(S) requests that retrieve the same pages and HTML documents as a user would fetch by operating a web browser manually ([HYPERLINK \l "6112910" 11]). On the other hand, after such requests have succeeded, data can be distilled, examined and applied to some sort of scripting/analytics. Most HTTP command line (CLI) client programs/libraries allow authentication and form submission, which is usually enough for most purposes. Although web scrapping seems the most compatible form of mechanized data-mining, we still face a minor problem: some LMS make huge use of Javascript for accessing resources and building routes to them. In this scenario, CLI web clients are not enough and should be superseded by what are known as headless web browsers, explained in previous studies (12], [HYPERLINK \l "Grigalis:jucs_20_2:unsupervised_structu" 13]). Such browsers are scriptable, run without any user interface, and best of all understand and can execute Javascript code without user intervention.

The result of a scrapping operation is usually an HTML file or a set of files of this kind, which should be processed afterwards (14]) in order to extract the desired monitoring information. As HTML is a descendant of XML, any XML parsing technique (XPath, XQuery, XSLT, etc.) and technology applies here, e.g., Nokogiri ([HYPERLINK \l "Hun13" 15]).

C. Raw database access

This is by far the most-often-seen method in the literature, which implies direct access to the system database. This approach has several advantages and disadvantages. The main advantage is speed, since no intermediaries, software layers or no other different APIs play a role in data retrieval (apart from the SQL engine and the APIs themselves). The most significant downside is possible database scheme migrations and incompatibilities as new versions of the server software are deployed.

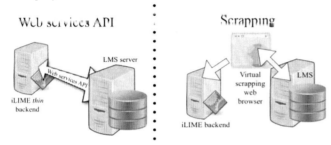

Fig. 2. Basic web monitoring techniques

These three techniques spring into action at some point or another of the student data-mining process, in different ways and with different goals. Some monitoring models, as seen in 16] and [HYPERLINK \l "Mazza04gismo:a" 17], make use of reports and logs derived from data contained in server temporary files. Other research efforts, such as the one presented in 18], have used closed-systems and setups, with their own specific monitoring methods and engines. The study presented in [HYPERLINK \l "5561329" 19] makes use of quiz results as input for a research recommender model. The authors of 20] and [HYPERLINK \l "6033004" 21] feed their recommenders with web-browsing behaviour. In22], the authors gain direct access to a Moodle instance database in order to boot their *Predictive a priori algorithm*. The model in [HYPERLINK \l "ElB10" 23] initially presents students with a test to identify his/her personality in Myers-Briggs dimensions. The authors in 24] suggest obtaining input data not only from the server and client sides, but also from proxy servers. In [HYPERLINK \l "Kardan:2012aa" 25], content recommendation needs each student to self-monitor him/herself: learners estimate different indexes themselves and compare them with actual values, which are retrieved by the system. The model presented in 26] uses the *AprioriAll* algorithm to immediately build sequences from server logs, which are used in conjunction with tags in order to deliver recommendations. The model in [HYPERLINK \l "conf/wec/WangH05" 27] also makes use of the AprioriAll

algorithm using only web logs. In 28], again, only web-browsing activities of learners are monitored, but these are then subdivided into *web content mining*, *web structure mining* and *web usage mining* realms.

We also find learning research software prototypes, like the PSLC Datashop initiative from the Pittsburgh Science of Learning Center [HYPERLINK \l "Stamper:2011:MED:2026506.2026609" 29], which has defined its own XML DTD schema as a logging scaffold for their *Tutor* learning research platform. Some approaches rather build a dedicated tool or patch applied to a LMS, as in 30] with the MOCLog project for Moodle.

The Experience API and other standardization proposals for the monitoring phase, presented below, advocate a completely new and cohesive approach to this critical phase in the recommendation/learning analytics workflow.

II. STANDARD SPECIFICATIONS FOR MONITORING

The aforementioned non-standardized approaches to user/learner monitoring can be applied on fully controlled scenarios and research projects. However, they turn out to be unsatisfactory in real academic environments managed by third-party institutions.

There exist a few proposals that aim at standardizing the monitoring and logging of user actions. Almost all are based on the *Resource Description Framework*, or RDF [HYPERLINK \l "Pan09" 31]. The idea behind RDF is something called the *triple*. A triple can really be condensed to a plain sentence structure:

- subject
- phrase that characterizes a relationship
- object.

Example: Daniel – *is the author of* – this paper.

Triples are extremely useful and simple, and provide a grammar for the so-called *semantic web*.

Also, some of these specifications include some sort of software and database back-end service, linked APIs and query language that allow learning platforms to send and store monitoring data and third-party learning analytics software to query and retrieve analysable data. We summarize here the most important and paradigmatic monitoring specs:

The **Caliper** framework/**Sensor** API was proposed by the IMS Global Consortium and follows the triple metaphor. It is built around the following concepts (32]): *Learning Metric Profiles* that provide an activity-centric focus to standardize actions and related context; *Learning Sensor API* and *Learning Events*, which drive tools and an associated analytics service solution; and finally, Learning Tool Interoperability (LTI), which enhances and integrates standardized learning measurements with tool interoperability.

IEEE 1484.11.1/IEEE 1484.11.2 ([HYPERLINK \l "IEE05" 33]) provides a complex data model structure for tracking information on student interactions with learning content. Additionally, an API allows digital educational content coming from the LMS and third-party services to query and share collected information.

JSON Activity Streams (34]) is the name of the specification published by IBM, Google, MySpace, Facebook, VMware and Microsoft. Its goal is to provide sufficient metadata about an activity such that a consumer of the data can present them to a user in a rich human-friendly format. It does not provide a logging service, just the specification of the message format.

Finally, we also have the **Experience API**, which will be addressed in the next section.

Security and privacy models can also be applied in all specs cited above. Network communications can be encrypted and the subject can be anything but the learner's real name. Learning analytics researchers and logging storage implementers are responsible for the ethical usage of the compiled info coming from student monitoring. As with any other area related to digital mining, trust, accountability and transparency must always prevail ([HYPERLINK \l "Par14" 35]).

III. THE EXPERIENCE API SPECIFICATION

The Experience API (or *xAPI* for short) is an eLearning monitoring specification developed by Rustici Software and the Advanced Distributed Learning Initiative (ADL), and is aimed at defining a data model for logging data about students' learning paths (36]). It also furnishes an API for sharing these data between remote systems, as we will see later. The Experience API allows, among other things, the tracking of games and simulations, real-world behaviour, learning paths and academic achievements. xAPI defines independent mechanisms, protocols, specifications, agreements and software tools for monitoring any imaginable scenario (Figure 3): from online campuses and student behaviour to workforce control ([HYPERLINK \l "6530268" 37]).

Fig. 3. Examples of usage of the Experience API

xAPI also uses JSON to transfer states/sentences to a central web service. This web service allows clients to read and write data in the form of *sentence objects* that share the foundations of the aforementioned triple scheme. In their simplest conception, sentences are in the form of *actor*, *verb* and *object/activity*, like the examples in Figure 4. A JSON xAPI message could resemble the following:

```
{"id": "3f2ef28f-ef1a-4a1f-9f5e",
 "actor": {
  "name": "Peter",
  "mbox": "mailto:some@new.user",
  "objectType": "Agent"
 },
 "verb": {
  "id": "http://.../verbs/solved",
  "display": {
   "und": "solved"
  }
 },
 "context": {
  "contextActivities": {
   "parent": [
    {
     "id": "http://../objects/problems",
     "objectType": "Activity"
    }
   ]
  }
 }
}}
```

More complex statement forms can be used and we will elaborate more on them in the next section. The set of verbs and objects an institution can work with is called *vocabulary*. Each institution can define its own vocabulary with no restriction as long as an URL links back each verb and object to a JSON stream describing it.

Fig. 4. Some examples of xAPI sentences

The Experience API was released, as version 1.0, in April 2013, and there are, as of today, over 100 adopters, projects and companies involved, such as those in Figure 5.

Fig. 5. Some adopters of the Experience API specification

The specification also contemplates a query API to help find logged statements, and performs some analytics (averages, aggregation, etc.) on the data. Finally, the Experience API is an open-source and free initiative, whose source code and specifications are open to anyone.

IV.   EXPERIENCE API LRS AS AN ELEARNING MONITORING ENGINE

The core of the Experience API is the Learning Record Store (LRS). The LRS is a specific module for data storage that allows an LMS (or any other social platform) to report tracking information on the learning experience. At any time, an LMS can send collected data over the network to an Experience API web service. An LRS is nothing more and nothing less than a wrapper or API software layer to a SQL database (initially, a PostgresSQL instance in the original Rustici implementation), as can be appreciated from Figure 6. This free LRS implementation was open-sourced by ADL (available at its Github repository) and is based on the Python computer language and on the publicly acclaimed Django web framework.

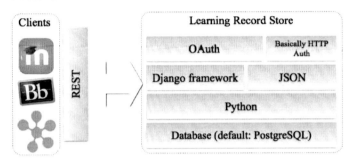

Fig. 6. Usual LRS software stack and interaction

The *learner (actor)*, *verb* and *object/activity* elements explained above are mandatory when talking to the LRS. However, they can be complemented with *result* and a *context* extra fields with additional information.

Students who interact with educational content via different systems or tools will leave traces in the LRS; each of these tools, if appropriately designed, will provide a totally different actor/user ID to preserve anonymity.

The *verb* element is a key part of an LRS communication, because it describes the action performed by the student. A URL must also be attached to the verb JSON property, pointing to its definition. This definition is composed of a name, a description, and a brief text suggesting plausible uses. In an eLearning environment, a verb is usually employed in its past tense form and could be something like: "read", "tried", "failed", "passed", "experienced", etc.

The *object/activity* part of the statement refers to "what" was experienced in the action defined in the verb, and usually corresponds to the learning activity (webinar, wiki, chat room, forum, mail message, etc.). Objects/activities must also embody a URL pointing to their rationale, which can include other information such as a description of the learning activity, verbs that can apply, possible results and usage suggestions.

The *result* component provides the denouement to the statement. It includes score, level of success and completion fields.

The context part adds more details to the overall statement,

like the relationship of the activity with other activities, its order in the learning stream, or the teacher's name.

To every element in a sentence (actor, verb, context, etc.) sent to the LRS can be added, if needed, any type of pair key/value with extra information. It is even possible to add localization information so that an element can be perfectly identified in all possible languages.

As introduced in Figure 6, an LRS must also implement REST calls for data transfer (PUT, POST, GET and DELETE). The Experience API can make use of either OAuth or HTTP Basic Authentication when communicating with the outside world, ensuring a certified and secured dialogue between clients (usually an LMS) and the LRS service.

One of the key aspects of the LRS architecture is that it can be implemented in shared cloud ecosystems, allowing communications from very different eLearning platforms and academic institutions. In other words, monitoring data can be uniformly stored, allowing rapid, vast and democratic access to learning analytics information. Also, as LRS servers can integrate data from many different sources and from the same user/learner in a harmonized way, recommender systems can reduce the effects of possible cold-start scenarios.

Some companies are beginning to offer corporate cloud LRS services at different price tiers: Rustici Software, Saltbox, Learning Locker, Biscue, Clear, Grassblade, among others. Some also include compelling online analytics tools.

There exist some free LRS *hosting* services but mainly for testing and technology promotion purposes, and not applicable for research or production environments. It is worth mentioning the service run by ADL (lrs.adlnet.gov/xAPI) and the one deployed by Rustici Software (demo.tincanapi.com).

V. THE LIME MODEL AND THE LRS

Now that we have reviewed the most prominent monitoring techniques and introduced a few recent efforts towards regulation, we should ask how a real recommender engine could work with and benefit from a specific RDF-based source. The Experience API and the LIME model, explained below, are chosen.

The LIME model, presented in 38], is a tutor-lecturer-crafted rule-based recommender grounded on four separate pedagogical components strongly evident in all stages of education (Figure 7):

☐ Learning, or what every learner needs to do in order to assimilate and build knowledge on his or her own.

☐ Interaction, or relationships established, activities and academic interaction between students, leading to the acquisition of knowledge and competencies.

☐ Mentoring, or what teachers/tutors give relevance to.

☐ Evaluation, or officially graded activities, in every single category above listed.

Lecturers-tutors must design a strategy for each of his/her courses. The model codifies this strategy for a course or class group by using settings and categories.

A *course setting* is the balance between *formal* and *informal* scenarios. In this context, *formal* means a regular academic programme with regular evaluation means (e.g. graded exams); *informal* means continuous evaluation and user activity inside the Learning Management System and every tool linked to it (e.g. Social Networks or repository). The system collects specific inputs from both settings, keeping an overall balance of 100%. For instance, if the designer requires just a *formal* setting, the balance should be *Informal*: 100% - *Formal*: 0%.

Furthermore, a learning scenario must be defined as the balance between the Learning, Interaction, Mentoring, and Evaluation, in combination with the Formal and Informal settings categories. In the LIME model, every category and setting are assigned with a specific weight (w_i), keeping an overall balance of 100%.

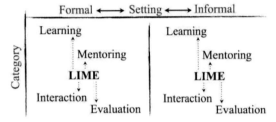

Fig. 7. Categories and settings in the LIME model

In the LIME model each input (action performed by a student in the eLearning platform or Social Network) is attributed a category and a weight, assigned by the teacher/tutor.

An example of model configuration for a specific site can be found in Figure 8. Based on these components, tutors can manually define and parameterize recommendation rules, which will only trigger a message to the student if conditions regarding categories, inputs and settings are met.

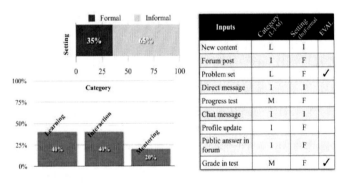

Fig. 8. Sample configuration of the LIME model for a specific course site

LIME is therefore a tutor-lecturer-crafted, rule-based recommender system for cloud-institutional learning environments (SPOCs or MOOCs), which contrasts with other recommendation paradigms reviewed in previous sections. LIME's goal is simply to improve learning efficiency, and to facilitate the learning itinerary of every student by a personalised recommendation set.

LIME can be fed from learner inputs in a variety of ways. However, our model can also be initialized with tracked data

stored in a xAPI LRS instance/server if we make some assumptions.

How can LIME inputs be built out of information stored in the LRS? A LIME model input has to define an action and a context in which a learner performs this action:

- participation in chat
- answer in main forum thread
- message to tutor
- resolution of problem set
- formal broadcast mail to mates
- ratio of emoticons used in communications
- ...

xAPI verbs and objects, taken in an isolated way, are not sufficient. However, a joint entity composed of a verb plus an xAPI object makes more sense in our model, as shown in Figure 9:

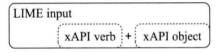

Fig. 9. LIME Inputs from xAPI sentences

As stated above, verbs and objects in the xAPI specification must be backed by JSON composites with information about meaning and usage tips. It is up to the implementer to define which verbs and objects best represent the scenario to be tracked and monitored. Let us take a look at the sample verbs and activities available on the official Experience API site (adlnet.gov/expapi). In Figure 10 are listed all the verbs and activities the LRS can store and their possible combinations to build a meaningful and compatible LIME input.

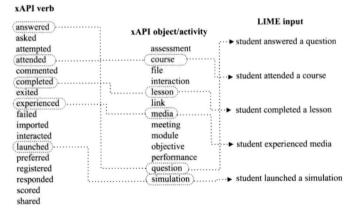

Fig. 10 From xAPI verbs and objects to LIME inputs

As explained in previous paragraphs and as part of the model configuration, each input should be assigned a weight (w_i), a category and a setting. These parameters should not reside on the LRS but on the LIME system's own configuration repository. In other words, LIME administrators should maintain an updated *equivalency list* between LRS vocabulary and LIME inputs. These inputs will then interplay with rules (Figure 11), which are, in turn, based on *predicate filtering*. Predicates are applied over collections of inputs and highly resemble W3C XQuery or ECMA LINQ, detailed in [HYPERLINK \l "Saigaonkar:2010:XFS:1858378.1858429" 39],40] and [HYPERLINK \l "Pardede:jucs_15_10:sqlxml_hierarchical_" 41].

Fig. 11: Predicate filtering in LIME

As LIME was developed as a Basic Learning Tool Interoperability (Basic LTI) application, this equivalency list can even be stored in the LMS database through the LTI Settings API specification, part of LTI 1.0 and above. The model thus remains free from external configuration files or own database management. In order to save this list, it is only necessary to send a POST HTTP request like the one in the following example:

```
POST http://server/imsblis/service/
id=832823923899238
lti_message_type=basic-lti-savesetting
lti_version=LTI-1p0
setting="participated+chat=message   in   chat
room; experienced+lesson=read text"
oauth_callback=about:blank
oauth_consumer_key=1213415
oauth_nonce=14c6211cc66d87644f0855511
oauth_signature=Ik1lkkZ1qfShYBYE+BhC
oauth_signature_method=HMAC-SHA1
oauth_timestamp=1338872426
oauth_version=1.0
```

It is important to notice that LMS must be LTI compatible and support the Settings API protocol.

VI. LRS DATA AGGREGATION AND LIME RULES

Once LRS sentences are stored and an agreement between LIME inputs and these has been established, we have all the necessary ingredients to trigger recommender rules and deliver recommendations to students, if applicable. However, rules in LIME cannot operate upon atomic and individual LRS records, but only upon averages and aggregated substantial data, which offer a more equalized view of the learner situation. An example of this aggregation procedure is presented in Figure 12:

Figure 12: Aggregation of LRS sentences

Mathematically:

$$(\text{LIME input})_i = \frac{\sum_{j=0}^{n} (\text{LRS statement})_j}{w_i}$$

These aggregation operations are covered by the xAPI standard as well. The Experience API provides a query language to easily data-mine an LRS. For instance, the following code collects all the times the user "John" has tried an exam, and returns an aggregated result:

```
stmts.where(
    'actor.name = "John" and ('+
        'verb.id =
"http://adlnet.gov/expapi/verbs/passed"'+
        ' or '+
        'verb.id =
"http://adlnet.gov/expapi/verbs/failed"'+
        ')')
```

The default (and so far only) implementation of this query language is the ADL.Collection API, written in Javascript and ready to be used in browsers or on the server-side with NodeJS. There are two versions of this API: CollectionSync and CollectionAsync. They are almost the same, but the Async version runs the queries in a separate worker thread. The downside of this is that the statements must be serialized and passed into the worker, which can be slow. On the other hand, the user interface is more responsive.

VII. CONCLUSION

This paper describes incipient technologies and steps taken towards the dissemination of standardized monitoring engines. The engine mainly underlined in this paper is the Experience API, or xAPI for short. xAPI has been designed to store user data in a simple, centric, standard, client agnostic and powerful way. We also discuss the suitability of recommender systems in general and of the LIME recommender model in particular. LIME is a rule-based recommendation model. Rules in LIME require inputs (e.g. learner data and actions taken) that can be obtained in a variety of ways, like user tracking and interaction, user performance, or user profile.

We also perform a survey of the most common monitoring techniques and how they have been implemented in previous research projects related to recommender systems and learning analytics in general. With this review we illustrate there is no agreed way on how to register learner events. All mentioned techniques incorporate a certain percentage of dependency on the system software being monitored.

Finally, we present the required adaptations and modifications that xAPI sentences need in order to build LIME-compatible inputs and how those can be aggregated and mined in order to feed system rules. On rule execution, our model delivers suggestions to students and learners. The xAPI spec atomizes learner actions in verbs and objects, which must be syntactically combined in order to obtain the aforementioned inputs. These combinations must be designed and listed by the tutor/teacher and handed over to our model. We suggest this equivalency list resides in the LMS's own database space, thanks to the LTI Settings API. The Experience API also offers native aggregation-statistical tools, which turn out to be of great help in this process.

ACKNOWLEDGMENT

This research is partially funded by UNIR Research (http://research.unir.net), Universidad Internacional de La Rioja (UNIR, http://www.unir.net), under the Research Support Strategy (2013-2015), Research Group TELSOCK.

VIII. REFERENCES

[1] G. Linden, B. Smith, and J. York, "Amazon.com recommendations: item-to-item collaborative filtering," Internet Computing, IEEE, vol. 7, no. 1, pp. 76-80, Jan 2003.

[2] F. Ricci, L. Rokach, B. Shapira, and P.B. Kantor, Recommender Systems Handbook.: Springer, 2010.

[3] Benjamin Marlin, "Modeling User Rating Profiles For Collaborative Filtering," in NIPS'03, 2003.

[4] J. Bobadilla, F. Ortega, A. Hernando, and A. Gutiérrez, "Recommender Systems Survey," Know.-Based Syst., vol. 46, pp. 109-132, Journal of Universal Computer Science 2013.

[5] M. Aberdour, "Open Source Learning Management Systems: Emerging open source LMS markets," 2007.

[6] Fran, Martin Ebner, Alexander Pohl, and Behnam Taraghi, "Interaction in Massive Courses," Journal of Universal Computer Science, vol. 20, no. 1, pp. 1-5, jan 2014.

[7] Y. Epelboin, "MOOC in Europe," UPMC-Sorbonne Université, 2013.

[8] Daniel Burgos, Colin Tattersall, and Rob Koper, "Representing Adaptive and Adaptable Units of Learning," in Computers and Education.: Springer Netherlands, 2007, pp. 41-56

[9] Jesus Bobadilla, Fernando Ortega, Antonio Hernando, and Javier Alcal, "Improving collaborative filtering recommender system results and performance using genetic algorithms," Knowledge-Based Systems, vol. 24, no. 8, pp. 1310-1316, 2011.

[10] M.AC. González, F.J.G. Penalvo, M.J.C. Guerrero, and M.A Forment, "Adapting LMS Architecture to the SOA: An Architectural Approach," in Internet and Web Applications and Services, 2009. ICIW '09. Fourth International Conference on, May 2009, pp. 322-327.

[11] S.K. Malik and S. A M Rizvi, "Information Extraction Using Web Usage Mining, Web Scrapping and Semantic Annotation," in Computational Intelligence and Communication Networks (CICN), 2011 International Conference on, Oct 2011, pp. 465-469.

[12] A Holmes and M. Kellogg, "Automating functional tests using Selenium," in Agile Conference, 2006, July 2006, pp. 6 pp.-275.

[13] Tomas Grigalis and Antanas , "Unsupervised Structured Data Extraction from Template-generated Web Pages," Journal of Universal Computer Science, vol. 20, no. 2, pp. 169-192, feb 2014

[14] H. Bosch et al., "Innovative filtering techniques and customized analytics tools," in Visual Analytics Science and Technology, 2009.

VAST 2009. IEEE Symposium on, 2009

[15] P. Hunter, Instant Nokogiri.: Packt Publishing Ltd., 2013.

[16] Angel A. Juan, Thanasis Daradoumis, Javier Faulin, and Fatos Xhafa, "SAMOS a Model for Monitoring Studentsand Groups; Activities in Collaborative eLearning," Int. J. Learn. Technol., vol. 4, no. 1/2, pp. 53-72, 2009.

[17] Riccardo Mazza and Christian Milani, "GISMO: a Graphical Interactive Student Monitoring Tool for Course Management Systems," in T.E.L.'04 Technology Enhanced Learning '04 International Conference. Milan, 2004, pp. 18-19.

[18] Jungsoon Yoo, Sung Yoo, Chris Lance, and Judy Hankins, "Student Progress Monitoring Tool Using Treeview," SIGCSE Bull., vol. 38, no. 1, pp. 373-377, 2006.

[19] S. Shishehchi, S.Y. Banihashem, and N.AM. Zin, "A proposed semantic recommendation system for e-learning: A rule and ontology based e-learning recommendation system," in Information Technology (ITSim), 2010 International Symposium in, vol. 1, June 2010, pp. 1-5.

[20] K. Takano and Kin Fun Li, "An Adaptive e-Learning Recommender Based on User's Web-Browsing Behavior," in P2P, Parallel, Grid, Cloud and Internet Computing (3PGCIC), 2010 International Conference on, Nov 2010, pp. 123-131.

[21] K. Takano and Kin Fun Li, "An adaptive learning book system based on user's study interest," in Communications, Computers and Signal Processing (PacRim), 2011 IEEE Pacific Rim Conference on, Aug 2011, pp. 842-847.

[22] Enrique García, Crist, Sebasti, and Carlosde Castro, "An architecture for making recommendations to courseware authors using association rule mining and collaborative filtering," User Modeling and User-Adapted Interaction, vol. 19, no. 1-2, pp. 99-132, 2009.

[23] El Hassan, A. and El Adani, M. El Bachari E., "Design of an Adaptive E- Learning Model Based on Learner's Personality," Ubiquitous Computing and Communication Journal, vol. 5, 2010.

[24] C. Romero and S. Ventura, "Educational data mining: A survey from 1995 to 2005," Expert Systems with Applications, vol. 33, no. 1, pp. 135-146, 2007.

[25] Ahmad A. Kardan, Nahid Ghassabzadeh Saryazdi, and Hamed Mirashk, "Learner Clustering and Association Rule Mining for Content Recommendation in Self-Regulated Learning," International Journal of Computer Science Research and Application, 2012.

[26] Boban Vesin, Mirjana Ivanovi, Aleksandra Kla, and Zoran Budimac, "Protus 2.0: Ontology-based semantic recommendation in programming tutoring system," Expert Systems with Applications, vol. 39, no. 15, pp. 12229-12246, 2012.

[27] Tong Wang and Pi lian He, "Web Log Mining by an Improved AprioriAll Algorithm.," in WEC (2), 2005, pp. 97-100.

[28] M. K. Khribi M. Jemni, "Toward a Hybrid Recommender System for E-Learning Personalization Based on Web Usage Mining Techniques and Information Retrieval," in World Conference on E-Learning in Corporate, Government, Healthcare, and Higher Education, 2017.

[29] John C. Stamper et al., "Managing the Educational Dataset Lifecycle with DataShop," in Proceedings of the 15th International Conference on Artificial Intelligence in Education, Berlin, Heidelberg, 2011, pp. 557-559.

[30] Riccardo Mazza, Marco Bettoni, Marco Far, and Luca Mazzola, "MOCLog--Monitoring Online Courses with log data," Proceedings of the 1st Moodle Research Conference, pp. 14-15, 2012.

[31] JeffZ. Pan, "Resource Description Framework," International Handbooks on Information Systems, 2009.

[32] IMS Global Learning Consortium Inc., "Learning Measurement for Analytics Whitepaper," 2013.

[33] IEEE, "Data Model for Content to Learning Management System Communication," IEEE Std 1484.11.1-2004, 2005.

[34] J and Atkins, M and Norris, W and Messina, C and Wilkinson, M and Dolin, R Snell, "JSON Activity Streams 1.0," 2011.

[35] Abelardo Pardo and George Siemens, "Ethical and privacy principles for learning analytics," British Journal of Educational Technology, vol. 45, no. 3, 2014.

[36] David Kelly and Kevin Thorn, "Should Instructional Designers Care About the Tin Can API?," eLearn, vol. 2013, no. 3, 2013.

[37] A del Blanco, A Serrano, M. Freire, I Martinez-Ortiz, and B. Fernandez-Manjon, "E-Learning standards and learning analytics. Can data collection be improved by using standard data models?," in Global Engineering Education Conference (EDUCON), 2013 IEEE, March 2013, pp. 1255-1261.

[38] Daniel Burgos, "L.I.M.E. A recommendation model for informal and formal learning, engaged," IJIMAI, pp. 79-86, 2013.

[39] Swati Saigaonkar and Madhuri Rao, "XML Filtering System Based on Ontology," in Proceedings of the 1st Amrita ACM-W Celebration on Women in Computing in India, New York, NY, USA, 2010, pp. 51:1--51:6.

[40] James Cheney, Sam Lindley, and Philip Wadler, "A Practical Theory of Language-integrated Query," SIGPLAN Not., vol. 48, no. 9, pp. 403-416, 2013.

[41] Eric Pardede, J. Wenny Rahayu, Ramanpreet Kaur Aujla, and David Taniar, "SQL/XML Hierarchical Query Performance Analysis in an XML-Enabled Database System," Journal of Universal Computer Science, vol. 15, no. 10, pp. 2058-2077, may 2009.

Permissions

All chapters in this book were first published in IJIMAI, by Imai-Software Research Group; hereby published with permission under the Creative Commons Attribution License or equivalent. Every chapter published in this book has been scrutinized by our experts. Their significance has been extensively debated. The topics covered herein carry significant findings which will fuel the growth of the discipline. They may even be implemented as practical applications or may be referred to as a beginning point for another development.

The contributors of this book come from diverse backgrounds, making this book a truly international effort. This book will bring forth new frontiers with its revolutionizing research information and detailed analysis of the nascent developments around the world.

We would like to thank all the contributing authors for lending their expertise to make the book truly unique. They have played a crucial role in the development of this book. Without their invaluable contributions this book wouldn't have been possible. They have made vital efforts to compile up to date information on the varied aspects of this subject to make this book a valuable addition to the collection of many professionals and students.

This book was conceptualized with the vision of imparting up-to-date information and advanced data in this field. To ensure the same, a matchless editorial board was set up. Every individual on the board went through rigorous rounds of assessment to prove their worth. After which they invested a large part of their time researching and compiling the most relevant data for our readers.

The editorial board has been involved in producing this book since its inception. They have spent rigorous hours researching and exploring the diverse topics which have resulted in the successful publishing of this book. They have passed on their knowledge of decades through this book. To expedite this challenging task, the publisher supported the team at every step. A small team of assistant editors was also appointed to further simplify the editing procedure and attain best results for the readers.

Apart from the editorial board, the designing team has also invested a significant amount of their time in understanding the subject and creating the most relevant covers. They scrutinized every image to scout for the most suitable representation of the subject and create an appropriate cover for the book.

The publishing team has been an ardent support to the editorial, designing and production team. Their endless efforts to recruit the best for this project, has resulted in the accomplishment of this book. They are a veteran in the field of academics and their pool of knowledge is as vast as their experience in printing. Their expertise and guidance has proved useful at every step. Their uncompromising quality standards have made this book an exceptional effort. Their encouragement from time to time has been an inspiration for everyone.

The publisher and the editorial board hope that this book will prove to be a valuable piece of knowledge for researchers, students, practitioners and scholars across the globe.

List of Contributors

Dr. José Miguel Castillo Chamorro
Pontifical University of Salamanca, Madrid –Spain

D. Rafael de Solís Montes
Superior School of Telecommunications, Polytechnic University in Madrid, Madrid –Spain

Frack Gechter
IRTES-SET, UTBM, Belfort Cedex, France

Bruno Ronzani
Oyez Digital Agency

Fabien Rioli
Tharsis Evolution

Rimvydas Skyrius
Economic Informatics Department, Vilnius University, Lithuania

Gėlytė Kazakevičienė
Economic Informatics Department, Vilnius University, Lithuania

Vytautas Bujauskas
Economic Informatics Department, Vilnius University, Lithuania

L. D. LLedo
Miguel Hernández University of Elche, Elche, Spain

A. Bertomeu
Miguel Hernández University of Elche, Elche, Spain

J. Díez
Miguel Hernández University of Elche, Elche, Spain

F. J. Badesa
Miguel Hernández University of Elche, Elche, Spain

R. Morales
Miguel Hernández University of Elche, Elche, Spain

J. M. Sabater
Miguel Hernández University of Elche, Elche, Spain

N. Garcia-Aracil
Miguel Hernández University of Elche, Elche, Spain

Vinay S Bhaskar
Human Resource Manager, Electro Equipment, Roorkee, India

Abhishek Kumar Singh
IIIT Allahabad

Jyoti Dhruw
Chhatrapati Shivaji Institute of Technology (CSIT, Durg, Chhattisgrah

Anubha Parashar
Maharshi Dayanand University, Rohtak

Mradula Sharma
MNNIT Alllahabad

Juan Carlos Piedra Calderón
Universidad Pontificia de Salamanca, Spain

J. Javier Rainer
Universidad Pontificia de Salamanca, Spain

Roberto Amadini
Department of Computer Science and Engineering/Lab. Focus INRIA. University of Bologna, Italy

Imane Sefrioui
Computer Science, Operational Research and Applied Statistics Lab. Faculty of Sciences, Abdelmalek Essaadi University, Tetuan, Morocco

Jacopo Mauro
Department of Computer Science and Engineering/Lab. Focus INRIA. University of Bologna, Italy

Maurizio Gabbrielli
Department of Computer Science and Engineering/Lab. Focus INRIA. University of Bologna, Italy

Sánchez Aparicio
Universidad Distrital Francisco José de Caldas, Bogotá, Colombia

Ismael Fernando
Universidad Distrital Francisco José de Caldas, Bogotá, Colombia

Romero Villalobos
Universidad Distrital Francisco José de Caldas, Bogotá, Colombia

Oswaldo Alberto
Universidad Distrital Francisco José de Caldas, Bogotá, Colombia

Krishna Asawa
Department of Computer Science Engineering and Information Technology Jaypee Institute of Information Technology, Noida, India

Priyanka Manchanda
Department of Computer Science Engineering and Information Technology Jaypee Institute of Information Technology, Noida, India

Pablo Seoane
Departament of Information and Communications Technologies, University of A Coruña, A Coruña, Spain

Marcos Gestal
Departament of Information and Communications Technologies, University of A Coruña, A Coruña, Spain

Julián Dorado
Departament of Information and Communications Technologies, University of A Coruña, A Coruña, Spain

Abílio Costa
Computer Science Department, School of Engineering (ISEP), Polytechnic of Porto, R. Dr. António Bernardino de Almeida 431, Porto, Portugal

João P. Pereira
Computer Science Department, School of Engineering (ISEP), Polytechnic of Porto, R. Dr. António Bernardino de Almeida 431, Porto, Portugal
Knowledge Engineering and Decision Support Group (GECAD), School of Engineering, Polytechnic of Porto, R. Dr. António Bernardino de Almeida 431, Porto, Portugal

Eugenio Gil
University Pontifical of Salamanca, Madrid Campus, Spain

Andrés G. Castillo Sanz
University Pontifical of Salamanca, Madrid Campus, Spain

Anthony G. Picciano
Graduate Center and Hunter College, City University of New York (CUNY)

Min Yuan
Utah State University

Mimi Recker
Utah State University

Giovanny Mauricio Tarazona Bermúdez
Faculty of Engineering, District University Francisco José de Caldas, Bogotá, Colombia

Luz Andrea Rodríguez Rojas
Faculty of Engineering, District University Francisco José de Caldas, Bogotá, Colombia

Cristina B Pelayo
Computer Science Department, University of Oviedo, Oviedo, Spain

Oscar Sanjuan Martínez
Computer Science Department, University of Oviedo, Oviedo, Spain

Daniel Burgos
UNIR Research, International University of La Rioja. Spain

Abdelhamid Zouhair
LIST Lab, The University of Abdelmalek Essaâdi, FST of Tangier, Morocco

El Mokhtar En-Naimi
LIST Lab, The University of Abdelmalek Essaâdi, FST of Tangier, Morocco

Benaissa Amami
LIST Lab, The University of Abdelmalek Essaâdi, FST of Tangier, Morocco

Hadhoum Boukachour
LITIS Lab, The University of Le Havre, France

Patrick Person
LITIS Lab, The University of Le Havre, France

Cyrille Bertelle
LITIS Lab, The University of Le Havre, France

Nobuyuki Teraura
Terrara Code Research Institute , Tokai, Japan

Kouichi Sakurai
Information Science and Electrical Enginerring, Kyushu University, Fukuoka, Japan

Juan Carlos Fernández Rodríguez
Bureau Veritas Centro Universitario, Madrid, Spain

José Javier Rainer Granados
Bureau Veritas Centro Universitario, Madrid, Spain

Fernando Miralles Muñoz
Universidad San Pablo CEU, Madrid, Spain

Paula A. Rodríguez
Departamento de Ciencias de la Computación y la Decisión, Universidad Nacional de Colombia-Medellín, Colombia
Departamento de Informática y Computación, Universidad Nacional de Colombia-Manizales, Colombia

Valentina Tabares
Departamento de Ciencias de la Computación y la Decisión, Universidad Nacional de Colombia-Medellín, Colombia
Departamento de Informática y Computación, Universidad Nacional de Colombia-Manizales, Colombia

Néstor D. Duque
Departamento de Informática y Computación, Universidad Nacional de Colombia-Manizales, Colombia

Demetrio A. Ovalle
Departamento de Ciencias de la Computación y la Decisión, Universidad Nacional de Colombia-Medellín, Colombia

Rosa M. Vicari
Instituto de Informática, Universidade Federal do Rio Grande do Sul, Brasil

Jamal Ahmad Dargham
Universiti Malaysia Sabah

Ali Chekima
Universiti Malaysia Sabah

Ervin Gubin Moung
Universiti Malaysia Sabah

Chuii Khim Chong
Mohd Saberi Mohamad
Safaai Deris
Mohd Shahir Shamsir
Yee Wen Choon
Lian En Chai
Llanos Tobarra
Communication and Control System Department, from Spanish University for Distance Education (Universidad Nacional de Educación a Distancia, UNED)

Salvador Ros
Communication and Control System Department, from Spanish University for Distance Education (Universidad Nacional de Educación a Distancia, UNED)

Roberto Hernández
Communication and Control System Department, from Spanish University for Distance Education (Universidad Nacional de Educación a Distancia, UNED)

Antonio Robles-Gómez
Communication and Control System Department, from Spanish University for Distance Education (Universidad Nacional de Educación a Distancia, UNED)

Agustín C. Caminero
Communication and Control System Department, from Spanish University for Distance Education (Universidad Nacional de Educación a Distancia, UNED)

Rafael Pastor
Communication and Control System Department, from Spanish University for Distance Education (Universidad Nacional de Educación a Distancia, UNED)

P Giuffra
Departament of Informatic and Statistics Federal University of Santa Catarina, Brasil

E Cecilia
Departament of Informatic and Statistics Federal University of Santa Catarina, Brasil

A. Silveira Ricardo
Departament of Informatic and Statistics Federal University of Santa Catarina, Brasil

Rafael León
Centre for Automation and Robotics UPM - CSIC Universidad Politécnica de Madrid, Spain

J. Javier Rainer
Centre for Automation and Robotics UPM - CSIC Universidad Politécnica de Madrid, Spain

José Manuel Rojo
Centre for Automation and Robotics UPM - CSIC Universidad Politécnica de Madrid, Spain

Ramón Galán
Centre for Automation and Robotics UPM - CSIC Universidad Politécnica de Madrid, Spain

Gabriel López-García
A. Javier Gallego-Sánchez
J. Luis Dalmau-Espert
Rafael Molina-Carmona
Patricia Compañ-Rosique
Elisa Boff
Universidade de Caxias do Sul (UCS) – Brazil

Eliseo Berni Reategui
Universidade Federal do Rio Grande do Sul (UFRGS) – Brazil

Santiago Planet
La Salle – Universitat Ramon Llull

Ignasi Iriondo
La Salle – Universitat Ramon Llull

Lucía Romero
Universidad Nacional del Litoral (UNL)

Milagros Gutiérrez
Facultad Regional Santa Fe, Universidad Tecnológica Nacional

María Laura Caliusco
Facultad Regional Santa Fe, Universidad Tecnológica Nacional

Bruno Correia
Computer Science Department, Universidad de Lisboa

Paulo Urbano
Computer Science Department, Universidad de Lisboa

Luís Moniz
Computer Science Department, Universidad de Lisboa

Friederike Wall
Alpen-Adria-Universität Klagenfurt, Austria

Alberto Corbi
UNIR Research, Universidad Internacional de La Rioja - UNIR

Daniel Burgos
UNIR Research, Universidad Internacional de La Rioja - UNIR

Printed by BoD™in Norderstedt, Germany